MW01627059

CORPUS OF EARLY ITALIAN PAINTINGS

IN NORTH AMERICAN PUBLIC COLLECTIONS:

THE SOUTH

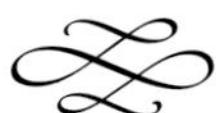

VOLUME 2

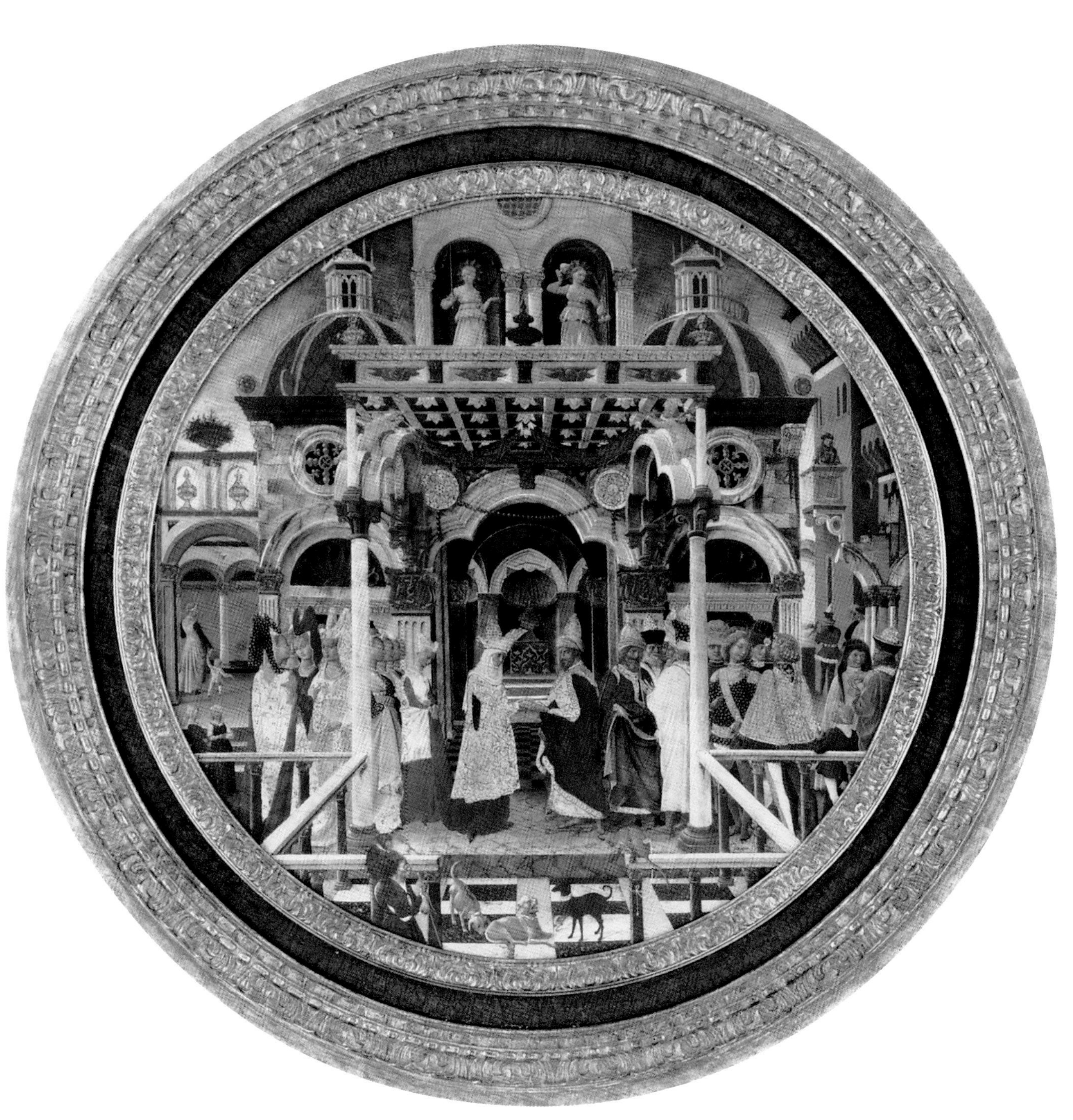

Corpus of Early Italian Paintings in North American Public Collections:

The South

VOLUME 2

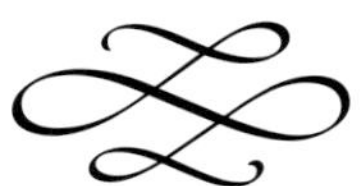

PERRI LEE ROBERTS

ANDREW LADIS, GENERAL EDITOR

GEORGIA MUSEUM OF ART ~ THE UNIVERSITY OF GEORGIA ~ ATHENS, GEORGIA

In loving memory of Samuel Roberts and Andrew Ladis.

©2009 GEORGIA MUSEUM OF ART, UNIVERSITY OF GEORGIA

PUBLISHED BY THE GEORGIA MUSEUM OF ART, UNIVERSITY OF GEORGIA. ALL RIGHTS RESERVED.

NO PART OF THIS BOOK MAY BE REPRODUCED WITHOUT THE WRITTEN CONSENT OF THE PUBLISHERS.

PRINTED IN CHINA IN AN EDITION OF 1,000 BY ASIA PACIFIC

DESIGNER AND PRODUCTION MANAGER:

Carol Haralson, *Haralson Design, Sedona, Arizona*

PROJECT EDITOR:

Cynthia A. Payne, *Special Assistant to the Director, Georgia Museum of Art*

ISBN 10: 0-915977-64-8

ISBN 13: 978-0-915977-64-2

LIBRARY OF CONGRESS CATALOGING-IN-PUBLICATION DATA

Roberts, Perri Lee.

Corpus of early Italian paintings in North American public collections. The South / Perri Lee Roberts; Andrew Ladis, general editor.

p. cm.

Includes bibliographical references and index.

ISBN-13: 978-0-915977-64-2

ISBN-10: 0-915977-64-8

1. Painting, Italian—13th century—Catalogs. 2. Painting, Italian—14th century—Catalogs. 3. Painting, Italian—15th century—Catalogs. 4. Painting—Southern States—Catalogs. 5. Art museums—Southern States—Catalogs. I. Ladis, Andrew, 1949–2007. II. Georgia Museum of Art. III. Title.

ND615.R623 2008

759.5074'75--dc22

2007014141

PARTIAL SUPPORT FOR THE EXHIBITIONS AND PROGRAMS AT THE GEORGIA MUSEUM OF ART IS PROVIDED BY THE W. NEWTON MORRIS CHARITABLE FOUNDATION, THE FRIENDS OF THE MUSEUM, AND THE GEORGIA COUNCIL FOR THE ARTS THROUGH THE APPROPRIATIONS OF THE GEORGIA GENERAL ASSEMBLY. THE COUNCIL IS A PARTNER AGENCY OF THE NATIONAL ENDOWMENT FOR THE ARTS. INDIVIDUALS, FOUNDATIONS, AND CORPORATIONS PROVIDE ADDITIONAL SUPPORT THROUGH THEIR GIFTS TO THE ARCH FOUNDATION AND THE UNIVERSITY OF GEORGIA FOUNDATION.

FRONTISPIECE: Ferrarese School, third quarter of the fifteenth century, *The Meeting of Solomon and the Queen of Sheba*. The Museum of Fine Arts, Houston, The Edith A. and Percy S. Straus Collection, 44.574.

CORPUS OF EARLY ITALIAN PAINTINGS

IN NORTH AMERICAN PUBLIC COLLECTIONS: THE SOUTH

VOLUME 2

CATALOGUE

FORT WORTH, TEXAS. KIMBELL ART MUSEUM *284*

GREENVILLE, SOUTH CAROLINA. BOB JONES UNIVERSITY MUSEUM & GALLERY *296*

HELENA, ARKANSAS. PHILLIPS COUNTY MUSEUM *360*

HOUSTON, TEXAS. THE MENIL COLLECTION *364*

HOUSTON, TEXAS. THE MUSEUM OF FINE ARTS, HOUSTON *366*

HOUSTON, TEXAS. SARAH CAMPBELL BLAFFER FOUNDATION *432*

JACKSONVILLE, FLORIDA. THE CUMMER MUSEUM OF ART & GARDENS *446*

LITTLE ROCK, ARKANSAS. THE ARKANSAS ARTS CENTER *458*

LOUISVILLE, KENTUCKY. THE SPEED ART MUSEUM *460*

MACON, GEORGIA. WESLEYAN COLLEGE *472*

MEMPHIS, TENNESSEE. MEMPHIS BROOKS MUSEUM OF ART *474*

MIAMI BEACH, FLORIDA. BASS MUSEUM OF ART *506*

MONTGOMERY, ALABAMA. HUNTINGDON COLLEGE, HOUGHTON MEMORIAL LIBRARY *520*

MONTGOMERY, ALABAMA. MONTGOMERY MUSEUM OF FINE ARTS *522*

NASHVILLE, TENNESSEE. VANDERBILT UNIVERSITY FINE ARTS GALLERY *524*

CORPUS OF EARLY ITALIAN PAINTINGS IN NORTH AMERICAN PUBLIC COLLECTIONS: THE SOUTH

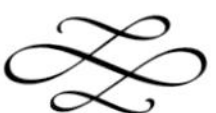

VOLUME 2

ANGELICO, FRA, C. 1400–1455; FLORENTINE

St. James Freeing Hermogenes (AP 1986.03) 26.8 X 23.8 CM, TEMPERA ON PANEL

FORT WORTH, TEXAS. KIMBELL ART MUSEUM

Miklòs Boskovits (1976; 1976) suggested that the painting came from the predella of an unidentified polyptych that had as its central panel the Madonna and Child, which may have been flanked by *St. James* (current location unknown; formerly, Minneapolis Institute of Arts, Minneapolis) and a representation of St. John the Baptist on the left, with either St. Francis or St. Dominic and an unidentified saint on the right. Everett P. Fahy (1987) hypothesized a predella for the altarpiece that included the *Naming of John the Baptist* (Museo di San Marco, Florence; 1499); the *Meeting of St. Dominic and St. Francis* (M. H. de Young Memorial Museum, San Francisco; 61.44-7); the *Dormition of the Virgin* (John G. Johnson Collection, Philadelphia Museum of Art, Philadelphia; 15); and *St. Agatha Rising from Her Tomb* (Feigen Collection, New York). Laurence B. Kanter (in Christiansen, Kanter, and Strehlke 1994) identified *Christ Blessing* and *Angels* (Galleria Sabauda, Turin; 103 and 104) as panels that might have belonged to the polyptych. With the notable exceptions of Giorgio Bonsanti (1998) and Carl Brandon Strehlke (2004), both of whom dated the work to the mid- to late 1420s, scholars have dated the altarpiece c. 1430 on the basis of stylistic similarities to Angelico's *St. Peter Martyr Altarpiece* (Museo di San Marco, Florence) of 1429 and his *Last Judgment* (Museo di San Marco, Florence) of 1431–1432.

The textual source for the scene is Jacobus de Voragine's *Golden Legend*. St. James the Greater is shown tapping the newly converted Philetus with his staff, thus empowering Philetus to free his former master, the magician Hermogenes, from the devils Hermogenes had sent to torment the saint. Following the magician's conversion, James gave him a pilgrim's staff as a talisman.

PROVENANCE

Ignazio Hugford (d. 1778), Florence (?); James-Alexandre, Comte de Pourtalès-Gorgier, Paris, acquired 1841; Hôtel Pourtalès-Gorgier, Paris, March 27, 1865, lot 15; Comte Lafond, Paris, 1865–1879; Comtesse Lafond, Paris; Thérèse Lafond, Duchesse des Cars, Paris; François, Duc des Cars, Paris, 1932; Duc des Cars, Paris, 1933; De Meeüs family, Belgium, early 1940s; private collection, Switzerland, late 1940s; Wildenstein, New York; Kimbell Art Museum, acquired 1986

BIBLIOGRAPHY

Roberto Longhi, "Fatti di Masolino e di Masaccio," *Critica d'Arte* 5 (1940): 175-76; John Pope-Hennessy, *Fra Angelico* (London: Phaidon Press, 1952), 9, 197; *Mostra delle opere di Fra Angelico: Nel quinto centenario della morte (1455–1955)* (Vatican: Direzione generale dei monumenti, musei e gallerie pontificie, 1955), 28; Giovanni Urbani, *Beato Angelico* (Milan: Mondadori, 1957), 87; Mario Salmi, *Il Beato Angelico* (Spoleto: Arti grafiche Panetto e Petrelli, 1958), 103; Mario Salmi, *Il Beato Angelico* (Rome: Edizione "Valori plastici," 1958), 110; Fern Rusk Shapley, *Paintings from the Samuel H. Kress Collection: Italian Schools*, vol. 1, *XIII–XV Century* (London: Phaidon Press, 1966), 97; Elsa Morante and Umberto Baldini, *L'opera completa dell'Angelico* (Milan: Rizzoli, 1970), 94-95, no. 36; John Pope-Hennessy, *Fra Angelico* (London: Phaidon Press, 1974), 18, 196; Miklòs Boskovits, *Un' adorazione dei magi e gli inizi dell'Angelico* (Riggisberg: Abegg-Stiftung Bern, 1976), 31; Miklòs Boskovits, "Appunti sull'Angelico," *Paragone* 27 (1976): 39; Galleria degli Uffizi, *Gli Uffizi: Catalogo generale* (Florence: Centro Di, 1980), 156; Umberto Baldini, *Beato Angelico* (Florence: Edizioni d'Arte Il Fiorino, 1986), 24; Edward P. Pillsbury and William Jordan, "Recent Painting Acquisitions—III: The Kimbell Art Museum," *Burlington Magazine* 124 (1987): 767-68; Everett P. Fahy, "The Kimbell Fra Angelico," *Apollo* 125 (1987): 178-83; *In Pursuit of Quality: The Kimbell Art Museum* (Fort Worth: Kimbell Art Museum, 1987), 156; *La chiesa e il convento di San Marco a Firenze* (Florence: Giunti, 1990), 73; Luciano Berti and Antonio Paolucci, eds., *L'età di Masaccio: Il primo Quattrocento a Firenze* (Milan: Electa, 1990), 228, no. 84; Carl Brandon Strehlke, "Fra Angelico and Early Florentine Renaissance Painting in the John G. Johnson Collection," *Philadelphia Museum of Art Bulletin* 88 (1993): 5-6; Miklòs Boskovits, *Immagini da meditare: Ricerche su dipinti di tema religioso nei secoli XII–XV* (Milan: Vita e Pensiero, 1994), 346-67; Keith Christiansen, Laurence B. Kanter, and Carl Brandon Strehlke, *Painting and Illumination in Early Renaissance Florence, 1300–1450* (New York: Metropolitan Museum of Art, 1994), 326-27, 332; John T. Spike, *Angelico* (Milan: Fabbri, 1996), 255-56, no. 114c; Giorgio Bonsanti, *Beato Angelico: Catalogo completo* (Florence: Octavo, 1998), 126, no. 31; Carl Brandon Strehlke, *Italian Paintings 1250–1450, in the John G. Johnson Collection and the Philadelphia Museum of Art* (Philadelphia: Philadelphia Museum of Art, 2004), 48; Laurence B. Kanter, *Reconstructing the Renaissance: "Saint James Freeing Hermogenes" by Fra Angelico* (New Haven and London: Yale University Press, 2008); Diane Cole Ahl, *Fra Angelico* (London: Phaidon, 2008), 227, no. 166.

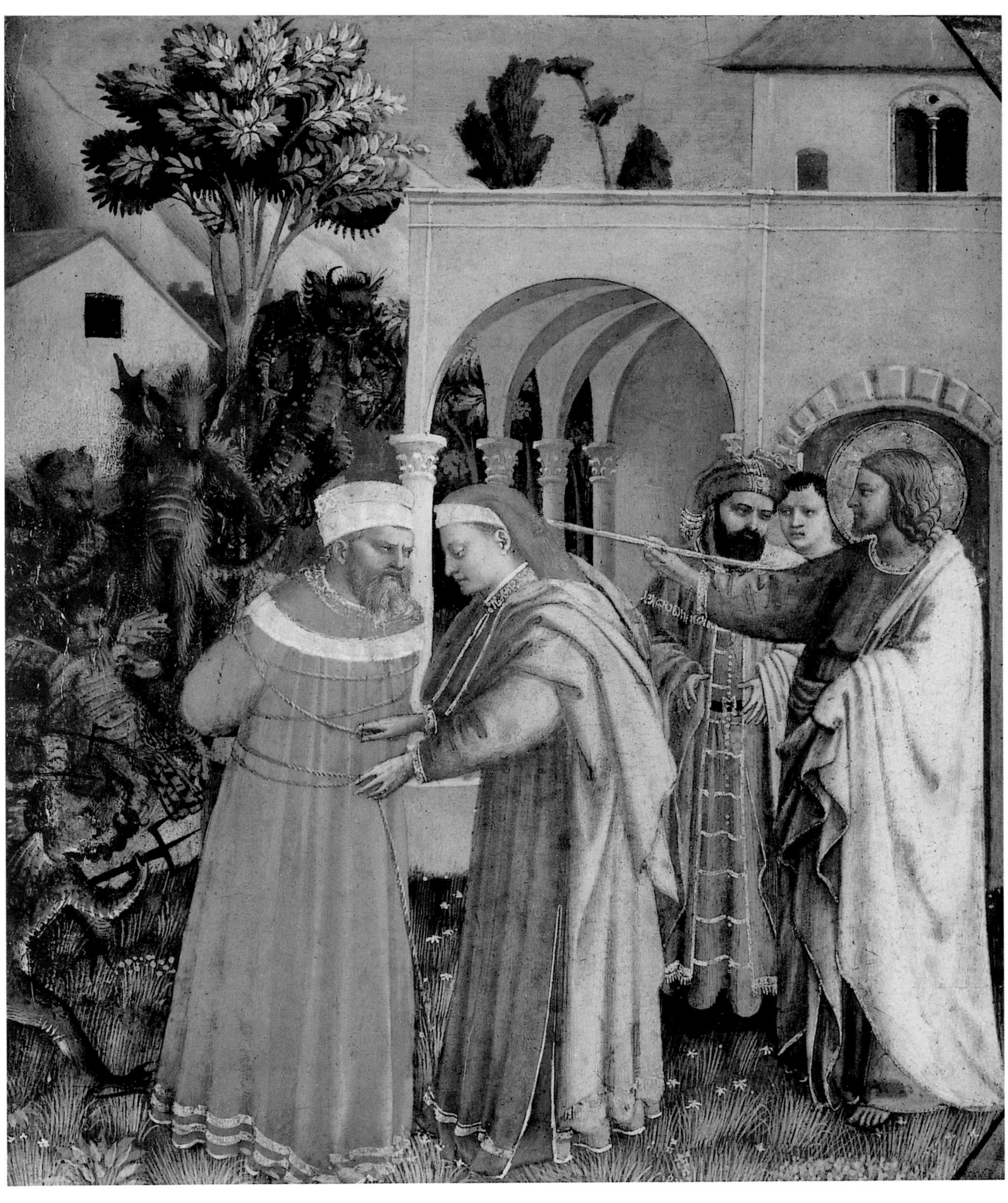

Fig. 148 Fra Angelico: *St. James Freeing Hermogenes*. Kimbell Art Museum, Fort Worth, Texas, AP 1986.03.

BELLINI, GIOVANNI, 1431/6–1516; VENETIAN

Christ Blessing (AP 1967.07) 59 X 47 CM, TEMPERA AND OIL ON PANEL

FORT WORTH, TEXAS. KIMBELL ART MUSEUM

Antonio Morassi (1958), who first attributed the work to Bellini, proposed a possible identification with the representation of the "Savior in the act of blessing" given by the artist as a votive offering to his parish church of Santo Stefano, Venice; the event was recorded by Carlo Ridolfi in *Le Maraviglie dell'arte* (Venice, 1648). This provenance is not universally accepted. Anchise Tempestini (1999) suggested the Kimbell painting may have been part of a *Noli me Tangere* scene, but no physical or compositional evidence supports the proposal. The date of the work has been debated. Rodolfo Pallucchini (1959), Fritz Heinemann (1962), and Stefano Bottari (1963) dated it c. 1490–1495, whereas Terisio Pignatti (1979) placed it c. 1500. The Museum acknowledges the latter date. Citing the influence of Antonello da Messina (c. 1430–1479) on the design of the drapery folds, Heinemann (1991) revised his earlier opinion, assigning the panel to 1475–1478, contemporary with Bellini's *Resurrection* (Staatliche Museen, Gemäldegalerie, Berlin; 1177 A).

Figures of Christ Blessing appear in other paintings by Bellini, but this particular interpretation of the imagery is unique within the artist's oeuvre. Christ is depicted as the savior triumphant over death. Several elements allude to the themes of death, resurrection, and salvation, including a solitary bird on a withered tree, a pair of rabbits, a shepherd with his flock, and a church bell tower. The holy women who were the first to discover the empty tomb after Christ's resurrection are present in the background.

PROVENANCE

Cunningham, England, by 1849; Richard Fisher, Esq., England; Mrs. Gunhilda Fisher, England; Sotheby's, London, June 11, 1958; Joseph H. Dasser, Zurich; Newhouse, New York; Kimbell Art Museum, acquired 1967

BIBLIOGRAPHY

Antonio Morassi, "Scoperta d'un Cristo Benedicente del Giambelliano," *Arte Veneta* 12 (1958): 45-52; Rodolfo Pallucchini, *Giovanni Bellini* (Milan: A. Martello, 1959), 88, 148; Fritz Heinemann, *Giovanni Bellini e i Belliniani*, 3 vols. (Venice: Neri Pozza, 1962), 1:57, no. 191bis; *Konstens Venedig* (Stockholm: Nationalmuseum, 1962), 62, no. 56; Stefano Bottari, ed., *Tutta la pittura di Giovanni Bellini*, 2 vols. (Milan: Rizzoli, 1963), 2:25; Luitpold Düssler, "Berichte: Schweden," *Pantheon* 21 (1963): 129; Giles Robertson, *Giovanni Bellini* (Oxford: Clarendon Press, 1968), 113; Terisio Pignatti, *L'opera completa di Giovanni Bellini* (Milan: Rizzoli, 1969), 103; Kimbell Art Museum, *Catalogue of the Collection* (Fort Worth: Kimbell Art Foundation, 1972), 30-32; Terisio Pignatti, *The Golden Century of Venetian Painting* (Los Angeles: Los Angeles County Museum of Art, 1979), 156, no. 3; Kimbell Art Museum, *Handbook of the Collection* (Fort Worth: Kimbell Art Foundation, 1981), 135; *In Pursuit of Quality: The Kimbell Art Museum* (Fort Worth: Kimbell Art Museum, 1987), 167; Fritz Heinemann, *Giovanni Bellini e i Belliniani*, 3 vols. (Venice: Neri Pozza, 1991), 3:26, no. 191bis; Anchise Tempestini, *Giovanni Bellini* (New York: Abbeville Press, 1999), 198, 230, no. 114.

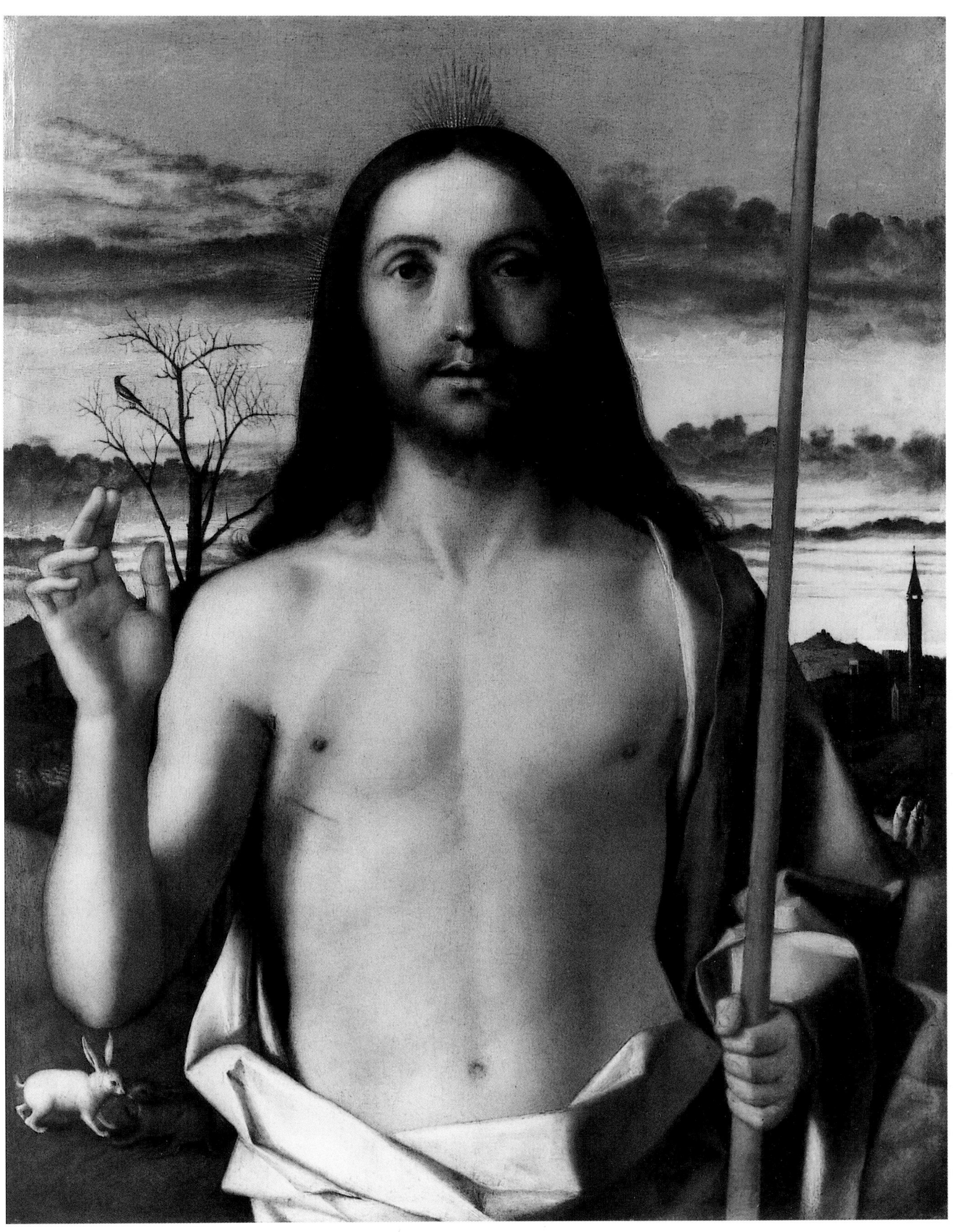

Fig. 149 Giovanni Bellini: *Christ Blessing*. Kimbell Art Museum, Fort Worth, Texas, AP 1967.07.

BELLINI, GIOVANNI, 1431/6–1516; VENETIAN

Madonna and Child (AP 1971.06) 82.5 X 58.4 CM, TEMPERA AND OIL ON PANEL

FORT WORTH, TEXAS. KIMBELL ART MUSEUM

The painting, a personal devotional image, is signed "IOANNES BELLINVS" on a *cartellino*, a small card rendered illusionistically, that appears to be attached to the front of the parapet. It is one of three half-length Madonnas by Bellini in which he employed the same composition with slight variations; the other works are in Santa Maria dell'Orto, Venice, and the Staatliche Museen, Gemäldegalerie, Berlin (10A). The majority of scholars have considered the painting autograph and have dated it early in the artist's career, c. 1470–1475, based on the obvious influence of Mantegna (c. 1431–1506) on the imagery. Only Anchise Tempestini (1999) considered it a later workshop copy of a work by the master.

The open book on the parapet alludes to Christ as the Word Incarnate.

PROVENANCE

Private collection, Bergamo, by 1866; Otto Mündler, Paris, by 1870; Prince Napoleon III, Paris, 1870–1872; Christie, Manson & Woods, London, May 9, 1872; private collection, Europe, to 1969; Kimbell Art Museum, acquired 1971

BIBLIOGRAPHY

Emile Galichon, "Jacopo, Gentile et Giovanni Bellini, Documents inédits trouvés par M. de Mas-Latrie," *Gazette des Beaux-Arts* 20 (1866): 286; Joseph A. Crowe and Giovanni B. Cavalcaselle, *A History of Painting in North Italy, Venice, Padua, Vicenza, Verona, Ferrara, Milan, Friuli, Brescia, from the Fourteenth to the Sixteenth Century*, 3 vols., ed. Tancred Borenius (London: John Murray, 1912), 1:151, no. 2; Georg Gronau, *Giovanni Bellini* (Stuttgart and Berlin: Deutsche Verlag-Anstalt, 1930), 206; "Eastlake's Travelling Agent," *Burlington Magazine* 83 (1943): 211; Rodolfo Pallucchini, ed., *Giovanni Bellini: Catalogo illustrato della mostra* (Venice: Alfieri, 1949), 122; Luitpold Düssler, *Giovanni Bellini* (Vienna: A. Schroll, 1949), 33; Fritz Heinemann, *Giovanni Bellini e i Belliniani*, 3 vols. (Venice: Neri Pozza, 1962), 1:6, no. 26; Stefano Bottari, ed., *Tutta la pittura di Giovanni Bellini*, 2 vols. (Milan: Rizzoli, 1963), 1:139; Kimbell Art Museum, *Catalogue of the Collection* (Fort Worth: Kimbell Art Foundation, 1972), 27-29; Kimbell Art Museum, *Handbook of the Collection* (Fort Worth: Kimbell Art Foundation, 1981), 134; *In Pursuit of Quality: The Kimbell Art Museum* (Fort Worth: Kimbell Art Museum, 1987), 166; Rona Goffen, *Giovanni Bellini* (New Haven: Yale University Press, 1989), 90, 289; Fritz Heinemann, *Giovanni Bellini e i Belliniani*, 3 vols. (Venice: Neri Pozza, 1991), 3:2, no. 26II; Anchise Tempestini, *Giovanni Bellini: Catalogo completo dei dipinti* (Florence: Cantini, 1992), 102; Anchise Tempestini, *Giovanni Bellini* (New York: Abbeville Press, 1999), 65, 68, 203, no. 37; Keith Christiansen, "Giovanni Bellini and the Practice of Devotional Painting," in *Giovanni Belllini and the Art of Devotion*, ed. Ronda Kasl (Indianapolis, Ind.: Indianapolis Museum of Art, 2004), 10-12, no. 5.

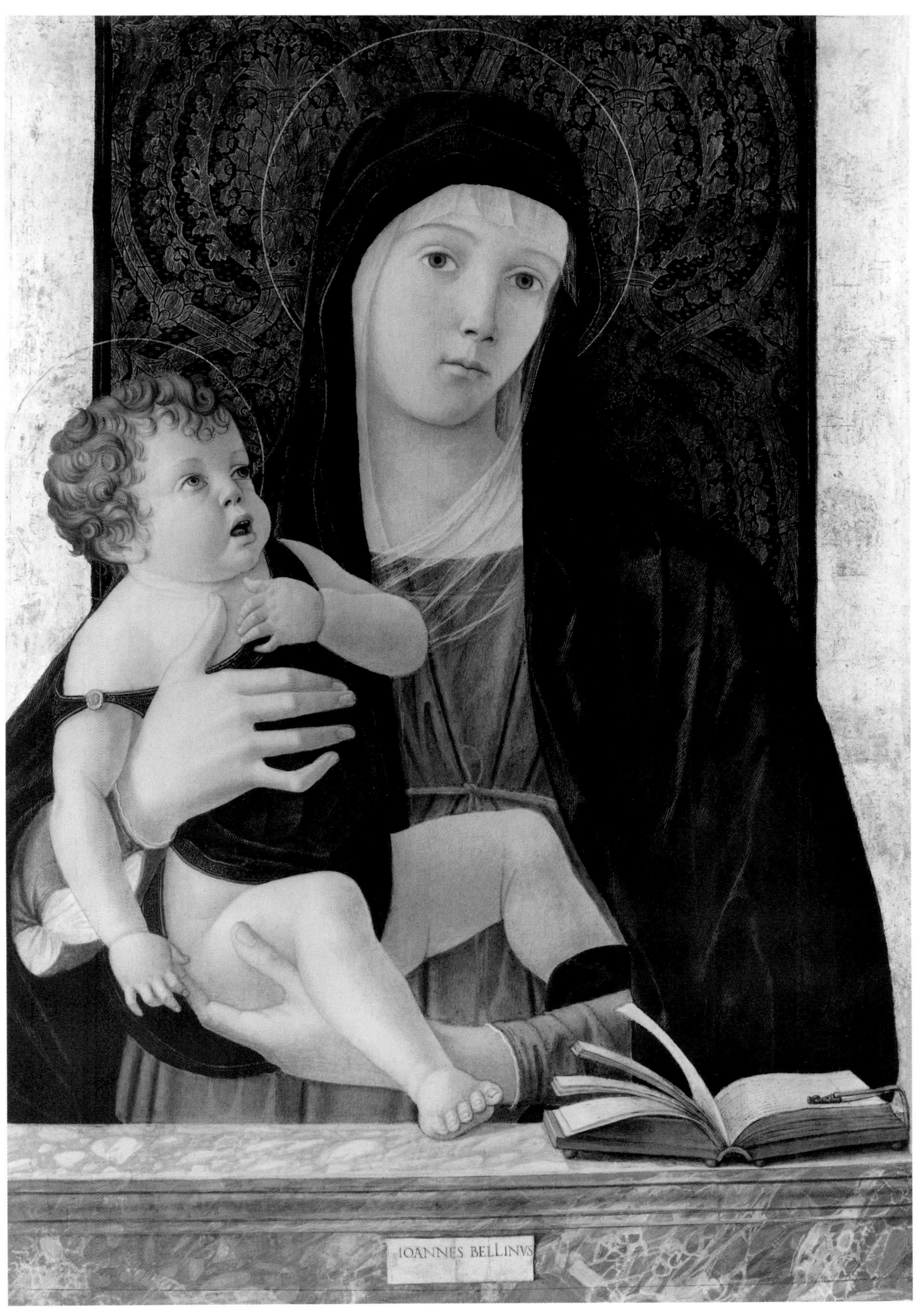

Fig. 150 Giovanni Bellini: *Madonna and Child*. Kimbell Art Museum, Fort Worth, Texas, AP 1971.06.

DUCCIO DI BUONINSEGNA, C. 1255–BEFORE 1319; SIENESE

Raising of Lazarus (AP 1975.01) 43.5 X 46.4 CM, TEMPERA ON PANEL

FORT WORTH, TEXAS. KIMBELL ART MUSEUM

With the notable exception of James H. Stubblebine (1977; 1979), who attributed the execution of the panel to Pietro Lorenzetti (active by 1306; died c. 1348) and located it on the narrow side of the altarpiece from which it came, scholars have considered the *Raising of Lazarus* to be an autograph work by Duccio; moreover, they located it to the far right end of the rear predella of his *Maestà* for the high altar of Siena Cathedral. X-radiographs have indicated that the painting was once part of a single plank that also incorporated *Christ and the Samaritan Woman* (Thyssen-Bornemisza Collection, Lugano; 1971.7) and *Jesus Opens the Eyes of a Man Born Blind* and the *Transfiguration* (National Gallery, London; 1140, 1330), in this order. As the last image on the rear predella, the *Raising of Lazarus* represented the culmination of the ministry of Christ. Notably, the panel evinces traces of one of the most extensive trecento underdrawings to have survived. A pentimento with the sarcophagus standing on end is visible in the lower right corner. The scene illustrates the miracle recounted in John 11:1-44. The iconography mirrors the Byzantine tradition, in which Lazarus emerges from a cave, in an upright position. The left-hand portion of the composition appears to derive from Guido da Siena's treatment of the subject (Pinacoteca Nazionale, Siena; 8) from c. 1275. The overlapping, cross-forming hands of Christ and Martha, Mary Magdalen's heaven-directed gesture, and the isolation of Lazarus, however, were invented by Duccio. The composition became the model for later Sienese depictions of the miracle.

PROVENANCE

Cathedral, Siena, 1311–1771; Sant'Ansano, Castelvecchio, Siena, 1771; Giuseppe and Maziale Dini, Colle Val d'Elsa, by 1879; Charles Fairfax Murray, Florence, 1886; Robert and Evelyn Benson, London, 1886; Duveen Brothers, New York, 1927; John D. Rockefeller, Jr., New York, 1927–1960; David Rockefeller, 1960; Kimbell Art Museum, acquired 1975

BIBLIOGRAPHY

Exhibition of Early Italian Art from 1300 to 1550 (London: New Gallery, Regent Street, 1893), 11; R. Langton Douglas, *Exhibition of Pictures of the School of Siena and Examples of the Minor Arts of That City* (London: Burlington Fine Arts Club, 1904), 43-44; Salomon Reinach, *Répertoire de peintures du Moyen-Âge et de la Renaissance (1280–1580)*, 6 vols. (Paris: E. Leroux, 1905), 1:383; Adolfo Venturi, *Storia dell'arte italiana*, vol. 5, *La pittura del Trecento e le sue origini* (Milan: U. Hoepli, 1907), 568, 570, 574; Joseph A. Crowe and Giovanni B. Cavalcaselle, *A New History of Painting in Italy from the II to the XVI Century*, ed. Edward Hutton, 3 vols. (London: Dent; New York: Dutton, 1908–1909), 1:11; 3:10 n. 5; Bernard Berenson, *The Central Italian Painters of the Renaissance* (New York and London: G. P. Putnam's Sons, 1909), 163; Roger Fry, "Exhibition of Old Masters at the Grafton Galleries," *Burlington Magazine* 20 (1911): 71; Curt H. Weigelt, *Duccio di Buoninsegna* (Leipzig: K. W. Hiersemann, 1911), 240-41; Tancred Borenius, *Catalogue of Italian Pictures at 16 South Street, Park Lane, London and Buckhurst in Sussex* (London: Chiswick Press, 1914), 3-4, no. 3; Raimond van Marle, *The Development of the Italian Schools of Painting*, vol. 2, *The Sienese School of the Late Fourteenth Century* (The Hague: M. Nijhoff, 1924), 35-36; R. Langton Douglas, "I dipinti senesi della Collezione Benson passati da Londra in America," *Rassegna d'Arte Senese* 5 (1927): 99-100; Henry Comstock, "Panels from Duccio's Majestas for America," *International Studio* 88 (1927): 68-69; F. E. Washburn Freund, "Die vier Duccios der Sammlung Benson," *Cicerone* 20 (1928): 333-36; Curt H. Weigelt, *Die sienesische Malerei des vierzehnten Jahrhunderts* (Florence: Pantheon, 1930), 13-14, 73, 86 n. 56; Bernard Berenson, *Italian Pictures of the Renaissance* (Oxford: Clarendon Press, 1932), 176; Bernard Berenson, *Pitture italiane del Rinascimento* (Milan: U. Hoepli, 1936), 152; *Catalogue of the Twentieth Anniversary Exhibition of the Cleveland Museum of Art* (Cleveland: Artcraft Printing Co., 1936), 55, no. 124; Duveen Brothers, *Duveen Pictures in Public Collections of America* (New York: William Bradford Press, 1941), nos. 6-8; Cesare Brandi, *Duccio* (Florence: Vallecchi, 1951), 144; Martin Davies, *The Earlier Italian Schools* (London: National Gallery, 1951), 135 n. 2; Pietro Toesca, *Il Trecento* (Turin: Unione Tipografico-Editrice Torinese, 1951), 501 n. 37, 505; Ernest T. DeWald, "Observations on Duccio's *Maestà*," in *Late Classical and Mediaeval Studies in Honor of Albert Mathias Friend, Jr.*, ed. Kurt Weitzmann (Princeton: Princeton University Press, 1955), 367; Enzo Carli, *Duccio di Buoninsegna* (Milan: A. Martello, 1961), 22, 30; Enzo Carli, *Duccio* (Milan: Fratelli Fabbri, 1964), 6; F. A. Cooper, "A Reconstruction of Duccio's *Maestà*," *Art Bulletin* 47 (1965): 156, 159, 170; Monika Cämmerer-George, *Die Rahmung der toskanischen Altarbilder im Trecento* (Strasbourg: P. H. Heitz, 1966), 144; Alessandro Parronchi, "Segnalazione Duccesca," *Antichità Viva* 5 (1966): 3, 5 n. 1; John White, *Art and Architecture in Italy, 1250–1400* (Harmondsworth: Penguin Books, 1966),

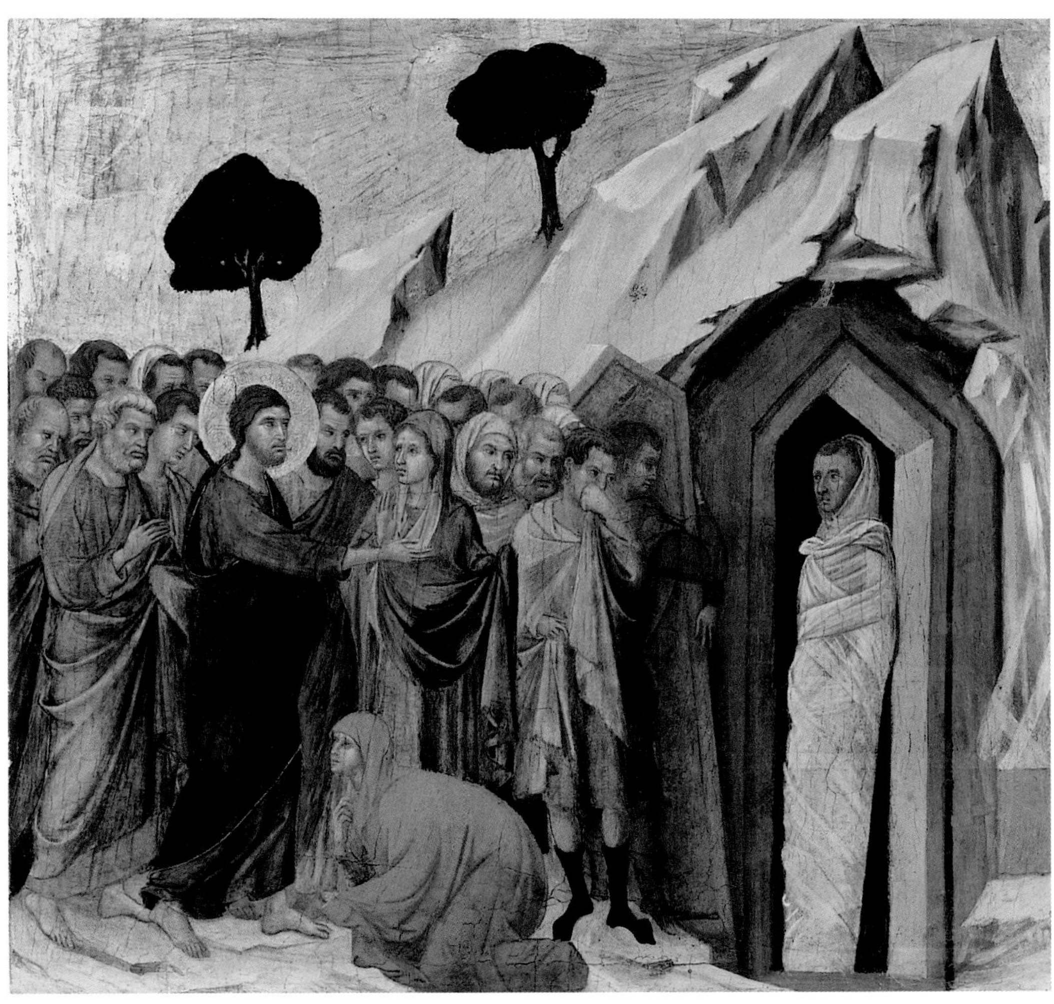

Fig. 151 Duccio di Buoninsegna: *Raising of Lazarus*. Kimbell Art Museum, Fort Worth, Texas, AP 1975.01.

153; Bernard Berenson, *Italian Pictures of the Renaissance: A List of the Principal Artists and Their Works with an Index of Places. Central Italian and North Italian Schools*, 3 vols. (London: Phaidon Press, 1968), 1:117; Enzo Carli, *I pittori senesi* (Siena: Monte dei Paschi di Siena, 1971), 56; Giulio Cattaneo and Edi Baccheschi, *L'opera completa di Duccio* (Milan: Rizzoli, 1972), 92, no. 87; Arno Preiser, *Das Entstehen und die Entwicklung der Predella in der italienischen Malerei* (Hildesheim and New York: Olms, 1973), 72-73, 78; John White, "Measurements, Design and Carpentry in Duccio's *Maestà*," *Art Bulletin* 55 (1973): 566; "A Duccio for the Kimbell Art Museum," *Apollo* 102 (1975): 224; James H. Stubblebine, "The Back Predella of Duccio's *Maestà*," in *Studies in Late Medieval and Renaissance Painting in Honor of Millard Meiss*, ed. Irving Lavin and John Plummer, 2 vols. (New York: New York University Press, 1977), 1:430, 435-36; John White, *Duccio: Tuscan Art and the Medieval Workshop* (London: Thames and Hudson, 1979), 122, 181 n. 4; Florens Deuchler, "Duccio Doctus: New Readings for the *Maestà*," *Art Bulletin* 61 (1979): 545-46; James H. Stubblebine, *Duccio di Buoninsegna and His School*, 2 vols. (Princeton: Princeton University Press, 1979), 1:31-33, 36-37; Enzo Carli, *La pittura senese del Trecento* (Milan: Electa, 1981), 49; Kimbell Art Museum, *Handbook of the Collection* (Fort Worth: Kimbell Art Foundation, 1981), 130; Florens Deuchler, *Duccio* (Milan: Electa, 1984), 66, 67, 139; Denys Sutton, "Aspects of British Collecting. Part IV," *Apollo* 122 (1985): 123; Ruth Wilkins Sullivan, "The Anointing in Bethany and Other Affirmations of Christ's Divinity in Duccio's Back Predella," *Art Bulletin* 67 (1985): 33-36, 47-48; *In Pursuit of Quality: The Kimbell Art Museum* (Fort Worth: Kimbell Art Museum, 1987), 146; Martin Davies and Dillian Gordon, *The Early Italian Schools before 1400* (London: National Gallery Publications, National Gallery, 1988), 18, 21; Ruth Wilkins Sullivan, "Duccio's *Raising of Lazarus* Reexamined," *Art Bulletin* 70 (1988): 374-87; Giovanna Ragionieri, *Duccio: Catalogo completo dei dipinti* (Florence: Cantini, 1989), 110; David Bromford, Jill Dunkerton, Dillian Gordon, et al., *Art in the Making: Italian Painting before 1400* (London: National Gallery, 1989), 72, 83, 86; Miklòs Boskovits, *Early Italian Painting, 1290–1470: The Thyssen-Bornemisza Collection* (London: Sotheby's Publications, 1990), 72-76; Andrea Weber, *Duccio di Buoninsegna about 1255–1319* (Cologne: Könemann, 1997), 67, no. 60; Enzo Carli, *Duccio* (Milan: Electa, 1999), 26; Luciano Bellosi, *Duccio, The Maestà* (New York: Thames and Hudson, 1999), 19.

MANTEGNA, ANDREA, C. 1431–1506; PADUAN

Holy Family with St. Elizabeth and the Infant St. John the Baptist (AP 1987.04) 62.9 x 51.3 CM, DISTEMPER AND OIL ON CANVAS

FORT WORTH, TEXAS. KIMBELL ART MUSEUM

Edmund P. Pillsbury and William Jordan (1987) compared the style and technique of this work with those in Mantegna's *Madonna della Vittoria* (Louvre, Paris; 369) and his *Holy Family* (Gemäldegalerie, Dresden; 51), both painted in the 1490s. Keith Christiansen (in Martineau and Boorsch 1992) argued for an earlier date, c. 1485–1488, before the artist's trip to Rome; this is the date endorsed by the Museum. In Christiansen's opinion, the Kimbell picture is contemporary with the inception of work on Mantegna's *Triumphs*, c. 1485–1494, and is one of his earliest devotional compositions with the Madonna and Child flanked by two or more saints. Furthermore, Christiansen proposed it as the painting commissioned by Eleonora of Aragon mentioned in a letter from Francesco Gonzaga in 1485; others have identified Eleonora's commission with the Dresden *Holy Family*. Umberto Baldini (1997) considered the Kimbell picture to be a late work by the artist.

PROVENANCE

Private collection, Marseilles, by 1909; Sotheby's, Monte Carlo, June 21, 1986, lot 17; private collection, Europe; Kimbell Art Museum, acquired 1987

BIBLIOGRAPHY

Tableaux anciens, du XIXe siècle (Monte Carlo: Sotheby's, 1986), no. 17, app. A; Edmund P. Pillsbury and William Jordan, "Recent Acquisitions III: The Kimbell Art Museum," *Burlington Magazine* 129 (1987): 767-76; *In Pursuit of Quality: The Kimbell Art Museum* (Fort Worth: Kimbell Art Museum, 1989), 162; Jane Martineau and Suzanne Boorsch, eds., *Andrea Mantegna* (Milan: Electa, 1992), 225, no. 51; Umberto Baldini, *Andrea Mantegna* (Florence: Edizioni d'Arte Il Fiorino, 1997), 184, 252; Alberta De Nicolò Salmazo, *Mantegna* (Milan: Electa, 1997), 148, no. 15; Paolo Biscottini, *Andrea Mantegna: Sacra famiglia con sant'Elisabetta e san Giovannino* (Milan: Museo diocesano, 2006).

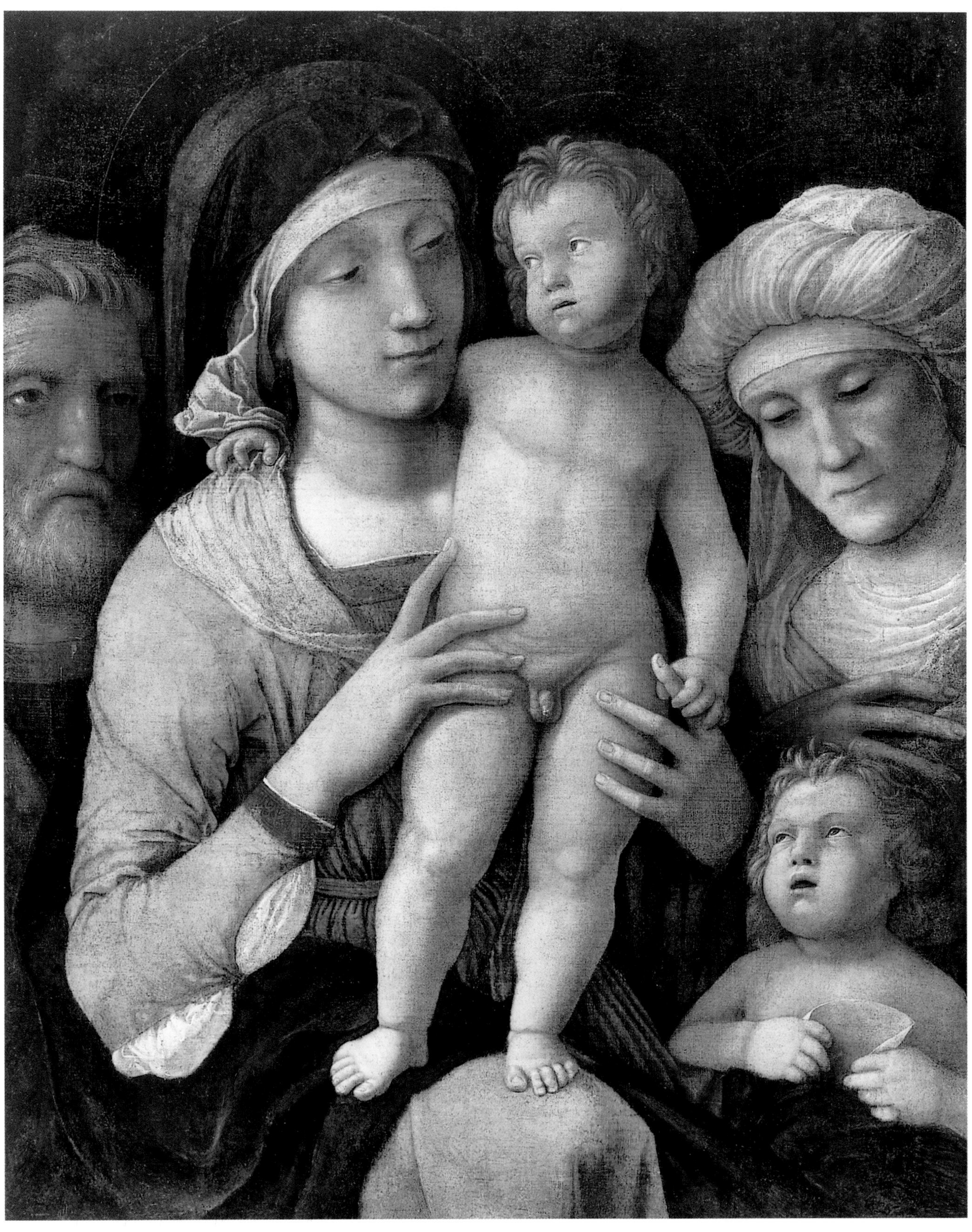

Fig. 152 Andrea Mantegna: *Holy Family with St. Elizabeth and the Infant St. John the Baptist.* Kimbell Art Museum, Fort Worth, Texas, AP 1987.04.

ROBERTI, ERCOLE DE', C. 1455–1496; FERRARESE

Brutus and Portia (AP 1986.05) 48.7 X 34.3 CM, TEMPERA ON PANEL

FORT WORTH, TEXAS. KIMBELL ART MUSEUM

The panel was one of a series of paintings depicting virtuous Roman women, which also included the *Wife of Hasdrubal and Her Children* (National Gallery of Art, Washington, D.C.; 1945) and the *Death of Lucrezia* (Galleria Estense, Modena; 178). The group served either as *spalliere* or decorated a large piece of furniture. It has been associated with *cassoni* made for Isabella d'Este on the occasion of her marriage. Joseph Manca (1986; 1992), however, proposed that the pictures most likely were made for Roberti's patroness, Eleonora of Aragon, who had a personal interest in the theme of famous women; the works may have been created for one of the smaller rooms in the Castello Vecchio in Ferrara, which Roberti decorated for the duchess between 1489 and 1493. Ruth Wilkins Sullivan (1994) reaffirmed this provenance, arguing that the series illustrated the motto of King Ferrante of Naples, Eleonora's father: "I prefer death to dishonor." Although several scholars have assigned *Brutus and Portia* to Ercole's shop, it has generally been considered an autograph work. In Manca's opinion (1992), the style of the work resembles that of the artist's *Ascent to Calvary* from the San Giovanni in Monte predella of 1482, but the Kimbell painting should be dated several years later. The Museum dates the work c. 1490.

The original textual source for the story, which was popularized by Boccaccio's *De Claris Mulieribus* (*Concerning Famous Women*) of c. 1360–1374, is Plutarch's *Life of Brutus* (xiii, 3-11). Portia displays a self-inflicted wound on her foot, rather than on her thigh as sources described, to her husband Brutus, in order to convince him that she is worthy of participating in his conspiracy against Julius Caesar; Brutus's reaction, as indicated in the panel, is displeasure.

PROVENANCE

John Hope Barton, Stapleton Park, Yorkshire, by 1868; Sir Herbert Cook, Bart., Doughty House, Richmond, Surrey, acquired 1920; Fitzwilliam Museum, Cambridge (on loan), late 1940s; Francis Cook, St. Aubin (Jersey), Channel Islands; Kimbell Art Museum, acquired 1986

BIBLIOGRAPHY

National Exhibition of Works of Art at Leeds 1868: Official Catalogue (Leeds: Edward Baines and Sons, 1868), 38, no. 514; Maurice W. Brockwell, "Exposition des Beaux-Arts du Burlington Club," *Gazette des Beaux-Art; Chronique des Arts* 2 (31 January 1921): 13-14; Roger Fry, "Pictures at the Burlington Fine Arts Club," *Burlington Magazine* 38 (1921): 137-38; William G. Constable, ed., *Exhibition of Italian Art, 1200–1900* (London: Royal Academy of Arts, 1930), 134, no. 213; William G. Constable, "Dipinti di raccolte inglesi alla mostra d'arte italiana a Londra," *Dedalo* 10 (1930): 730; David L. Balniel and Kenneth Clark, eds., *A Commemorative Catalogue of the Exhibition of Italian Art Held in the Galleries of the Royal Academy, Burlington House, London, January–March, 1930*, 2 vols. (London: Oxford University Press, 1931), 1:74, no. 213; Maurice W. Brockwell, *Abridged Catalogue of the Pictures at Doughty House, Richmond, Surrey in the Collection of Sir Herbert Cook, Bart.* (London: Heinemann, 1932), 23-25; *Catalogo della esposizione della pittura ferrarese del Rinascimento* (Venice: C. Ferrari, 1933), 54; Roberto Longhi, *Officina ferrarese* (Rome: Edizioni d'Italia, 1934), 58; Bernard Berenson, *Pitture italiane del Rinascimento* (Milan: U. Hoepli, 1936), 417; Sergio Ortolani, *Cosmè Tura, Francesco del Cossa, Ercole de' Roberti* (Milan: U. Hoepli, 1941), 189; Benedict Nicolson, *The Painters of Ferrara: Cosmè Tura, Francesco del Cossa, Ercole de' Roberti, and Others* (London: Elek, 1950), 15, 20; Mario Salmi, *Ercole de' Roberti* (Milan: Silvana editoriale d'arte, 1960), 43; Rosemarie Molajoli, *L'opera completa di Cosmè Tura e i grandi pittori ferraresi del suo tempo: Francesco Cossa e Ercole de' Roberti* (Milan: Rizzoli, 1974), 98, no. 120; Silla Zamboni, *Pittori di Ercole I d'Este* (Milan: Silvana, 1975), 13, 54-55; Fern Rusk Shapley, *Catalogue of the Italian Paintings* (Washington, D.C.: National Gallery of Art, 1979), 408-10; Andrea Bacchi, "Tre artisti nella Bologna dei Bentivoglio: Appunti su un mostra," *Antichità Viva* 87 (1986): 289; Joseph Manca, "The Life and Art of Ercole de' Roberti" (Ph.D. diss., Columbia University, 1986), 175-78, 292-96; Catherine Turrill, "Ercole de' Roberti's Altarpieces for the Lateran Canons" (Ph.D. diss., University of Delaware, 1986), 323-24; Edmund P. Pillsbury and William Jordan, "Recent Painting Acquisitions—III: The Kimbell Art Museum," *Burlington Magazine* 129 (1987): 768-69; *In Pursuit of Quality: The Kimbell Art Museum* (Fort Worth: Kimbell Art Museum, 1987), 164; Joseph Manca, *The Art of Ercole de' Roberti* (Cambridge: Cambridge University Press, 1992), 59-61, 136-37, cat. 17b; Andrea De Marchi, "Un geniale anacronista, nel solco di Ercole,"

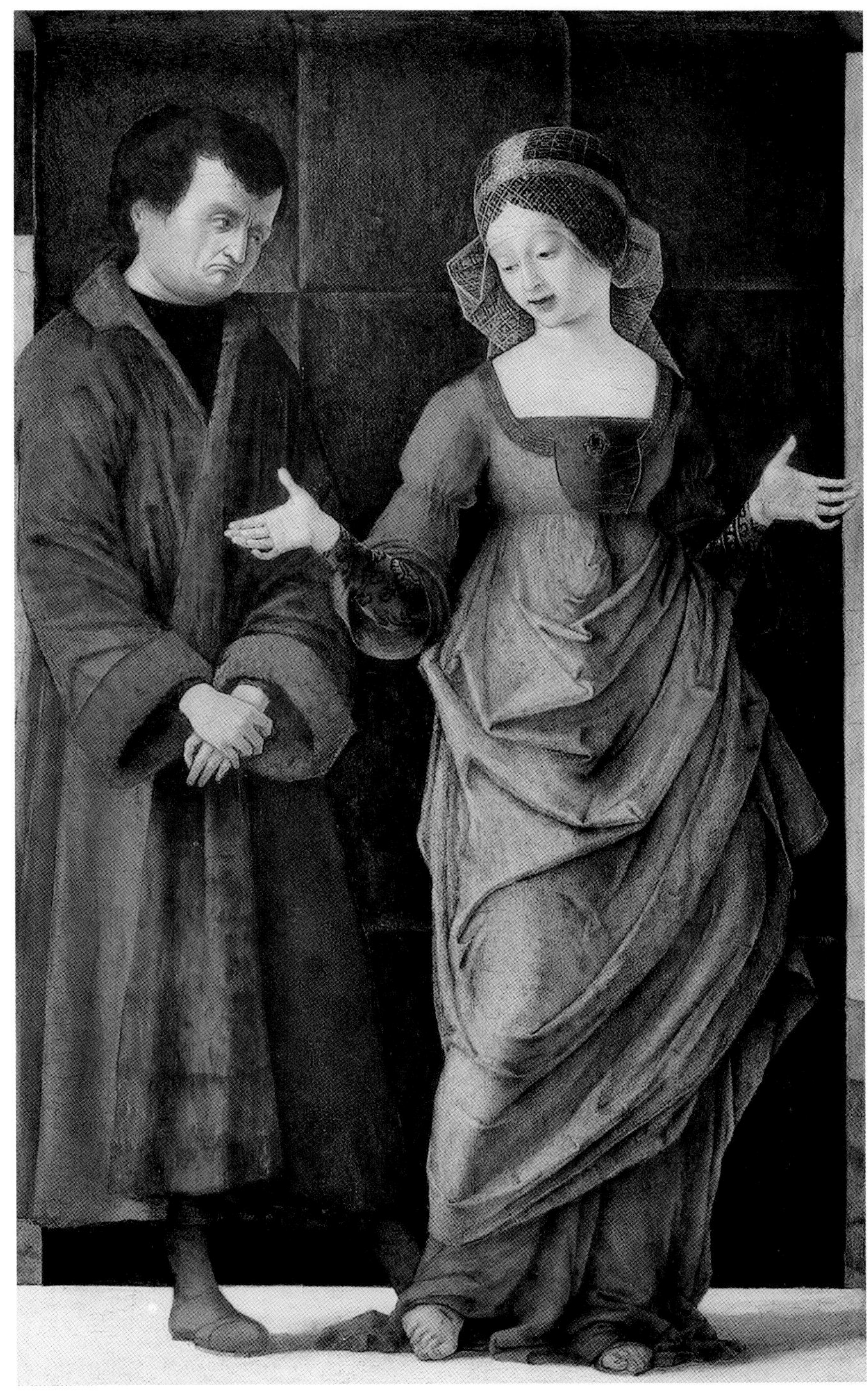

Fig. 153 Ercole de' Roberti: *Brutus and Portia*. Kimbell Art Museum, Fort Worth, Texas, AP 1986.05.

Annale della Scuola Normale Superiore di Pisa 22 (1992): 1069; Ruth Wilkins Sullivan, "Three Ferrarese Panels on the Theme of 'Death Rather than Dishonor,' and the Neapolitan Connection," *Zeitschrift für Kunstgeschichte* 57 (1994): 601-25; Monica Molteni, *Ercole de' Roberti* (Milan: Silvana, 1995), 176-77, no. 40; Denise Allen and Luke Syson, *Ercole de' Roberti: The Renaissance in Ferrara* (London: Burlington Magazine, 1999), xxxii–xxxiii; Luke Syson and Dora Thornton, *Objects of Virtue, Art in Renaissance Italy* (London: British Museum Press, 2001), 19-20; Miklòs Boskovits and David Alan Brown et al., *Italian Paintings of the Fifteenth Century* (Washington, D.C.: National Gallery of Art, 2003), 608; Andrea Bayer, ed., *Art and Love in Renaissance Italy* (New York: Metropolitan Museum of Art; New Haven: Yale University Press, 2008), 309-11, no. 142.

ALAMANNO, PIETRO, C. 1430–1497/8; MARCHIGIAN

Madonna and Child with Saints (61.273) 165.1 X 199.4 CM (INCLUDING FRAME), TEMPERA ON PANEL

GREENVILLE, SOUTH CAROLINA. BOB JONES UNIVERSITY MUSEUM & GALLERY

The artist's signature, "PETRVS ALEMANVS PINXIT," is inscribed at the bottom of the central panel. The altarpiece is largely intact, lacking only the predella, which must have been lost when the work was removed from San Giacomo Apostolo, the church for which it was created. Raimond van Marle (1934) noted its absence. The composition derives from the work of Carlo Crivelli (c. 1430–1495 [?]), although Alamanno simplified the imagery; the Madonna and Child resemble the same figures in Crivelli's altarpiece of the *Madonna and Child with Four Music-Making Angels* (Galleria Nazionale delle Marche, Urbino; 1990 DE225). The Greenville work's excellence of execution suggests that it was created between 1475 and 1483, when Alamanno was at the height of his career.

St. Stephen and St. James flank the Virgin on her right, St. John the Evangelist and St. Sebastian on her left; the Man of Sorrows appears in the pinnacle above. The inclusion of James in a position of honor to the Christ Child's right was prompted by the dedication of San Giacomo Apostolo. The apple on the Virgin's throne alludes to the original sin of mankind that was redeemed by the incarnation and sacrifice of Christ.

PROVENANCE

San Giacomo Apostolo, Ascoli, to c. 1907; Edmond Foulc and Duval Foulc, Paris, 1927; private collection, New York, by 1934; Wildenstein & Co., New York, 1962; Bob Jones University Museum & Gallery (Bob Jones University Collection), acquired 1962

BIBLIOGRAPHY

Giambattista Carducci, *Su le memorie e i monumenti di Ascoli nel Piceno* (Fermo: Saverio Del-Monte, 1853), 172; "Alamanno, Pietro," in Ulrich Thieme and Felix Becker, eds., *Allgemeines Lexikon der bildenden Künstler von der Antike bis zur Gegenwart*, 37 vols. (Leipzig: E. A. Seemann, 1907), 1:167; Joseph A. Crowe and Giovanni B. Cavalcaselle, *A History of Painting in North Italy, Venice, Padua, Vicenza, Verona, Ferrara, Milan, Friuli, Brescia, from the Fourteenth to the Sixteenth Century*, 3 vols., ed. Tancred Borenius (New York: Charles Scribner's Sons, 1912), 1:98 n. 5; Henri Leman, *La Collection Foulc, objets d'art du Moyen Âge et de la Renaissance*, 2 vols. (Paris: Les Beaux-arts, 1927), 1:10-11, no. 3; Luigi Serra, *L'arte nelle Marche: Il periodo del Rinascimento* (Rome: Arti grafiche evaristo armani, 1934), 402; Raimond van Marle, *The Development of the Italian Schools of Painting*, vol. 15, *The Renaissance Painters of Central and Southern Italy* (The Hague: M. Nijhoff, 1934), 89-90; *Religious Art: An Exhibition of Fourteenth, Fifteenth, Sixteenth, and Seventeeth Century Paintings* (Baltimore: Baltimore Museum of Art, 1938), no. 12; Bernard Berenson, *Italian Pictures of the Renaissance: A List of the Principal Artists and Their Works with an Index of Places. Venetian School*, 2 vols. (New York: Phaidon, 1957), 1:3; Alfred Scharf, *The Bob Jones University Collection of Religious Paintings*, vol. 1, *Italian and French Paintings* (Greenville, S.C.: Bob Jones University, 1962), 37; Henry R. Hope, "The Bob Jones University Religious Art Collection," *Art Journal* 25 (1965–1966): 156; Pietro Zampetti, *Paintings from the Marches: Gentile to Raphael* (London: Phaidon, 1971), 188; Burton B. Fredericksen and Federico Zeri, *Census of Pre-Nineteenth-Century Italian Paintings in North American Public Collections* (Cambridge, Mass.: Harvard University Press, 1972), 3, 583; D. Stephen Pepper, *Bob Jones University Collection of Religious Art: Italian Paintings* (Greenville, S.C.: Bob Jones University, 1984), 3-4; Pietro Zampetti, *Pittura nelle Marche*, vol. 1, *Dalle origini al primo Rinascimento* (Florence: Nardini, 1988), 340.

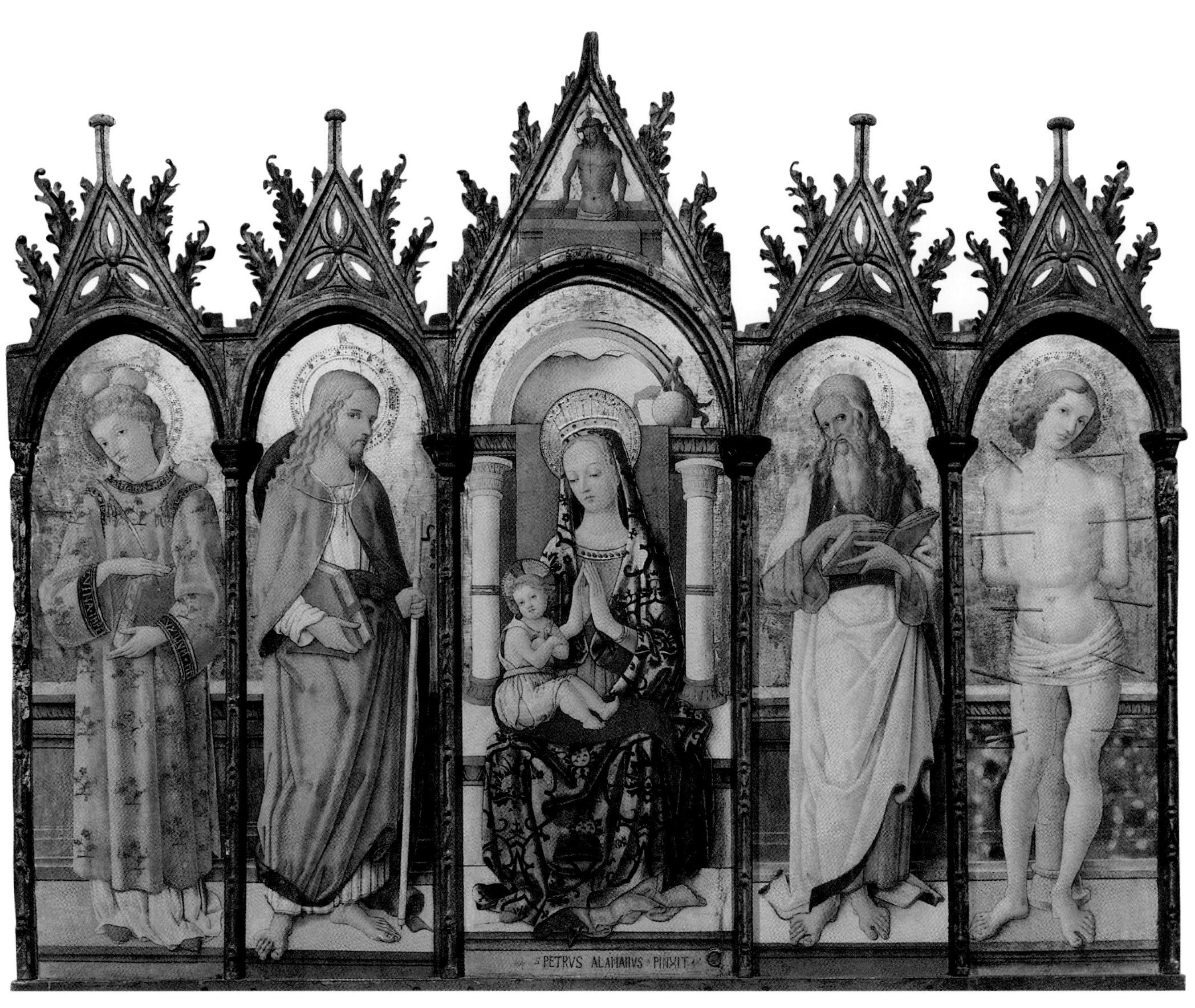

Fig. 154 Pietro Alamanno: *Madonna and Child with Saints*. Bob Jones University Museum & Gallery, Greenville, South Carolina, 61.273.

BERGAMASQUE SCHOOL, LATE FIFTEENTH CENTURY

Annunciation (51.17) 188.6 x 184.2 CM, TEMPERA ON PANEL

GREENVILLE, SOUTH CAROLINA. BOB JONES UNIVERSITY MUSEUM & GALLERY

Hans Tietze and Erica Tietze-Conrat (1954) attributed this large altarpiece to an early-sixteenth-century central Italian painter. Federico Zeri (cited in Scharf 1962) ascribed the work to the little-known Constantino Zelli from Viterbo (active 1501–1517). Mauro Natale (cited in Pepper 1984) argued for the anonymous late-fifteenth-century Bergamasque painter responsible for the *Adoration of the Christ Child with St. Sebastian and St. Roch* (Bagatti-Valsecchi Collection, Milan) and the *Nativity* (parish church, Piario [Bergamo]), the latter dated 1496 (?). Natale (1991) subsequently assigned the painting to the Piedmontese Master of Castelnuovo Scrivia (active 1509–1517), whose eponymous work is the *Man of Sorrows with St. Anthony Abbot and St. Christopher* (San Ignazio, Castelnuovo Scrivia).

The color and style of the habits worn by the two monks and their abbot identify them as Benedictines or Augustinians, not Dominicans as noted by D. Stephen Pepper (1984). The depiction of them as witnesses to the Annunciation suggests that the painting was commissioned as a votive offering for their monastery. The setting and the dog to the lower left appear to derive from Albrecht Dürer's prints of the *Annunciation* and *Visitation* in the *Life of the Virgin* series of 1510.

PROVENANCE

Otto Kahn, New York; Hammer Galleries, New York; Bob Jones University Museum & Gallery (Bob Jones University Collection), acquired 1951

BIBLIOGRAPHY

Hans Tietze and Erica Tietze-Conrat, *The Bob Jones University Collection of Religious Paintings* (Greenville, S.C.: Bob Jones University, 1954), 40; Alfred Scharf, *The Bob Jones University Collection of Religious Paintings*, vol. 1, *Italian and French Paintings* (Greenville, S.C.: Bob Jones University, 1962), 162; Burton B. Fredericksen and Federico Zeri, *Census of Pre-Nineteenth-Century Italian Paintings in North American Public Collections* (Cambridge, Mass.: Harvard University Press, 1972), 213, 582; D. Stephen Pepper, *Bob Jones University Collection of Religious Art: Italian Paintings* (Greenville, S.C.: Bob Jones University, 1984), 28; Maura Natale, ed., *Pittura italiana dal '300 al '500* (Milan: G. Mondadori, 1991), 11, 20 n. 6.

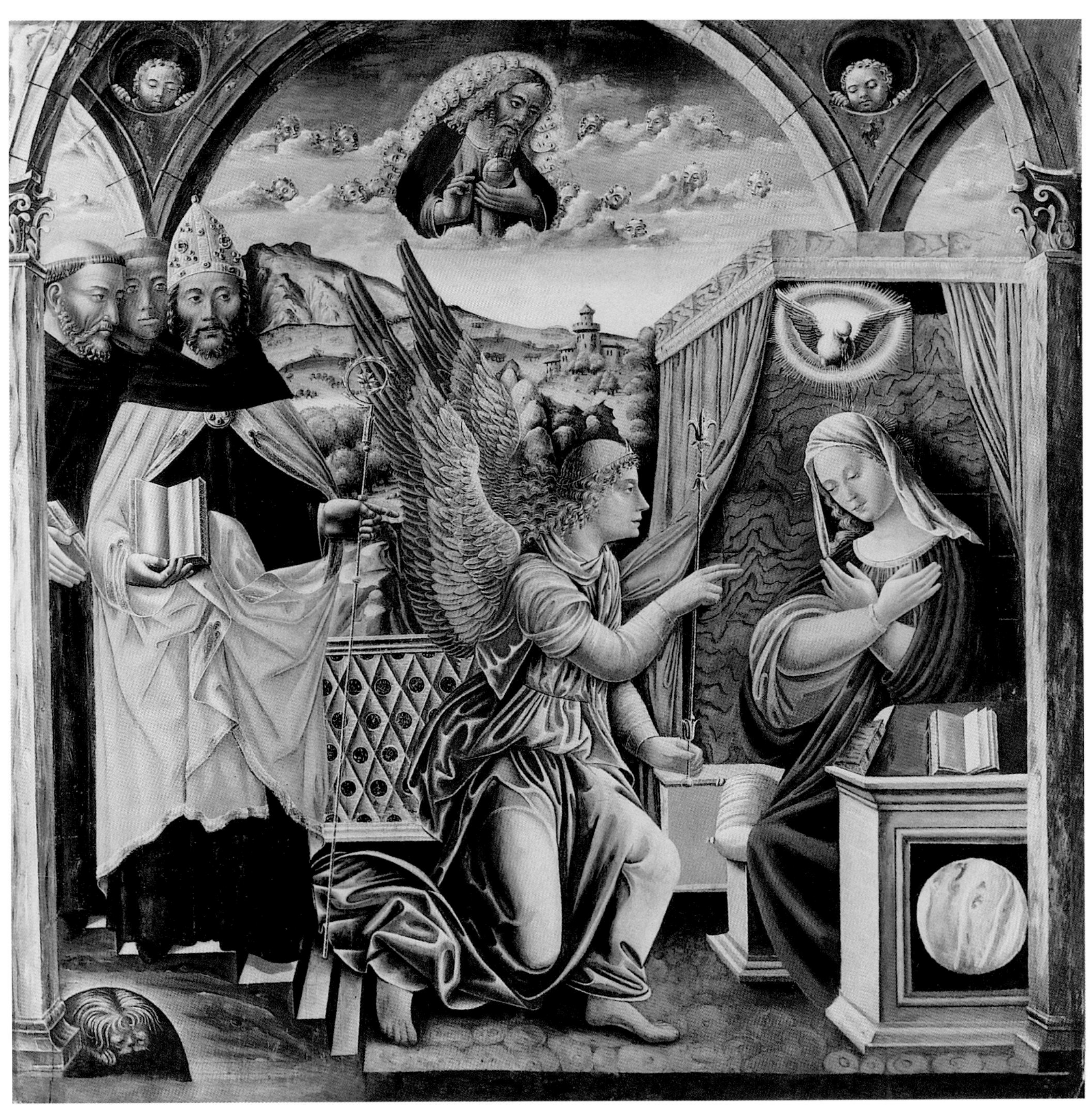

Fig. 155 Bergamasque School, late fifteenth century: *Annunciation*. Bob Jones University Museum & Gallery, Greenville, South Carolina, 51.17.

BICCI DI LORENZO, 1373–1452; FLORENTINE

Madonna and Child with St. Anne and Angels (57.111) 93 x 63.8 CM, TEMPERA ON PANEL

GREENVILLE, SOUTH CAROLINA. BOB JONES UNIVERSITY MUSEUM & GALLERY

Devotional images such as this, depicting St. Anne enthroned with the Madonna and Child, are sometimes known by the descriptive phrases *Sant'Anna Metterza* and *Annaselbdritt* (St. Anne triplicated), because three generations are present. The image symbolizes the genealogy of the Incarnation and emphasizes Anne's role as progenitrix, as well as the miraculous births of Mary and Christ. The nursing Virgin in the Greenville work, a feature unique in the various representations of the subject, calls attention to the humanity of Christ.

The painting is one of a handful of representations of *Sant'Anna Metterza* produced in Tuscany from the mid-fourteenth century through the early sixteenth century. The original location of this votive image is unknown, but it was probably produced for a venue in Florence, as St. Anne was considered a patron saint of the city. The main features of the composition—the poses and placements of the Madonna and St. Anne, the brocaded cloth of honor, and the foreshortened throne—obviously derive from Masolino and Masaccio's *St. Anne Metterza* (Uffizi, Florence; 8386) of c. 1424–1425, which presumably was painted for the Florentine church of Sant'Ambrogio.

PROVENANCE

Polizzo, Paris; Robert Lehman, New York; Julius Weitzner, New York; Bob Jones University Museum & Gallery (Bob Jones University Collection), acquired 1957

BIBLIOGRAPHY

Roberto Longhi, "Fatti di Masolino e di Masaccio," *Critica d'Arte* 5 (1940): 153; Alfred Scharf, *The Bob Jones University Collection of Religious Paintings*, vol. 1, *Italian and French Paintings* (Greenville, S.C.: Bob Jones University, 1962), 42; Bernard Berenson, *Italian Pictures of the Renaissance: A List of the Principal Artists and Their Works with an Index of Places. Florentine School*, 2 vols. (London: Phaidon Press, 1963), 1:29; Burton B. Fredericksen and Federico Zeri, *Census of Pre-Nineteenth-Century Italian Paintings in North American Public Collections* (Cambridge, Mass.: Harvard University Press, 1972), 28, 582; Bruce Cole, *Masaccio and the Art of Early Renaissance Florence* (Bloomington: Indiana University Press, 1980), 194-95; D. Stephen Pepper, *Bob Jones University Collection of Religious Art: Italian Paintings* (Greenville, S.C.: Bob Jones University, 1984), 6-7; Timothy Verdon, "La Sant'Anna Metterza: Riflessioni, domande, ipotesi," *Gli Uffizi. Studi e Ricerche* 5 (1984): 33, 36.

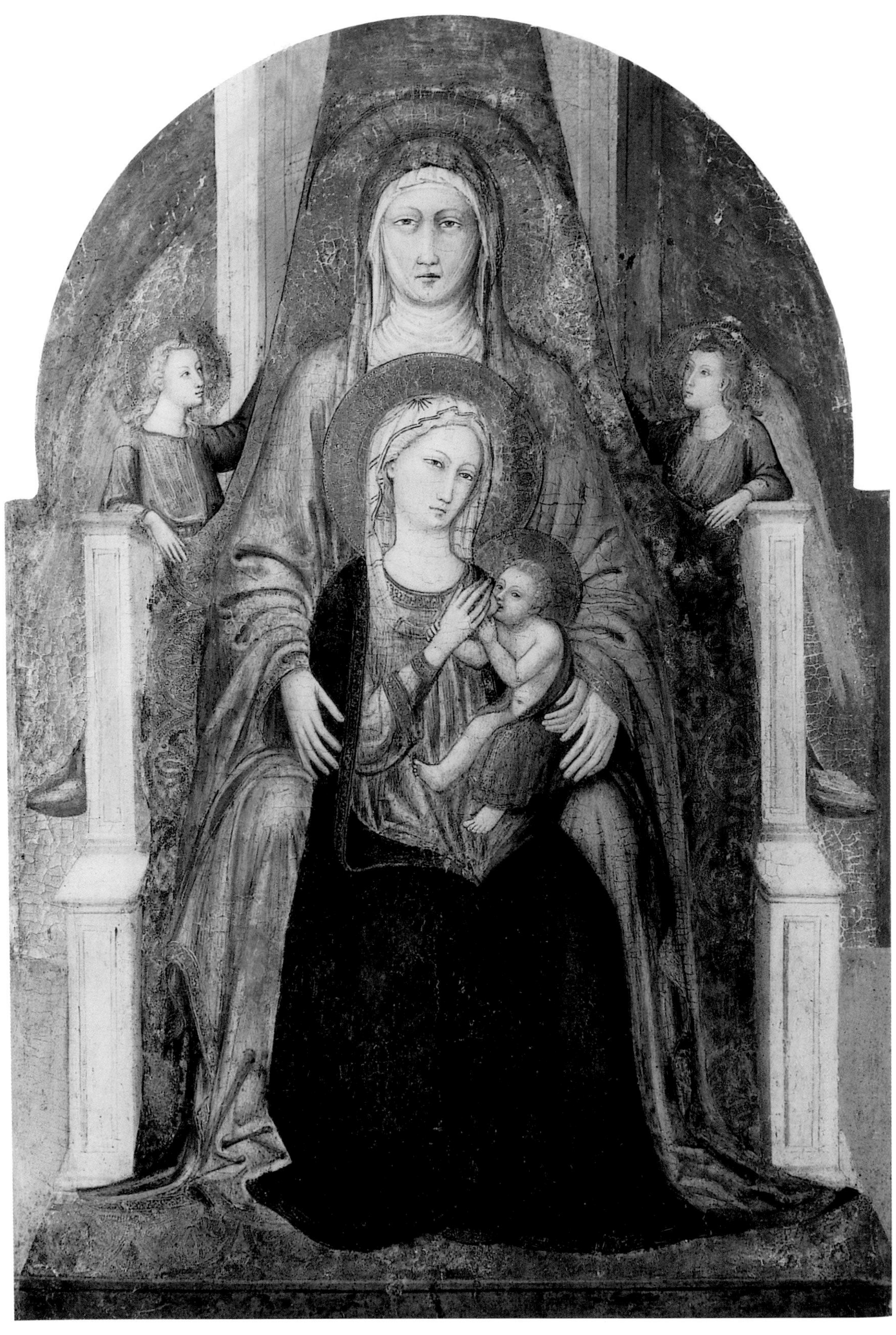

Fig. 156 Bicci di Lorenzo: *Madonna and Child with St. Anne and Angels*. Bob Jones University Museum & Gallery, Greenville, South Carolina, 57.111.

BICCI DI LORENZO, 1373–1452; FLORENTINE

Madonna and Child with St. John the Baptist and St. James (51.11) 80.6 X 43.8 CM, TEMPERA ON PANEL

GREENVILLE, SOUTH CAROLINA. BOB JONES UNIVERSITY MUSEUM & GALLERY

This small devotional altarpiece, the frame of which is original, is a work of high quality that dates to the period 1423–1433, according to Miklòs Boskovits (1990). The imagery and style are comparable to those of Bicci di Lorenzo's *Madonna and Child Enthroned with Simone Guiducci di Specchio* (Museo della Collegiata, Empoli; 18), dated 1423.

The Virgin, whose halo is inscribed "AVE MARIA" ("Hail Mary"), is depicted as the Madonna of Humility, suspended in heaven within a *mandorla* of cherubim and seraphim. The model for this image, emphasizing both the Virgin's humility and divinity, appears to have been a lost painting by Orcagna (1315/20–1368) or Jacopo di Cione (1320/30–before 1400), dating to the third quarter of the fourteenth century. The goldfinch for which the Christ Child reaches symbolizes the Passion.

PROVENANCE

Private collection, Florence; Pedulli Galleries, Florence; Grosvenor Backus, Englewood, N.J.; Aquavella Galleries, New York; Bob Jones University Museum & Gallery (Bob Jones University Collection), acquired 1951

BIBLIOGRAPHY

Mary Logan Berenson, "Opere inedite di Bicci di Lorenzo," *Rassegna d'Arte* 10 (1915): 212-13; Raimond van Marle, *The Development of the Italian Schools of Painting*, vol. 9, *Late Gothic Painting in Tuscany* (The Hague: M. Nijhoff, 1927), 25; Alfred Scharf, *The Bob Jones University Collection of Religious Paintings*, vol. 1, *Italian and French Paintings* (Greenville, S.C.: Bob Jones University, 1962), 29; Bernard Berenson, *Italian Pictures of the Renaissance: A List of the Principal Artists and Their Works with an Index of Places. Florentine School*, 2 vols. (London: Phaidon Press, 1963), 1:29; Brigitte Klesse, *Seidenstoffe in der italienischen Malerei des vierzehnten Jahrhunderts* (Bern: Stämpfli, 1967), 480, no. 515; Burton B. Fredericksen and Federico Zeri, *Census of Pre-Nineteenth-Century Italian Paintings in North American Public Collections* (Cambridge, Mass.: Harvard University Press, 1972), 28, 582; D. Stephen Pepper, *Bob Jones University Collection of Religious Art: Italian Paintings* (Greenville, S.C.: Bob Jones University, 1984), 5-6; Miklòs Boskovits, *Early Italian Painting, 1290–1470: The Thyssen-Bornemisza Collection* (London: Sotheby's Publications, 1990), 46 n. 9.

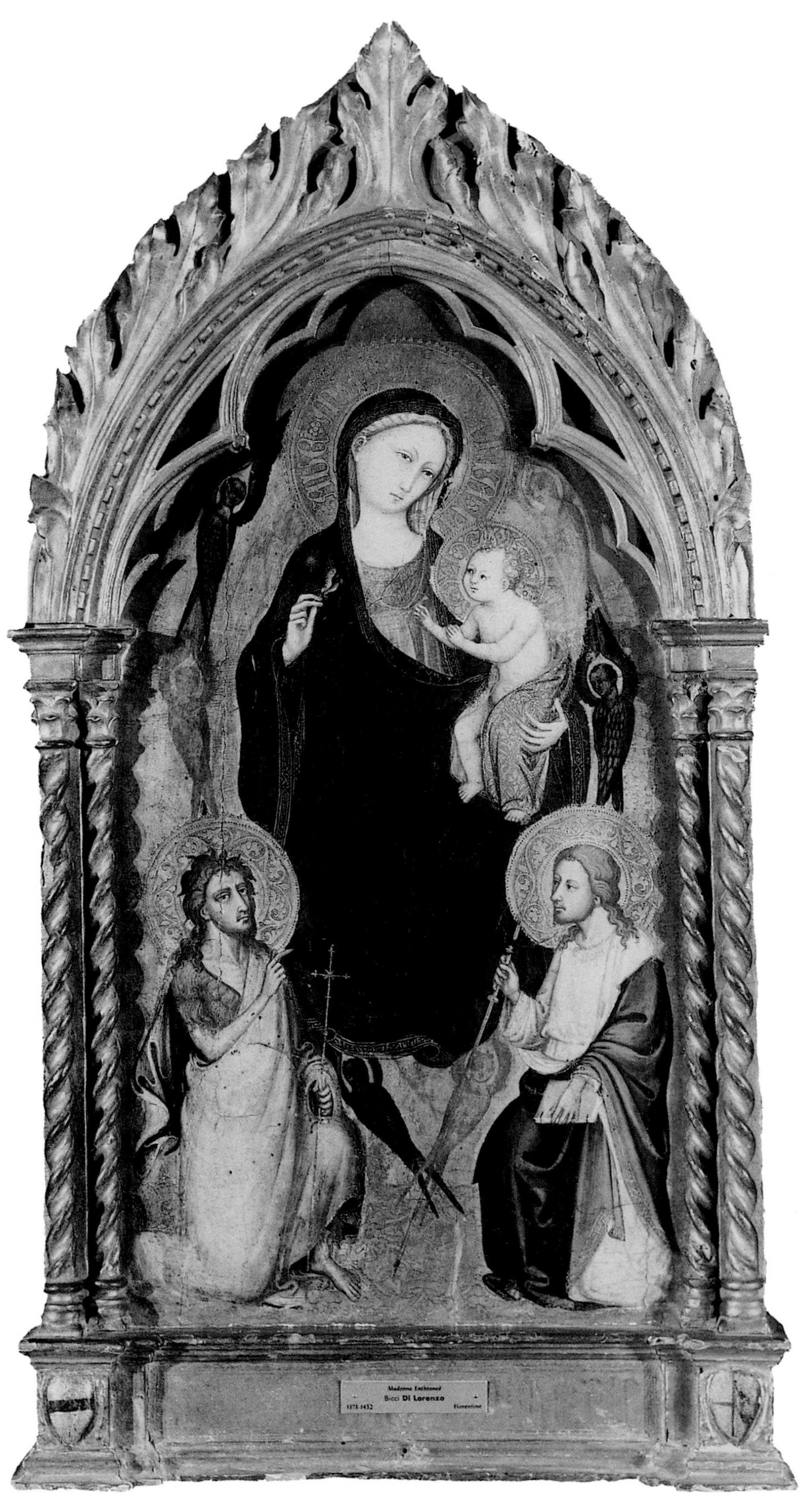

Fig. 157 Bicci di Lorenzo: *Madonna and Child with St. John the Baptist and St. James*. Bob Jones University Museum & Gallery, Greenville, South Carolina, 51.11.

BOTTICELLI, SANDRO, 1444/5–1510; FLORENTINE

Madonna and Child with an Angel (52.23) 96.5 CM (DIAMETER), TEMPERA ON PANEL

GREENVILLE, SOUTH CAROLINA. BOB JONES UNIVERSITY MUSEUM & GALLERY

Except for its architectural setting, this work replicates almost exactly the *Madonna and Child with an Angel* (current location unknown; formerly, Lord D'Abernon, Stoke D'Abernon), attributed to Botticelli's workshop or school. Two other versions of the composition are recorded, one with an additional angel, both angels holding lilies, and an architectural setting (Chigi-Saracini Collection, Siena; 243), the other with the Baptist added at the right (current location unknown). Burton B. Fredericksen and Federico Zeri (1972) assigned the painting to Botticelli's school, shop, or studio, whereas D. Stephen Pepper (1984) and Everett P. Fahy (cited in Townsend 1994) considered the work autograph. Fahy dated the work c. 1490. The *tondo*, which probably hung in a domestic setting, typifies Botticelli's late devotional works.

Inscribed on the open book held by the angel is the *Magnificat*, the canticle praising the Virgin from Luke 1:46-55: "MAGNIFICAT: ANIMA MEA / DOMINVM ET" (verso); "DEPOSVIT POTENTES / DE SEDE" (recto) ("My soul magnifies the Lord, and my spirit rejoices in God my savior; . . . he has put down the mighty from their thrones").

PROVENANCE

Private collection, Florence (?), to c. 1890; Douglas Freshfield, England; Thomas Agnew and Sons, London, 1902; T. J. Blakeslee, London; Catholina Lambert Collection, Paterson, N.J.; American Art Association, New York, February 21, 1916, lot 329; Boice Thompson, Yonkers, N.Y.; Julius Weitzner, New York, 1952; Bob Jones University Museum & Gallery (Bob Jones University Collection), acquired 1952

BIBLIOGRAPHY

Illustrated Catalogue of the Valuable Paintings and Sculptures by Old and Modern Masters Forming the Famous Catholina Lambert Collection (New York: American Art Association, 1916), no. 329; Hans Tietze and Erica Tietze-Conrat, *The Bob Jones University Collection of Religious Paintings* (Greenville, S.C.: Bob Jones University, 1954), 30-31; Alfred Scharf, *The Bob Jones University Collection of Religious Paintings*, vol. 1, *Italian and French Paintings* (Greenville, S.C.: Bob Jones University, 1962), 44-45; Burton B. Fredericksen and Federico Zeri, *Census of Pre-Nineteenth-Century Italian Paintings in North American Public Collections* (Cambridge, Mass.: Harvard University Press, 1972), 34, 582; Ronald W. Lightbown, *Sandro Botticelli*, 2 vols. (Berkeley: University of California Press, 1978), 2:142; D. Stephen Pepper, *Bob Jones University Collection of Religious Art: Italian Paintings* (Greenville, S.C.: Bob Jones University, 1984), 7-8; Dario A. Covi, *The Inscription in Fifteenth-Century Florentine Painting* (New York: Garland Press, 1986), 527-38; Luciano Bellosi and Alessandro Angelini, eds., *Sassetta e i pittori toscani tra XIII e XV secolo* (Florence: Studio per edizioni scelte, 1986), 62; Richard P. Townsend, *Botticelli to Tiepolo: Three Centuries of Italian Painting from Bob Jones University* (Tulsa: Philbrook Museum of Art, 1994), 110.

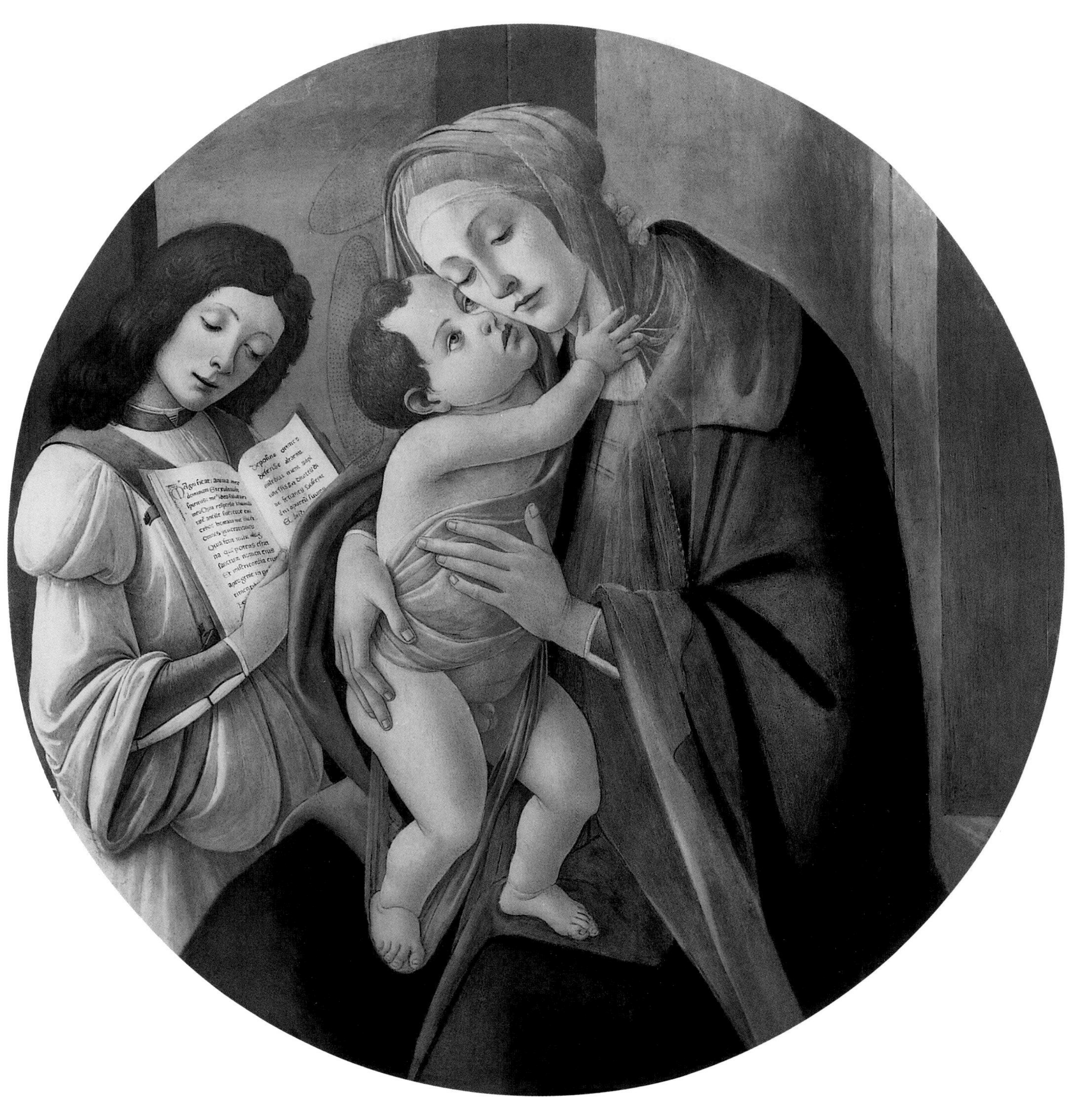

Fig. 158 Sandro Botticelli: *Madonna and Child with an Angel.* Bob Jones University Museum & Gallery, Greenville, South Carolina, 52.23.

CATENA, VINCENZO DI BIAGIO, C. 1470–1531; VENETIAN

Holy Family with St. John the Baptist (65.375.27) 111.8 X 157.5 CM, OIL ON CANVAS

GREENVILLE, SOUTH CAROLINA. BOB JONES UNIVERSITY MUSEUM & GALLERY

The painting is one of three related compositions by Catena that appear to derive from works by Jacopo Palma il vecchio (c. 1479–1528), in the opinion of Giles Robertson (1954), or from a lost work by Giovanni Bellini (1431/6–1516), according to Fritz Heinemann (1962). The other two versions, in the Norton Simon Museum, Pasadena (F.1965.1.014.P), and the Martin von Wagner Museum, Würzburg, omit the figure of the Baptist; they are of lesser merit and are probably workshop productions. Robertson and Heinemann (1962) initially doubted the autograph quality of the painting in Greenville, but they later changed their minds (Robertson, cited in Pepper 1984; Heinemann 1991). Robertson dated the work c. 1518/9.

The orb held by the Christ Child alludes to his role as Savior of the world. The quails symbolize divine providence, referring to the birds that God provided to the Israelites during their forty years in the wilderness, as Exodus 16 recounts.

PROVENANCE

Earl of Caledon, London; Christie, Manson & Woods, London, June 9, 1939, lot 9; William Permain, London; David Koetser, New York, 1965; Bob Jones University Museum & Gallery (Bob Jones University Collection), acquired 1965

BIBLIOGRAPHY

Gustav F. Waagen, *Galleries and Cabinets of Art in Great Britain* (London: John Murray, 1857), 147; Giles Robertson, *Vincenzo Catena* (Edinburgh: Edinburgh University Press, 1954), 73, app. 1, no. 5; Fritz Heinemann, *Giovanni Bellini e i Belliniani*, 3 vols. (Venice: Neri Pozza, 1962), 1:26, no. 100a; *Bob Jones University Collection of Religious Art, Fourteenth Anniversary, 1951–1965* (Greenville, S.C.: Bob Jones University, 1965); Donald and Kathleen Weil-Garris Posner, "More on the Bob Jones University Collection of Religious Art," *Art Journal* 26 (1966–1967): 145; Beneth A. Jones, *Bob Jones University Supplement to the Catalogue of the Art Collection: Paintings Acquired, 1963–1968* (Greenville, S.C.: Bob Jones University, 1968), 12; Burton B. Fredericksen and Federico Zeri, *Census of Pre-Nineteenth-Century Italian Paintings in North American Public Collections* (Cambridge, Mass.: Harvard University Press, 1972), 49, 583; D. Stephen Pepper, *Bob Jones University Collection of Religious Art: Italian Paintings* (Greenville, S.C.: Bob Jones University, 1984), 41; Fritz Heinemann, *Giovanni Bellini e i Belliniani*, 3 vols. (Venice: Neri Pozza, 1991), 3:12, no. 100a, 103; Richard P. Townsend, *Botticelli to Tiepolo: Three Centuries of Italian Painting from Bob Jones University* (Tulsa: Philbrook Museum of Art, 1994), 124-25.

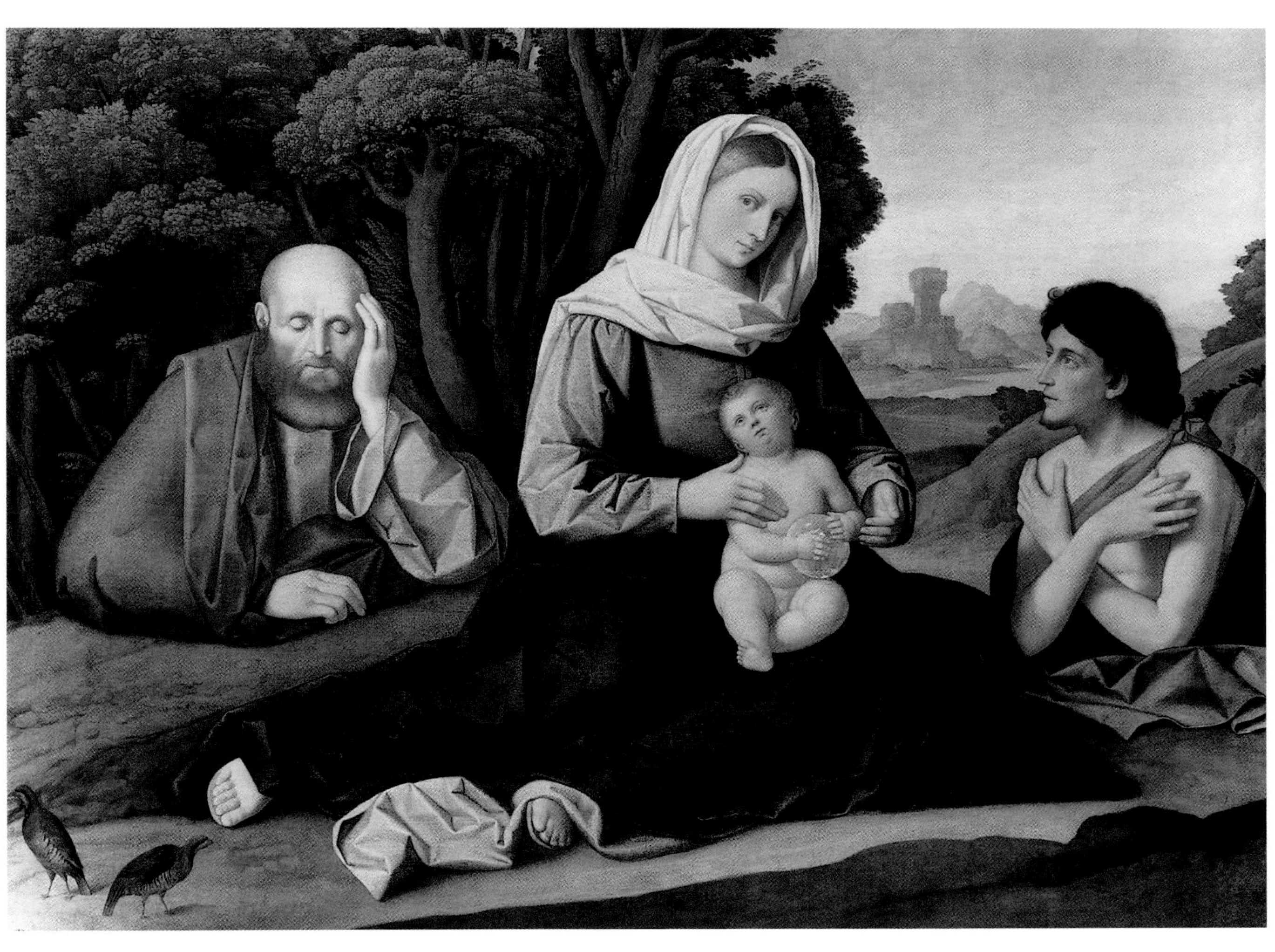

Fig. 159 Vincenzo di Biagio Catena: *Holy Family with St. John the Baptist*. Bob Jones University Museum & Gallery, Greenville, South Carolina, 65.375.27.

FIORENZO DI LORENZO, C. 1445–C. 1525; UMBRIAN

Christ on the Cross (61.265) 62.2 X 42.2 CM, OIL ON PANEL

GREENVILLE, SOUTH CAROLINA. BOB JONES UNIVERSITY MUSEUM & GALLERY

The painting was considered similar in style to Fiorenzo's *Crucifixion with St. Jerome and St. Christopher* (Borghese Gallery, Rome; 377) by D. Stephen Pepper (1984). He dated it early in Fiorenzo's career, before 1500, while Filippo Todini (1989) believed it was a late work and from the master's shop. Andrea De' Marchi (1993 correspondence; Museum files) tentatively reattributed the panel to Giovanni Santi (1430/40–1494), dating it to the early 1480s; he compared it to the artist's *Adoration of the Christ Child with St. Sebastian and St. Lawrence* (Luise and Fred Mond, New York). He also noted that the figure of Christ derives from Perugino's *Crucifixion with St. Jerome, St. Francis, and the Blessed Colombini* (Uffizi, Florence; 3254) from 1485–1490.

The size, format, and subject matter of the painting suggest that it served as a personal devotional image. The inscription on the cross, "I N R I," is an acronym for *Jesus Nazarenus Rex Judaeorum* (Jesus of Nazareth, the King of the Jews).

PROVENANCE

Philip Lehman, New York, by 1928; Robert Lehman, New York; Bob Jones University Museum & Gallery (Bob Jones University Collection), acquired 1960

BIBLIOGRAPHY

Robert Lehman, *The Philip Lehman Collection, New York* (Paris: Calmann-Lévy Éditeurs, 1928), no. 71; *The Lehman Collection, New York* (Cincinnati: Cincinnati Art Museum, 1959), 18, no. 88; Alfred Scharf, *The Bob Jones University Collection of Religious Paintings*, vol. 1, *Italian and French Paintings* (Greenville, S.C.: Bob Jones University, 1962), 46; Bernard Berenson, *Italian Pictures of the Renaissance: A List of the Principal Artists and Their Works with an Index of Places. Central Italian and North Italian Schools*, 3 vols. (London: Phaidon Press, 1968), 1:134; Burton B. Fredericksen and Federico Zeri, *Census of Pre-Nineteenth-Century Italian Paintings in North American Public Collections* (Cambridge, Mass.: Harvard University Press, 1972), 71, 582; D. Stephen Pepper, *Bob Jones University Collection of Religious Art: Italian Paintings* (Greenville, S.C.: Bob Jones University, 1984), 8; Filippo Todini, *La pittura umbra: Dal Duecento al primo Cinquecento*, 2 vols. (Milan: Longanesi & Co., 1989), 1:67.

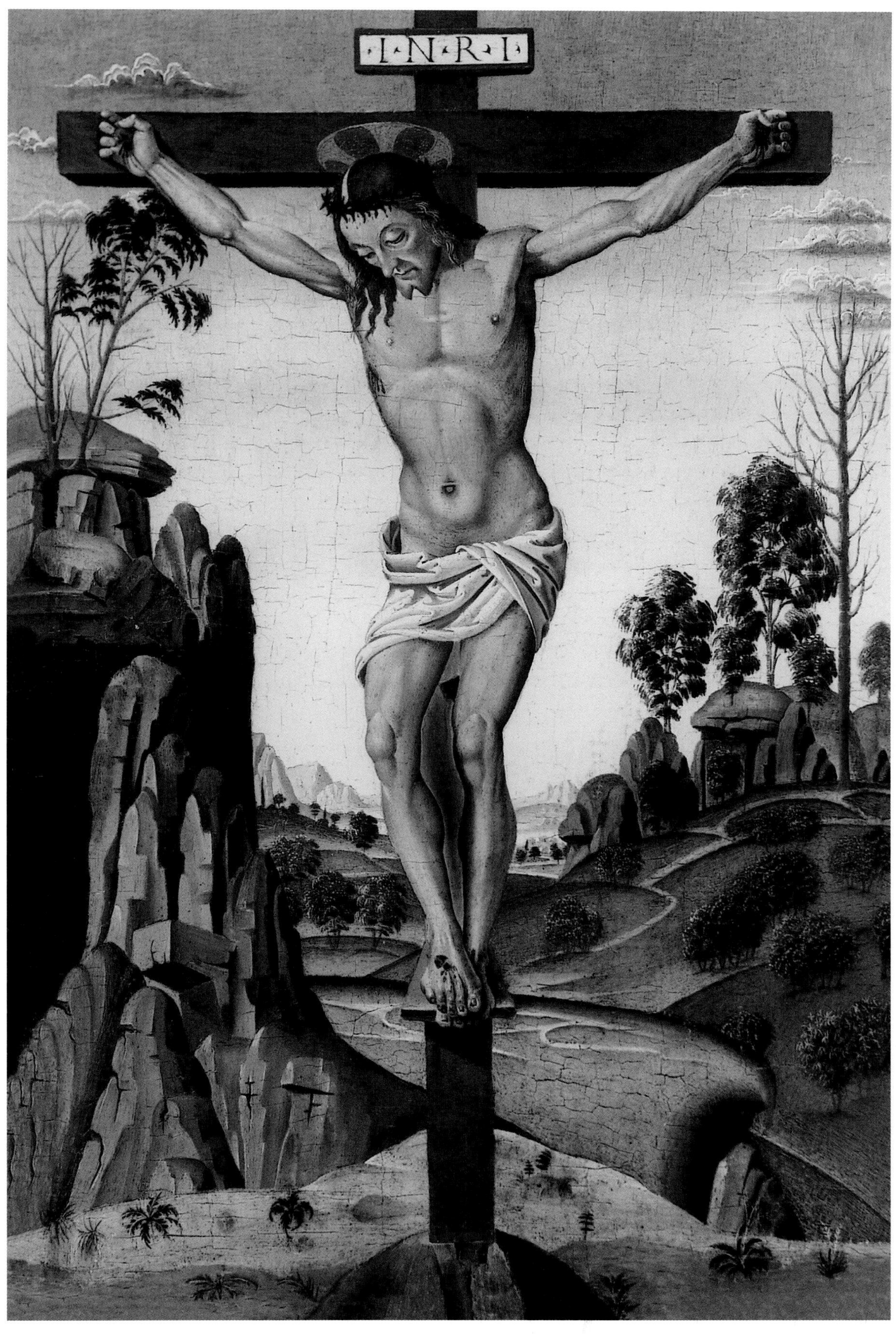

Fig. 160 Fiorenzo di Lorenzo: *Christ on the Cross*. Bob Jones University Museum & Gallery, Greenville, South Carolina, 61.265.

FRANCESCO DI VANNUCCIO, ACTIVE 1356–1389; SIENESE

Crucifix (57.97) 191.8 X 161.3 CM, TEMPERA ON PANEL

GREENVILLE, SOUTH CAROLINA. BOB JONES UNIVERSITY MUSEUM & GALLERY

The crucifix is the largest of several painted by Francesco di Vannuccio. Considered one of his finest works, it is similar in style to his processional cross in the Staatliche Museen, Gemäldegalerie, Berlin (10962B), signed and dated 1380.

The Virgin Mary and St. John the Evangelist appear on the lateral terminals, at the left and right, respectively; St. Mary Magdalen is at the base of the cross.

PROVENANCE

Elia Volpi, Palazzo Davanzati, Florence; American Art Association, New York, November 27, 1916, lot 1039; Mrs. Richard Mortimer, Tuxedo Park, N.J.; Jacques Seligman and Company, New York, 1956; Bob Jones University Museum & Gallery (Bob Jones University Collection), acquired 1956

BIBLIOGRAPHY

Richard Offner, "Works and Style of Francesco di Vannuccio," *Art in America* 20 (1932): 90, 96, 110, 111, 113; Cesare Brandi, "Francesco di Vannuccio e Paolo di Giovanni Fei," *Bollettino Senese di Storia Patria* 4 (1933): 30-31; John Pope-Hennessy, "A Diptych by Francesco di Vannuccio," *Burlington Magazine* 90 (1948): 138; "Accessions," *Art Quarterly* 20 (1957): 222; Carlo Volpe, "Deux panneaux de Benedetto di Bindo," *Revue des Arts* 8 (1958): 176; Alfred Scharf, *The Bob Jones University Collection of Religious Paintings*, vol. 1, *Italian and French Paintings* (Greenville, S.C.: Bob Jones University, 1962), 16; Henry R. Hope, "The Bob Jones University Religious Art Collection," *Art Journal* 25 (1965–1966): 157; Bernard Berenson, *Italian Pictures of the Renaissance: A List of the Principal Artists and Their Works with an Index of Places. Central Italian and North Italian Schools*, 3 vols. (London: Phaidon Press, 1968), 1:145; Burton B. Fredericksen and Federico Zeri, *Census of Pre-Nineteenth-Century Italian Paintings in North American Public Collections* (Cambridge, Mass.: Harvard University Press, 1972), 74, 582; *Early Italian Paintings and Works of Art, 1300–1480* (London: Matthiesen Fine Art Ltd., 1983), 32; D. Stephen Pepper, *Bob Jones University Collection of Religious Art: Italian Paintings* (Greenville, S.C.: Bob Jones University, 1984), 26-27; Miklòs Boskovits, *Frühe italienische Malerei: Gemäldegalerie Berlin, Katalog der Gemälde* (Berlin: Gebr. Mann, 1988), 36; Mojmír S. Frinta, *Punched Decoration on Late Medieval Panel and Miniature Painting*, pt. 1 (Prague: Maxdorf, 1998), 232, 386, 387, 427, 429; Sylvia Ferrari and Jean-Claude Bloch, *Trente-trois primitifs italiens: De 1310 à 1500, du sacré au profane* (Paris: G. Sarti, 1999), 78; Perri Lee Roberts, Bruce Cole, and Hayden B. J. Maginnis, *Sacred Treasures: Early Italian Paintings from Southern Collections* (Athens, Ga.: Georgia Museum of Art, 2002), 25-27, 94-96.

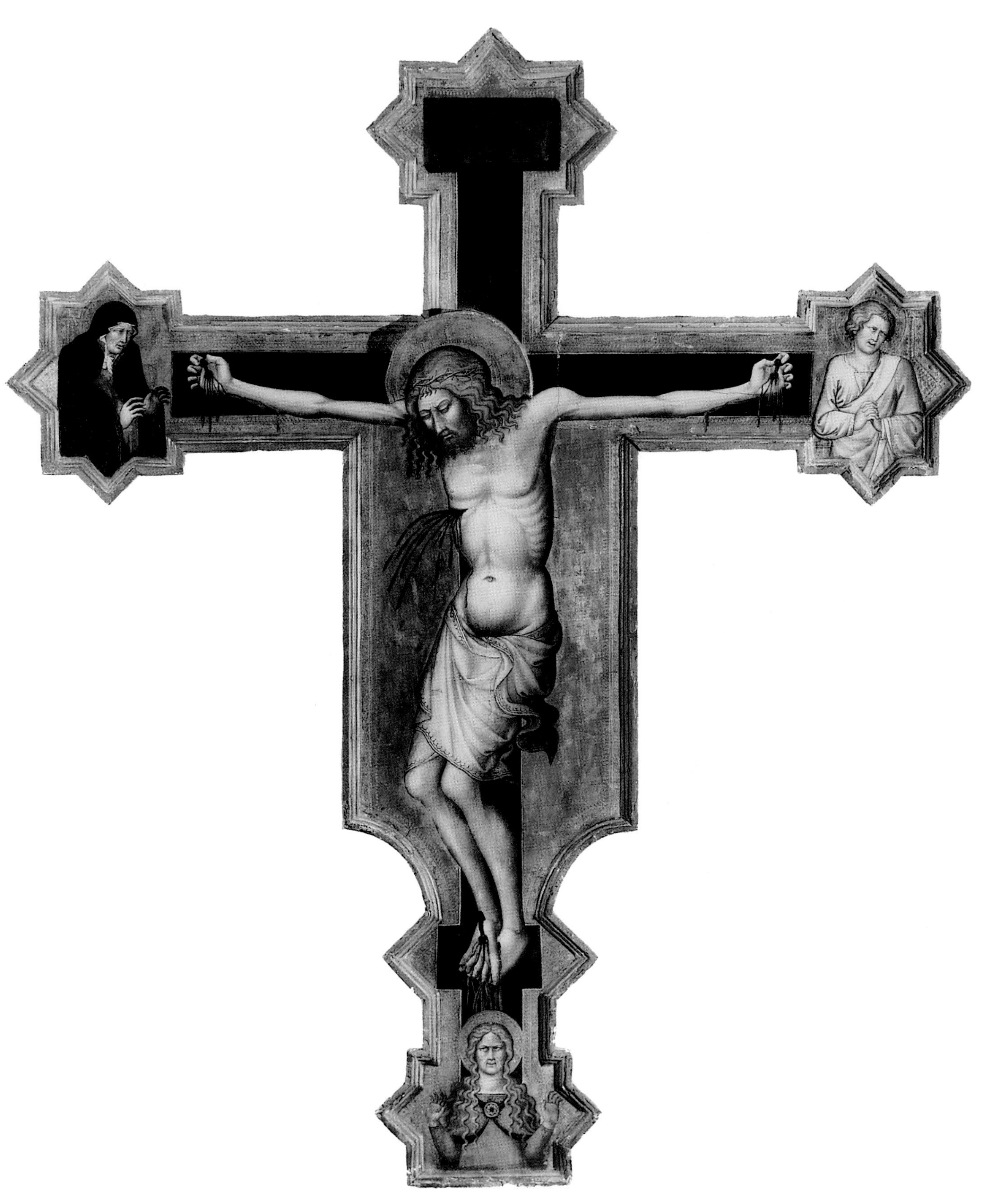

Fig. 161 Francesco di Vannuccio: *Crucifix*. Bob Jones University Museum & Gallery, Greenville, South Carolina, 57.97.

GERINI, NICCOLÒ DI PIETRO, ACTIVE 1368–1415; FLORENTINE

Madonna and Child with Saints (59.176) 127 X 193 CM (INCLUDING FRAME), TEMPERA ON PANEL

GREENVILLE, SOUTH CAROLINA. BOB JONES UNIVERSITY MUSEUM & GALLERY

The work is a rare example of an intact altarpiece. Mary Magdalen and St. Bartholomew are to the Virgin's right, St. John the Baptist and St. Francis to her left. In the pinnacles, from left to right, are an anonymous prophet, the Annunciate Angel, Christ Blessing, the Annunciate Virgin, and another anonymous prophet. Five scenes from the life of the Magdalen constitute the predella: from left to right, Christ at supper with Simon the Pharisee (Luke 7:36-50), Christ in the house of Martha and Mary (Luke 10:38-42), the Assumption of the Magdalen, the Last Communion of the Magdalen, and the Burial of the Magdalen. Given the prominence of the Magdalen, the altarpiece was surely made for a Tuscan chapel or church dedicated to the saint. Miklòs Boskovits (1975) dated the work 1375–1380.

PROVENANCE

Lord Somers, Eastnor Castle, England; Wildenstein and Co., New York; Bob Jones University Museum & Gallery (Bob Jones University Collection), acquired 1959

BIBLIOGRAPHY

Commemorative Exhibition of the Art Treasures of the Midlands (Birmingham: Birmingham Museum and Art Gallery, 1934), no. 268; "Accessions," *Art Journal* 19 (1959–1960): 170; Alfred Scharf, *The Bob Jones University Collection of Religious Paintings*, vol. 1, *Italian and French Paintings* (Greenville, S.C.: Bob Jones University, 1962), 23; Bernard Berenson, *Italian Pictures of the Renaissance: A List of the Principal Artists and Their Works with an Index of Places. Florentine School*, 2 vols. (London: Phaidon Press, 1963), 1:160; Burton B. Fredericksen and Federico Zeri, *Census of Pre-Nineteenth-Century Italian Paintings in North American Public Collections* (Cambridge, Mass.: Harvard University Press, 1972), 81, 582; Miklòs Boskovits, *Pittura fiorentina alla vigilia del Rinascimento, 1370–1400* (Florence: Edam, 1975), 309; Richard Offner and Hayden B. J. Maginnis, *A Critical and Historical Corpus of Florentine Painting: A Legacy of Attributions* (New York: Institute of Fine Arts, New York University, 1981), 82; D. Stephen Pepper, *Bob Jones University Collection of Religious Art: Italian Paintings* (Greenville, S.C.: Bob Jones University, 1984), 148-49; John M. Nolan, Carl B. Strehlke, Barbara Deimling, and Yvonne Szafran, *Discovering a Pre-Renaissance Master: Tommaso del Mazza* (Greenville, S.C.: Bob Jones University, 2009), 28-29, 76-77.

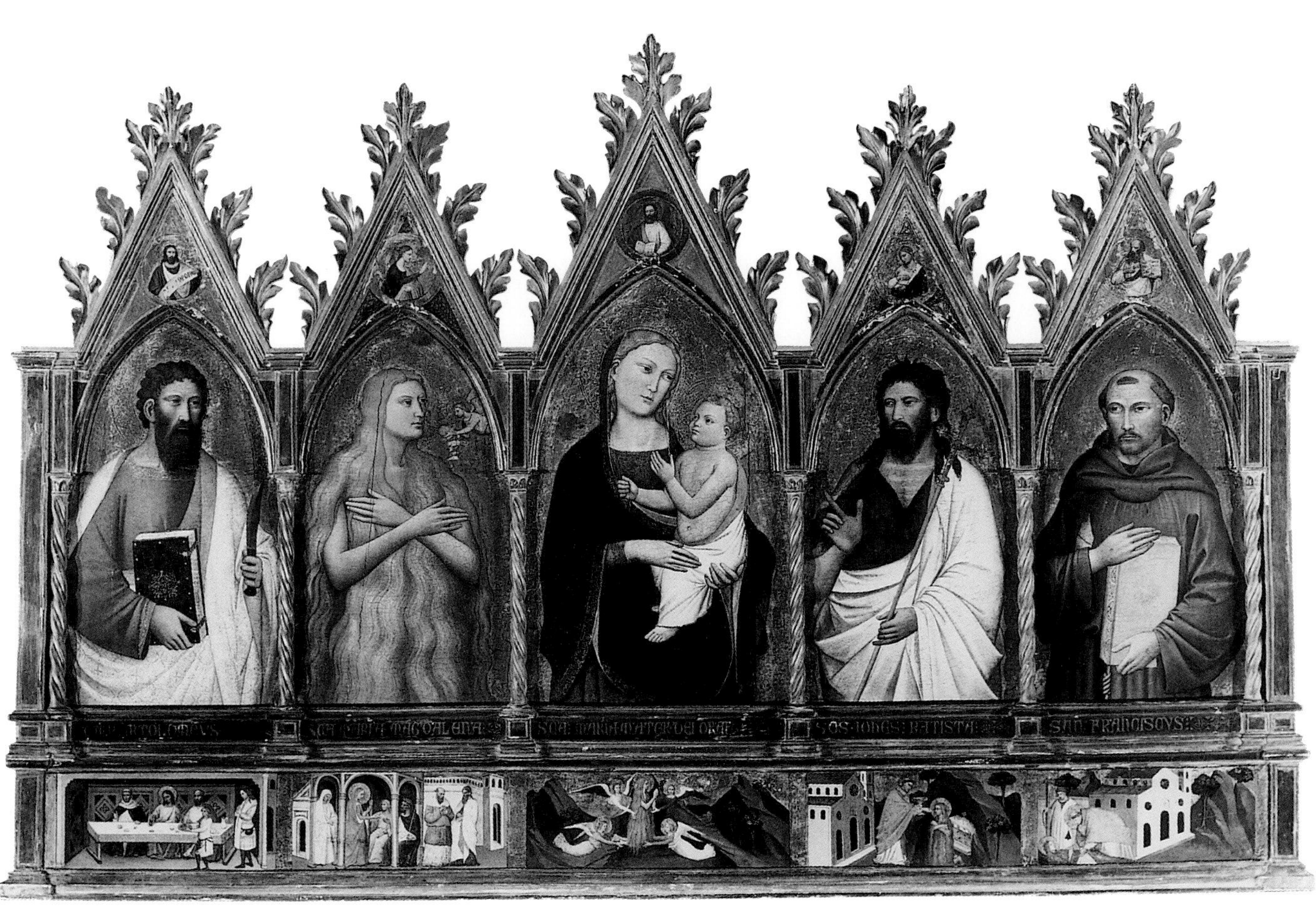

Fig. 162 Niccolò di Pietro Gerini: *Madonna and Child with Saints*. Bob Jones University Museum & Gallery, Greenville, South Carolina, 59.176.

GUIDACCIO DA IMOLA, ACTIVE 1463–1481; ROMAGNOL

Coronation of the Virgin (57.100) 215.9 X 256.5 CM, TEMPERA AND OIL ON PANEL

GREENVILLE, SOUTH CAROLINA. BOB JONES UNIVERSITY MUSEUM & GALLERY

The painting is signed and dated on a *cartellino*, a small piece of paper painted illusionistically, near the base of the throne: "Hoc opus fecit antonius / alias ghuidacius imolensis / ano dni 1470 die IX mensis / octebris: deo gratias" ("This work was made by Antonio, known as Guidaccio da Imola, 9 October 1470; thanks be to God") (author's translation). As the only signed and dated work by Antonio da Imola, this large altarpiece has guided the identification of his oeuvre. Both Alfred Scharf (1962) and D. Stephen Pepper (1984) assumed that the painting was commissioned for Sant'Agostino, Forlì, but there are no documents supporting its presence there prior to 1794.

Among the saints on the left (from front to back, left to right) are Francis of Assisi, Paul, Peter Martyr, John the Baptist, Augustine, and Peter (?); on the right are Mary Magdalen, Catherine of Alexandria, Lucy, Agatha (?), and Anne (?). The unidentified male martyr who kneels at Mary's immediate left and holds an unusually large palm frond may be the dedicatory saint of the chapel or church for which the work was painted.

PROVENANCE

Sant'Agostino, Forlì, by 1794; Count Lovatelli, Ravenna, c. 1898; R. T. Crawshay, Esq., Rome; Major W. R. Crawshay, England; Sotheby's, London, February 18, 1953, lot 89; Frank T. Sabin, London, 1955; William Hallsborough Ltd., London, 1957; Bob Jones University Museum & Gallery (Bob Jones University Collection), acquired 1957

BIBLIOGRAPHY

Joseph A. Crowe and Giovanni B. Cavalcaselle, *Storia della pittura in Italia dal secolo II al secolo XVI*, 11 vols. (Florence: Le Monnier, 1898), 8:277; "Antonio da Imola," in Ulrich Thieme and Felix Becker, eds., *Allgemeines Lexikon der bildenden Künstler von der Antike bis zur Gegenwart*, 37 vols. (Leipzig: E. A. Seemann, 1907), 1:596-97; Joseph A. Crowe and Giovanni B. Cavalcaselle, *A History of Painting in Italy, Umbria, Florence and Siena, from the Second to the Sixteenth Century*, 6 vols., ed. Tancred Borenius (London: John Murray, 1914), 5:34 n. 2; Rezio Buscaroli, *La pittura romagnola del Quattrocento* (Faenza: Fratelli Lega, 1931), 399; Rezio Buscaroli, *Melozzo e il melozzismo* (Bologna: Athena, 1955), 60-61; "Trade News—Antonio da Imola," *The Connoisseur* 134 (1955): 285; Alfred Scharf, *The Bob Jones University Collection of Religious Paintings*, vol. 1, *Italian and French Paintings* (Greenville, S.C.: Bob Jones University, 1962), 39; Henry R. Hope, "The Bob Jones University Religious Art Collection," *Art Journal* 25 (1965–1966): 156; Burton B. Fredericksen and Federico Zeri, *Census of Pre-Nineteenth-Century Italian Paintings in North American Public Collections* (Cambridge, Mass.: Harvard University Press, 1972), 11, 582; D. Stephen Pepper, *Bob Jones University Collection of Religious Art: Italian Paintings* (Greenville, S.C.: Bob Jones University, 1984), 4-5; Federico Zeri, ed., *La pittura in Italia. Il Quattrocento*, 2 vols. (Milan: Electa, 1986), 1:248; Anna Tambini, "Guidaccio da Imola e le influenze Padovane nella pittura Emiliano-Romagnola del Quattrocento," *Paragone* 38 (1987): 51-52; Giordano Viroli, "Appunti su pittura e scultura a Forlì tra Quattro e Cinquecento," in *Melozzo da Forlì: La sua città e il suo tempo*, ed. Marina Foschi and Luciana Prati (Milan: Leonardo arte, 1994), 214; Mojmír S. Frinta, *Punched Decoration on Late Medieval Panel and Miniature Painting*, pt. 1 (Prague: Maxdorf, 1998), 496.

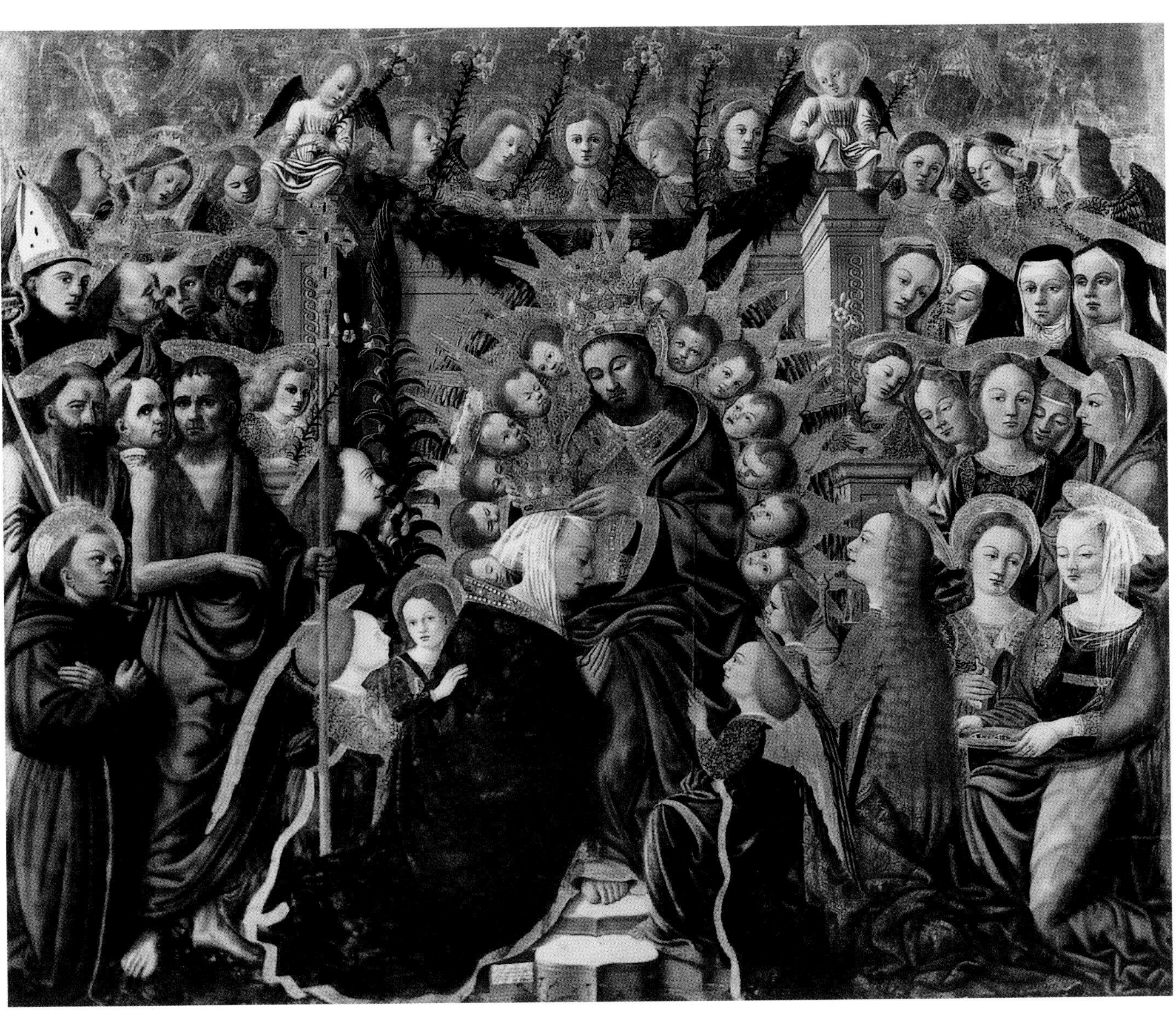

Fig. 163 Guidaccio da Imola: *Coronation of the Virgin*. Bob Jones University Museum & Gallery, Greenville, South Carolina, 57.100.

LORENZO DI BICCI, C. 1350–C. 1427; FLORENTINE

St. Lucy and St. Mary Magdalen; St. James Major (PINNACLE) (63.334.32); *St. Luke and St. Christopher; St. Francis* (PINNACLE) (63.334.33) 130.2 X 49.5 CM (EACH), TEMPERA ON PANEL

GREENVILLE, SOUTH CAROLINA. BOB JONES UNIVERSITY MUSEUM & GALLERY

Formerly attributed to Niccolò di Tommaso (c. 1343–c. 1405), the panels were reassigned to Lorenzo di Bicci by Federico Zeri (cited in Pepper 1984). Zeri identified them as the wings of a triptych that had as its central panel *St. Catherine of Alexandria with Six Female Virtues* (current location unknown; formerly, D. Van Hadeln, Florence). Miklòs Boskovits (1975) dated the Greenville works 1400–1405.

Burton B. Fredericksen and Federico Zeri (1972), as well as Boskovits, identified the figure currently recognized as St. Luke as St. John the Evangelist. The female figure flanking Mary Magdalen has been identified as St. Lucy because of the lamp she holds, although she does not usually appear with a book.

PROVENANCE

Lord Somers, Eastnor Castle, England; Wildenstein Gallery, New York, 1963; Bob Jones University Museum & Gallery (Bob Jones University Collection), acquired 1963

BIBLIOGRAPHY

Beneth A. Jones, *Bob Jones University Supplement to the Catalogue of the Art Collection: Paintings Acquired, 1963–1968* (Greenville, S.C.: Bob Jones University, 1968), 9; Burton B. Fredericksen and Federico Zeri, *Census of Pre-Nineteenth-Century Italian Paintings in North American Public Collections* (Cambridge, Mass.: Harvard University Press, 1972), 583; Miklòs Boskovits, *Pittura fiorentina alla vigilia del Rinascimento, 1370–1400* (Florence: Edam, 1975), 334; Richard Offner and Hayden B. J. Maginnis, *A Critical and Historical Corpus of Florentine Painting: A Legacy of Attributions* (New York: Institute of Fine Arts, New York University, 1981), 40; D. Stephen Pepper, *Bob Jones University Collection of Religious Art: Italian Paintings* (Greenville, S.C.: Bob Jones University, 1984), 14; Mojmír S. Frinta, *Punched Decoration on Late Medieval Panel and Miniature Painting*, pt. 1 (Prague: Maxdorf, 1998), 513, 519; John M. Nolan, Carl B. Strehlke, Barbara Deimling, and Yvonne Szafran, *Discovering a Pre-Renaissance Master: Tommaso del Mazza* (Greenville, S.C.: Bob Jones University, 2009), 29.

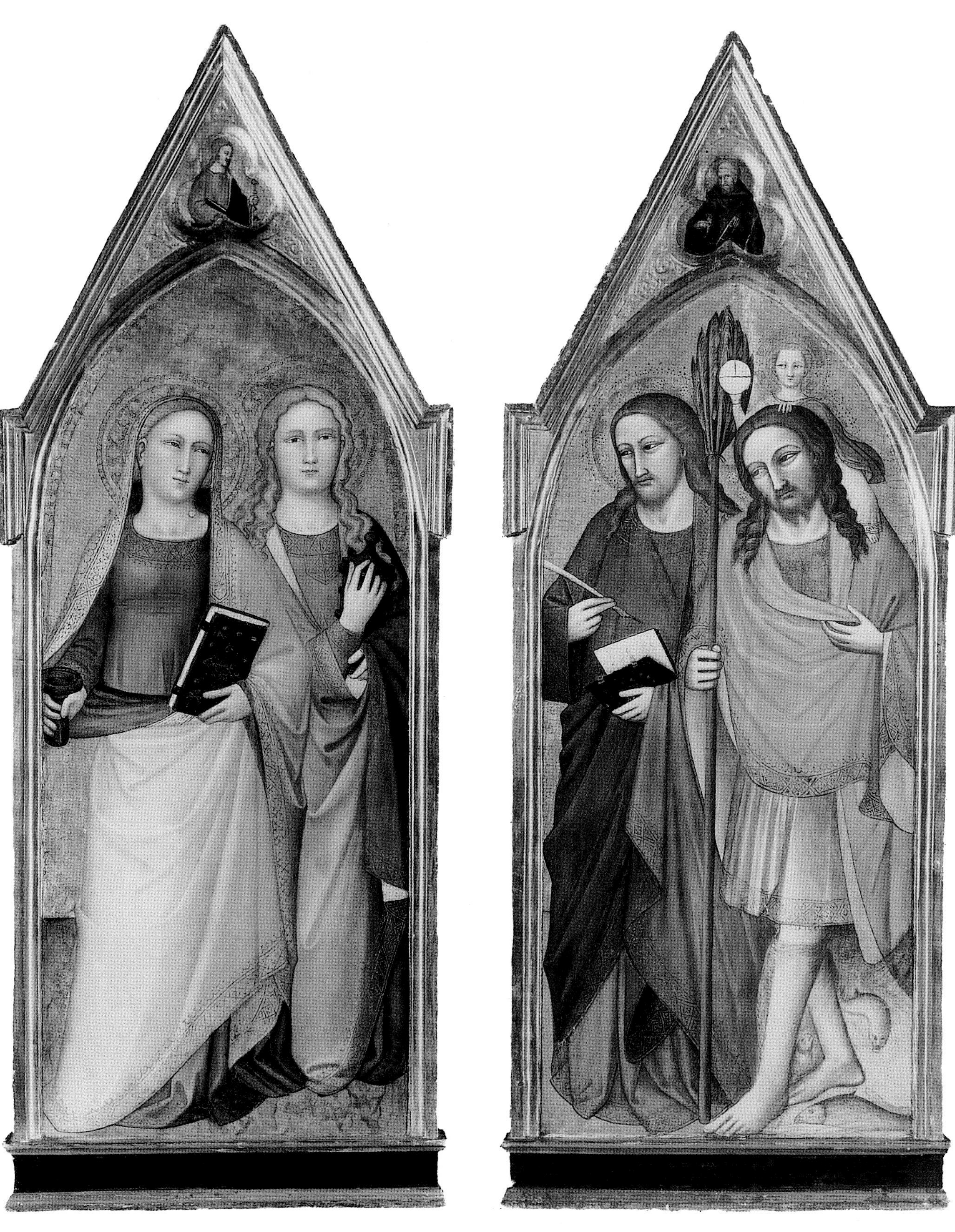

Fig. 164 (left) Lorenzo di Bicci: *St. Lucy and St. Mary Magdalen; St. James Major*. Bob Jones University Museum & Gallery, Greenville, South Carolina, 63.334.32.

Fig. 165 (right) Lorenzo di Bicci: *St. Luke and St. Christopher; St. Francis*. Bob Jones University Museum & Gallery, Greenville, South Carolina, 63.334.33.

LORENZO DI NICCOLÒ, ACTIVE 1392–1412; FLORENTINE

Holy Trinity (51.14) 85.1 X 30.5 CM, TEMPERA ON PANEL

GREENVILLE, SOUTH CAROLINA. BOB JONES UNIVERSITY MUSEUM & GALLERY

The panel was probably the center of a triptych, which would have resembled Nardo di Cione's *Holy Trinity* altarpiece of 1365 (Accademia, Florence; 3258). Its back has a painted border and a partially damaged cross-shaped pattern within a diamond, mirroring the appearance of the frames in Agnolo Gaddi's frescoes illustrating the Legend of the True Cross in the chancel of Santa Croce, Florence (c. 1385–1387). The painting has always been attributed to Lorenzo di Niccolò, who was sometimes erroneously referred to as Lorenzo di Niccolò Gerini. D. Stephen Pepper (1984) dated the work c. 1395 on the basis of stylistic similarities with the artist's *Crucifixion* (San Domenico, Prato).

The Trinity, represented as the Throne of Grace or Throne of Mercy, was an image of salvation, instilling in the viewer the hope of his own resurrection through the mercy of God the Father, the sacrifice of Christ, and the grace of the Holy Ghost. In most other Tuscan images of this genre, God the Father is seated or enthroned; Lorenzo di Niccolò's unusual standing figure anticipates that in Masaccio's *Trinity* (Santa Maria Novella, Florence) from c. 1426–1428.

PROVENANCE

Private collection, Florence, 1915; Pedulli Galleries, Florence; Ercole Canessa Collection, Paris and New York; American Art Association, Anderson Galleries, New York, March 29, 1930, lot 89; Grosvenor Backus, Englewood, N.J.; E. and A. Silberman Gallery, New York, 1951; Bob Jones University Museum & Gallery (Bob Jones University Collection), acquired 1951

BIBLIOGRAPHY

Millard Meiss, *Painting in Florence and Siena after the Black Death* (Princeton: Princeton University Press, 1951), 35, no. 86; Hans Tietze and Erica Tietze-Conrat, *The Bob Jones University Collection of Religious Paintings* (Greenville, S.C.: Bob Jones University, 1954), 20; Alfred Scharf, *The Bob Jones University Collection of Religious Paintings*, vol. 1, *Italian and French Paintings* (Greenville, S.C.: Bob Jones University, 1962), 24; Joseph Polzer, "The Anatomy of Masaccio's *Holy Trinity*," *Jahrbuch der Berliner Museen* 93 (1971): 49; Burton B. Fredericksen and Federico Zeri, *Census of Pre-Nineteenth-Century Italian Paintings in North American Public Collections* (Cambridge, Mass.: Harvard University Press, 1972), 80, 582; D. Stephen Pepper, *Bob Jones University Collection of Religious Art: Italian Paintings* (Greenville, S.C.: Bob Jones University, 1984), 15; Paul Joannides, *Masaccio and Masolino: A Complete Catalogue* (London: Phaidon, 1993), 359; Mojmír S. Frinta, *Punched Decoration on Late Medieval Panel and Miniature Painting*, pt. 1 (Prague: Maxdorf, 1998), 211.

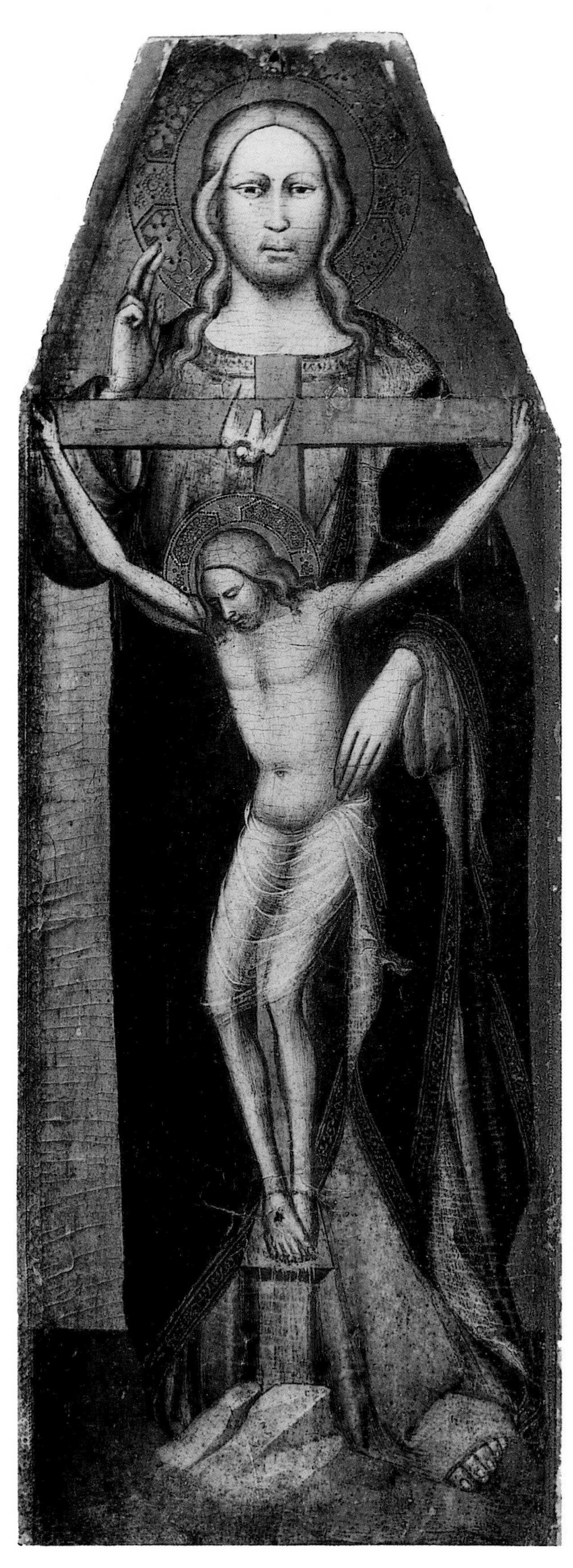

Fig. 166 Lorenzo di Niccolò: *Holy Trinity*. Bob Jones University Museum & Gallery, Greenville, South Carolina, 51.14.

MAINERI, GIAN FRANCESCO DE, ACTIVE 1489–1506; ATTRIBUTED; FERRARESE

Head of St. John the Baptist (63.301.3) 43.2 X 31.8 CM, OIL ON PANEL

GREENVILLE, SOUTH CAROLINA. BOB JONES UNIVERSITY MUSEUM & GALLERY

Published by Bernard Berenson (1907) as the work of Andrea Solario (c. 1465–1524), the painting was assigned to Antonio Solario (active 1502–1514) by the Museum in 1968. Burton B. Fredericksen and Federico Zeri (1972) endorsed the latter attribution. D. Stephen Pepper (1984) reattributed the panel to Gian Francesco de Maineri, and it is currently exhibited by the Museum as his. David Alan Brown (1987) revived Berenson's opinion.

This personal devotional image is one of many derivatives of Maineri's *Head of the Baptist* (Brera, Milan; 819).

PROVENANCE

Dr. Gustavo Frizzoni, Milan, by 1907; Eugene J. Carpenter, 1917; Minneapolis Institute of Arts, acquired 1935; Mr. and Mrs. Julius Weitzner, New York, by 1963; Bob Jones University Museum & Gallery (Bob Jones University Collection), acquired 1963

BIBLIOGRAPHY

Wilhelm Suida, "Die Spätwerke des Bartolommeo Suardi, genannt Bramantino," *Jahrbuch der Kunsthistorischen Sammlungen des allerhöchsten Kaiserhaus* 26 (1906–1907): 309; Bernard Berenson, *North Italian Painters of the Renaissance* (New York and London: G. P. Putnam's Sons, 1907), 411; Kurt Badt, *Andrea Solario, sein Leben und seine Werke* (Leipzig: Klinkhardt & Biermann, 1914), 174; Bernard Berenson, *Italian Pictures of the Renaissance: A List of the Principal Artists and Their Works with an Index of Places. Central Italian and North Italian Schools*, 3 vols. (London: Phaidon Press, 1968), 1:410; Beneth A. Jones, *Bob Jones University Supplement to the Catalogue of the Art Collection: Paintings Acquired, 1963–1968* (Greenville, S.C.: Bob Jones University, 1968), 12; Burton B. Fredericksen and Federico Zeri, *Census of Pre-Nineteenth-Century Italian Paintings in North American Public Collections* (Cambridge, Mass.: Harvard University Press, 1972), 190, 583; D. Stephen Pepper, *Bob Jones University Collection of Religious Art: Italian Paintings* (Greenville, S.C.: Bob Jones University, 1984), 72; David Alan Brown, *Andrea Solario* (Milan: Electa, 1987), 165, 198 n. 60.

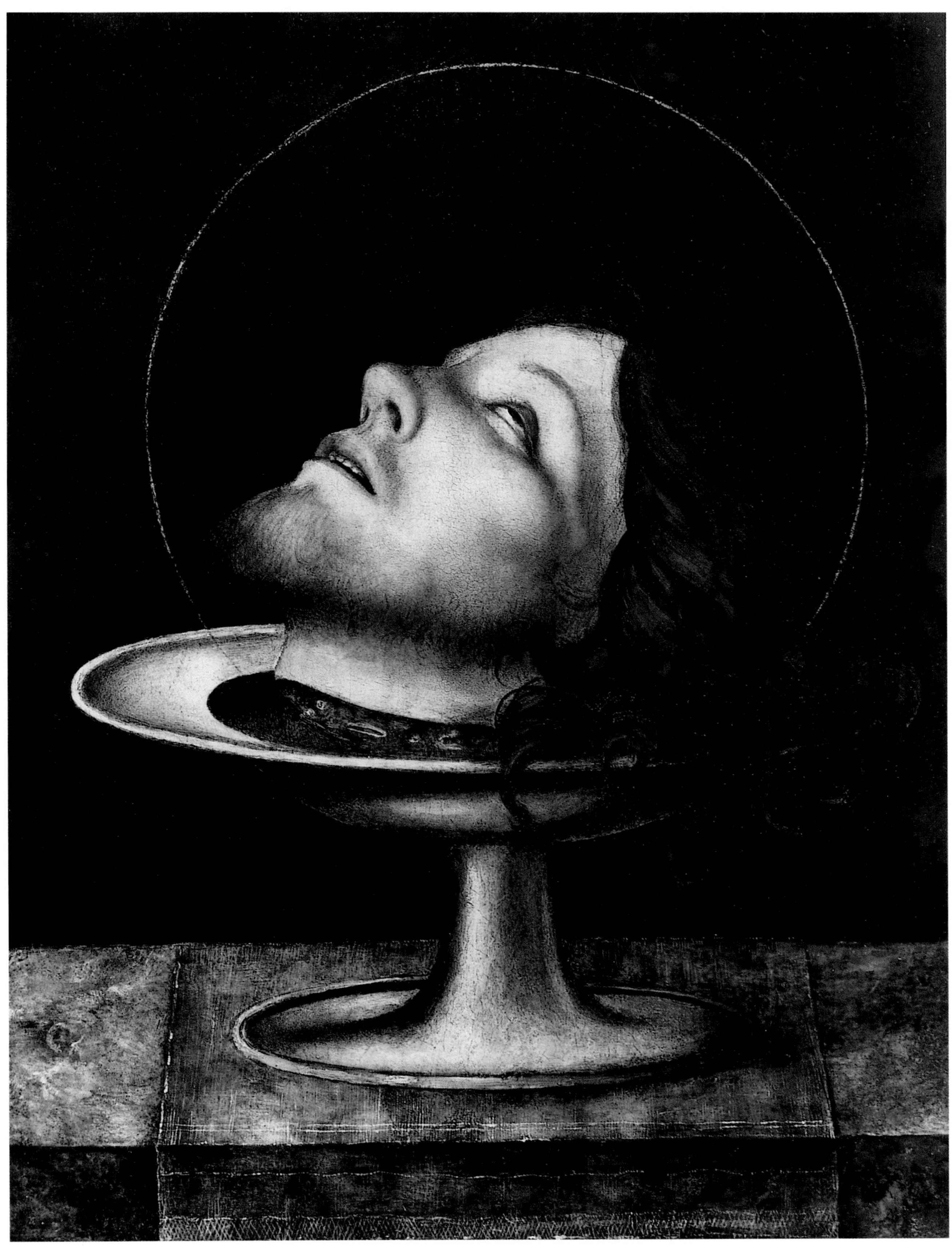

Fig. 167 Gian Francesco de Maineri (attributed): *Head of St. John the Baptist*. Bob Jones University Museum & Gallery, Greenville, South Carolina, 63.301.3.

MASTER OF BENABBIO, ACTIVE C. 1469; LUCCHESE

Madonna and Child with St. Michael the Archangel, St. John the Evangelist, St. Blaise, and St. Peter (61.272)

205.1 X 193 CM (INCLUDING FRAME), TEMPERA ON PANEL

GREENVILLE, SOUTH CAROLINA. BOB JONES UNIVERSITY MUSEUM & GALLERY

The frame is inscribed with the names of the saints and the date 1469; although the lettering has been renewed, it presumably preserves the original inscription. Published as the work of an unknown Tuscan painter ("Accessions" 1961), the panel was assigned to the fifteenth-century Lucchese School by Burton B. Fredericksen and Federico Zeri (1972). Roberto Longhi (cited in Pepper 1984) attributed it to the Master of Benabbio, a minor Lucchese painter responsible for the *Madonna and Child with Saints* (Santa Maria della Assunta, Benabbio, Bagni di Lucca). This master was subsequently identified as Baldassare di Biagio del Firenze (1453–1484) (Zeri 1986).

Massimo Ferretti (1978) identified this triptych as the work on the altar of San Michele, Antraccoli, Lucca, described in an inventory of the contents of the church; Ferretti suggested that the predella with the twelve apostles that was joined to a polyptych by Mariotto di Nardo (active 1394–1424) (current location unknown; formerly, Massimo Collection, Rome) originally belonged to the San Michele altarpiece. He noted that St. Michael, who appears on the left wing, looking out toward the viewer, was the dedicatory saint of the church at Antraccoli. The Christ Child holds a rose, symbolizing the Virgin's purity; the object in his other hand may be a piece of fruit.

PROVENANCE

San Michele, Antraccoli, Lucca; Countess Schaffgotsch, Schloss Niederleis, Austria; Rosenberg and Stiebel, New York; Bob Jones University Museum & Gallery (Bob Jones University Collection), acquired 1961

BIBLIOGRAPHY

"Accessions," *Art Quarterly* 24 (1961): 394; Alfred Scharf, *The Bob Jones University Collection of Religious Paintings*, vol. 1, *Italian and French Paintings* (Greenville, S.C.: Bob Jones University, 1962), 34; Burton B. Fredericksen and Federico Zeri, *Census of Pre-Nineteenth-Century Italian Paintings in North American Public Collections* (Cambridge, Mass.: Harvard University Press, 1972), 232, 582; Massimo Ferretti, "Percorso lucchese," *Annali della Scuola Normale Superiore di Pisa* 5 (1975): 1034; Massimo Ferretti, "Di nuovo sul percorso lucchese," *Annali della Scuola Normale Superiore di Pisa* 8 (1978): 1243; D. Stephen Pepper, *Bob Jones University Collection of Religious Art: Italian Paintings* (Greenville, S.C.: Bob Jones University, 1984), 17; Federico Zeri, ed., *La pittura in Italia. Il Quattrocento*, 2 vols. (Milan: Electa, 1986), 1:308; 2:688.

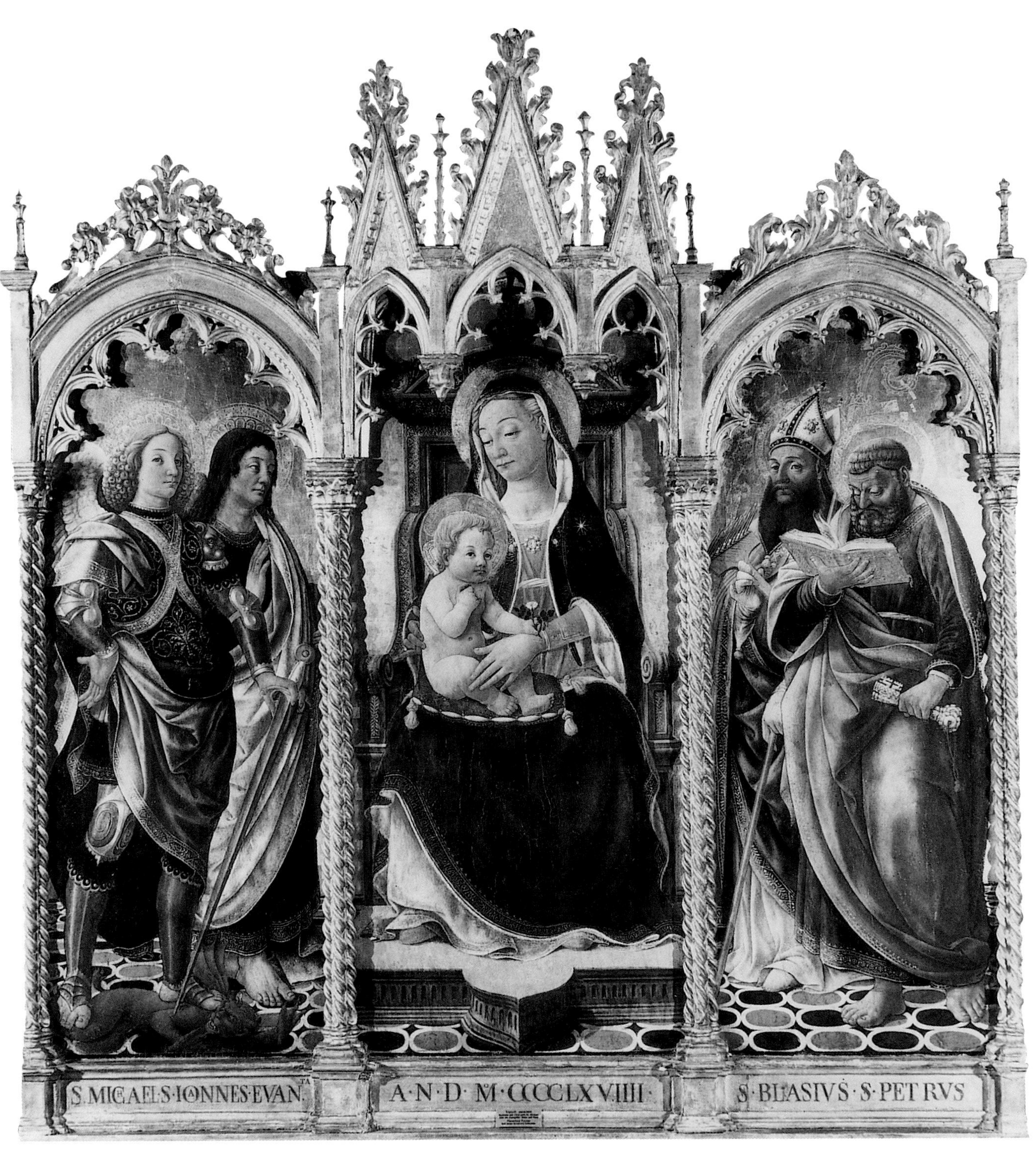

Fig. 168 Master of Benabbio: *Madonna and Child with St. Michael the Archangel, St. John the Evangelist, St. Blaise, and St. Peter*. Bob Jones University Museum & Gallery, Greenville, South Carolina, 61.272.

MASTER OF THE BORGHESE TONDO, ACTIVE 1450–1500; FLORENTINE

Nativity (52.27) 99.1 X 79.4 CM, TEMPERA ON PANEL

GREENVILLE, SOUTH CAROLINA. BOB JONES UNIVERSITY MUSEUM & GALLERY

Hans Tietze and Erica Tietze-Conrat (1954) attributed the painting to Davide Ghirlandaio (1452–1525); Burton B. Fredericksen and Federico Zeri (1972) assigned it to Bastiano Mainardi (1466–1513). D. Stephen Pepper (1984) endorsed Everett P. Fahy's reattribution (1976) to the Master of the Borghese Tondo.

This devotional altarpiece brings together various features of Domenico Ghirlandaio's Adorations, including the *Adoration of the Shepherds* (Santa Trinità, Florence) from 1485 and the *Adoration of the Shepherds* (Pinacoteca, Museo dello Spedale degli Innocenti, Florence) from 1488.

PROVENANCE

Baron Raoul Kuffner, Castle Dioszegh, Hungary/Czechoslovakia; Parke-Bernet, New York, November 18, 1948, lot 31; Julius Weitzner, New York, 1952; Bob Jones University Museum & Gallery (Bob Jones University Collection), acquired 1952

BIBLIOGRAPHY

Hans Tietze and Erica Tietze-Conrat, *The Bob Jones University Collection of Religious Paintings* (Greenville, S.C.: Bob Jones University, 1954), 36; Alfred Scharf, *The Bob Jones University Collection of Religious Paintings,* vol. 1, *Italian and French Paintings* (Greenville, S.C.: Bob Jones University, 1962), 52; Burton B. Fredericksen and Federico Zeri, *Census of Pre-Nineteenth-Century Italian Paintings in North American Public Collections* (Cambridge, Mass.: Harvard University Press, 1972), 117, 582; Everett P. Fahy, *Some Followers of Domenico Ghirlandajo* (New York: Garland Press, 1976), 168; D. Stephen Pepper, *Bob Jones University Collection of Religious Art: Italian Paintings* (Greenville, S.C.: Bob Jones University, 1984), 18, no. 11.

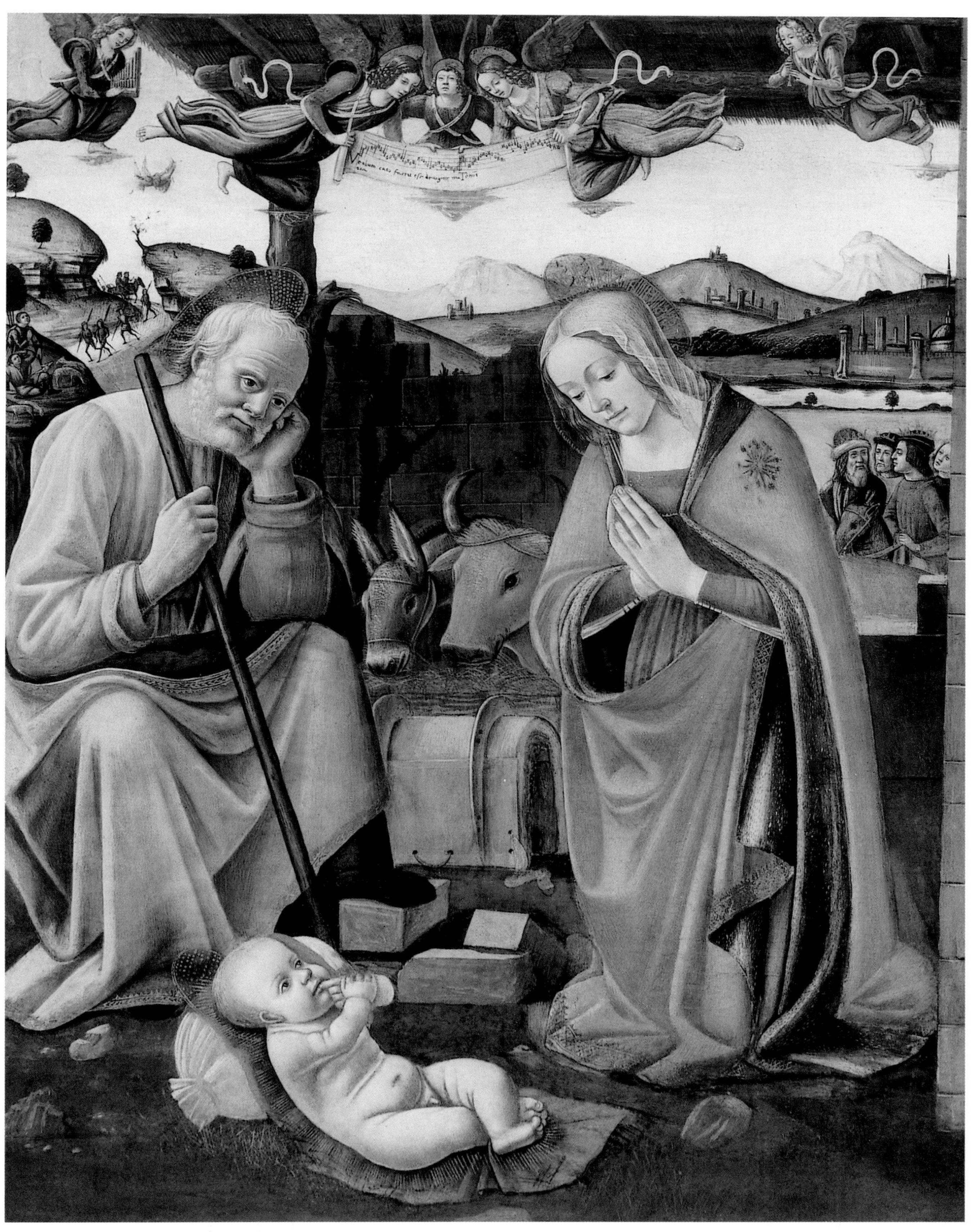

Fig. 169 Master of the Borghese Tondo: *Nativity*. Bob Jones University Museum & Gallery, Greenville, South Carolina, 52.27.

MASTER OF THE BORGO ALLA COLLINA, ACTIVE 1400–1425; FLORENTINE

Madonna and Child (51.13) 118.1 X 54.6 CM, TEMPERA ON PANEL

GREENVILLE, SOUTH CAROLINA. BOB JONES UNIVERSITY MUSEUM & GALLERY

The painting was published by Hans Tietze and Erica Tietze-Conrat (1954) as the work of the Master of the Bambino Vispo (active early fifteenth century), now generally identified as Gherardo Starnina (c. 1360–before 1413). Everett P. Fahy (cited in Pepper 1984) reassigned it to a follower or pupil of Starnina, the Master of the Borgo alla Collina, whose eponymous work is the *Mystic Marriage of St. Catherine Altarpiece* (San Donato, Borgo alla Collina, Casentino) of 1423.

The Christ Child holds a goldfinch, symbolizing the Passion. He makes a gesture of blessing, perhaps toward the supplicant or saints who appeared on the right wing of the unidentified triptych from which the panel comes. The triptych probably resembled the master's *Madonna and Child with Angels and Saints* (Galleria Doria Pamphili, Rome).

PROVENANCE

E. and A. Silberman Gallery, New York, 1951; Bob Jones University Museum & Gallery (Bob Jones University Collection), acquired 1951

BIBLIOGRAPHY

Hans Tietze and Erica Tietze-Conrat, *The Bob Jones University Collection of Religious Paintings* (Greenville, S.C.: Bob Jones University, 1954), 22; Alfred Scharf, *The Bob Jones University Collection of Religious Paintings*, vol. 1, *Italian and French Paintings* (Greenville, S.C.: Bob Jones University, 1962), 26; Brigitte Klesse, *Seidenstoffe in der italienischen Malerei des vierzehnten Jahrhunderts* (Bern: Stämpfli, 1967), 308, no. 227; Burton B. Fredericksen and Federico Zeri, *Census of Pre-Nineteenth-Century Italian Paintings in North American Public Collections* (Cambridge, Mass.: Harvard University Press, 1972), 126, 582; Richard Fremantle, *Florentine Gothic Painters from Giotto to Masaccio: A Guide to Painting in and near Florence, 1300 to 1450* (London: Secker & Warburg, 1975), 441-42; D. Stephen Pepper, *Bob Jones University Collection of Religious Art: Italian Paintings* (Greenville, S.C.: Bob Jones University, 1984), 18-19.

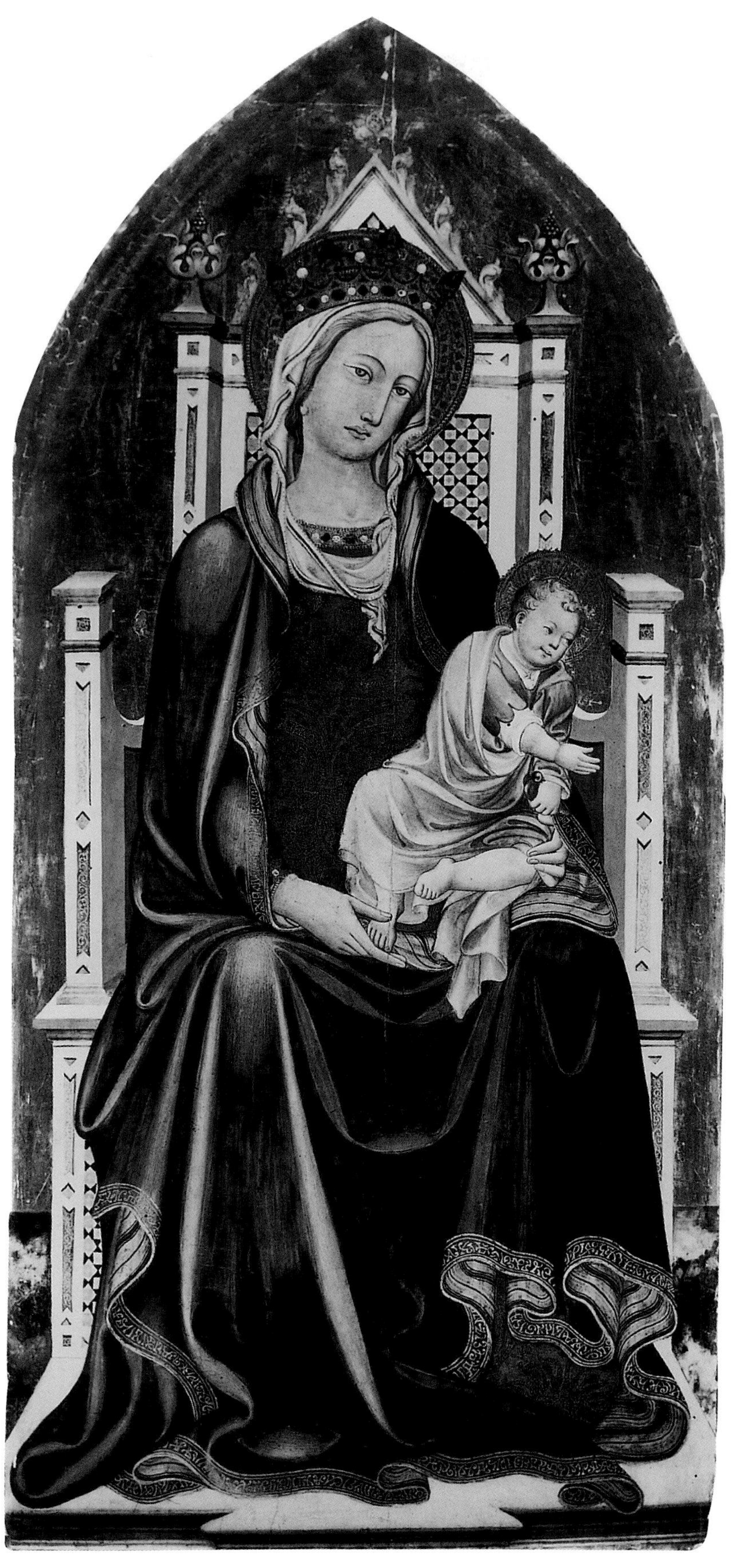

Fig. 170 Master of the Borgo alla Collina: *Madonna and Child*. Bob Jones University Museum & Gallery, Greenville, South Carolina, 51.13.

MASTER OF THE FIESOLE EPIPHANY, ACTIVE 1450–1500; FLORENTINE

Madonna and Child with St. Paul and St. Augustine (52.59) 125.7 X 148.6 CM, TEMPERA ON PANEL

GREENVILLE, SOUTH CAROLINA. BOB JONES UNIVERSITY MUSEUM & GALLERY

Exhibited in 1911 (*A Descriptive and Illustrated Catalogue*) as the work of Alesso Baldovinetti (c. 1425–1499), the painting was attributed by Bernard Berenson (1932) to the Master of San Miniato (active 1460–1480). Hans Tietze and Erica Tietze-Conrat (1954) ascribed it to Francesco Botticini (1446–1497), whereas Alfred Scharf (1962) followed Berenson's lead. Everett P. Fahy (1967) reassigned it to the Master of the Fiesole Epiphany, whose eponymous work is the *Adoration of the Magi with St. Paul, St. Francis, and St. John the Baptist* (on deposit, Gallerie Fiorentine, Florence; formerly, San Francesco, Fiesole). Fahy later (1976) tentatively identified the master as Filippo di Giuliano, who is recorded as Jacopo del Sellaio's collaborator in 1473 and 1480; no extant works by Filippo di Giuliano have been identified positively. A similar painting, also assigned by Fahy to Filippo, is the *Madonna and Child Enthroned with St. Bernard, St. Mary Magdalen, St. Benedict, and Bishop* (Philadelphia Museum of Art; 58). Burton B. Fredericksen and Federico Zeri (1972) revived the Tietzes' attribution to Francesco Botticini, assigning the Greenville work to his shop, studio, or school. D. Stephen Pepper (1984) endorsed the authorship of the Master of the Fiesole Epiphany.

This altarpiece presents a typical fifteenth-century Florentine *sacra conversazione*, based on a formula developed early in the century by such painters as Angelico (c. 1400–1455), Domenico Veneziano (c. 1400–1461), and Filippo Lippi (c. 1406–1469).

PROVENANCE

Judge Alexander C. Humphrey, Glennew, Ky., by 1911; Kleinberger Galleries, New York, 1911; Julius Weitzner, New York, 1951; Bob Jones University Museum & Gallery (Bob Jones University Collection), acquired 1951

BIBLIOGRAPHY

A Descriptive and Illustrated Catalogue of 150 Paintings of Old Masters of the Dutch, Flemish, German, Italian, Spanish and French Schools (New York: Kleinberger Galleries, 1911), 160, no. 127; Bernard Berenson, *Italian Pictures of the Renaissance* (Oxford: Clarendon Press, 1932), 348; Hans Tietze and Erica Tietze-Conrat, *The Bob Jones University Collection of Religious Paintings* (Greenville, S.C.: Bob Jones University, 1954), 34; Alfred Scharf, *The Bob Jones University Collection of Religious Paintings*, vol. 1, *Italian and French Paintings* (Greenville, S.C.: Bob Jones University, 1962), 49; Bernard Berenson, *Italian Pictures of the Renaissance: A List of the Principal Artists and Their Works with an Index of Places. Florentine School*, 2 vols. (London: Phaidon Press, 1963), 1:146; Everett P. Fahy, "Some Early Italian Pictures in the Gambier Parry Collection," *Burlington Magazine* 109 (1967): 133-34; Burton B. Fredericksen and Federico Zeri, *Census of Pre-Nineteenth-Century Italian Paintings in North American Public Collections* (Cambridge, Mass.: Harvard University Press, 1972), 34, 582; Everett P. Fahy, *Some Followers of Domenico Ghirlandajo* (New York: Garland Press, 1976), 169; D. Stephen Pepper, *Bob Jones University Collection of Religious Art: Italian Paintings* (Greenville, S.C.: Bob Jones University, 1984), 19.

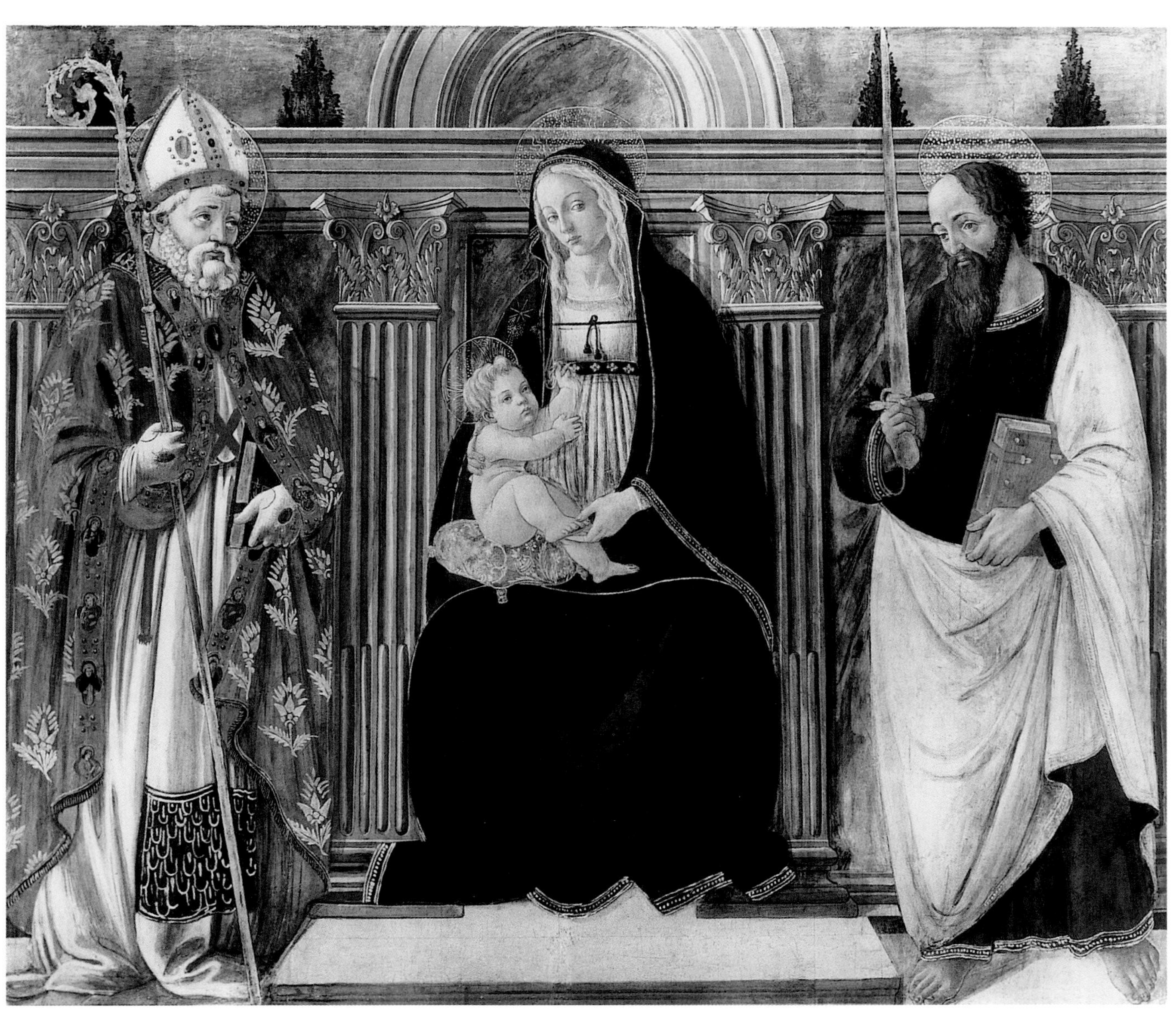

Fig. 171 Master of the Fiesole Epiphany: *Madonna and Child with St. Paul and St. Augustine.* Bob Jones University Museum & Gallery, Greenville, South Carolina, 52.59.

MASTER OF THE GREENVILLE TONDO, ACTIVE SIXTEENTH CENTURY; UMBRIAN

Madonna and Child with Angels (59.192) 103.5 CM (DIAMETER), OIL ON PANEL

GREENVILLE, SOUTH CAROLINA. BOB JONES UNIVERSITY MUSEUM & GALLERY

Published as the work of Sinibaldo Ibi (1475–1550) by Willy Burger (1929), this devotional *tondo* was reattributed to the studio of Pietro Perugino (c. 1450–1523) by Alfred Scharf (1962). Burton B. Fredericksen and Federico Zeri (1972) ascribed it to a follower of Perugino. Everett P. Fahy (cited in Pepper 1984) identified this close follower as the Master of the Greenville Tondo. The design is similar to that of Perugino's *Madonna and Child Enthroned with Saints* (Pinacoteca Vaticana, Rome; 224). The cartoon for the Greenville *Madonna and Child* was employed in reverse for the master's *Madonna and Child in a Landscape* (Strossmayer Gallery, Zagreb; 32/93).

PROVENANCE

Private collection, Cologne; Kleinberger Galleries, New York, 1929; S. Aram, New York, 1959; Bob Jones University Museum & Gallery (Bob Jones University Collection), acquired 1959

BIBLIOGRAPHY

Willy Burger, "A Tondo by Sinibaldo Ibi," *Burlington Magazine* 55 (1929): 87-88; "Accessions of American and Canadian Museums," *Art Quarterly* 23 (1960): 400; Alfred Scharf, *The Bob Jones University Collection of Religious Paintings*, vol. 1, *Italian and French Paintings* (Greenville, S.C.: Bob Jones University, 1962), 55; Burton B. Fredericksen and Federico Zeri, *Census of Pre-Nineteenth-Century Italian Paintings in North American Public Collections* (Cambridge, Mass.: Harvard University Press, 1972), 161, 583; D. Stephen Pepper, *Bob Jones University Collection of Religious Art: Italian Paintings* (Greenville, S.C.: Bob Jones University, 1984), 20, 317-18; Pietro Scarpellini, *Perugino* (Milan: Electa, 1984), 311; Filippo Todini, *La pittura umbra: Dal Duecento al primo Cinquecento*, 2 vols. (Milan: Longanesi & Co., 1989), 1:197; Joseph A. Becherer, *Pietro Perugino: Master of the Italian Renaissance* (New York: Rizzoli International; Grand Rapids, Mich.: Grand Rapids Art Museum, 1997), 119; Roberta J. M. Olson, *The Florentine Tondo* (Oxford and New York: Oxford University Press, 2000), 262.

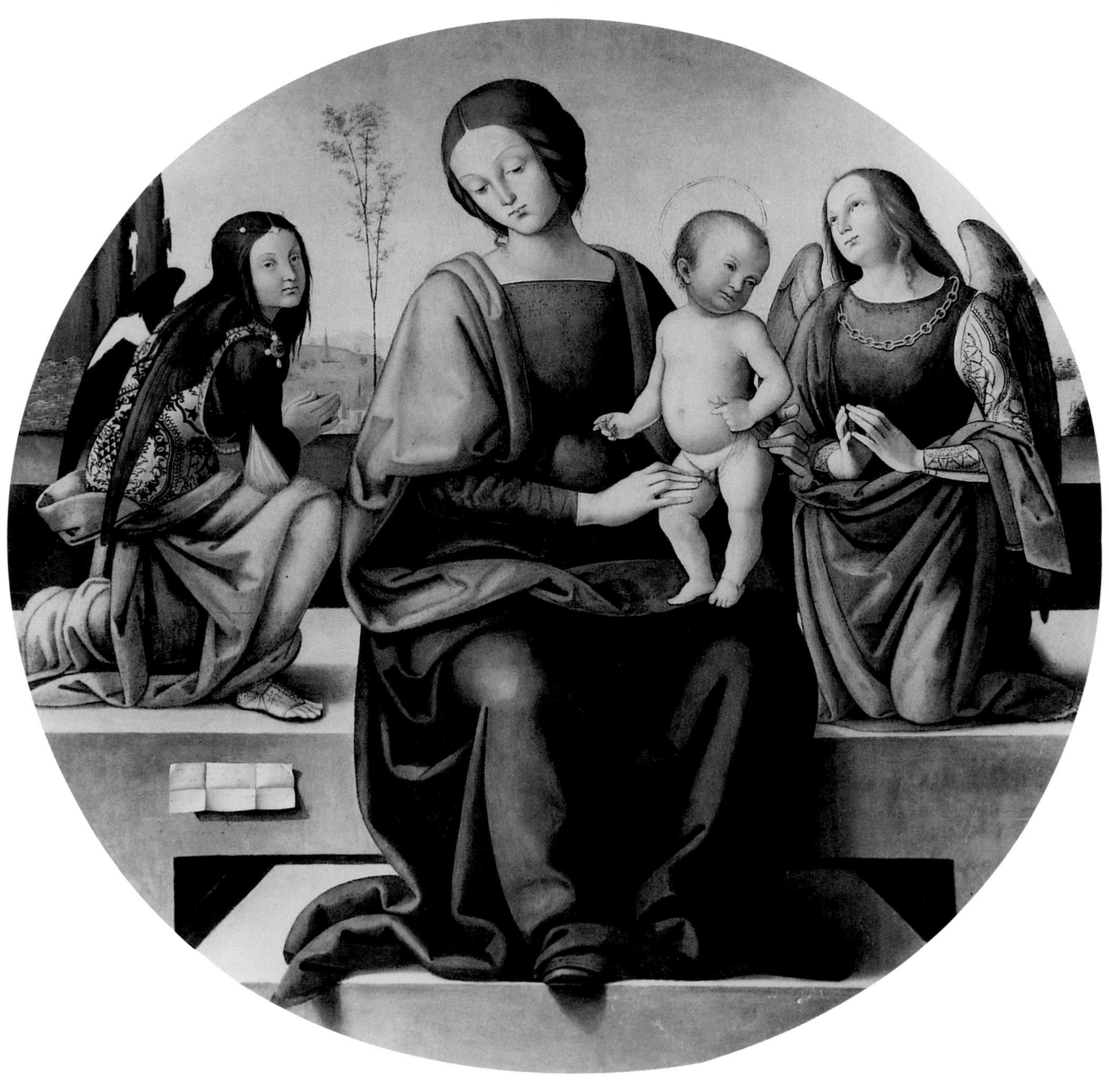

Fig. 172 Master of the Greenville Tondo: *Madonna and Child with Angels*. Bob Jones University Museum & Gallery, Greenville, South Carolina, 59.192.

MASTER OF SAN FILIPPO, 1500–1550; LUCCHESE

Madonna and Child with the Infant St. John the Baptist and Angels (51.9) 61 CM (DIAMETER), TEMPERA ON PANEL

GREENVILLE, SOUTH CAROLINA. BOB JONES UNIVERSITY MUSEUM & GALLERY

Hans Tietze and Erica Tietze-Conrat (1954) assigned the work to Raffaello Botticini (1477–after 1520), while Alfred Scharf (1962) attributed it to Raffaellino del Garbo (c. 1466–1524); Burton B. Fredericksen and Federico Zeri (1972) considered it to be in the manner of Raffaellino del Garbo. Mauro Natale (1980) identified the artist as the Master of San Filippo, a follower of Raffaellino who was active in Lucca in the first half of the sixteenth century and whose eponymous work is the altarpiece of the *Madonna and Child with St. Philip and St. James* (San Filippo, Lucca). The Master of San Filippo has since been identified as Ansano di Michele Ciampanti (1501–1532) (Zeri 1986).

The Madonna and Child of this devotional *tondo* appear to derive from Filippino Lippi's *Nerli Altarpiece* (Santo Spirito, Florence) from c. 1488.

PROVENANCE

Hapsburg family, Royal Palace, Buda, Hungary; Count Ambrozy Migaszy, 1868; E. and A. Silberman Gallery, New York, 1951; Bob Jones University Museum & Gallery (Bob Jones University Collection), acquired 1951

BIBLIOGRAPHY

Hans Tietze and Erica Tietze-Conrat, *The Bob Jones University Collection of Religious Paintings* (Greenville, S.C.: Bob Jones University, 1954), 32; Alfred Scharf, *The Bob Jones University Collection of Religious Paintings*, vol. 1, *Italian and French Paintings* (Greenville, S.C.: Bob Jones University, 1962), 57; Burton B. Fredericksen and Federico Zeri, *Census of Pre-Nineteenth-Century Italian Paintings in North American Public Collections* (Cambridge, Mass.: Harvard University Press, 1972), 171, 582; Mauro Natale, "Note sulla pittura lucchese alla fine del Quattrocento: Il Maestro di Stratonice e il Maestro di San Filippo," *The J. Paul Getty Museum Journal* 8 (1980): 60; D. Stephen Pepper, *Bob Jones University Collection of Religious Art: Italian Paintings* (Greenville, S.C.: Bob Jones University, 1984), 21; Federico Zeri, ed., *La pittura in Italia. Il Quattrocento*, 2 vols. (Milan: Electa, 1986), 2:693; Marilena Tamassia, *Collezioni d'arte tra Ottocento e Novecento: Jacquier fotografi a Firenze, 1870–1935* (Naples: Electa, 1995), 24.

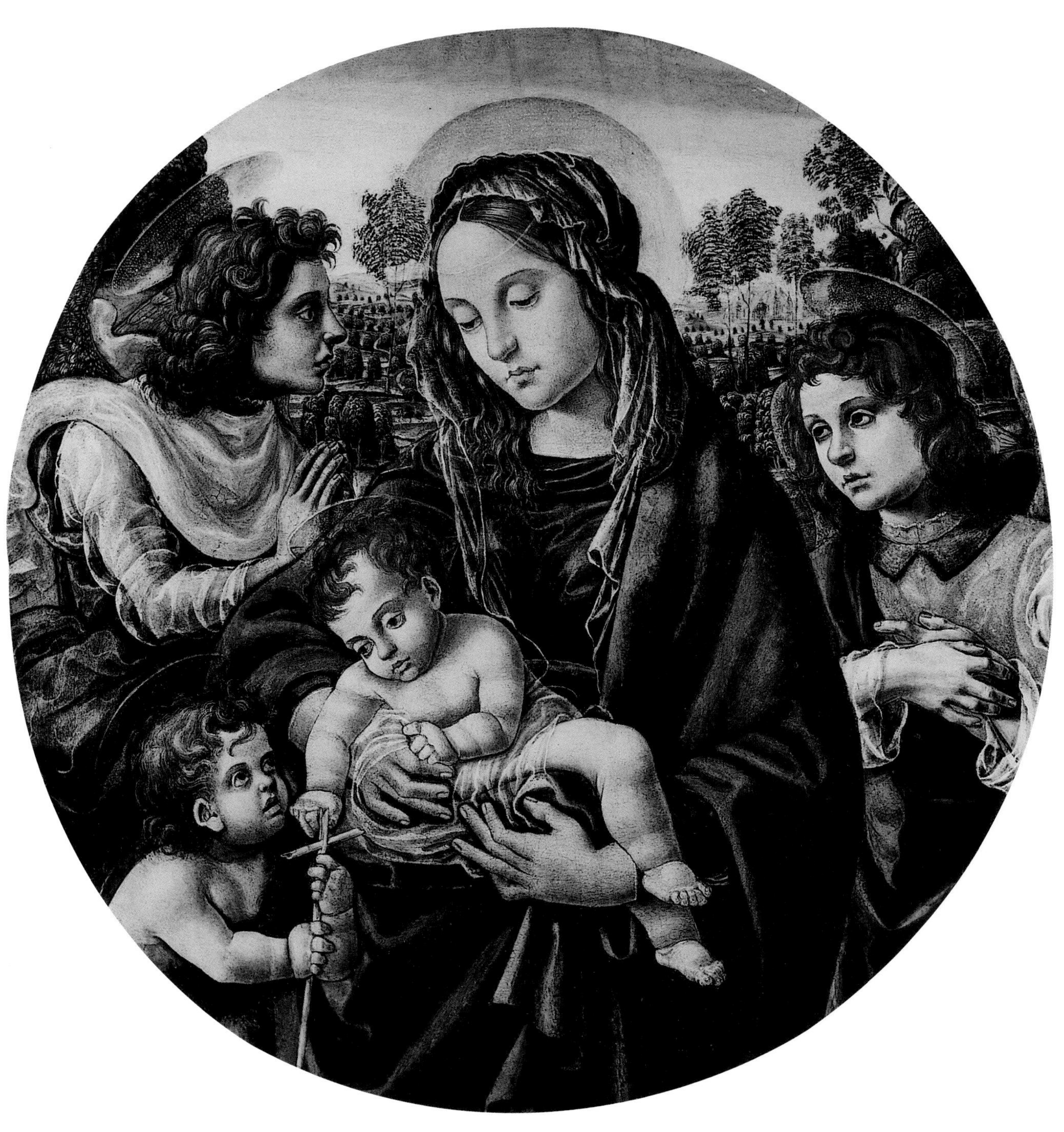

Fig. 173 Master of San Filippo: *Madonna and Child with the Infant St. John the Baptist and Angels.* Bob Jones University Museum & Gallery, Greenville, South Carolina, 51.9.

MASTER OF SAN SILVESTRO, ACTIVE FOURTEENTH CENTURY; VENETIAN

Madonna and Child with a Donor (57.113) 80 x 49.8 CM, TEMPERA ON PANEL

GREENVILLE, SOUTH CAROLINA. BOB JONES UNIVERSITY MUSEUM & GALLERY

The painting was originally the central panel of a polyptych created for an unidentified Franciscan church. Formerly attributed to Niccolò di Pietro (active 1394–1430) by Alfred Scharf (1962), the work was assigned by Miklòs Boskovits (cited in Pepper 1984) to the Venetian Master of San Silvestro, whose eponymous work is the *Madonna and Child with St. James and St. Nicholas* (San Silvestro, Venice). Burton B. Fredericksen and Federico Zeri (1972) ascribed it to an anonymous late-fourteenth-century Venetian artist.

The Virgin is crowned as Queen of Heaven and has a star on her shoulder, referring to her Hebrew name Miriam, meaning "Star of the Sea." The Christ Child is blessing not only the kneeling Franciscan, but, by implication, the monastic community for which the work was commissioned.

PROVENANCE

Robert Lehman, New York; Julius Weitzner, New York, 1957; Bob Jones University Museum & Gallery (Bob Jones University Collection), acquired 1957

BIBLIOGRAPHY

Luigi Coletti, *Pittura veneta del Quattrocento* (Novara: Istituto geografico De Agostini, 1953), pl. l; Alfred Scharf, *The Bob Jones University Collection of Religious Paintings*, vol. 1, *Italian and French Paintings* (Greenville, S.C.: Bob Jones University, 1962), 18; Burton B. Fredericksen and Federico Zeri, *Census of Pre-Nineteenth-Century Italian Paintings in North American Public Collections* (Cambridge, Mass.: Harvard University Press, 1972), 245, 582; D. Stephen Pepper, *Bob Jones University Collection of Religious Art: Italian Paintings* (Greenville, S.C.: Bob Jones University, 1984), 23.

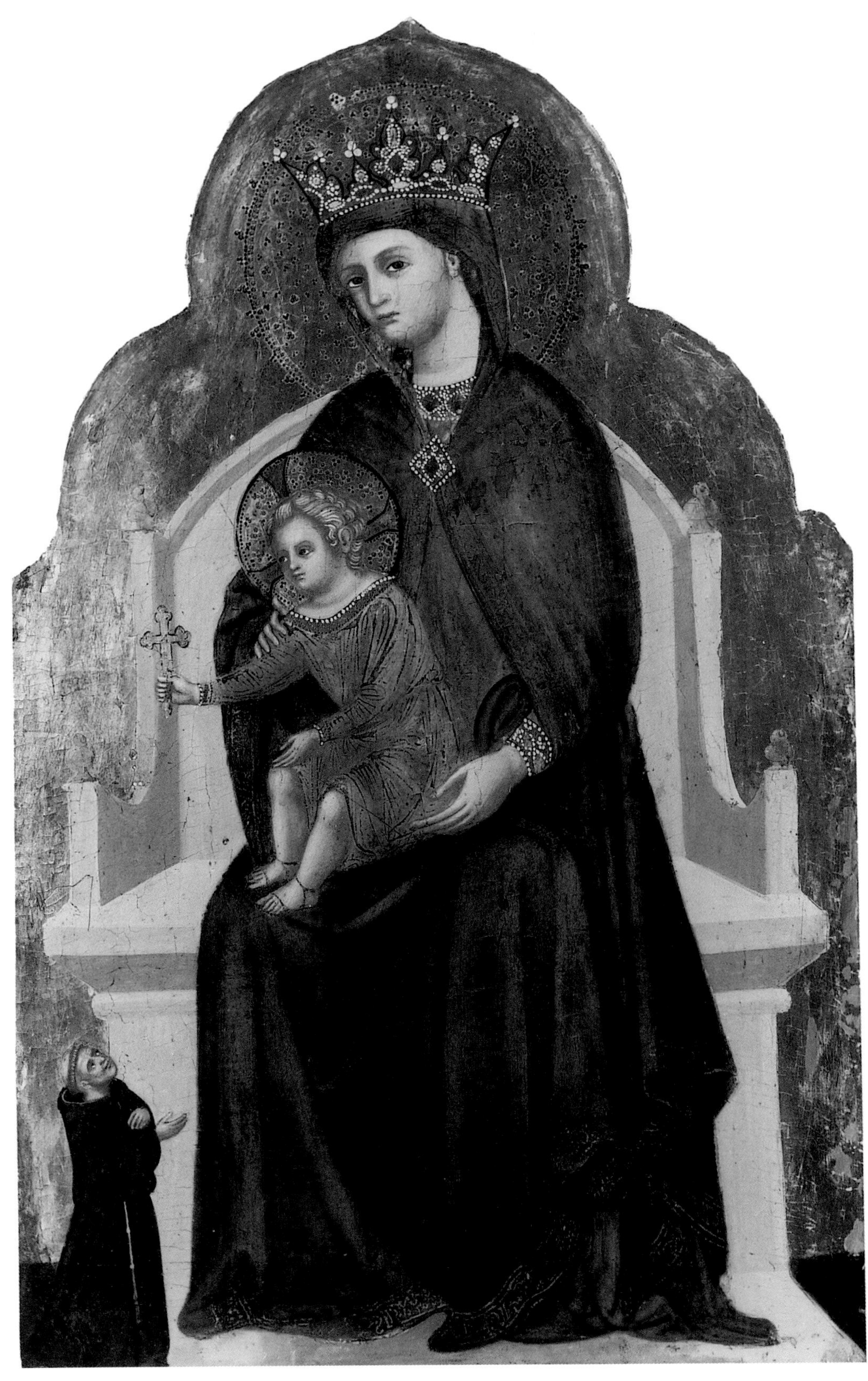

Fig. 174 Master of San Silvestro: *Madonna and Child with a Donor*. Bob Jones University Museum & Gallery, Greenville, South Carolina, 57.113.

MASTER OF STAFFOLO, ACTIVE FIFTEENTH CENTURY; MARCHIGIAN

Madonna and Child with Saints (53.39) 179.1 x 164.5 CM (OVERALL), TEMPERA ON PANEL

GREENVILLE, SOUTH CAROLINA. BOB JONES UNIVERSITY MUSEUM & GALLERY

Recognized as a work of the School of the Marches by earlier scholars, this triptych was attributed by Burton B. Fredericksen and Federico Zeri (1972) to the Marchigian Master of Staffolo, whose eponymous work is the polyptych in the church of San Francesco, Staffolo. Miklòs Boskovits (cited in Pepper 1984) endorsed the attribution. Subsequently, Zeri (cited in Pepper 1984) described the painting as being near, but distinct from, the work of the Master of Staffolo, coining the designation Master of the Bob Jones University Altar for its anonymous creator.

The Virgin is flanked on the left by St. Jerome and on the right by St. Augustine. In the pinnacles are St. Gregory, the Crucifixion, and St. Ambrose. The saints are the four pre-eminent Latin Fathers of the Church.

PROVENANCE

Ashburnham Collection, England; Sotheby's, London, June 24, 1953, lot 6; D. Koetser, London; Bob Jones University Museum & Gallery (Bob Jones University Collection), acquired 1953

BIBLIOGRAPHY

Hans Tietze and Erica Tietze-Conrat, *The Bob Jones University Collection of Religious Paintings* (Greenville, S.C.: Bob Jones University, 1954), 25; Alfred Scharf, *The Bob Jones University Collection of Religious Paintings*, vol. 1, *Italian and French Paintings* (Greenville, S.C.: Bob Jones University, 1962), 30; Burton B. Fredericksen and Federico Zeri, *Census of Pre-Nineteenth-Century Italian Paintings in North American Public Collections* (Cambridge, Mass.: Harvard University Press, 1972), 137, 582; D. Stephen Pepper, *Bob Jones University Collection of Religious Art: Italian Paintings* (Greenville, S.C.: Bob Jones University, 1984), 23-24; Mojmír S. Frinta, *Punched Decoration on Late Medieval Panel and Miniature Painting*, pt. 1 (Prague: Maxdorf, 1998), 386.

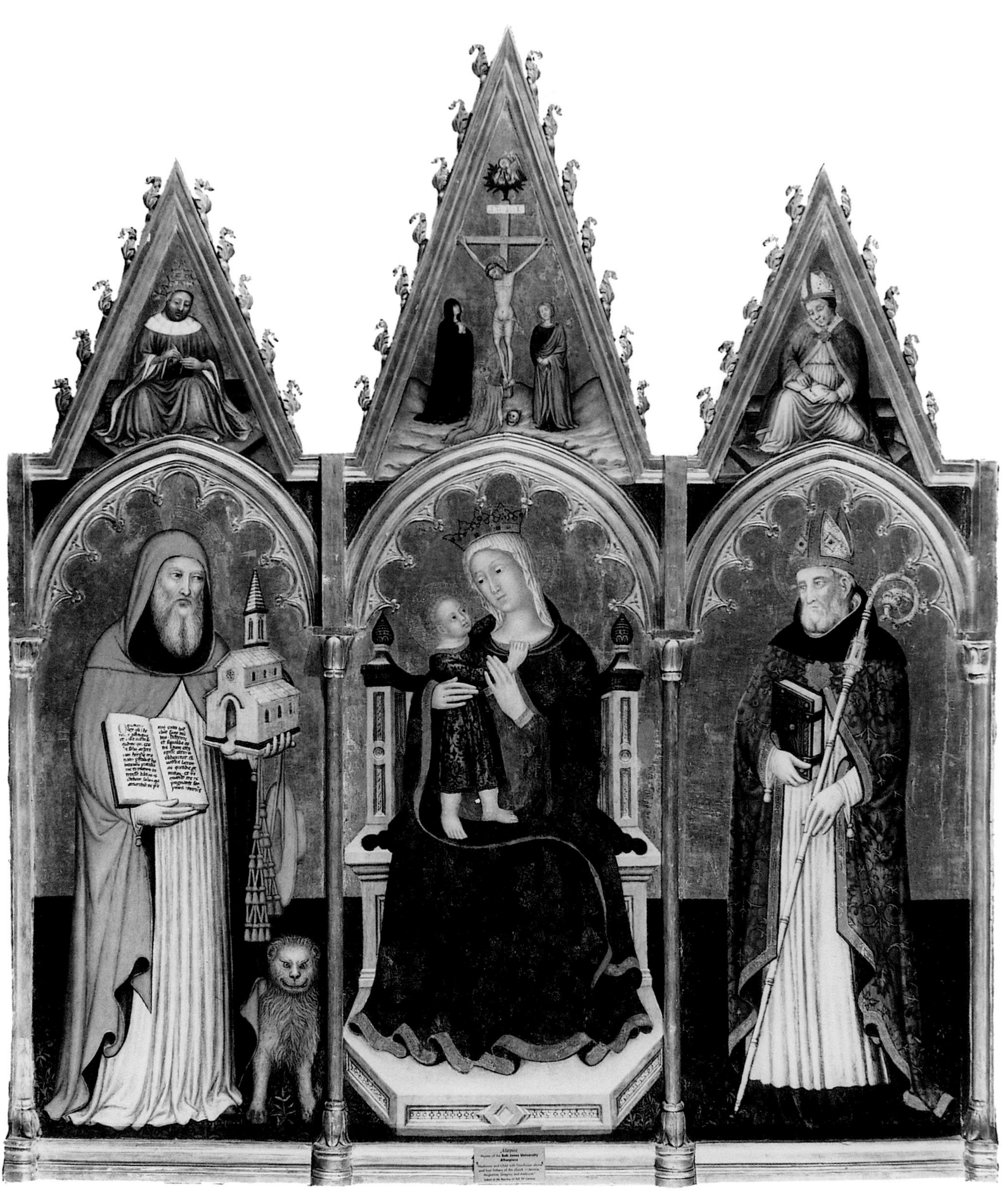

Fig. 175 Master of Staffolo: *Madonna and Child with Saints*. Bob Jones University Museum & Gallery, Greenville, South Carolina, 53.39.

MAZZA, TOMMASO DEL, ACTIVE LATE FOURTEENTH CENTURY; FLORENTINE

St. Paul and a Deacon Saint; St. Bartholomew (gable) (51.4); *St. Jude and St. John the Evangelist; St. Francis of Assisi* (gable) (51.5) 121.9 x 50.8 CM (EACH), TEMPERA ON PANEL

GREENVILLE, SOUTH CAROLINA. BOB JONES UNIVERSITY MUSEUM & GALLERY

The paintings were attributed to Giovanni del Biondo (active 1356; died 1399) by Hans Tietze and Erica Tietze-Conrat (1954). Federico Zeri (1959) assigned them to the Master of Santa Verdiana (active c. 1370–c. 1415), who has since been identified as the Florentine painter Tommaso del Mazza. The panels are the right and left wings of a triptych, the central portion of which Barbara Deimling (1991) identified as the *Annunciation* (J. Paul Getty Museum, Los Angeles; 71.PB.21). Miklòs Boskovits (1975) dated the works 1380–1385, whereas Deimling (1991) placed them in the final years of the artist's career.

The anonymous deacon saint is Stephen or Lawrence.

PROVENANCE

E. and A. Silberman Gallery, New York; Bob Jones University Museum & Gallery (Bob Jones University Collection), acquired 1951

BIBLIOGRAPHY

Hans Tietze and Erica Tietze-Conrat, *The Bob Jones University Collection of Religious Paintings* (Greenville, S.C.: Bob Jones University, 1954), 16; Federico Zeri, "Il Maestro di Santa Verdiana," in *Studies in the History of Art* (London: Phaidon Press, 1959), 35; Alfred Scharf, *The Bob Jones University Collection of Religious Paintings,* vol. 1, *Italian and French Paintings* (Greenville, S.C.: Bob Jones University, 1962), 20; Luciano Bellosi, "Da Spinello a Lorenzo Monaco," *Paragone* 16 (1965): 34; Miklòs Boskovits, "Der Meister der Santa Verdiana," *Mitteilungen des Kunsthistorischen Institutes in Florenz* 13 (1967): 43-44, 58; Burton B. Fredericksen and Federico Zeri, *Census of Pre-Nineteenth-Century Italian Paintings in North American Public Collections* (Cambridge, Mass.: Harvard University Press, 1972), 138, 582; Miklòs Boskovits, *Pittura fiorentina alla vigilia del Rinascimento, 1370–1400* (Florence: Edam, 1975), 30, 384; Richard Fremantle, *Florentine Gothic Painters from Giotto to Masaccio: A Guide to Painting in and near Florence, 1300 to 1450* (London: Secker & Warburg, 1975), 297; Richard Offner and Hayden B. J. Maginnis, *A Critical and Historical Corpus of Florentine Painting. A Legacy of Attributions* (New York: Institute of Fine Arts, New York University, 1981), 45; D. Stephen Pepper, *Bob Jones University Collection of Religious Art: Italian Paintings* (Greenville, S.C.: Bob Jones University, 1984), 20-21; Barbara Deimling, "Il Maestro di Santa Verdiana: Un polittico disperso e il problema dell'identificazione," *Arte Cristiana* 79 (1991): 406; Simona Pasquinucci and Barbara Deimling, *Tradition and Innovation in Florentine Trecento Painting: Giovanni Bonsi, Tommaso del Mazza* (Florence: Giunti, 2000), 123, 124, 309, 314-16; John M. Nolan, Carl B. Strehlke, Barbara Deimling, and Yvonne Szafran, *Discovering a Pre-Renaissance Master: Tommaso del Mazza* (Greenville, S.C.: Bob Jones University, 2009), 9, 18, 25-27, 51-55, 58-68, 82-83.

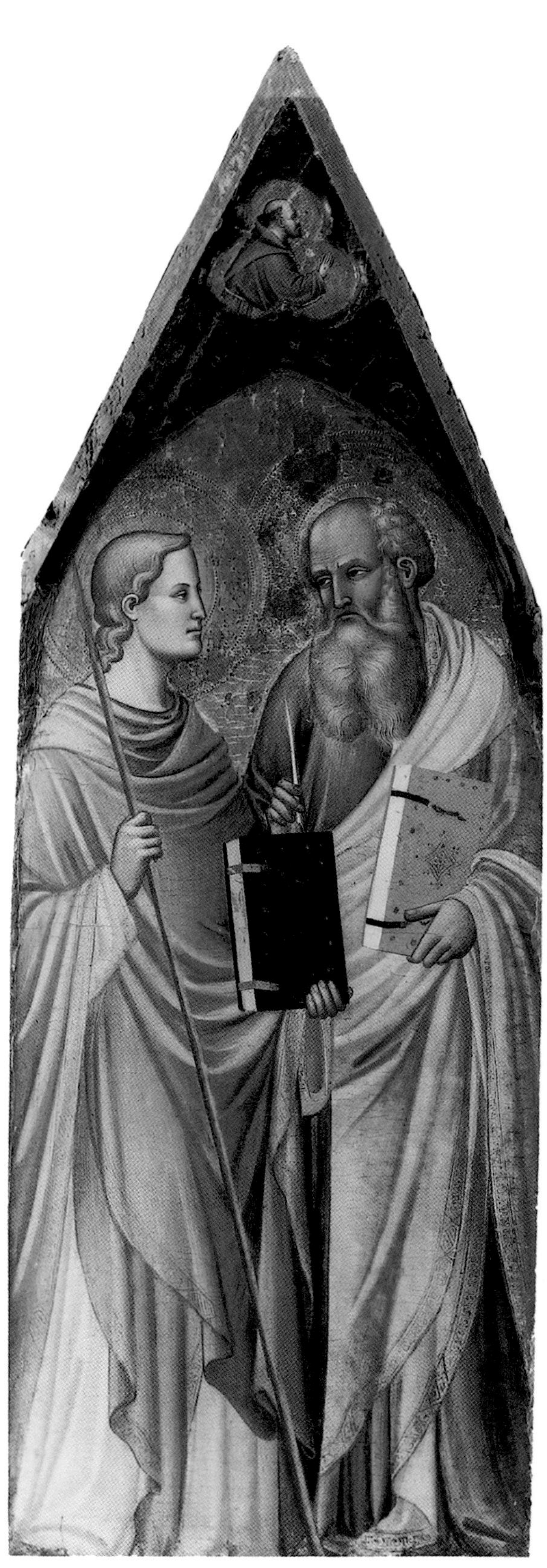

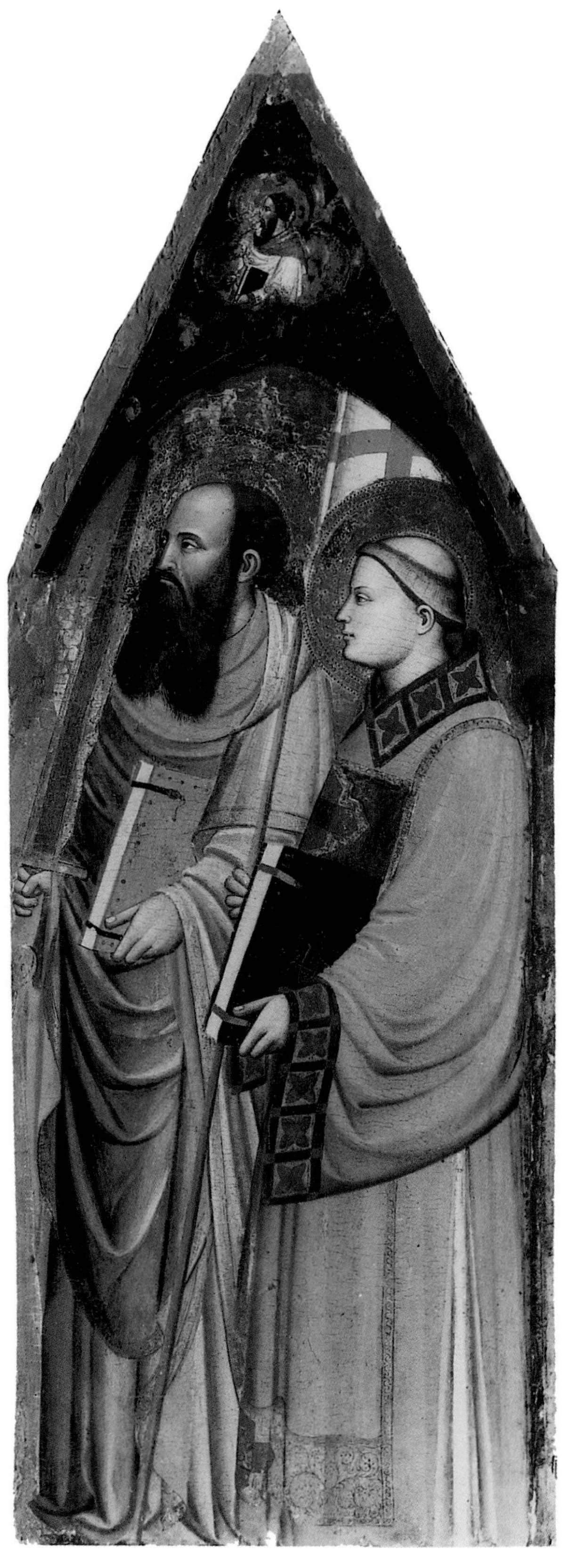

Fig. 176 Tommaso del Mazza: *St. Jude and St. John the Evangelist; St. Francis of Assisi* (left). *St. Paul and a Deacon Saint; St. Bartholomew* (right).
Bob Jones University Museum & Gallery, Greenville, South Carolina, 51.5 (left), 51.4 (right).

MAZZA, TOMMASO DEL, ACTIVE LATE FOURTEENTH CENTURY; FLORENTINE

St. Peter; St. Anthony Abbot (63.331.29) 97.5 X 42.7 CM (WITH FRAME), TEMPERA ON PANEL

GREENVILLE, SOUTH CAROLINA. BOB JONES UNIVERSITY MUSEUM & GALLERY

Originally exhibited as a work from the circle of Orcagna (1315/20–1368) (*An Exhibition of Italian Panels* 1965), the panel was reattributed to Lorenzo di Bicci (c. 1350–1427) when it entered the Bob Jones University Collection (in Beneth A. Jones 1968). Burton B. Fredericksen and Federico Zeri (1972), however, assigned it to the Master of the San Niccolò Altarpiece (active second half of the fourteenth century). Miklòs Boskovits (1975) and D. Stephen Pepper (1984) associated it with the work of the Master of Santa Verdiana (active c. 1370–c. 1415), who has since been identified as the Florentine painter Tommaso del Mazza. Boskovits suggested that the painting may have been the left wing of a polyptych, flanking the *Madonna and Child Enthroned* (current location unknown; formerly, Lazzaroni Collection, Paris), because of the panels' shared stylistic characteristics and identical punchmarks in the aureoles and margins. Barbara Deimling (1991) initially found this reconstruction problematic, since the St. Peter in the extensively reworked Greenville painting is so much smaller than the Madonna in the Paris panel. She subsequently (in Pasquinucci and Deimling 2000) endorsed Boskovits's reconstruction and proposed *St. Francis of Assisi* (private collection, London) as the right wing of the triptych. Deimling dated the altarpiece 1375–1380.

PROVENANCE

Lord Somers, Eastnor Castle, England; Wildenstein Gallery, New York, 1953; Bob Jones University Museum & Gallery (Bob Jones University Collection), acquired 1963

BIBLIOGRAPHY

An Exhibition of Italian Panels and Manuscripts from the Thirteenth and Fourteenth Centuries in Honor of Richard Offner, April 9 to June 6, 1965 (Hartford: Wadsworth Atheneum, 1965), 14, no. 6; Brigitte Klesse, *Seidenstoffe in der italienischen Malerei des vierzehnten Jahrhunderts* (Bern: Stämpfli, 1967), 388, no. 361; Beneth A. Jones, *Bob Jones University Supplement to the Catalogue of the Art Collection: Paintings Acquired, 1963–1968* (Greenville, S.C.: Bob Jones University, 1968), 9; Burton B. Fredericksen and Federico Zeri, *Census of Pre-Nineteenth-Century Italian Paintings in North American Public Collections* (Cambridge, Mass.: Harvard University Press, 1972), 136, 583; Miklòs Boskovits, *Pittura fiorentina alla vigilia del Rinascimento, 1370–1400* (Florence: Edam, 1975), 106, 229 n. 90, 230; D. Stephen Pepper, *Bob Jones University Collection of Religious Art: Italian Paintings* (Greenville, S.C.: Bob Jones University, 1984), 21; Federico Zeri, ed., *La pittura in Italia. Il Quattrocento*, 2 vols. (Milan: Electa, 1986), 2:630; Barbara Deimling, "Il Maestro di Santa Verdiana: Un polittico disperso e il problema dell'identificazione," *Arte Cristiana* 79 (1991): 405, 406; Simona Pasquinucci and Barbara Deimling, *Tradition and Innovation in Florentine Trecento Painting: Giovanni Bonsi, Tommaso del Mazza* (Florence: Giunti, 2000), 128, 129, 203-5; John M. Nolan, Carl B. Strehlke, Barbara Deimling, and Yvonne Szafran, *Discovering a Pre-Renaissance Master: Tommaso del Mazza* (Greenville, S.C.: Bob Jones University, 2009), 4, 5, 20, 27, 72-73.

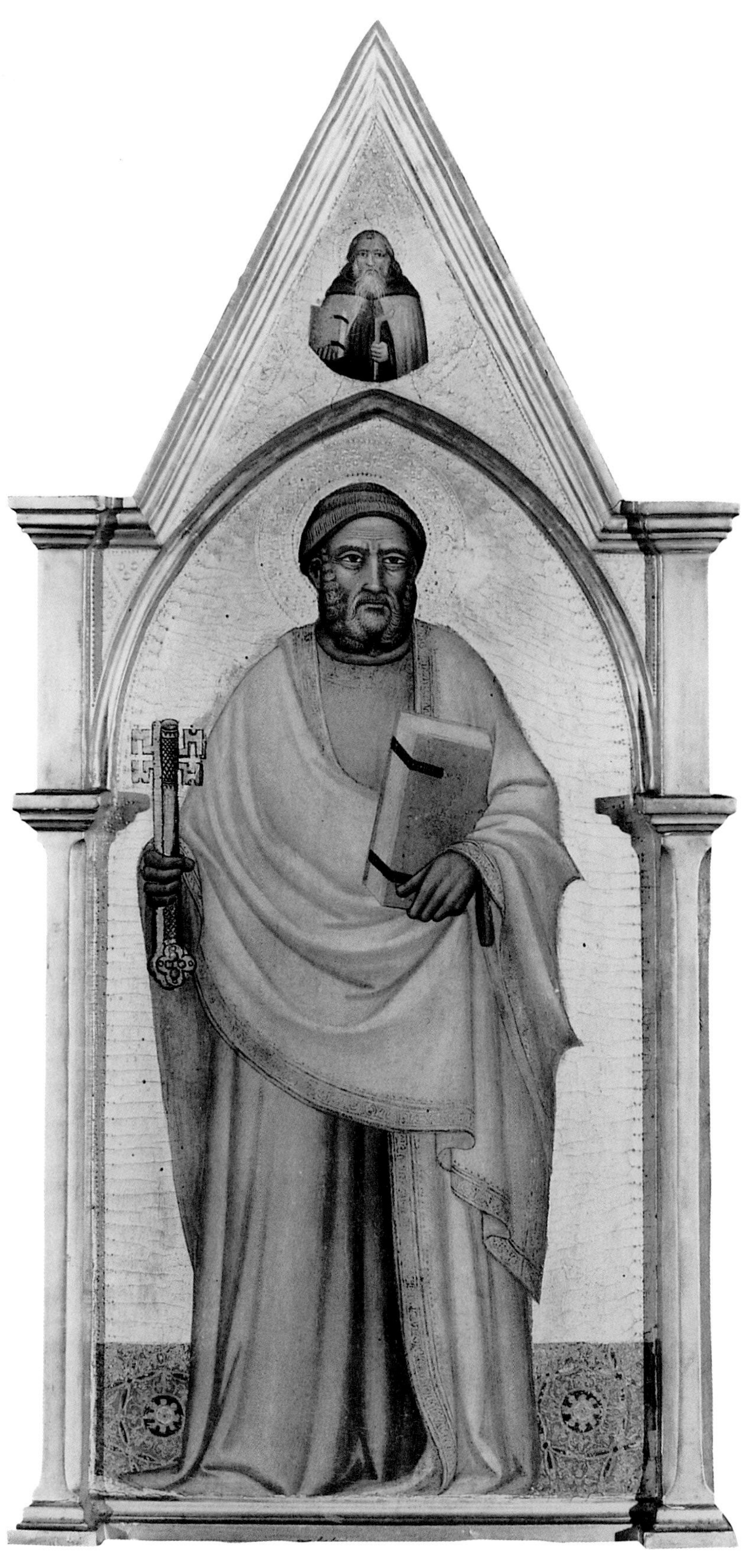

Fig. 177 Tommaso del Mazza: *St. Peter; St. Anthony Abbot*. Bob Jones University Museum & Gallery, Greenville, South Carolina, 63.331.29.

NORTH ITALIAN SCHOOL, LATE FIFTEENTH CENTURY

Ecce Homo (65.358.10) 95.9 X 70.5 CM, OIL ON CANVAS

GREENVILLE, SOUTH CAROLINA. BOB JONES UNIVERSITY MUSEUM & GALLERY

The painting probably served as a personal devotional image. When it entered the collection of Bob Jones University (in Beneth A. Jones 1968), it was assigned to the Lombard painter Giovanni Donato Montorfano (1440–1510). Burton B. Fredericksen and Federico Zeri (1972) maintained this attribution, but D. Stephen Pepper (1984) noted that it has not been widely accepted.

The scorpion that appears on the flag and on the escutcheon above the entrance to Pilate's palace symbolizes evil; its presence in this context may allude to Revelation 9:5: " . . . their torture was like the torture of the scorpion, when it stings a man," thereby likening the suffering inflicted on Christ by Pilate and the jeering crowd to that caused by the venomous creature. The Flagellation of Christ is depicted at the left of the canvas, within the palace. In the foreground, from left to right, are John the Evangelist, an unidentified female saint, the Virgin Mary, Mary Magdalen, and St. Peter. The composition may be based on a late-fifteenth-century northern European print.

PROVENANCE

Mr. and Mrs. Jack Linsky, New York, 1965; Bob Jones University Museum & Gallery (Bob Jones University Collection), acquired 1965

BIBLIOGRAPHY

Beneth A. Jones, *Bob Jones University Supplement to the Catalogue of the Art Collection: Paintings Acquired, 1963–1968* (Greenville, S.C.: Bob Jones University, 1968), 9; Burton B. Fredericksen and Federico Zeri, *Census of Pre-Nineteenth-Century Italian Paintings in North American Public Collections* (Cambridge, Mass.: Harvard University Press, 1972), 144, 583; D. Stephen Pepper, *Bob Jones University Collection of Religious Art: Italian Paintings* (Greenville, S.C.: Bob Jones University, 1984), 33.

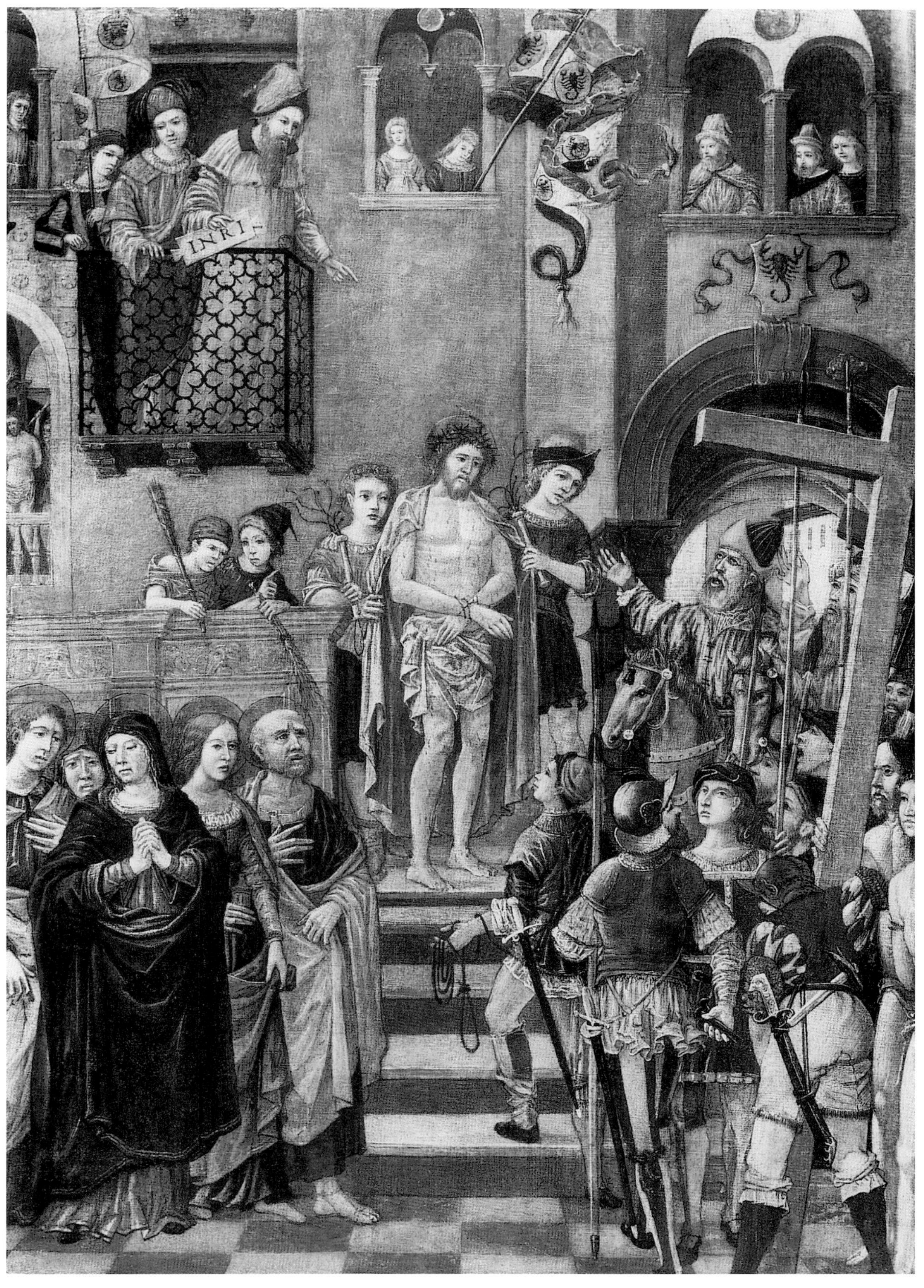

Fig. 178 North Italian School, late fifteenth century: *Ecce Homo*. Bob Jones University Museum & Gallery, Greenville, South Carolina, 65.358.10.

PALMEZZANO, MARCO, C. 1460–1539; ROMAGNOL

Christ Bearing the Cross (59.208) 55.6 X 46.4 CM, OIL ON PANEL

GREENVILLE, SOUTH CAROLINA. BOB JONES UNIVERSITY MUSEUM & GALLERY

The painting, a devotional image, has been accepted generally as a work by Marco Palmezzano, based on stylistic affinities with his *Communion of the Apostles* (Pinacoteca Civica, Forlì; 122). There are a number of other versions of the subject attributed to Palmezzano, including works in the Rheinisches Landesmuseum, Bonn (209); the Pinacoteca Civica, Brescia (110); the Czartoryski Collection, National Museum, Cracow; the Pinacoteca Comunale, Faenza (87); and the Pinacoteca Civica, Forlì (116).

PROVENANCE

Barbiano Palace, near Bologna; Jack Linsky, New York; Bob Jones University Museum & Gallery (Bob Jones University Collection), acquired 1959

BIBLIOGRAPHY

"Acquisitions," *Art Journal* 20 (1961): 158; Alfred Scharf, *The Bob Jones University Collection of Religious Paintings*, vol. 1, *Italian and French Paintings* (Greenville, S.C.: Bob Jones University, 1962), 66; Bernard Berenson, *Italian Pictures of the Renaissance: A List of the Principal Artists and Their Works with an Index of Places. Central Italian and North Italian Schools*, 3 vols. (London: Phaidon Press, 1968), 1:315; Burton B. Fredericksen and Federico Zeri, *Census of Pre-Nineteenth-Century Italian Paintings in North American Public Collections* (Cambridge, Mass.: Harvard University Press, 1972), 155, 583; D. Stephen Pepper, *Bob Jones University Collection of Religious Art: Italian Paintings* (Greenville, S.C.: Bob Jones University, 1984), 91.

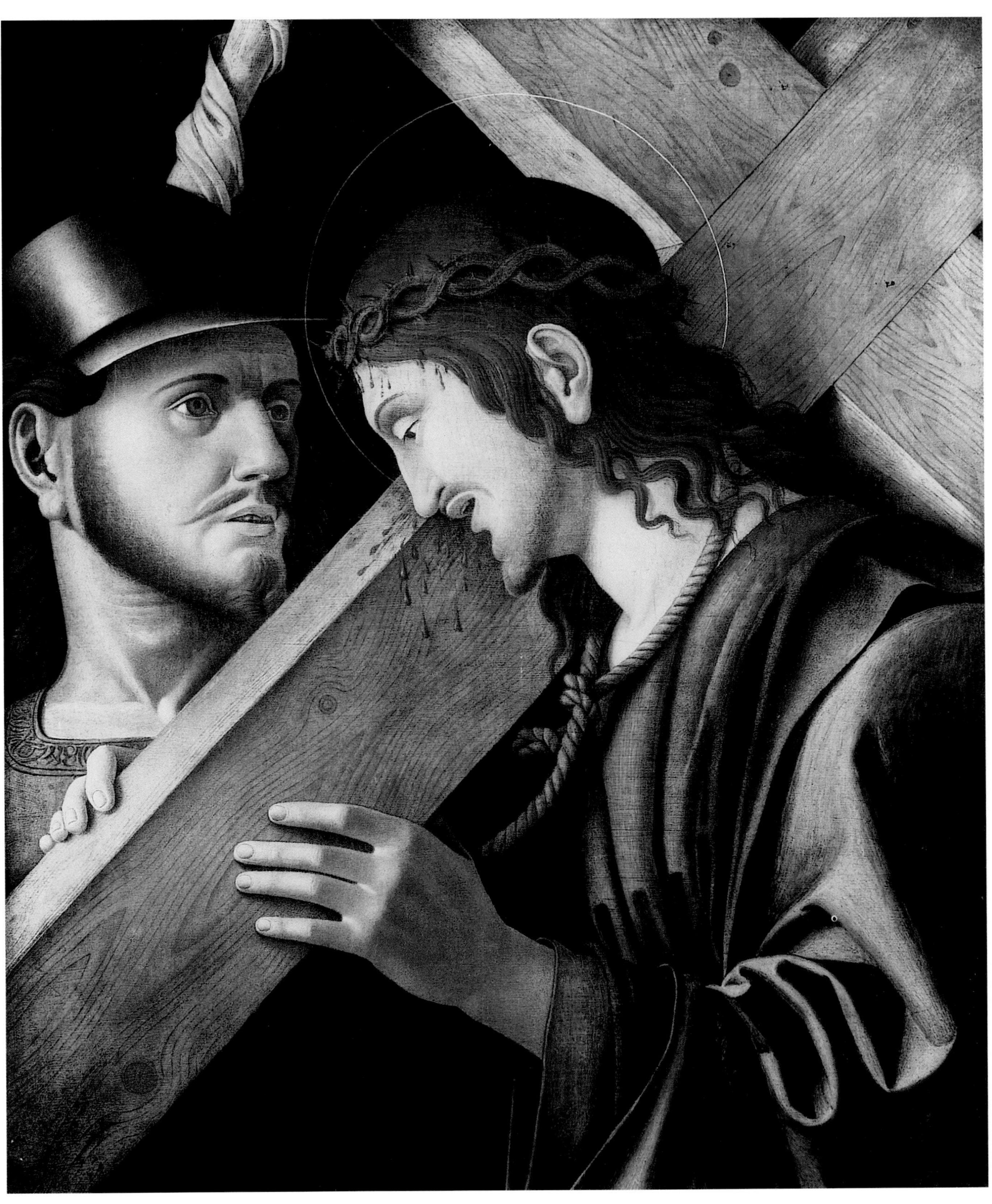

Fig. 179 Marco Palmezzano: *Christ Bearing the Cross*. Bob Jones University Museum & Gallery, Greenville, South Carolina, 59.208.

PREVITALI, ANDREA, C. 1470–1528; ATTRIBUTED; BERGAMASQUE

Madonna and Child (53.42) 12.7 X 10.2 CM, OIL ON CANVAS

GREENVILLE, SOUTH CAROLINA. BOB JONES UNIVERSITY MUSEUM & GALLERY

The painting has been attributed to various north Italian artists in the circle of Giovanni Bellini (1431/6–1516). Hans Tietze and Erica Tietze-Conrat (1954) ascribed it to Andrea Previtali, Fritz Heinemann (1962) to Altobello Melone (active 1497–1517), and Alfred Scharf (1962) to an anonymous sixteenth-century painter from northern Italy. Burton B. Fredericksen and Federico Zeri (1972) also assigned it to a northern Italian painter, of the fifteenth century, however. D. Stephen Pepper (1984) revived the attribution to Previtali.

According to Heinemann, this small devotional painting is one of twelve, by various artists, deriving from a lost work by Giovanni Bellini.

PROVENANCE

Manfrin, Venice; private collection, Vienna; E. and A. Silberman Gallery, New York; Bob Jones University Museum & Gallery (Bob Jones University Collection), acquired 1953

BIBLIOGRAPHY

Hans Tietze and Erica Tietze-Conrat, *The Bob Jones University Collection of Religious Paintings* (Greenville, S.C.: Bob Jones University, 1954), 38; Fritz Heinemann, *Giovanni Bellini e i Belliniani*, 3 vols. (Venice: Neri Pozza, 1962), 1:12, no. 41c; Alfred Scharf, *The Bob Jones University Collection of Religious Paintings*, vol. 1, *Italian and French Paintings* (Greenville, S.C.: Bob Jones University, 1962), 60; Burton B. Fredericksen and Federico Zeri, *Census of Pre-Nineteenth-Century Italian Paintings in North American Public Collections* (Cambridge, Mass.: Harvard University Press, 1972), 234, 582; D. Stephen Pepper, *Bob Jones University Collection of Religious Art: Italian Paintings* (Greenville, S.C.: Bob Jones University, 1984), 97.

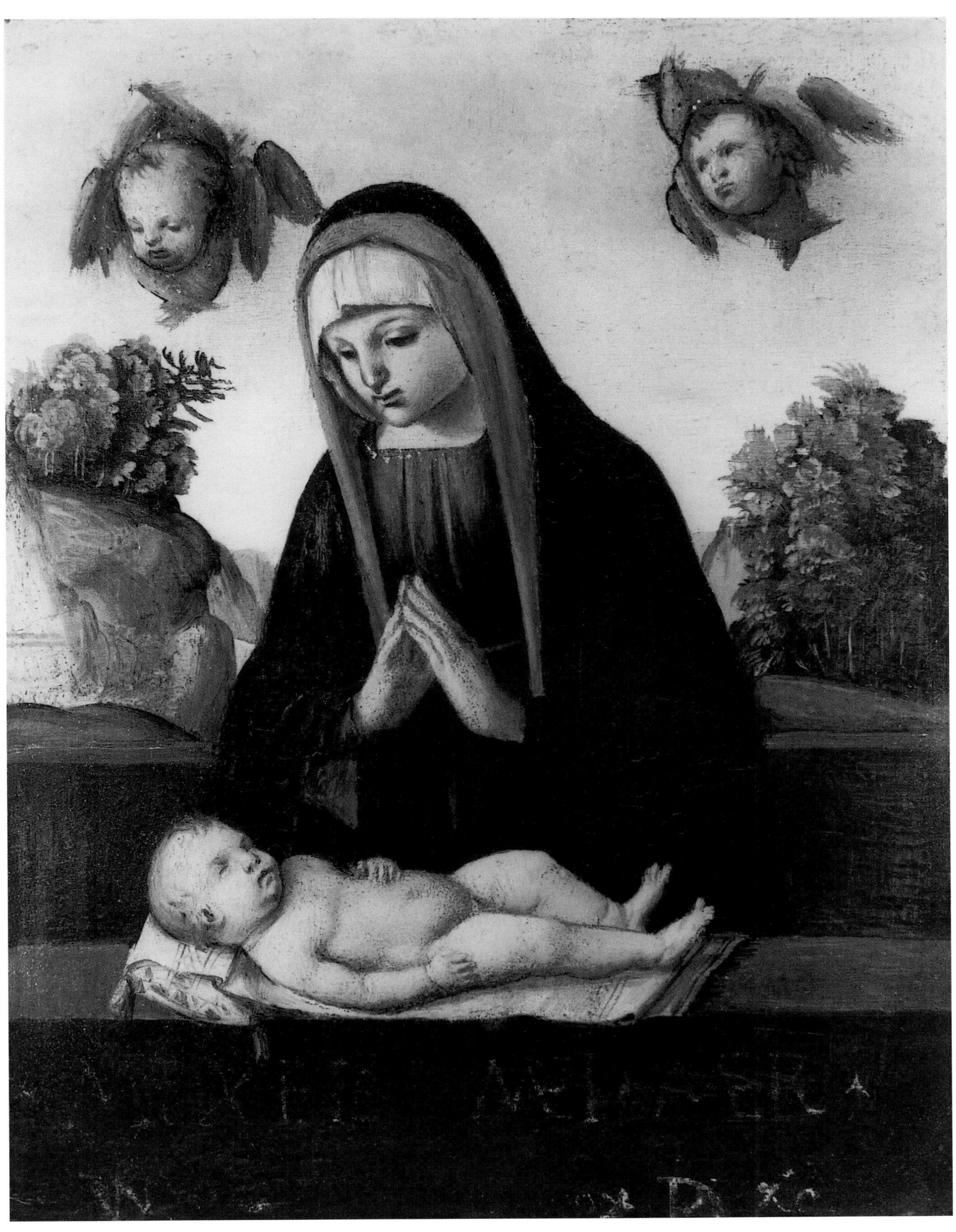

Fig. 180 Andrea Previtali (attributed): *Madonna and Child*. Bob Jones University Museum & Gallery, Greenville, South Carolina, 53.42.

PSEUDO PIER FRANCESCO FIORENTINO, ACTIVE SECOND HALF OF THE FIFTEENTH CENTURY; FLORENTINE

Madonna and Child with St. John the Baptist and an Angel (51.8) 79.4 CM (DIAMETER), TEMPERA ON PANEL

GREENVILLE, SOUTH CAROLINA. BOB JONES UNIVERSITY MUSEUM & GALLERY

The composition of the painting was inspired by Filippo Lippi's representations of the Adoration of the Child from the 1450s. The artist derived the figures of the Madonna and Child from Lippi's *Annalena Altarpiece* (Uffizi, Florence; 8350) of c. 1455 and the angel from works by Francesco Pesellino (1422 [?]–1457). Roberta J. M. Olson (2000) considered the panel to be one of the earliest *tondi* produced after Lippi popularized the format. A *tondo* attributed to Lippi–Pesellino imitators (San Martino, Sinnalunga) has a similar composition and the same Virgin, Christ Child, and John the Baptist figures.

Hans Tietze and Erica Tietze-Conrat (1954) attributed this devotional work, intended for a domestic setting, to Pseudo Pier Francesco Fiorentino. Burton B. Fredericksen and Federico Zeri (1972) assigned it to Lippi–Pesellino imitators, a group of mid-fifteenth-century Florentine artists who apparently shared a workshop in which they emulated the compositions of the two masters. Everett P. Fahy (Frick Art Reference Library Artists List) gave the painting to the Master of the Scandicci Lamentation (active sixteenth century). The Museum maintains the attribution to Pseudo Pier Francesco Fiorentino.

The unicorn in the background of the Greenville panel and the white lilies held by the angel allude to the purity of the Virgin.

PROVENANCE

Harry Payne Whitney, New York; Julius Weitzner, New York; Bob Jones University Museum & Gallery (Bob Jones University Collection), acquired 1951

BIBLIOGRAPHY

Hans Tietze and Erica Tietze-Conrat, *The Bob Jones University Collection of Religious Paintings* (Greenville, S.C.: Bob Jones University, 1954), 28; Alfred Scharf, *The Bob Jones University Collection of Religious Paintings*, vol. 1, *Italian and French Paintings* (Greenville, S.C.: Bob Jones University, 1962), 42; Burton B. Fredericksen and Federico Zeri, *Census of Pre-Nineteenth-Century Italian Paintings in North American Public Collections* (Cambridge, Mass.: Harvard University Press, 1972), 134, 582; D. Stephen Pepper, *Bob Jones University Collection of Religious Art: Italian Paintings* (Greenville, S.C.: Bob Jones University, 1984), 24; Roberta J. M. Olson, *The Florentine Tondo* (Oxford and New York: Oxford University Press, 2000), 175; Perri Lee Roberts, Bruce Cole, and Hayden B. J. Maginnis, *Sacred Treasures: Early Italian Paintings from Southern Collections* (Athens, Ga.: Georgia Museum of Art, 2002), 156-58.

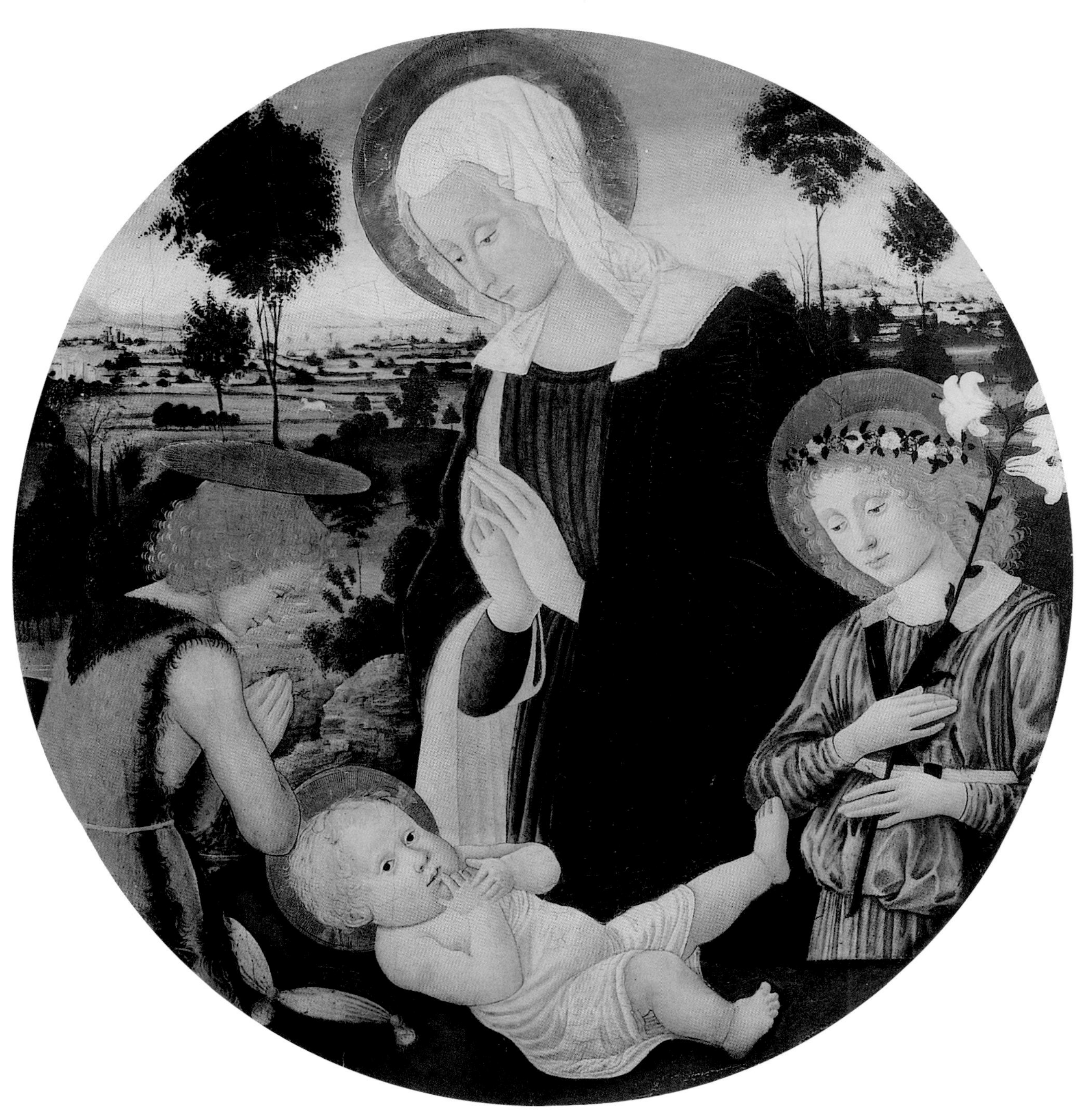

Fig. 181 Pseudo Pier Francesco Fiorentino: *Madonna and Child with St. John the Baptist and an Angel.* Bob Jones University Museum & Gallery, Greenville, South Carolina, 51.8.

SCACCO, CRISTOFORO, ACTIVE LATE FIFTEENTH CENTURY; VERONESE

God the Father (55.69) 43.2 x 67.3 CM (OVAL), TEMPERA ON PANEL

GREENVILLE, SOUTH CAROLINA. BOB JONES UNIVERSITY MUSEUM & GALLERY

The painting was acquired as a work by Luca Signorelli (c. 1450–1523) ("Accessions" 1957), but it was reattributed to Cristoforo Scacco by Federico Zeri (cited in Scharf 1962), who determined that it came from the same altarpiece as the artist's *St. John the Baptist* (Musée Calvet, Avignon; 22676). The panel was part of the apex of the altarpiece's Coronation of the Virgin scene, which resembled the central portion of Scacco's triptych of the *Coronation* (Museo di Capodimonte, Naples; 64). Rinaldo Naldi (1986) dated the painting c. 1500.

PROVENANCE

E. & A. Silberman Gallery, New York, 1955; Bob Jones University Museum & Gallery (Bob Jones University Collection), acquired 1955

BIBLIOGRAPHY

"Accessions," *Art Quarterly* 20 (1957): 320; Alfred Scharf, *The Bob Jones University Collection of Religious Paintings*, vol. 1, *Italian and French Paintings* (Greenville, S.C.: Bob Jones University, 1962), 65; Bernard Berenson, *Italian Pictures of the Renaissance: A List of the Principal Artists and Their Works with an Index of Places. Central Italian and North Italian Schools*, 3 vols. (London: Phaidon Press, 1968), 1:387; Burton B. Fredericksen and Federico Zeri, *Census of Pre-Nineteenth-Century Italian Paintings in North American Public Collections* (Cambridge, Mass.: Harvard University Press, 1972), 184, 582; D. Stephen Pepper, *Bob Jones University Collection of Religious Art: Italian Paintings* (Greenville, S.C.: Bob Jones University, 1984), 24-25; Rinaldo Naldi, "Riconsiderando Cristoforo Scacco," *Prospettiva* 45 (1986): 49, 55 n. 65.

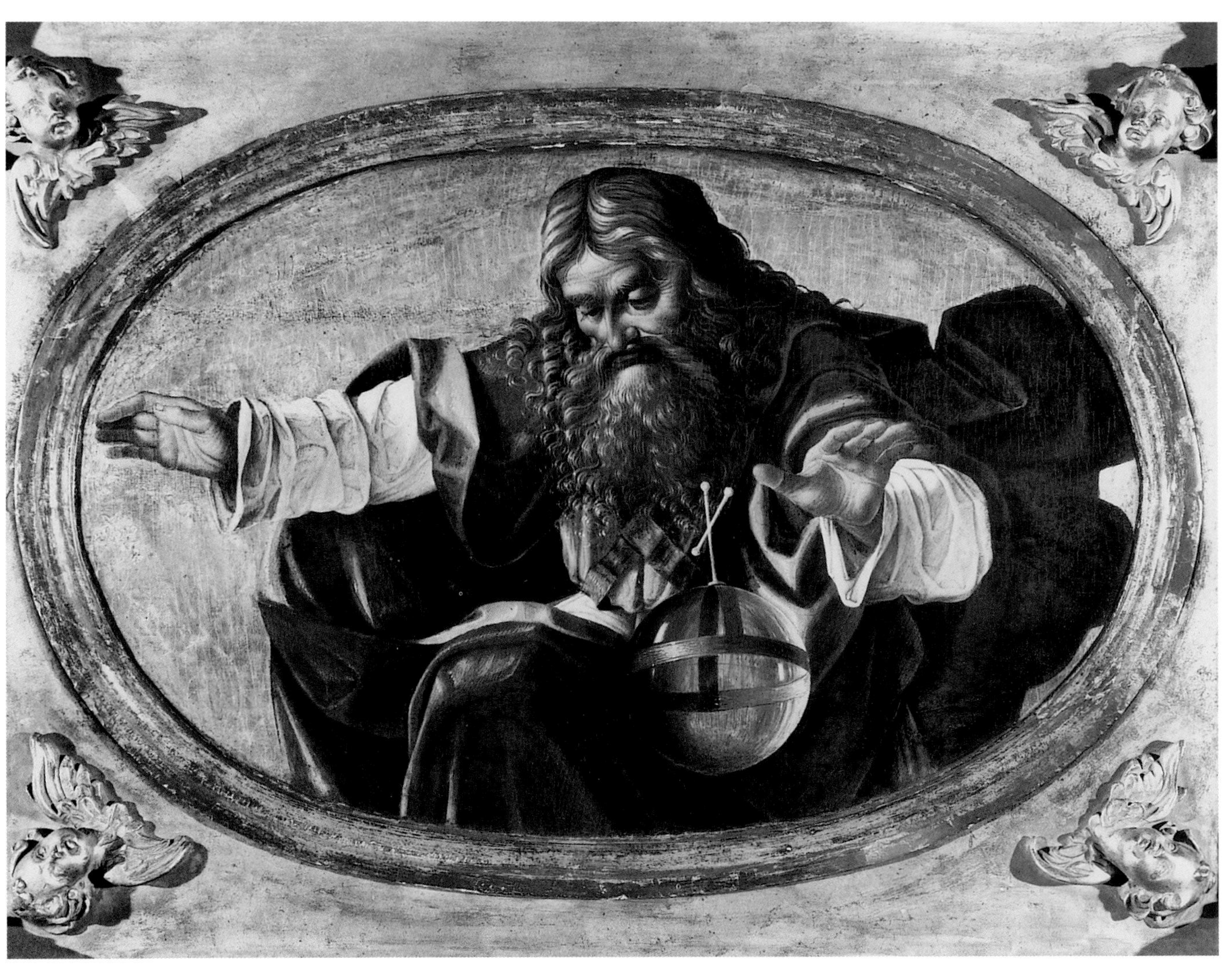

Fig. 182 Cristoforo Scacco: *God the Father*. Bob Jones University Museum & Gallery, Greenville, South Carolina, 55.69.

SICILIAN SCHOOL, FOURTEENTH CENTURY

Bishop Saint with Christ and Donor (68.431.2) 172.7 X 99.1 CM, TEMPERA ON PANEL

GREENVILLE, SOUTH CAROLINA. BOB JONES UNIVERSITY MUSEUM & GALLERY

Edward B. Garrison (1949) attributed the panel to the mid-fourteenth-century Venetian Master of Sts. Placidus and Benefactus; he noted that the painting was badly damaged, its shape probably indicating an original architectonic setting, perhaps over an altar. Burton B. Fredericksen and Federico Zeri (1972) assigned the work to southern Italy. Miklòs Boskovits (cited in Pepper 1984) endorsed the latter attribution and specified a Sicilian point of origin. D. Stephen Pepper dated the work c. 1340.

"ABBAS JANNUS DE QUERCIS" ("Abbot Gianus da Quercia") is inscribed near the kneeling Benedictine monk. The painting is a votive image, most likely commissioned to commemorate the election of the donor to an abbacy and his benediction by the diocesan bishop. Christ and the panel's bishop saint, perhaps Bonifilius, the abbot bishop of Foligno, represent the source of the patron's ecclesiastical authority. Notably, all three figures hold similar crosiers.

PROVENANCE

Bellini, Florence, by 1935; M. Adolphe Stoclet, Brussels; Central Picture Galleries, 1968; Bob Jones University Museum & Gallery (Bob Jones University Collection), acquired 1968

BIBLIOGRAPHY

Edward B. Garrison, *Italian Romanesque Panel Painting* (Florence: Leo S. Olschki, 1949), 223, no. 607; Beneth A. Jones, *Bob Jones University Supplement to the Catalogue of the Art Collection: Paintings Acquired, 1963–1968* (Greenville, S.C.: Bob Jones University, 1968), 9; Burton B. Fredericksen and Federico Zeri, *Census of Pre-Nineteenth-Century Italian Paintings in North American Public Collections* (Cambridge, Mass.: Harvard University Press, 1972), 241, 582; D. Stephen Pepper, *Bob Jones University Collection of Religious Art: Italian Paintings* (Greenville, S.C.: Bob Jones University, 1984), 32-33; Marilena Tamassia, *Collezioni d'arte tra Ottocento e Novecento: Jacquier fotografi a Firenze, 1870–1935* (Naples: Electa, 1995), 182, no. 50201.

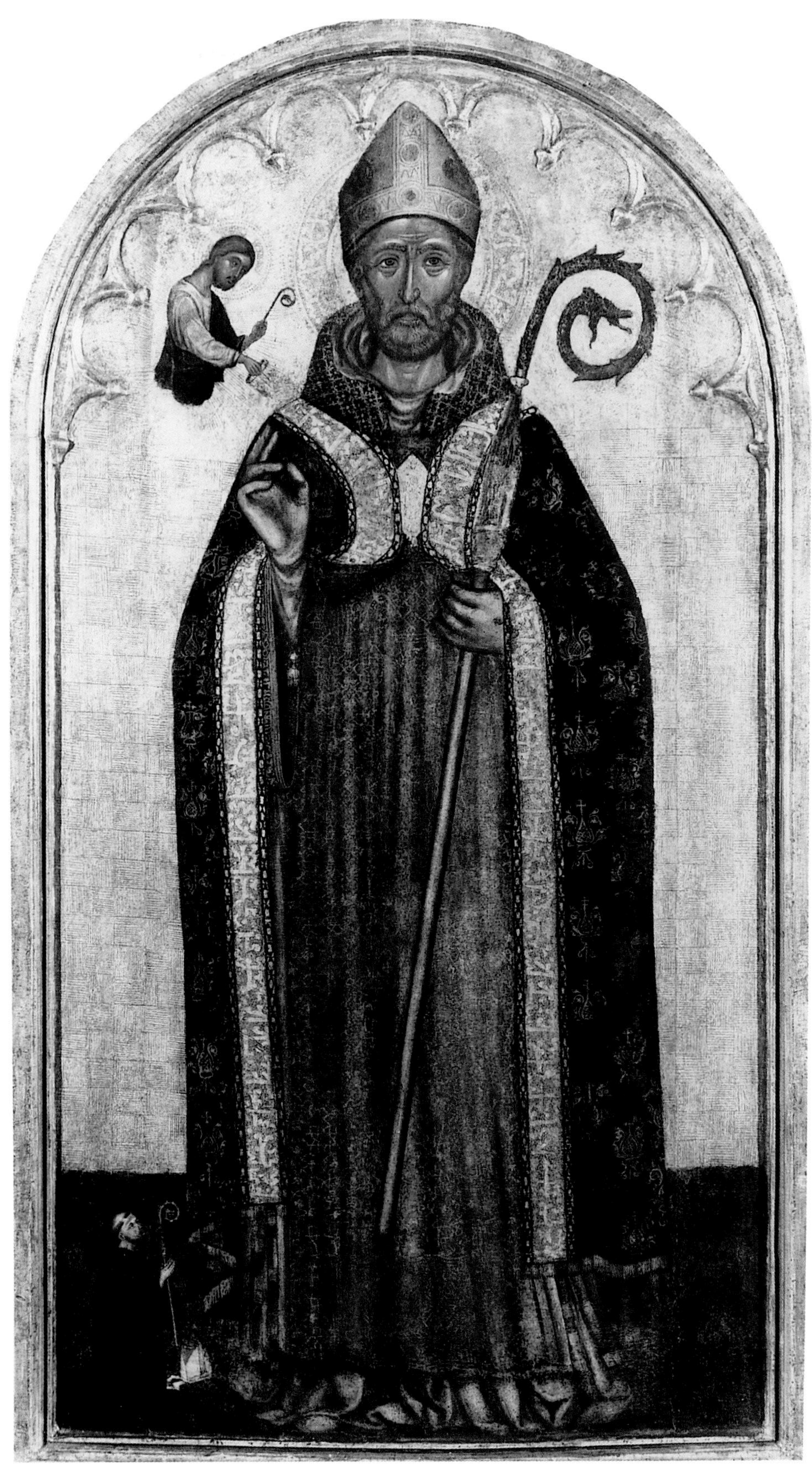

Fig. 183 Sicilian School, fourteenth century: *Bishop Saint with Christ and Donor*. Bob Jones University Museum & Gallery, Greenville, South Carolina, 68.431.2.

SIGNORELLI, LUCA, C. 1450–1523; WORKSHOP; UMBRIAN

Flagellation of Christ (62.283) 36.8 X 92.7 CM, TEMPERA ON PANEL

GREENVILLE, SOUTH CAROLINA. BOB JONES UNIVERSITY MUSEUM & GALLERY

The painting has generally been considered a product of Signorelli's shop, part of the predella of an unidentified altarpiece. Its composition is a variant of the *Flagellation* in the predella of Signorelli's *Santa Margherita Altarpiece* (Museo Diocesano, Cortona) from 1502. Laurence B. Kanter (1989) attributed the work to Francesco Signorelli, Luca's nephew and primary shop assistant (active 1520; died 1539), who was responsible for many of his uncle's major commissions after 1513. Kanter also suggested that the painting may have come from the same altarpiece as the *Doubting Thomas* (central panel) and the *Madonna and Child with St. John the Baptist and St. Jerome* (lunette), both at Santa Maria Assunta, Cortona. Miklòs Boskovits (2003) proposed that the panel may have come from the same predella as Signorelli's *Crucifixion* (National Gallery, Washington, D.C.; 1952.5.75), possibly a part of the altarpiece for Sant'Agostino, Matelica (Macerata).

PROVENANCE

Stefano Bardini, Florence, acquired 1902; American Art Galleries, New York, April 23, 1918, lot 451; Bruno Tartaglia, Rome; Acquavella Galleries, New York; Bob Jones University Museum & Gallery (Bob Jones University Collection), acquired 1962

BIBLIOGRAPHY

Mostra di Luca Signorelli: Catalogo (Florence: L'Arte della Stampa, 1953), 118, no. 63; Mario Salmi, *Luca Signorelli* (Munich: Wilhelm Goldman, 1955), 64; Alfred Scharf, *The Bob Jones University Collection of Religious Paintings*, vol. 1, *Italian and French Paintings* (Greenville, S.C.: Bob Jones University, 1962), 51; Bernard Berenson, *Italian Pictures of the Renaissance: A List of the Principal Artists and Their Works with an Index of Places. Central Italian and North Italian Schools*, 3 vols. (London: Phaidon Press, 1968), 1:397; Burton B. Fredericksen and Federico Zeri, *Census of Pre-Nineteenth-Century Italian Paintings in North American Public Collections* (Cambridge, Mass.: Harvard University Press, 1972), 187, 583; D. Stephen Pepper, *Bob Jones University Collection of Religious Art: Italian Paintings* (Greenville, S.C: Bob Jones University, 1984), 110; Laurence B. Kanter, "The Late Works of Luca Signorelli and His Followers 1498–1559" (Ph.D. diss., New York University, 1989), 310; Miklòs Boskovits, *Italian Paintings of the Fifteenth Century* (Washington, D.C.: National Gallery of Art, 2003), 645.

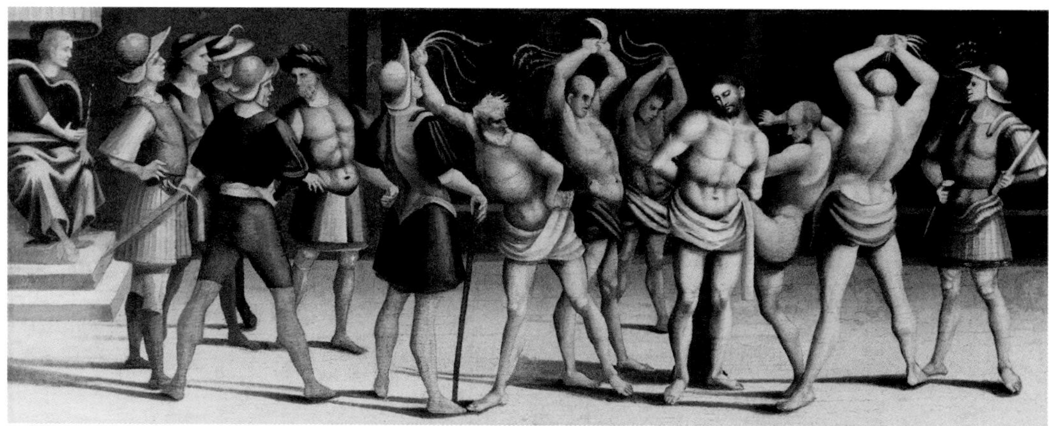

Fig. 184 (above and facing, detail) Luca Signorelli (workshop): *Flagellation of Christ*. Bob Jones University Museum & Gallery, Greenville, South Carolina, 62.283.

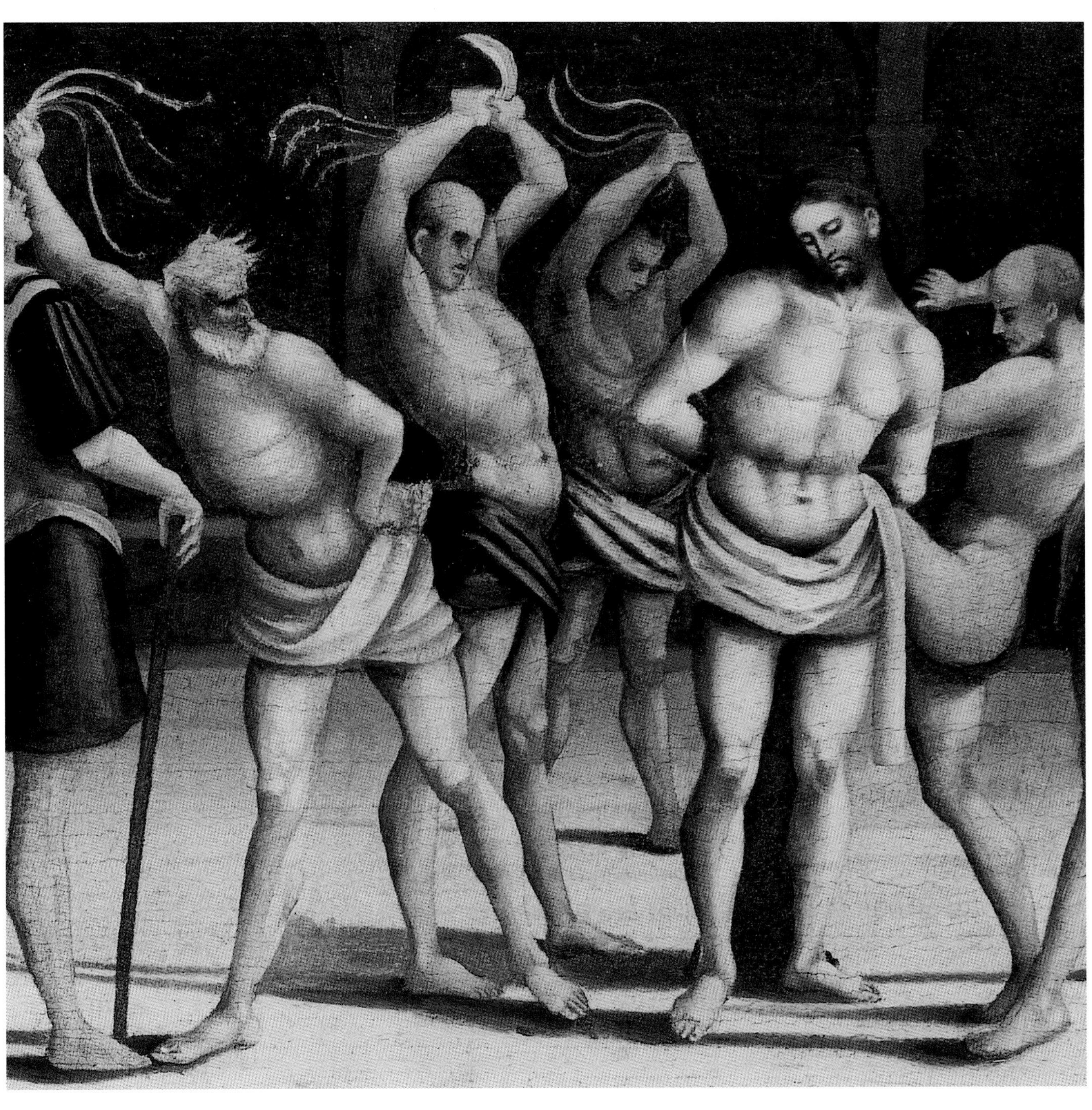

SOLARIO, ANDREA, C. 1465–1524; MILANESE

Christ of Derision (66.390) 58.7 X 44.5 CM, OIL ON PANEL

GREENVILLE, SOUTH CAROLINA. BOB JONES UNIVERSITY MUSEUM & GALLERY

Scholars have considered the painting an autograph work by Andrea Solario, with the notable exception of David Alan Brown (1987), who saw it as another artist's copy of Solario's composition.

This personal devotional image is one of a dozen variant copies of Solario's signed *Ecce Homo* (Philadelphia Museum of Art, Philadelphia; J274) of c. 1507–1509. The painting lacks the drops of blood on the forehead, chest, and arms of Christ that are found in the original.

PROVENANCE

Julius Weitzner, New York, 1966; Bob Jones University Museum & Gallery (Bob Jones University Collection), acquired 1966

BIBLIOGRAPHY

"Acquisitions," *Art Journal* 26 (1966): 55; Beneth A. Jones, *Bob Jones University Supplement to the Catalogue of the Art Collection: Paintings Acquired, 1963–1968* (Greenville, S.C.: Bob Jones University, 1968), 11; Burton B. Fredericksen and Federico Zeri, *Census of Pre-Nineteenth-Century Italian Paintings in North American Public Collections* (Cambridge, Mass.: Harvard University Press, 1972), 77, 583; D. Stephen Pepper, *Bob Jones University Collection of Religious Art: Italian Paintings* (Greenville, S.C.: Bob Jones University, 1984), 113; David Alan Brown, *Andrea Solario* (Milan: Electa, 1987), 213, no. 50.

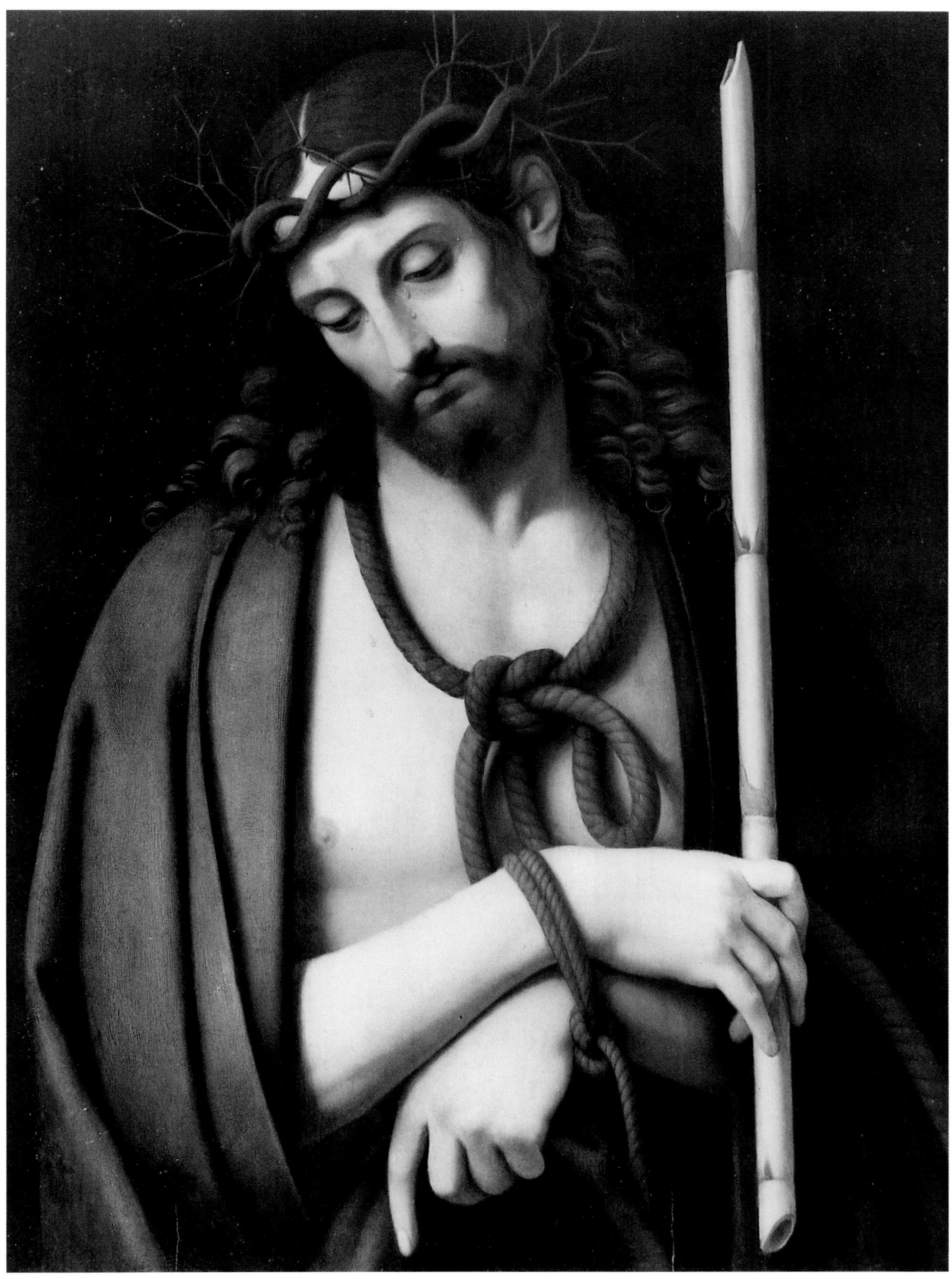

Fig. 185 Andrea Solario: *Christ of Derision*. Bob Jones University Museum & Gallery, Greenville, South Carolina, 66.390.

VIVARINI, BARTOLOMEO, ACTIVE C. 1440; DIED AFTER 1500; VENETIAN

Christ Showing His Wounds (57.112) 46.4 X 76.5 CM, TEMPERA ON PANEL

GREENVILLE, SOUTH CAROLINA. BOB JONES UNIVERSITY MUSEUM & GALLERY

Published by Adolfo Venturi (1900) as the work of Bartolomeo Vivarini, the painting was identified by Rodolfo Pallucchini (1962) as a panel from the upper register of an unidentified polyptych dating to the mid-1490s. It was probably located directly above the central panel; a similar juxtaposition may be found in Bartolomeo's altarpiece for the Certosa of Padua (San Antonio Abate, Lussingrande), signed and dated 1475.

The Man of Sorrows wears a crown of thorns and displays the wounds in his hands and side. Other references to the Passion include the arms of the cross, the cloth of honor, and the mourning angels.

PROVENANCE

Count Albani, Bergamo; Crespi Collection, Milan; Galerie Georges Petit, Paris, June 4, 1914, lot 63; Achillito Chiesa, Milan; American Art Association, New York, April 16, 1926, lot 10; Julius Weitzner, New York; Robert Lehman, New York; Bob Jones University Museum & Gallery (Bob Jones University Collection), acquired 1957

BIBLIOGRAPHY

Adolfo Venturi, *La Galleria Crespi in Milano* (Milan: Hoepli, 1900), 55-56; Lionello Venturi, *Le origini della pittura veneziana, 1300–1500* (Venice: Istituto Veneto di arti grafiche, 1907), 182; Bernard Berenson, *Italian Pictures of the Renaissance: A List of the Principal Artists and Their Works with an Index of Places. Venetian School*, 2 vols. (New York: Phaidon, 1957), 1:202; Alfred Scharf, *The Bob Jones University Collection of Religious Paintings*, vol. 1, *Italian and French Paintings* (Greenville, S.C.: Bob Jones University, 1962), 33; Rodolfo Pallucchini, *I Vivarini: Antonio, Bartolomeo, Alvise* (Venice: Neri Pozza, 1962), 128; Burton B. Fredericksen and Federico Zeri, *Census of Pre-Nineteenth-Century Italian Paintings in North American Public Collections* (Cambridge, Mass.: Harvard University Press, 1972), 211, 582; D. Stephen Pepper, *Bob Jones University Collection of Religious Art: Italian Paintings* (Greenville, S.C.: Bob Jones University, 1984), 27.

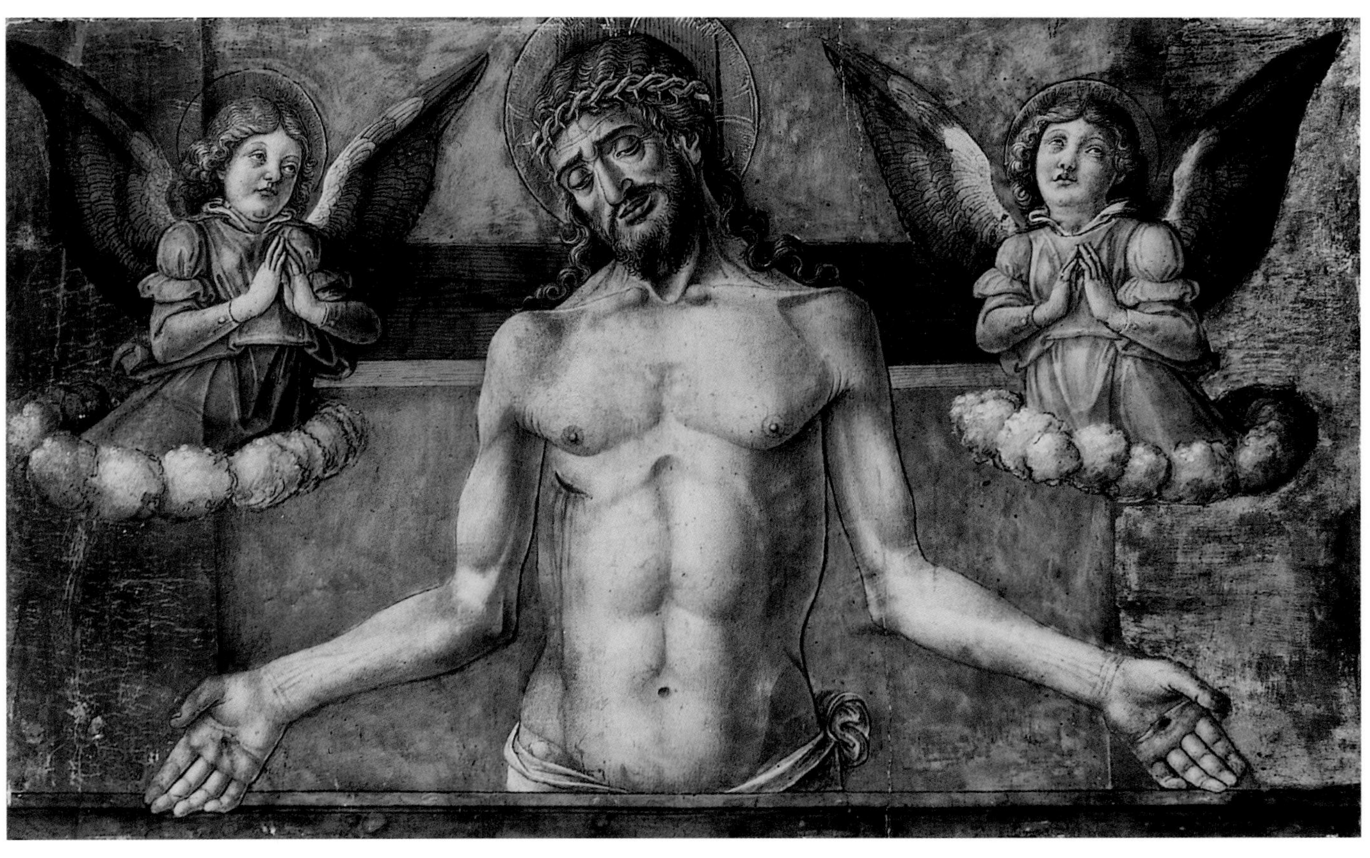

Fig. 186 Bartolomeo Vivarini: *Christ Showing His Wounds*. Bob Jones University Museum & Gallery, Greenville, South Carolina, 57.112.

BOCCACCINO, BOCCACCIO, BEFORE 1466–1525; CREMONESE

Madonna and Child (A 368B; K 1056) 62.9 X 50.8 CM, OIL ON CANVAS

HELENA, ARKANSAS. PHILLIPS COUNTY MUSEUM

Roberto Longhi (1934) observed that the painting's figure types and poses were influenced by Raphael's *Sistine Madonna* (Gemäldegalerie, Dresden; 93) from 1513 and his *Madonna della Sedia* (Palazzo Pitti, Florence; 151) from 1514. The attribution to Boccaccino has been accepted universally, as has a date late in his career. Marco Tanzi (1991) placed the painting in the year of the artist's death, after he completed his frescoes in the Cathedral of Cremona.

PROVENANCE

Private collection, Rome; Count Alessandro Contini-Bonacossi, Florence; Samuel H. Kress, New York, acquired 1936; Phillips County Museum, acquired 1938

BIBLIOGRAPHY

Roberto Longhi, *Officina ferrarese* (Rome: Edizioni d'Italia, 1934), 120; Roberto Longhi, *Officina ferrarese 1934* (Florence: Sansoni, 1956), 71; Alfredo Puerari, *Boccaccino* (Milan: Ceschina, 1957), 176-78; Bernard Berenson, *Italian Pictures of the Renaissance: A List of the Principal Artists and Their Works with an Index of Places. Central Italian and North Italian Schools*, 3 vols. (London: Phaidon Press, 1968), 1:53; Fern Rusk Shapley, *Paintings from the Samuel H. Kress Collection: Italian Schools*, vol. 2, *XV–XVI Century* (London: Phaidon Press, 1968), 85; Burton B. Fredericksen and Federico Zeri, *Census of Pre-Nineteenth-Century Italian Paintings in North American Public Collections* (Cambridge, Mass.: Harvard University Press, 1972), 30, 585; Marco Tanzi, *Boccaccio Boccaccino* (Soncino: Edizioni dei Soncino, 1991), 25-46.

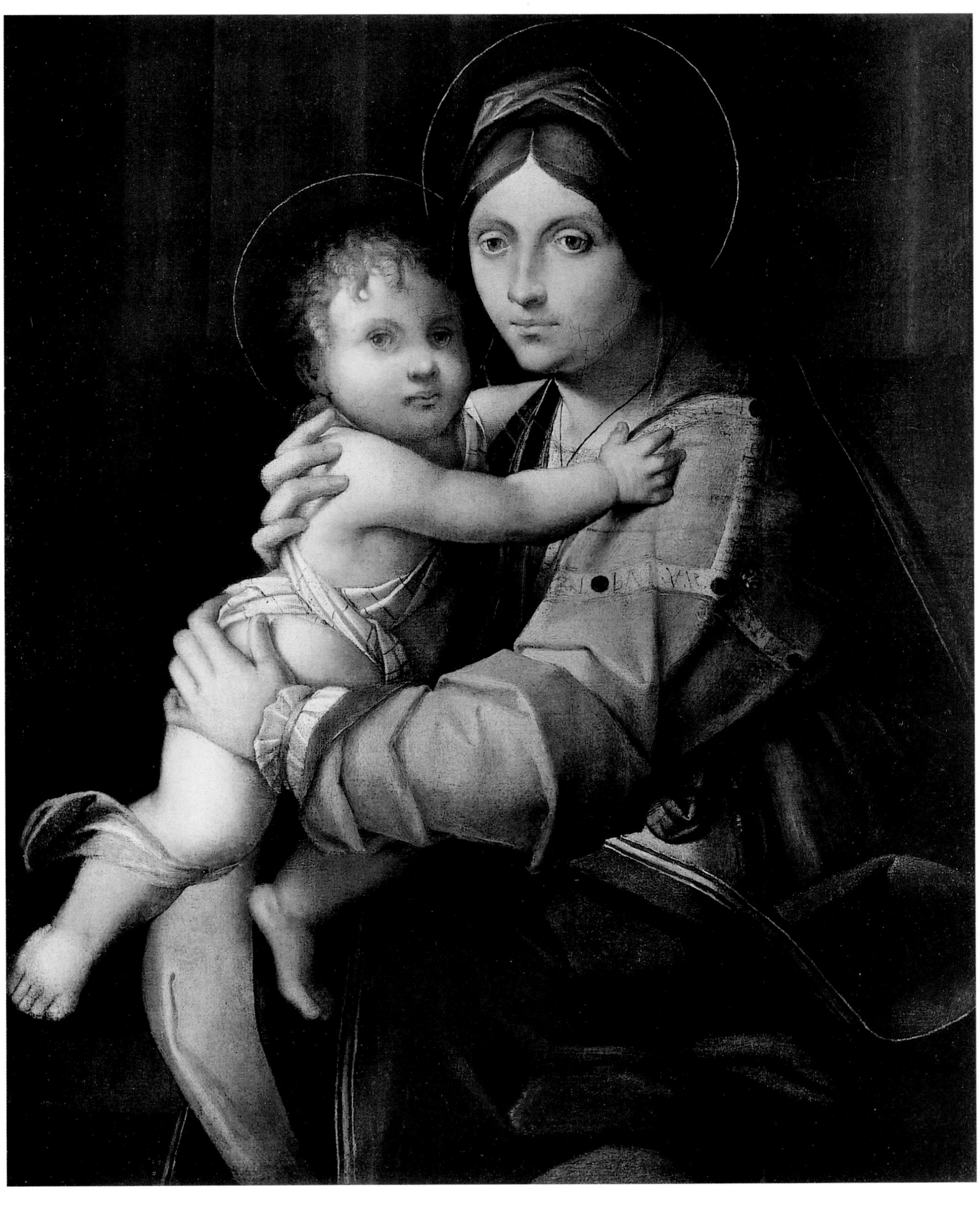

Fig. 187 Boccaccio Boccaccino: *Madonna and Child*. Phillips County Museum, Helena, Arkansas, A 368b.

FALCONETTO, GIAN MARIA, C. 1468–1535; ATTRIBUTED; VERONESE

St. Onophrius and St. John the Baptist (A 368A; K 120) 111.2 X 60.7 CM, TEMPERA ON PANEL

HELENA, ARKANSAS. PHILLIPS COUNTY MUSEUM

The panel was originally the right wing of an unidentified altarpiece, similar in format and style to Falconetto's *Madonna and Child with Saints* (San Fermo Maggiore, Verona). Roberto Longhi (cited in Shapley 1968) suggested that the background may have been inspired by a northern European engraving. Shapley dated the work to the end of the 1400s or the beginning of the 1500s.

Inscribed above St. Onophrius is "S [O]NOFRIVS," above the Baptist, "S IOHES BA," and on the Baptist's scroll, "ECCE AGNVS DEI" ("Here is the Lamb of God"), from John 1:29.

PROVENANCE

Count Alessandro Contini-Bonacossi, Rome; Samuel H. Kress, New York, acquired 1930; Phillips County Museum, acquired 1934

BIBLIOGRAPHY

Fern Rusk Shapley, *Paintings from the Samuel H. Kress Collection: Italian Schools*, vol. 2, *XV–XVI Century* (London: Phaidon Press, 1968), 94; Burton B. Fredericksen and Federico Zeri, *Census of Pre-Nineteenth-Century Italian Paintings in North American Public Collections* (Cambridge, Mass.: Harvard University Press, 1972), 68, 585.

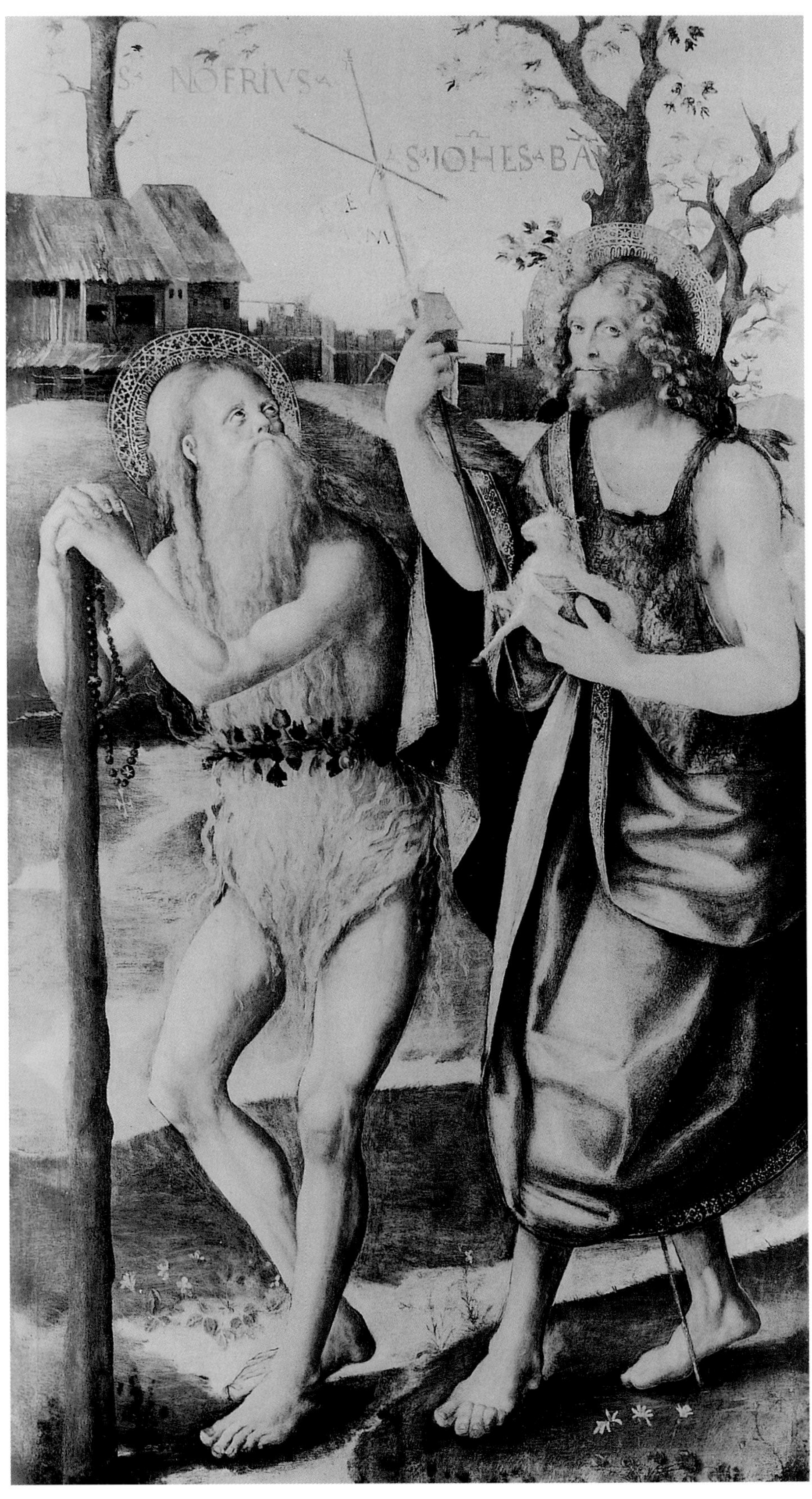

Fig. 188 Gian Maria Falconetto (attributed): *St. Onophrius and St. John the Baptist.* Phillips County Museum, Helena, Arkansas, A 368a.

BEMBO, BONIFACIO, ACTIVE 1447–1478; DIED BEFORE 1482; LOMBARD

Banquet Scene (78-026-E [CA 6047]); *Mounted Knight in Tournament Attire* (78-027-E [CA 6347])
23.5 X 34.3 CM (78-026-E); 23.5 X 36.8 CM (78-027-E), OIL ON PANEL

HOUSTON, TEXAS. THE MENIL COLLECTION

Charles Sterling (Collection files) associated the paintings with the twenty-nine panels depicting scenes from Genesis on the coffered ceiling of the Casa Meli, Cremona (Pinacoteca Ala Ponzone, Museo Civico, Cremona; 46–73). He observed that the Menil works, although somewhat smaller than those in Cremona, have similar Gothic surrounds and demonstrate the same technique of outlining the human figures with touches of light color against a dark background; moreover, the aristocratic garments, hats, and headdresses are comparable. Despite their secular subject matter, Sterling suggested that the Menil panels were originally part of the Casa Meli ensemble, which he attributed to Bonifacio Bembo.

These secular scenes evince the chivalric subject matter typically found in the shallow *caselle* (coffers) of Cremonese ceilings in the second half of the fifteenth century.

PROVENANCE

Arthur Sambon, Paris, c. 1929 (?); François Lepage, Marché Vernaison, Paris; Menil Foundation, Houston, acquired 1960; Menil Collection, acquired 1987

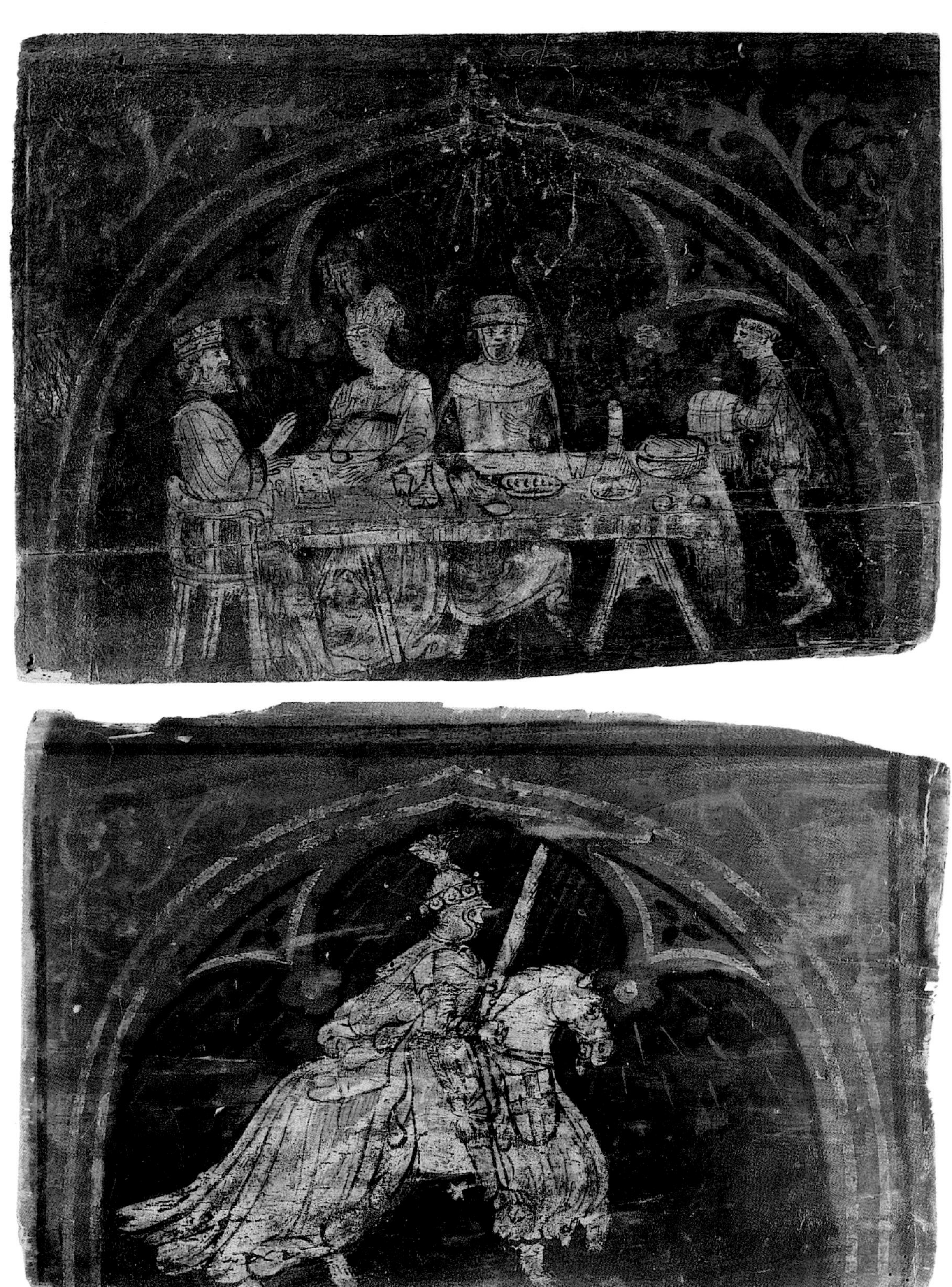

Fig. 189 (top) Bonifacio Bembo: *Banquet Scene*. The Menil Collection, Houston, 78-026-E (CA 6047).

Fig. 190 (bottom) Bonifacio Bembo: *Mounted Knight in Tournament Attire*. The Menil Collection, Houston, 78-027-E (CA 6347).

ALLEGRETTO DI NUZIO, C. 1315–1373; FABRIANESE

Saints and Angels (44.568; 44.569) 107.9 x 50.9 cm (44.568); 107.6 x 50.9 cm (44.569), tempera on panel

HOUSTON, TEXAS. THE MUSEUM OF FINE ARTS, HOUSTON

It has long been recognized in the literature that these panels originally flanked a representation of the Coronation of the Virgin similar in appearance to the *Coronation* altarpiece (Accademia, Florence; 3449) attributed to Bernardo Daddi (active c. 1280–1348). The saints and angels, originally full-length figures, represent the congregation of the blessed in paradise, as they witness the crowning of the Virgin as Queen of Heaven. The group includes Apostles, Martyrs, Virgins, and Confessors, all of whom are mentioned in the liturgy for the feast of All Saints. On one panel (44.568), from front to back, left to right, are Mary Magdalen, St. Lawrence, an unidentifiable female saint, St. Elizabeth of Hungary, St. Anthony of Padua (?), two unidentifiable female saints, St. Clare of Assisi, and two angels. On the other panel (44.569) are St. Louis of Toulouse, St. Catherine of Alexandria, St. Paul, St. Anthony Abbot, an unidentifiable bishop saint, St. Jerome, St. Dominic, St. Ursula, and two angels.

Iconographic and physical evidence supports the reconstruction of the altarpiece proposed by Federico Zeri (1975) uniting the Houston works with the *Coronation of the Virgin* (Southampton City Art Gallery) in a pentaptych. Noting the prominence of St. Francis in the reconstruction and the presence of four saints in the front rows who were titulars of churches in Fabriano, Zeri suggested that the altarpiece may have been painted for the now-destroyed church of San Francesco, Fabriano. Raimond van Marle (1924; 1925) published the Houston panels as the work of Jacopo di Cione (1320/30–before 1400), although he cited the unpublished opinions of Richard Offner and F. Mason Perkins that they were by Allegretto di Nuzio. Offner's and Perkins's attribution was endorsed by Lionello Venturi (1931) and thereafter was accepted. Emphasizing the influence of Nardo di Cione (c. 1320–1365/6) on the paintings, Offner (1947) and Alessandro Marabottini (1951–1952) dated the works c. 1360–1370. Zeri alone suggested the collaboration of Francescuccio Ghissi (active 1359–1374), dating the altarpiece c. 1370.

PROVENANCE

D'Atri, Paris, c. 1922; Jugo Jandolo, Rome; Enrico Testa, Florence; Edith A. and Percy S. Straus, New York, 1922–1945; Edith A. and Percy S. Straus Collection, The Museum of Fine Arts, Houston, acquired 1945

BIBLIOGRAPHY

Raimond van Marle, *The Development of the Italian Schools of Painting*, vol. 3, *The Florentine School of the Fourteenth Century* (The Hague: M. Nijhoff, 1924), 497, 599; Raimond van Marle, *The Development of the Italian Schools of Painting*, vol. 5, *The Local Schools of Central and Southern Italy of the Fourteenth Century* (The Hague: M. Nijhoff, 1925), 152-53; Lionello Venturi, *Pitture italiane in America* (Milan: U. Hoepli, 1931), pl. 89; Bernard Berenson, *Italian Pictures of the Renaissance* (Oxford: Clarendon Press, 1932), 400; Lionello Venturi, *Italian Paintings in America*, 3 vols. (New York: E. Wyhe, 1933), 1:pl. 109; Bernard Berenson, *Pitture italiane del Rinascimento* (Milan: U. Hoepli, 1936), 344; Richard Offner, "The Straus Collection Goes to Houston—Comments on Its More Important Objects," *Art News* 44 (1945): 21-22; *Catalogue of the Edith A. and Percy S. Straus Collection* (Houston: Museum of Fine Arts, 1945), 11, nos. 8, 9; Luigi Coletti, *I primitivi*, vol. 2, *I Senesi e i Giotteschi* (Novara: Istituto geografico De Agostini, 1946), 68 n. 148; Richard Offner, *A Critical and Historical Corpus of Florentine Painting*, sec. 3, vol. 5, *Master of S. Martino alla Palma; Assistant of Daddi; Master of the Fabriano Altarpiece* (New York: New York University Press, 1947), 179; Alessandro Marabottini, "Allegretto Nuzi," *Rivista d'Arte* 27 (1951–1952): 43-44; Bernard Berenson, *Italian Pictures of the Renaissance: A List of the Principal Artists and Their Works with an Index of Places. Central Italian and North Italian Schools*, 3 vols. (London: Phaidon Press, 1968), 1:303; Burton B. Fredericksen and Federico Zeri, *Census of Pre-Nineteenth-Century Italian Paintings in North American Public Collections* (Cambridge, Mass.: Harvard University Press, 1972), 4, 586; Federico Zeri, "Un'ipotesi sui rapporti tra Allegretto Nuzi e Francescuccio Ghisi," *Antichità Viva* 14 (1975): 3-7; *Southampton Art Gallery Collection: Illustrated Inventory of Paintings, Drawings, and Sculpture* (Southampton: Southampton Art Gallery, 1980), 62; *The Museum of Fine Arts, Houston: A Guide to the Collection* (Houston: Museum of Fine Arts, 1981), 23, no. 40; Martin Davies and Dillian Gordon, *The Early Italian Schools before 1400* (London: National Gallery Publications, National Gallery, 1988), 2; Erling S. Skaug, *Punch*

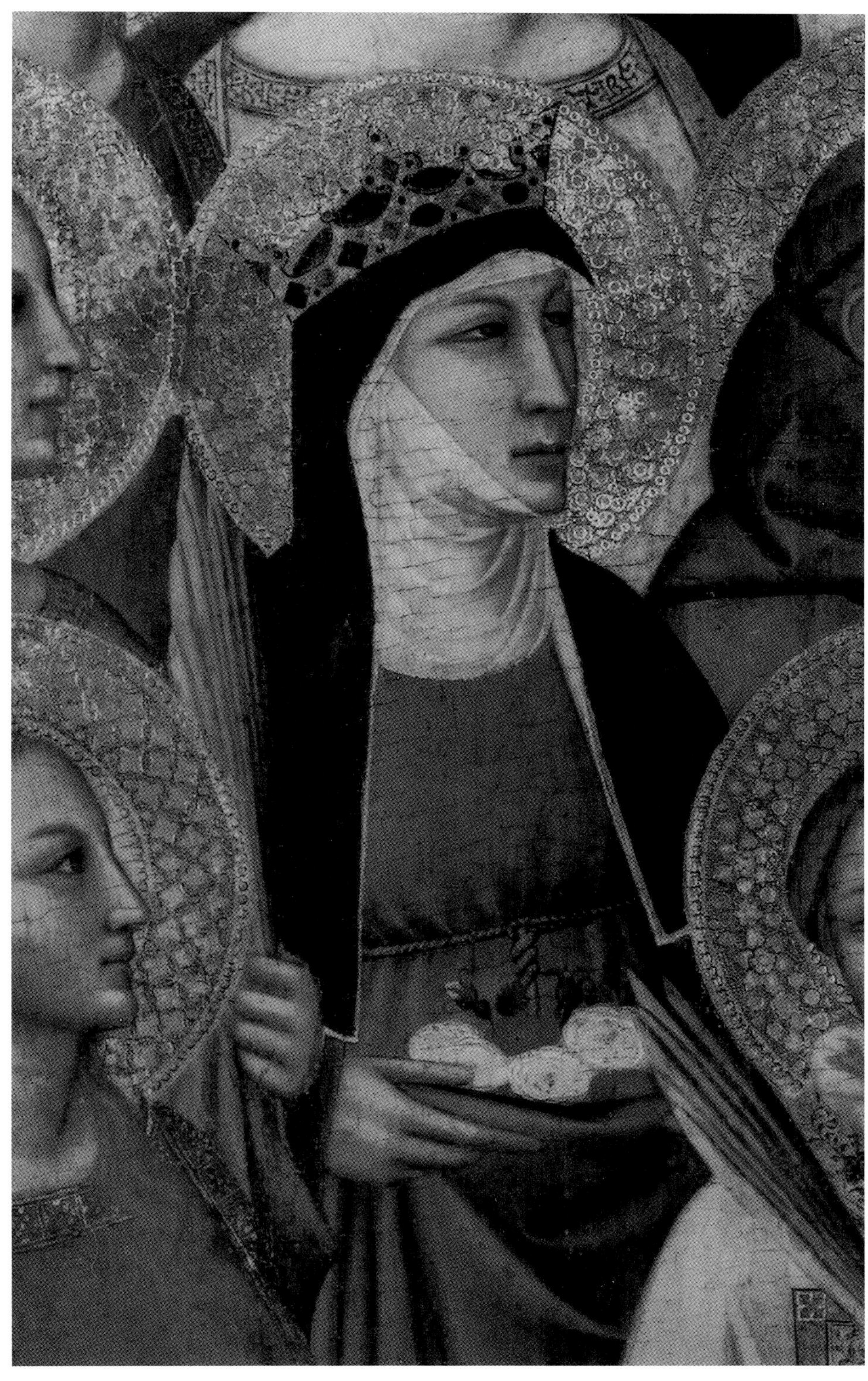

Fig. 191 (detail) Allegretto di Nuzio: *Saints and Angels.* The Museum of Fine Arts, Houston, The Edith A. and Percy S. Straus Collection, 44.568.

Marks from Giotto to Fra Angelico, 2 vols. (Oslo: IIC-Nordic Group, 1994), 1:143; Carolyn C. Wilson, *Italian Paintings XIV–XVI Centuries in the Museum of Fine Arts, Houston* (Houston: Museum of Fine Arts, 1996), 53-66; Mojmír S. Frinta, *Punched Decoration on Late Medieval Panel and Miniature Painting*, pt. 1 (Prague: Maxdorf, 1998), 295, 306, 330, 352, 474.

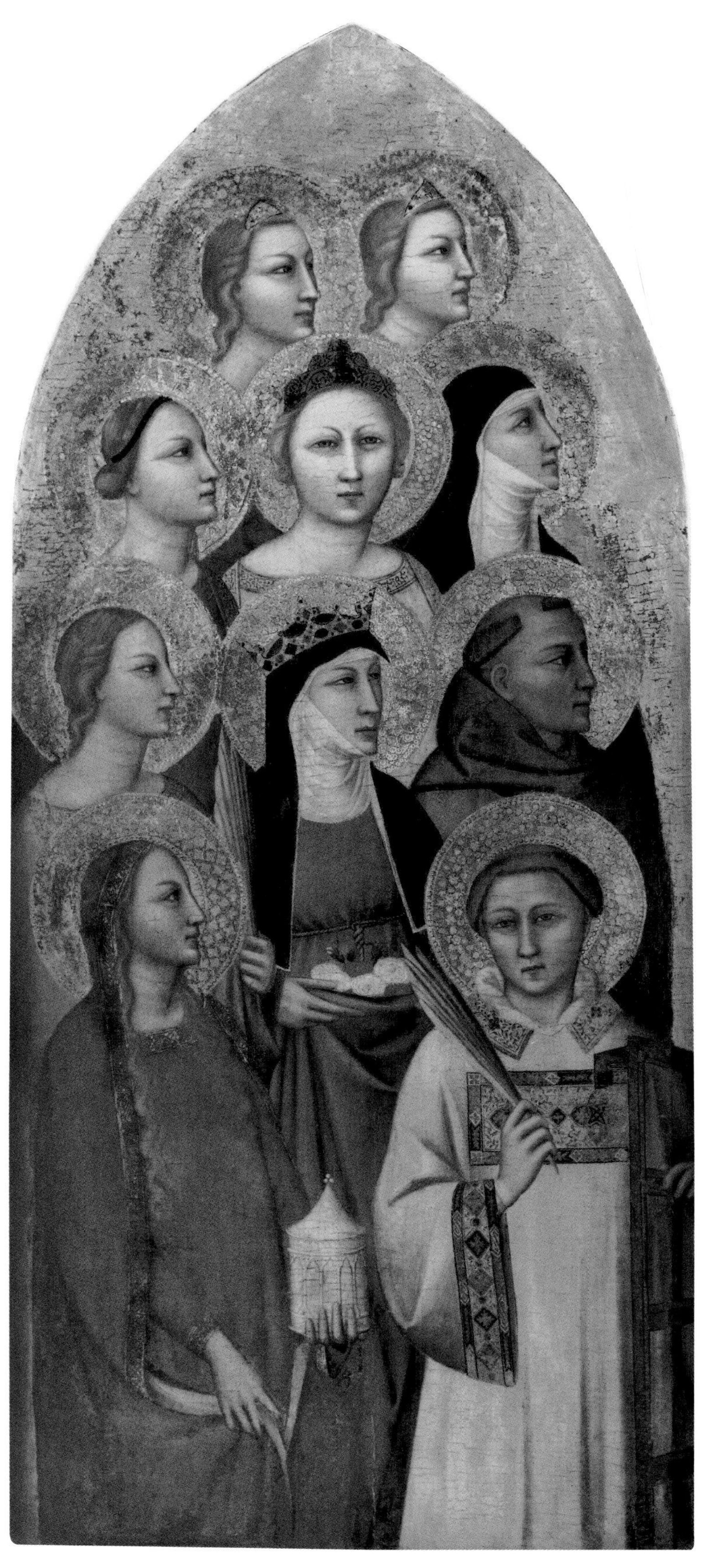

Fig. 191 Allegretto di Nuzio: *Saints and Angels*. The Museum of Fine Arts, Houston, The Edith A. and Percy S. Straus Collection, 44.568.

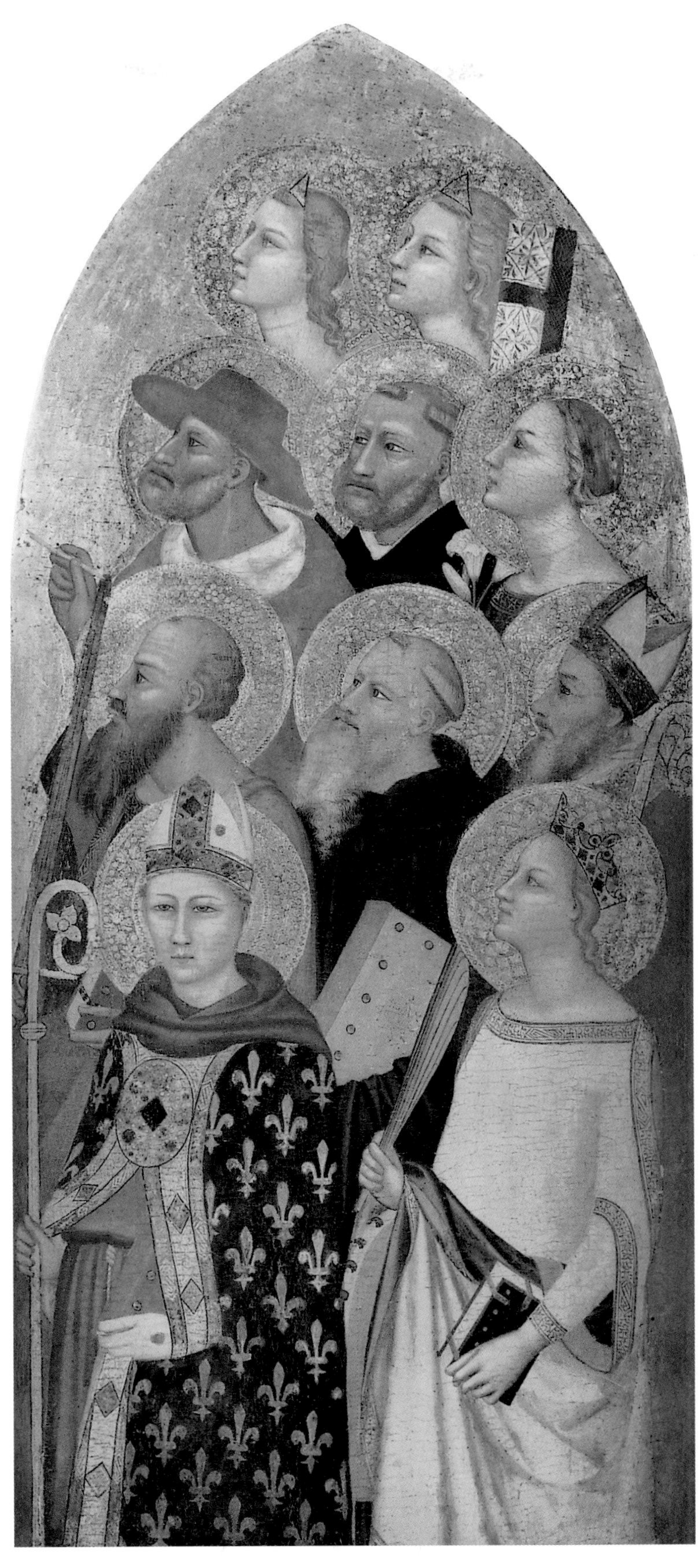

Fig. 192 Allegretto di Nuzio: *Saints and Angels*. The Museum of Fine Arts, Houston, The Edith A. and Percy S. Straus Collection, 44.569.

ANDREA DA FIRENZE (ANDREA DI BONAIUTO), ACTIVE 1346; DIED 1379; FLORENTINE

St. Bartholomew (44.556); *St. Agnes* (44.557); *St. Elizabeth of Hungary* (44.558); *St. Nicholas of Bari* (44.559)
87.2 x 22.1 CM (44.556); 86.2 x 28.9 CM (44.557); 87.2 x 28.9 CM (44.558); 86.2 x 28.6 CM (44.559),
TEMPERA ON PANEL

HOUSTON, TEXAS. THE MUSEUM OF FINE ARTS, HOUSTON

The panels were originally part of a large, unidentified polyptych; as the figures' orientations indicate, *St. Agnes* and *St. Bartholomew* probably appeared to the left of a larger image of the Madonna and Child enthroned, which would have been flanked by *St. Nicholas* and *St. Elizabeth* on the right. With this arrangement in mind, Carolyn C. Wilson (1996) concluded that Bartholomew was the titular saint of the chapel for which the altarpiece was commissioned, since he gazes out at the viewer and would have been to the Christ Child's immediate right. Listed by Bernard Berenson (1932) as the work of Jacopo di Cione (1320/30–before 1400), the Houston panels were reattributed by Richard Offner (1945) to a close follower of Andrea da Firenze. In the *Catalogue of the Edith A. and Percy S. Straus Collection* (1945), they were assigned to Andrea da Firenze; this attribution was followed thereafter. As Wilson and others suggested, the saints compare in style to Andrea's figures in the Spanish Chapel (Santa Maria Novella, Florence); she proposed that they had been executed by the artist, or under his direct supervision, in the mid-1360s.

The names of the saints are inscribed on their haloes: "SANTO BARTOLO," "SANTA ANGNIESA," "SANT[A] [ ] A[ ]ETA," and "SANTO NICHOLO."

PROVENANCE

Osvald Sirén, Stockholm; Edward Hutton, London; Edith A. and Percy S. Straus, New York, 1925–1945; Edith A. and Percy S. Straus Collection, The Museum of Fine Arts, Houston, acquired 1945

BIBLIOGRAPHY

Bernard Berenson, *Italian Pictures of the Renaissance* (Oxford: Clarendon Press, 1932), 275; Richard Offner, "The Straus Collection Goes to Texas—Comments on Its More Important Objects," *Art News* 44 (1945): 22; *Catalogue of the Edith A. and Percy S. Straus Collection* (Houston: Museum of Fine Arts, 1945), 10, nos. 4-7; Millard Meiss, *Painting in Florence and Siena after the Black Death* (Princeton: Princeton University Press, 1951), 47 n. 143; Bernard Berenson, *Italian Pictures of the Renaissance: A List of the Principal Artists and Their Works with an Index of Places. Florentine School*, 2 vols. (London: Phaidon Press, 1963), 1:104; Burton B. Fredericksen and Federico Zeri, *Census of Pre-Nineteenth-Century Italian Paintings in North American Public Collections* (Cambridge, Mass.: Harvard University Press, 1972), 7, 586; Miklòs Boskovits, *Pittura fiorentina alla vigilia del Rinascimento, 1370–1400* (Florence: Edam, 1975), 278; Richard Offner and Hayden B. J. Maginnis, *A Critical and Historical Corpus of Florentine Painting: A Legacy of Attributions* (New York: Institute of Fine Arts, New York University, 1981), 63; Johannes Tripps, "Andrea Bonaiuti: Pisaner Fresken, Tafel- und Glasmalerei" (Ph.D. diss., University of Heidelberg, 1988), 51-52, 223, no. 12; Erling S. Skaug, *Punch Marks from Giotto to Fra Angelico*, 2 vols. (Oslo: IIC-Nordic Group, 1994), 1:162-63; Carolyn C. Wilson, *Italian Paintings XIV–XVI Centuries in the Museum of Fine Arts, Houston* (Houston: Museum of Fine Arts, 1996), 69-78.

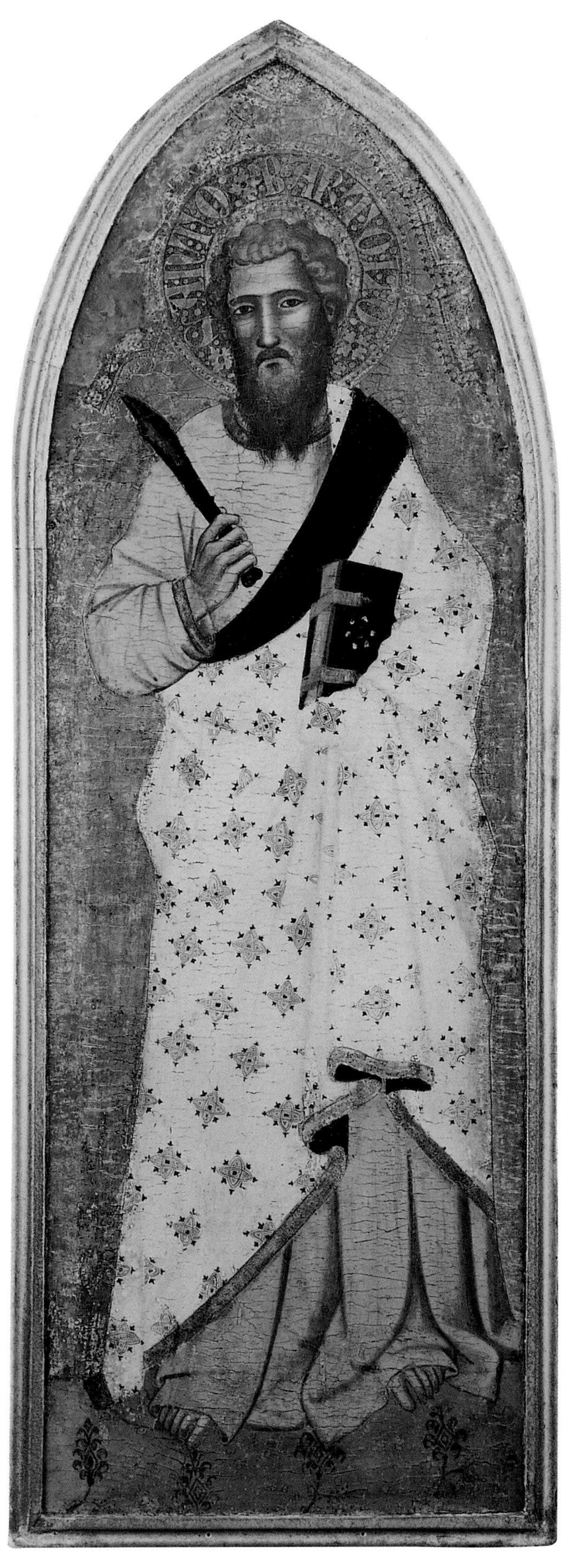

Fig. 193 Andrea da Firenze (Andrea di Bonaiuto): *St. Bartholomew*. The Museum of Fine Arts, Houston, The Edith A. and Percy S. Straus Collection, 44.556.

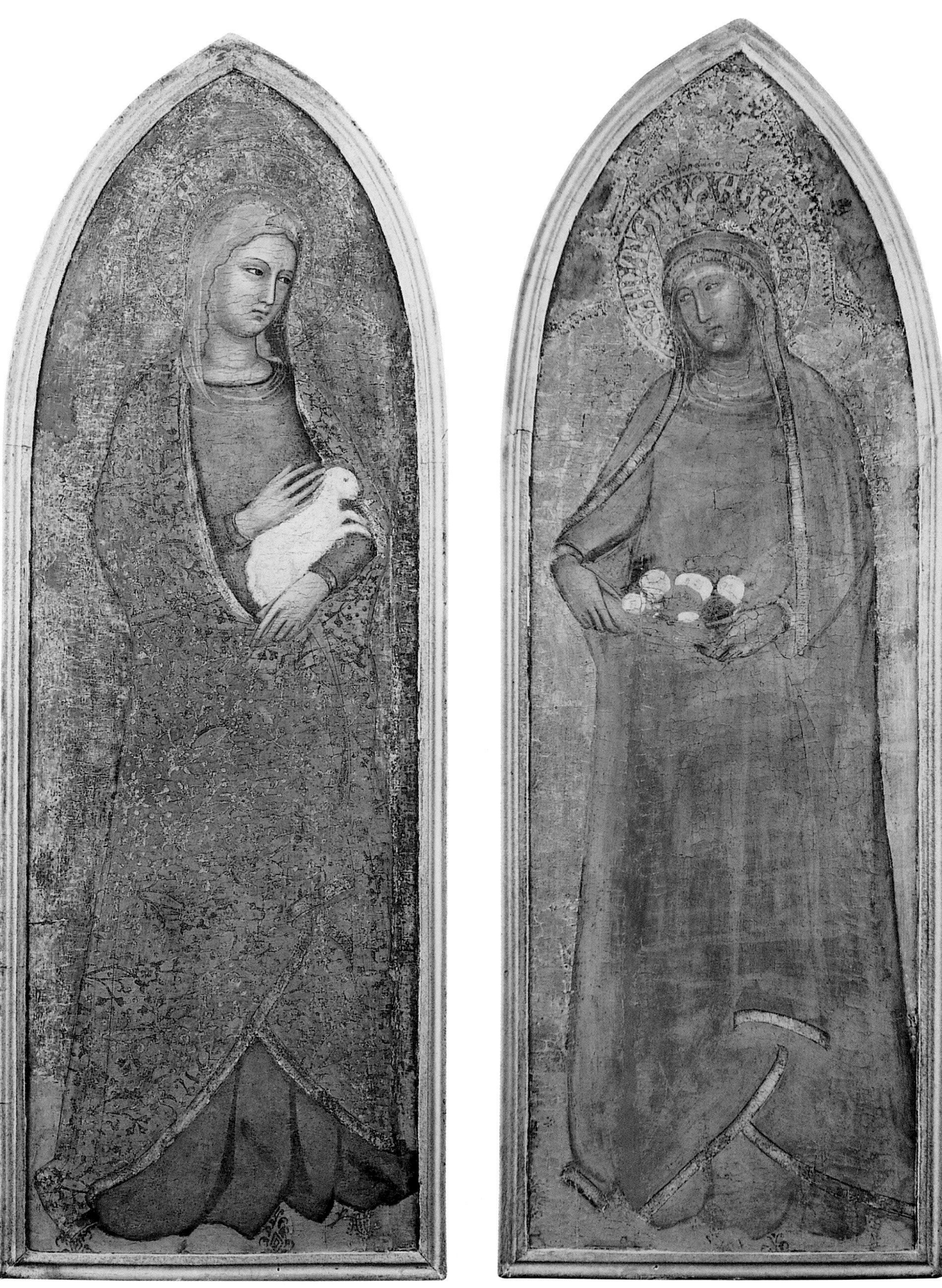

Fig. 194 Andrea da Firenze (Andrea di Bonaiuto): *St. Agnes*. The Museum of Fine Arts, Houston, The Edith A. and Percy S. Straus Collection, 44.557.
Fig. 195 Andrea da Firenze (Andrea di Bonaiuto): *St. Elizabeth of Hungary*. The Museum of Fine Arts, Houston, The Edith A. and Percy S. Straus Collection, 44.558.

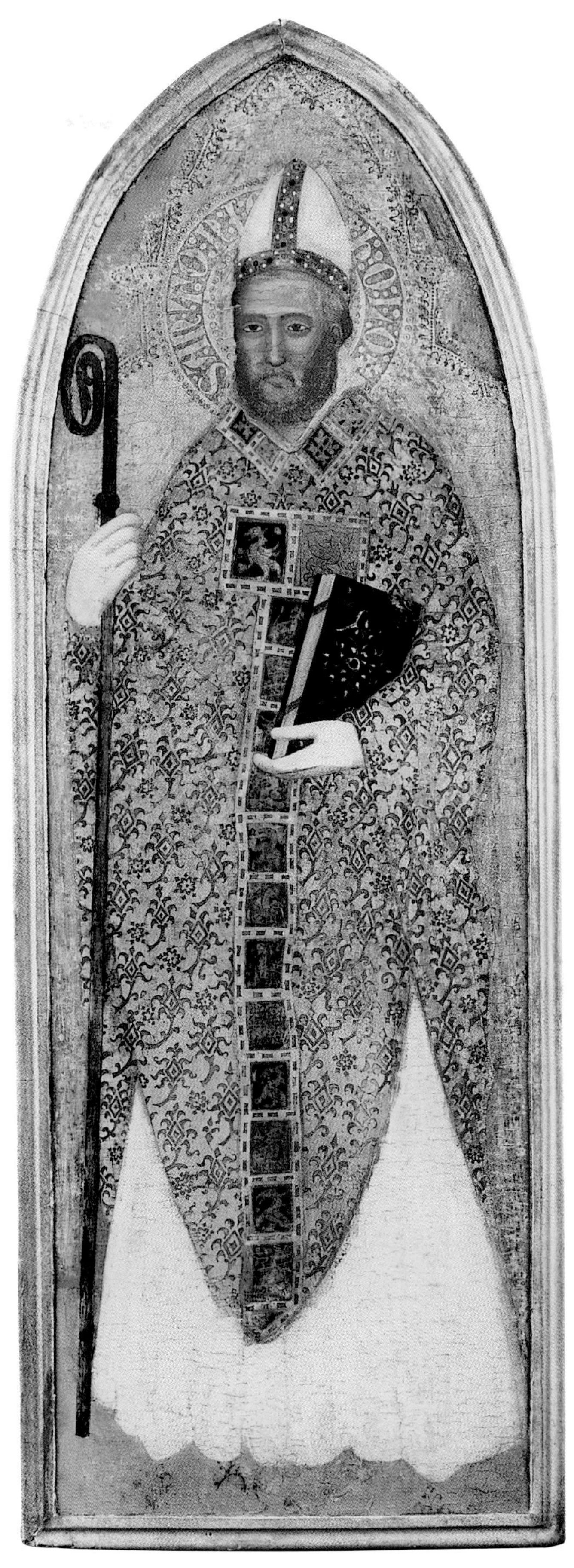

Fig. 196 Andrea da Firenze (Andrea di Bonaiuto): *St. Nicholas of Bari*. The Museum of Fine Arts, Houston, The Edith A. and Percy S. Straus Collection, 44.559.

ANGELICO, FRA, C. 1400–1455; FLORENTINE

St. Anthony Abbot Shunning the Mass of Gold (44.550) 19.7 X 28 CM, TEMPERA ON PANEL

HOUSTON, TEXAS. THE MUSEUM OF FINE ARTS, HOUSTON

Since its original publication in 1924 (Frida Schottmüller), the painting has been attributed to Fra Angelico, to his workshop, or to a follower of the artist, for example Zanobi Strozzi (1412–1468), and dated between c. 1435 and 1440. In Carolyn C. Wilson's opinion (1995; 1996), it was part of a larger devotional assemblage designed by Fra Angelico and executed with the assistance of his workshop. The Houston work has long been recognized as a predella panel; in 1976, however, Miklòs Boskovits suggested a location beneath Fra Angelico's *St. Anthony Abbot* (T. Robert and Katherine States Burke Collection), which itself has been described as the wing of an unidentified altarpiece. Wilson (1995; 1996) demonstrated that Boskovits's reconstruction is supported by a Florentine engraving of *St. Anthony Abbot with Eleven Scenes From His Life* (Museo Civico, Pavia), c. 1460–1470, which appears to be based on designs originating in Fra Angelico's shop. Giorgio Bonsanti (1998), who considered the Houston painting to be an autograph work by the master, dating to the early 1440s, also accepted the reconstruction.

The panel illustrates an episode from St. Athanasius's life of St. Anthony Abbot, recounted also in Jacobus de Voragine's *Golden Legend*, in which Anthony fled from a mass of gold placed in his path by the Devil; the temptation led him to seek refuge on a mountain, where he remained for twenty years. Wilson (1995) observed that the theme of good versus evil is reflected in the setting; the dark, rocky foreground with the Devil's gold contrasts markedly with the sunny, green fields of the background, toward which the saint is escaping.

PROVENANCE

Friedrich Wilhelm IV, Hohenzollern; Count Franz von Ingenheim, Reisewitz bei Friedenthal-Giesmanndorf, Silesia; Count Marczel von Nemes, Munich; K. W. Bachstitz Gallery, The Hague and New York, by 1925; Edith A. and Percy S. Straus, New York, 1930–1945; Edith A. and Percy S. Straus Collection, The Museum of Fine Arts, Houston, acquired 1945

BIBLIOGRAPHY

Frida Schottmüller, *Fra Angelico: Des Meisters Gemälde* (Stuttgart: Deutsche verlags-anstalt, 1924), 252; "St. Anthony's Flight to the Convent by Fra Angelico da Fiesole," *Bulletin of the Bachstitz Gallery* 9-10 (1925): 98; "Fra Giovanni da Fiesole," *Bulletin of the Bachstitz Gallery*, n.s., 1 (1929): 16-17; F. W. Hudig, "Art in Holland," *Parnassus* 1 (1929): 19; Bernard Berenson, *Italian Pictures of the Renaissance* (Oxford: Clarendon Press, 1932), 22; Daniel C. Rich, ed., *Catalogue of a Century of Progress Exhibition of Paintings and Sculpture* (Chicago: Lakeside Press, 1933), 13, no. 81; Lionello Venturi, *Italian Paintings in America*, 3 vols. (New York: E. Wyhe, 1933), 2:pl. 178; Bernard Berenson, *Pitture italiane del Rinascimento* (Milan: U. Hoepli, 1936), 19; George H. McCall, *Catalogue of European Paintings and Sculpture from 1300–1800* (New York: Publishers Printing Co., 1939), 3, no. 4; Malcolm Vaughan, "Old Masters at the Fair," *Parnassus* 11 (1939): 10; Richard Offner, "The Straus Collection Goes to Texas—Comments on Its More Important Objects," *Art News* 44 (1945): 20, 22-23; *Catalogue of the Edith A. and Percy S. Straus Collection* (Houston: Museum of Fine Arts, 1945), 13, no. 14; Charles David Cuttler, "The Temptations of Saint Anthony in Art from Earliest Times to the First Quarter of the XVI Century" (Ph.D. diss., New York University, 1952), 65; John Pope-Hennessy, *Fra Angelico* (London: Phaidon Press, 1952), 176; "The Connoisseur's Diary: Fra Angelico," *Connoisseur* 547 (1955): 49; *Mostra delle opere di Fra Angelico: Nel quinto centenario della morte, 1455–1955* (Vatican: Direzione generale dei monumenti, musei e gallerie pontificie, 1955), no. 23; Mario Salmi, *Mostra delle opere del Beato Angelico: Nel quinto centenario della morte, 1455–1955* (Florence: Museo di San Marco, 1955), no. 26; Milton Gendel, "Summer Events: Rome," *Art News* 54 (1955): 52; Luciano Berti, "Mostra del Beato Angelico," *Bollettino d'Arte* 40 (1955): 282; Innocenzo Taurisano, *Beato Angelico* (Rome: Fratelli Palombi, 1955), 173; Mario Salmi, *Il Beato Angelico* (Rome: Valori plastici, 1958), 24, 105-6; Luciano Berti, "Miniature dell'Angelico (e altro)—II," *Acropoli* 3 (1963): 38 n. 108; Bernard Berenson, *Italian Pictures of the Renaissance: A List of the Principal Artists and Their Works with an Index of Places. Florentine School*, 2 vols. (London: Phaidon Press, 1963), 1:14; Elsa Morante and Umberto Baldini, *L'opera completa dell'Angelico* (Milan: Rizzoli, 1970), 97-98, no. 51; Burton B. Fredericksen and Federico Zeri, *Census of Pre-Nineteenth-Century Italian Paintings in North American Public Collections* (Cambridge, Mass.: Harvard University Press, 1972), 9, 586; John Pope-Hennessy,

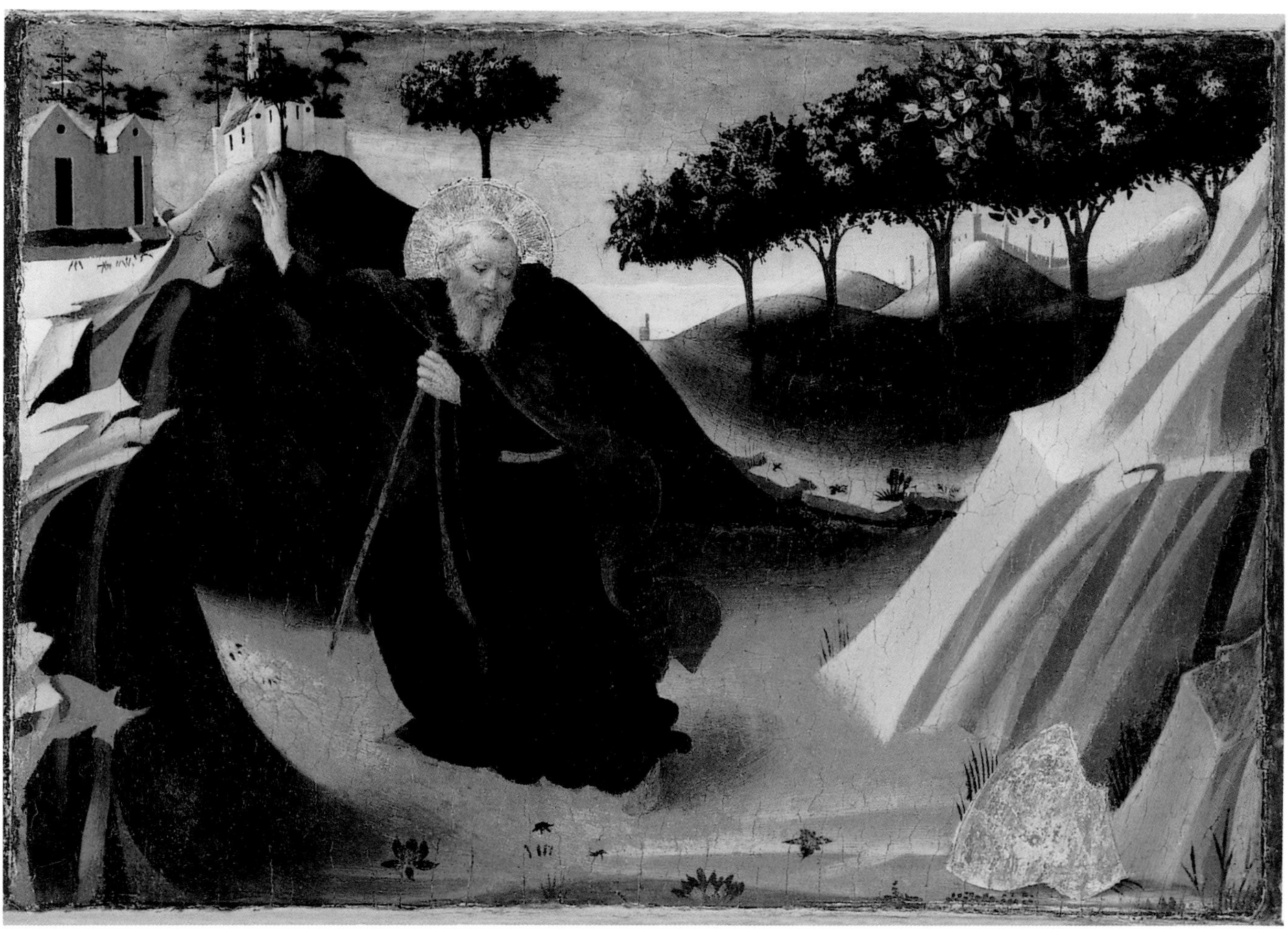

Fig. 197 Fra Angelico: *St. Anthony Abbot Shunning the Mass of Gold*. The Museum of Fine Arts, Houston, The Edith A. and Percy S. Straus Collection, 44.550.

Fra Angelico (London: Phaidon Press, 1974), 227; Miklòs Boskovits, "Appunti sull'Angelico," *Paragone* 27 (1976): 43, 52 n. 27; Diane E. Cole, "Fra Angelico: His Role in Quattrocento Painting and Problems of Chronology," 2 vols. (Ph.D. diss., University of Virginia, 1977), 2:476, 500, 503-4, 530-32, no. 96, 567; *The Museum of Fine Arts, Houston: A Guide to the Collection* (Houston: Museum of Fine Arts, 1981), 24, no. 43; Keith Christiansen, "Workshop of Fra Angelico (Guido di Pietro)," in *Notable Acquisitions, 1983–1984* (New York: Metropolitan Museum of Art, 1984), 61; Jan van der Marck, *In Quest of Excellence: Civic Pride, Patronage, Connoisseurship* (Miami: Center for the Fine Arts, 1984), 100-1; *Beato Angelico: Miscellanea di studi* (Rome: Pontificia commissione centrale per l'arte sacra in Italia, 1984), 355; John Pope-Hennessy, *The Robert Lehman Collection*, vol. 1, *Italian Paintings* (New York: Metropolitan Museum of Art; Princeton: Princeton University Press, 1987), 105; Elisabeth de Boissard and Valérie LaVergne-Durey, *Chantilly, Musée Condé, Peintures de l'école italienne/ XIVe-XVIe siècles* (Paris: Ministère de la Culture, 1988), 46-47; Keith Christiansen, Laurence B. Kanter, and Carl Brandon Strehlke, *Painting in Renaissance Siena, 1420–1500* (New York: Metropolitan Museum of Art, 1988), 120; Peter C. Marzio, *A Permanent Legacy: 150 Works from the Collection of the Museum of Fine Arts, Houston* (New York: Hudson Hills Press, 1989), 104-5; Carl Brandon Strehlke, "Fra Angelico and Early Florentine Renaissance Painting in the John G. Johnson Collection at the Philadelphia Museum of Art," *Philadelphia Museum of Art Bulletin* 88 (1993): 20; Carolyn C. Wilson, "Fra Angelico: New Light on a Lost Work," *Burlington Magazine* 137 (1995): 737-40; John T. Spike, *Angelico* (Milan: Fabbri, 1996), 253-55, no. 113e; Carolyn C. Wilson, *Italian Paintings XIV–XVI Centuries in the Museum of Fine Arts, Houston* (Houston: Museum of Fine Arts, 1996), 130-45; Giorgio Bonsanti, *Beato Angelico: Catalogo completo* (Florence: Octavo, 1998), 132-33, no. 43; Edgar Peters Bowron and Mary G. Morton, *Masterworks of European Painting in the Museum of Fine Arts, Houston* (Princeton: Princeton University Press, 2000), 7-9; Perri Lee Roberts, Bruce Cole, and Hayden B. J. Maginnis, *Sacred Treasures: Early Italian Paintings from Southern Collections* (Athens, Ga.: Georgia Museum of Art, 2002), 130-34: Laurence Kanter and Pia Palladino, *Fra Angelico* (New York: Metropolitan Museum of Art and Yale University Press, 2005), 104.

BARTOLOMEO VENETO, ACTIVE 1502; DIED 1531; VENETIAN

Portrait of a Man (44.573) 70.8 X 54.6 CM, OIL ON PANEL

HOUSTON, TEXAS. THE MUSEUM OF FINE ARTS, HOUSTON

Gustav F. Waagen (1854) reported that the panel was attributed to Titian (c. 1488–1576) when it resided in the Mayo Collection and also to Titian when it was in the collection of Robert S. Holford. Bernard Berenson (1895) and Adolfo Venturi (1899) reattributed it to Bartolomeo Veneto; this opinion has been accepted ever since. The work resembles Bartolomeo's portraits of young noblemen in the National Gallery of Art, Washington, D.C. (368), and the Galleria Nazionale d'Arte Antica, Palazzo Barberini, Rome, the latter dated 1520. All three feature a bust-length presentation, with the sitter turning to the left; the men are richly and fashionably attired and wear hats with medals or badges. Although no trace remains of the date that once appeared on the *cartellino* in the Houston panel, reported in the early literature as 1520 or 1512, the Museum dates it "possibly 1512." The majority of scholars, however, believe it typifies Bartolomeo's mature style of the 1520s–1530s.

The early literature identifies the sitter as Massimiliano Sforza (1492–1530), duke of Milan; there is no visual or documentary evidence, however, to support the identification. The sitter's fashionable attire and attributes, the sword and cap-badge, attest to his patrician status. The badge features a large ox with wings, the emblem of St. Luke, and signifies membership in an unidentified student club, religious confraternity, or honorary association dedicated to the saint. According to Carolyn C. Wilson (1996), the painting exemplifies the many portraits of young men in fashionable dress, holding swords and wearing caps with brooches as personal emblems, produced in northern Italy and Germany in the second decade of the sixteenth century.

PROVENANCE

Mayo della Porta, Milan; Robert S. Holford, Westonbirt, Gloucestershire, by 1854; Sir George Lindsay Holford, Dorchester House, London, 1892–1927; Christie, Manson & Woods, London, July 15, 1927, lot 128; Thomas Agnew & Sons, New York and London; Mr. and Mrs. Edwin S. Bayer, New York and Paris, 1928–1933; Galerie Jean Charpentier, Paris, May 19, 1933, lot 4; Seligmann, Rey and Co., New York; Edith A. and Percy S. Straus, New York, 1933–1945; Edith A. and Percy S. Straus Collection, The Museum of Fine Arts, Houston, acquired 1945

BIBLIOGRAPHY

Gustav F. Waagen, "Mr. Holford's Collection," in *Treasures of Art in Great Britain*, 3 vols. (London: John Murray, 1854), 2:197; *Works by the Old Masters and by Deceased Masters of the British School* (London: Royal Academy of Arts, 1893), 33, no. 143; *Early Italian Art from 1300 to 1550* (London: The New Gallery, 1893), 47, no. 253; Costanza Jocelyn Ffoulkes, "Le esposizioni d'arte italiana a Londra," *Archivio Storico dell'Arte* 7 (1894): 254; Bernard Berenson, *The Venetian Painters of the Renaissance* (New York: G. P. Putnam's Sons, 1895), 81; Adolfo Venturi, "Bartolomeo Veneto," *L'Arte* 2 (1899): 454; Federico Hermanin, "Bartolomeo Veneto e Alberto Dürer," *L'Arte* 3 (1900): 157; Adolfo Venturi, *La Galleria Crespi in Milano* (Milan: Hoepli, 1900), 89, 91; *Early Venetian Pictures and Other Works of Art* (London: Burlington Fine Arts Club, 1912), 66-67, no. 32; Joseph A. Crowe and Giovanni B. Cavalcaselle, *A History of Painting in North Italy, Venice, Padua, Vicenza, Verona, Ferrara, Milan, Friuli, Brescia from the Fourteenth to the Sixteenth Century*, 3 vols., ed. Tancred Borenius (London: John Murray, 1912), 1:300; Adolfo Venturi, *Storia dell'arte italiana*, vol. 7/4, *La pittura del Quattrocento* (Milan: U. Hoepli, 1915), 698-99; Salomon Reinach, *Répertoire de peintures du Moyen-Âge et de la Renaissance (1280–1580)*, 6 vols. (Paris: E. Leroux, 1918), 4:93; "Italian Paintings," *Bulletin of the Metropolitan Museum of Art* 15 (1920): 159; *Catalogue of Pictures and Other Objects of Art Selected from the Collection of Mr. Robert Holford (1808–1892) Mainly from Westonbirt in Gloucestershire* (London: Burlington Fine Arts Club, 1921), 15, no. 96; Georg Swarzenski, "Bartolomeo Veneto und Lucrezia Borgia," *Städel-Jahrbuch* 2 (1922): 67; Robert H. Benson, ed., *The Holford Collection* (Oxford: Oxford University Press, 1924), 50, no. 24; *An Exhibition of Paintings by Old Masters of the Venetian School* (New York: Thomas Agnew & Sons, Inc., 1927), no. 19; "Venetian Art Exhibition at Agnew Galleries," *Art News* 26 (1927): 3; Ernst Michalski, "Zur Problematik des Bartolomeo Veneto, I, II," *Zeitschrift für bildenden Kunst* 61 (1927): 283, 286, 301-2, 307-8; Frank Jewett Mather, Jr., "Some Old Masters of Venice," *The Arts* 13 (1928): 20; August L. Mayer, "Zur Bildniskunst des Bartolomeo Veneto," *Pantheon* 2 (1928): 571, 574; *Loan Exhibition of Primitives* (New York:

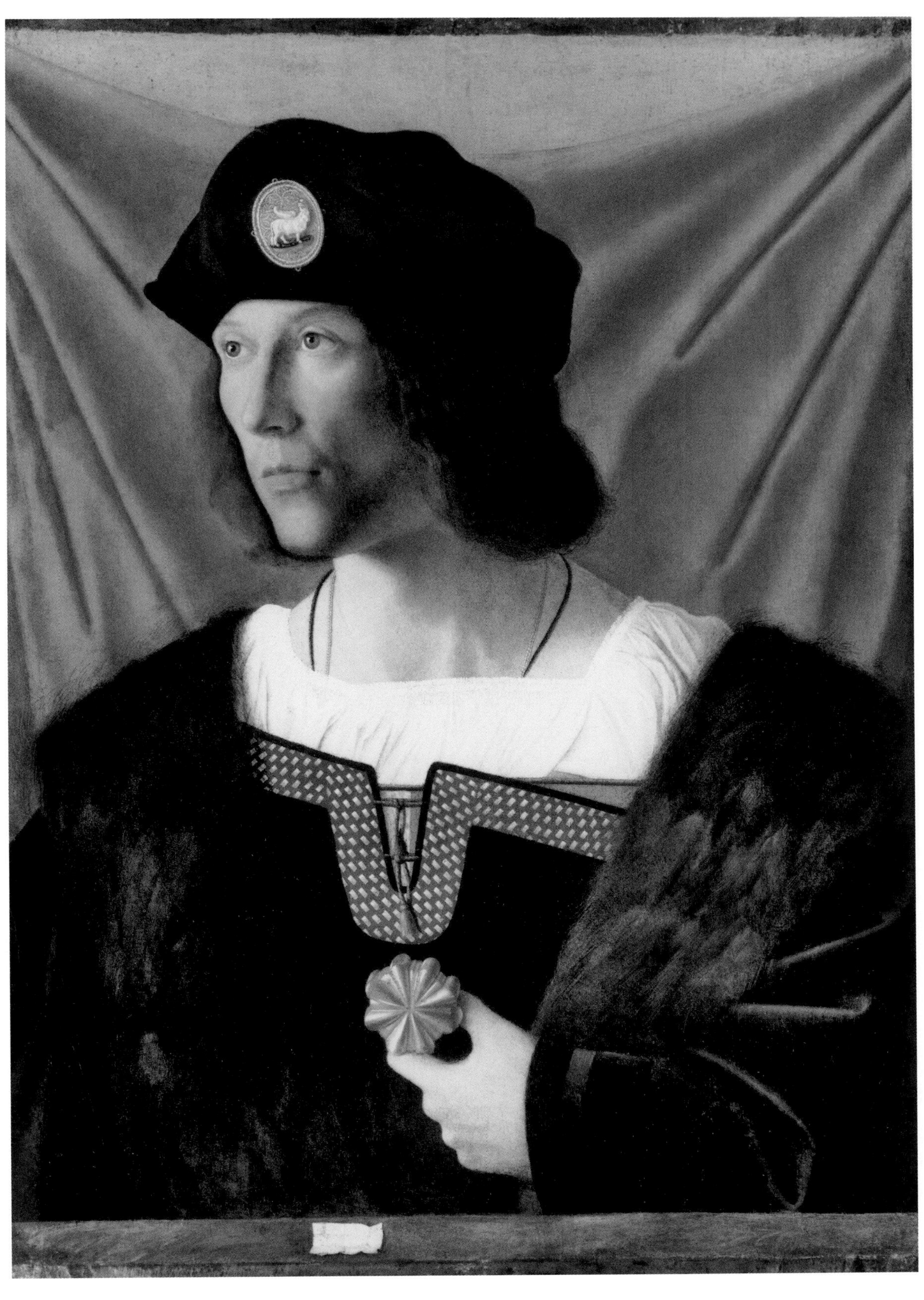

Fig. 198 (above and overleaf, detail) Bartolomeo Veneto: *Portrait of a Man*. The Museum of Fine Arts, Houston, The Edith A. and Percy S. Straus Collection, 44.573.

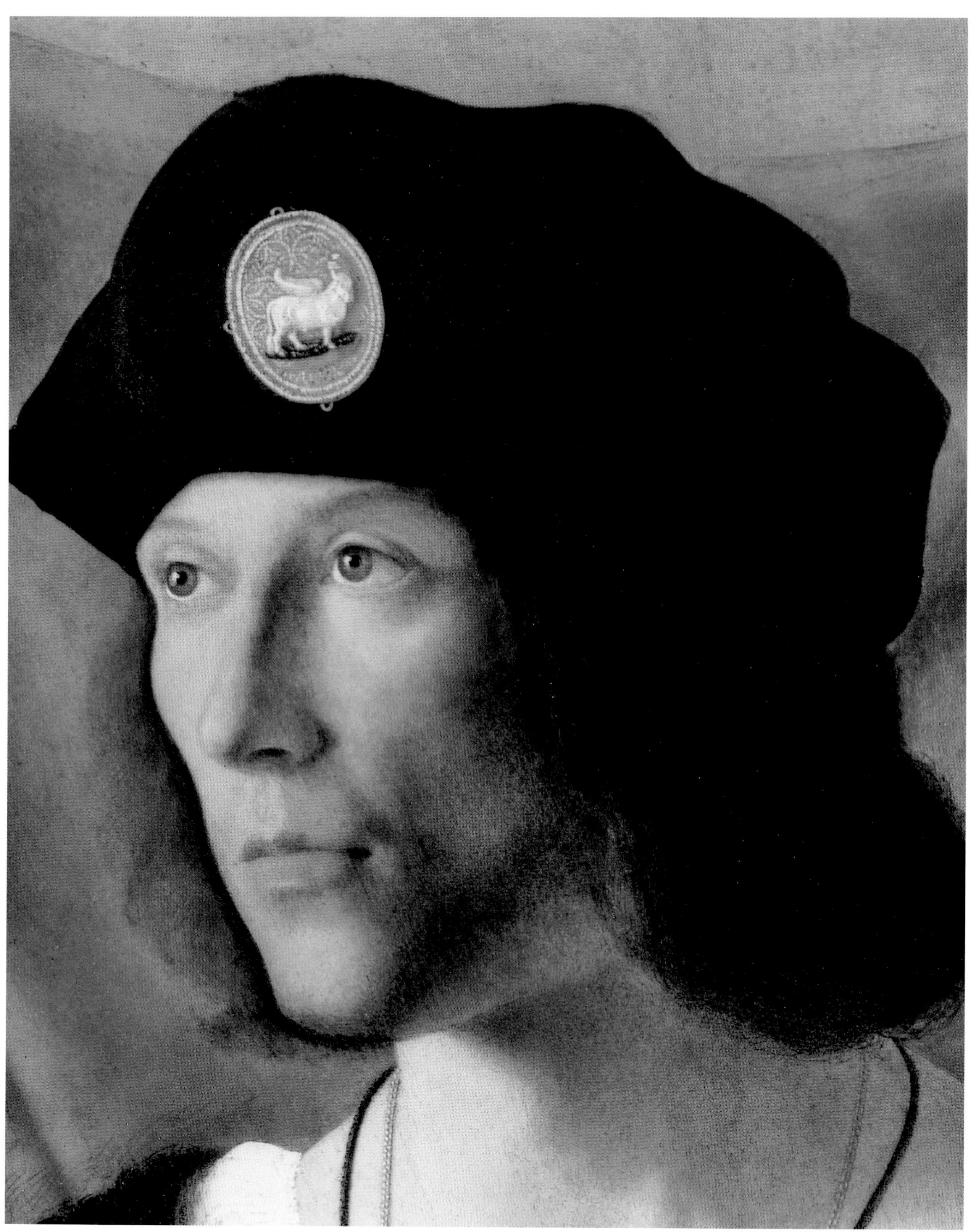

M. Knoedler and Co., 1929), no. 1; Harry Adsit Bull, Jr., "Exhibitions," *International Studio* 17 (1929): 71; André de Hevesy, "Um Bartolomeo Veneto," *Pantheon* 7 (1931): 227-28; Ernst Michalski, "Zur Stilkritik des Bartolomeo Veneto," *Zeitscrift für bildende Kunst* 65 (1931–1932): 177-78, 179, 181, 182; Bernard Berenson, *Italian Pictures of the Renaissance* (Oxford: Clarendon Press, 1932), 52; Lionello Venturi, *Italian Paintings in America*, 3 vols. (New York: E. Wyhe, 1933) 3:pl. 475; Bernard Berenson, *Pitture italiane del Rinascimento* (Milan: U. Hoepli, 1936), 44; Alfred M. Frankfurter, "Important Italian Paintings Recently Added to American Collections, II," *Art News* 34 (1936): 5; Malcolm Vaughan, "Old Masters at the Fair," *Parnassus* 11 (1939): 11; George H. McCall, *Catalogue of European Paintings and Sculpture from 1300–1800* (New York: Publishers Printing Co., 1939), 4, no. 6; Helen Comstock, "Bartolomeo Veneto's *Portrait of a Youth*," *Connoisseur* 107 (1941): 260; Richard Offner, "The Straus Collection Goes to Texas—Comments on Its More Important Objects," *Art News* 44 (1945): 21, 23, 30; *Catalogue of the Edith A. and Percy S. Straus Collection* (Houston: Museum of Fine Arts, 1945), 18, no. 24; Bernard Berenson, *Italian Pictures of the Renaissance: A List of the Principal Artists and Their Works with an Index of Places. Venetian School*, 2 vols. (New York: Phaidon, 1957), 1:12; Nolfo di Carpegna, ed., *Catalogue of the National Gallery, Barberini Palace, Rome* (Rome: Lorenzo del Turco, 1964), 18; Luisa Cogliati Arano, *Andrea Solario* (Milan: E. T. I., 1965), 42; J. W. Goodison and G. H. Robertson, *Catalogue of Paintings*, vol. 2, *Italian Schools* (Cambridge: Fitzwilliam Museum, 1967), 8 n. 4; Fern Rusk Shapley, *Paintings from the Samuel H. Kress Collection: Italian Schools*, vol. 2, *XV–XVI Century* (London: Phaidon Press, 1968), 164; Burton B. Fredericksen and Federico Zeri, *Census of Pre-Nineteenth-Century Italian Paintings in North American Public Collections* (Cambridge, Mass.: Harvard University Press, 1972), 17, 586; Creighton Gilbert, "Bartolommeo Veneto and His Portrait of a Lady," *National Gallery of Canada Bulletin* 20 (1973): 14 n. 15, 16; *Chefs-d'oeuvre des musées des États-Unis: De Giorgione à Picasso* (Paris: Musée Marmottan, 1976), no. 7; Fern Rusk Shapley, *Catalogue of the Italian Paintings*, 2 vols. (Washington, D.C.: National Gallery of Art, 1979), 1:27; A. Vesey B. Norman, *The Rapier and Small-Sword, 1460–1820* (London: Arms and Armour Press, 1980), 239; *The Museum of Fine Arts, Houston: A Guide to the Collection* (Houston: Museum of Fine Arts, 1981), 38, no. 71; Caterina Bon, *Laboratorio di restauro 2*, ed. Dante Bernini (Rome: Fratelli Palombi, 1988), 103-4; Peter C. Marzio, *A Permanent Legacy: 150 Works from the Collection of the Museum of Fine Arts, Houston* (New York: Hudson Hills Press, 1989), 126-27; *Pinacoteca di Brera. Scuola veneta* (Milan: Electa, 1990), 19; Yvonne Hackenbroch, *Enseignes* (Florence: Studio per Edizioni Scelte, 1996), 104; Carolyn C. Wilson, *Italian Paintings XIV–XVI Centuries in the Museum of Fine Arts, Houston* (Houston: Museum of Fine Arts, 1996), 306-14; Laura Pagnotta, *Bartolomeo Veneto: L'opera completa* (Florence: Centro Di, 1997), 90-91, 233-35, no. 31; Edgar Peters Bowron and Mary G. Morton, *Masterworks of European Painting in the Museum of Fine Arts, Houston* (Princeton: Princeton University Press, 2000), 32-34.

BELLINI, GIOVANNI, 1431/6–1516; ATTRIBUTED; VENETIAN

Virgin and Child (44.552) 82 X 63.8 CM, TEMPERA ON PANEL

HOUSTON, TEXAS. THE MUSEUM OF FINE ARTS, HOUSTON

Since its original publication, this panel has generally been considered an autograph work, despite the fact that it was extensively overpainted. Even after it was conserved in 1954, with the removal of the overpainting, its authenticity as a work by Bellini was maintained by scholars, including Fritz Heinemann (1962) and Terisio Pignatti (1969). Carolyn C. Wilson (1996) suggested that the panel is either an irreparably damaged but autograph work of c. 1460–1470 or a later freehand copy of an early Bellini by a close follower. She compared the physically active Christ Child and his relationship to the Madonna to the content of Bellini's *Madonna and Child* (Staatliche Museen, Gemäldegalerie, Berlin; 117) and his *Madonna "Lochis"* (Accademia Carrara, Bergamo; 167).

The painting served as a devotional image. The Christ Child holds a goldfinch, symbolizing his Passion. The marble slabs in front of and behind the figures suggest the walls of a sarcophagus and may have been intended as another allusion to Christ's future sacrifice.

PROVENANCE

Publio Podio, Bologna; Alverà, Venice; Edith A. and Percy S. Straus, New York, 1922–1945; Edith A. and Percy S. Straus Collection, The Museum of Fine Arts, Houston, acquired 1945

BIBLIOGRAPHY

Loan Exhibition of the Arts of the Italian Renaissance (New York: Metropolitan Museum of Art, 1923), 13, no. 41; Bryson Burroughs, "Loan Exhibition of the Arts of the Italian Renaissance," *Bulletin of the Metropolitan Museum of Art* 18 (1923): 200; Dudley Poore, "Italian Renaissance Exhibition," *The Arts* 3 (1923): 410; Bryson Burroughs, "Landscape in Italy in the Fifteenth Century," *Bulletin of the Metropolitan Museum of Art* 18 (1923): 200; Raimond van Marle, "Representation of Great Italian Masters in American Collections Very Inferior to That of Other Schools," *Art News* 28 (1930): 21; Georg Gronau, *Giovanni Bellini* (Stuttgart and Berlin: Deutsche Verlag-Anstalt, 1930), 203-4, 222; Raimond van Marle, *The Development of the Italian Schools of Painting*, vol. 17, *The Renaissance Painters of Venice: Antonio Vivarini, the Bellini, Cima, Basaiti* (The Hague: M. Nijhoff, 1935), 245; Luitpold Dussler, *Giovanni Bellini* (Frankfurt am Main: Prestel-Verlag, 1935), 157, 158; Carlo Gamba, *Giovanni Bellini* (Milan: U. Hoepli, 1937), 54; *Catalogue of the Edith A. and Percy S. Straus Collection* (Houston: Museum of Fine Arts, 1945), 17, no. 22; Herbert Friedmann, *The Symbolic Goldfinch: Its History and Significance in European Devotional Art* (New York: Pantheon Books, 1946), 83; Fritz Heinemann, *Giovanni Bellini e i Belliniani*, 3 vols. (Venice: Neri Pozza, 1962), 1:4, no. 15; Terisio Pignatti, *L'opera completa di Giovanni Bellini* (Milan: Rizzoli, 1969), 87, no. 20; Burton B. Fredericksen and Federico Zeri, *Census of Pre-Nineteenth-Century Italian Paintings in North American Public Collections* (Cambridge, Mass.: Harvard University Press, 1972), 22, 586; Fritz Heinemann, *Giovanni Bellini e i Belliniani*, 3 vols. (Venice: Neri Pozza, 1991), 3:1-2, no. 15; Jean Paris, *L'atelier Bellini* (Paris: Lagune, 1995), 204; Marilena Tamassia, *Collezioni d'arte tra Ottocento e Novecento: Jacquier fotografi a Firenze, 1870–1935* (Naples: Electa, 1995), 208; Carolyn C. Wilson, *Italian Paintings XIV–XVI Centuries in the Museum of Fine Arts, Houston* (Houston: Museum of Fine Arts, 1996), 202-13.

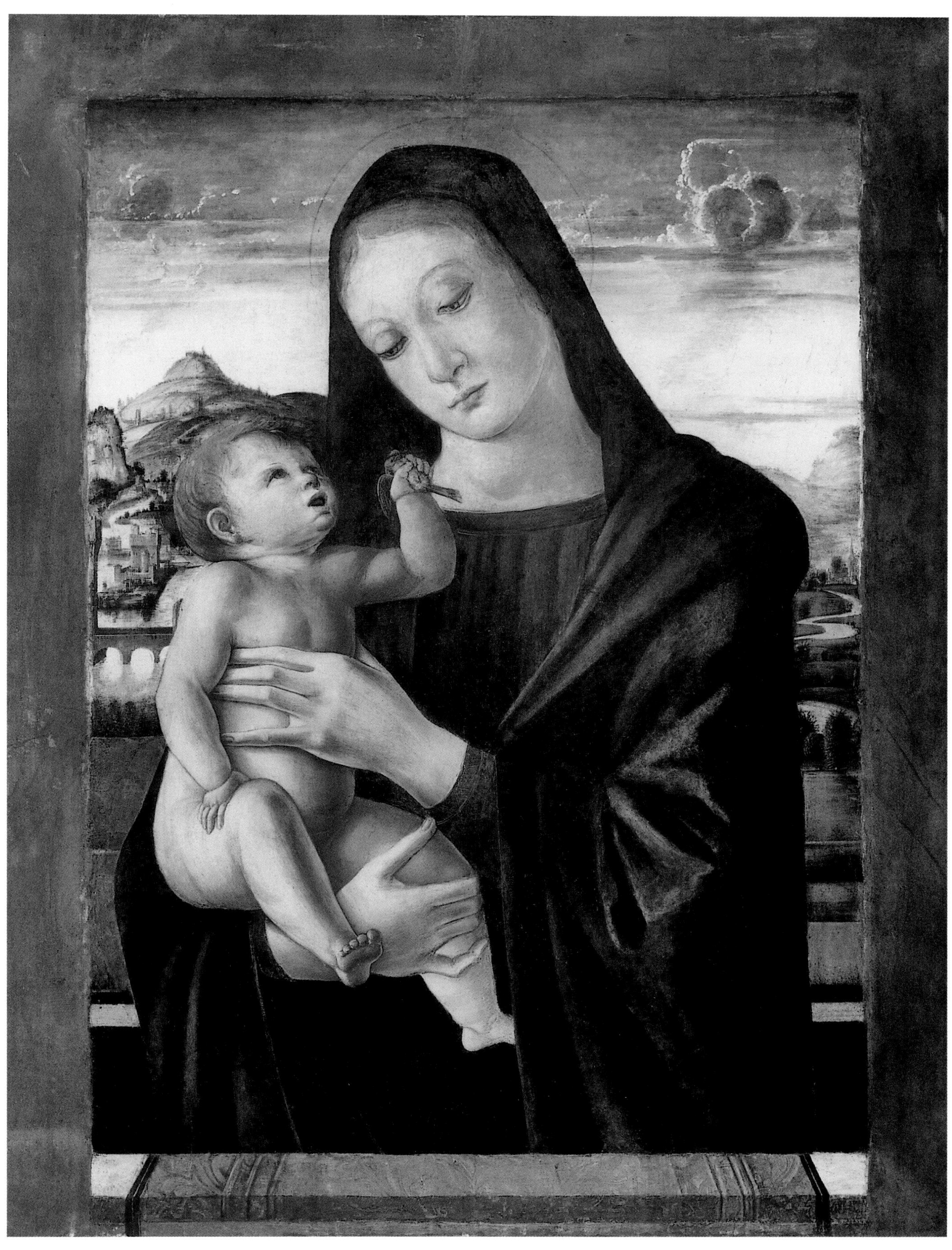

Fig. 199 Giovanni Bellini (attributed): *Virgin and Child*. The Museum of Fine Arts, Houston, The Edith A. and Percy S. Straus Collection, 44.552.

BELLINIANO, VITTORE, ACTIVE 1507; DIED 1529; ATTRIBUTED; VENETIAN

Portrait of Two Young Men (44.553) 45.7 X 63.2 CM, OIL ON CANVAS

HOUSTON, TEXAS. THE MUSEUM OF FINE ARTS, HOUSTON

Carolyn C. Wilson (1996) observed that the unidentified young men sport hairstyles and the clothing of fashionable Venetian gentlemen of the late fifteenth and early sixteenth centuries. Early in the picture's history, the sitters were identified as Giovanni (1431/6–1516) and Gentile Bellini (c. 1429–1507); the identification has been dismissed, based on a comparison with authentic portraits of the Bellini. The work is important, as it is one of the oldest surviving examples of early-sixteenth-century Venetian half-length double portraits, evincing a format that probably derives from a lost original by Giovanni Bellini. The Houston painting has long been associated with a bust-length double portrait in the Louvre (101), which depicts the same sitters in reversed positions and silhouetted against a landscape background. A copy of the Louvre painting, executed by an unidentified artist, is in the Museum of Fine Arts, Boston (50.3412). Although scholars have debated the priority of the Houston and Paris paintings, it is now generally thought that they derive from the same lost prototype, most likely a double portrait by Giovanni Bellini. Several copies of each bust, shown individually, exist, including the *Portrait of a Young Man* (Dionysios Mouszakis Collection, Athens).

The attribution of the work has been discussed at length, often in conjunction with the Louvre painting cited above. When the painting was in the collection of the Kaiser Friedrich Museum, it was assigned to the school of Giovanni Bellini. Joseph A. Crowe and Giovanni B. Cavalcaselle (1871) proposed it as an early work of Giovanni Cariani (c. 1485–after 1547); this attribution has been endorsed by a number of scholars up to the present. Georg Gronau (cited in Ludwig 1905) reattributed it to Vittore Belliniano, based on the similar appearance of its subjects and the supplicant depicted in the artist's signed and dated *Crucifixion* (Accademia Carrara, Bergamo; 400) of 1518. A handful of specialists considered the paintings in Houston and Paris as autograph works by Giovanni Bellini. Wilson found the attribution to Belliniano entirely plausible, in light of his role as a student of the master; she suggested a date for the painting of c. 1515, when Belliniano was still closely associated with the older artist.

PROVENANCE

Edward Solly, London, to 1821; Kaiser Friedrich Museum, Berlin, 1822–1921; Achillito Chiesa, Milan, by 1925; American Art Galleries, New York, November 27, 1925, pt. 1, lot 56; Edith A. and Percy S. Straus, New York, 1925–1944; Edith A. and Percy S. Straus Collection, The Museum of Fine Arts, Houston, acquired 1945

BIBLIOGRAPHY

Gustav F. Waagen, *Verzeichniss der Gemälde-Sammlung des Königlichen Museums zu Berlin* (Berlin: W. Moeser & Kühn, 1845), 6, no. 12; Claudius Tarral, *Observations sur le classement actuel des tableaux du Louvre et analyse critique du nouveau catalogue* (Paris: P. Dupont, 1850), 18; Frédéric Villot, *Notice des tableaux exposés dans les galeries du musée impérial du Louvre* (Paris: Vinchon, 1852), 34, no. 69; Joseph A. Crowe and Giovanni B. Cavalcaselle, *A History of Painting in North Italy, Venice, Padua, Vicenza, Verona, Ferrara, Milan, Friuli, Brescia, from the Fourteenth to the Sixteenth Century*, 2 vols. (London: John Murray, 1871), 1:134; Julius Meyer and Wilhelm von Bode, *Beschreibendes Verzeichniss der Während des Umbaues Ausgestelten Gemälde* (Berlin: C. Berg & von Holten, 1878), 26-27, no. 12; *Königliche Museen zu Berlin, beschreibendes Verzeichniss der Gemälde*, ed. Julius Meyer (Berlin: Weidemann, 1883), 37-38, no. 12; Jean Guiffrey, "Le double portrait vénitien du Musée du Louvre," *Revue de l'Art Ancien et Moderne* 10 (1901): 291 n. 1; Emil Jacobsen, "Italienische Gemälde im Louvre," *Repertorium für Kunstwissenschaft* 25 (1902): 182; Gustav Ludwig, "Archivalische Beiträge zur Geschichte der venezianischen Malerei," *Jahrbuch der königlich preuszischen Kunstsammlungen* 26 (1905): 73; Hans Posse, ed., *Die Gemäldegalerie des Kaiser-Friedrich-Museums*, vol. 1, *Die romanischen Länder: Byzanz, Italien, Spanien, Frankreich* (Berlin: J. Bard, 1909), 117, no. 12; Joseph A. Crowe and Giovanni B. Cavalcaselle, *A History of Painting in North Italy, Venice, Padua, Vicenza, Verona, Ferrara, Milan, Friuli, Brescia, from the Fourteenth to the Sixteenth Century*, 3 vols., ed. Tancred Borenius (London: John Murray, 1912), 1:135; Claude Phillips, "Some Portraits by Cariani," *Burlington Magazine* 24 (1913): 157-58; Seymour de Ricci, *Description raisonée des peintures du Louvre*, vol. 1, *Écoles étrangères: Italie et Espagne* (Paris: Imprimerie de l'Art, 1913), 17; Bernard Berenson, *Venetian Painting in America: The Fifteenth Century* (London: Bell, 1916), 261; Lionel Cust, "Notes on Pictures in the Royal Collections,"

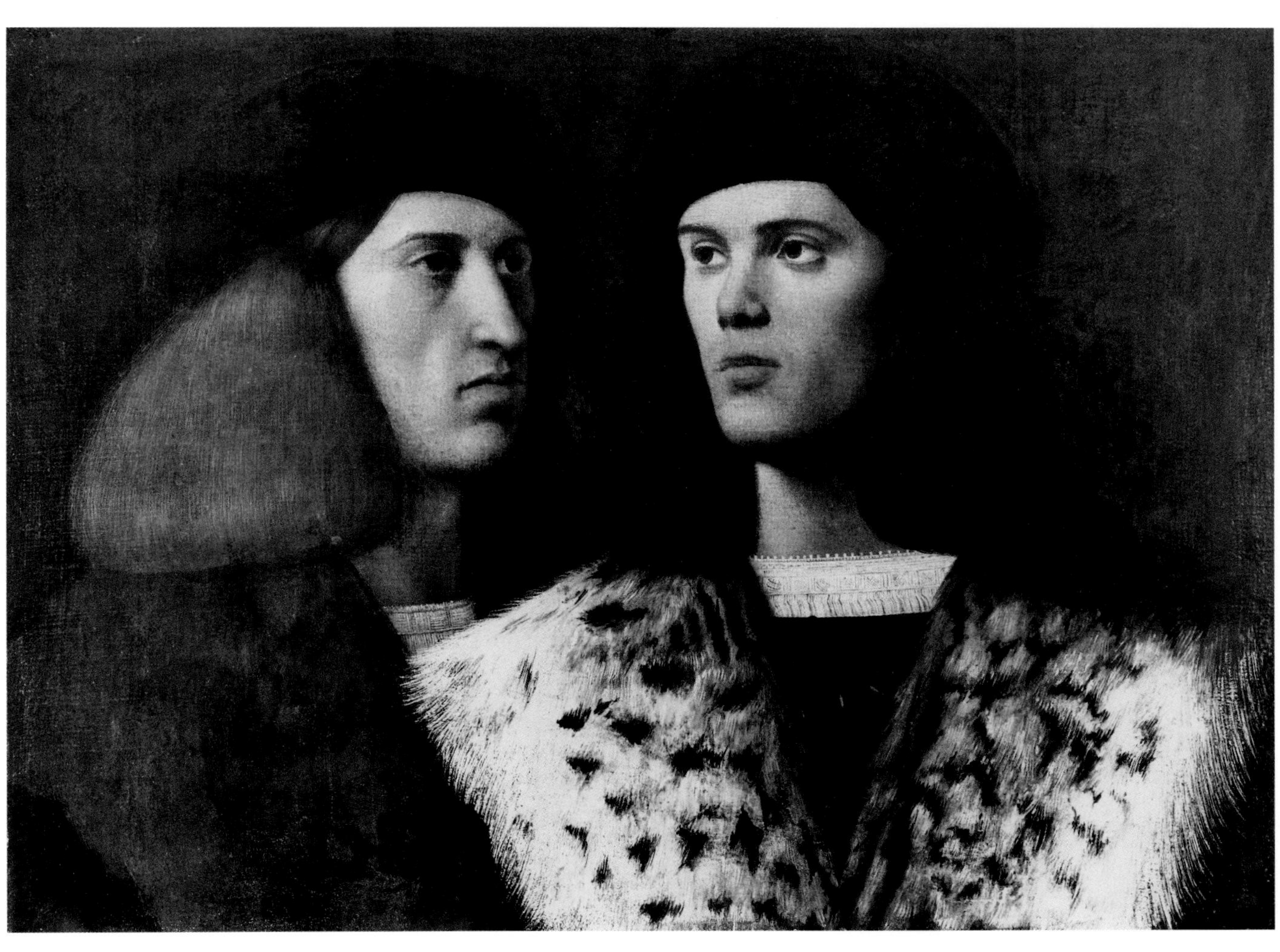

Fig. 200 (above and overleaf, detail): Vittore Belliniano (attributed): *Portrait of Two Young Men*. The Museum of Fine Arts, Houston, The Edith A. and Percy S. Straus Collection, 44.553.

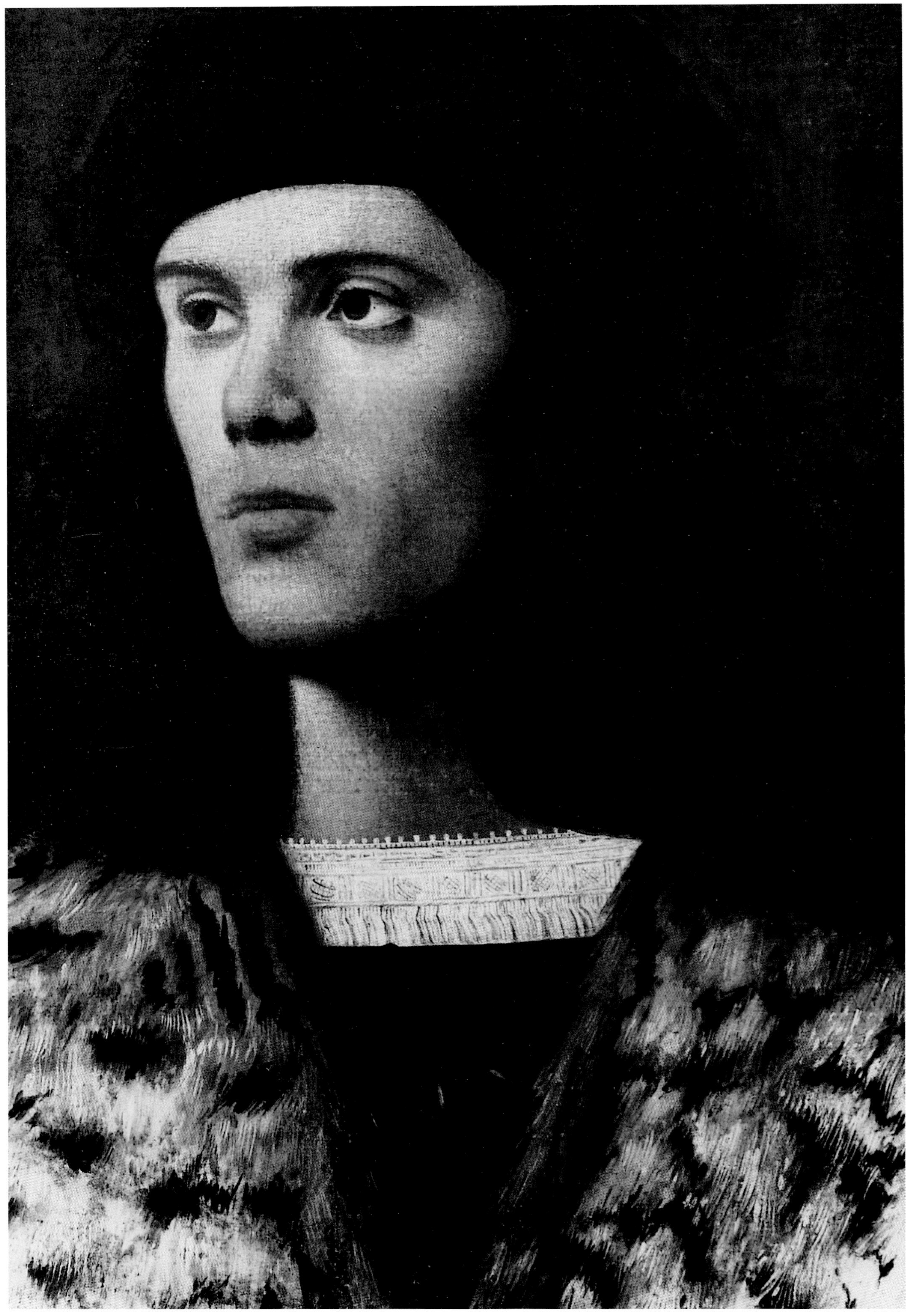

Burlington Magazine 19 (1916): 204; Louis Hautecoeur, *La peinture au Musée du Louvre: Écoles italiennes XIII, XIV, XV siècles* (Paris: L'Illustration, 1925), 88; *The Collection of Achillito Chiesa*, vol. 1, *Flemish and Dutch Paintings of the XV, XVI, XVII Centuries; Italian Primitives and Renaissance Examples* (New York: American Art Association, Inc., 1925), no. 56; Louis Hautecoeur, *École italienne et école espagnole* (Paris: Musées Nationaux, 1926), 40; Roberto Longhi, "Cartella tizianesca," *Vita Artistica* 2 (1927): 223; Bernard Berenson, *Italian Pictures of the Renaissance* (Oxford: Clarendon Press, 1932), 72; Günter Troche, "Giovanni Cariani als Bildnismaler," *Pantheon* 9 (1932): 7 n. 3; Günter Troche, "Giovanni Cariani," *Jahrbuch der preussischen Kunstsammlungen* 55 (1934): 102 n. 1, 120, no. 12; Bernard Berenson, *Pitture italiane del Rinascimento* (Milan: U. Hoepli, 1936), 62; Carlo Gamba, *Giovanni Bellini* (Milan: U. Hoepli, 1937), 174; Malcolm Vaughan, "Old Masters at the Fair," *Parnassus* 11 (1939): 11; George H. McCall, *Catalogue of European Paintings and Sculpture from 1300–1800* (New York: Publishers Printing Co., 1939), 6-7, no. 10; *Catalogue of the Edith A. and Percy S. Straus Collection* (Houston: Museum of Fine Arts, 1945), 17-18, no. 23; Luitpold Dussler, *Giovanni Bellini* (Vienna: A. Schroll, 1949), 72; Luciano Gallina, *Giovanni Cariani: Materiale per uno studio* (Bergamo: Documenti lombardi, 1954), 122, 126; Bernard Berenson, *Italian Pictures of the Renaissance: A List of the Principal Artists and Their Works with an Index of Places. Venetian School*, 2 vols. (New York: Phaidon, 1957), 1:31; Fritz Heinemann, *Giovanni Bellini e i Belliniani*, 3 vols. (Venice: Neri Pozza, 1962), 1:200, S. 804; Cecil Gould, "Lorenzo Lotto and the Double Portrait: Transformations of the Della Torre Picture," *Saggi e Memorie di Storia dell'Arte* 5 (1966): 45 n. 2; Burton B. Fredericksen and Federico Zeri, *Census of Pre-Nineteenth-Century Italian Paintings in North American Public Collections* (Cambridge, Mass.: Harvard University Press, 1972), 23, 586; Sarah Wilk, *The Sculpture of Tullio Lombardo: Studies in Sources and Meaning* (New York: Garland Press, 1978), 313; Gian Alberto Dell'Acqua, *I pittori bergamaschi dal XIII al XIX secolo*, vol. 3, *Il Cinquecento* (Bergamo: Poligrafiche Bolis, 1980), pt. 1, 292; *Museum of Fine Arts, Houston: A Guide to the Collection* (Houston: Museum of Fine Arts, 1981), 32, no. 59; *Catalogue sommaire illustré des peintures du Musée du Louvre*, vol. 2, *Italie, Espagne, Allemagne, Grande-Bretagne et divers*, ed. Arnauld Bréjon de Lavergnée and Dominique Thiébaut (Paris: Editions de la Réunion des musées nationaux, 1981), 161, no. 101; Rodolfo Pallucchini and Francesco Rossi, *Giovanni Cariani* (Milan: Cinisello, 1983), 135-36, 279, 298, no. A41; Giorgio Fossaluzza, "Vittore Belliniano, Fra' Marco Pensaben e Giovan Girolamo Savoldo: La 'Sacra Conversazione' in San Niccolò a Treviso," *Studi Trevisani* 2 (1985): 51 n. 26; Rona Goffen, *Giovanni Bellini* (New Haven: Yale University Press, 1989), 320 n. 51; Fritz Heinemann, *Giovanni Bellini e i Belliniani*, 3 vols. (Venice: Neri Pozza, 1991), 3:71, S. 804; *Le siècle de Titien*, ed. Michel Laclotte and Giovanna Nepi Sciré (Paris: Editions de la Réunion des musées nationaux, 1993), 272, no. 5; Alison Luchs, *Tullio Lombardo and Ideal Portrait Sculpture in Renaissance Venice, 1490–1530* (Cambridge and New York: Cambridge University Press, 1995), 163 n. 59; Carolyn C. Wilson, *Italian Paintings XIV–XVI Centuries in the Museum of Fine Arts, Houston* (Houston: Museum of Fine Arts, 1996), 315-22.

BENVENUTO DI GIOVANNI, C. 1436–C. 1518; SIENESE

St. Francis (70.36) 23.5 X 26.7 CM, TEMPERA ON PANEL

HOUSTON, TEXAS. THE MUSEUM OF FINE ARTS, HOUSTON

The painting is one of six similar panels formerly exhibited together in the Robert Lehman Collection, including also: *Christ as Salvator Mundi* and *St. Dominic* (formerly, Nelson-Atkins Museum of Art, Kansas City, Missouri); *St. Peter Martyr* (Yale University Art Gallery, New Haven; 140); *St. Bernardino of Siena* (Robert Lehman Collection, The Metropolitan Museum of Art, New York; 1975.1.53); and *St. Anthony of Padua* (current location unknown). The pictures were probably cut from a horizontal predella, which originally featured a seventh saint; the lost figure may have been St. Thomas Aquinas or St. Catherine of Siena. The paintings have been dated c. 1474–1475, based on their stylistic affinities with Benvenuto's *biccherna* panel, *Allegory of Good Government* (Archivio di Stato, Siena), dated 1474, and his altarpiece from San Michele Arcangelo, Montepertuso, dated 1475. Maria Cristina Bandera (1974) proposed that the representations of the saints were originally part of the same altarpiece as the six pilaster panels depicting full-length saints in the Kress Collection (K 1744), at Bucknell University, Lewisburg, Pennsylvania, and the New Orleans Museum of Art, New Orleans. John Pope-Hennessy (1987) thought that both sets of panels may have come from Benvenuto's altarpiece in San Domenico, Siena, completed by the end of 1478.

St. Francis holds a staff surmounted by a crucifix, symbolizing his devotion to the Passion. He opens his habit to reveal one of the stigmata, corresponding to the wound made in Christ's side during his ordeal on the cross.

PROVENANCE

Santinover Galleries, New York; Robert Lehman, New York, 1920–c. 1945/6; Maurice W. Newton or A. Merriman Paff; Parke-Bernet Galleries, New York, October 22, 1970, lot 2; The Museum of Fine Arts, Houston, acquired 1970

BIBLIOGRAPHY

Bernard Berenson, *Italian Pictures of the Renaissance* (Oxford: Clarendon Press, 1932), 77; Raimond van Marle, *The Development of the Italian Schools of Painting*, vol. 16, *The Renaissance Painters of Tuscany* (The Hague: M. Nijhoff, 1937), 416; Burton B. Fredericksen and Darrell D. Davisson, *Benvenuto di Giovanni, Girolamo di Benvenuto: Their Altarpieces in the J. Paul Getty Museum* (Malibu: J. Paul Getty Museum, 1966), 25-27; Charles Seymour, *Early Italian Paintings in the Yale University Art Gallery* (New Haven: Yale University Press, 1970), 188; J. L. Schrader, "Recent Acquisitions: A Quattrocento Sienese Saint Francis," *The Museum of Fine Arts, Houston Bulletin* 2 (1971): 18-21; Maria Cristina Bandera, "Qualche osservazione su Benvenuto di Giovanni," *Antichità Viva* 13 (1974): 8, 16 n. 24; Maria Cristina Bandera, "Variazioni ai cataloghi Berensoniani di Benvenuto di Giovanni," in *Scritti di storia dell'arte in onore di Ugo Procacci*, 2 vols., ed. Maria Grazia Ciardi Dupré and Paolo Dal Poggetto (Milan: Electa, 1977), 1:312; John Pope-Hennessy, *The Robert Lehman Collection*, vol. 1, *Italian Paintings* (New York: Metropolitan Museum of Art; Princeton: Princeton University Press, 1987), 164; Carolyn C. Wilson, *Italian Paintings XIV–XVI Centuries in the Museum of Fine Arts, Houston* (Houston: Museum of Fine Arts, 1996), 180-88; Maria Cristina Bandera Viani, *Benvenuto di Giovanni* (Milan: Federico Motta, 1999), 104-6, 229, no. 38.

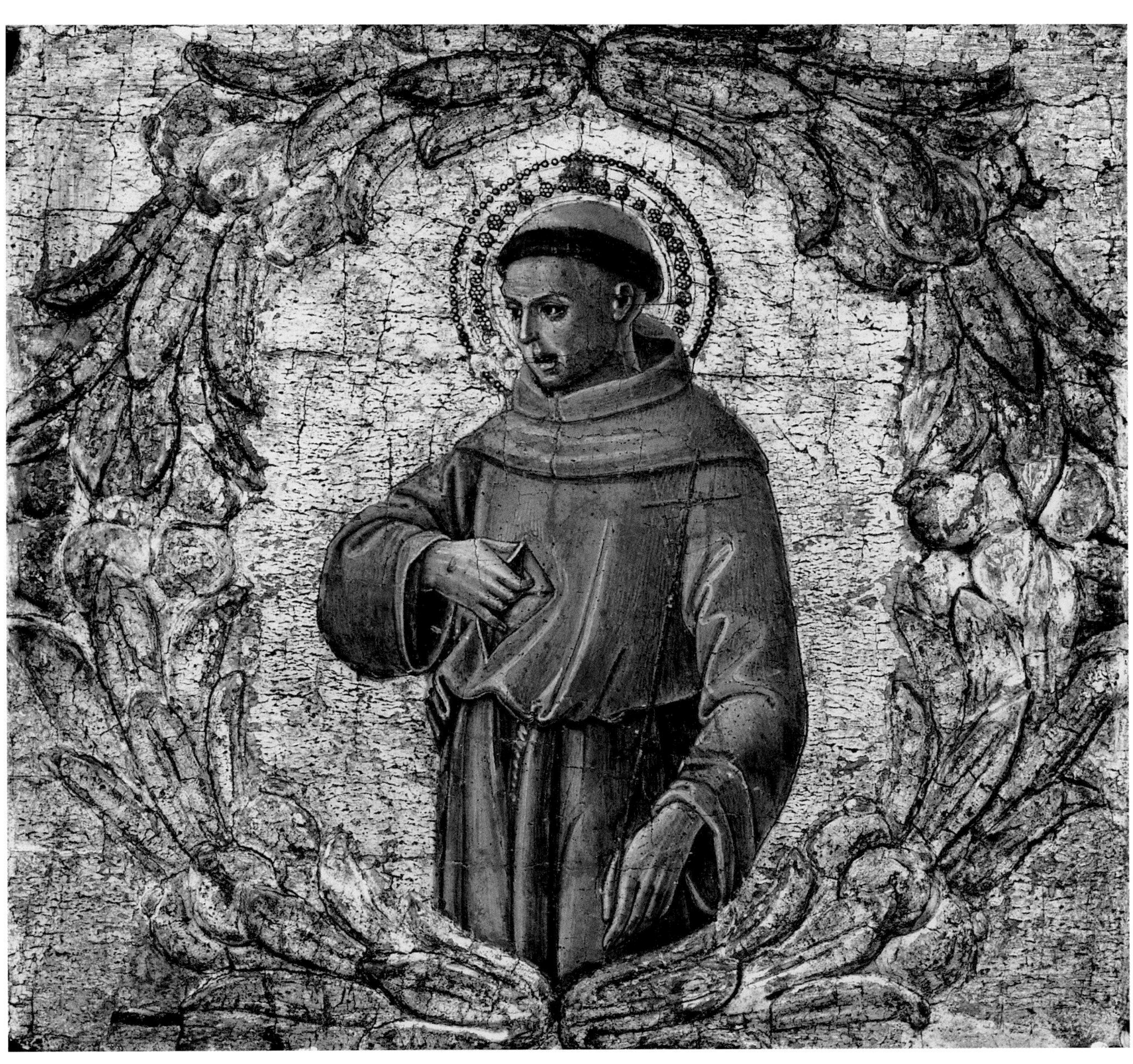

Fig. 201 Benvenuto di Giovanni: *St. Francis*. The Museum of Fine Arts, Houston; Gift of Mrs. Harry C. Hanszen, 70.36.

BERTUCCI, GIOVANNI BATTISTA, I, C. 1465–1516; FAVENTINE

St. Thomas Aquinas (64.34) 138.3 X 54.4 CM, TEMPERA ON PANEL

HOUSTON, TEXAS. THE MUSEUM OF FINE ARTS, HOUSTON

Martin Davies (1951) was the first scholar to recognize that *St. Thomas Aquinas* originally constituted the left-hand panel of Bertucci's *Manfredi Altarpiece* for San Andrea in Vineis, Faenza, which had as its central image the *Madonna and Child in Glory* (National Gallery, London; 282); on the right was *St. John the Evangelist* (Sarah Campbell Blaffer Foundation, Houston; 78.22). The altarpiece was commissioned by Clarice Manfredi, a Dominican tertiary, in 1512 and, presumably, was completed before the artist's death in 1516.

Thomas Aquinas was the titular saint of the chapel in which the painting was originally located. He is shown with four traditional attributes: a book; a brooch representing a blazing sun; a model of a church; and a lily. According to Carolyn C. Wilson (1996), the golden rays emanating from the cloud at the upper right allude to the divine inspiration that informed Thomas's writings.

PROVENANCE

Chapel of St. Thomas Aquinas, San Andrea in Vineis, Faenza, to 1759 (?); Hercolani family, Bologna, by 1770–after 1828; Mr. Earle, Leamington, 1856; Christie's, London, July 9, 1948, lot 99; Spencer A. Samuels and Co., Ltd., New York; Sarah Campbell Blaffer, Houston, acquired 1964; The Robert Lee Blaffer Memorial Collection, The Museum of Fine Arts, Houston, acquired 1964

BIBLIOGRAPHY

Giovanni G. Bottari and Stefano Ticozzi, *Raccolta di lettere sulla pittura, scultura ed architettura scritte da' più celebri personaggi dei secoli XV, XVI, e XVII* (Milan: G. Silvestri, 1822), 103-4; Carlo Grigioni, *La pittura faentina dalle origini alla metà del Cinquecento* (Faenza: Fratelli Lega, 1936), 294, 315; Martin Davies, *The Earlier Italian Schools* (London: National Gallery, 1951), 182, 183 n. 3; Burton B. Fredericksen and Federico Zeri, *Census of Pre-Nineteenth-Century Italian Paintings in North American Public Collections* (Cambridge, Mass.: Harvard University Press, 1972), 27, 587; *Museum of Fine Arts, Houston: A Guide to the Collection* (Houston: Museum of Fine Arts, 1981), 40, no. 75; Terisio Pignatti, *Five Centuries of Italian Painting, 1300–1800: From the Collection of the Sarah Campbell Blaffer Foundation* (Houston: Sarah Campbell Blaffer Foundation, 1985), 67-68; Carolyn C. Wilson, *Italian Paintings XIV–XVI Centuries in the Museum of Fine Arts, Houston* (Houston: Museum of Fine Arts, 1996), 292-98.

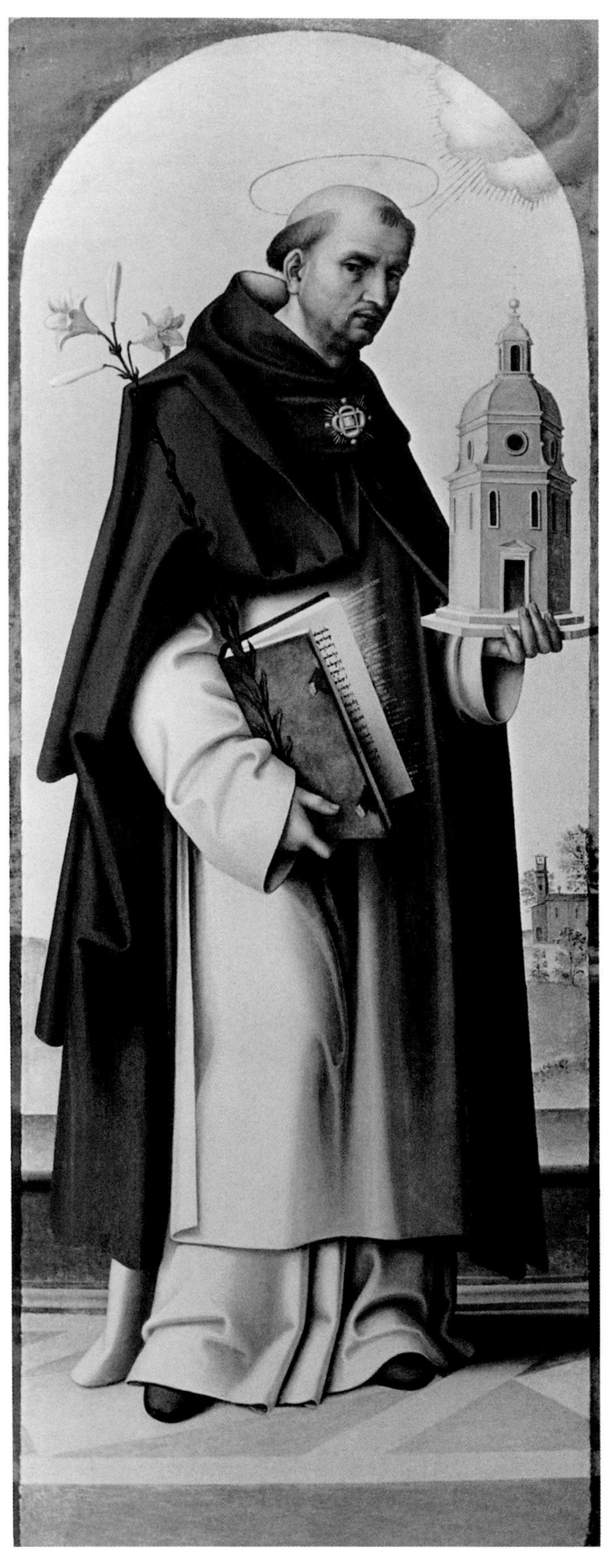

Fig. 202 Giovanni Battista Bertucci I: *St. Thomas Aquinas*. The Museum of Fine Arts, Houston, The Robert Lee Blaffer Memorial Collection; Gift of Sarah Campbell Blaffer, 64.34.

CATENA, VINCENZO DI BIAGIO, C. 1470–1531; VENETIAN

Virgin and Child with St. John the Baptist and St. Joseph (61.61; K 1104) 76.8 X 104 CM, OIL ON CANVAS

HOUSTON, TEXAS. THE MUSEUM OF FINE ARTS, HOUSTON

The painting was sold in 1929 as the work of Cima da Conegliano (c. 1459–1517), but, by 1935, it was attributed to Catena (according to William E. Suida 1953). The latter attribution was generally accepted thereafter by scholars, with the notable exceptions of Terisio Pignatti (1955), who suggested Pier Maria Pennacchi (1464–1514/5), and Fritz Heinemann (1962), who concurred. Heinemann later (1991) favored Catena, dating the work c. 1510. Most scholars placed it later in the artist's career, c. 1525, contemporary with his two representations of the *Supper at Emmaus* (Count Alessandro Contini-Bonacossi Bequest, Uffizi, Florence; Accademia Carrara, Bergamo; 390). Giles Robertson (1954) first noted the affinities between the saints' heads in the Houston work and those of the apostles in the *Supper* scenes.

The composition for this devotional painting follows Giovanni Bellini's (1431/6–1516) *sacra conversazione* format, found, for example, in his Giovannelli *Madonna and Child with Saints John the Baptist and Mary Magdalene* (Accademia, Venice; 881). The small book that the Virgin holds is probably a psalter.

PROVENANCE

Col. Sir Wyndham Murray, London, to 1929; Christie, Manson and Woods, London, March 15, 1929, lot 96; A. L. Nicholson, London, 1929; George H. Winterbottom, London, 1929–1935; Christie, Manson and Woods, London, December 20, 1935, lot 101; W. H. G. Turner; Count Alessandro Contini-Bonacossi, Florence; Samuel H. Kress Collection, New York, acquired 1937; Honolulu Academy of Arts, Honolulu, Hawaii, 1938–1952, on loan; The Museum of Fine Arts, Houston, acquired 1953

BIBLIOGRAPHY

William E. Suida, *The Samuel H. Kress Collection at the Museum of Fine Arts of Houston* (Houston: Museum of Fine Arts, 1953), no. 7; Giles Robertson, *Vincenzo Catena* (Edinburgh: Edinburgh University Press, 1954), 34, 64, no. 41, 66, 72; Terisio Pignatti, "Vincenzo Catena," *Arte Veneta* 9 (1955): 232; Bernard Berenson, *Italian Pictures of the Renaissance: A List of the Principal Artists and Their Works with an Index of Places. Venetian School*, 2 vols. (New York: Phaidon, 1957), 1:62; Fritz Heinemann, *Giovanni Bellini e i Belliniani*, 3 vols. (Venice: Neri Pozza, 1962), 1:131, S. 276; Fern Rusk Shapley, *Paintings from the Samuel H. Kress Collection: Italian Schools*, vol. 2, *XV–XVI Century* (London: Phaidon Press, 1968), 155-56; Burton B. Fredericksen and Federico Zeri, *Census of Pre-Nineteenth-Century Italian Paintings in North American Public Collections* (Cambridge, Mass.: Harvard University Press, 1972), 49, 587; Fern Rusk Shapley, *Paintings from the Samuel H. Kress Collection: Italian Schools*, vol. 3, *XVI–XVIII Century* (London: Phaidon Press, 1973), 393; *The Museum of Fine Arts, Houston: A Guide to the Collection* (Houston: Museum of Fine Arts, 1981), 38-39, no. 72; Fritz Heinemann, *Giovanni Bellini e i Belliniani*, 3 vols. (Venice: Neri Pozza, 1991), 3:48, 72, S. 276, 104; Carolyn C. Wilson, *Italian Paintings XIV–XVI Centuries in the Museum of Fine Arts, Houston* (Houston: Museum of Fine Arts, 1996), 336-40; Edgar Peters Bowron and Mary G. Morton, *Masterworks of European Painting in the Museum of Fine Arts, Houston* (Princeton: Princeton University Press, 2000), 34-36.

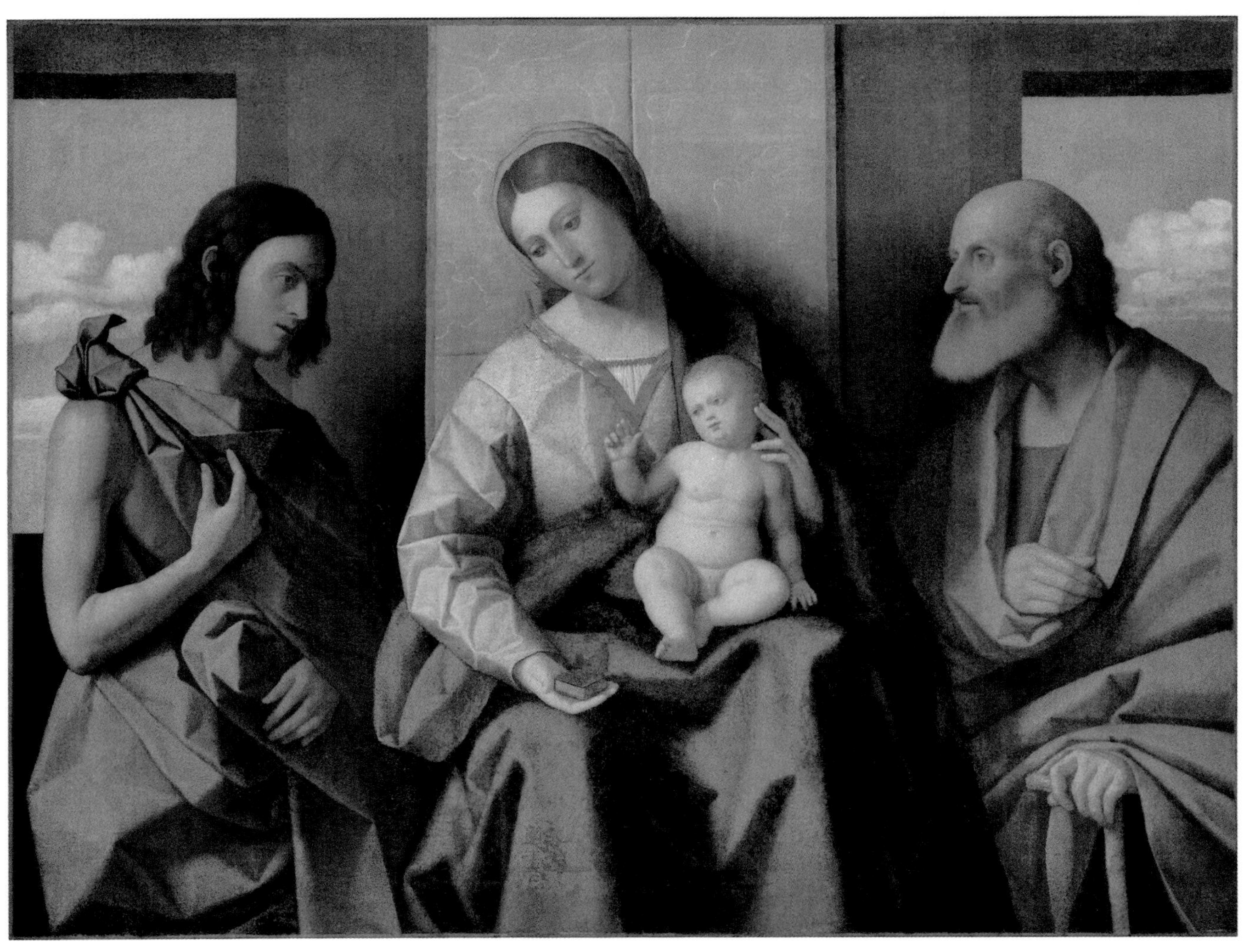

Fig. 203 Vincenzo di Biagio Catena: *Virgin and Child with St. John the Baptist and St. Joseph*. The Museum of Fine Arts, Houston, The Samuel H. Kress Collection, 61.61.

FERRARESE SCHOOL, THIRD QUARTER OF THE FIFTEENTH CENTURY

The Meeting of Solomon and the Queen of Sheba (44.574) 92.3 CM (DIAMETER), TEMPERA ON PANEL

HOUSTON, TEXAS. THE MUSEUM OF FINE ARTS, HOUSTON

This work is one of the most distinguished surviving birth salvers (*deschi da parto*) from northern Italy in the fifteenth century. It is particularly noteworthy for its elaborate architectural setting, the employment of a single vanishing point, the complexity of the figural relationships, the profusion of naturalistic detail, and the extensive use of tooled gold leaf and *sgraffitto* in the clothing and headdresses. Carolyn C. Wilson (1996) observed that the composition is so similar to Lorenzo Ghiberti's in his panel of the *Meeting of Solomon and the Queen of Sheba* (Baptistry, east doors, Florence; 1425–1452) that the painter must have known the sculptural work first-hand or through a close intermediate source, such as a Florentine birth salver with the same subject. William Rankin (1907) associated the Houston panel with Domenico Veneziano (c. 1400–1461); the attribution was accepted by a number of scholars, including Bernard Berenson (1932; 1936) and the author of the *Catalogue of the Edith A. and Percy S. Straus Collection* (1945). Other artists have been proposed as well, including Alesso Baldovinetti (c. 1425–1499) and Matteo di Giovanni (c. 1430–1495), but most specialists have followed Georg Pudelko (1934) in assigning the *tondo* to the School of Ferrara. In Wilson's opinion, the appearance of the figures, certain motifs, and the color scheme recall the work of Francesco del Cossa (c. 1425–c. 1477); she therefore ascribed the panel to his circle, c. 1470–1473.

The scene illustrates the visit of the Queen of Sheba to the court of King Solomon, as recounted in 1 Kings 10:1-13 and 2 Chronicles 9:1-12. The meeting of the rulers symbolized the marriage of Christ and the Church. The theme also alluded to the reconciliation of the Greek and Latin churches at the Council of Florence-Ferrara in 1438–1439. The Queen of Sheba's acknowledgment of Solomon's superior wisdom led to the choice of the subject for fifteenth-century marriage chests and birth salvers. In 1927, the reverse was described by Henri Leman as having a double escutcheon within a wreath of leaves and flowers; this coat-of-arms was obliterated when the panel was thinned shortly thereafter.

PROVENANCE

Prince Michele di Demetrio Boutourlin, Conte Russo, Florence; Edmond Foulc, Paris, by 1894, to 1916; Duval-Foulc, Paris, 1916–1927; Wildenstein and Co., New York; Edith A. and Percy S. Straus, New York, 1930–1945; Edith A. and Percy S. Straus Collection, The Museum of Fine Arts, Houston, acquired 1945

BIBLIOGRAPHY

Eugène Müntz, "Les plateaux d'accouchées et la peinture sur meuble du IVe au XVIe siècle," *Monuments et mémoires* 1 (1894): 221; Gaston Mignon, "La collection de M. Edmond Foulc," *Les Arts* 1 (1902): 14; William Rankin, "Cassone Fronts in American Collections—VI," *Burlington Magazine* 12 (1907): 64; Attilio Schiaparelli, *La casa fiorentina e i suoi arredi nei secoli XIV e XV*, 2 vols. (Florence: G. C. Sansoni, 1908), 1:285; 2:82 n. 241; A. Pératé, "Le triomphe de l'amour: Plateau d'accouchée," *Catalogue raisonné de la collection Martin Le Roy*, 5 vols. (Paris: M. M. Durand, Chartres, 1909), 5:17-18; Paul Schubring, *Cassoni: Truhen und Truhenbilder der italienischen Frührenaissance*, 2 vols. (Leipzig: K. W. Hiersemann, 1923), 1:361-62; Henri Leman, *La collection Foulc, objets d'art du Moyen Âge et de la Renaissance*, 2 vols. (Paris: Les Beaux-Arts, 1927), 1:12; Bernard Berenson, *Three Essays in Method* (Oxford: Clarendon Press, 1927), 19; A. L. Mayer and O. von Falke, "Die Sammlung Foulc," *Pantheon* 2 (1928): 491; Ella S. Seple, "Recent Acquisitions in America," *Burlington Magazine* 60 (1932): 110; Bernard Berenson, *Italian Pictures of the Renaissance* (Oxford: Clarendon Press, 1932), 172; Lionello Venturi, *Italian Paintings in America*, 3 vols. (New York: E. Wyhe, 1933), 2:pl. 292; Georg Pudelko, "Studien über Domenico Veneziano," *Mitteilungen des Kunsthistorischen Institutes in Florenz* 4 (1934): 199; Bernard Berenson, *Pitture italiane del Rinascimento* (Milan: U. Hoepli, 1936), 149; Mario Salmi, *Paolo Uccello, Andea del Castagno, Domenico Veneziano* (Rome: Valori plastici, 1936), 67-69, 100, 125, 141, no. 174; Richard Offner, "The Straus Collection Goes to Houston—Comments on Its Most Important Objects," *Art News* 44 (1945): 16, 23; *Catalogue of the Edith A. and Percy S. Straus Collection* (Houston: Museum of Fine Arts, 1945), 13-14, no. 14; *Diamond Jubilee Exhibition: Masterpieces of Painting* (Philadelphia: Philadelphia Museum of Art, 1950), no. 17; *Masterpieces from Museums and Private Collections* (New York: Wildenstein and Company, 1951), no. 3; Roberto Longhi, "Il 'Maestro di Pratovecchio,'" *Paragone* 35 (1952): 34; Luigi Coletti, *Pittura veneta del Quattrocento* (Novara: Istituto geografico De Agostini, 1953), xxvi; *Religious Painting, 15th–19th Century* (New York: Brooklyn Museum,

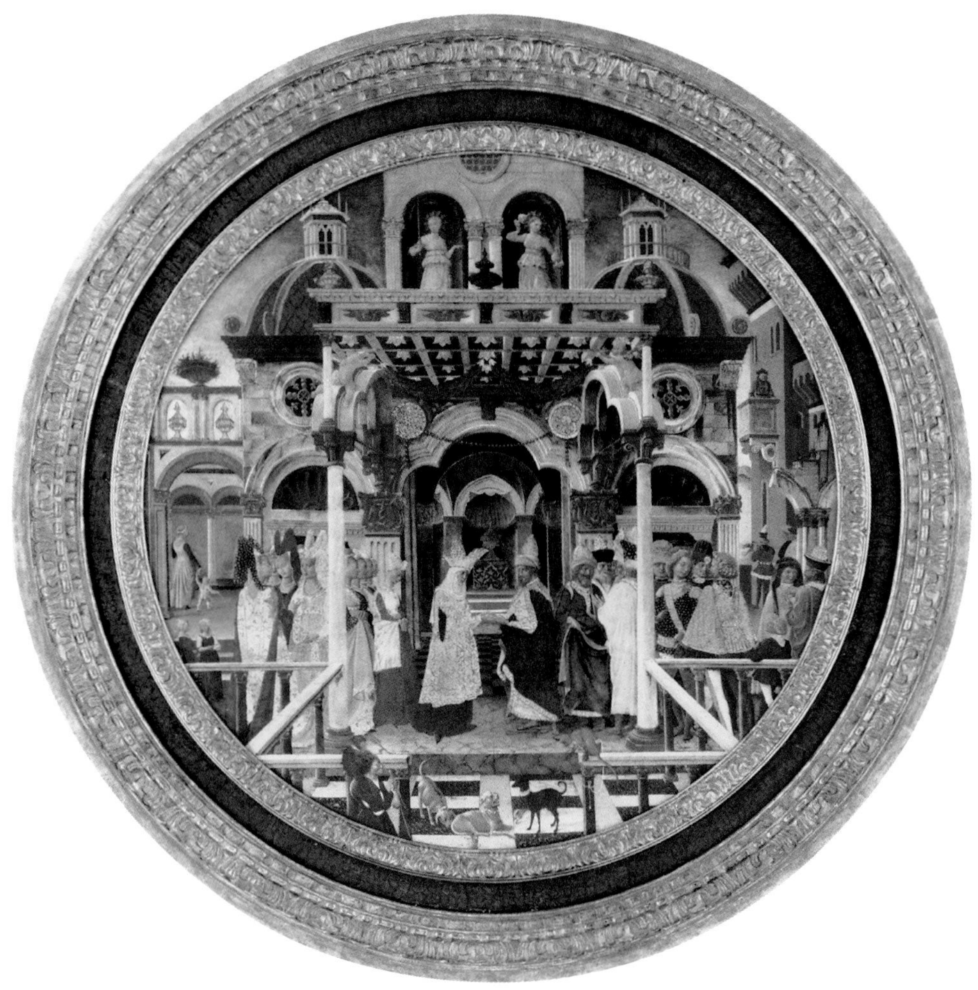

Fig. 204 Ferrarese School, third quarter of the fifteenth century: *The Meeting of Solomon and the Queen of Sheba.* The Museum of Fine Arts, Houston, The Edith A. and Percy S. Straus Collection, 44.574.

1956), no. 2; Carlo Volpe, "In margine a un Filippo Lippi," *Paragone* 7 (1956): 45; James Fasanelli, "An Italian 'Nativity Salver,'" *Virginia Museum of Fine Arts Members' Bulletin* 19/4 (1958); *Decorative Arts of the Italian Renaissance, 1400–1600* (Detroit: Detroit Institute of Arts, 1958), 35, no. 51; Bernard Berenson, *Italian Pictures of the Renaissance: A List of the Principal Artists and Their Works with an Index of Places. Florentine School*, 2 vols. (London: Phaidon Press, 1963), 1:61; André Chastel, *The Studios and Styles of the Renaissance: Italy 1460–1500* (New York: Thames and Hudson, 1966), 16; Burton B. Fredericksen and Federico Zeri, *Census of Pre-Nineteenth-Century Italian Paintings in North American Public Collections* (Cambridge, Mass.: Harvard University Press, 1972), 216, 586; Hellmut Wohl, *The Paintings of Domenico Veneziano, ca. 1410-1461* (Oxford: Phaidon, 1980), 156, no. 28; Anne Jacobson-Schute, "'Trionfo delle donne': Tematiche di rovesciamento dei ruoli nella Firenze rinascimentale," *Quaderni Storici* 15 (1980): 480; *The Museum of Fine Arts, Houston: A Guide to the Collection* (Houston: Museum of Fine Arts, 1981), 28, no. 51; Diane Cole Ahl, "Renaissance Birth Salvers and the Richmond 'Judgment of Solomon,'" *Studies in Iconography* 7-8 (1981–1982): 164 n. 12; Alessandra Uguccioni, *Salomone e la regina di Saba: La pittura di cassone a Ferrara presenze nei musei americani* (Ferrara: G. Corbo, 1988), 25-54 and passim; Peter C. Marzio, *A Permanent Legacy: 150 Works from the Collection of the Museum of Fine Arts, Houston* (New York: Hudson Hills Press, 1989), 114-15; Joseph Manca, "A Ferrarese Painter of the Quattrocento," *Gazette des Beaux-Arts* 116 (1990): 157-72; *Le muse e il principe: Arte di corte nel Rinascimento padano*, ed. Alessandra Mottola Molfino and Mauro Natale (Modena: F. C. Panini, 1991), 303, 304, 360-62; Carolyn C. Wilson, *Italian Paintings XIV–XVI Centuries in the Museum of Fine Arts, Houston* (Houston: Museum of Fine Arts, 1996), 214-29; Graham Hughes, *Renaissance Cassoni: Masterpieces of Early Italian Art* (Sussex: Starcity Publishing, 1997), 231; Edgar Peters Bowron and Mary G. Morton, *Masterworks of European Painting in the Museum of Fine Arts, Houston* (Princeton: Princeton University Press, 2000), 16-18; Andrea Bayer, ed., *Art and Love in Renaissance Italy* (New York: Metropolitan Museum of Art; New Haven: Yale University Press, 2008), 159-61, no. 73.

FLORENTINE SCHOOL, THIRD QUARTER OF THE FOURTEENTH CENTURY

Nativity (44.570.2); *Christ on the Cross with the Virgin, St. John, and St. Mary Magdalen* (44.570.1)
29.5 X 12.9 CM (44.570.2); 30.2 X 12.9 CM (44.570.1), TEMPERA ON PANEL

HOUSTON, TEXAS. THE MUSEUM OF FINE ARTS, HOUSTON

Richard Offner (1945) identified the two panels as the shutters of a small, portable tabernacle, the central part of which was the *Madonna and Child Enthroned with Six Saints and Four Angels* (Statens Museum for Kunst, Copenhagen; 3479). The lost gables probably depicted Gabriel and the Annunciate Virgin on the left and right, respectively. *Christ on the Cross* evinces traditional imagery, whereas the *Nativity*, as noted by Carolyn C. Wilson (1996), is notable for its stark simplicity.

Controverting earlier attributions to Orcagna (1315/20–1368) (*International Studio* 1929) and Jacopo di Cione (1320/30–before 1400) (Bernard Berenson 1931; 1932; 1936), Offner ascribed them to a follower of Orcagna, whom he later (in Offner and Maginnis 1981) identified as the Nardesque Master of the Statens Madonna. Burton B. Fredericksen and Federico Zeri (1972) also considered the paintings to be by an Orcagna follower, while Miklòs Boskovits (1975) saw them as some of the first works by Andrea da Firenze (Andrea di Bonaiuto; active 1346; died 1379), dating from the early 1360s. In Wilson's opinion, the style of the Copenhagen and Houston panels is not in keeping with that of Andrea da Firenze's documented oeuvre; she assigned the reconstructed triptych to an artist in the circle of Orcagna and Nardo di Cione (c. 1320–1365/6), c. 1360–1380.

PROVENANCE

Private collection, Karlsruhe, by 1922; Leo Blumenreich, Berlin; R. Langton Douglas, London; Edith A. and Percy S. Straus, New York, 1928–1945; Edith A. and Percy S. Straus Collection, The Museum of Fine Arts, Houston, acquired 1945

BIBLIOGRAPHY

"A Diptych by Andrea Orcagna," *International Studio* 92 (1929): 54; Bernard Berenson, "Quadri senza casa: Il Trecento fiorentino, II," *Dedalo* 11 (1931): 1042, 1044; Bernard Berenson, *Italian Pictures of the Renaissance* (Oxford: Clarendon Press, 1932), 275; Bernard Berenson, *Pitture italiane del Rinascimento* (Milan: U. Hoepli, 1936), 236; Richard Offner, "The Straus Collection Goes to Texas—Comments on Its More Important Objects," *Art News* 44 (1945): 19; *Catalogue of the Edith A. and Percy S. Straus Collection* (Houston: Museum of Fine Arts, 1945), 10, no. 3; *Katalog over aeldre malerier* (Copenhagen: Statens Museum for Kunst, 1946), 137; Hans D. Gronau, "Review of 'Florentine Painting and Its Social Background,'" *Burlington Magazine* 90 (1948): 298; Edmund B. Nielsen, "Report on the Collections: A Reconstruction of the Copenhagen-Straus Triptych," *Museum of Fine Arts of Houston Bulletin* 20 (1958); Harald Olsen, *Italian Paintings and Sculpture in Denmark* (Copenhagen: Munksgaard, 1961), 22, 81; Bernard Berenson, *Italian Pictures of the Renaissance: A List of the Principal Artists and Their Works with an Index of Places. Florentine School*, 2 vols. (London: Phaidon Press, 1963), 1:104; Burton B. Fredericksen and Federico Zeri, *Census of Pre-Nineteenth-Century Italian Paintings in North American Public Collections* (Cambridge, Mass.: Harvard University Press, 1972), 152, 586; Miklòs Boskovits, *Pittura fiorentina alla vigilia del Rinascimento, 1370–1400* (Florence: Edam, 1975), 32, 201 n. 96, 278; Richard Offner and Hayden B. J. Maginnis, *A Critical and Historical Corpus of Florentine Painting: A Legacy of Attributions* (New York: Institute of Fine Arts, New York University, 1981), 25-26; Eugenio Marino, "L'affresco 'La Vergine dalla radice di Iesse' di Andrea Bonaiuti in S. Domenico di Pistoia," *Memorie Domenicane* 13 (1982): 63 n. 191, 70 n. 206; Johannes Tripps, "Andrea Bonaiuti: Pisaner Fresken, Tafel- und Glasmalere" (Ph.D. diss., University of Heidelberg, 1988), 22-24, 223, no. 12; Erling S. Skaug, *Punch Marks from Giotto to Fra Angelico*, 2 vols. (Oslo: IIC-Nordic Group, 1994), 1:162; 2:chart 6.7; Carolyn C. Wilson, *Italian Paintings XIV–XVI Centuries in the Museum of Fine Arts, Houston* (Houston: Museum of Fine Arts, 1996), 79-90; Mojmír S. Frinta, *Punched Decoration on Late Medieval Panel and Miniature Painting*, pt. 1 (Prague: Maxdorf, 1998), 210, 509.

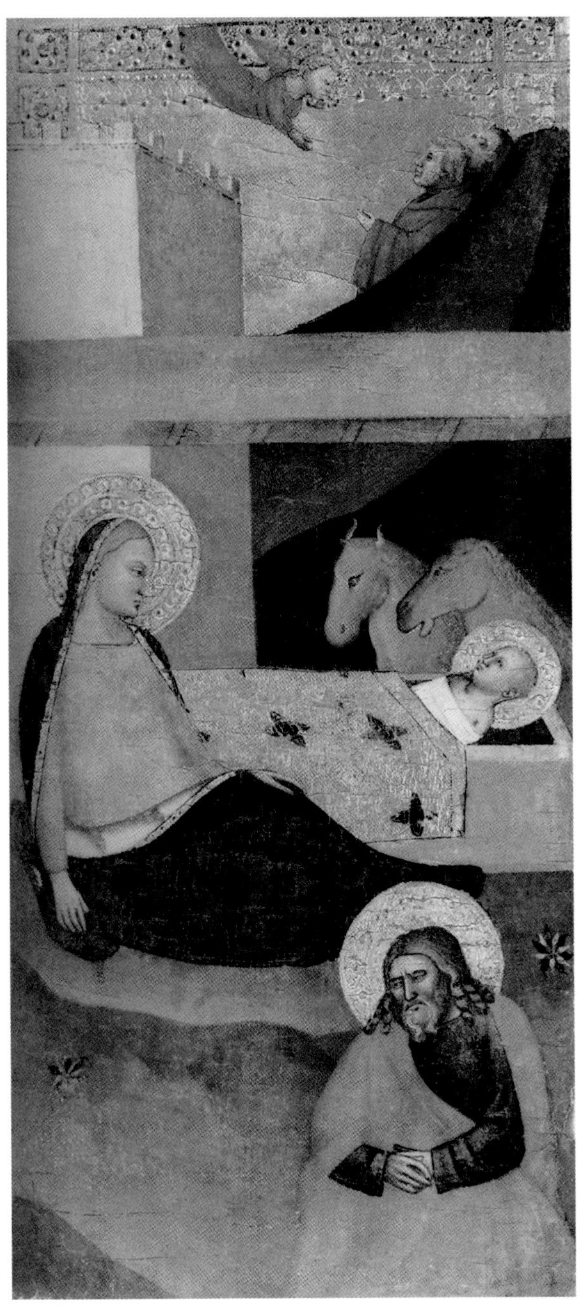

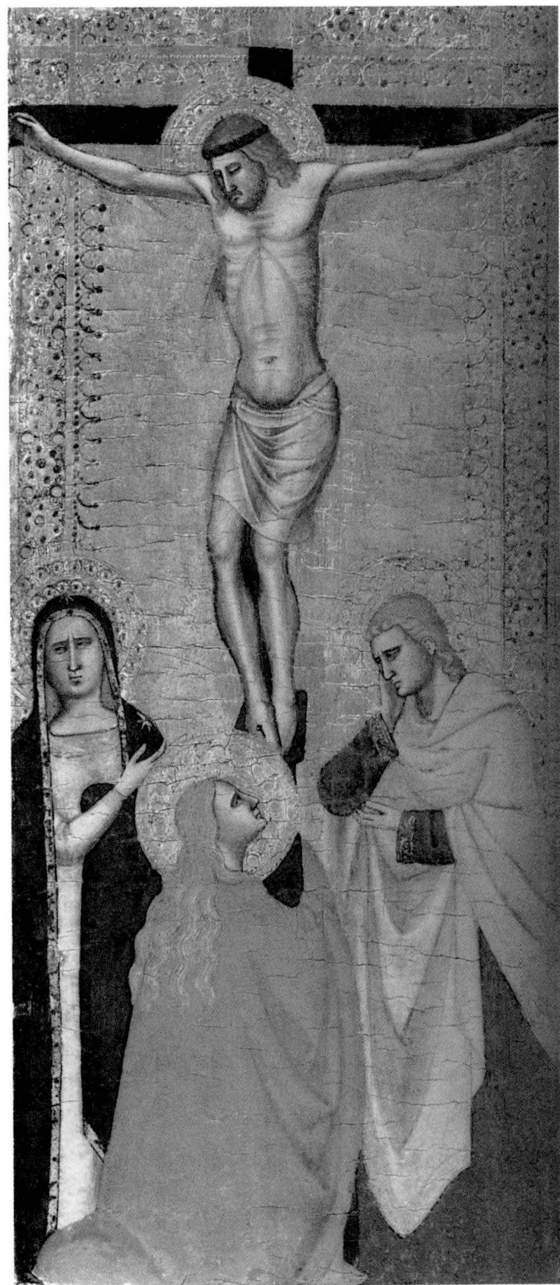

Fig. 205 (left) Florentine School, third quarter of the fourteenth century: *Nativity*. The Museum of Fine Arts, Houston, The Edith A. and Percy S. Straus Collection, 44.570.2.

Fig. 206 (right) Florentine School, third quarter of the fourteenth century: *Christ on the Cross with the Virgin, St. John, and St. Mary Magdalen*. The Museum of Fine Arts, Houston, The Edith A. and Percy S. Straus Collection, 44.570.1.

FLORENTINE SCHOOL, LATE FOURTEENTH OR EARLY FIFTEENTH CENTURY

Virgin and Child (57.43) 48.9 X 34 CM, TEMPERA ON PANEL

HOUSTON, TEXAS. THE MUSEUM OF FINE ARTS, HOUSTON

The panel is in poor condition, with extensive areas of damage and repainting throughout. Originally published by Charles Oulmont (1917–1918) as the work of Gentile da Fabriano (c. 1370–1427), it was ascribed by Burton B. Fredericksen and Federico Zeri (1972) to a follower of Gentile. Carlo L. Ragghianti (1972) and Keith Christiansen (1982) dismissed both attributions, the latter observing that the panel closely resembles examples of Bohemian painting of the late fourteenth century. Miklòs Boskovits (cited in Wilson 1996) considered the work Italian and tentatively associated it with the Marchigian painter Arcangelo di Cola da Camerino (active 1416–1429). Carolyn C. Wilson (1996) attributed it to the Bohemian or Italian School, dating from the late fourteenth or early fifteenth century. The Museum assigns the work to the Florentine School of the fifteenth century.

PROVENANCE

Girolamo Palumbo, Rome, 1916; M.-F. Gentili di Giuseppe, Paris, 1917–1918; Sotheby's, London, June 9, 1955, lot 78; Mark J. Millard; The Museum of Fine Arts, Houston, acquired 1957

BIBLIOGRAPHY

Charles Oulmont, "Collection M.-F. Gentili di Giuseppe," *Les Arts* 14 (1917–1918): 14; "Accessions of American and Canadian Museums," *Art Quarterly* 23 (1960): 89; Burton B. Fredericksen and Federico Zeri, *Census of Pre-Nineteenth-Century Italian Paintings in North American Public Collections* (Cambridge, Mass.: Harvard University Press, 1972), 79, 587; Carlo L. Ragghianti, "Pertinenze francesi nel Cinquecento," *Critica d'Arte* 19 (1972): 87; Keith Christiansen, *Gentile da Fabriano* (Ithaca: Cornell University Press, 1982), 121; Carolyn C. Wilson, *Italian Paintings XIV–XVI Centuries in the Museum of Fine Arts, Houston* (Houston: Museum of Fine Arts, 1996), 380-82.

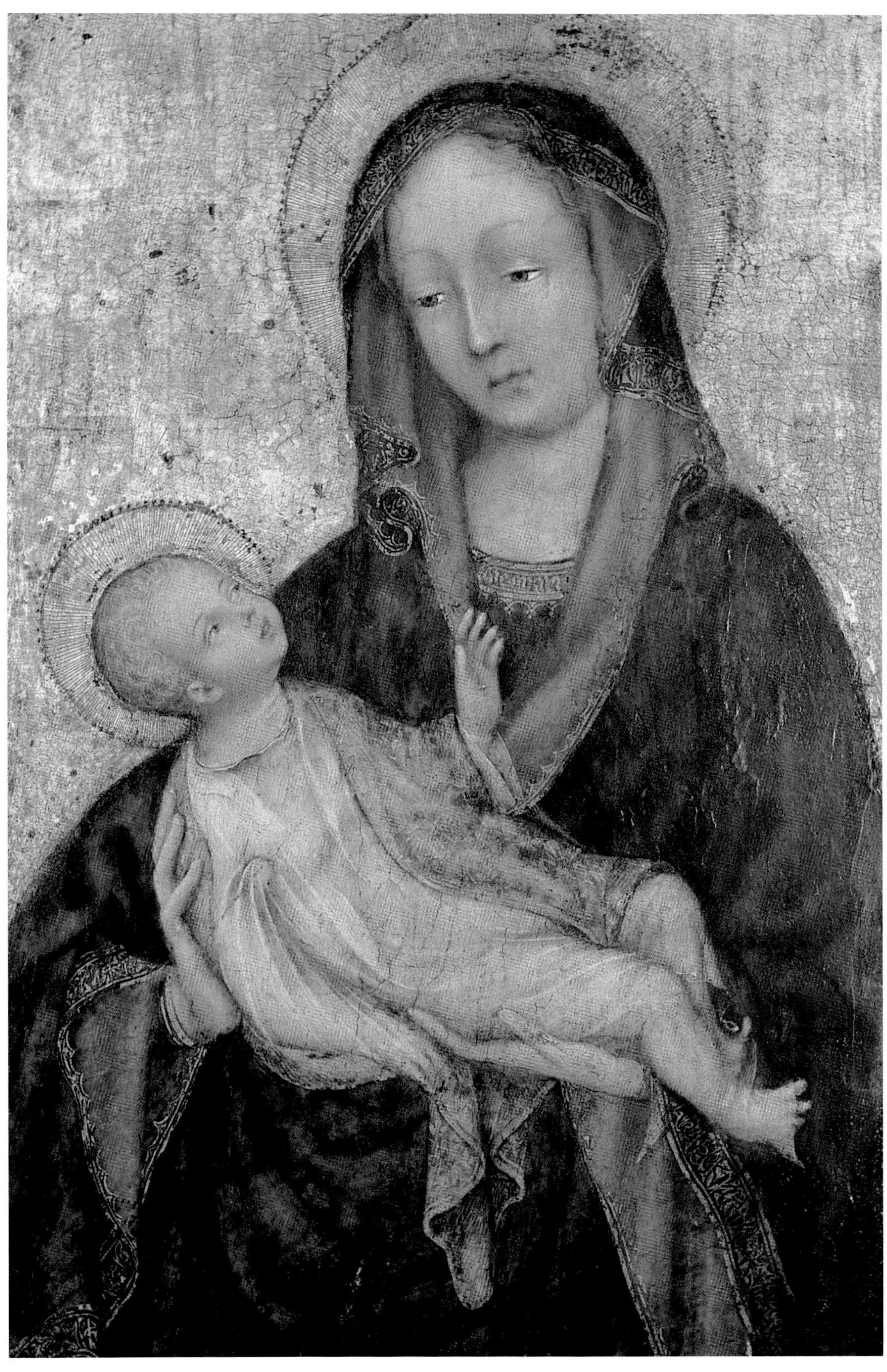

Fig. 207 Florentine School, late fourteenth or early fifteenth century: *Virgin and Child*. The Museum of Fine Arts, Houston; Gift of Mr. Mark J. Millard, 57.43.

FLORENTINE SCHOOL, LAST QUARTER OF THE FIFTEENTH CENTURY

Portrait of a Young Man with a Pink (55.88) 37.7 x 30.8 CM, TEMPERA ON PANEL

HOUSTON, TEXAS. THE MUSEUM OF FINE ARTS, HOUSTON

The relationship of the sitter to the background landscape, his pose, and the attribute of the pink, which was common to Netherlandish portraits of the period, suggest a northern model for the work. According to Carolyn C. Wilson (1996), Hans Memling's *Portrait of a Man* (Palazzo Vecchio, Florence), dating to the 1470s, is the painting most like the Houston portrait among those that may have been available in Florence. The sitter holds a pink, a variety of red carnation that symbolizes earthly love. Its prominence here suggests that the portrait was commissioned to commemorate the betrothal of the sitter.

Exhibited in 1920 at the Burlington Fine Arts Club, London, as a work by Piero di Cosimo (1462–1521), the painting was attributed to Cosimo Rosselli (1439–1507) by Hans D. Gronau (1931). This opinion was generally accepted by scholars, including Burton B. Fredericksen and Federico Zeri (1972), with some reservations, however, due to the damaged state of the sitter's face. Wilson and Roberta Bartoli (1999) suggested that the portrait may be by Rosselli's colleague and collaborator, Biagio d'Antonio (1446–1516). Arthur Blumenthal (2001) assigned the work to an unknown Florentine painter because he did not find the drawing or style of the painting comparable to those of Rosselli's known portraits. The Museum dates the work c. 1475–1485.

PROVENANCE

Private collection, London; Ernest James Wythes, Coppel Hall, Essex, 1920–1921; M. Knoedler and Co., New York, 1955; Sarah Campbell Blaffer, Houston, 1955; Robert Lee Blaffer Memorial Collection, The Museum of Fine Arts, Houston, acquired 1988

BIBLIOGRAPHY

Catalogue of a Collection of Pictures and English Furniture of the Chippendale Period (London: Burlington Fine Arts Club, 1920), 6, no. 6; Hans D. Gronau, "Zwei unpublizierte Porträts von Cosimo Rosselli," *Pantheon* 7 (1931): 155-56; "Rosselli, Cosimo," in *Allgemeines Lexikon der bildenden Künstler von der Antike bis zur Gegenwart*, 37 vols., ed. Ulrich Thieme and Felix Becker (Leipzig: E. A. Seemann, 1935), 29:36; *Italian Renaissance and Baroque Art* (New York: M. Knoedler and Co., 1947), 5, no. 7; *Burlington Magazine* 97 (1955): xi; "Accessions of American and Canadian Museums," *Art Quarterly* 15 (1955): 307; Bernard Berenson, *Italian Pictures of the Renaissance: A List of the Principal Artists and Their Works with an Index of Places. Florentine School*, 2 vols. (London: Phaidon Press, 1963), 1:190; Burton B. Fredericksen and Federico Zeri, *Census of Pre-Nineteenth-Century Italian Paintings in North American Public Collections* (Cambridge, Mass.: Harvard University Press, 1972), 178, 586; *The Museum of Fine Arts, Houston: A Guide to the Collection* (Houston: Museum of Fine Arts, 1981), 28, no. 52; Carolyn C. Wilson, *Italian Paintings XIV–XVI Centuries in the Museum of Fine Arts, Houston* (Houston: Museum of Fine Arts, 1996), 146-49; Roberta Bartoli, *Biagio d'Antonio* (Milan: Federico Motta, 1999), 239, no. 14; Arthur Blumenthal, *Cosimo Rosselli: Painter of the Sistine Chapel* (Winter Park, Fla.: George D. and Harriet W. Cornell Fine Arts Museum, Rollins College, 2001), 155-59, no. 17.

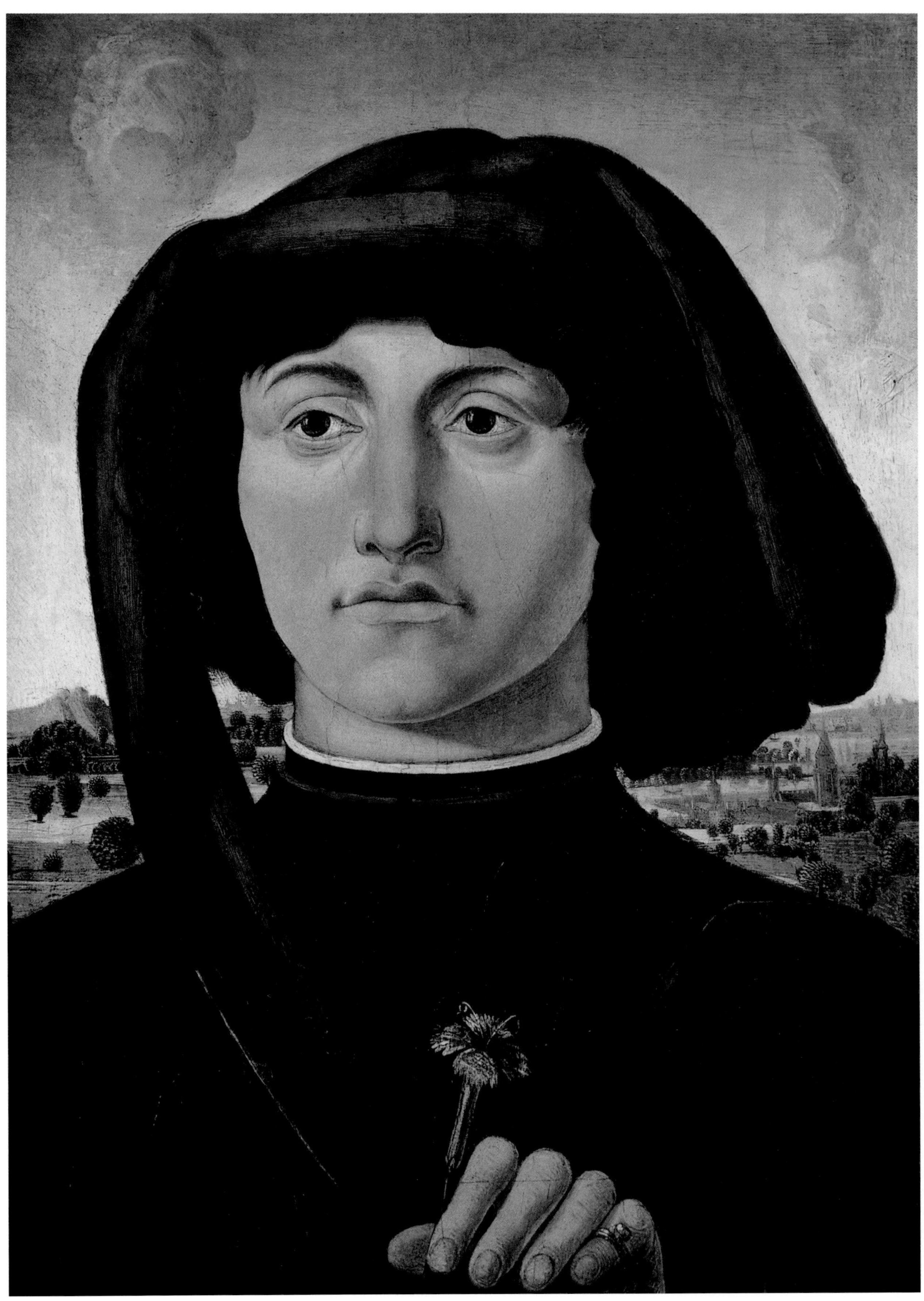

Fig. 208 Florentine School, last quarter of the fifteenth century: *Portrait of a Young Man with a Pink*. The Museum of Fine Arts, Houston, The Robert Lee Blaffer Memorial Collection; Gift of Sarah Campbell Blaffer, 55.88.

FUNGAI, BERNARDINO, 1460–1516; SIENESE

The Beloved of Enalus Sacrificed to Poseidon and Spared (44.560) 51.7 x 201.9 CM,
TEMPERA AND OIL ON PANEL

HOUSTON, TEXAS. THE MUSEUM OF FINE ARTS, HOUSTON

When F. Mason Perkins published this painting in 1913, he identified its subject as the rescue of Hippo. Carolyn C. Wilson (1995; 1996) persuasively argued that, instead, it represents the obscure Greek myth of Enalus, who was enamored of the maiden selected for sacrifice to Poseidon by colonists bound for Lesbos; the representation does not, however, entirely or precisely illustrate texts of the story known in the Renaissance. Enalus is presumably the well-dressed young man with raised hand to the left of the main mast of the ship. His beloved, a young, blond woman in a red dress shot with gold, appears three times, from right to left: she is suspended in the air, having been cast overboard; she swims with dolphin escorts, under the protection of Poseidon; and she arrives safely ashore, where she is welcomed by richly clad ladies who may represent nereids.

The size, format, and subject matter of the painting led Wilson (1995) to identify it as a framed *spalliera*, rather than a *cassone* panel, as previously had been thought. She hypothesized that it was originally one in a series of narrative works created for the walls of a bedchamber or the study of a newly married Sienese couple. F. Mason Perkins's initial attribution (1913) to Fungai has never been questioned, but the date of the painting has been disputed. Richard Offner (1945) located it late in the artist's career, c. 1510, while Laurence B. Kanter (in Christiansen, Kanter, and Strehlke 1988) considered it an early work, from c. 1498. Wilson (1995) proposed a time close to that of Fungai's signed and dated *San Niccolò al Carmine Altarpiece* (Pinacoteca Nazionale, Siena) of 1512.

PROVENANCE

Baron Maurice de Rothschild, Paris, by 1913; Edward A. Faust, St. Louis, Mo., by 1929; Wildenstein & Co., New York, 1938; Edith A. and Percy S. Straus, New York, 1938–1945; Edith A. and Percy S. Straus Collection,The Museum of Fine Arts, Houston, acquired 1945

BIBLIOGRAPHY

F. Mason Perkins, "Alcuni dipinti senesi poco sconosciuti o inediti," *Rassegna d'Arte* 13 (1913): 125-26; Paul Schubring, *Cassoni: Truhen und Truhenbilder der italienischen Frührenaissance* (Leipzig: K. W. Hiersemann, 1915), 334-35, no. 483; Piero Misciatelli, "Cassoni senesi," *La Diana* 4 (1929): 124; Bernard Berenson, "Lost Works of the Sienese Masters, Pt. III," *International Studio* 98 (1931): 21; Bernard Berenson, *Italian Pictures of the Renaissance* (Oxford: Clarendon Press, 1932), 212; F. Mason Perkins, "Two Panel Pictures by Bernardino Fungai," *Apollo* 15 (1932): 145; Bernard Berenson, *Pitture italiane del Rinascimento* (Milan: U. Hoepli, 1936), 183; Raimond van Marle, *The Development of the Italian Schools of Painting*, vol. 16, *The Renaissance Painters of Tuscany* (The Hague: M. Nijhoff, 1937), 481; Arthur M. Hind, *Early Italian Engraving*, 7 vols. (London: B. Quaritch, 1938), 1:51; Richard Offner, "The Straus Collection Goes to Texas—Comments on Its Most Important Objects," *Art News* 44 (1945): 19; *Catalogue of the Edith A. and Percy S. Straus Collection* (Houston: Museum of Fine Arts, 1945), 16, no. 20; Pèleo Bacci, *Bernardino Fungai, pittore senese, 1460–1516* (Siena: Lazzeri, 1947), 20; Alfred Scharf, *A Catalogue of Pictures and Drawings from the Collection of Sir Thomas Merton* (London: Chiswick Press, 1950), 22; Enzo Carli, "Dipinti senesi nel Museo di Houston," *Antichità Viva* 4 (1963): 24-25; Bernard Berenson, *Italian Pictures of the Renaissance: A List of the Principal Artists and Their Works with an Index of Places. Central Italian and North Italian Schools*, 3 vols. (London: Phaidon Press, 1968), 1:150; Burton B. Fredericksen and Federico Zeri, *Census of Pre-Nineteenth-Century Italian Paintings in North American Public Collections* (Cambridge, Mass.: Harvard University Press, 1972), 76, 586; *The Museum of Fine Arts, Houston: A Guide to the Collection* (Houston: Museum of Fine Arts, 1981), 30, no. 55; Liubov Faenson, *Italian Cassoni from the Art Collections of Soviet Museums* (Leningrad: Aurora Art Publishers, 1983), nos. 15-19; Bruce Cole, *Sienese Painting in the Age of the Renaissance* (Bloomington: Indiana University Press, 1985), 144; Keith Christiansen, Laurence B. Kanter, and Carl Brandon Strehlke, *Painting in Renaissance Siena, 1420–1500* (New York: Metropolitan Museum of Art, 1988), 352, 357-58; Damian M. Charboneau, "The Fungai Altarpiece in Santa Maria dei Servi in Siena (1498–1501): Rare Exhibit Reunites Lost Predella Pieces," *Studi Storici*

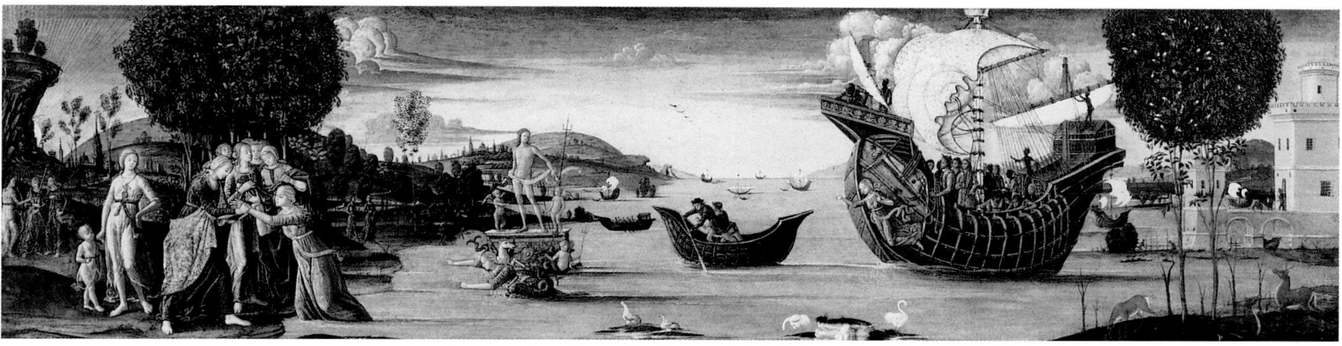

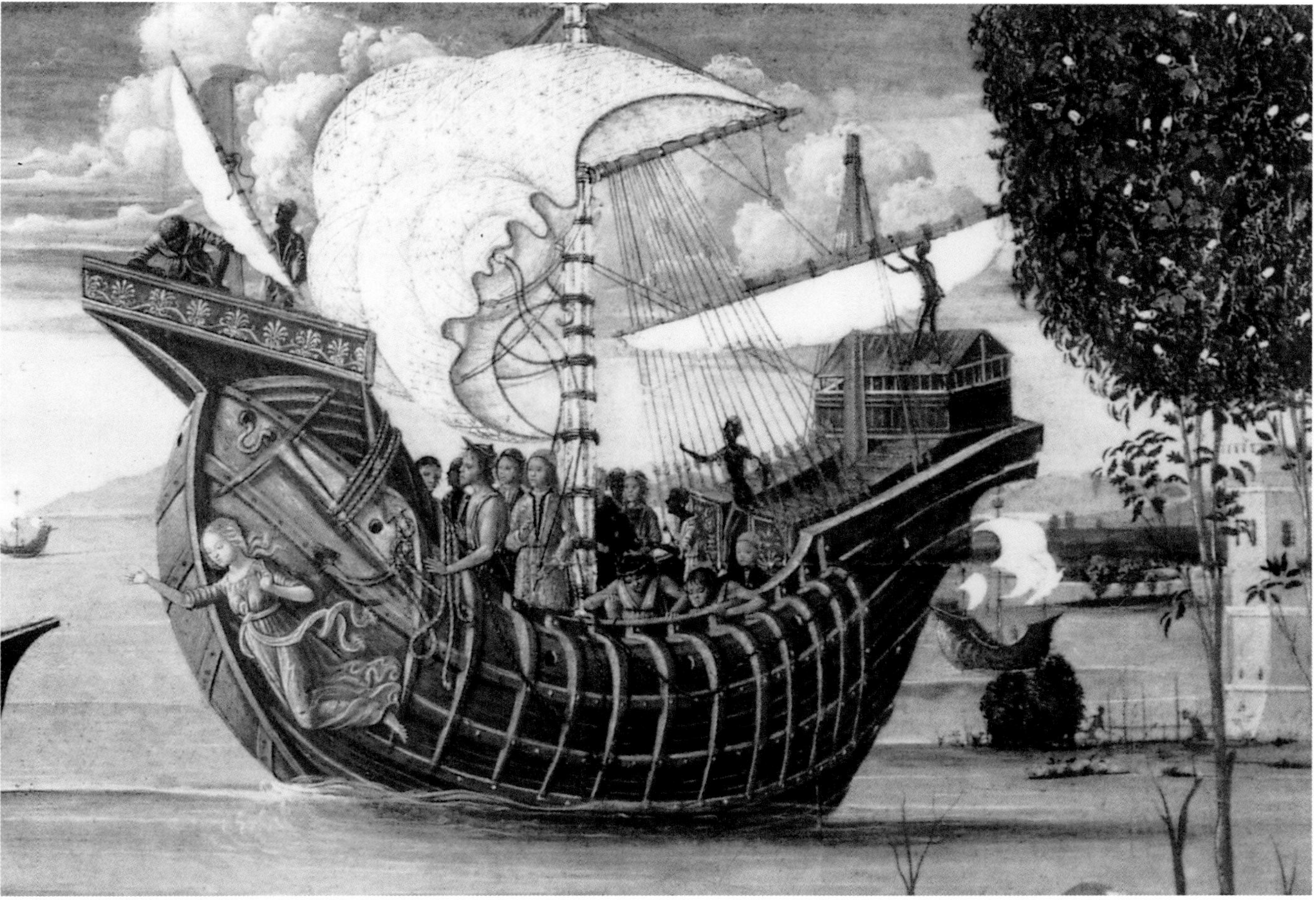

Fig. 209 (top; bottom, detail) Bernardino Fungai: *The Beloved of Enalus Sacrificed to Poseidon and Spared*. The Museum of Fine Arts, Houston, The Edith A. and Percy S. Straus Collection, 44.560.

dell'Ordine dei Servi di Maria 39/1-2 (1989): 163; Carolyn C. Wilson, "Bernardino Fungai and a Theme of Human Sacrifice," *Antichità Viva* 34 (1995): 29-42; Carolyn C. Wilson, *Italian Paintings XIV–XVI Centuries in the Museum of Fine Arts, Houston* (Houston: Museum of Fine Arts, 1996), 257-65; Edgar Peters Bowron and Mary G. Morton, *Masterworks of European Painting in the Museum of Fine Arts, Houston* (Princeton: Princeton University Press, 2000), ix.

GIOVANNI DI PAOLO, ACTIVE C. 1420; DIED 1482; SIENESE

St. Clare Rescuing a Child Mauled by a Wolf (44.571) 20.6 X 28.1 CM, TEMPERA ON PANEL

HOUSTON, TEXAS. THE MUSEUM OF FINE ARTS, HOUSTON

The painting is one of four surviving panels by Giovanni di Paolo illustrating the life of St. Clare. The others are the *Investiture of St. Clare* and *St. Clare Rescuing the Shipwrecked* (Staatliche Museen, Gemäldegalerie, Berlin; 2170 and 2171) and *St. Clare Blessing the Loaves before Pope Innocent IV* (Yale University Art Gallery, New Haven; 1871.59). Carl Brandon Strehlke (in Christiansen, Kanter, and Strehlke 1988) suggested that the panels, together with a centrally placed Crucifixion scene, originally constituted the predella of the artist's altarpiece of the *Madonna and Child Enthroned with Saints Peter Damian, Thomas, Clare, and Ursula* (Pinacoteca Nazionale, Siena; 191). Carolyn C. Wilson (1996; 1996) questioned the reconstruction on the grounds of both altarpiece convention and Clarissan iconography, proposing instead that the works were part of an extensive life cycle on a reliquary cabinet or *vita retable*. Accepted as an autograph work by Giovanni since 1930, the Houston painting has been dated c. 1455–1460, on the basis of stylistic affinities with his narrative panels from the *St. Nicholas of Tolentino Altarpiece* (Montepulciano) of 1456.

The panel provides the only surviving illustration of a posthumous miracle performed by St. Clare of Assisi, for which there is no known textual source. A wolf has maimed a young boy; his mother prays to St. Clare, asking her to rescue her son. The saint, who appears in the sky, responds by causing the wolf to die.

PROVENANCE

Sir John Peter Boileau, Bart., Ketteringham Hall, Norfolk, by 1854; Sir Frederick Raymond Boileau, Bart., Ketteringham, Norfolk; Henry Harris, London, by 1930; Edward Hutton, London; Edith A. and Percy S. Straus, New York, 1931–1945; Edith A. and Percy S. Straus Collection, The Museum of Fine Arts, Houston, acquired 1945

BIBLIOGRAPHY

Gustav F. Waagen, *Treasures of Art in Great Britain*, 3 vols. (London: John Murray, 1854), 3:428; *Catalogue of the Art Treasures of the United Kingdom Collected at Manchester in 1857* (London: Bradbury and Evans, 1857), 17, no. 60; Joseph A. Crowe and Giovanni B. Cavalcaselle, *A History of Painting in Italy, Umbria, Florence and Siena, from the Second to the Sixteenth Century*, 6 vols., ed. Tancred Borenius (London: John Murray, 1914), 5:173; "Opere d'arte senesi alla mostra di Londra," *Bullettino Senese di Storia Patria* 1 (1930): 160, no. 25; David L. Balniel and Kenneth Clark, eds., *A Commemorative Catalogue of the Exhibition of Italian Art Held in the Galleries of the Royal Academy, Burlington House, London, January–March, 1930* (London: Oxford University Press, 1931), 35, no. 104; Paolo D'Ancona, Irene Cattaneo, and Fernanda Wittgens, *L'arte italiana*, vol. 2, *Il Rinascimento* (Florence: R. Bemporad & Figlio, 1932), 65; Marialuisa Gengaro, "Giovanni di Paolo," *La Diana* 5 (1932): 28; Bernard Berenson, *Italian Pictures of the Renaissance* (Oxford: Clarendon Press, 1932), 246; Bernard Berenson, *Pitture italiane del Rinascimento* (Milan: U. Hoepli, 1936), 212; John Pope-Hennessy, *Giovanni di Paolo, 1403–1483* (London: Chatto & Windus, 1937), 78-80, 173; George H. McCall and William R. Valentiner, *Catalogue of European Paintings and Sculpture from 1300–1800* (New York: Publishers Printing Co., 1939), 73, no. 148; William R. Valentiner and Alfred M. Frankfurter, *Masterpieces of Art: Exhibition at the New York World's Fair, 1939* (New York: The Art News, 1939), no. 148; Richard Offner, "The Straus Collection Goes to Texas—Comments on Its Most Important Objects," *Art News* 44 (1945): 18-19; "Recent Important Acquisitions of American Collections," *Art Quarterly* 8 (1945): 245; *Catalogue of the Edith A. and Percy S. Straus Collection* (Houston: Museum of Fine Arts, 1945), 15, no. 18; *Landscape: An Exhibition of Paintings* (New York: Brooklyn Museum, 1945), 15, no. 3; Cesare Brandi, *Giovanni di Paolo* (Florence: F. Le Monnier, 1947), 84; Enzo Carli, "Dipinti senesi nel Museo di Houston," *Antichità Viva* 2 (1963): 17-18; *Verzeichnis der ausgestellten Gemälde des 13. bis 18. Jahrhunderts im Museum Dahlem* (Berlin: Staatliche Museen, 1964), 53; Bernard Berenson, *Italian Pictures of the Renaissance: A List of the Principal Artists and Their Works with an Index of Places. Central Italian and North Italian Schools*, 3 vols. (London: Phaidon Press, 1968), 1:177; Charles Seymour, *Early Italian Paintings in the Yale University Art Gallery*

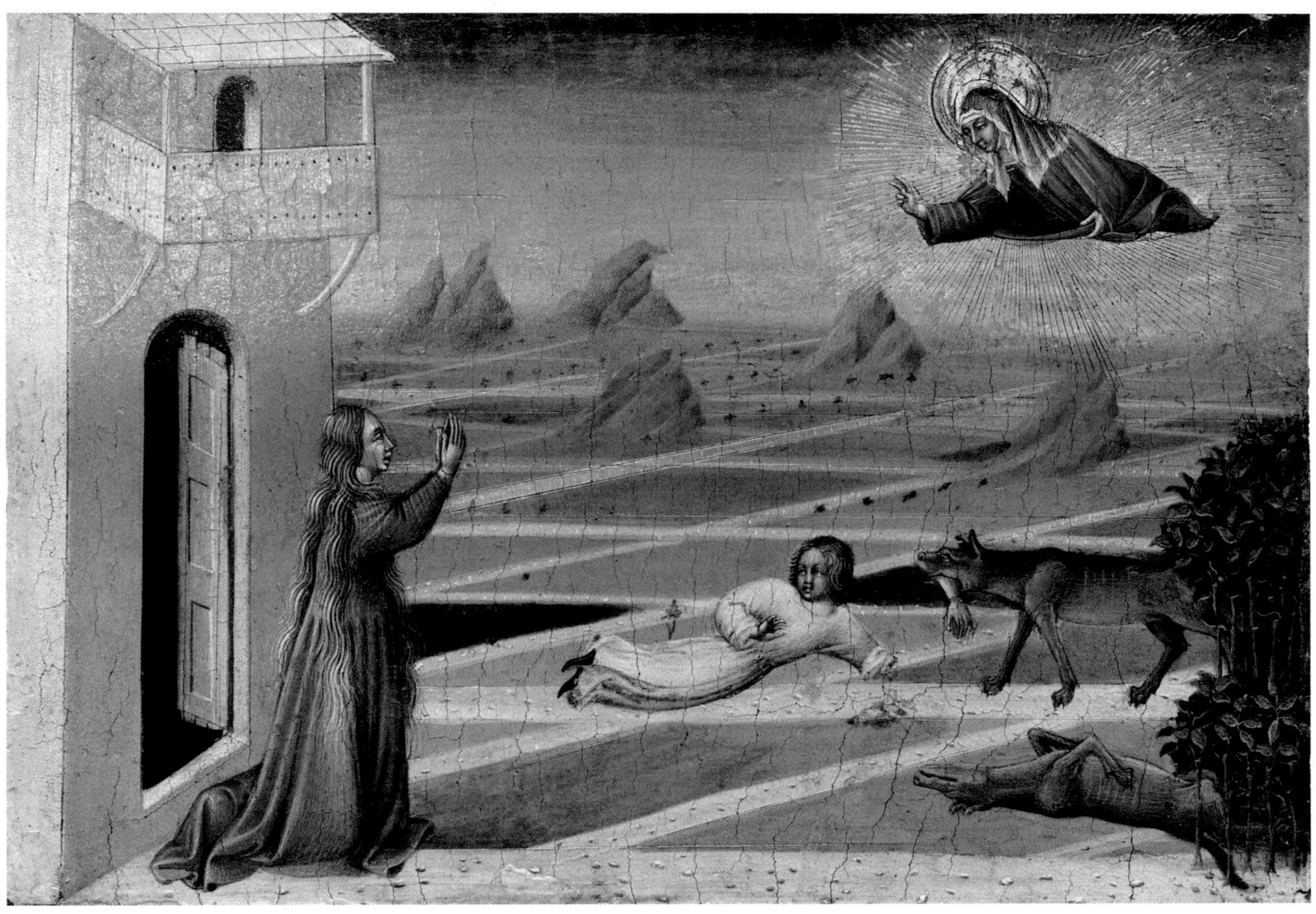

Fig. 210 Giovanni di Paolo: *St. Clare Rescuing a Child Mauled by a Wolf.* The Museum of Fine Arts, Houston, The Edith A. and Percy S. Straus Collection, 44.571.

(New Haven: Yale University Press, 1970), 197; Burton B. Fredericksen and Federico Zeri, *Census of Pre-Nineteenth-Century Italian Paintings in North American Public Collections* (Cambridge, Mass.: Harvard University Press, 1972), 89, 586; *The Museum of Fine Arts, Houston: A Guide to the Collection* (Houston: Museum of Fine Arts, 1981), 26; John Pope-Hennessy, "Giovanni di Paolo," *Metropolitan Museum of Art Bulletin* 46 (1988): 17; Keith Christiansen, Laurence B. Kanter, and Carl Brandon Strehlke, *Painting in Renaissance Siena, 1420–1500* (New York: Metropolitan Museum of Art, 1988), 204-7, no. 34b; Peter C. Marzio, *A Permanent Legacy: 150 Works from the Collection of the Museum of Fine Arts, Houston* (New York: Hudson Hills Press, 1989), 106; Carolyn C. Wilson, *Italian Paintings XIV–XVI Centuries in the Museum of Fine Arts, Houston* (Houston: Museum of Fine Arts, 1996), 166-69; Carolyn C. Wilson, "Iconography in Giovanni di Paolo's Altarpieces: The Case of the Houston Panels," *Arte Cristiana* 84 (1996): 425-29; Edgar Peters Bowron and Mary G. Morton, *Masterworks of European Painting in the Museum of Fine Arts, Houston* (Princeton: Princeton University Press, 2000), 12-14; Perri Lee Roberts, Bruce Cole, and Hayden B. J. Maginnis, *Sacred Treasures: Early Italian Paintings from Southern Collections* (Athens, Ga.: Georgia Museum of Art, 2002), 27, 148-51.

GIOVANNI DI PAOLO, ACTIVE C. 1420; DIED 1482; SIENESE

St. John the Baptist (53.2); *St. Catherine of Alexandria* (53.3) 104.3 x 46.8 CM (53.2); 104.6 x 44.4 CM (53.3), TEMPERA ON PANEL

HOUSTON, TEXAS. THE MUSEUM OF FINE ARTS, HOUSTON

John Pope-Hennessy (1937) published the paintings as early works by Giovanni di Paolo and proposed them as the two parts of the left wing of an altarpiece that had the *Madonna and Child* (Monte dei Paschi, Siena; formerly, Via delle Terme tabernacle) as its central panel and *St. Matthew and St. Francis of Assisi* (Metropolitan Museum of Art, New York; 1888.3.111) as its right wing. He identified the ensemble with the Houston-Siena-New York altarpiece painted for the Fondi family in 1436 for the church of San Francesco, Siena. His reconstruction was universally accepted, but most scholars, beginning with Cesare Brandi (1949), rejected the hypothesized provenance. Andrea De Marchi (1992) suggested a predella for the reconstituted altarpiece with the following panels: the *Nativity* (Pinacoteca Vaticana, Rome; 132); the *Adoration of the Magi* (Cleveland Museum of Art; 42.536); the *Presentation in the Temple* (Metropolitan Museum of Art, New York; 41.100.4); the *Annunciation* (National Gallery of Art, Washington, D.C.; 334, K 412); and the *Crucifixion* (Staatliche Museen, Gemäldegalerie, Berlin; 1112C). Carolyn C. Wilson (1996; 1996) dated the Houston paintings c. 1435–1440, possibly 1436.

The names of the saints appear on their halos: "SANCTA KATERINA" and "SANCTVS IOHANNES BATISTA." The figure of Catherine was adapted from that of Mary Magdalen in Gentile da Fabriano's *Quaratesi Altarpiece* of 1425; John's figure derives from a similar figure of the saint kneeling in Sassetta's *Madonna of the Snow* (Count Alessandro Contini-Bonacossi Bequest, Uffizi, Florence), of 1430–1432.

PROVENANCE

Dikran Kelekian, Paris; Charles D. Kelekian, New York; M. Knoedler and Co., New York; Robert Lee Blaffer Memorial Collection, The Museum of Fine Arts, Houston, acquired 1953

BIBLIOGRAPHY

John Pope-Hennessy, *Giovanni di Paolo, 1403–1483* (London: Chatto & Windus, 1937), 12-14, 147; Henry B. Wehle, *A Catalogue of Italian, Spanish, and Byzantine Paintings* (New York: Metropolitan Museum of Art, 1940), 87-88; Cesare Brandi, "Giovanni di Paolo," *Le Arti* 3 (1941): 241-42, 244 n. 34; Cesare Brandi, *Giovanni di Paolo* (Florence: F. Le Monnier, 1947), 18-20, 83, 120; John Pope-Hennessy, "*Giovanni di Paolo* by Cesare Brandi," *Burlington Magazine* 89 (1947): 138; Cesare Brandi, *Quattrocentisti senesi* (Milan: Hoepli, 1949), 260; "Reviews and Previews: Old Masters (Knoedler; to March 8)," *Art News* 49 (1950): 45; "Painting," *Denver Art Museum Winter Quarterly* (1950): 6-7; Helen Comstock, "The Connoisseur in America: The Blaffer Collection in Houston," *Connoisseur* 133 (1954): 209; Enzo Carli, "Dipinti senesi nel Museo di Houston," *Antichità Viva* 2 (1963): 20; Bernard Berenson, *Italian Pictures of the Renaissance: A List of the Principal Artists and Their Works with an Index of Places. Central Italian and North Italian Schools*, 3 vols. (London: Phaidon Press, 1968), 1:177; Enzo Carli, *I pittori senesi* (Siena: Monte dei Paschi di Siena, 1971), 172; Burton B. Fredericksen and Federico Zeri, *Census of Pre-Nineteenth-Century Italian Paintings in North American Public Collections* (Cambridge, Mass.: Harvard University Press, 1972), 89, 586; Piero Torriti, *La Pinacoteca Nazionale di Siena: I dipinti dal XII al XV secolo* (Genoa: Sagep, 1977), 306; Federico Zeri and Elizabeth E. Gardner, *Italian Paintings: Sienese and Central Italian Schools* (New York: Metropolitan Museum of Art, 1980), 19-20; *The Museum of Fine Arts, Houston: A Guide to the Collection* (Houston: Museum of Fine Arts, 1981), 25, no. 45; Francesco Gurrieri, ed., *La sede storica del Monte dei Paschi di Siena* (Siena: Le Monnier, 1988), 308, 312; John Pope-Hennessy, "Giovanni di Paolo," *Metropolitan Museum of Art Bulletin* 46/2 (1988): 10; Keith Christiansen, Laurence B. Kanter, and Carl Brandon Strehlke, *Painting in Renaissance Siena, 1420–1500* (New York: Metropolitan Museum of Art, 1988), 176-78; *The Early Sienese Paintings in Holland*, ed. Henk W. van Os et al. (Florence: Centro Di; The Hague: G. Schwartz, 1989), 70; Andrea De Marchi, *Gentile da Fabriano: Un viaggio nella pittura italiana alla fine del gotico* (Milan: Federico Motta, 1992), 211, no. 33, 34; John Pope-Hennessy, *Paradiso: The Illuminations to Dante's Divine Comedy by Giovanni di Paolo* (London: Thames & Hudson, 1993), 26; Carolyn C. Wilson, *Italian Paintings XIV–XVI Centuries in the Museum of Fine Arts, Houston* (Houston: Museum of Fine Arts, 1996), 156-65; Carolyn C. Wilson, "Iconography in Giovanni di Paolo's Altarpieces: The Case of the Houston Panels," *Arte Cristiana* 84 (1996): 420-25.

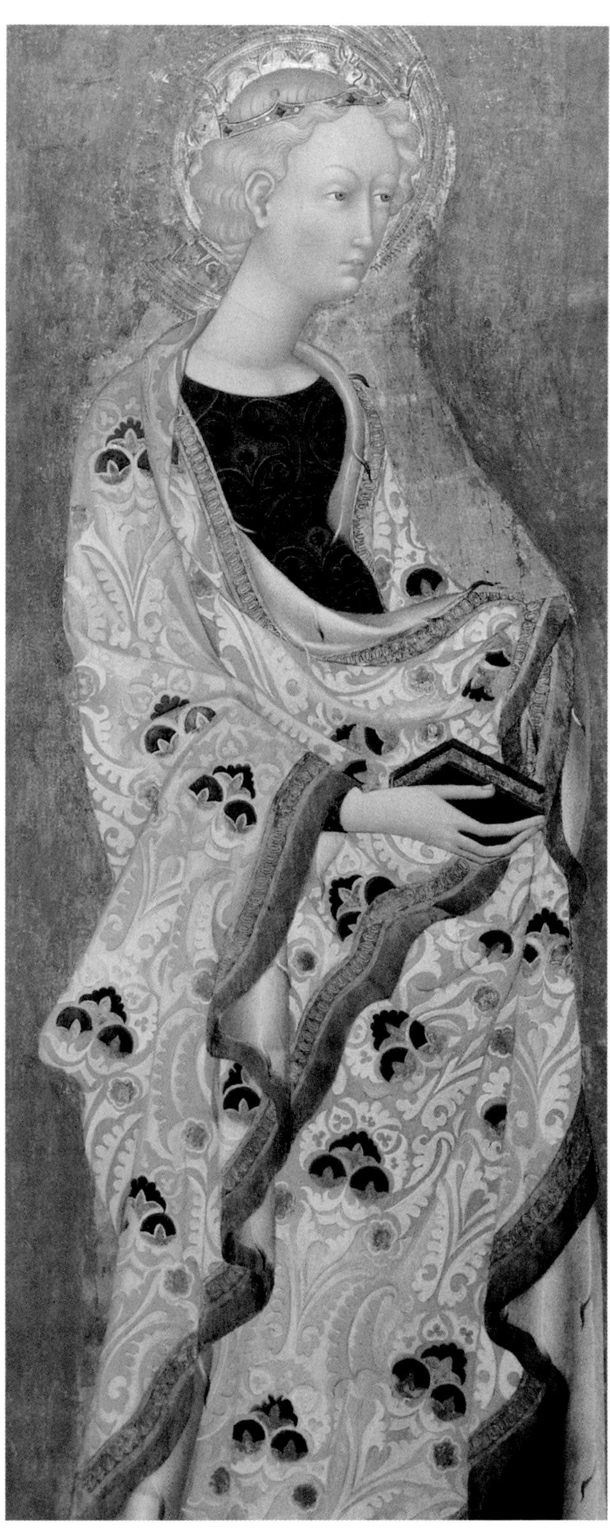

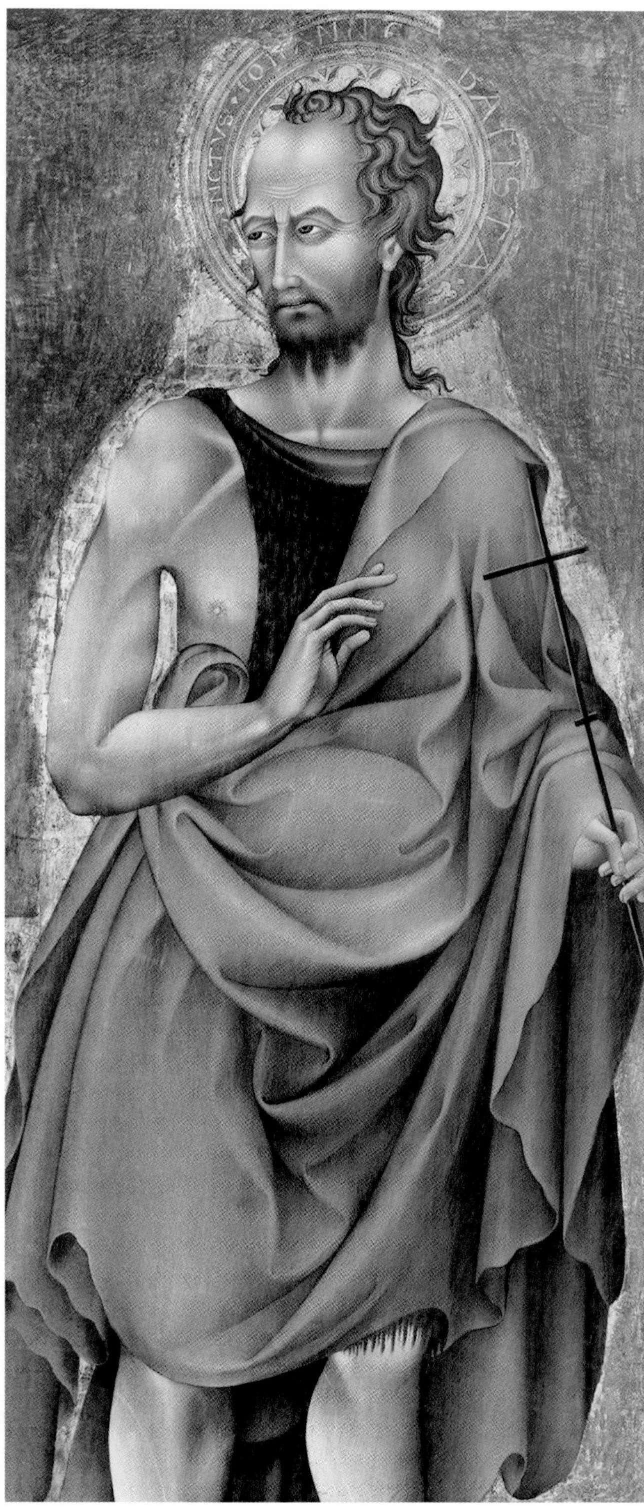

Fig. 211 (left) Giovanni di Paolo: *St. Catherine of Alexandria*. The Museum of Fine Arts, Houston, The Robert Lee Blaffer Memorial Collection; Gift of Sarah Campbell Blaffer, 53.3.

Fig. 212 (right) Giovanni di Paolo: *St. John the Baptist*. The Museum of Fine Arts, Houston, The Robert Lee Blaffer Memorial Collection; Gift of Sarah Campbell Blaffer, 53.2.

LOMBARD SCHOOL, THIRD QUARTER OF THE FIFTEENTH CENTURY

St. Anthony Abbot and St. John the Baptist with a Donor (34.124; K 202A); *St. Margaret and St. Catherine of Alexandria with a Donatrix* (34.125; K 202B) 163.9 x 57.2 CM (EACH), TEMPERA ON PANEL

HOUSTON, TEXAS. THE MUSEUM OF FINE ARTS, HOUSTON

The paintings originally constituted the lateral panels of a polyptych that had as a centerpiece the *Enthroned Madonna and Child* (private collection; formerly, Finarte, Milan, sold 1971). The decorative quality of the works typifies courtly Lombard taste in the early fifteenth century, but the attribution and dating have proven problematic. William E. Suida (1953) attributed the Houston panels to the Lombard artist Fermo da Caravaggio Stella (active 1519–1562), c. 1495. Federico Zeri (1958), who reconstructed the altarpiece to which the panels belonged, dismissed this attribution, proposing instead a provincial master working outside of Milan but within Lombardy. On the basis of the clothing of the supplicants, Zeri dated the panels 1475–1485. Roberto Longhi, Adolfo Venturi, and Giuseppe Fiocco (cited in Shapley 1968) assigned the paintings to Giovanni della Chiesa (active 1494–1512), whereas Fern Rusk Shapley considered them provincial works of the Lombard School, c. 1485. Burton B. Fredericksen and Federico Zeri (1972) listed them as products of both the fifteenth-century Lombard School and Giovanni della Chiesa.

The haloes of the saints display pastiglia lettering indicating their identities: "SANCTVS ANTONIVS"; "SANCTVS JOHANES BABTISTA"; "SANCTA MARGARITA OR(A)"; and "SANCTA KHATERINA OR." The banderole held by the Baptist is inscribed "ECCE AGNVS DEI ECCE QVI" ("Behold the Lamb of God, who takes away . . . "), from John 1:29. The depiction of Catherine's wheel, her attribute, in miniature and mounted on a long axle is unusual, but not unique, in Lombard painting, according to Carolyn C. Wilson (1996). The profile representations of the unidentified donors reflect a custom in Lombard portraiture that was initiated by the Duke and Duchess of Milan in the *Pala Sforzesca* (Brera, Milan). Wilson noted that the placement of supplicants to the right and left of the Madonna's throne, as in the Brera *pala*, was standard for the representation of married couples in Lombard painting during the second half of the fifteenth century; their proximity to the saints, probably name-saints and intermediaries in this context, was also conventional.

PROVENANCE

Henri Haro, Paris, to 1911; Hôtel Drouot, Paris, December 13, 1911, lots 95 and 96; Marczell von Nemes, Munich, 1911–1931; Mensing, Cassirer, and Helbring, Munich, June 16, 1931, lot 22; Count Alessandro Contini-Bonacossi, Florence; Samuel H. Kress, New York, acquired 1932; The Museum of Fine Arts, Houston, acquired 1934

BIBLIOGRAPHY

"Houston Reviews Its Fruits," *The American Magazine of Art* 28 (1935): 177; "Early Italian Work Recently Presented to Houston Museum," *Art News* 33 (1935): 12; William E. Suida, *The Samuel H. Kress Collection at the Museum of Fine Arts of Houston* (Houston: Museum of Fine Arts, 1953), nos. 1, 2; Federico Zeri, "Due pannelli nel Museo di Houston," *Paragone* 9 (1958): 66-69; Giovanni A. dell'Acqua, ed., *Arte lombarda dai Visconti agli Sforza* (Milan: Silvana, 1959), 130, nos. 412, 413; Fern Rusk Shapley, *Paintings from the Samuel H. Kress Collection: Italian Schools*, vol. 2, *XV–XVI Century* (London: Phaidon Press, 1968), 12-13; Burton B. Fredericksen and Federico Zeri, *Census of Pre-Nineteenth-Century Italian Paintings in North American Public Collections* (Cambridge, Mass.: Harvard University Press, 1972), 52, 231, 586; Carolyn C. Wilson, *Italian Paintings XIV–XVI Centuries in the Museum of Fine Arts, Houston* (Houston: Museum of Fine Arts, 1996), 230-36.

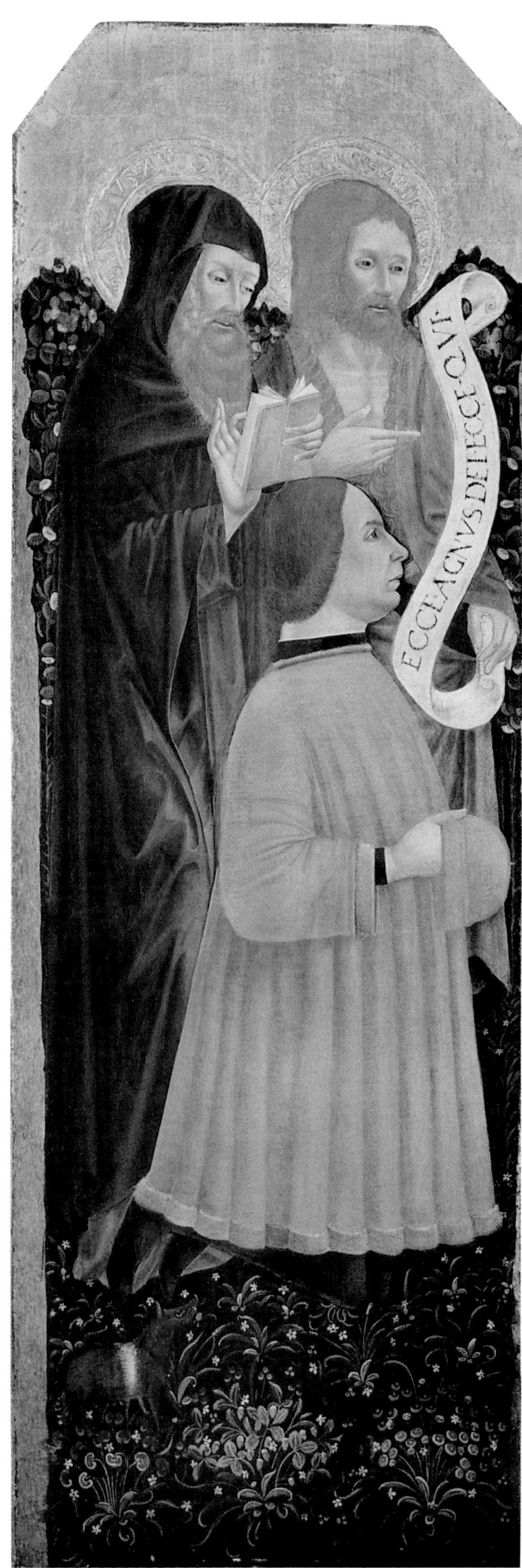

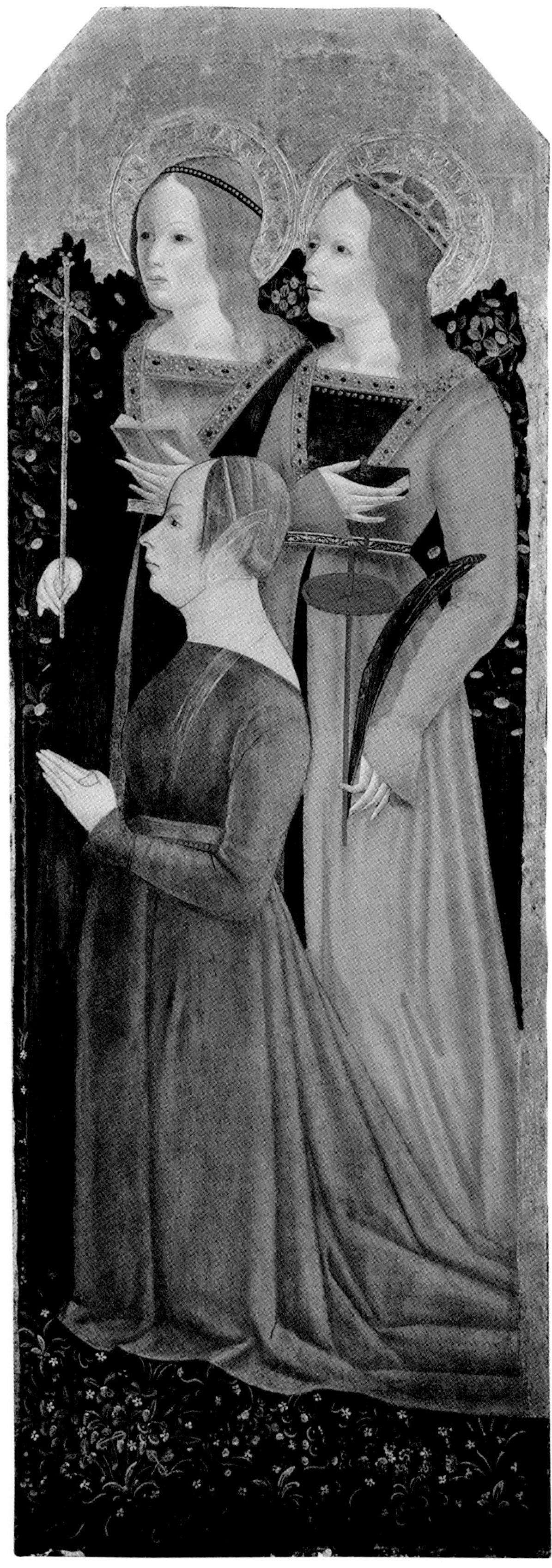

Fig. 213 (left) Lombard School, third quarter of the fifteenth century: *St. Anthony Abbot and St. John the Baptist with a Donor*. The Museum of Fine Arts, Houston, The Samuel H. Kress Collection, 34.124.

Fig. 214 (right) Lombard School, third quarter of the fifteenth century: *St. Margaret and St. Catherine of Alexandria with a Donatrix*. The Museum of Fine Arts, Houston, The Samuel H. Kress Collection, 34.125.

LORENZO MONACO, C. 1370–1425; WORKSHOP; FLORENTINE

St. Michael and the Archangel Gabriel (44.567B); *St. Francis and the Annunciate Virgin* (44.567A)
116 X 35.5 CM (EACH), TEMPERA ON PANEL

HOUSTON, TEXAS. THE MUSEUM OF FINE ARTS, HOUSTON

The shapes and iconography of the panels, as well as the use of geometric patterns on their reverses, suggest that they were originally the hinged wings of a portable triptych or recessed tabernacle, although they are much larger than other surviving shutters. The tabernacle to which the panels were attached until 1985, seen in the photograph, seems to be of the eighteenth century, with early-twentieth-century embellishments. The attribution of the paintings to Lorenzo Monaco, first proposed by Vincenzo Golzio (1927), has been accepted by a majority of scholars, who generally date the works to the 1420s. The one notable exception is Marvin Eisenberg (1989), who considers them to be by a provincial imitator of Lorenzo Monaco in the early 1420s employing a pastiche of motifs from the master. Carolyn C. Wilson (1996) assigned the paintings to the workshop of Lorenzo Monaco or to a follower.

PROVENANCE

Giuseppe Grassi, Rome; Edith A. and Percy S. Straus, New York, 1925–1945; Edith A. and Percy S. Straus Collection, The Museum of Fine Arts, Houston, acquired 1945

BIBLIOGRAPHY

Vincenzo Golzio, "Lorenzo Monaco e una sua nuova opera," *Corriere d'Italia* 22 (16 September 1927): 3; Raimond van Marle, *The Development of the Italian Schools of Painting*, vol. 9, *Late Gothic Painting in Tuscany* (The Hague: M. Nijhoff, 1927), 150-51, 153; Vincenzo Golzio, *Lorenzo Monaco: L'unificazione della tradizione senese con la fiorentina e il Gotico* (Rome: Biblioteca d'arte, 1931), 32-33; Bernard Berenson, *Italian Pictures of the Renaissance* (Oxford: Clarendon Press, 1932), 300; Bernard Berenson, *Pitture italiane del Rinascimento* (Milan: U. Hoepli, 1936), 258; Richard Offner, "The Straus Collection Goes to Houston—Comments on Its Most Important Objects," *Art News* 44 (1945): 22; *Catalogue of the Edith A. and Percy S. Straus Collection* (Houston: Museum of Fine Arts, 1945), 12-13, no. 13; Mirella Levi D'Ancona, "Matteo Torelli," *Commentari* 9 (1958): 252, 255, 257; Burton B. Fredericksen and Federico Zeri, *Census of Pre-Nineteenth-Century Italian Paintings in North American Public Collections* (Cambridge, Mass.: Harvard University Press, 1972), 111, 586; Miklòs Boskovits, *Pittura fiorentina alla vigilia del Rinascimento, 1370–1400* (Florence: Edam, 1975), 347; Luciano Bellosi, "Due note in margine a Lorenzo Monaco miniatore: Il 'Maestro del Codice Squarcialupi' e il poco probabile Matteo Torelli," in *Studi di storia dell'arte in memoria di Mario Rotili*, 2 vols. (Benevento: Banca sannitica, 1984), 1:311; Marvin Eisenberg, *Lorenzo Monaco* (Princeton: Princeton University Press, 1989), 195; Keith Christiansen, Laurence B. Kanter, and Carl Brandon Strehlke, *Painting and Illumination in Early Renaissance Florence, 1300–1450* (New York: Metropolitan Museum of Art, 1994), 259, 260-61 n. 1; Carolyn C. Wilson, *Italian Paintings XIV–XVI Centuries in the Museum of Fine Arts, Houston* (Houston: Museum of Fine Arts, 1996), 122-27.

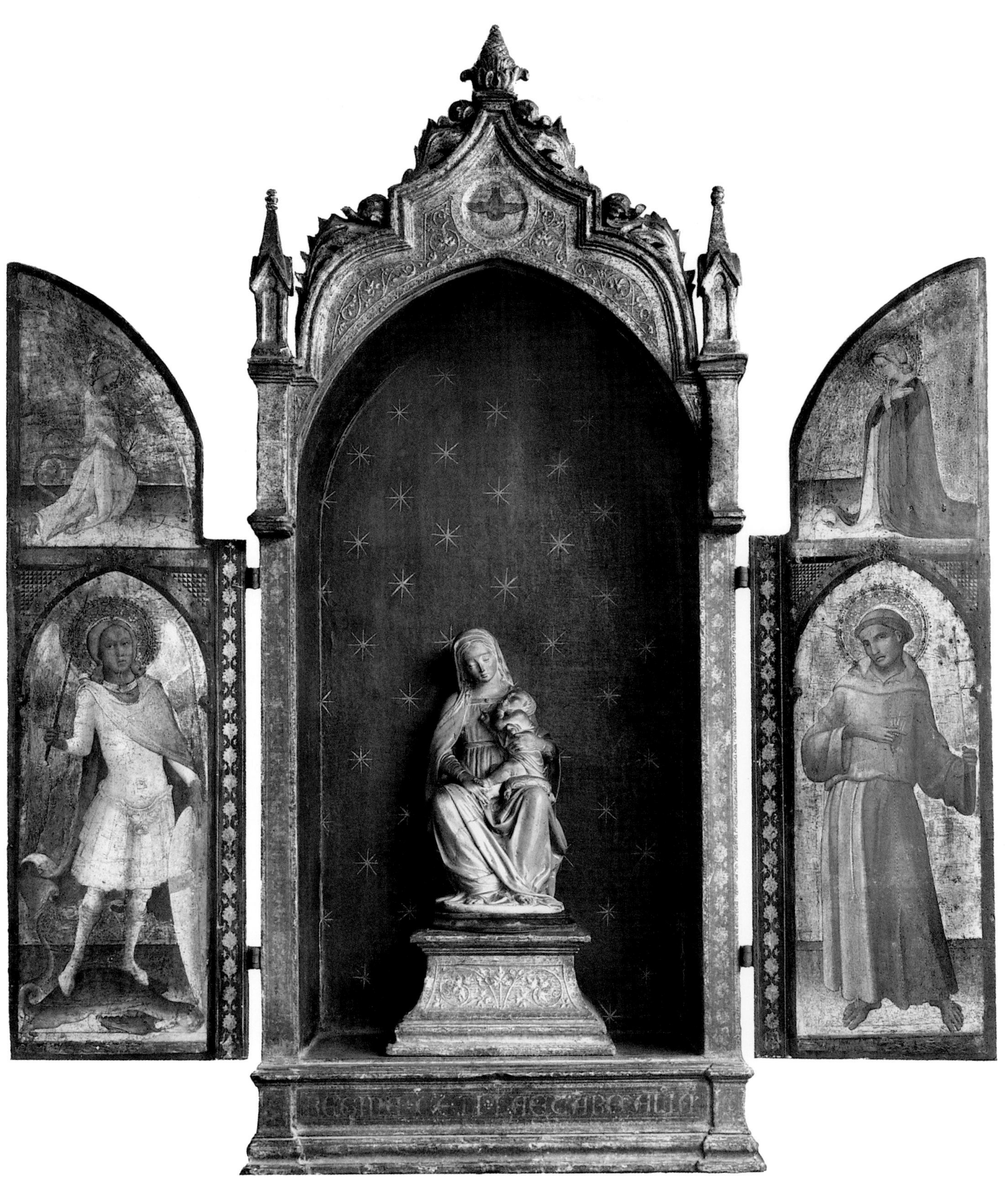

Fig. 215 Lorenzo Monaco (workshop): *St. Michael and the Archangel Gabriel* (left); *St. Francis and the Annunciate Virgin* (right). The Museum of Fine Arts, Houston, The Edith A. and Percy S. Straus Collection, 44.567B, 44.567A.

MASTER OF THE GOLDEN GATE, ACTIVE FOURTEENTH CENTURY; FLORENTINE

The Meeting of Anna and Joachim at the Golden Gate (44.561) 30.2 X 34.8 CM, TEMPERA ON PANEL

HOUSTON, TEXAS. THE MUSEUM OF FINE ARTS, HOUSTON

The painting was part of the predella of an unidentified altarpiece, one of several panels illustrating the life of the Virgin; these also included the *Nativity with the Adoration of the Shepherds* (current location unknown; formerly, Western European Museum, Kiev) and the *Adoration of the Magi* (Fogg Art Museum, Cambridge; 1930.201). Published in the Chillingworth sale catalogue (1922) as Florentine School, c. 1360, the Houston picture was attributed to Jacopo di Cione (1320/30–before 1400) by Raimond van Marle (1931) and Bernard Berenson (1932). When it entered the Straus Collection and, thereafter, the Museum of Fine Arts, Houston, it was ascribed to Agnolo Gaddi (active 1369; died 1396). Richard Offner (1945) rejected his authorship, assigning the panel to an anonymous painter influenced by Orcagna (1315/20–1368) and Jacopo di Cione who became known in subsequent literature as the Master of the Golden Gate. Miklòs Boskovits (1975) reassigned the oeuvre of this artist to another anonymous Cionesque painter, the Master of the Ashmolean Predella (active c. 1365–c. 1390), whose eponymous work is the *Birth of the Virgin* (Ashmolean Museum, Oxford; A74); the opinion was endorsed by Laurence B. Kanter (in Christiansen, Kanter, and Strehlke 1994). Carolyn C. Wilson (1996) maintained the distinction between the Master of the Golden Gate and the Master of the Ashmolean Predella, noting, however, that the former was somewhat dependent upon the latter; she dated the panel 1370–1390. The panel depicts the meeting of Mary's parents, Joachim and Anna, at the Golden Gate, an event generally understood as the moment of the Virgin's conception. The subject is common in fourteenth-century Florentine painting, and the couple's restrained embrace follows pictorial convention. Wilson observed that the Houston panel's composition resembles that of the fresco in the Chiostrino dei Morti, Santa Maria Novella, Florence, and may reflect the artist's direct knowledge of the latter or a mutual source.

PROVENANCE

Rudolf Chillingworth, Nuremberg; Galerie Fischer, Lucerne, September 5, 1922, lot 100; Kaufman, Munich; Edward Hutton, 1926; Edith A. and Percy S. Straus, New York, 1927–1945; Edith A. and Percy S. Straus Collection, The Museum of Fine Arts, Houston, acquired 1945

BIBLIOGRAPHY

Catalogue de la collection Chillingworth. Tableaux anciens, XIIIe–XVIIe siècles (Lucerne: Galerie Fischer, 1922), 35, no. 100; Raimond van Marle, *The Development of the Italian Schools of Painting*, vol. 3, *The Florentine School of the Fourteenth Century* (The Hague: M. Nijhoff, 1931), 506; Bernard Berenson, *Italian Pictures of the Renaissance* (Oxford: Clarendon Press, 1932), 275; Bernard Berenson, *Pitture italiane del Rinascimento* (Milan: U. Hoepli, 1936), 236; Richard Offner, "The Straus Collection Goes to Texas—Comments on Its Most Important Objects," *Art News* 44 (1945): 19, 21; *Catalogue of the Edith A. and Percy S. Straus Collection* (Houston: Museum of Fine Arts, 1945), 11-12, no. 11; Millard Meiss, *Painting in Florence and Siena after the Black Death* (Princeton: Princeton University Press, 1951), 26 n. 51; Bernard Berenson, *Italian Pictures of the Renaissance: A List of the Principal Artists and Their Works with an Index of Places. Florentine School*, 2 vols. (London: Phaidon Press, 1963), 1:104; *An Exhibition of Italian Panels & Manuscripts from the Thirteenth and Fourteenth Centuries in Honor of Richard Offner* (Hartford: Wadsworth Atheneum, 1965), 15, no. 9; Burton B. Fredericksen and Federico Zeri, *Census of Pre-Nineteenth-Century Italian Paintings in North American Public Collections* (Cambridge, Mass.: Harvard University Press, 1972), 129, 586; Miklòs Boskovits, *Pittura fiorentina alla vigilia del Rinascimento, 1370–1400* (Florence: Edam, 1975), 372, 374; *Chefs-d'oeuvre des musées des États-Unis: De Giorgione à Picasso* (Paris: Musée Marmottan, 1976), no. 1; Christopher Lloyd, *A Catalogue of the Earlier Italian Paintings in the Ashmolean Museum* (Oxford: Clarendon Press, 1977), 140; Richard Offner and Hayden B. J. Maginnis, *A Critical and Historical Corpus of Florentine Painting: A Legacy of Attributions* (New York: Institute of Fine Arts, New York University, 1981), 7; Miklòs Boskovits, *Dipinti italiani del XIV e XV secolo in una raccolta milanese: Catalogo* (Milan: Silvana, 1987), 24; Keith Christiansen, Laurence B. Kanter, and Carl Brandon Strehlke, *Painting and Illumination in Early Renaissance Florence, 1300–1450* (New York: Metropolitan Museum of Art, 1994), 193; Carolyn C. Wilson, *Italian Paintings XIV–XVI Centuries in the Museum of Fine Arts, Houston* (Houston: Museum of Fine Arts, 1996), 92-100; Edgar Peters Bowron and Mary G. Morton, *Masterworks of European Painting in the Museum of Fine Arts, Houston* (Princeton: Princeton University Press, 2000), 5-6.

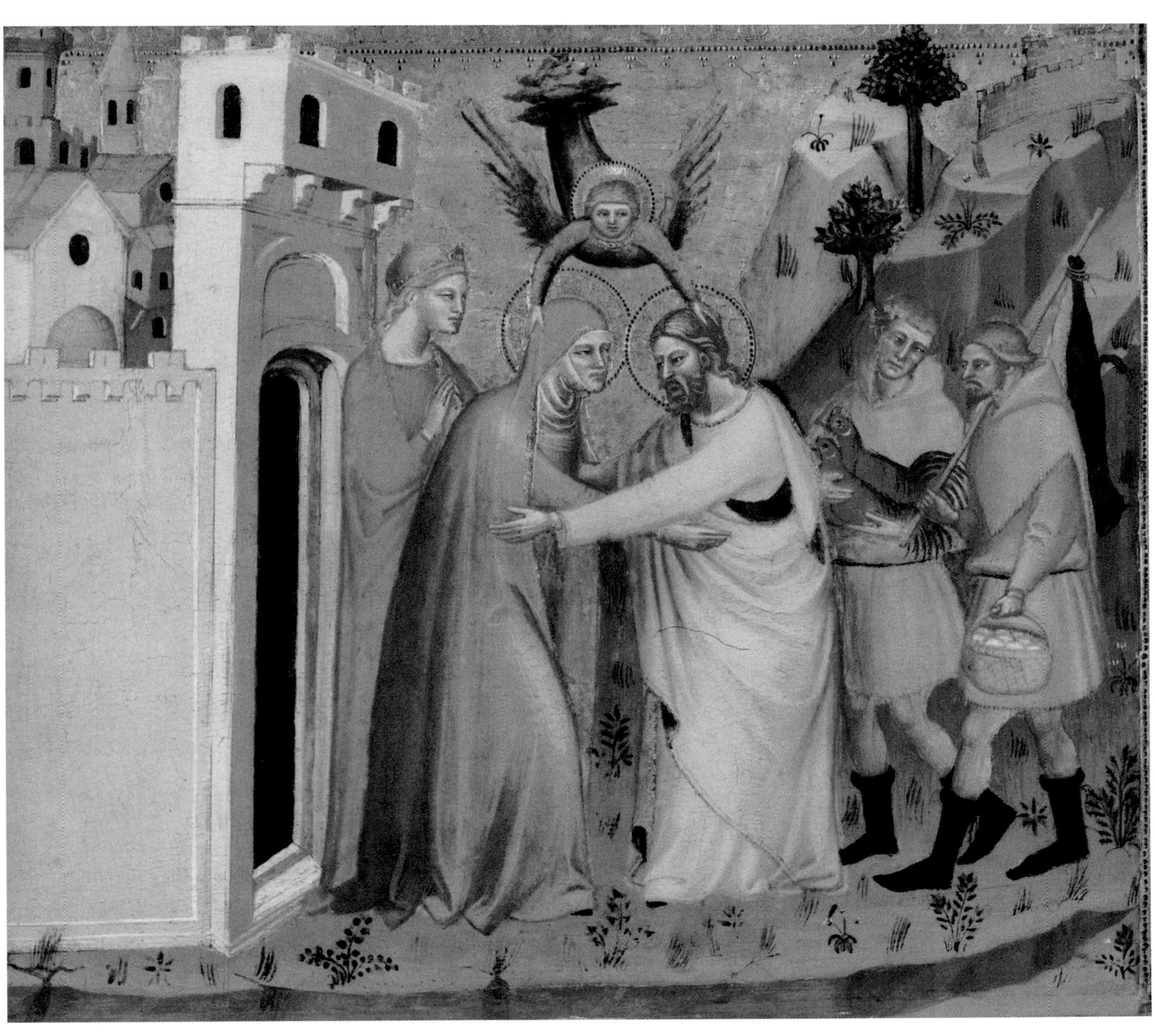

Fig. 216 Master of the Golden Gate: *The Meeting of Anna and Joachim at the Golden Gate*. The Museum of Fine Arts, Houston, The Edith A. and Percy S. Straus Collection, 44.561.

MASTER OF THE SIENESE STRAUS MADONNA, ACTIVE C. 1340–1360; SIENESE

Virgin and Child (44.564) 81.5 X 44.4 CM, TEMPERA ON PANEL

HOUSTON, TEXAS. THE MUSEUM OF FINE ARTS, HOUSTON

The imagery and size of the panel suggest that it was the central component of a large altarpiece, flanked on each side by two or three slightly smaller panels with three-quarter-length images of saints. Curt Weigelt (1931) and Richard Offner (1945) suggested that *St. Agnes* (Worcester Art Museum; 23.35) and *St. John the Evangelist* (Yale University Art Gallery, New Haven; 43.239) may have been part of the same altarpiece as the Houston panel. Both John Pope-Hennessy (1946) and Martin Davies (cited in *European Paintings in the Collection of the Worcester Art Museum* 1974) dismissed the association of the Worcester panel on grounds of dissimilarity of dimensions and proportions. A triangular pinnacle with the half-length figure of a bishop saint (Museum of Fine Arts, Boston; 51.738) may also have belonged to the altarpiece. Since its original publication, the Houston panel has been associated with Simone Martini (c. 1284–1344), his workshop, or his followers, but a more specific attribution has proven problematic. Suggestions have included Donato Martini (died 1347), Barna da Siena (active c. 1330–1350), Lippo Memmi (active 1317–c. 1350), the Master of the Palazzo Venezia Madonna (active early to mid-fourteenth century), and Federigo Memmi (active 1345). The currently favored pseudonym for the anonymous author is the Master of the Sienese Straus Madonna.

Dorothy C. Shorr (1954) recognized this painting as the earliest surviving depiction in trecento Sienese painting of the Christ Child offering his finger to an open-mouthed goldfinch, an action she identified as an allusion to the eucharistic sacrifice.

PROVENANCE

R. Langton Douglas, London; Edith A. and Percy S. Straus, New York, 1923–1945; Edith A. and Percy S. Straus Collection, The Museum of Fine Arts, Houston, acquired 1945

BIBLIOGRAPHY

Raimond van Marle, *The Development of the Italian Schools of Painting*, vol. 2, *The Sienese School of the Late Fourteenth Century* (The Hague: M. Nijhoff, 1924), 226, 607; Raimond van Marle, "Unknown Paintings by Simone Martini and His Followers—I," *Apollo* 4 (1926): 163; Lionello Venturi, *Pitture italiane in America* (Milan: U. Hoepli, 1931), pl. 76; Curt Weigelt, "Minor Simonesque Masters," *Apollo* 14 (1931): 11; Bernard Berenson, *Italian Pictures of the Renaissance* (Oxford: Clarendon Press, 1932), 360; George H. Edgell, *A History of Sienese Painting* (New York: Dial Press, 1932), 83 n. 20; Lionello Venturi, *Italian Paintings in America*, 3 vols. (New York: E. Wyhe, 1933), 1:pl. 95; Bernard Berenson, *Pitture italiane del Rinascimento* (Milan: U. Hoepli, 1936), 309; Anna Maria Gabrielli, "Ancora del Barna pittore delle storie del nuovo testamento nella Collegiata di S. Gimignano," *Bullettino Senese di Storia Patria* 7 (1936): 129; Richard Offner, "The Straus Collection Goes to Houston—Comments on Its Most Important Objects," *Art News* 44 (1945): 17; *Catalogue of the Edith A. and Percy S. Straus Collection* (Houston: Museum of Fine Arts, 1945), 9, no. 1; John Pope-Hennessy, "Barna, the Pseudo-Barna and Giovanni d'Asciano," *Burlington Magazine* 88 (1946): 36-37; Millard Meiss, *Painting in Florence and Siena after the Black Death* (Princeton: Princeton University Press, 1951), 21 n. 28; Dorothy C. Shorr, *The Christ Child in Devotional Images in Italy during the XIV Century* (New York: G. Wittenborn, 1954), 176; Enzo Carli, *La pittura senese* (Milan: Electa, 1955), 150; Millard Meiss, "Nuovi dipinti e vecchi problemi," *Rivista d'Arte* 5 (1955): 143; Federico Zeri, "La riapertura della Alte Pinakothek di Monaco," *Paragone* 95 (1957): 66; Carlo Volpe, "Precisazioni sul 'Barna' e sul 'Maestro di Palazzo Venezia'," *Arte Antica e Moderna* 10 (1960): 152, 157 n. 14; Enzo Carli, "Ancora de Memmi a San Gimignano," *Paragone* 159 (1963): 35, 43 n. 12; Enzo Carli, "Dipinti senese nel Museo di Houston," *Antichità Viva* 1 (1963): 15, 17; Olga A. Nygren, *Barna da Siena* (Stockholm: Söderström, 1963), 85; Brigitte Klesse, *Seidenstoffe in der italienischen Malerei des vierzehnten Jahrhunderts* (Bern: Stämpfli, 1967), 244, no. 1366, 254, no. 145b; Bernard Berenson, *Italian Pictures of the Renaissance: A List of the Principal Artists and Their Works with an Index of Places. Central Italian and North Italian Schools*, 3 vols. (London: Phaidon Press, 1968), 1:404; Henk W. van Os, *Marias Demut und Verherrlichung in der sienesischen Malerei 1300–1450* ('s-Gravenhage: Ministerie van Cultuur, 1969), 165 n. 54; Charles Seymour, *Early Italian Paintings in the Yale*

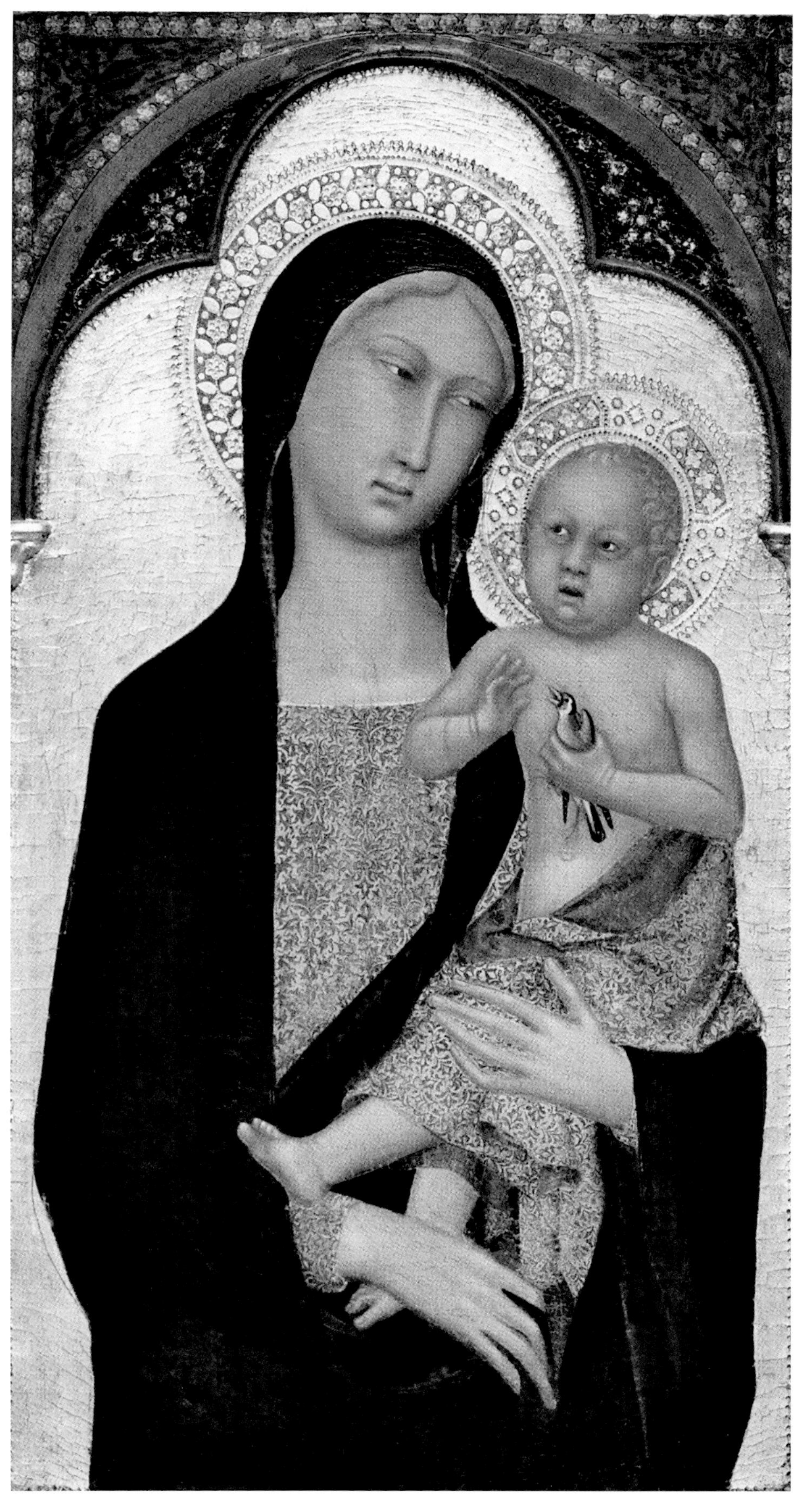

Fig. 217 (above and detail, page 415) Master of the Sienese Straus Madonna: *Virgin and Child*. The Museum of Fine Arts, Houston, The Edith A. and Percy S. Straus Collection, 44.564.

University Art Gallery (New Haven: Yale University Press, 1970), 69; Sebastiana Delogu Ventroni, *Barna da Siena* (Pisa: Giardini, 1972), 43, 50-51, 62-63; Burton B. Fredericksen and Federico Zeri, *Census of Pre-Nineteenth-Century Italian Paintings in North American Public Collections* (Cambridge, Mass.: Harvard University Press, 1972), 122, 586; *European Paintings in the Collection of the Worcester Art Museum* (Worcester: Worcester Art Museum, 1974), 456; Cristina De Benedictis, "Naddo Cecccarelli," *Commentari* 25 (1974): 152; Cristina De Benedictis, "Il polittico della passione di Simone Martini e una proposta per Donato," *Antichità Viva* 15 (1976): 4, 8; Piero Torriti, *La Pinacoteca Nazionale di Siena: I dipinti dal XII al XV secolo* (Genoa: Sagep, 1977), 90; Antonino Caleca, "Tre polittici di Lippo Memmi: Un'ipotesi sul Barna e la bottega di Simone di Lippo, 2," *Critica d'Arte* 42 (1977): 75; Hayden B. J. Maginnis, "The Literature of Sienese Trecento Painting 1945–1975," *Zeitschrift für Kunstgeschichte* 40 (1977): 287-89; Cristina De Benedictis, *La pittura senese 1330–1370* (Florence: Salimbeni libreria editrice, 1979), 43; Giuliano Ercoli, "Nuovi studi sulla pittura senese del Trecento: Un libro, un mostra e qualche riflessione," *Antichità Viva* 18 (1979): 8; Denys Sutton, "Robert Langton Douglas, III," *Apollo* 109 (1979): 190-91; Federico Zeri and Elizabeth E. Gardner, *Italian Paintings: Sienese and Central Italian Schools* (New York: Metropolitan Museum of Art, 1980), 54; Enzo Carli, *La pittura senese del Trecento* (Milan: Electa, 1981), 125; *The Museum of Fine Arts, Houston: A Guide to the Collection* (Houston: Museum of Fine Arts, 1981), 22, no. 38; Alessandro Bagnoli and Luciano Berti, eds., *Simone Martini e "chompagni"* (Florence: Centro Di, 1985), 110; Enrico Castelnuovo, ed., *La pittura in Italia. Il Duecento e il Trecento*, 2 vols. (Milan: Electa, 1986), 1:344; Miklòs Boskovits, *Frühe italienische Malerei: Gemäldegalerie Berlin, Katalog der Gemälde* (Berlin: Gebr. Mann, 1988), 55; Laurence B. Kanter, *Italian Paintings in the Museum of Fine Arts, Boston*, vol. 1, *13th–15th Century* (Boston: Museum of Fine Arts, 1994), 95-96; Carolyn C. Wilson, *Italian Paintings XIV–XVI Centuries in the Museum of Fine Arts, Houston* (Houston: Museum of Fine Arts, 1996), 24-37; Mojmír S. Frinta, *Punched Decoration on Late Medieval Panel and Miniature Painting*, pt. 1 (Prague: Maxdorf, 1998), 309, 420, 516; Edgar Peters Bowron and Mary G. Morton, *Masterworks of European Painting in the Museum of Fine Arts, Houston* (Princeton: Princeton University Press, 2000), 2-4; Victor M. Schmidt, *Painted Piety, Panel Paintings for Personal Devotion in Tuscany, 1250–1400* (Florence: Centro Di, 2005), 225.

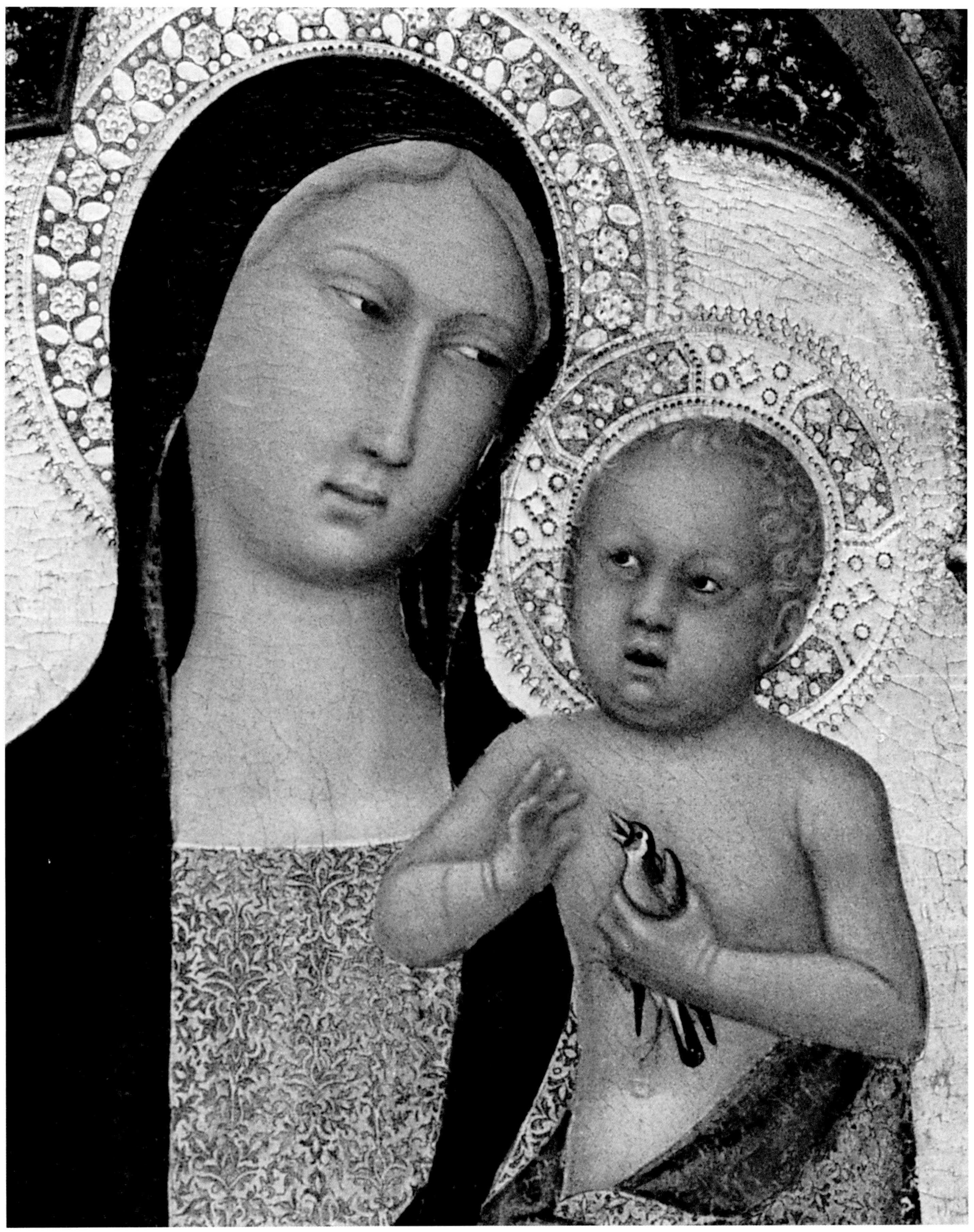

MASTER OF THE STRAUS MADONNA, ACTIVE LATE FOURTEENTH–EARLY FIFTEENTH CENTURY; FLORENTINE

Virgin and Child (44.565) 90.1 X 48.2 CM, TEMPERA ON PANEL

HOUSTON, TEXAS. THE MUSEUM OF FINE ARTS, HOUSTON

The tabernacle frame is original; its base is inscribed "AVE MARIA GRATIA PLENA DOMI" ("Hail Mary, O favored one, the Lord is with you"), from Luke 1:28. The small altarpiece, created for a domestic setting, is the eponymous work of this master, whose career was first reconstructed by Roberto Longhi (1928). Miklòs Boskovits (1975) observed that the composition repeats, with minor variations, his earlier *Madonna and Child* (Aartbisschoppelijk Museum, Utrecht; 2824), from c. 1385–1390; he dated the Houston painting 1395–1400, like the *Madonna of Humility* (Museo Nazionale del Bargello, Florence; 2016) and the *Madonna and Child Enthroned with St. Dominic, St. James, St. Lawrence, St. Peter Martyr, and Two Donors* (Museo Diocesano di Cestello, Florence). Carolyn C. Wilson (1996), on the other hand, found it closest to the artist's *San Giuseppe Triptych* (San Giuseppe, Florence), his Lanz *Madonna* (Rijksdienst Beeldende Kunst, The Hague), his *San Lorenzo in Galiga Polyptych* (Museo Diocesano di Cestello, Florence), and his *Quinto Annunciation* (Santo Stefano al Ponte, Florence); she dated the painting c. 1395–1400.

The Christ Child holds a goldfinch, a symbol of the Passion, and wears a red coral pendant, representing the cross by virtue of its shape. The Virgin's pointing gesture recalls that of John the Baptist indicating the Lamb of God and, thus, also alludes to Christ's sacrifice. Wilson suggested that the composition may have been inspired by the reputedly miracle-working fresco of the *Madonna and Child* in the main cloister of Santa Maria Novella, Florence, which she attributes to a Sienese painter of the 1330s.

PROVENANCE

Carlo Pini, c. 1898; James Kerr-Lawson, Settignano; Edward Hutton, London; Edith A. and Percy S. Straus, New York, 1926–1945; Edith A. and Percy S. Straus Collection, The Museum of Fine Arts, Houston, acquired 1945

BIBLIOGRAPHY

Tancred Borenius, "A Madonna by the Compagno di Agnolo," *Burlington Magazine* 40 (1922): 233; Raimond van Marle, *The Development of the Italian Schools of Painting*, vol. 9, *Late Gothic Painting in Tuscany* (The Hague: M. Nijhoff, 1927), 88, 92; Roberto Longhi, "Ricerche su Giovanni di Francesco," *Pinacoteca* 1 (1928): 34; Ugo Procacci, "Opere inedite alla Mostra del Tesoro di Firenze Sacra," *Rivista d'Arte* 15 (1933): 230 n. 2, 244 n. 1; Richard Offner, "The Mostra del Tesoro di Firenze Sacra—II," *Burlington Magazine* 63 (1933): 170 n. 14; Roberto Salvini, "Per la cronologia e per il catalogo di un discepolo di Agnolo Gaddi," *Bollettino d'Arte* 29 (1935): 294 n. 11; *Catalogue of the Edith A. and Percy S. Straus Collection* (Houston: Museum of Fine Arts, 1945), 12, no. 12; Cesare Brandi, *Quattrocentisti senesi* (Milan: Hoepli, 1949), 187 n. 21; Federico Zeri, "Il Maestro di Santa Verdiana," *Studies in the History of Art: Dedicated to William E. Suida on His Eightieth Birthday* (London: Phaidon Press, 1959), 40; D. A. Fabbi, "Appunti d'archivio: Artisti fiorentini nel territorio di Norcia," *Rivista d'Arte* 9 (1959): 117; *The International Style: The Arts in Europe around 1400* (Baltimore: Walters Art Gallery, 1962), 22; Bernard Berenson, *Italian Pictures of the Renaissance: A List of the Principal Artists and Their Works with an Index of Places. Florentine School*, 2 vols. (London: Phaidon Press, 1963), 1:215; Denys Sutton, ed., *The Art of Painting in Florence and Siena from 1250 to 1500* (London: Wildenstein, 1965), 9; Fern Rusk Shapley, *Paintings from the Samuel H. Kress Collection: Italian Schools*, vol. 1, *XIII–XV Century* (London: Phaidon Press, 1966), 41; J. Byam Shaw, *Paintings by Old Masters at Christ Church, Oxford* (London: Phaidon, 1967), 36, 37; Miklòs Boskovits, "Der Meister der Santa Verdiana: Beiträge zur Geschichte der florentinischen Malerei um die Wende des 14. und 15. Jahrhunderts," *Mitteilungen des Kunsthistorischen Institutes in Florenz* 13 (1967): 48; Brigitte Klesse, *Seidenstoffe in der italienischen Malerei des vierzehnten Jahrhunderts* (Bern: Stämpfli, 1967), 351, no. 276; Burton B. Fredericksen and Federico Zeri, *Census of Pre-Nineteenth-Century Italian Paintings in North American Public Collections* (Cambridge, Mass.: Harvard University Press, 1972), 137, 586; David Wilkins, "A Florentine Diptych," *Carnegie Magazine* 47 (1973): 158; Carnegie Institute, *Catalogue of Painting Collection* (Pittsburgh: Carnegie Institute, 1973), 112; Henk W. van Os and Marian Prakken, *The Florentine Paintings in Holland 1300–1500* (Maarssen: G. Schwartz, 1974), 89, 90; Richard Fremantle, *Florentine Gothic Painters from Giotto to Masaccio: A Guide to Painting in and near Florence, 1300 to 1450* (London: Secker & Warburg, 1975), 305; Miklòs Boskovits, *Pittura fiorentina alla vigilia del Rinascimento, 1370–1400* (Florence: Edam, 1975), 138, 364; Federico Zeri, *Italian Paintings in the Walters Art Gallery*, 2 vols.

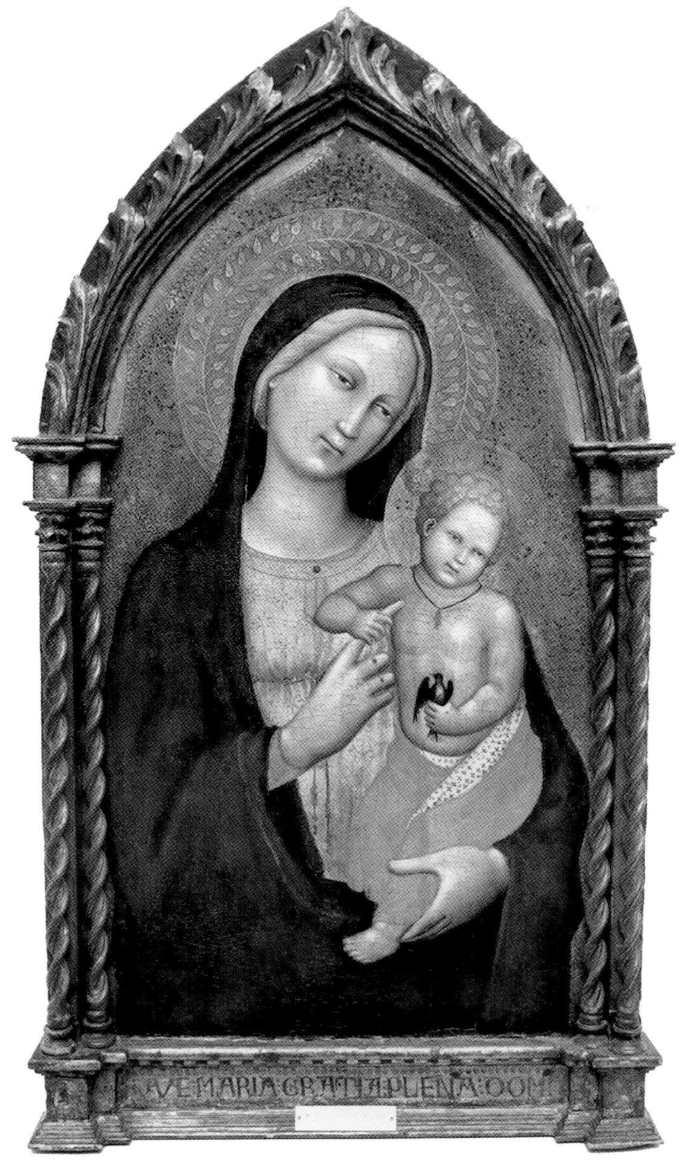

Fig. 218 Master of the Straus Madonna: *Virgin and Child.* The Museum of Fine Arts, Houston, The Edith A. and Percy S. Straus Collection, 44.565.

(Baltimore: Walters Art Gallery, 1976), 1:27; Michel Laclotte and Elisabeth Mognetti, *Avignon-Musée du Petit Palais. Peinture italienne* (Paris: Musées nationaux, 1976), no. 141; *Chefs-d'oeuvre des musées des États-Unis: De Giorgione à Picasso* (Paris: Musée Marmottan, 1976), no. 2; Bruce Cole, *Masaccio and the Art of Early Renaissance Florence* (Bloomington: Indiana University Press, 1980), 62; *The Museum of Fine Arts, Houston: A Guide to the Collection* (Houston: Museum of Fine Arts, 1981), 23, no. 41; David McTavish, ed., *The Arts of Italy in Toronto Collections, 1300–1800* (Toronto: Art Gallery of Ontario, 1981), 25; Carlo Volpe, ed., *Early Italian Paintings and Works of Art, 1300–1480: In Aid of the Friends of the Fitzwilliam Museum* (London: Matthiesen Fine Art Ltd., 1983), 44; *Arte in Valnerina e nello Spoletino, Emergenza e tutela permanente* (Rome: Multigrafica, 1983), 44; Miklòs Boskovits, ed., *The Martello Collection: Paintings, Drawings, and Miniatures from the XIVth to the XVIIIth Centuries* (Florence: Centro Di, 1985), 104; Federico Zeri, ed., *La pittura in Italia. Il Quattrocento*, 2 vols. (Milan: Electa, 1986), 1:342; Angelo Tartuferi, "Qualche considerazione sul Maestro della Madonna Straus e due tavole inedite," *Arte Cristiana* 75 (1987): 161, 162; Peter C. Marzio, *A Permanent Legacy: 150 Works from the Collection of the Museum of Fine Arts, Houston* (New York: Hudson Hills Press, 1989), 98; Marvin Eisenberg, *Lorenzo Monaco* (Princeton: Princeton University Press, 1989), 187; Luciano Berti and Antonio Paolucci, eds., *L'età di Masaccio: Il primo Quattrocento a Firenze* (Milan: Electa, 1990), 80; Miklòs Boskovits, *The Martello Collection: Further Paintings, Drawings, and Miniatures, 13th–18th Century* (Florence: Centro Di, 1992), 132; Erling S. Skaug, *Punch Marks from Giotto to Fra Angelico*, 2 vols. (Oslo: IIC-Nordic Group, 1994), 1:270; Laurence B. Kanter, *Italian Paintings in the Museum of Fine Arts, Boston*, vol. 1, *13th–15th Century* (Boston: Museum of Fine Arts, 1994), 95-96; Carolyn C. Wilson, *Italian Paintings XIV–XVI Centuries in the Museum of Fine Arts, Houston* (Houston: Museum of Fine Arts, 1996), 104-17; Mojmír S. Frinta, *Punched Decoration on Late Medieval Panel and Miniature Painting*, pt. 1 (Prague: Maxdorf, 1998), 510; Edgar Peters Bowron and Mary G. Morton, *Masterworks of European Painting in the Museum of Fine Arts, Houston* (Princeton: Princeton University Press, 2000), ix.

NICCOLÒ DI BUONACCORSO, ACTIVE 1356; DIED 1388; SIENESE

St. Anthony Abbot Preaching; Christ on the Cross with the Virgin and St. John; St. Anthony Abbot and the Centaur (44.555) 29.2 X 98.7 CM, TEMPERA ON PANEL

HOUSTON, TEXAS. THE MUSEUM OF FINE ARTS, HOUSTON

The original function of the panel is unknown. Bernard Berenson (1932) identified the author as Andrea di Bartolo (active by 1389; died 1428). Richard Offner (1945) reattributed the painting to Niccolò di Buonaccorso. Both Anna Marie Doré (cited in *L'art gothique siennois* 1983) and Carolyn C. Wilson (1996) expressed reservations about this attribution. Wilson observed that the style of painting has little in common with Niccolò's manner; she also suggested that more than one artist may have participated in the panel's creation. In contrast, Pia Palladino (1997) reaffirmed the panel as an autograph, late work by Niccolò, contemporary with his *Maestà* (Staatliche Museen, Gemäldegalerie, Berlin; 1100).

PROVENANCE

Edward Hutton, London, 1929; Edith A. and Percy S. Straus, New York, 1929–1945; Edith A. and Percy S. Straus Collection, The Museum of Fine Arts, Houston, acquired 1945

BIBLIOGRAPHY

Bernard Berenson, *Italian Pictures of the Renaissance* (Oxford: Clarendon Press, 1932), 8; John Pope-Hennessy, *Sassetta* (London: Chatto & Windus, 1939), 71-72; Richard Offner, "The Straus Collection Goes to Texas," *Art News* 44 (1945): 17-18; *Catalogue of the Edith A. and Percy S. Straus Collection* (Houston: Museum of Fine Arts, 1945), 11, no. 10; Enzo Carli, "Dipinti senesi nel Museo di Houston," *Antichità Viva* 1 (1963): 17-19; Burton B. Fredericksen and Federico Zeri, *Census of Pre-Nineteenth-Century Italian Paintings in North American Public Collections* (Cambridge, Mass.: Harvard University Press, 1972), 149, 586; Arno Preiser, *Das Entstehen und die Entwicklung der Predella in der italienischen Malerei* (Hildesheim and New York: Olms, 1973), 316; Michel Laclotte and Elisabeth Mognetti, *Avignon—musée du Petit Palais. Peinture italienne* (Paris: Musées nationaux, 1976), nos. 302, 303; *L'art gothique siennois: Enluminure, peinture, orfèvrerie, sculpture* (Florence: Centro Di, 1983), 262-63; John Pope-Hennessy, *The Robert Lehman Collection*, vol. 1, *Italian Paintings* (New York: Metropolitan Museum of Art; Princeton: Princeton University Press, 1987), 106; Carolyn C. Wilson, *Italian Paintings XIV–XVI Centuries in the Museum of Fine Arts, Houston* (Houston: Museum of Fine Arts, 1996), 42-50; Pia Palladino, *Art and Devotion in Siena after 1350: Luca di Tommé and Niccolò di Buonaccorso* (San Diego: Timken Museum of Art, 1997), 72; Mojmír S. Frinta, *Punched Decoration on Late Medieval Panel and Miniature Painting*, pt. 1 (Prague: Maxdorf, 1998), 274, 477.

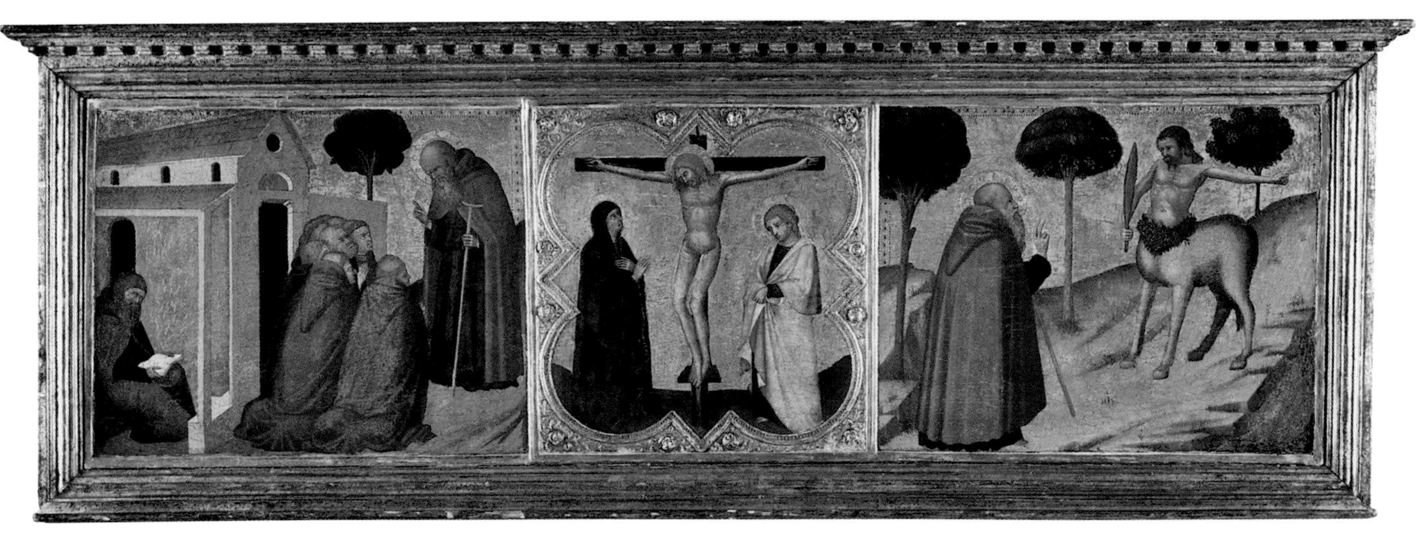

Fig. 219 Niccolò di Buonaccorso: *St. Anthony Abbot Preaching; Christ on the Cross with the Virgin and St. John; St. Anthony Abbot and the Centaur*. The Museum of Fine Arts, Houston, The Edith A. and Percy S. Straus Collection, 44.555.

RAFFAELLINO DEL GARBO, C. 1444/5–1510; FLORENTINE

Bust of a Young Woman (44.554) 38.7 X 24.8 CM, TEMPERA ON PANEL

HOUSTON, TEXAS. THE MUSEUM OF FINE ARTS, HOUSTON

Since its entry into the collection of the Kaiser-Friedrich Museum, the portrait has been considered by most scholars a product of Sandro Botticelli's (1444/5–1510) shop or school. Bernard Berenson (1909; 1932; 1936; 1963), however, attributed it to Raffaellino del Garbo; his attribution was tentatively accepted by Jean Lipman (1936) and endorsed by the Museum of Fine Arts, Houston (*The Museum of Fine Arts* 1981). Carolyn C. Wilson (1996) definitively rejected the authorship of Raffaellino and assigned the painting to a Florentine follower of Botticelli, c. 1485–1490.

Wilson noted that the woman's distinctive hairstyle was fashionable in Florence from c. 1485 to 1490 and appears in a number of portraits from the period. The depiction of female sitters in profile was a convention of Florentine portraiture in the Quattrocento, although additional formats were employed by the last quarter of the century. While the picture was once labeled as a likeness of Lucrezia Tornabuoni, the mother of Lorenzo de' Medici, the sitter's identity has not, in reality, been determined. The portrait is not individualized, evincing instead the generalized facial features common to representations of contemporary women. The simplicity of the clothing argues against this as a depiction of a member of a prominent Florentine family.

PROVENANCE

Kaiser-Friedrich Museum, Berlin, acquired 1829; Kurt Glogowski, Berlin, c. 1922; Sotheby's, London, June 9, 1932, lot 84; Arnold Seligmann, Rey and Co., New York, 1932; Edith A. and Percy S. Straus, New York, 1932–1945; Edith A. and Percy S. Straus Collection, The Museum of Fine Arts, Houston, acquired 1945

BIBLIOGRAPHY

Gustav F. Waagen, *Verzeichniss der Gemälde-Sammlung des Königlichen Museums zu Berlin* (Berlin: W. Moeser & Kühn, 1845), 26; Julius Meyer and Wilhelm von Bode, *Beschreibendes Verzeichniss der während des Umbaues ausgestelten Gemälde* (Berlin: C. Berg & von Holten, 1878), 46; George N. Plunkett, *Sandro Botticelli* (London: G. Bell and Sons, 1900), 107; Richard Davey, *The Work of Botticelli* (London: G. Newnes; New York: F. Warne, 1903), xvii; Joseph A. Crowe and Giovanni B. Cavalcaselle, *A New History of Painting in Italy from the II to the XVI Century*, 3 vols., ed. Edward Hutton (London: Dent; New York: Dutton, 1909), 2:412; Bernard Berenson, *The Florentine Painters of the Renaissance* (New York and London: G. P. Putnam's Sons, 1909), 136; Adolfo Venturi, *Storia dell'arte italiana*, vol. 7/1, *La pittura del Quattrocento* (Milan: U. Hoepli, 1911), 642 n. 1; Wilhelm von Suida, "Ein Bildnis von Bastiano Mainardi," *Pantheon* 5 (1930): 5; Bernard Berenson, *Italian Pictures of the Renaissance* (Oxford: Clarendon Press, 1932), 478; Bernard Berenson, *Pitture italiane del Rinascimento* (Milan: U. Hoepli, 1936), 411; Jean Lipman, "The Florentine Profile Portrait in the Quattrocento," *Art Bulletin* 18 (1936): 102; Richard Offner, "The Straus Collection Goes to Texas—Comments on Its More Important Objects," *Art News* 44 (1945): 21, 23; *Catalogue of the Edith A. and Percy S. Straus Collection* (Houston: Museum of Fine Arts, 1945), 16, no. 19; Bernard Berenson, *Italian Pictures of the Renaissance: A List of the Principal Artists and Their Works with an Index of Places. Florentine School*, 2 vols. (London: Phaidon Press, 1963), 1:187; Carlo Bo and Gabriele Mandel, *L'opera completa del Botticelli* (Milan: Rizzoli, 1967), 90; Burton B. Fredericksen and Federico Zeri, *Census of Pre-Nineteenth-Century Italian Paintings in North American Public Collections* (Cambridge, Mass.: Harvard University Press, 1972), 34, 586; Ronald W. Lightbown, *Sandro Botticelli*, 2 vols. (Berkeley: University of California Press, 1978), 2:156, no. C75; *Museum of Fine Arts, Houston: A Guide to the Collection* (Houston: Museum of Fine Arts, 1981), 41, no. 77; Roberto Bellucci et al, "Il ritratto di giovanne donna della Galleria Palatina di Firenze," *O.P.D. Restauro* (1988): 72 n. 3; Marco Ciatti, "Ancora sulla 'Bella Simonetta,'" *O.P.D. Restauro* (1989): 126; Carolyn C. Wilson, *Italian Paintings XIV–XVI Centuries in the Museum of Fine Arts, Houston* (Houston: Museum of Fine Arts, 1996), 150-53; Edgar Peters Bowron and Mary G. Morton, *Masterworks of European Painting in the Museum of Fine Arts, Houston* (Princeton: Princeton University Press, 2000), 24-26.

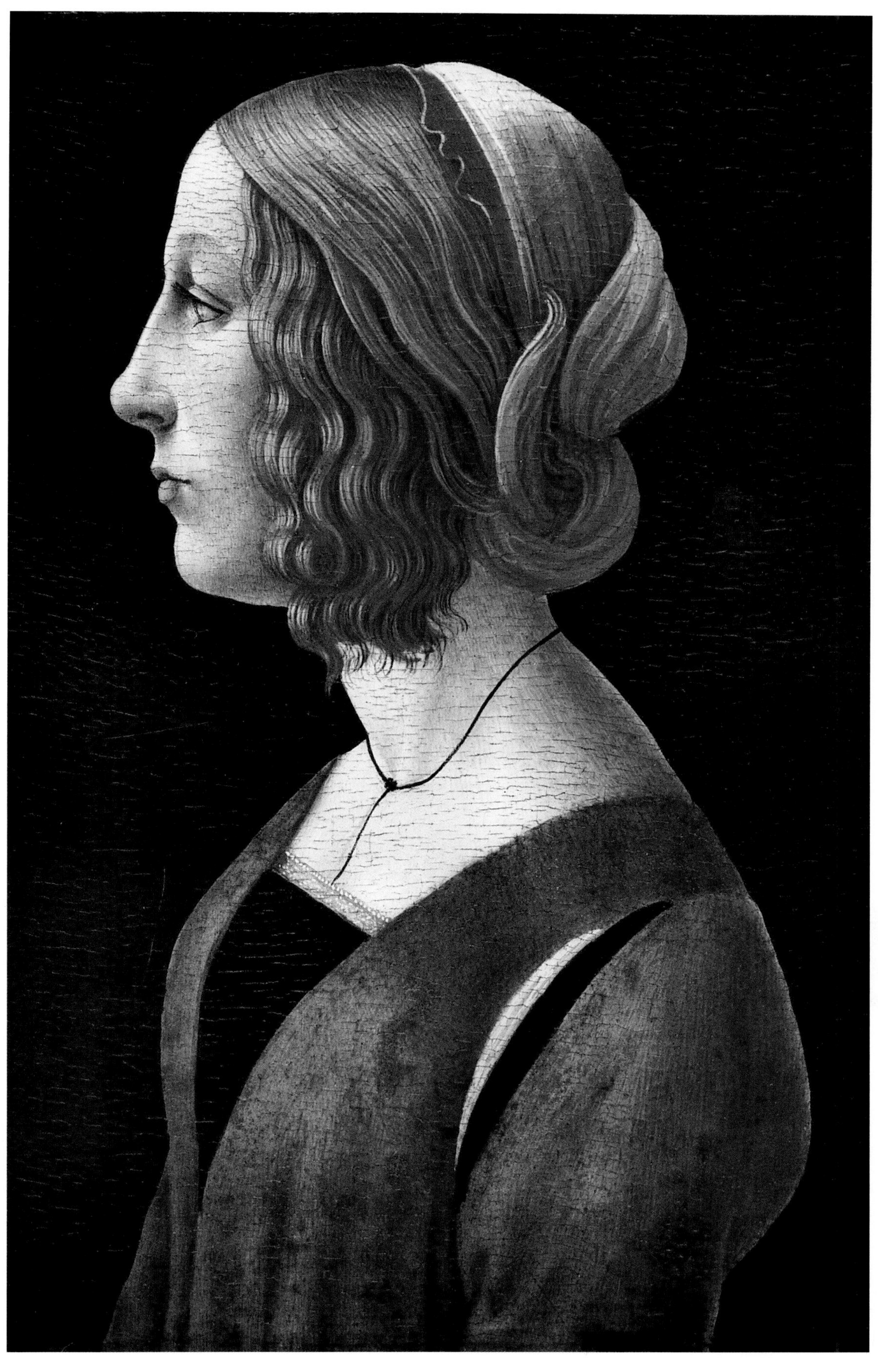

Fig. 220 Raffaellino del Garbo: *Bust of a Young Woman*. The Museum of Fine Arts, Houston, The Edith A. and Percy S. Straus Collection, 44.554.

ROMANO, ANTONIAZZO, ACTIVE AFTER 1461; DIED 1508/9; ROMAN

Virgin and Child with Donor (44.551) 47.6 X 37.9 CM, TEMPERA ON PANEL

HOUSTON, TEXAS. THE MUSEUM OF FINE ARTS, HOUSTON

The painting has always been considered an autograph work of high quality. Repeated, with variations, in at least ten workshop copies, the composition derives from Antoniazzo's more monumental representations of the Madonna and Child. Carolyn C. Wilson (1996) dated the work c. 1480 on the basis of its marked similarity to the artist's signed altarpiece in San Pietro, Fondi, from 1476–1479; the correspondences include the overall composition, the presence of the supplicant, the Madonna's facial features, the pose of her right hand, and the punch motif in the haloes.

The scale, format, and inclusion of the supplicant suggest that the painting was a personal devotional image. The Christ Child holds a goldfinch symbolizing his Passion. Wilson noted that the crossed position of Christ's legs is unusual, not only in Antoniazzo's oeuvre, but in contemporary half-length images of the Madonna and Child in general. She hypothesized that the posture may have been inspired by that of the Christ Child in the medieval apse mosaic of Santa Maria Nova in Rome, as well as by medieval Lombard sculpture in the city.

PROVENANCE

Enrico Testa, Rome and Florence, 1921; Edith A. and Percy S. Straus, New York, 1921–1945; Edith A. and Percy S. Straus Collection, The Museum of Fine Arts, Houston, acquired 1945

BIBLIOGRAPHY

Loan Exhibition of the Arts of the Italian Renaissance (New York: Metropolitan Museum of Art, 1923), 8, no. 24; Bryson Burroughs, "Loan Exhibition of the Arts of the Italian Renaissance," *Bulletin of the Metropolitan Museum of Art* 8 (1923): 108; Roberto Longhi, "In favore di Antoniazzo Romano," *Vita Artistica* 2 (1927): 232-33; Bernard Berenson, *Italian Pictures of the Renaissance* (Oxford: Clarendon Press, 1932), 27; Raimond van Marle, *The Development of the Italian Schools of Painting*, vol. 15, *The Renaissance Painters of Central and Southern Italy* (The Hague: M. Nijhoff, 1934), 258; Bernard Berenson, *Pitture italiane del Rinascimento* (Milan: U. Hoepli, 1936), 23; *Mostra di Melozzo e del Quattrocento romagnolo* (Bologna: Stabilimenti Poligrafici, 1938), 39; *Catalogue of the Edith A. and Percy S. Straus Collection* (Houston: Museum of Fine Arts, 1945), 16-17, no. 21; Herbert Friedmann, *The Symbolic Goldfinch: Its History and Significance in European Devotional Art* (Washington, D.C.: Pantheon Books, 1946), 105; Francesco Negri Arnoldi, "Madonne giovanili di Antoniazzo Romano," *Commentari* 15 (1964): 211 n. 9; Francesco Negri Arnoldi, "Maturità di Antoniazzo," *Commentari* 16 (1965): 242-43 n. 9; Antonio Boschetto, "Due opere di Antoniazzo Romano," *Paragone* 18 (1967): 86; Bernard Berenson, *Italian Pictures of the Renaissance: A List of the Principal Artists and Their Works with an Index of Places. Central Italian and North Italian Schools*, 3 vols. (London: Phaidon Press, 1968), 1:15; Ilaria Toesca, "Una scheda per Antoniazzo," *Paragone* 19 (1968): 64; Burton B. Fredericksen and Federico Zeri, *Census of Pre-Nineteenth-Century Italian Paintings in North American Public Collections* (Cambridge, Mass.: Harvard University Press, 1972), 11, 586; Gisela Noehles-Doerk, "Antoniazzo Romano: Studien zur Quattrocentomalerei in Rom" (Ph.D. diss., Westfälischen Wilhelms-Universität zu Münster, 1973), 183-84, no. 27; Giuseppe Palumbo, *Collezione Federico Mason Perkins* (Assisi: Sacro convento di S. Francesco, 1973), 59; Maria Letizia Casanova Uccella, *Arte a Gaeta: Dipinti dal XII al XVIII secolo* (Florence: Centro Di, 1976), 54; Gregory Hedberg, "Antoniazzo Romano and His School" (Ph.D. diss., New York University, 1980), 34, 54, 95 n. 242, 165, nos. 15, 171, 182, 212, 214, 218-19, 226-28; Federico Zeri and Elizabeth E. Gardner, *Italian Paintings: Sienese and Central Italian Schools* (New York: Metropolitan Museum of Art, 1980), 3; *The Museum of Fine Arts, Houston: A Guide to the Collection* (Houston: Museum of Fine Arts, 1981), 29-30, no. 54; Sandra Vasco Rocca, "La pittura," in *Fondi e la signoria dei Caetani*, ed. Francesco Negri Arnoldi, Amalia Pacia, and Sandra Vasco Rocca (Rome: De Lucca, 1981), 74, 76; Anna Cavallaro, "Antoniazzo Romano e le confraternite del quattrocento Roma," *Ricerche per la storia religiosa di Roma* 5 (1984): 345; Antonio Paolucci, *Antoniazzo Romano: Catalogo completo dei dipinti* (Florence: Cantini, 1992), 50, no. 9; Vitaliano Tiberia, *Antoniazzo Romano: Per il Cardinale Bessarione a Roma* (Todi: Ediart, 1992), 77; Anna Cavallaro, *Antoniazzo Romano e gli antoniazzeschi: Una generazione di pittori nella Roma del Quattrocento* (Udine: Campanotto, 1992), 61, 69-70, 187-88, no. 11, 224-26; Carolyn C. Wilson, *Italian Paintings XIV–XVI Centuries in the Museum of Fine Arts, Houston* (Houston: Museum of Fine Arts, 1996), 244-54; Edgar Peters Bowron and Mary G. Morton, *Masterworks of European Painting in the Museum of Fine Arts, Houston* (Princeton: Princeton University Press, 2000), 22-24.

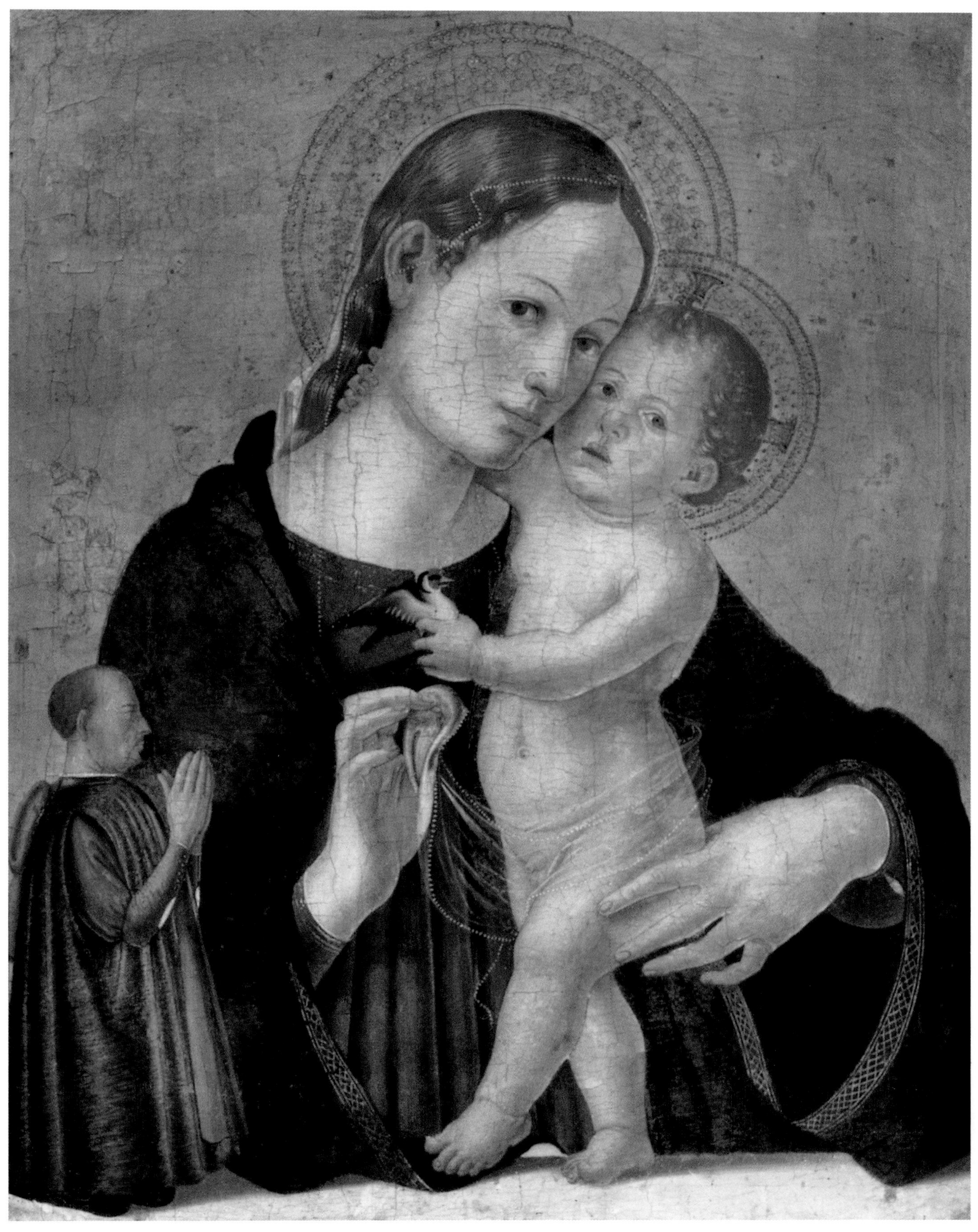

Fig. 221 Antoniazzo Romano: *Virgin and Child with Donor*. The Museum of Fine Arts, Houston, The Edith A. and Percy S. Straus Collection, 44.551.

SANO DI PIETRO, 1405–1481; SIENESE

Virgin and Child with St. Jerome, St. Bernardino of Siena, and Six Angels (44.572) 59.7 X 40.6 CM, TEMPERA ON PANEL

HOUSTON, TEXAS. THE MUSEUM OF FINE ARTS, HOUSTON

The panel is one of numerous small devotional paintings of the Madonna and Child produced by Sano and his shop, many of which may have decorated monastic cells. The artist frequently employed the cartoon used for the mother and son in small and large works. The entire composition, including both saints, is repeated, with minor variations, in several other works: Lowe Art Museum, University of Miami, Coral Gables (K 286); Robert Lehman Collection, Metropolitan Museum of Art, New York (1975.1.43); and Kingsley Porter Collection, Fogg Art Museum, Cambridge (1962.284). The inclusion of the Franciscan reformer St. Bernardino of Siena (died 1444; canonized 1450) suggests that the original owner was affiliated with or sympathetic toward the Observant movement. Carolyn C. Wilson (1996) dated the painting to the 1460s, primarily on the basis of Bernardino's appearance, which conforms to Sano's later, more stylized portrayals of the saint.

Inscribed on the Madonna's halo is "AVE GRATIA PLENA do[minus] . . ." ("Hail, O favored one, the Lord [is with you]"), from Luke 1:28; on the Christ Child's halo is ". . . SVM VER . . ." ("[I am the way, and] the truth, [and the life]"), from John 14:6. "YHS," the abbreviation of the name of Jesus in Greek, appears in the center of the tablet held by St. Bernardino; along its top and bottom edges are "INE GESU" and "LECTAT," a corrupted reference to ". . . at the name of Jesus every knee should bow," from Philippians 2:10. The pressing together of the faces of the Madonna and Child derives from the Byzantine *Glykophilousa* or *Eleousa* ("affectionate Virgin") type of image. The star on her shoulder refers to her Hebrew name, Miriam, which means "Star of the Sea." The cherries held by the Christ Child allude to Paradise and represent the sweet rewards of the blessed. The tablet displaying the sacred monogram of Christ is Bernardino's usual attribute.

PROVENANCE

Newman, Florence (?); Edith A. and Percy S. Straus, New York, 1925–1945; Edith A. and Percy S. Straus Collection, The Museum of Fine Arts, Houston, acquired 1945

BIBLIOGRAPHY

Bernard Berenson, *Italian Pictures of the Renaissance* (Oxford: Clarendon Press, 1932), 500; Bernard Berenson, *Pitture italiane del Rinascimento* (Milan: U. Hoepli, 1936), 430; *Catalogue of the Edith A. and Percy S. Straus Collection* (Houston: Museum of Fine Arts, 1945), 15, no. 17; Richard Offner, "The Straus Collection Goes to Houston—Comments on Its Most Important Objects," *Art News* 44 (1945): 19; Enzo Carli, "Dipinti senesi nel Museo di Houston," *Antichità Viva* 2 (1963): 20, 24; Burton B. Fredericksen and Federico Zeri, *Census of Pre-Nineteenth-Century Italian Paintings in North American Public Collections* (Cambridge, Mass.: Harvard University Press, 1972), 181, 586; *The Museum of Fine Arts, Houston: A Guide to the Collection* (Houston: Museum of Fine Arts, 1981), 25-26, no. 46; John Pope-Hennessy, *The Robert Lehman Collection*, vol. 1, *Italian Paintings* (New York: Metropolitan Museum of Art; Princeton: Princeton University Press, 1987), 146; Carolyn C. Wilson, *Italian Paintings XIV–XVI Centuries in the Museum of Fine Arts, Houston* (Houston: Museum of Fine Arts, 1996), 173-78; Mojmír S. Frinta, *Punched Decoration on Late Medieval Panel and Miniature Painting*, pt. 1 (Prague: Maxdorf, 1998), 222, 345; Edgar Peters Bowron and Mary G. Morton, *Masterworks of European Painting in the Museum of Fine Arts, Houston* (Princeton: Princeton University Press, 2000), 14-16.

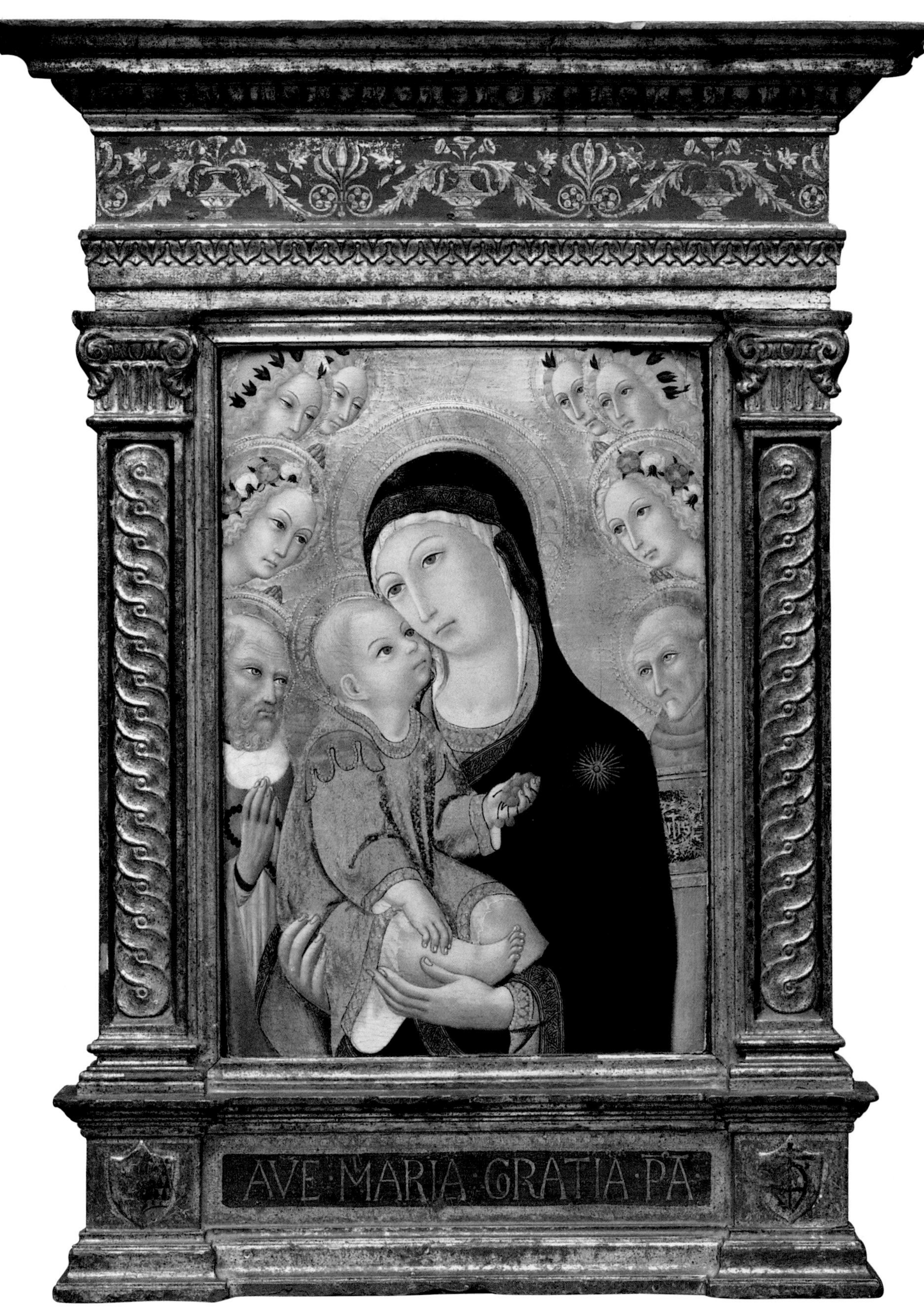

Fig. 222 Sano di Pietro: *Virgin and Child with St. Jerome, St. Bernardino of Siena, and Six Angels.* The Museum of Fine Arts, Houston, The Edith A. and Percy S. Straus Collection, 44.572.

SIENESE SCHOOL, SECOND QUARTER OF THE FOURTEENTH CENTURY

Virgin and Child with St. Francis, St. Clare, and Two Angels (44.566) 47.5 x 21.3 CM, TEMPERA ON PANEL

HOUSTON, TEXAS. THE MUSEUM OF FINE ARTS, HOUSTON

This small, autonomous panel originally served as the focus of private devotion. The presence of St. Francis and St. Clare suggests that the original owner had a particular affection for or devotion to the Franciscan Order. The work has long been associated with the circle of Simone Martini (c. 1284–1344), and numerous suggestions have been made regarding a specific attribution. The panel entered the Straus Collection (*Catalogue of the Edith A. and Percy S. Straus Collection* 1945) as the work of Lippo Memmi (active 1317–c. 1350). Enzo Carli (1963) noted its similarity to the monumental *Madonna and Child with Angels* (Berenson Collection, Villa I Tatti, Settignano), attributed to the Master of the Palazzo Venezia Madonna (active early to mid-fourteenth century). Miklòs Boskovits (1988) also associated the work with this painter, comparing it to his small *Madonna and Child with Four Saints* (Staatliche Museen, Gemäldegalerie, Berlin; 1071A). Carolyn C. Wilson (1996) distinguished the Houston panel from these works by the Master of the Palazzo Venezia Madonna on the basis of its more linear style and assigned it to a Sienese follower of Simone Martini and Lippo Memmi, c. 1340–1350.

The Virgin has a star on her shoulder, which refers to her Hebrew name, Miriam, meaning "Star of the Sea." St. Francis and St. Clare wear the traditional brown habits and cord belts of the Franciscan Order. Francis holds a cross, alluding to the miracle of the stigmata and his identification with the crucified Christ. Clare holds a lamp, recalling Thomas of Celano's (c. 1200–c. 1255) description of her as the source of "a most shining light for womankind" and his identification of her with a lamp on its stand, which "gives light to all in the house" (Matthew 5:15).

PROVENANCE

Private collection, Scotland; Edward Hutton, London; Edith A. and Percy S. Straus, New York, 1929–1944; Edith A. and Percy S. Straus Collection, The Museum of Fine Arts, Houston, acquired 1944

BIBLIOGRAPHY

George H. McCall and William R. Valentiner, *Catalogue of European Paintings and Sculpture from 1300–1800* (New York: Publishers Printing Co., 1939), 125, no. 257; William R. Valentiner and Alfred M. Frankfurter, *Masterpieces of Art: Exhibition at the New York World's Fair, 1939* (New York: The Art News, 1939), no. 257; *Catalogue of the Edith A. and Percy S. Straus Collection* (Houston: Museum of Fine Arts, 1945), 9, no. 1; Enzo Carli, "Dipinti senesi nel museo di Houston," *Antichità Viva* 2 (1963): 15, 17; Bernard Berenson, *Italian Pictures of the Renaissance: A List of the Principal Artists and Their Works with an Index of Places. Central Italian and North Italian Schools*, 3 vols. (London: Phaidon Press, 1968), 1:405; Burton B. Fredericksen and Federico Zeri, *Census of Pre-Nineteenth-Century Italian Paintings in North American Public Collections* (Cambridge, Mass.: Harvard University Press, 1972), 122, 586; *The Museum of Fine Arts, Houston: A Guide to the Collection* (Houston: Museum of Fine Arts, 1981), 22, no. 39; Miklòs Boskovits, *Frühe italienische Malerei: Gemäldegalerie Berlin, Katalog der Gemälde* (Berlin: Gebr. Mann, 1988), 115; Carolyn C. Wilson, *Italian Paintings XIV–XVI Centuries in the Museum of Fine Arts, Houston* (Houston: Museum of Fine Arts, 1996), 38-41; Mojmír S. Frinta, *Punched Decoration on Late Medieval Panel and Miniature Painting*, pt. 1 (Prague: Maxdorf, 1998), 205, 339, 353, 493, 502; Perri Lee Roberts, Bruce Cole, and Hayden B. J. Maginnis, *Sacred Treasures: Early Italian Paintings from Southern Collections* (Athens, Ga.: Georgia Museum of Art, 2002), 24, 70-72.

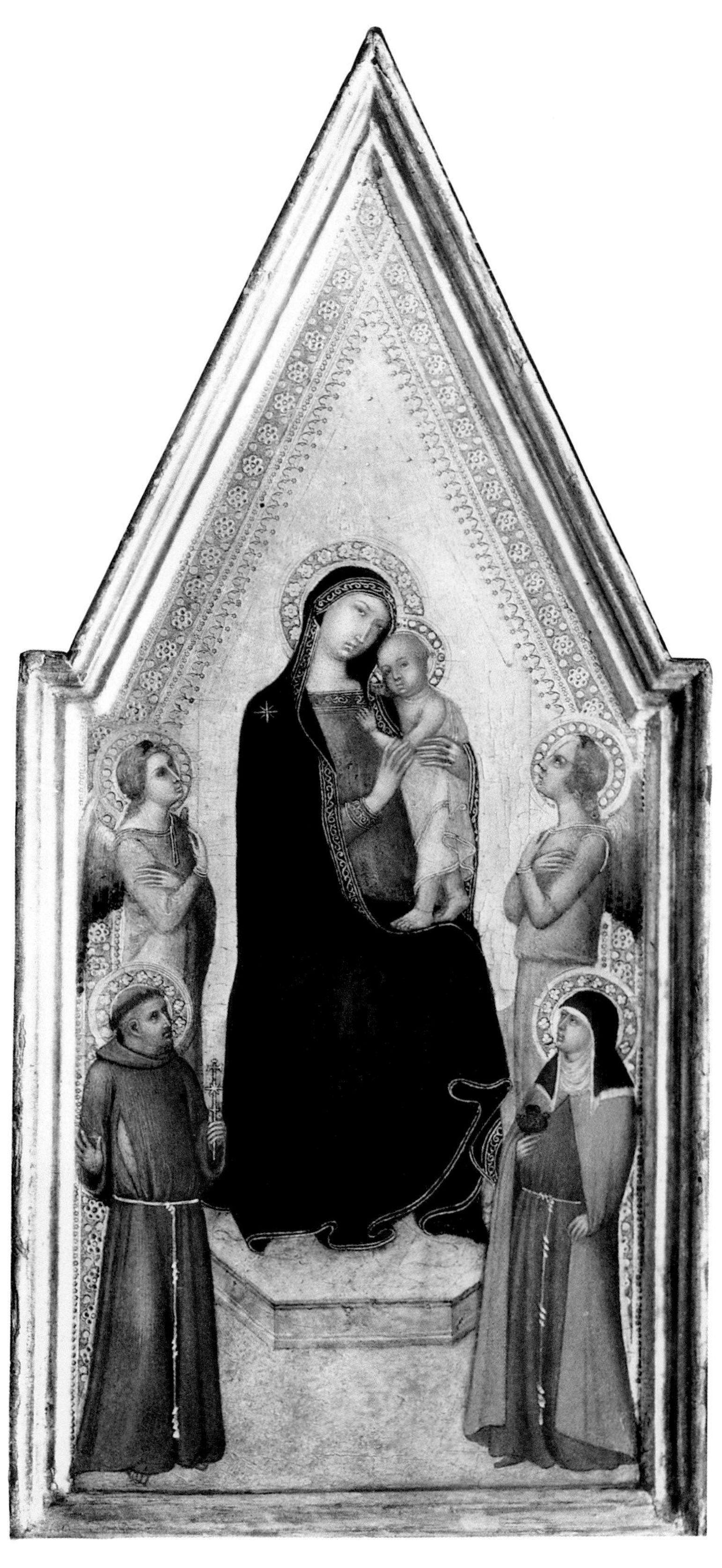

Fig. 223 Sienese School, second quarter of the fourteenth century: *Virgin and Child with St. Francis, St. Clare, and Two Angels.* The Museum of Fine Arts, Houston, The Edith A. and Percy S. Straus Collection, 44.566.

VIVARINI, ANTONIO, C. 1415–1476/84; VENETIAN

Virgin and Child (44.575) 88 X 43.8 CM, TEMPERA ON PANEL

HOUSTON, TEXAS. THE MUSEUM OF FINE ARTS, HOUSTON

The attribution of the painting to Antonio Vivarini by F. Mason Perkins (1927) has been accepted universally. The work probably served as the lower central panel of a multi-tiered polyptych, similar in appearance and size to the artist's signed altarpiece in Poreč (Croatia) of c. 1440. Federico Zeri (1971) hypothesized that the Houston painting was flanked by panels depicting St. Christopher, St. Nicholas, St. James, and St. Anthony Abbot (current location unknown); he placed the commission early in Antonio's career, contemporary with the *Poreč Polyptych*. Carolyn C. Wilson (1996) supported this reconstruction and dating, noting the similiarity of dimensions, of the punched decoration of the haloes, and of the representations of the Christ Child in the St. Christopher and Madonna panels. She conjectured that Antonio's frontal depiction of the Madonna, who adores a wakeful child, may have derived from a lost composition by Jacopo Bellini (c. 1400–1470/1).

PROVENANCE

David John Carnegie, Earl of Northesk, Ethie Castle, Arbroath, Scotland, to c. 1918; Cavalieri Angiolo and Aldo Rambaldi, Bologna, to 1924; Girardi Giraldi, Florence; Edith A. and Percy S. Straus, New York, 1925–1945; Edith A. and Percy S. Straus Collection, The Museum of Fine Arts, Houston, acquired 1945

BIBLIOGRAPHY

F. Mason Perkins, "A Painting by Antonio Vivarini," *Art in America* 16 (1927): 12-16; Wart Arslan, "Una Madonna di Antonio Vivarini," *Rivista d'Arte* 12 (1930): 543; Lionello Venturi, *Pitture italiane in America* (Milan: U. Hoepli, 1931), pl. 255; Bernard Berenson, *Italian Pictures of the Renaissance* (Oxford: Clarendon Press, 1932), 599; Lionello Venturi, *Italian Paintings in America*, 3 vols. (New York: E. Wyhe, 1933), 2:pl. 336; Raimond van Marle, *The Development of the Italian Schools of Painting*, vol. 17, *The Renaissance Painters of Venice: Antonio Vivarini, the Bellini, Cima, Basaiti* (The Hague: M. Nijhoff, 1935), 21, 24; Bernard Berenson, *Pitture italiane del Rinascimento* (Milan: U. Hoepli, 1936), 515; George H. McCall, *Catalogue of European Paintings and Sculpture from 1300–1800* (New York: Publishers Printing Co., 1939), 197, no. 403; *Catalogue of the Edith A. and Percy S. Straus Collection* (Houston: Museum of Fine Arts, 1945), 14, no. 16; Luigi Coletti, *Pittura veneta del Quattrocento* (Novara: Istituto geografico de' Agostini, 1953), 28; Jack Key Flanagan, "Report of the Conservator," *The Museum of Fine Arts of Houston: Bulletin of the Museum* 17 (1955); Suzanne Sulzberger, "Variation sur un thème iconographique: 'La Vierge et l'Enfant a mi-corps'," in *Venezia e l'Europa: Atti del XVIII Congresso Internazionale di Storia dell'Arte* (Venice: Arte veneta, 1956), 231; Bernard Berenson, *Italian Pictures of the Renaissance. A List of the Principal Artists and Their Works with an Index of Places. Venetian School*, 2 vols. (New York: Phaidon, 1957), 1:198; Rodolfo Pallucchini, *I Vivarini: Antonio, Bartolomeo, Alvise* (Venice: Neri Pozza, 1962), 18, 101; Giles Robertson, *Giovanni Bellini* (Oxford: Clarendon Press, 1968), 37; Federico Zeri, "Un 'San Girolamo' firmato di Giovanni d'Alemagna," in *Studi di storia dell'arte in onore di Antonio Morassi* (Venice: Alfieri, 1971), 44-45; Burton B. Fredericksen and Federico Zeri, *Census of Pre-Nineteenth-Century Italian Paintings in North American Public Collections* (Cambridge, Mass.: Harvard University Press, 1972), 211, 586; *The Museum of Fine Arts, Houston: A Guide to the Collection* (Houston: Museum of Fine Arts, 1981), 24-25, no. 44; John Steer, *Alvise Vivarini, His Art and Influence* (Cambridge and New York: Cambridge University Press, 1982), 5 n. 9, 43 n. 20; Francesco Federico Manicini, ed., *Pinacoteca comunale di Città di Castello* (Perugia: Electa, 1987), 151; Carolyn C. Wilson, *Italian Paintings XIV-XVI Centuries in the Museum of Fine Arts, Houston* (Houston: Museum of Fine Arts, 1996), 192-200; Mojmír S. Frinta, *Punched Decoration on Late Medieval Panel and Miniature Painting*, pt. 1 (Prague: Maxdorf, 1998), 437.

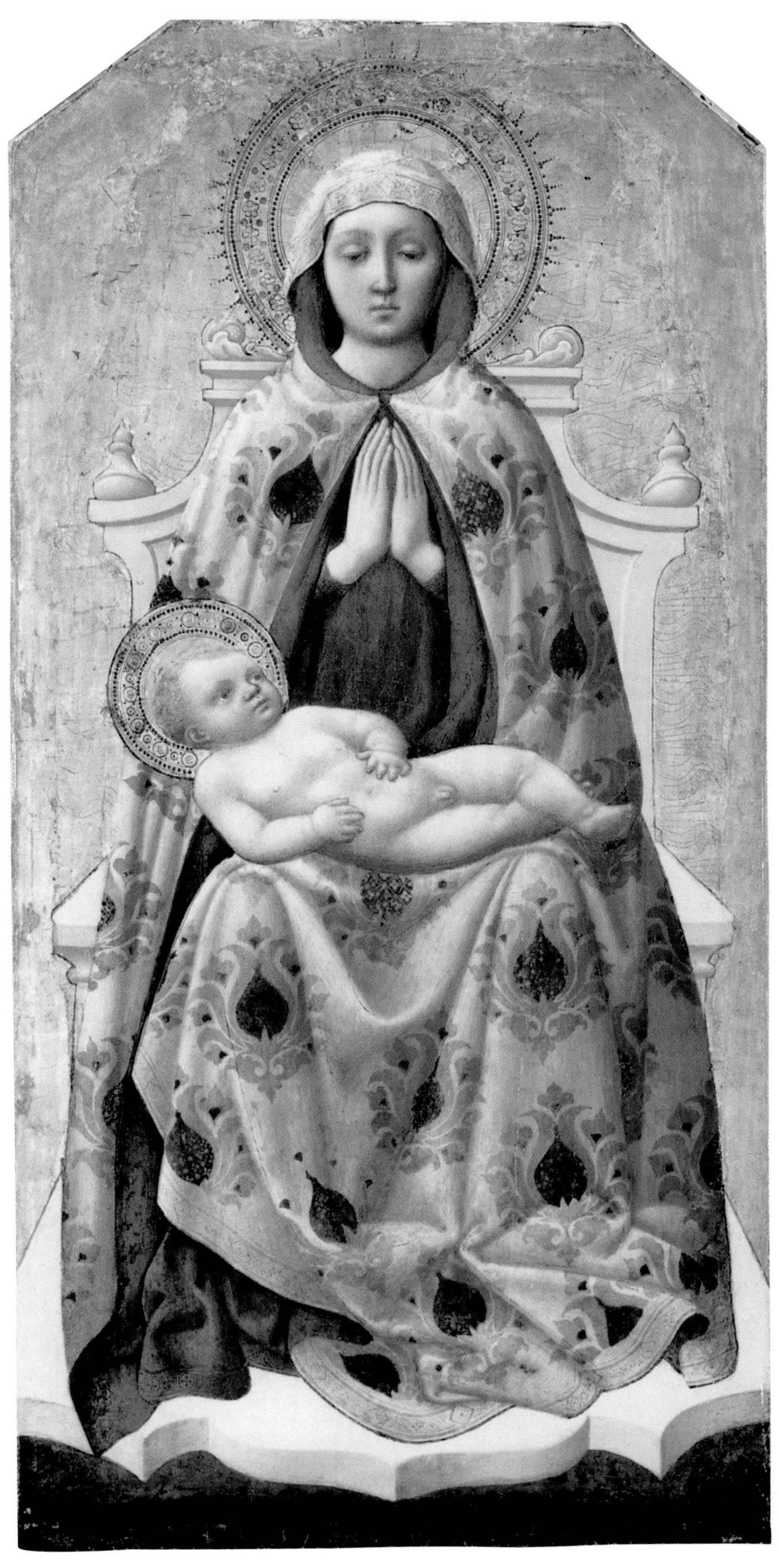

Fig. 224 Antonio Vivarini: *Virgin and Child*. The Museum of Fine Arts, Houston, The Edith A. and Percy S. Straus Collection, 44.575.

ZAGANELLI, BERNARDINO DI BOSIO, 1460/70–1510/2; ATTRIBUTED; ROMAGNOL

Virgin and Child Enthroned with St. Michael, St. Catherine of Alexandria, St. Cecilia, and St. Jerome (78.1)

25.1 X 20.3 CM, OIL ON PANEL

HOUSTON, TEXAS. THE MUSEUM OF FINE ARTS, HOUSTON

The attribution of this personal devotional image is uncertain. Philip Pouncey (1977) assigned it to either Bernardino or Francesco Zaganelli (c. 1470–c. 1532), dating it to the early 1490s. Andrea Ugolini (1991), Andrea De Marchi (1994), and Raffaella Zama (1994) gave it to Bernardino's pupil Girolamo Marchesi (1471/81–1540/50). Carolyn C. Wilson (1996) emphasized stylistic affinities with Bernardino's signed *St. Sebastian* (National Gallery, London; 1092) of c. 1505–1506, his *Madonna and Child with Mary Magdalen and St. Catherine* (private collection, Turin), and his *Penitent Magdalen in the Wilderness* (Musée du Petit Palais, Avignon; 20214). She noted, however, that the Houston panel might represent the collaboration of Bernardino and Girolamo and be dated c. 1506–1512.

Wilson observed that the composition of this small painting reflects a format used in monumental Ferrarese altarpieces, in which the Madonna is elevated on an elaborate throne, silhouetted against a landscape, and accompanied by saints. Wilson also noted that the Madonna and Child emulate figures by Perugino (c. 1450–1523), for example, those found in his altarpieces for Santa Maria Nuova, Fano (*in situ*), and for Santa Maria delle Grazie, Senigallia (Palazzo Comunale).

PROVENANCE

Private collection, Switzerland, to 1977; Sotheby, Parke-Bernet and Co., London, April 6, 1977, lot 9A; Julius H. Weitzner, London; The Museum of Fine Arts, Houston, acquired 1977

BIBLIOGRAPHY

Philip Pouncey, "Saleroom Discoveries: An Unknown Zaganelli," *Burlington Magazine* 119 (1977): 376, 379; *The Museum of Fine Arts, Houston: A Guide to the Collection* (Houston: Museum of Fine Arts, 1981), 30-31, no. 56; Peter C. Marzio, *A Permanent Legacy: 150 Works from the Collection of the Museum of Fine Arts, Houston* (New York: Hudson Hills Press, 1989), 118; Giovanni Romano, ed., *Da Biduino ad Algardi: Pittura e scultura a confronto* (Turin: U. Allemandi, 1990), 113; Andrea Ugolini, "Per Gerolamo Marchesi: Della 'concezione' di Pesaro alla 'Madonna in gloria' di Lugo," *Arte Cristiana* 80 (1991): 27; Andrea De Marchi, "Bernardino Zaganelli inedito: Due 'Facies Christi'," *Prospettiva* 75-76 (1994): 129, 134 n. 32; Raffaella Zama, *Gli Zaganelli: Francesco e Bernardino, pittori: Catalogo generale* (Rimini: Luisè, 1994), 27, 29; Carolyn C. Wilson, *Italian Paintings XIV–XVI Centuries in the Museum of Fine Arts, Houston* (Houston: Museum of Fine Arts, 1996), 282-89; Edgar Peters Bowron and Mary G. Morton, *Masterworks of European Painting in the Museum of Fine Arts, Houston* (Princeton: Princeton University Press, 2000), 26-28.

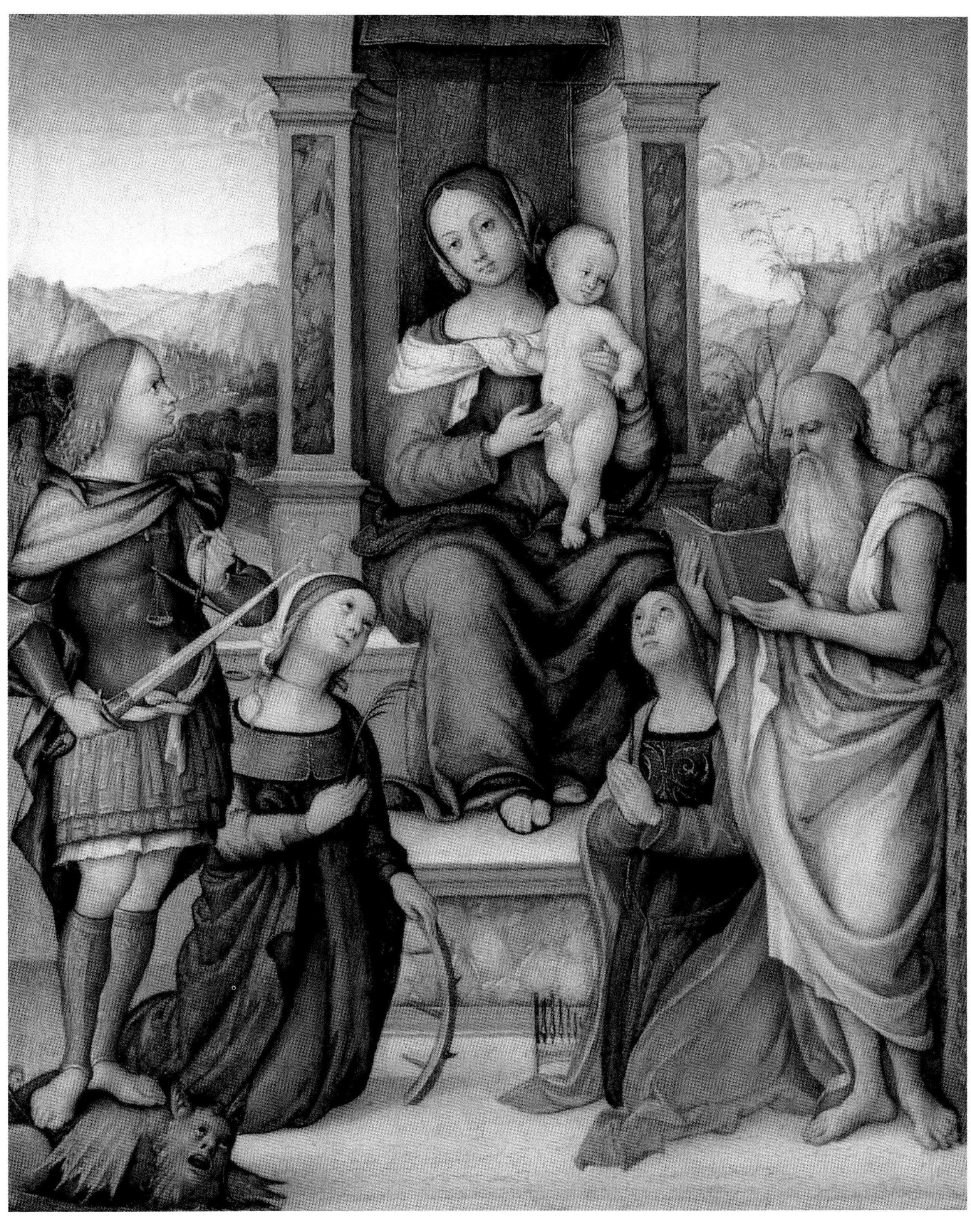

Fig. 225 Bernardino di Bosio Zaganelli (attributed): *Virgin and Child Enthroned with St. Michael, St. Catherine of Alexandria, St. Cecilia, and St. Jerome.* The Museum of Fine Arts, Houston; Gift of Alice Hanszen, 78.1.

BARTOLOMEO VENETO, ACTIVE 1502; DIED 1531; VENETIAN

Portrait of a Lady (1984.26) 57.5 X 44.5 CM, OIL ON PANEL

HOUSTON, TEXAS. SARAH CAMPBELL BLAFFER FOUNDATION

Donald Garstang (1984) dated the work to the 1520s. Laura Pagnotta (1997) placed it a few years earlier, 1518–1520, on the basis of artistic style and the clothing worn by the sitter. The portrait resembles Bartolomeo's *Lady Playing a Lute as St. Cecilia* (Isabella Stewart Gardner Museum, Boston), dated 1520. Another version of the Houston portrait, in which the sitter casts a shadow to the right, is in the Brooklyn Museum of Art (21.79).

Clovis Whitfield (1982) identified the sitter as Cecilia Gallerani (born 1473/4), a mistress of Duke Ludovico il Moro, on the basis of her resemblance to the woman in Leonardo's *Lady with an Ermine* (Czartoryski Museum, Cracow; 180) of c. 1483. He suggested that attributes associated with the Magdalen may have been added to the painting, at the sitter's request, after Ludovico's death in 1508. Patricia Rubin (1982) argued against the identification, noting that the panel is an allegorical portrayal of a woman in the guise of a saint, one of many such works painted by Bartolomeo. The jar, the age and melancholic expression of the sitter, and the modesty of the clothing, in comparison with garments in other portraits by the artist, may be associated with the penitent Magdalen and perhaps refer to the sitter's name. Pagnotta considered the work to be a portrait of a reformed courtesan, perhaps Cecilia Gallerani, citing the execution of the veil in yellow, a color used to distinguish prostitutes in the sixteenth century.

PROVENANCE

Count Paolo Thaon de Revel, Turin, by c. 1800; private collection, Turin; P. & D. Colnaghi, Ltd., London, acquired 1982; Sarah Campbell Blaffer Foundation, acquired 1984

BIBLIOGRAPHY

Clovis Whitfield, *Discoveries from the Cinquecento* (London: Colnaghi & Co., 1982), 8, no. 3; Patricia Rubin, "London, Cinquecento at Colgnaghi's [*sic*]," *Burlington Magazine* 124 (1982): 645; Donald Garstang, ed., *Art, Commerce, Scholarship: A Window into the Art World, Colnaghi 1760 to 1984* (London: Colnaghi, 1984), 66, no. 2; Terisio Pignatti, *Five Centuries of Italian Painting, 1300–1800: From the Collection of the Sarah Campbell Blaffer Foundation* (Houston: Sarah Campbell Blaffer Foundation, 1985), 76; Anne C. Junkerman, "*Bellissima donna*: An Interdisciplinary Study of Venetian Sensuous Half-Length Images of the Early Sixteenth Century" (Ph.D. diss., University of California, Berkeley, 1988), 460, no. 7; Laura Pagnotta, *Bartolomeo Veneto: L'opera completa* (Florence: Centro Di, 1997), 93, 213-14, no. 27.

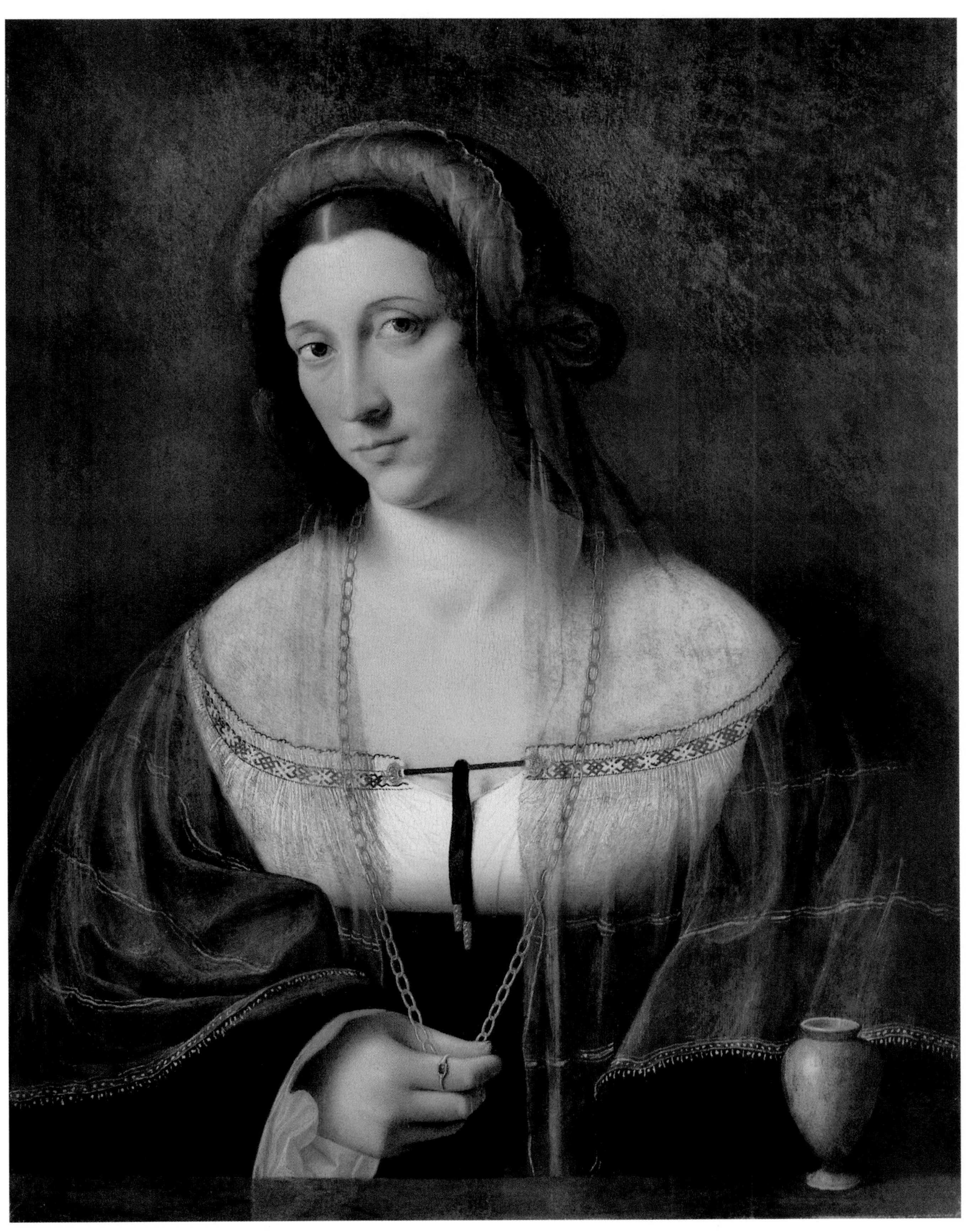

Fig. 226 Bartolomeo Veneto: *Portrait of a Lady*. Sarah Campbell Blaffer Foundation, Houston, Texas, 1984.26.

BERTUCCI, GIOVANNI BATTISTA, I, C. 1465–1516; FAVENTINE

St. John the Evangelist (1978.22) 129.5 X 53.5 CM, TEMPERA ON PANEL

HOUSTON, TEXAS. SARAH CAMPBELL BLAFFER FOUNDATION

Exhibited in 1886 at the Royal Academy, London, as a work of the Roman School, the panel was reattributed to Giovanni Bertucci when displayed at the Burlington Fine Arts Club in 1906 (according to Carolyn C. Wilson 1996). Martin Davies (1951) identified it as the right wing of an altarpiece that had the *Madonna and Child in Glory* (National Gallery, London; 282) as its central panel and *St. Thomas Aquinas* (Museum of Fine Arts, Houston; 64.34) as its left wing. The three works have identical parapets, and the edges of their marble floors are treated in a similar fashion; in addition, each of the adult figures holds a lily, symbolizing chastity. Davies associated the reconstructed altarpiece with the documented polyptych commissioned from Bertucci on 21 April 1512 by Sister Clarice Mandredi of the Third Order of St. Dominic. The polyptych was intended for the Chapel of St. Thomas Aquinas in the Dominican church of San Andrea in Vineis, Faenza, and it was completed by the time of the artist's death, in 1516.

PROVENANCE

Chapel of St. Thomas Aquinas, San Andrea in Vineis, Faenza, to 1759 (?); Hercolani family, Bologna, by 1770–after 1828; Count Cini, Rome; Lord Aldenham, acquired 1846; Sotheby's, London, February 24, 1937, lot 123; Jacob M. Heimann, New York, by 1949; Central Casino, Inc., New York; Sarah Campbell Blaffer Foundation, acquired 1966

BIBLIOGRAPHY

Giovanni G. Bottari and Stefano Ticozzi, *Raccolta di lettere sulla pittura, scultura ed architettura scritte da' più celebri personaggi dei secoli XV, XVI, e XVII* (Milan: G. Silvestri, 1822), 103-4; Carlo Grigioni, *La pittura faentina dalle origini alla metà del Cinquecento* (Faenza: Fratelli Lega, 1936), 294, 315; Martin Davies, *The Earlier Italian Schools* (London: National Gallery, 1951), 182-83; *The Museum of Fine Arts, Houston: A Guide to the Collection* (Houston: Museum of Fine Arts, 1981), 40, no. 75; Terisio Pignatti, *Five Centuries of Italian Painting, 1300–1800: From the Collection of the Sarah Campbell Blaffer Foundation* (Houston: Sarah Campbell Blaffer Foundation, 1985), 68; Carolyn C. Wilson, *Italian Paintings XIV–XVI Centuries in the Museum of Fine Arts, Houston* (Houston: Museum of Fine Arts, 1996), 293-96.

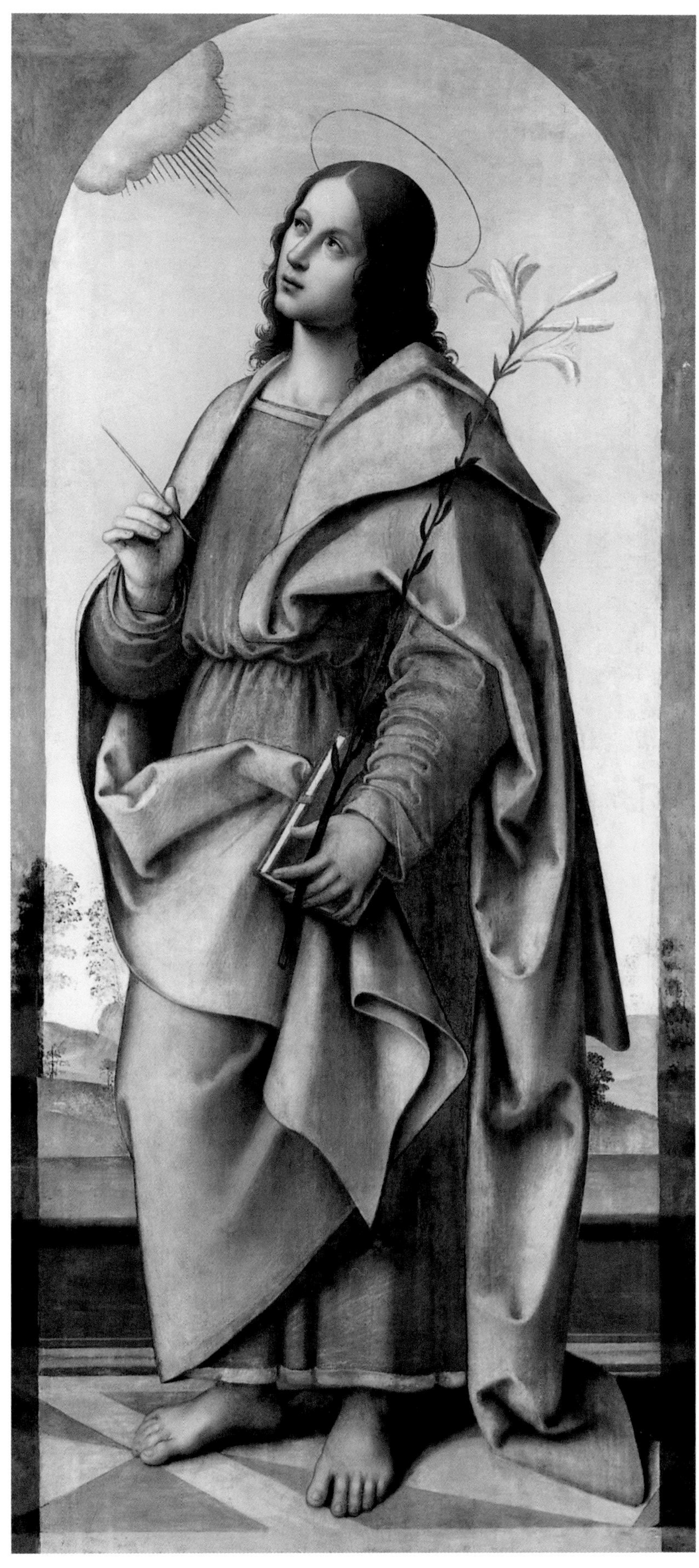

Fig. 227 Giovanni Battista Bertucci I: *St. John the Evangelist*. Sarah Campbell Blaffer Foundation, Houston, Texas, 1978.22.

BOTTICELLI, SANDRO, 1444/5–1510; FLORENTINE

Adoration of the Christ Child (1974.2) 120.7 CM (DIAMETER), TEMPERA ON PANEL

HOUSTON, TEXAS. SARAH CAMPBELL BLAFFER FOUNDATION

Scholars have debated the attribution of the *tondo*. Geza de Francovich (1927) assigned it to Bastiano Mainardi (1466–1513). Raimond van Marle (1931) endorsed this opinion, but R. Langton Douglas (1945; 1946) identified the panel as the work of Piero di Cosimo (1462–1521). Everett P. Fahy (cited in Pignatti 1985) and Laurence B. Kanter (cited in Jeromack 1996) considered it to be an autograph, late work by Botticelli. The Foundation dates it c. 1500.

The Adoration of the Shepherds appears to the right of the Holy Family. The Flight into Egypt is in the background. A sleeping Christ Child is seldom seen in Florentine painting, and this example is unique within Botticelli's oeuvre. The implication that Christ will awaken, an allusion to his victory over death, would have encouraged the worshipper's hopes regarding his or her own salvation and resurrection.

PROVENANCE

Quincy Adams Shaw, Boston; Duveen Brothers, New York, c. 1922–1942; Norton Simon Foundation, Pasadena; Sarah Campbell Blaffer Foundation, acquired 1974

BIBLIOGRAPHY

Geza de Francovich, "Sebastiano Mainardi," *Cronache d'Arte* 4 (1927): 182; Raimond van Marle, *The Development of the Italian Schools of Painting*, vol. 3, *The Florentine School of the Fourteenth Century* (The Hague: M. Nijhoff, 1931), 196; R. Langton Douglas, "*The Fall of Man* by Piero di Cosimo," *Burlington Magazine* 86 (1945): 137; R. Langton Douglas, *Piero di Cosimo* (Chicago: University of Chicago Press, 1946), 22, 44, 50-51, 65-66, 86-87, 114, 140; Terisio Pignatti, *Five Centuries of Italian Painting, 1300–1800: From the Collection of the Sarah Campbell Blaffer Foundation* (Houston: Sarah Campbell Blaffer Foundation, 1985), 40-42; Paul Jeromack, "Just Another Ficherelli . . . or a Unique Early Vermeer?" *Art News* 95 (1996): 130; Laurence B. Kanter, Hilliard T. Goldfarb, and James Hankins, *Botticelli's Witness: Changing Style in a Changing Florence* (Boston: Isabella Stewart Gardner Museum, 1997), 40.

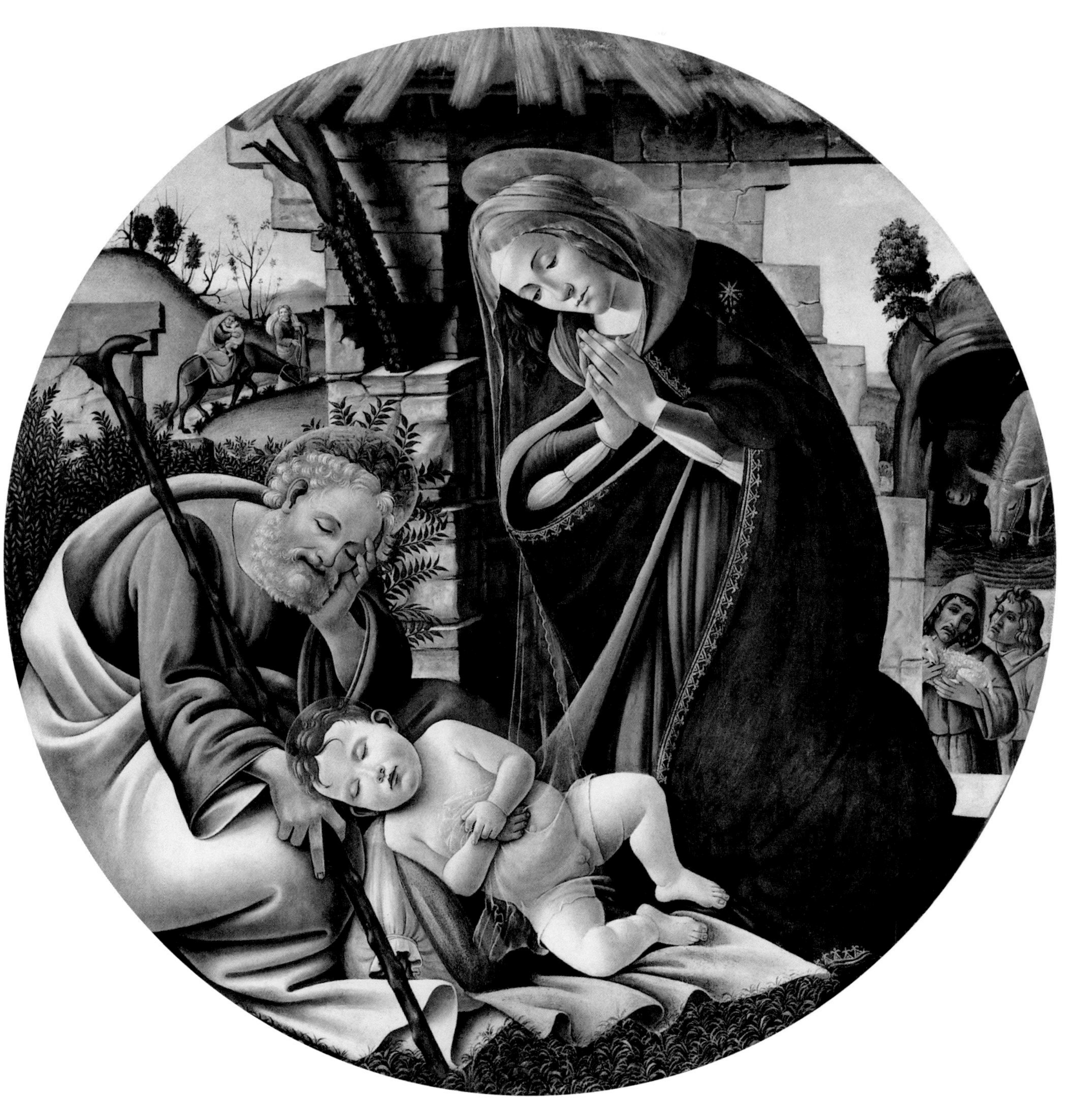

Fig. 228 Sandro Botticelli: *Adoration of the Christ Child*. Sarah Campbell Blaffer Foundation, Houston, Texas, 1974.2.

DADDI, BERNARDO, ACTIVE C. 1280–1348; FLORENTINE

Madonna and Child (1979.21) 90.2 X 50.8 CM, TEMPERA ON PANEL

HOUSTON, TEXAS. SARAH CAMPBELL BLAFFER FOUNDATION

Attributed by Bernard Berenson (1931) to Bernardo Daddi, the painting was reassigned to the artist's workshop by Richard Offner (1934). It was originally the central panel of an unidentified polyptych, which probably was similar in appearance to Daddi's *San Pancrazio Altarpiece* (Uffizi, Florence; 8345) of c. 1336. The Christ Child holds a goldfinch, which symbolizes his Passion.

PROVENANCE

Manfred, Count von Ingenheim, Ober-Rengersdorf, Germany; Duveen Brothers, New York; Norton Simon Foundation, Pasadena; Sarah Campbell Blaffer Foundation, acquired 1979

BIBLIOGRAPHY

Bernard Berenson, "Quadri senza casa: Il Trecento fiorentino, I," *Dedalo* 11 (1931): 973, 978; Richard Offner, *A Critical and Historical Corpus of Florentine Painting*, sec. 3, vol. 4, *Bernardo Daddi, His Shop and Following* (New York: College of Fine Arts, New York University, 1934), 118; Herbert Friedmann, *The Symbolic Goldfinch, Its History and Significance in European Devotional Art* (New York: Pantheon Books, 1946), 71-72, 143; Terisio Pignatti, *Five Centuries of Italian Painting, 1300–1800: From the Collection of the Sarah Campbell Blaffer Foundation* (Houston: Sarah Campbell Blaffer Foundation, 1985), 26; Richard Offner, *A Critical and Historical Corpus of Florentine Painting: The Fourteenth Century*, sec. 3, vol. 3, *The Works of Bernardo Daddi*, ed. Miklòs Boskovits (Florence: Giunti, 1989), 81, 150; Mojmír S. Frinta, *Punched Decoration on Late Medieval Panel and Miniature Painting*, pt. 1 (Prague: Maxdorf, 1998), 382, 411.

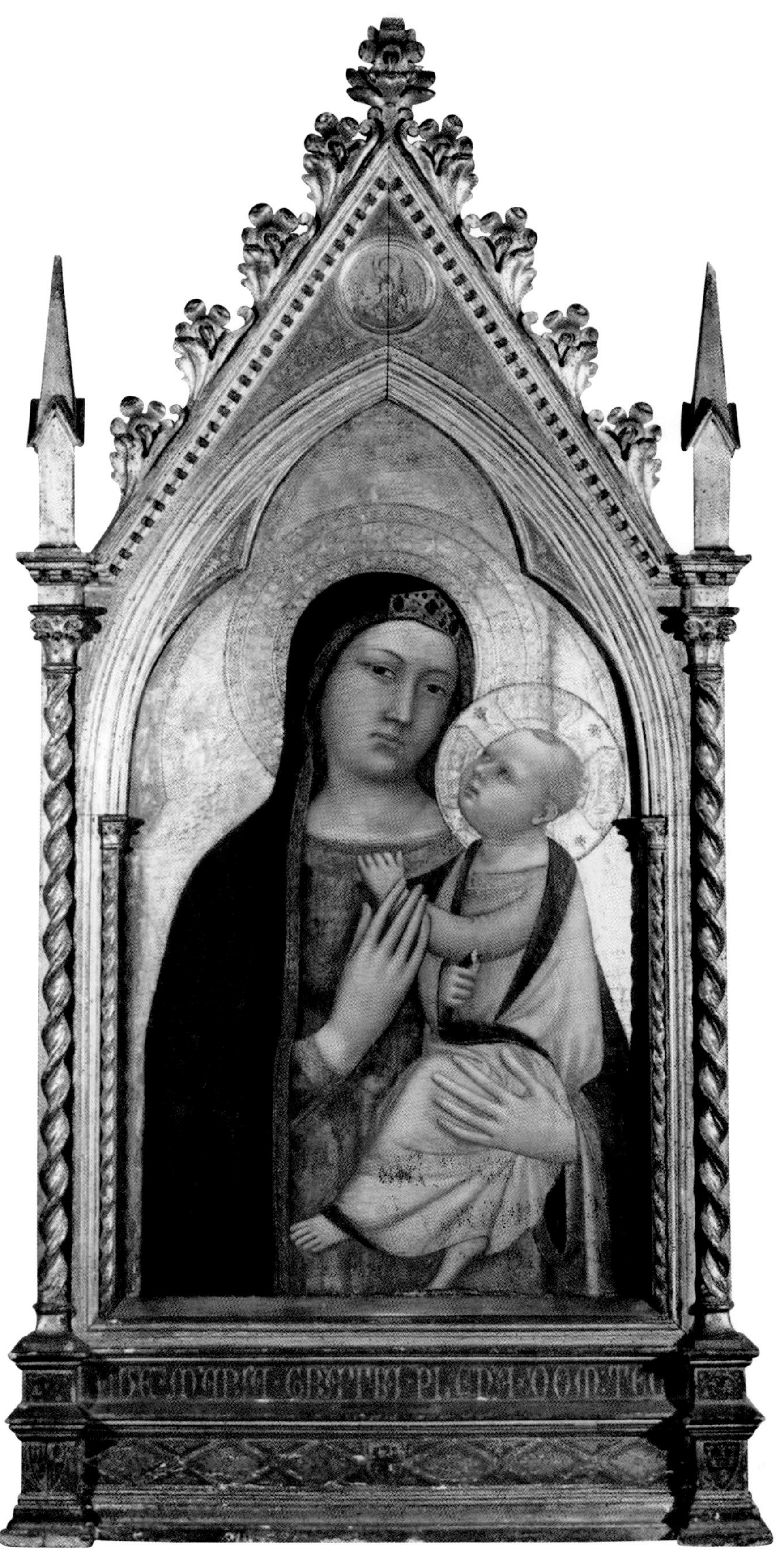

Fig. 229 Bernardo Daddi: *Madonna and Child*. Sarah Campbell Blaffer Foundation, Houston, Texas, 1979.21.

MANTEGNA, ANDREA, C. 1431–1506; PADUAN; COPY

Descent into Limbo (1979.17) 71.1 X 55.9 CM, OIL AND TEMPERA ON PANEL

HOUSTON, TEXAS. SARAH CAMPBELL BLAFFER FOUNDATION

Giuseppe Fiocco (1937) published the panel as the work of Mantegna, attributing the landscape background to Correggio (c. 1489–1534). Most scholars, with the notable exception of Terisio Pignatti (1985), rejected Fiocco's opinion while recognizing that the composition was mirrored in drawings and prints depicting the Descent associated with Mantegna. Jay A. Levenson, Konrad Oberhuber, and Jacquelyn L. Sheehan (1973) considered the painting to be a copy of a lost drawing by Mantegna. Keith Christiansen (in Martineau and Boorsch 1992) identified the Houston panel as one of two, perhaps contemporary, painted copies of a much admired work by Mantegna, the *Descent into Limbo* (Barbara Piasecka Johnson Collection, Princeton, N.J.) of c. 1492; the larger, weaker copy is in Bologna (Pinacoteca Nazionale; 268).

Christ's descent into Limbo, which followed his death and preceded his resurrection, was first recounted in early Christian apocryphal literature and was transmitted to late medieval and Renaissance readers by Jacobus de Voragine's *Golden Legend*. The devils and the splintered gates of Hell that usually appear in Italian depictions of the event have been eliminated by Mantegna. The identities of the figures whom Christ is liberating are not readily apparent, but the group on the left surely includes Adam and Eve.

PROVENANCE

Count Valier, Asolo, Italy; Cecil Amelia Blaffer Foundation; Sarah Campbell Blaffer Foundation, acquired 1979

BIBLIOGRAPHY

Giuseppe Fiocco, *Mantegna* (Milan: U. Hoepli, 1937), 77; Erika Tietze-Conrat, *Mantegna: Paintings, Drawings, Engravings* (London: Phaidon Press, 1955), 198; Giovanni Paccagnini, *Andrea Mantegna* (Milan: Silvana, 1961), 169, 175; Maria Bellonci and Nina Garavaglia, *L'opera completa del Mantegna* (Milan: Rizzoli, 1967), 98, no. 34; Jay A. Levenson, Konrad Oberhuber, and Jacquelyn L. Sheehan, *Early Italian Engravings from the National Gallery of Art* (Washington, D.C.: National Gallery of Art, 1973), 208; Terisio Pignatti, *Five Centuries of Italian Painting, 1300–1800: From the Collection of the Sarah Campbell Blaffer Foundation* (Houston: Sarah Campbell Blaffer Foundation, 1985), 58-61; Jane Martineau and Suzanne Boorsch, eds., *Andrea Mantegna* (Milan: Electa, 1992), 269-71; Umberto Baldini, Valter Curzi, and Cecilia Prete, *Andrea Mantegna* (Florence: Edizioni d'arte Il Fiorino, 1997), 255.

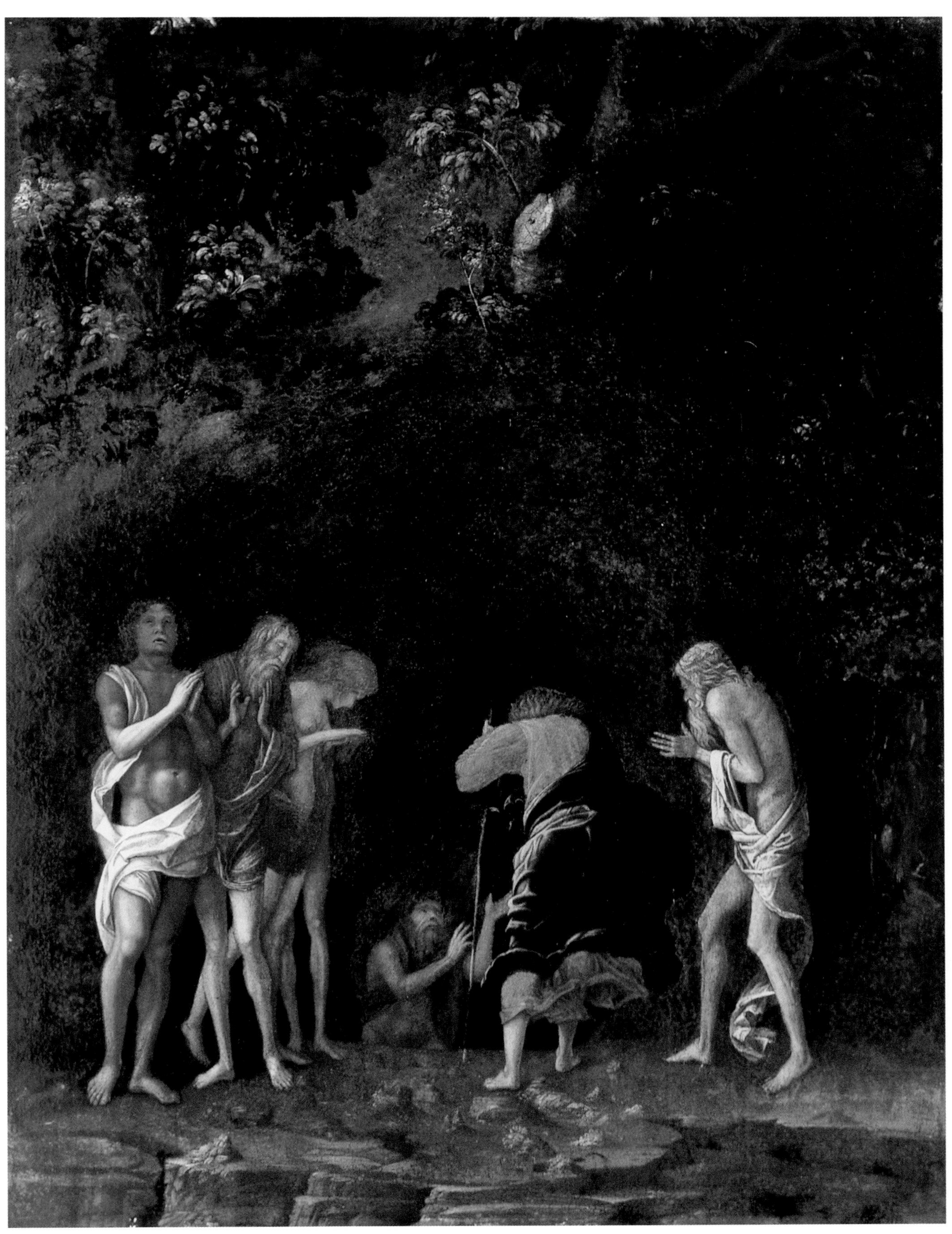

Fig. 230 Andrea Mantegna (copy): *Descent into Limbo*. Sarah Campbell Blaffer Foundation, Houston, Texas, 1979.17.

MASTER OF THE PALA SFORZESCA, ACTIVE C. 1490–C. 1500; MILANESE

Madonna and Child with St. Roch and a Donor (1983.3) 86.4 X 68 CM, OIL ON PANEL

HOUSTON, TEXAS. SARAH CAMPBELL BLAFFER FOUNDATION

The artist responsible for this votive painting is the Milanese follower of Leonardo known as the Master of the Pala Sforzesca, whose eponymous work is in the Brera, Milan. Woldemar von Seidlitz (1906) identified this master as Ambrogio de' Predis (c. 1455–after 1508), Bernard Berenson (1907) as Bernardino de' Conti (c. 1470–c. 1522). The relationship of the supplicant to both the saint and the Christ Child closely recalls that of Ludovico Sforza to St. Louis of Toulouse and to the Christ Child in the *Pala Sforzesca*. Martin Davies (1961) considered the Houston work to be close in style to the master's *Madonna and Child with Saints and Donors* (National Gallery, London; 4444), which he dated c. 1490.

Considered one of the primary protectors of the sick, St. Roch is depicted as an intercessor for the unidentified supplicant, who either hopes to be spared infection or gives thanks for his escape. The Virgin's face and posture derive from Leonardo's Madonna in the *Virgin of the Rocks* (Louvre, Paris; 777) of 1483–1486. Terisio Pignatti (1985) noted that a silverpoint drawing for the Houston Madonna is in the British Museum, London (128); at one time the drawing was attributed to Leonardo.

PROVENANCE

G. Cora, Turin and Florence; P. & D. Colnaghi, Ltd., London; Sarah Campbell Blaffer Foundation, acquired 1983

BIBLIOGRAPHY

Francesco Malaguzzi Valeri, "Il Maestro della Pala Sforzesca," *Rassegna d'Arte* 5 (1905): 46; Woldemar von Seidlitz, *Ambrogio Preda und Leonardo da Vinci* (Vienna: Tempsky; Leipzig: Freytag, 1906), 3; Bernard Berenson, *North Italian Painters of the Renaissance* (New York: G. P. Putnam's Sons, 1907), 199; Francesco Malaguzzi Valeri, *Catalogo della R. Pinacoteca di Brera* (Bergamo: Istituto italiano d'Arti Grafiche, 1908), 206; Adolfo Venturi, *Storia dell'arte italiana*, vol. 7/iv, *La pittura del Quattrocento* (Milan: U. Hoepli, 1915), 1043-44; William Suida, *Leonardo und sein Kreis* (Munich: F. Bruckmann, 1929), 182; "Meister des Pala Sforzesca," in *Allgemeines Lexikon der bildenden Künstler von der Antike bis zur Gegenwart*, ed. Ulrich Thieme and Felix Becker, 37 vols. (Leipzig: E. A. Seemann, 1950), 37:262; Martin Davies, *The Earlier Italian Schools* (London: National Gallery, 1961), 369; Bernard Berenson, *Italian Pictures of the Renaissance: A List of the Principal Artists and Their Works with an Index of Places. Central Italian and North Italian Schools*, 3 vols. (London: Phaidon Press, 1968), 1:256; Terisio Pignatti, *Five Centuries of Italian Painting, 1300–1800: From the Collection of the Sarah Campbell Blaffer Foundation* (Houston: Sarah Campbell Blaffer Foundation, 1985), 71-72; Kendall Curlee, *The Sforza Court: Milan in the Renaissance, 1450–1535* (Austin, Tex.: Archer M. Huntington Art Gallery, University of Texas at Austin, 1988), 18, no. 4; Mina Gregori, ed., *Pittura in Brianza e in Valsassina: Dall'alto medioevo al neoclassicismo* (Milan: Cassa di risparmio delle provincie Lombarde, 1993), 256-57; Pietro C. Marani, "The Master of the Pala Sforzesca," in *The Legacy of Leonardo: Painters in Lombardy 1490–1530* (Milan: Skira Editore, 1998), 180, 182.

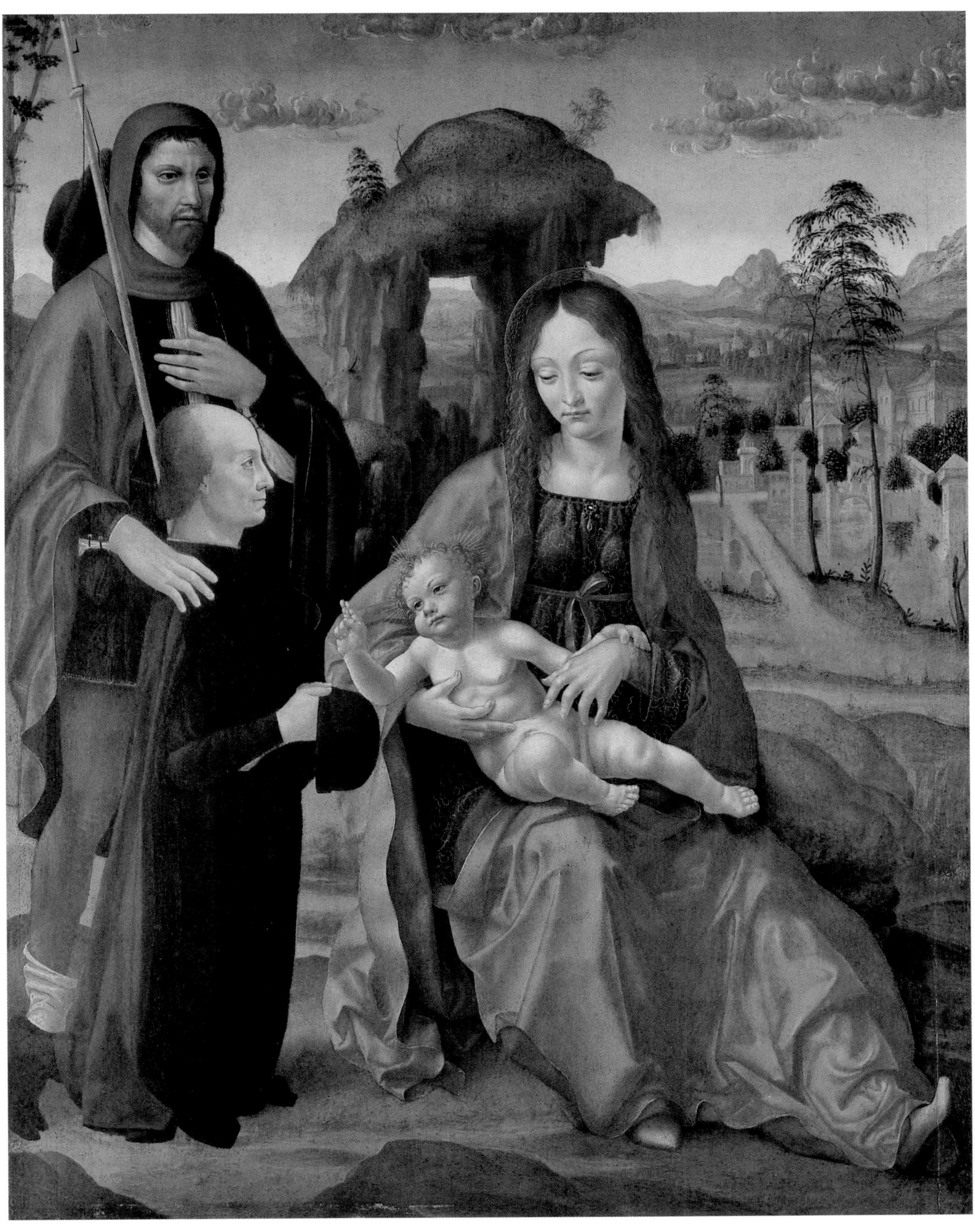

Fig. 231 Master of the Pala Sforzesca: *Madonna and Child with St. Roch and a Donor*. Sarah Campbell Blaffer Foundation, Houston, Texas, 1983.3.

PINTURICCHIO, BERNARDINO, C. 1452–1513; UMBRIAN

Madonna and Child with St. John the Baptist and St. Sebastian (1979.27) 29.2 X 21.6 CM, TEMPERA ON PANEL

HOUSTON, TEXAS. SARAH CAMPBELL BLAFFER FOUNDATION

Inscribed on the triumphal arch, between the reliefs beneath its coffered vault, are the Roman numerals "MCDLXXXXII" (1492). Since the time of its original publication (in Evelyn M. Phillipps 1901), this small personal devotional panel, remarkable for its minute, naturalistic detail, has been accepted as an autograph work of Pinturicchio. Sabine Poeschel (1999) was alone in assigning it to the artist's workshop. The authenticity of the inscribed date, misread by Adolfo Venturi (1913) as 1497, is supported by the comparability of the style of the painting to that of the artist's frescoes in the Borgia Apartment in the Vatican Palace, from 1492–1494.

The Virgin nurses the Christ Child, signifying his humanity and the spiritual nourishment provided by the Church. The penitent St. John appears in the background, along with a representation of St. Sebastian's martyrdom.

PROVENANCE

Prince Pio Falcò of Savoy, Mombello, Como, Italy; Spencer A. Samuels & Co., New York; Cecil Amelia Blaffer Foundation; Sarah Campbell Blaffer Foundation, acquired 1979

BIBLIOGRAPHY

Evelyn M. Phillipps, *Pintoricchio* (London: G. Bell, 1901), 157; Corrado Ricci, *Pintoricchio (Bernardino di Betto of Perugia), His Life, Work, and Time* (London: William Heinemann; Philadelphia: J. B. Lippincott Co., 1902), 151-52; Adolfo Venturi, *Storia dell'arte italiana*, vol. 7/ii, *La pittura del Quattrocento* (Milan: U. Hoepli, 1913), 661; Umberto Gnoli, *Pittori e miniatori nell'Umbria* (Spoleto: C. Argentieri, 1923), 296; Bernard Berenson, *Italian Pictures of the Renaissance* (Oxford: Clarendon Press, 1932), 459; Raimond van Marle, *The Development of the Italian Schools of Painting*, vol. 14, *The Renaissance Painters of Umbria* (The Hague: M. Nijhoff, 1933), 287; Bernard Berenson, *Italian Pictures of the Renaissance: A List of the Principal Artists and Their Works with an Index of Places. Central Italian and North Italian Schools*, 3 vols. (London: Phaidon Press, 1968), 1:344; Terisio Pignatti, *Five Centuries of Italian Painting, 1300–1800: From the Collection of the Sarah Campbell Blaffer Foundation* (Houston: Sarah Campbell Blaffer Foundation, 1985), 64-66; Filippo Todini, *La pittura umbra: Dal Duecento al primo Cinquecento*, 2 vols. (Milan: Longanesi & Co., 1989), 1:290-91; Michael J. Miller, "A Madonna and Child from Pintoricchio's Sienese Period," *The Bulletin of the Cleveland Museum of Art* 78 (1991): 332-34; Cristina Acidini Luchinat, *Pintoricchio* (Florence: Scala, 1999), 28; Sabine Poeschel, *Alexander Maximus: Das Bildprogramm des Appartamento Borgia im Vatikan* (Weimar: Verlag und Datenbank für Geisteswissenschaften, 1999), 141.

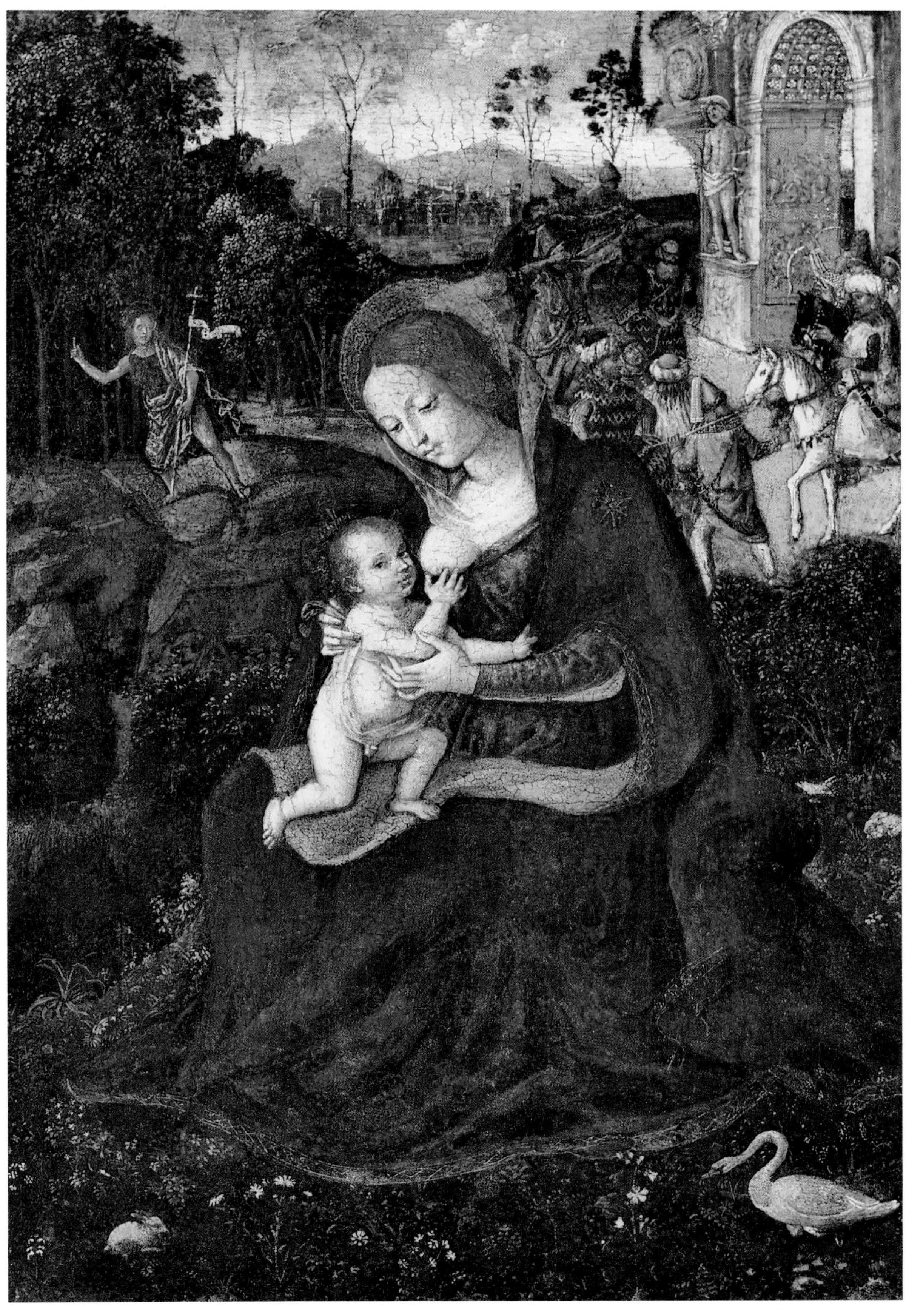

Fig. 232 Bernardino Pinturicchio: *Madonna and Child with St. John the Baptist and St. Sebastian*. Sarah Campbell Blaffer Foundation, Houston, Texas, 1979.27.

ANDREA DI BARTOLO, ACTIVE BY 1389; DIED 1428; SIENESE

Annunciation (C.133) 47.5 X 45 CM, TEMPERA ON PANEL

JACKSONVILLE, FLORIDA. THE CUMMER MUSEUM OF ART & GARDENS

The painting was attributed tentatively to Andrea di Bartolo by Millard Meiss, who dated it c. 1390 (Museum files). The punchwork and figure style relate it to Andrea's *Annunciation* on the spandrels of the *Madonna and Child Enthroned with Fourteen Saints* (Yale University Art Museum, New Haven; 43.248); his *Archangel Gabriel* (current location unknown; formerly, Belle da Costa Greene, New York) and *Annunciate Angel* (Pushkin Museum, Moscow); and his *Angel and Virgin Annunciate* (private collection, Milan).

The shape, size, and subject matter of the painting suggest that it was originally part of the superstructure of a polyptych, located above a central panel with the Madonna and Child and crowned with a pinnacle; a comparable arrangement is found in Andrea Vanni's altarpiece for Santo Stefano alla Lizza, Siena, of c. 1400. The use of ultramarine, an expensive pigment, for the Virgin's mantle implies that the Cummer panel was part of a major commission.

PROVENANCE

Arcade Gallery, London, 1956; Mrs. Ninah M. H. Cummer, Jacksonville, Fla., acquired 1956; The Cummer Museum of Art & Gardens (Cummer Gallery of Art), acquired 1958

BIBLIOGRAPHY

Cummer Gallery of Art, *Catalogue of Paintings and Other Art Objects* (Jacksonville, Fla.: Cummer Gallery of Art, 1962), 52; Federico Zeri, "Da Spinello a Andrea di Bartolo," *Diario di lavoro I* (Bergamo: Emblema, 1971), 31-32; Burton B. Fredericksen and Federico Zeri, *Census of Pre-Nineteenth-Century Italian Paintings in North American Public Collections* (Cambridge, Mass.: Harvard University Press, 1972), 6, 588; Miklòs Boskovits, ed., *Dipinti italiani del XIV e XV secolo in una raccolta milanese: Catalogo* (Milan: Silvana, 1987), 44-46.

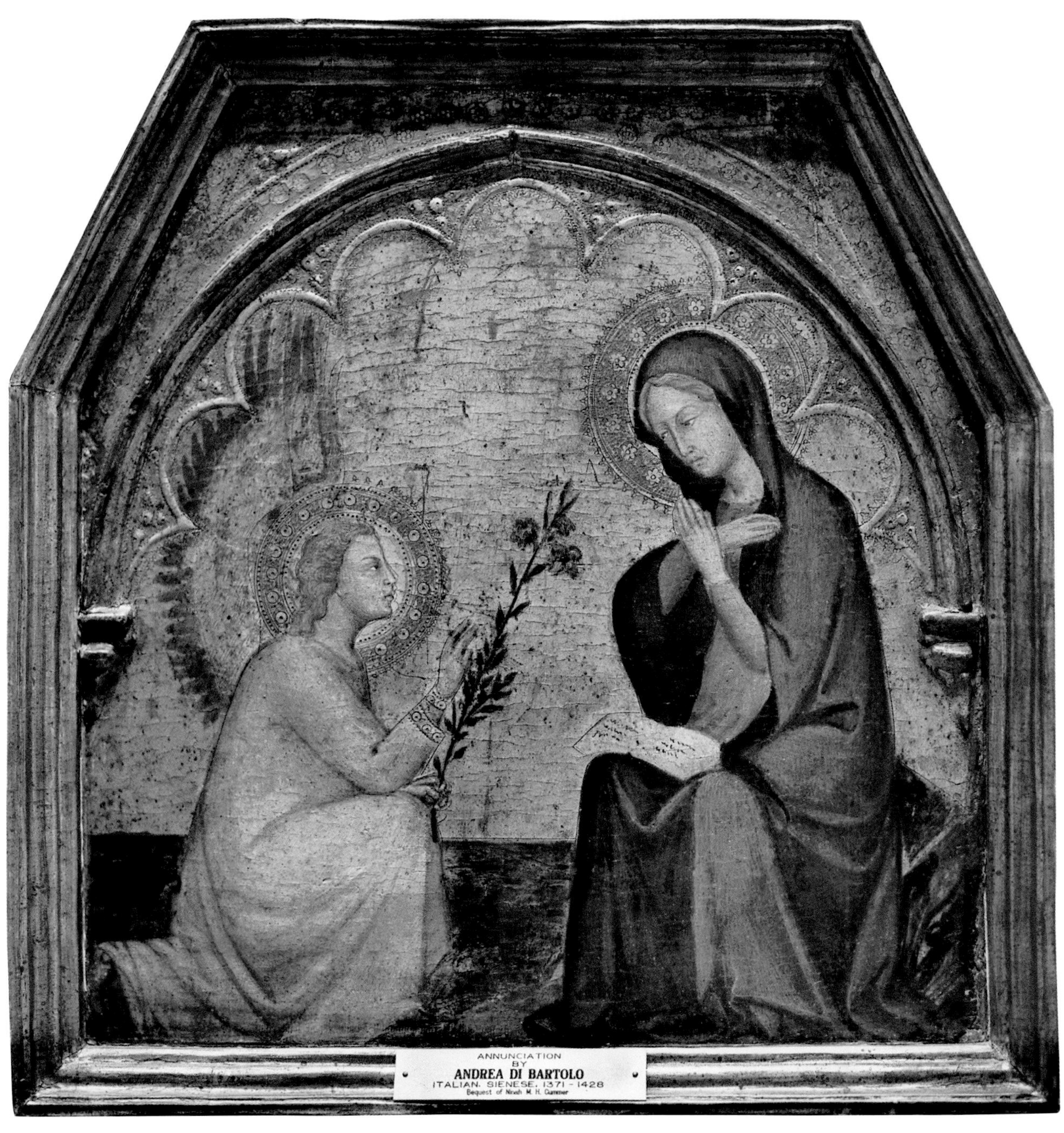

Fig. 233 Andrea di Bartolo: *Annunciation*. The Cummer Museum of Art & Gardens, Jacksonville, Florida, C.133.

BATTISTA DA VICENZA, C. 1404–1438; VICENZAN

St. Bartholomew (C.139.1); *Apostle Saint* (C.139.2) 18.7 X 13 CM (EACH), TEMPERA ON PANEL

JACKSONVILLE, FLORIDA. THE CUMMER MUSEUM OF ART & GARDENS

These small paintings were probably part of a series of Apostle portraits on the pinnacles of a large, unidentified polyptych. Attributed to Battista da Vicenza by William E. Suida (Museum files), they are comparable in style to the artist's sixteen pinnacle panels (Museo Civico, Vicenza; A20a–c, A22a–c) from his polyptych depicting St. John the Baptist for the Cathedral of Vicenza, c. 1395.

PROVENANCE

Alphonse L. Lovencon, New York, 1936; Mr. and Mrs. Arthur Gerrish Cummer, Jacksonville, Fla., 1936–1943; Mrs. Ninah M. H. Cummer, Jacksonville, Fla., 1943–1958; The Cummer Museum of Art & Gardens (Cummer Gallery of Art), acquired 1958

BIBLIOGRAPHY

Cummer Gallery of Art, *Catalogue of Paintings and Other Art Objects* (Jacksonville, Fla.: Cummer Gallery of Art, 1961), 52; Burton B. Fredericksen and Federico Zeri, *Census of Pre-Nineteenth-Century Italian Paintings in North American Public Collections* (Cambridge, Mass.: Harvard University Press, 1972), 20, 588.

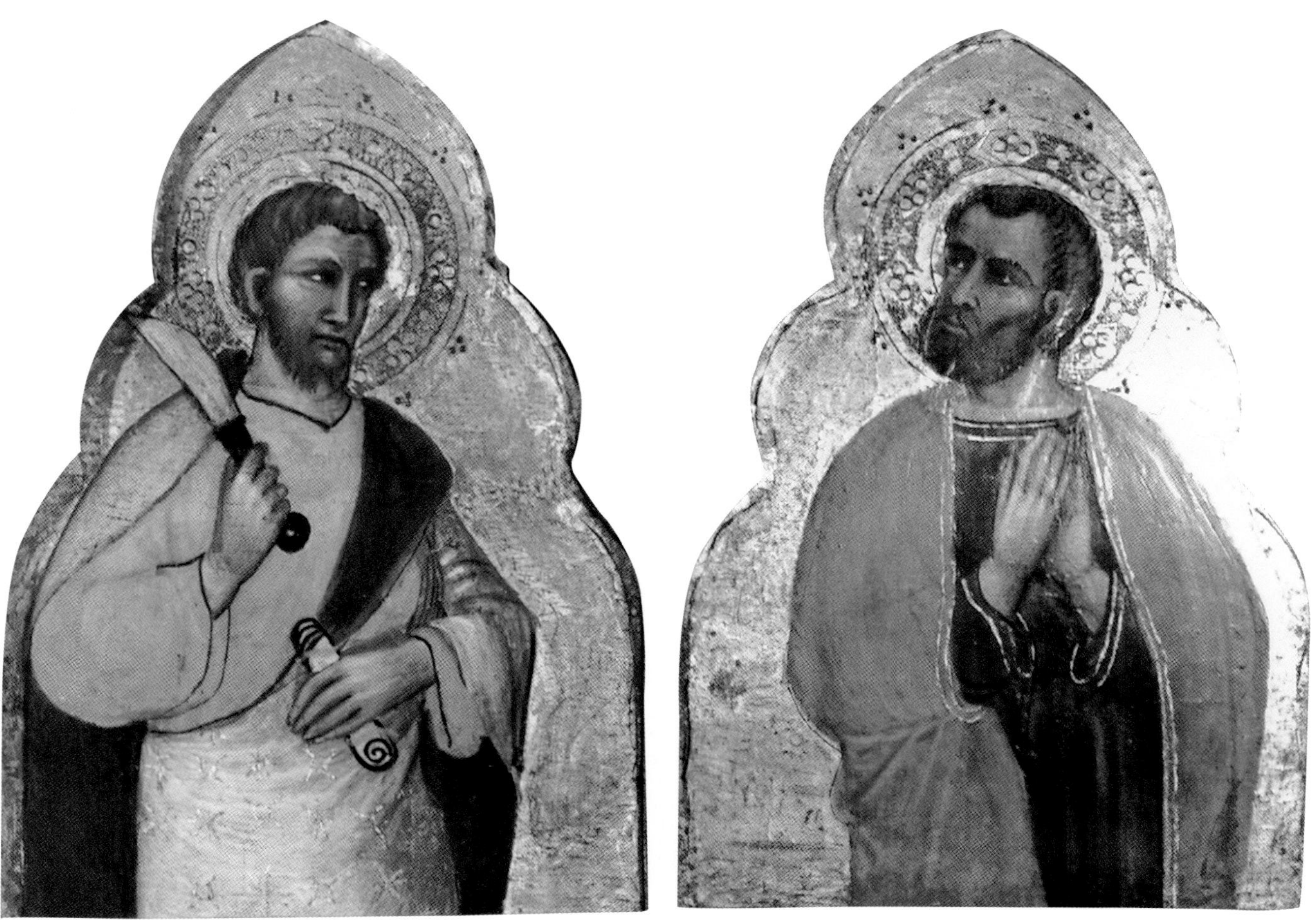

Fig. 234 (left) Battista da Vicenza: *St. Bartholomew*. The Cummer Museum of Art & Gardens, Jacksonville, Florida, C.139.1.
Fig. 235 (right) Battista da Vicenza: *Apostle Saint*. The Cummer Museum of Art & Gardens, Jacksonville, Florida, C.139.2.

BOTTICINI, RAFFAELLO, 1477–AFTER 1520; FLORENTINE

Madonna and Child (C.143) 85 CM (DIAMETER), OIL ON PANEL

JACKSONVILLE, FLORIDA. THE CUMMER MUSEUM OF ART & GARDENS

Until its restoration in 1959, the panel, overpainted, was thought to be a free copy of Raphael's *Belle Jardinière* (Louvre, Paris; 602) of 1508; Gustav F. Waagen (1854) considered it to be by Perugino's student Domenico Alfani (1479/80–1549/57). For a photograph of the work before restoration, see Christian von Holst (1974, pl. 163). Following the cleaning, the painting was reattributed to Francesco Granacci (1469–1543) by William E. Suida and Ulrich Middeldorf (cited in Von Holst). The current attribution to Raffaello Botticini was first proposed by Federico Zeri (1968) and endorsed by Everett P. Fahy (1976). The composition derives from the *'Panciatichi and Benson' Tondo* (Cincinnati Art Museum; 1948.201), which was executed by Raffaello's father, Francesco (1446–1497). The Jacksonville panel is one of many *tondi* with the Madonna and Child painted by the artist between 1500 and 1515 that served as private devotional images for domestic interiors.

PROVENANCE

Mr. Harford, Blaise Castle, Gloucestershire; Arcade Gallery, London, 1955; Mrs. Ninah M. H. Cummer, Jacksonsville, Fla., 1955–1958; The Cummer Museum of Art & Gardens (Cummer Gallery of Art), acquired 1958

BIBLIOGRAPHY

Gustav F. Waagen, *Treasures of Art in Great Britain*, 3 vols. (London: John Murray, 1854), 3:193; Cummer Gallery of Art, *Catalogue of Paintings and Other Art Objects* (Jacksonville, Fla.: Cummer Gallery of Art, 1961), 56; *Cummer Gallery of Art: The DeEtte Holden Cummer Museum Foundation* (Jacksonville, Fla.: Cummer Gallery of Art, 1965), 13; Federico Zeri, "Raffaello Botticini," *Gazette des Beaux-Arts* 72 (1968): 170; Burton B. Fredericksen and Federico Zeri, *Census of Pre-Nineteenth-Century Italian Paintings in North American Public Collections* (Cambridge, Mass.: Harvard University Press, 1972), 35, 588; Christian von Holst, *Francesco Granacci* (Munich: F. Bruckmann, 1974), 193, no. 158; Everett P. Fahy, *Some Followers of Domenico Ghirlandajo* (New York: Garland Press, 1976), 212.

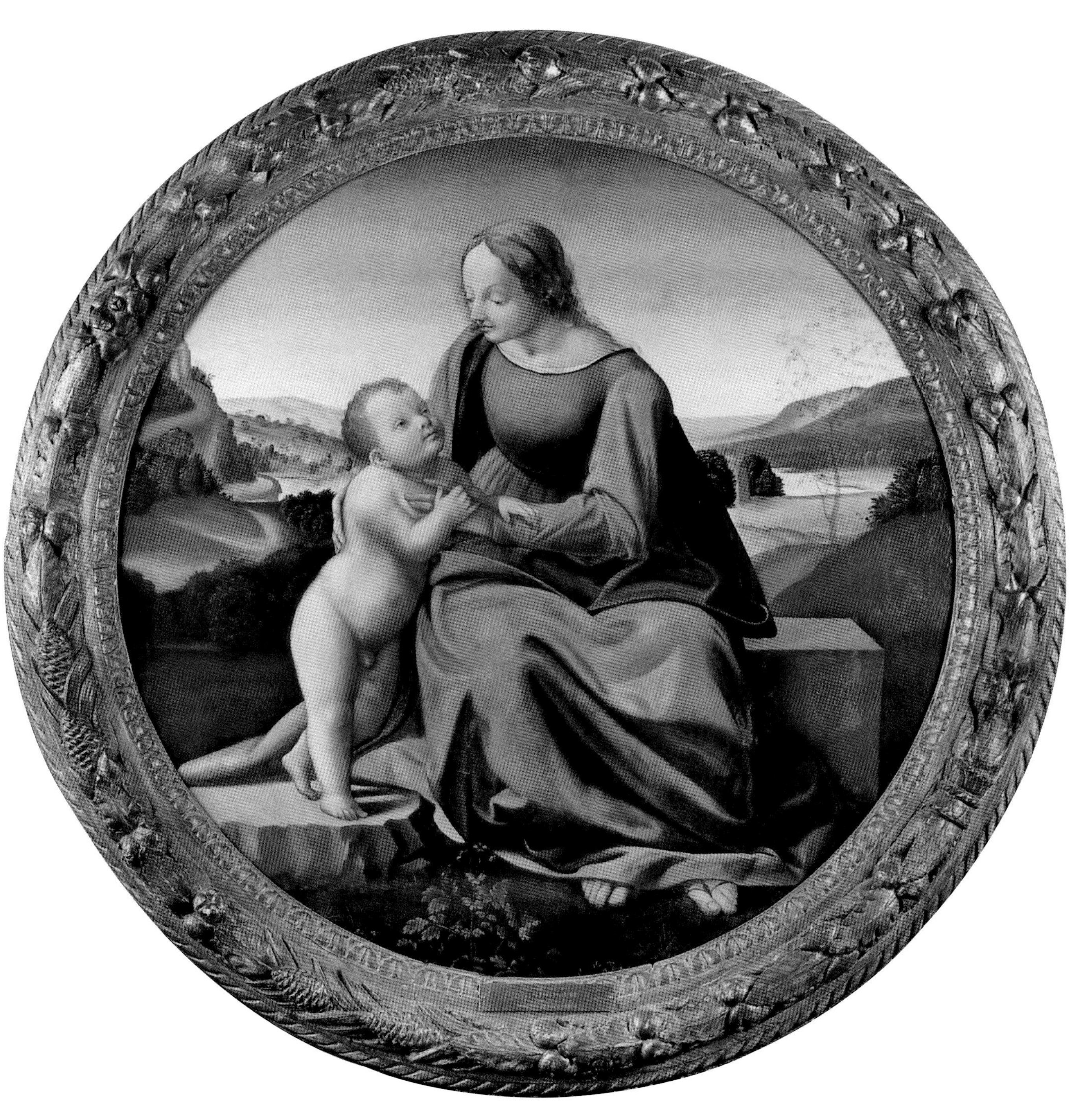

Fig. 236 Raffaello Botticini: *Madonna and Child*. The Cummer Museum of Art & Gardens, Jacksonville, Florida, C.143.

FRANCIA, FRANCESCO, C. 1450-1517; WORKSHOP; BOLOGNESE

Madonna and Child with the Infant St. John the Baptist (C.140) 62.5 X 52.5 CM, TEMPERA ON PANEL

JACKSONVILLE, FLORIDA. THE CUMMER MUSEUM OF ART & GARDENS

The panel was attributed to Giacomo Francia (c. 1486–1557) when it entered the Cummer Gallery of Art. Burton B. Fredericksen and Federico Zeri (1972) reassigned it to the workshop of Francesco Francia. Emilio Negro and Nicosetta Roio (1998) found that it resembled Francesco's late works, suggesting he may have been responsible for the design, turning over the execution to members of his shop. One of his sons, Giacomo or Giulio (1487–1540), may have participated. Similar shop works from the 1510s, in terms of style and composition, include the *Madonna and Child with St. Catherine of Alexandria* (formerly, Philadelphia Museum of Art; sold, Christie's, New York, January 10, 1980), the *Madonna and Child* (Hermitage, St. Petersburg; 199), and the *Madonna and Child* (Pinacoteca Vaticana, Rome; 643).

On the scroll near St. John is the repainted inscription ". . . CCE.AGN . . ." ("Behold, the lamb [of God]"), from John 1:29. The painting is a personal devotional work, probably intended for a domestic setting.

PROVENANCE

Count Cini, Rome, to 1846; Henry Hucks Gibbs, Esq., by 1894; Lord Aldenham, London; Sotheby's, London, February 23, 1937, lot 107; Paul Wengraf, Vienna, 1937; Mr. and Mrs. Arthur Gerrish Cummer, Jacksonville, Fla., 1937–1943; Mrs. Ninah M. H. Cummer, Jacksonville, Fla., 1943–1958; The Cummer Museum of Art & Gardens (Cummer Gallery of Art), acquired 1958

BIBLIOGRAPHY

Adolfo Venturi and Robert Benson, *Exhibition of Pictures, Drawings and Photographs of Works of the School of Ferrara-Bologna, 1440–1540* (London: Burlington Fine Arts Club, 1894), 9, no. 26; Cummer Gallery of Art, *Catalogue of Paintings and Other Art Objects* (Jacksonville, Fla.: Cummer Gallery of Art, 1961), 55; *Cummer Gallery of Art: The DeEtte Holden Cummer Museum Foundation* (Jacksonville, Fla.: Cummer Gallery of Art, 1965), 14; Burton B. Fredericksen and Federico Zeri, *Census of Pre-Nineteenth-Century Italian Paintings in North American Public Collections* (Cambridge, Mass.: Harvard University Press, 1972), 588; Nicosetta Roio, "Giacomo e Giulio Raibolini detti i Francia," in *Pittura bolognese del '500*, 2 vols., ed. V. Fortunati Pietrantonio (Bologna: Grafis, 1986), 1:36; Emilio Negro and Nicosetta Roio, *Francesco Francia e la sua scuola* (Modena: Poligrafico Artioli, 1998), 236-37, no. 143.

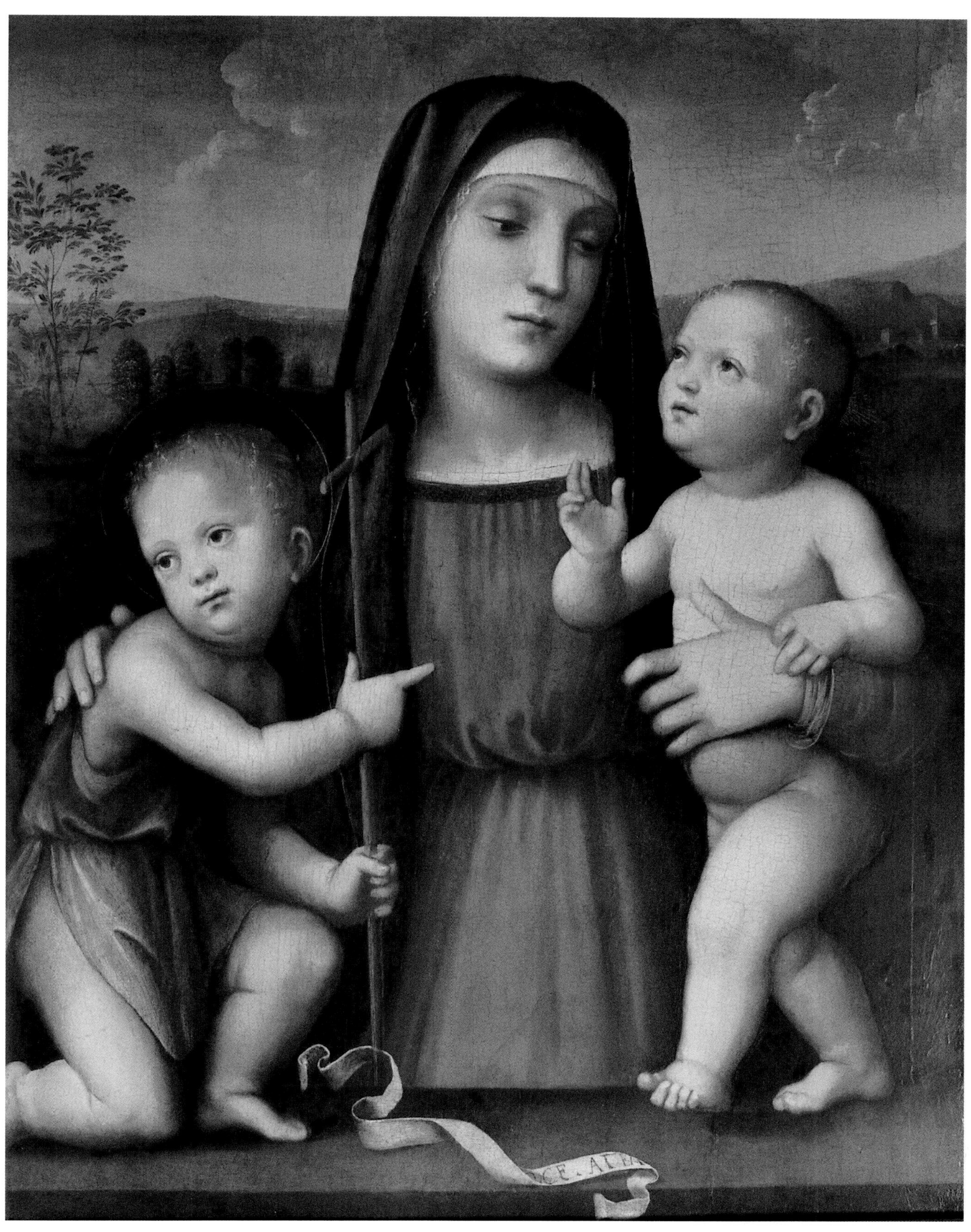

Fig. 237 Francesco Francia (workshop): *Madonna and Child with the Infant St. John the Baptist*. The Cummer Museum of Art & Gardens, Jacksonville, Florida, C.140.

GADDI, AGNOLO, ACTIVE 1369; DIED 1396; FLORENTINE

Madonna and Child with Angels (C.130.1) 86.3 x 51.9 CM, TEMPERA ON PANEL

JACKSONVILLE, FLORIDA. THE CUMMER MUSEUM OF ART & GARDENS

The painting served as a small devotional altarpiece. Originally attributed to the Master of the Madonnas (*Catalogue of Paintings* 1961), it was assigned to the workshop of Agnolo Gaddi by Burton B. Fredericksen and Federico Zeri (1972). Miklòs Boskovits (1975) and Bruce Cole (1977) considered it an autograph work dating to the late years of Agnolo's career, 1390–1396. Cole compared the Virgin to the Madonnas in Gaddi's *Madonna and Child Enthroned with Ten Angels* (Count Alessandro Contini-Bonacossi Bequest, Uffizi, Florence) and his Prato lunette (Cappella del Sacro Cingolo, Cathedral, Prato). The image refers to several of the Virgin Mary's roles: the Madonna of Humility; the nourishing mother, and, by implication, the Church; and the Queen of Heaven.

PROVENANCE

Sir Godfrey Llewellyn, Tredilion Park, Abergavenny, Wales; Arcade Gallery, London, 1952; Mrs. Ninah M. H. Cummer, Jacksonville, Fla., 1952–1958; The Cummer Museum of Art & Gardens (Cummer Gallery of Art), acquired 1958

BIBLIOGRAPHY

Cummer Gallery of Art, *Catalogue of Paintings and Other Art Objects* (Jacksonville, Fla.: Cummer Gallery of Art, 1961), 57; *Cummer Gallery of Art: The DeEtte Holden Cummer Museum Foundation* (Jacksonville, Fla.: Cummer Gallery of Art, 1965), 11; Burton B. Fredericksen and Federico Zeri, *Census of Pre-Nineteenth-Century Italian Paintings in North American Public Collections* (Cambridge, Mass.: Harvard University Press, 1972), 76, 588; Miklòs Boskovits, *Pittura fiorentina alla vigilia del Rinascimento, 1370–1400* (Florence: Edam, 1975), 300; Bruce Cole, *Agnolo Gaddi* (Oxford and New York: Clarendon Press, 1977), 41, 83; Sylvia Ferrari and Jean-Claude Bloch, *Trente-trois primitifs italiens: De 1310 à 1500, du sacré au profane* (Paris: G. Sarti, 1999), 90; Aaron De Groft et al., *The Cummer Museum of Art & Gardens, Jacksonville, Florida* (Jacksonville, Fla.: Cummer Museum of Art & Gardens, 2000), 10; Perri Lee Roberts, Bruce Cole, and Hayden B. J. Maginnis, *Sacred Treasures: Early Italian Paintings from Southern Collections* (Athens, Ga.: Georgia Museum of Art, 2002), 110-13.

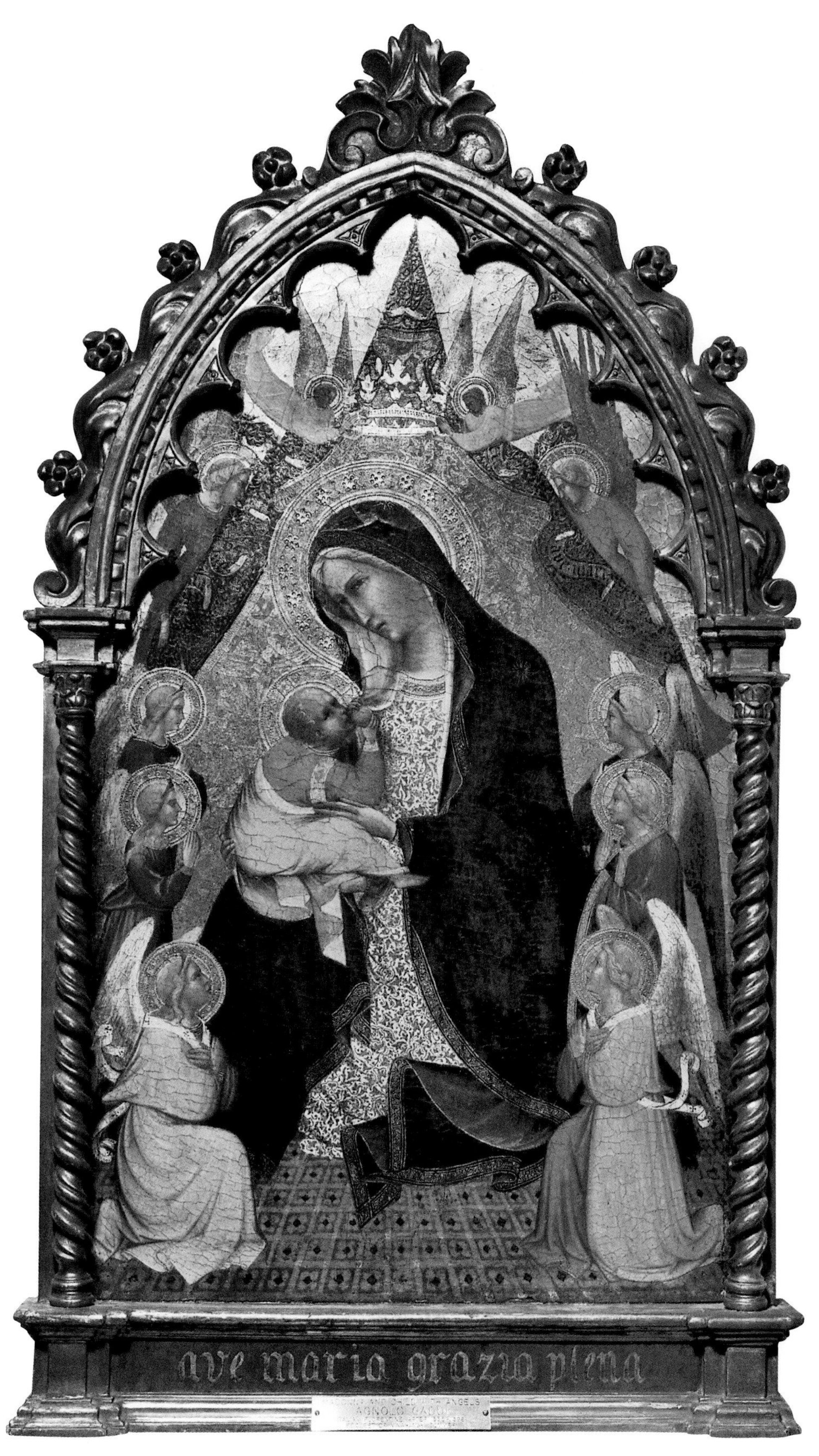

Fig. 238 Agnolo Gaddi: *Madonna and Child with Angels*. The Cummer Museum of Art & Gardens, Jacksonville, Florida, C.130.1.

PSEUDO PIER FRANCESCO FIORENTINO, ACTIVE SECOND HALF OF THE FIFTEENTH CENTURY; FLORENTINE

Madonna and Child with the Infant St. John the Baptist (AP 68.16) 69.9 X 42.5 CM, TEMPERA WITH OIL ON PANEL

JACKSONVILLE, FLORIDA. THE CUMMER MUSEUM OF ART & GARDENS

The Madonna and Child derive from Francesco Pesellino's (1422 [?]–1457) *Madonna* (Musée des Beaux-Arts, Lyons, 1997.4; formerly, Aynard Collection, Lyons), in which the figures appear before a shell niche. The creator of the Cummer panel produced many versions of this composition, with either a rose hedge or simply gold as a backdrop; among the most similar are Madonnas in the John G. Johnson Collection, Philadelphia Museum of Art (41) and the Walters Art Gallery, Baltimore (37.736). In a few instances, as here and in the variant in the Ionides Collection, Victoria and Albert Museum, London (99), the Christ Child is given a round object, perhaps a pomegranate seed or cherry, to justify the position of his hands. The young St. John does not appear in the Lyons *Madonna*, but the Cummer's Baptist may be based on a figure in another of Pesellino's or Filippo Lippi's (c. 1406–1469) paintings.

The imagery and size of the painting suggest that it served as a personal devotional image in a domestic setting.

PROVENANCE

Robert Simms, St. Petersburg, Fla., 1968; The Cummer Museum of Art & Gardens (Cummer Gallery of Art), acquired 1968

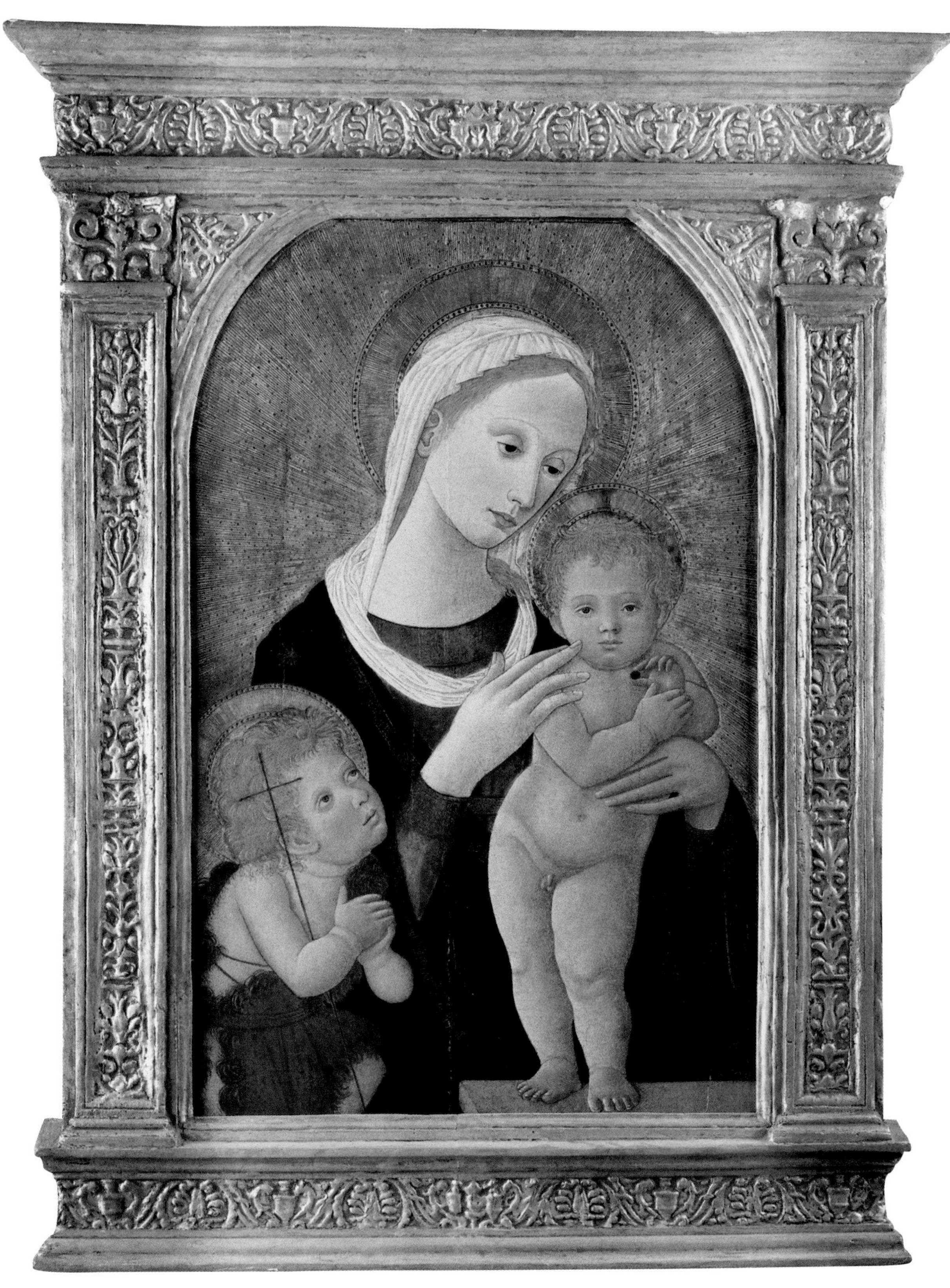

Fig. 239 Pseudo Pier Francesco Fiorentino: *Madonna and Child with the Infant St. John the Baptist*. The Cummer Museum of Art & Gardens, Jacksonville, Florida, AP 68.16.

CENNI DI FRANCESCO DI SER CENNI, ACTIVE 1369–1415; FLORENTINE

Martyrdom of St. Stephen (39.2; K 1016) 26.4 x 50.5 CM, TEMPERA ON PANEL

LITTLE ROCK, ARKANSAS. THE ARKANSAS ARTS CENTER

The work was part of the predella panel of an unidentified altarpiece, c. 1400, that must have depicted St. Stephen on one of its wings. Attributed to Lorenzo di Niccolò (active 1392–1412) by Fern Rusk Shapley (1966) and to Cenni di Francesco, 1370–1375, by Miklòs Boskovits (1975), the painting was reassigned by Hayden B. J. Maginnis (in Offner and Maginnis 1981) to the Rohoncz Master, a follower of the Cioni who worked in the second half of the fourteenth century.

The panel illustrates the stoning of the first Christian martyr, described in Acts 7:55-58. Stephen kneels, simultaneously seeing "the heavens opened, and the son of man standing on the right hand of God." Members of the Sanhedrin, who tried and convicted the saint, are gathered at the right, outside the walls of Jerusalem. Among them is the bald and bearded Saul, who became the Apostle Paul upon his conversion to Christianity. Shown with a sword, the instrument of his own future martyrdom, Saul consented to the death of Stephen and witnessed his execution.

PROVENANCE

Count Alessandro Contini-Bonacossi, Florence; Samuel H. Kress, New York, acquired 1936; The Arkansas Arts Center (Museum of Fine Arts), acquired 1938

BIBLIOGRAPHY

Alfred M. Frankfurter, "Kress Gifts to Eight Cities, Italian Paintings of Three Centuries in the South and West," *Art News* 37 (1939): 10; *Catalog* (Little Rock, Ark.: Museum of Fine Arts, 1945), 53, no. 231; Bernard Berenson, *Italian Pictures of the Renaissance: A List of the Principal Artists and Their Works with an Index of Places. Florentine School*, 2 vols. (London: Phaidon Press, 1963), 1:47; Fern Rusk Shapley, *Paintings from the Samuel H. Kress Collection: Italian Schools*, vol. 1, *XIII–XV Century* (London: Phaidon Press, 1966), 45; Burton B. Fredericksen and Federico Zeri, *Census of Pre-Nineteenth-Century Italian Paintings in North American Public Collections* (Cambridge, Mass.: Harvard University Press, 1972), 51, 591; Miklòs Boskovits, *Pittura fiorentina alla vigilia del Rinascimento, 1370–1400* (Florence: Edam, 1975), 289; Richard Offner and Hayden B. J. Maginnis, *A Critical and Historical Corpus of Florentine Painting: A Legacy of Attributions* (New York: Institute of Fine Arts, New York University, 1981), 51; Irma B. Jaffe and Yvonne Korshak, *Selections from the Permanent Collection of the Arkansas Arts Center Foundation* (Little Rock, Ark.: Arkansas Arts Center, 1983), 12, no. 1; Marvin Eisenberg, *The "Confraternity Altarpiece" by Mariotto di Nardo: The Coronation of the Virgin and the Life of Saint Stephen* (Tokyo: National Museum of Western Art, 1998), 45; Perri Lee Roberts, Bruce Cole, and Hayden B. J. Maginnis, *Sacred Treasures: Early Italian Paintings from Southern Collections* (Athens, Ga.: Georgia Museum of Art, 2002), 82-84.

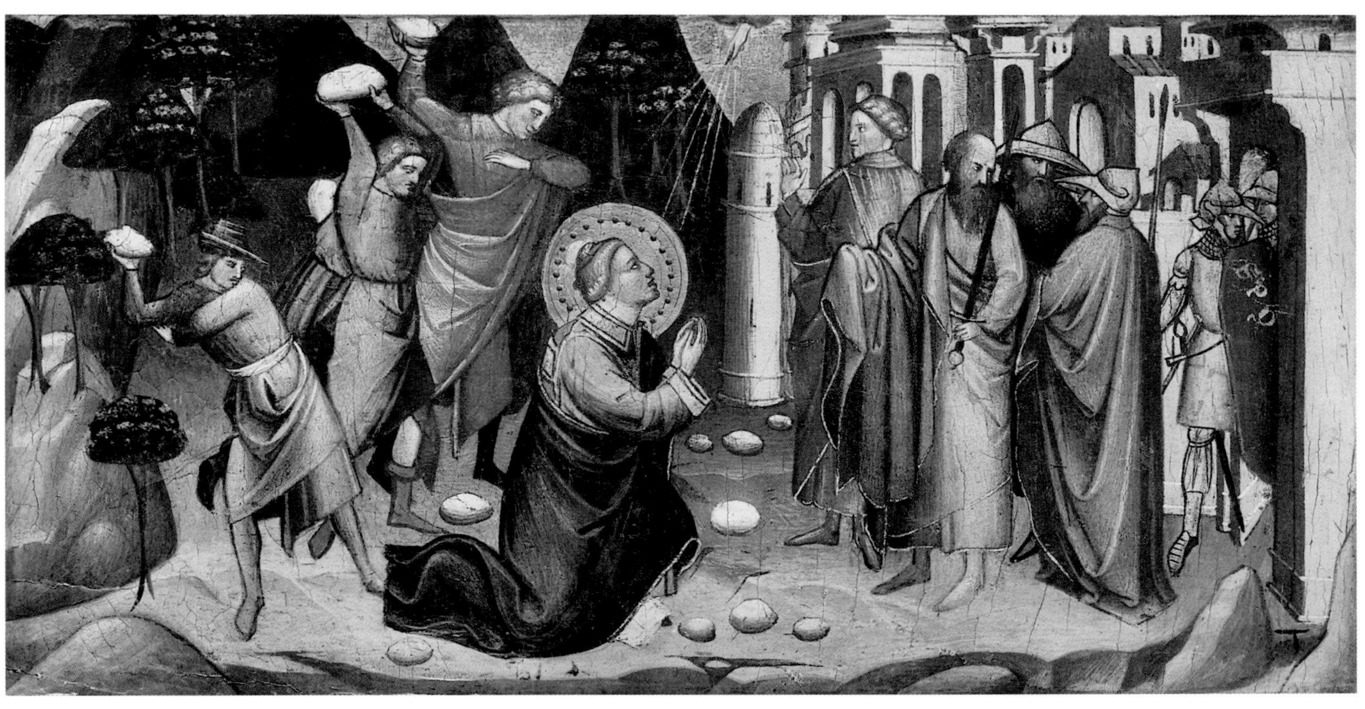

Fig. 240 Cenni di Francesco di Ser Cenni: *Martyrdom of St. Stephen*. The Arkansas Arts Center Foundation; Gift of the Kress Collection, 1939, 39.2.

DADDI, BERNARDO, ACTIVE C. 1280–1348; WORKSHOP; FLORENTINE

St. James Major (1941.105); *St. Catherine of Alexandria* (1941.106) 95 x 34 CM (EACH), TEMPERA ON PANEL

LOUISVILLE, KENTUCKY. THE SPEED ART MUSEUM

Richard Offner (1958) identified the works as the right-hand panels, now reduced, of a polyptych that had as its centerpiece the *Madonna and Child* (current location unknown; reproduced in Offner). The format of the altarpiece resembled that of Bernardo Daddi's *San Pancrazio Polyptych* (Uffizi, Florence; 1890, 8345), from 1335–1340. Offner attributed the Louisville panels to a Daddi follower of the mid-1340s. Burton B. Fredericksen and Federico Zeri (1972) assigned them to Daddi's school, shop, or studio. The Museum dates them to the mid-1340s.

PROVENANCE

George Blumenthal, New York; Walter Blumenthal, New York; French and Co., New York, acquired 1939; Preston Pope Satterwhite, Louisville, c. 1939–1948; The Speed Art Museum (J. B. Speed Art Museum), acquired 1949

BIBLIOGRAPHY

J. B. Speed Art Museum, *Handbook of the Preston Pope Satterwhite Collection* (Louisville, Ky.: J. B. Speed Memorial Museum, 1940), no. 3; Richard Offner, *A Critical and Historical Corpus of Florentine Painting*, sec. 3, vol. 8, *Workshop of Bernardo Daddi* (New York: Institute of Fine Arts, New York University, 1958), 114; Burton B. Fredericksen and Federico Zeri, *Census of Pre-Nineteenth-Century Italian Paintings in North American Public Collections* (Cambridge, Mass.: Harvard University Press, 1972), 62, 593; John F. Martin, ed., *J. B. Speed Art Museum Handbook* (Louisville, Ky.: J. B. Speed Art Museum, 1973), 44; *A Checklist of Drawings, Paintings, and Sculpture in the J. B. Speed Art Museum: 1927–1977* (Louisville, Ky.: J. B. Speed Art Museum, 1978), 42; Miklòs Boskovits, *A Critical and Historical Corpus of Florentine Painting*, sec. 3, vol. 3, *Works Attributed to Bernardo Daddi* (Florence: Giunti, 1989), 82; Erling S. Skaug, *Punch Marks from Giotto to Fra Angelico*, 2 vols. (Oslo: IIC-Nordic Group, 1994), 1:103; Mojmír S. Frinta, *Punched Decoration on Late Medieval Panel and Miniature Painting*, pt. 1 (Prague: Maxdorf, 1998), 382, 445; Perri Lee Roberts, Bruce Cole, and Hayden B. J. Maginnis, *Sacred Treasures: Early Italian Paintings from Southern Collections* (Athens, Ga.: Georgia Museum of Art, 2002), 62-64; Ruth H. Cloudman, *The Speed Art Museum: Highlights from the Collection* (New York and London: Merrell, 2007), 58.

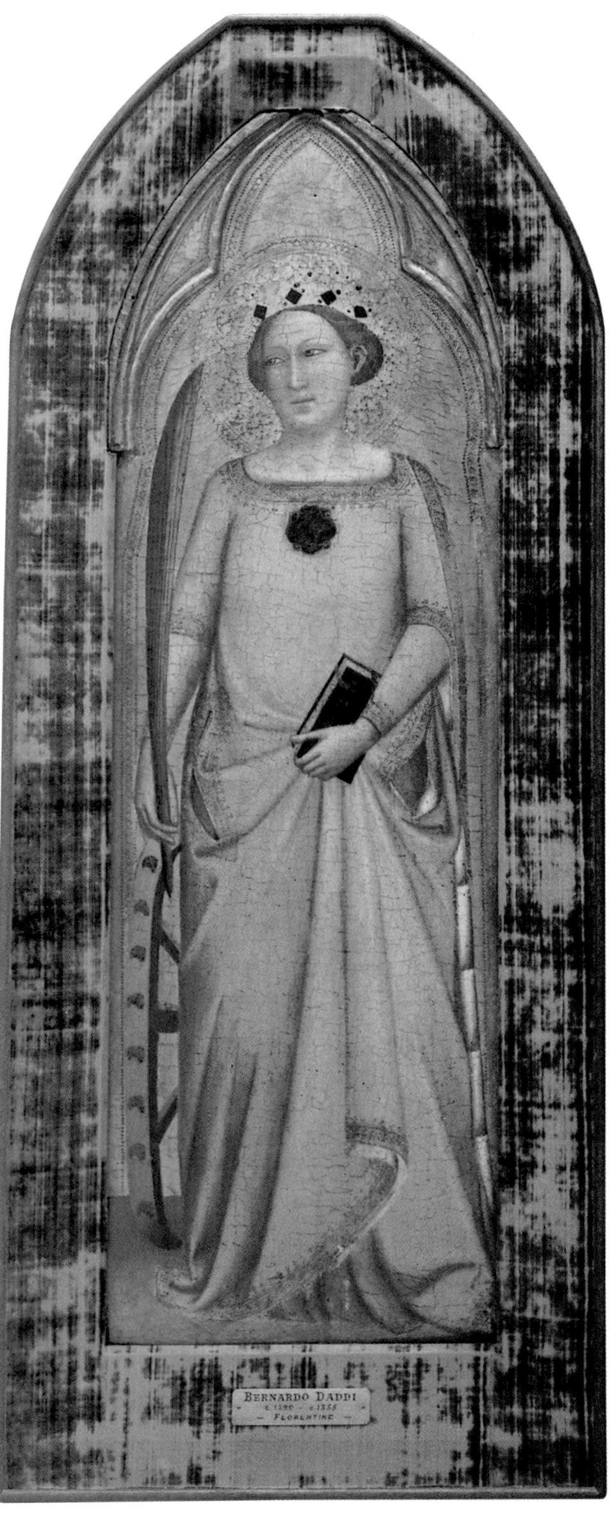

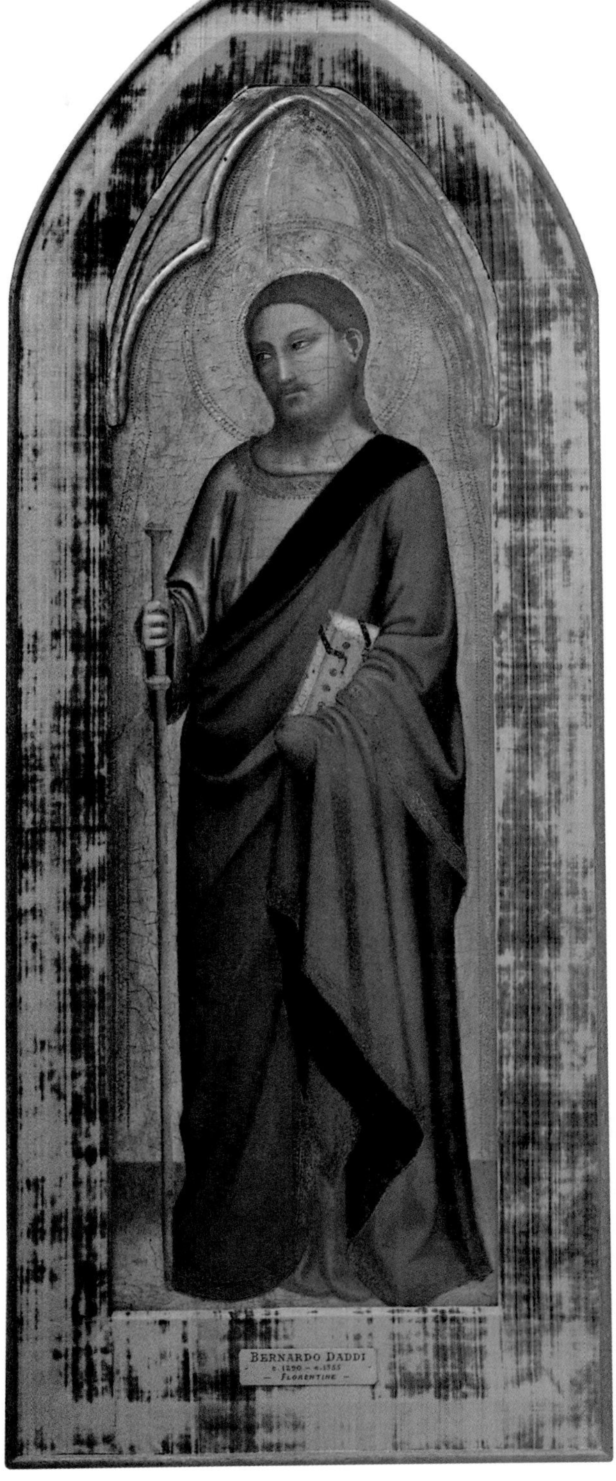

Fig. 241 (left) Bernardo Daddi (workshop): *St. Catherine of Alexandria*. Collection of the Speed Art Museum, Louisville, Kentucky; Gift of Preston Pope Satterwhite, 1941.106.

Fig. 242 (right) Bernardo Daddi (workshop): *St. James Major*. Collection of the Speed Art Museum, Louisville, Kentucky; Gift of Preston Pope Satterwhite, 1941.105.

FOPPA, VINCENZO, C. 1427–C. 1515; BRESCIAN

St. John the Baptist (1966.18) 58.7 X 21.3 CM, TEMPERA AND OIL ON PANEL

LOUISVILLE, KENTUCKY. THE SPEED ART MUSEUM

The size of the panel, its subject matter and pavement pattern, and the orientation of the saint's figure suggest the work is the left wing, now reduced, of a triptych with the enthroned Madonna and Child flanked by saints; it would have resembled Foppa's *Fornari Altarpiece* (Pinacoteca, Savona; 28), dated 1489. The Louisville painting appears to be a late work, as the style of the Baptist corresponds to that of St. George on the verso of Foppa's Orzinuovi Banner (Pinacoteca Tosio Martinengo, Brescia; 129) of 1514.

The banderole bears the inscription "AGNVS . . . DOLIT. . . MOND," a corrupted and fragmentary reference to "Ecce agnus Dei, ecce qui tollit peccatum mundi" ("Behold the Lamb of God, who takes away the sin of the world!"), from John 1:29.

PROVENANCE

Chalandon, France; Paul Drey Gallery, New York; The Speed Art Museum (J. B. Speed Art Museum), acquired 1967

BIBLIOGRAPHY

J. B. Speed Art Museum Bulletin 26 (1967): 9; Bernard Berenson, *Italian Pictures of the Renaissance: A List of the Principal Artists and Their Works with an Index of Places. Central Italian and North Italian Schools*, 3 vols. (London: Phaidon Press, 1968), 1:137; Burton B. Fredericksen and Federico Zeri, *Census of Pre-Nineteenth-Century Italian Paintings in North American Public Collections* (Cambridge, Mass.: Harvard University Press, 1972), 72, 593.

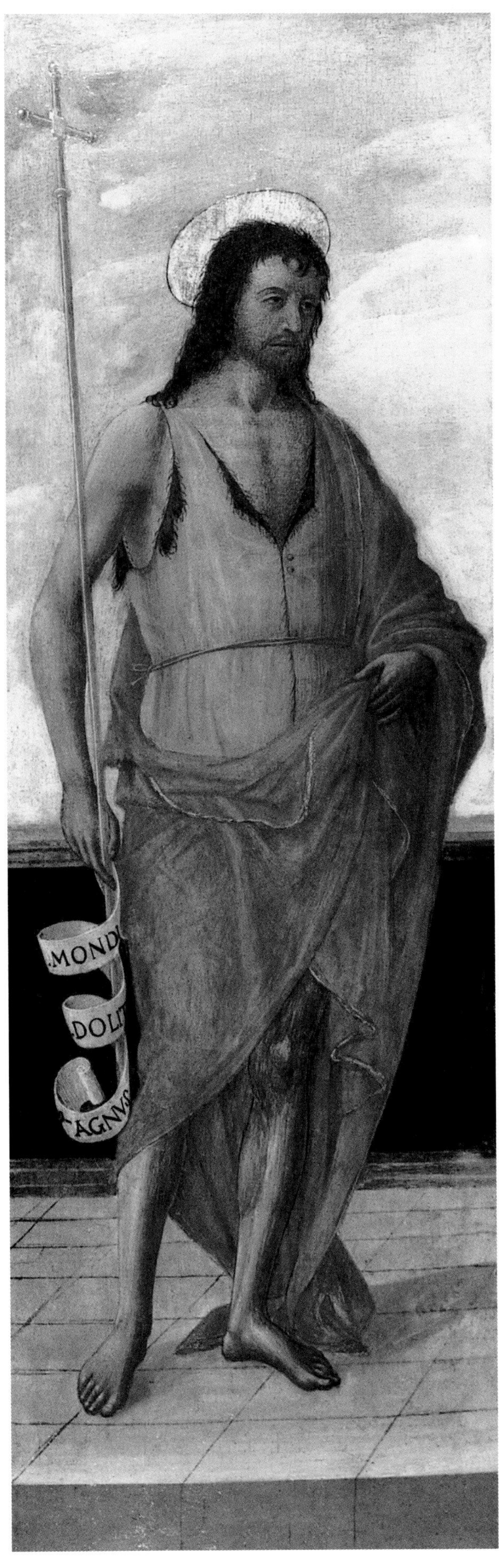

Fig. 243 Vincenzo Foppa: *St. John the Baptist*. Collection of the Speed Art Museum, Louisville, Kentucky; Gift of Mrs. Berry V. Stoll, 1966.18.

ITALIAN SCHOOL, FOURTEENTH CENTURY

Madonna and Child Enthroned (1973.15) 42.5 x 21.6 CM (CENTER); 48.8 x 11.9 CM (EACH WING), TEMPERA ON PANEL

LOUISVILLE, KENTUCKY. THE SPEED ART MUSEUM

The work is a small, portable altarpiece, dated by the Museum c. 1360. Andrew Ladis (Museum files) attributed it to the Florentine Master of San Martino a Mensola (active 1372–1395). The composition and style of the central panel recall the master's *Madonna and Child with Four Angels* (Acton Collection, Florence), dated 1385.

The Madonna is flanked by St. John the Baptist to the left, St. Catherine of Alexandria to the right. St. Anthony Abbot and a bishop saint appear on the left wing, while the Crucifixion, with the Virgin and St. John the Evangelist, appears on the right. The Annunciate Angel and the Annunciate Virgin appear on the pinnacles of the wings. The angel's greeting to the Virgin, "AVE MARIA GR . . ." ("Hail, O favored one . . ."), from Luke 1:28, appears on the base of the tabernacle. The coats-of-arms have not been identified.

PROVENANCE

Newhouse Galleries, New York; The Speed Art Museum (J. B. Speed Art Museum), acquired 1973

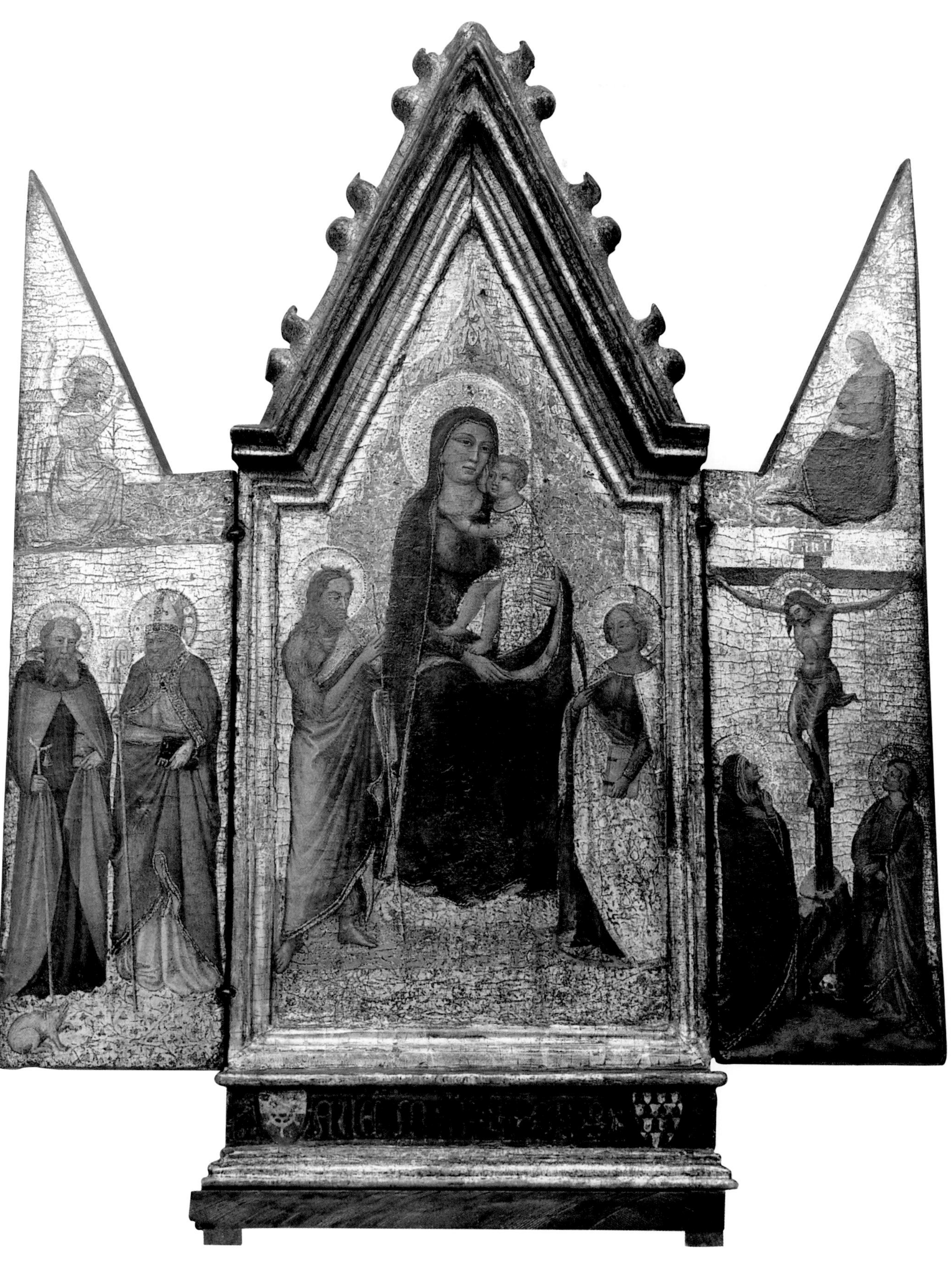

Fig. 244 Italian School, fourteenth century: *Madonna and Child Enthroned*. Collection of the Speed Art Museum, Louisville, Kentucky; Museum purchase, Preston Pope Satterwhite Fund, 1973.15.

ITALIAN SCHOOL, MID–FOURTEENTH CENTURY

St. Blaise and St. Peter (2005.5.1) 97.8 X 46.7 CM, TEMPERA ON PANEL

LOUISVILLE, KENTUCKY. THE SPEED ART MUSEUM

The painting has not yet been attributed definitively, but the Museum believes that it is Florentine in origin, dating from the third quarter of the fourteenth century. Everett P. Fahy (Museum files) suggested a possible attribution to Giovanni Bonsi (active 1351–1375) or Andrea da Firenze (Andrea di Bonaiuto; active 1346; died 1379). Miklòs Boskovits (Museum files) believed the panel may have come from a follower of Andrea da Firenze known as the Master of the Lazzaroni Madonna (active 1395–1400), whose eponymous work was formerly in the Lazzaroni Collection, Paris (current location unknown).

The Virgin Annunciate appears in a roundel above the saints. The panel, which originally served as the right-hand wing of an unidentified triptych, has been reduced along the bottom edge. The saints were three-quarter- or full-length figures and probably flanked an image of the Madonna and Child enthroned. The left-hand wing would have had a roundel with the Annunciate Angel above a similarly posed pair of saints.

PROVENANCE

Jane Mengel Allen, Louisville, Ky., by 1964–1986; Mary Hillery Bryant Jacobs, 1986–2002; Farnsworth Dudley Bryant and Elizabeth R. Bryant; The Speed Art Museum, acquired 2005

BIBLIOGRAPHY

Allen R. Hite Art Institute, *Italian Painting: 1300–1600* (Louisville, Ky.: University of Louisville, 1964), n.p.

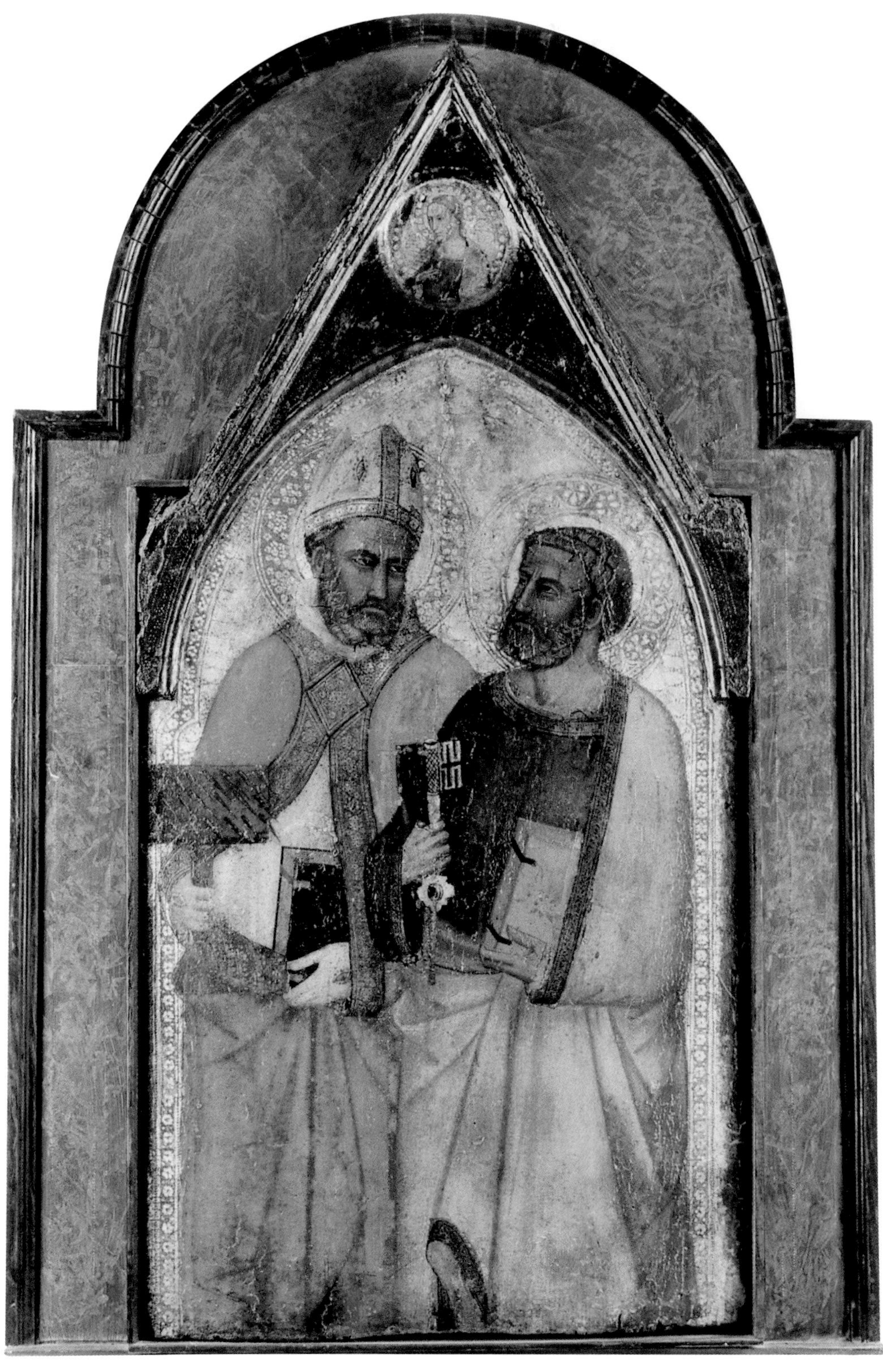

Fig. 245 Italian School, mid-fourteenth century: *St. Blaise and St. Peter*. Collection of the Speed Art Museum, Louisville, Kentucky; Donated in memory of Jane Mengel Allen, Jr., by heirs of Mary Hillery Bryant Jacobs, 2005.5.1.

PREVITALI, ANDREA, C. 1470–1528; BERGAMASQUE

Virgin and Child with St. Sebastian and St. Roch (1959.7) 37 X 58.7 CM, OIL ON PANEL

LOUISVILLE, KENTUCKY. THE SPEED ART MUSEUM

The panel's attribution has been contested. Acquired by the Museum as the product of a fifteenth-century Venetian painter, it was subsequently ascribed to Andrea Previtali and was listed as such by Burton B. Fredericksen and Federico Zeri (1972). Fritz Heinemann (1962) doubted the attribution, later (1991) assigning the work to another follower of Giovanni Bellini, Agostino Facheris (1500–after 1552).

The small size of the painting and the inclusion of saints invoked as protection against plague indicate it probably served as a personal devotional and votive image. The composition reprises Bellini's formula for the *sacra conversazione*, in which a half-length representation of the Madonna and Child, flanked by two saints, is silhouetted against a cloth of honor and a landscape. Heinemann (1962) erroneously listed the work as a copy of Bellini's Northbrook *Madonna* (High Museum of Art, Atlanta; 58.33, K 2188) of c. 1510.

PROVENANCE

Mrs. Albert Anson Bigelow; The Speed Art Museum (J. B. Speed Art Museum), acquired 1959

BIBLIOGRAPHY

J. B. Speed Art Museum Bulletin 20 (1959); Paul S. Harris, *Fourteen Seasons of Art Accessions in Kentucky, 1947 to 1960* (Louisville, Ky.: J. B. Speed Art Museum, 1960), no. 122; Fritz Heinemann, *Giovanni Bellini e i Belliniani*, 3 vols. (Venice: Neri Pozza, 1962), 1:20, no. 591; Burton B. Fredericksen and Federico Zeri, *Census of Pre-Nineteenth-Century Italian Paintings in North American Public Collections* (Cambridge, Mass.: Harvard University Press, 1972), 170, 448; Fritz Heinemann, *Giovanni Bellini e i Belliniani*, 3 vols. (Venice: Neri Pozza, 1991), 3:10, no. 591.

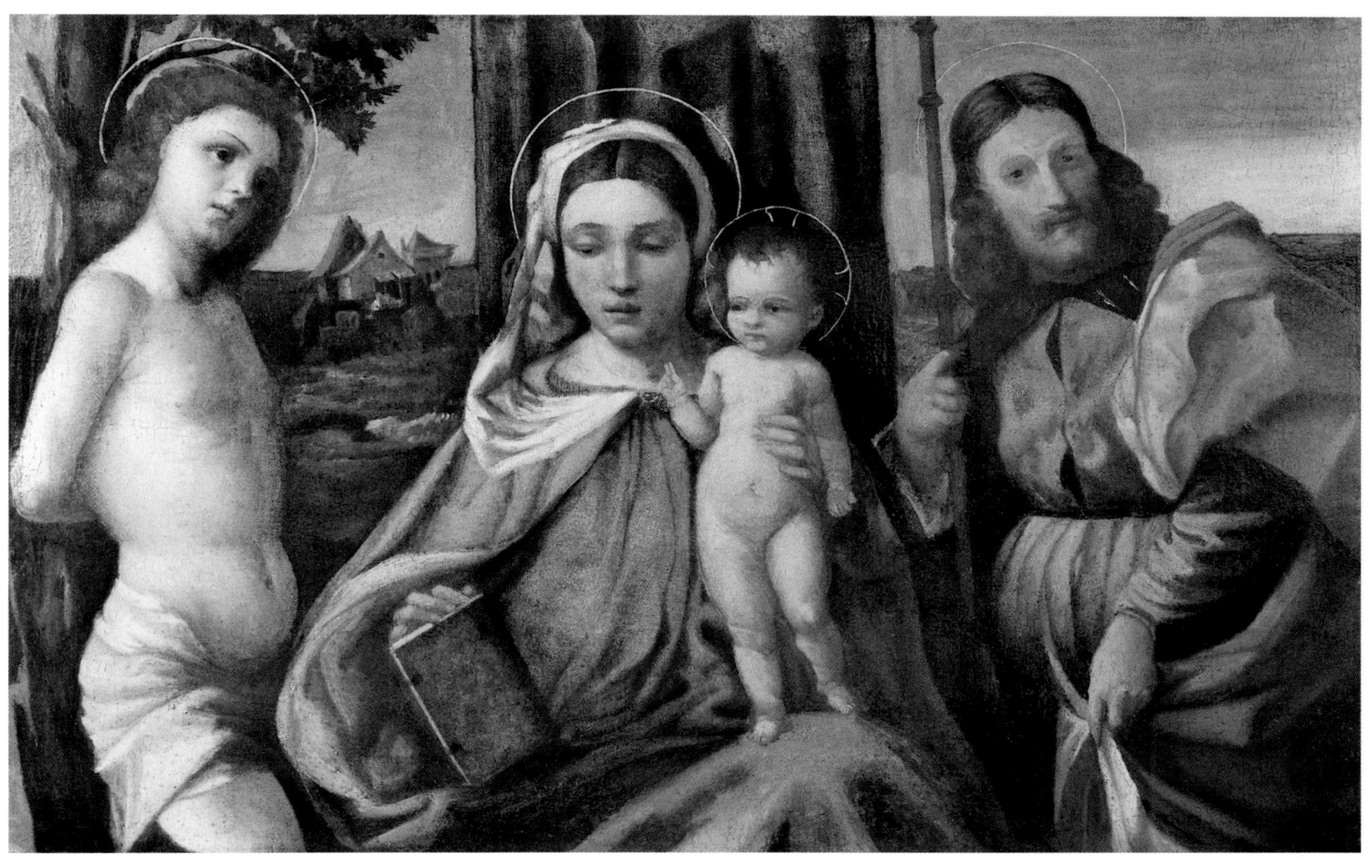

Fig. 246 Andrea Previtali: *Virgin and Child with St. Sebastian and St. Roch*. Collection of the Speed Art Museum, Louisville, Kentucky; Gift of Mrs. Albert Anson Bigelow, 1959.7.

SANO DI PIETRO, 1405–1481, AND WORKSHOP; SIENESE

Madonna and Child with Two Angels (2005.5.2) 52.1 X 41.4 CM, TEMPERA ON PANEL

LOUISVILLE, KENTUCKY. THE SPEED ART MUSEUM

The Louisville painting is a typical product of Sano di Pietro's workshop, which created over one hundred such small panels with the Madonna and Child intended to inspire private devotions and spiritual contemplation.

The Annunciate Angel's greeting to the Virgin Mary, "AVE GRATIA PLENA" ("Hail, O favored one [the Lord is with you]"), from Luke 1:28, is inscribed on her halo. On her left shoulder is the *Stella Maris* (Star of the Sea), referring to the meaning of her Hebrew name, Miriam. The Christ Child holds either an apple, alluding to his role as redeemer, or a pomegranate, symbolizing the Resurrection.

PROVENANCE

Mr. and Mrs. Arthur D. Allen, Louisville, Ky., c. 1924–after 1946; Jane Mengel Allen, Louisville, Ky., by 1964–1986; Mary Hillery Bryant Jacobs, 1986–2002; Farnsworth Dudley Bryant and Elizabeth R. Bryant; The Speed Art Museum, acquired 2005

BIBLIOGRAPHY

Allen R. Hite Art Institute, *Italian Painting: 1300–1600* (Louisville, Ky.: University of Louisville, 1964), n.p.; Bernard Berenson, *Italian Pictures of the Renaissance: A List of the Principal Artists and Their Works with an Index of Places. Central Italian and North Italian Schools*, 3 vols. (London: Phaidon Press, 1968), 1:376; Mary Bryan Hood et al., *Christianity and the Visual Arts: Kentucky Collections* (Owensboro, Ky.: Owensboro Museum of Fine Arts, 1986), 47, nos. 18, 52.

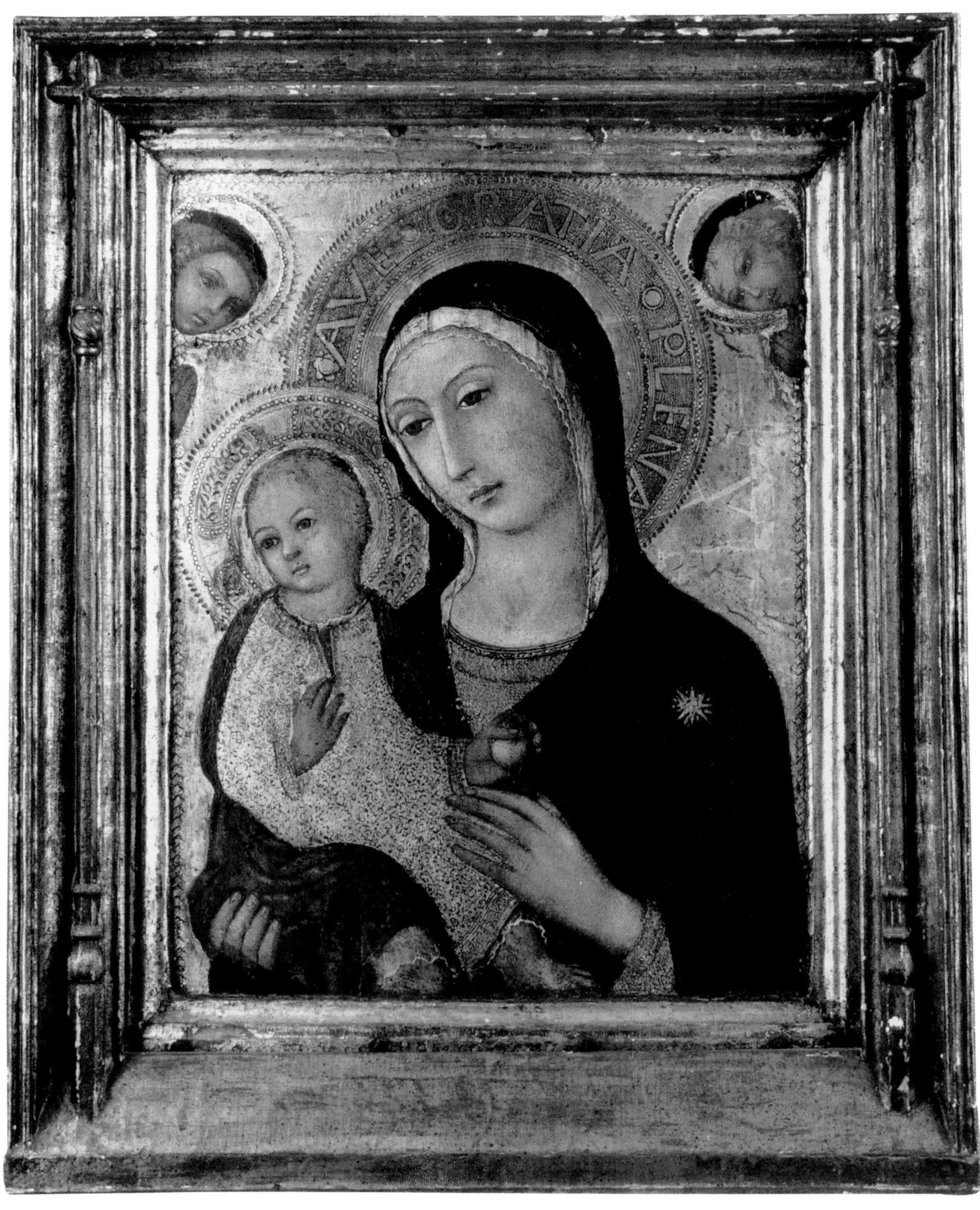

Fig. 247 Sano di Pietro (and workshop): *Madonna and Child with Two Angels*. Collection of the Speed Art Museum, Louisville, Kentucky; Donated in memory of Jane Mengel Allen, Jr., by heirs of Mary Hillery Bryant Jacobs, 2005.5.2.

CIMA DA CONEGLIANO, GIOVANNI BATTISTA, C. 1459–1517; VENETIAN

Madonna and Child (K 1069) 51.8 X 46.7 CM, TEMPERA ON PANEL

MACON, GEORGIA. WESLEYAN COLLEGE

Most scholars have attributed the panel to Cima, dating it to the middle of his career. The notable exception is Peter Humfrey (1983), who believed it to be only partially by the artist. It is one of at least five similar pictures associated with Cima and his workshop, of which the Johnson *Madonna* (John G. Johnson Collection, Philadelphia Museum of Art; 176) of c. 1485–1486 is the earliest.

The composition of this devotional painting derives from works by Giovanni Bellini (1431/6–1516) and his shop, for example, the *Madonna and Child in a Landscape* (National Gallery of Art, Washington, D.C.; K 479) and the *Madonna and Child* (Ball State University, Muncie, Ind.; K 1905).

PROVENANCE

Stefano Bardini, Florence; Christie, Manson & Woods, London, May 30, 1902, lot 648; Eugenio Ventura, Florence; Galleria Scopinich, Milan, April 6, 1932, lot 29; Count Alessandro Contini-Bonacossi, Florence; Samuel H. Kress, New York, acquired 1935; Wesleyan College, acquired 1936

BIBLIOGRAPHY

Bernard Berenson, *Venetian Painting in America* (New York: Frederic Fairchild Sherman, 1916), 186-205; Raimond van Marle, *The Development of the Italian Schools of Painting*, vol. 17, *The Renaissance Painters of Venice: Antonio Vivarini, the Bellini, Cima, Basaiti* (The Hague: M. Nijhoff, 1935), 397; Bernard Berenson, *Italian Pictures of the Renaissance: A List of the Principal Artists and Their Works with an Index of Places. Venetian School*, 2 vols. (New York: Phaidon, 1957), 1:66; Luigi Coletti, *Cima da Conegliano* (Venice: Neri Pozza, 1959), nos. 4, 5; Fern Rusk Shapley, *Paintings from the Samuel H. Kress Collection: Italian Schools*, vol. 2, *XV–XVI Century* (London: Phaidon Press, 1968), 60; Burton B. Fredericksen and Federico Zeri, *Census of Pre-Nineteenth-Century Italian Paintings in North American Public Collections* (Cambridge, Mass.: Harvard University Press, 1972), 53, 593; Peter Humfrey, *Cima da Conegliano* (Cambridge and New York: Cambridge University Press, 1983), 117; Bruce Cole, *Venetian Paintings of the Renaissance* (Athens, Ga.: Georgia Museum of Art, 1991), 43-44.

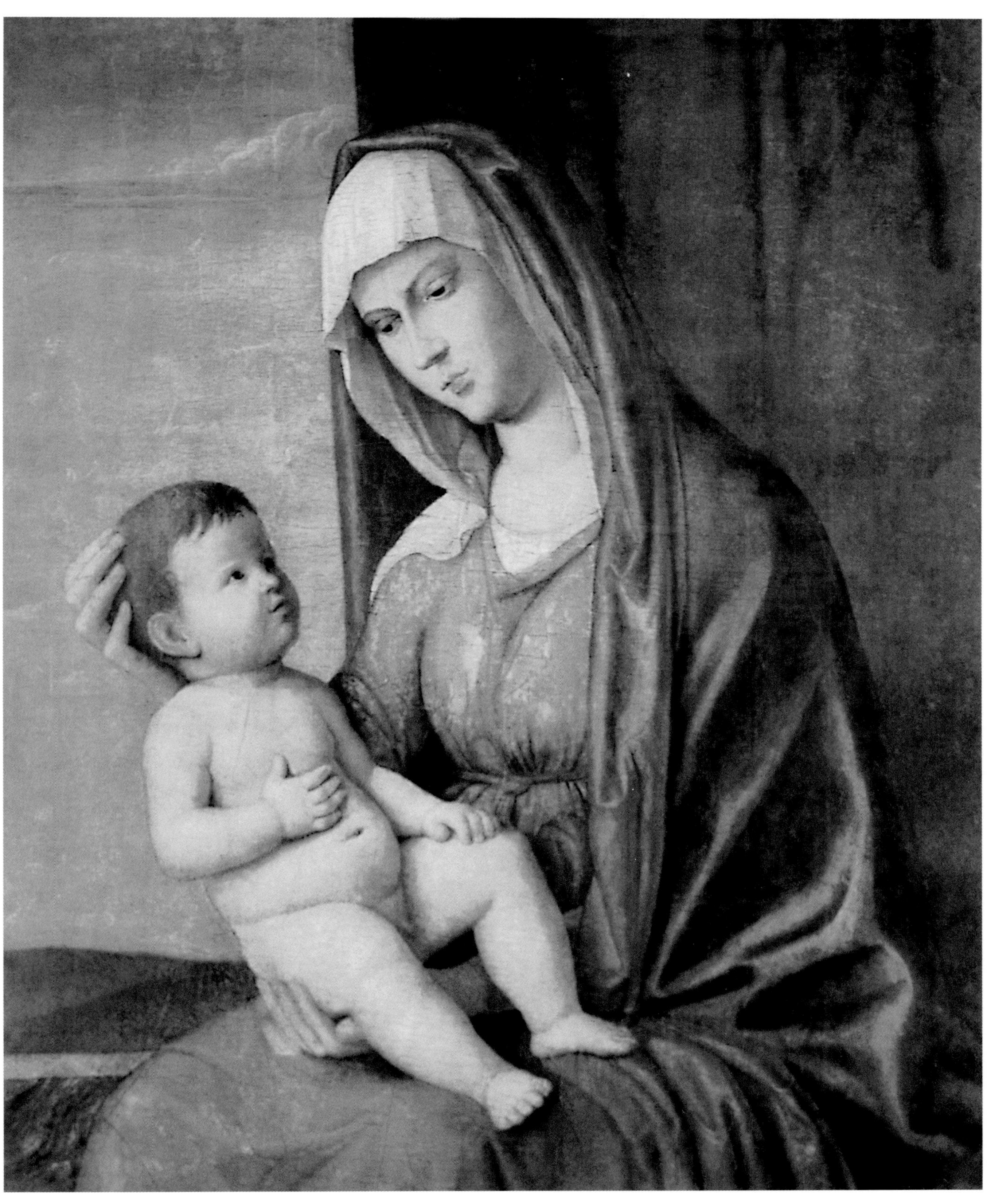

Fig. 248 Giovanni Battista Cima da Conegliano: *Madonna and Child*. Wesleyan College, Macon, Georgia; Gift of Samuel H. Kress, K 1069.

ANDREA DI NICCOLÒ, C. 1445–C. 1525; ATTRIBUTED; SIENESE

Pietà (61.192; K 290) 51.2 X 41.3 CM, TEMPERA ON PANEL

MEMPHIS, TENNESSEE. MEMPHIS BROOKS MUSEUM OF ART

The attribution of the painting has long been at issue. Early scholars, for example, Bernard Berenson (1936), Giorgio Vigni (1937), and Raimond van Marle (1937), assigned it to Vecchietta (c. 1412–1480). Citing the opinion of Millard Meiss, William E. Suida (1958) reattributed it to Andrea di Niccolò, c. 1500. Gertrude Coor (1961) and Federico Zeri (1964) believed it was much closer in style to the work of Benvenuto di Giovanni (1436–c. 1518). This opinion was endorsed by Burton B. Fredericksen and Darrell D. Davisson (1966) and Roberto Bartalini (1993), but it was dismissed by Maria Cristina Bandera Viani (1999). Fredericksen and Zeri (1972) came to accept the attribution to Andrea di Niccolò.

The grieving figures include, from left to right, St. Rosalie, St. John the Evangelist, St. Ursula, St. Agnes, the Virgin Mary, St. Margaret, St. Jerome, St. Francis, and Mary Magdalen. The small size of the panel and its subject matter suggest that the work served in a private, penitential capacity, or that it was a bierhead, as Berenson (1968) suggested. The postures and gestures of Christ, the Virgin, John, and Mary Madgalen are unusual, perhaps influenced by Vecchietta's work in the frescoed *Lamentation* (Museo del Seminario Arcivescovile, Monteriggioni) of c. 1445–c. 1448, formerly in the Martinozzi Chapel in San Francesco, Siena.

PROVENANCE

Karl Neumann, Barmen-Elberfeld, Germany, 1933; Count Alessandro Contini-Bonacossi, Florence; Samuel H. Kress, New York, acquired 1934; National Gallery of Art, Washington, D.C., exhibited 1941–1951; Memphis Brooks Museum of Art (Brooks Memorial Art Gallery), acquired 1961

BIBLIOGRAPHY

Bernard Berenson, *Pitture italiane del Rinascimento* (Milan: U. Hoepli, 1936), 508; Giorgio Vigni, *Lorenzo di Pietro detto il Vecchietta* (Florence: G. C. Sansoni, 1937), 89; Raimond van Marle, *The Development of the Italian Schools of Painting*, vol. 16, *The Renaissance Painters of Tuscany* (The Hague: M. Nijhoff, 1937), 244; National Gallery of Art, *Preliminary Catalogue of Paintings and Sculpture* (Washington, D.C.: National Gallery of Art, 1941), 209, no. 257; William E. Suida, *The Samuel H. Kress Collection, Brooks Memorial Art Gallery* (Memphis, Tenn.: Brooks Memorial Art Gallery, 1958), 12; Gertrude Coor, *Neroccio de' Landi, 1447–1500* (Princeton: Princeton University Press, 1961), 202-3; Federico Zeri, "Appunti nel Lindenau-Museum di Altenburg," *Bollettino d'Arte* 49 (1964): 48; Burton B. Fredericksen and Darrell D. Davisson, *Benvenuto di Giovanni, Girolamo di Benvenuto: Their Altarpieces in the J. Paul Getty Museum* (Malibu: J. Paul Getty Museum, 1966), 26, 35; *The Samuel H. Kress Collection* (Memphis, Tenn.: Brooks Memorial Art Gallery, 1966), 16-17; Fern Rusk Shapley, *Paintings from the Samuel H. Kress Collection: Italian Schools*, vol. 1, *XIII–XV Century* (London: Phaidon Press, 1966), 152; Bernard Berenson, *Italian Pictures of the Renaissance: A List of the Principal Artists and Their Works with an Index of Places. Central Italian and North Italian Schools*, 3 vols. (London: Phaidon Press, 1968), 1:445; Burton B. Fredericksen and Federico Zeri, *Census of Pre-Nineteenth-Century Italian Paintings in North American Public Collections* (Cambridge, Mass.: Harvard University Press, 1972), 7, 595; Fern Rusk Shapley, *Paintings from the Samuel H. Kress Collection: Italian Schools*, vol. 3, *XVI–XVIII Century* (London: Phaidon Press, 1973), 387; Sally Palmer Thomason, *Painting and Sculpture Collection: Memphis Brooks Museum of Art* (Memphis, Tenn.: Memphis Brooks Museum of Art, 1984), 39; Roberto Bartalini, "I. Il tempo di Pio II," in *Francesco di Giorgio e il Rinascimento a Siena 1450–1500*, ed. Luciano Bellosi (Milan: Electa, 1993), 97, 99; Mojmír S. Frinta, *Punched Decoration on Late Medieval Panel and Miniature Painting*, pt. 1 (Prague: Maxdorf, 1998), 50, 61, 106; Maria Cristina Bandera Viani, *Benvenuto di Giovanni* (Milan: Federico Motta, 1999), 42, 68 n. 143, 249-50, no. 14; Arnold Victor Coonin, "The Allure of Romanino's *Mystic Marriage of Saint Catherine*," in *Old Masters in Context: Romanino's Mystic Marriage of Saint Catherine*, ed. Arnold Victor Coonin (Memphis: Memphis Brooks Museum of Art, 2003), 9-10.

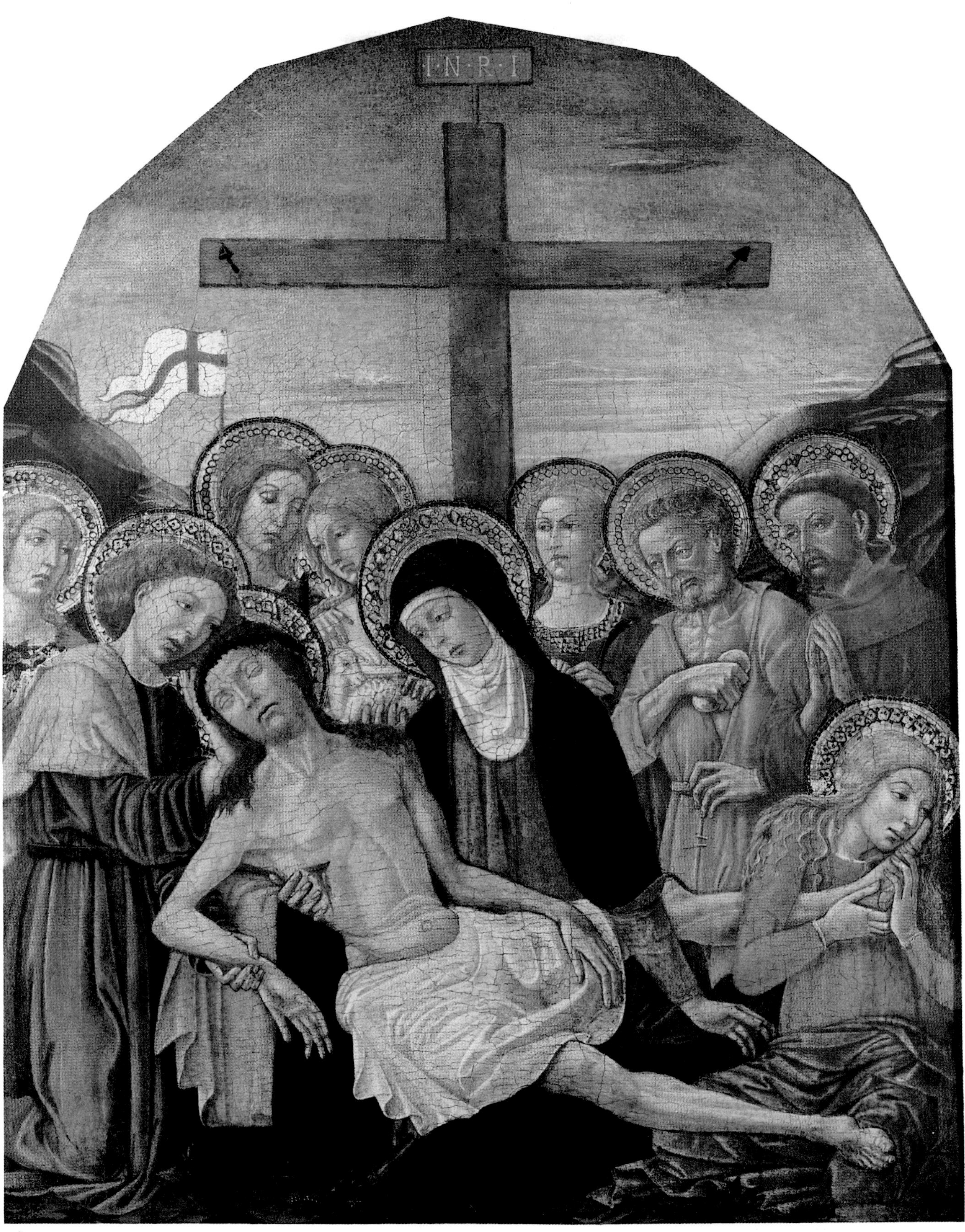

Fig. 249 Andrea di Niccolò (attributed): *Pietà*. Collection of Memphis Brooks Museum of Art, Memphis, Tennessee; Gift of the Samuel H. Kress Foundation, 61.192.

BOTTICINI, FRANCESCO, 1446–1497; ATTRIBUTED; FLORENTINE

Madonna and Child (61.206; K 1723) 81 x 66.7 CM, TEMPERA ON PANEL

MEMPHIS, TENNESSEE. MEMPHIS BROOKS MUSEUM OF ART

According to William E. Suida (1958), when the panel, from an unidentified altarpiece, appeared on the market in 1886, it was catalogued as a work by Masaccio (1401–1428). Later, Sidney F. Sabin (1937) attributed it to Filippo Lippi (c. 1406–1469). Suida gave it to a Florentine master, c. 1475, probably Francesco Botticini. Fern Rusk Shapley (1966), noting the influence of Filippo Lippi and the Carrand Master (also known as the Master of the Bargello Tondo; active first half of the fifteenth century), assigned it to the Florentine School in the second half of the fifteenth century. Burton B. Fredericksen and Federico Zeri (1972) endorsed Shapley's categorization.

The painting is a fragment of a larger composition that probably included standing saints on each side of the Virgin's throne. The image of the nursing Madonna was common in medieval and Renaissance painting; it emphasized the humanity of Christ and symbolized the nourishment provided by the Church.

PROVENANCE

Carlo del Chiaro, Florence (?); Prince Demidoff, Palazzo San Donato, Florence (?); William Graham, London, by 1884; Christie, Manson & Woods, London, April 9, 1886, lot 326; W. Lockett Agnew, London; Hon. J. F. Cheetham, Dunkinfield Lodge, Bournemouth; Christie, Manson & Woods, London, June 15, 1923, lot 82; Frank T. Sabin, London, by 1932; Count Alessandro Contini-Bonacossi, Florence; Samuel H. Kress, New York, acquired 1950; Memphis Brooks Museum of Art (Brooks Memorial Art Gallery), acquired 1961

BIBLIOGRAPHY

Algernon Graves, *Century of Loan Exhibitions 1813–1912*, 5 vols. (London: Graves, 1913–1915), 2:726; Sidney F. Sabin, *Gems of Painting* (London: Frank T. Sabin, 1937); "A Double Benefaction," *Arts Magazine* 34 (1958): 34; William E. Suida, *The Samuel H. Kress Collection, Brooks Memorial Art Gallery* (Memphis, Tenn.: Brooks Memorial Art Gallery, 1958), 26; Bernard Berenson, *Italian Pictures of the Renaissance: A List of the Principal Artists and Their Works with an Index of Places. Florentine School*, 2 vols. (London: Phaidon Press, 1963), 1:221; *The Samuel H. Kress Collection* (Memphis, Tenn.: Brooks Memorial Art Gallery, 1966), 32; Fern Rusk Shapley, *Paintings from the Samuel H. Kress Collection: Italian Schools*, vol. 1, *XIII–XV Century* (London: Phaidon Press, 1966), 119; Burton B. Fredericksen and Federico Zeri, *Census of Pre-Nineteenth-Century Italian Paintings in North American Public Collections* (Cambridge, Mass.: Harvard University Press, 1972), 221, 595; Sally Palmer Thomason, *Painting and Sculpture Collection: Memphis Brooks Museum of Art* (Memphis, Tenn.: Memphis Brooks Museum of Art, 1984), 35; Mojmír S. Frinta, *Punched Decoration on Late Medieval Panel and Miniature Painting*, pt. 1 (Prague: Maxdorf, 1998), 133, 137.

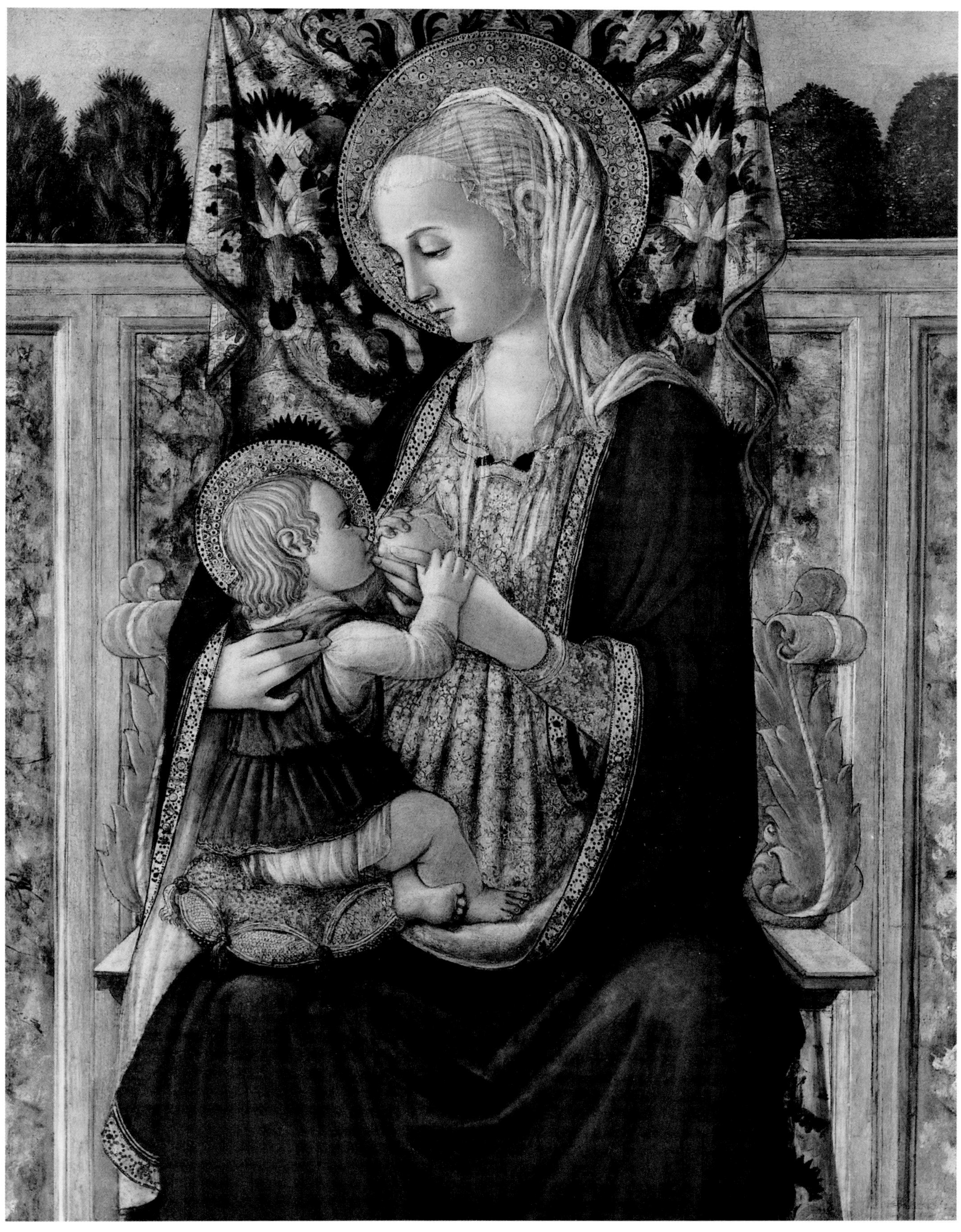

Fig. 250 Francesco Botticini (attributed), *Madonna and Child*. Collection of Memphis Brooks Museum of Art, Memphis, Tennessee; Gift of the Samuel H. Kress Foundation, 61.206.

CIMA DA CONEGLIANO, GIOVANNI BATTISTA, C. 1459–1517; VENETIAN

Enthroned Madonna and Child with Two Virgin Martyrs (61.211; K 2070) 59.7 X 43.8 CM, TEMPERA ON PANEL

MEMPHIS, TENNESSEE. MEMPHIS BROOKS MUSEUM OF ART

The artist's signature appears on a *cartellino*, a simulated piece of paper, at the lower left: "Joañis . baptista . Coneglian . opus." As Fern Rusk Shapley (1968) and Peter Humfrey (1983) observed, the composition is a pastiche of elements from other works by Cima. The Virgin derives from his signed *Madonna and Child with St. Jerome and St. John the Baptist* (National Gallery of Art, Washington, D.C.; 33); St. Catherine repeats in reverse the Catherine in his altarpiece in the cathedral of Conegliano; St. Christina reprises the representation of Christina in the *Madonna with Saints* (Hage Collection, Nivaagaard); and the base of the throne echoes that in the *Zermen Altarpiece* (Accademia, Venice; 658). Scholars have generally placed the work early in the artist's career, c. 1490–1495. Humfrey considered it to be a product of Cima's shop, dating to the later portion of the master's career.

The figures to the left and right, respectively, are the virgin martyrs St. Catherine of Alexandria and St. Christina. The small size of the panel and the subject matter suggest use as a personal devotional image, perhaps by a female patron, given the inclusion of two female saints.

PROVENANCE

Private collection, Paris, by c. 1950; Count Alessandro Contini-Bonacossi, Florence; Samuel H. Kress, New York, acquired 1954; Memphis Brooks Museum of Art (Brooks Memorial Art Gallery), acquired 1961

BIBLIOGRAPHY

William E. Suida, *The Samuel H. Kress Collection, Brooks Memorial Art Gallery* (Memphis, Tenn.: Brooks Memorial Art Gallery, 1958), 36; Luigi Coletti, *Cima da Conegliano* (Venice: Neri Pozza, 1959), 74; Rodolfo Pallucchini, "Giunte al catalogo di Cima da Conegliano," *Arte Antica e Moderna* 13-16 (1961): 186-87; Luigi Menegazzi, ed., *Cima da Conegliano* (Venice: Neri Pozza, 1962), 4, 25; *The Samuel H. Kress Collection* (Memphis, Tenn.: Brooks Memorial Art Gallery, 1966), 42; Fern Rusk Shapley, *Paintings from the Samuel H. Kress Collection: Italian Schools*, vol. 2, *XV–XVI Century* (London: Phaidon Press, 1968), 59; Burton B. Fredericksen and Federico Zeri, *Census of Pre-Nineteenth-Century Italian Paintings in North American Public Collections* (Cambridge, Mass.: Harvard University Press, 1972), 53, 595; Luigi Menegazzi, *Cima da Conegliano* (Treviso: Canova, 1981), 88; Peter Humfrey, *Cima da Conegliano* (Cambridge and New York: Cambridge University Press, 1983), 118, no. 77; Sally Palmer Thomason, *Painting and Sculpture Collection: Memphis Brooks Museum of Art* (Memphis, Tenn.: Memphis Brooks Museum of Art, 1984), 37; Arnold Victor Coonin, "The Allure of Romanino's *Mystic Marriage of Saint Catherine*," in *Old Masters in Context: Romanino's Mystic Marriage of Saint Catherine*, ed. Arnold Victor Coonin (Memphis, Tenn.: Memphis Brooks Museum of Art, 2003), 5-6.

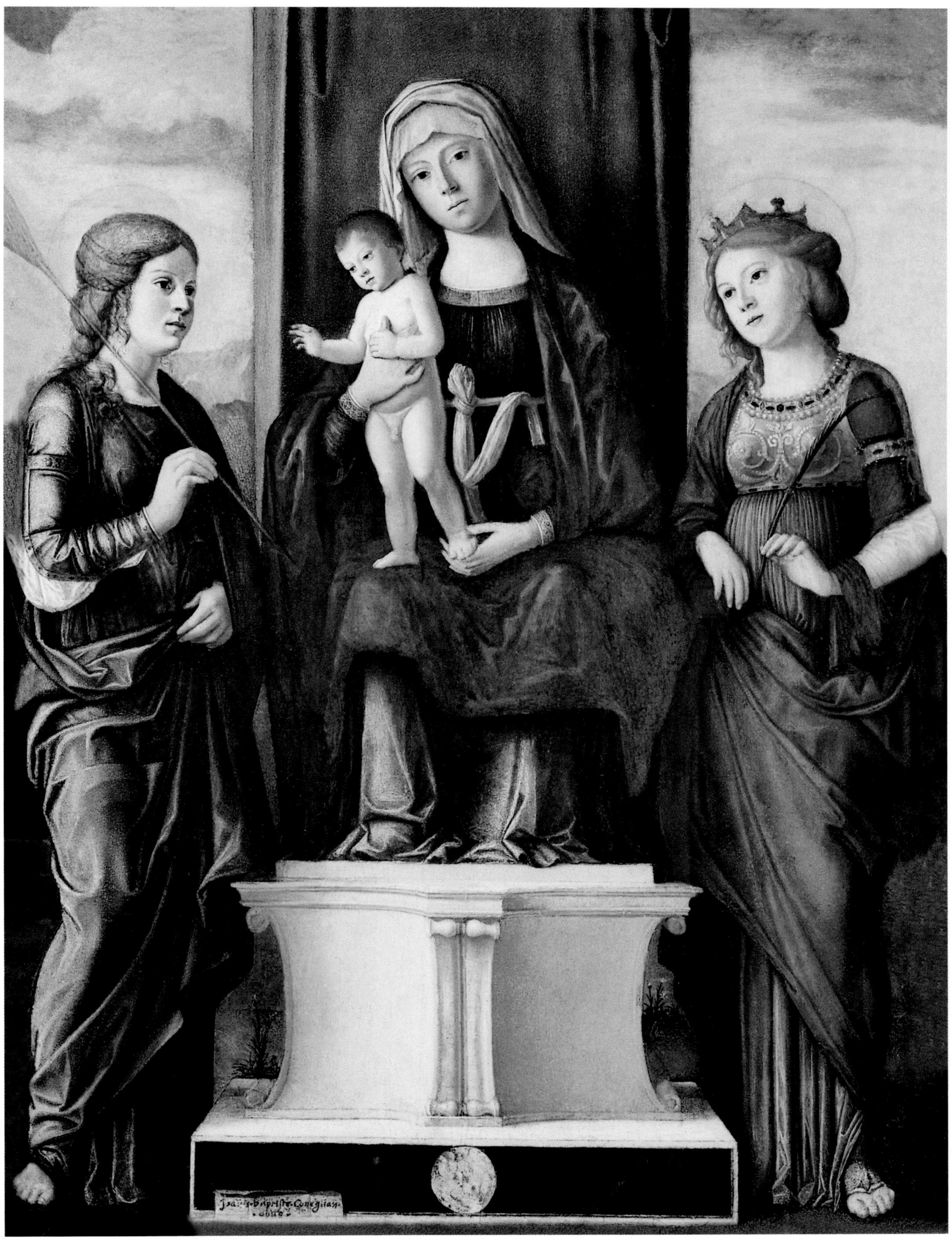

Fig. 251 Giovanni Battista Cima da Conegliano: *Enthroned Madonna and Child with Two Virgin Martyrs*. Collection of Memphis Brooks Museum of Art, Memphis, Tennessee; Gift of the Samuel H. Kress Foundation, 61.211.

COSTA, LORENZO DI OTTAVIO, C. 1460–1535; FERRARESE-BOLOGNESE

St. Paul (61.194; K 466) 34.3 X 26.3 CM, TEMPERA ON PANEL

MEMPHIS, TENNESSEE. MEMPHIS BROOKS MUSEUM OF ART

Roberto Longhi (1940) published the painting as a late work from Costa's Mantuan period, c. 1510–1515. Noting Correggio's (c. 1489–1534) influence on Costa's treatment of chiaroscuro effects, Andrea Ugolini (1987) refined the date to c. 1511–1515.

Paul, the apostle to the Gentiles, appears with his traditional attributes, a book and a sword. Contemporary representations of the saint preaching to the crowds in Athens during one of his missions to Greece employ the same pointing gesture. The small size of the panel and its subject matter suggest that it was used for the private devotions of someone whose name or patron saint was Paul.

PROVENANCE

D. Botto, Milan; Achillito Chiesa, Milan; Count Alessandro Contini-Bonacossi, Florence; Samuel H. Kress, New York, acquired 1936; National Gallery of Art, Washington, D.C., exhibited 1941–1951; Memphis Brooks Museum of Art (Brooks Memorial Art Gallery), acquired 1961

BIBLIOGRAPHY

Roberto Longhi, *Ampliamenti nell'officina ferrarese di Roberto Longhi* (Florence: G. C. Sansoni, 1940), 19-20; National Gallery of Art, *Preliminary Catalogue of Paintings and Sculpture* (Washington, D.C.: National Gallery of Art, 1941), 47, no. 364; Roberto Longhi, *Officina ferrarese 1934* (Florence: Sansoni, 1956), 145; Alfredo Puerari, *Boccaccino* (Milan: Ceschina, 1957), 164; William E. Suida, *The Samuel H. Kress Collection, Brooks Memorial Art Gallery* (Memphis, Tenn.: Brooks Memorial Art Gallery, 1958), 52; *The Samuel H. Kress Collection* (Memphis, Tenn.: Brooks Memorial Art Gallery, 1966), 60; Ranieri Varese, *Lorenzo Costa* (Milan: Silvana, 1967), 55, 76; Bernard Berenson, *Italian Pictures of the Renaissance: A List of the Principal Artists and Their Works with an Index of Places. Central Italian and North Italian Schools*, 3 vols. (London: Phaidon Press, 1968), 1:97; Fern Rusk Shapley, *Paintings from the Samuel H. Kress Collection: Italian Schools*, vol. 2, *XV–XVI Century* (London: Phaidon Press, 1968), 65-66; Burton B. Fredericksen and Federico Zeri, *Census of Pre-Nineteenth-Century Italian Paintings in North American Public Collections* (Cambridge, Mass.: Harvard University Press, 1972), 57, 595; Sally Palmer Thomason, *Painting and Sculpture Collection: Memphis Brooks Museum of Art* (Memphis, Tenn.: Memphis Brooks Museum of Art, 1984), 44; Andrea Ugolini, "Lorenzo Costa da Bologna a Mantova," *Prospettiva* 48 (1987): 82; Marilena Tamassia, *Collezioni d'arte tra Ottocento e Novecento: Jacquier fotografi a Firenze, 1870–1973* (Naples: Electa, 1995), 232, no. 52035.

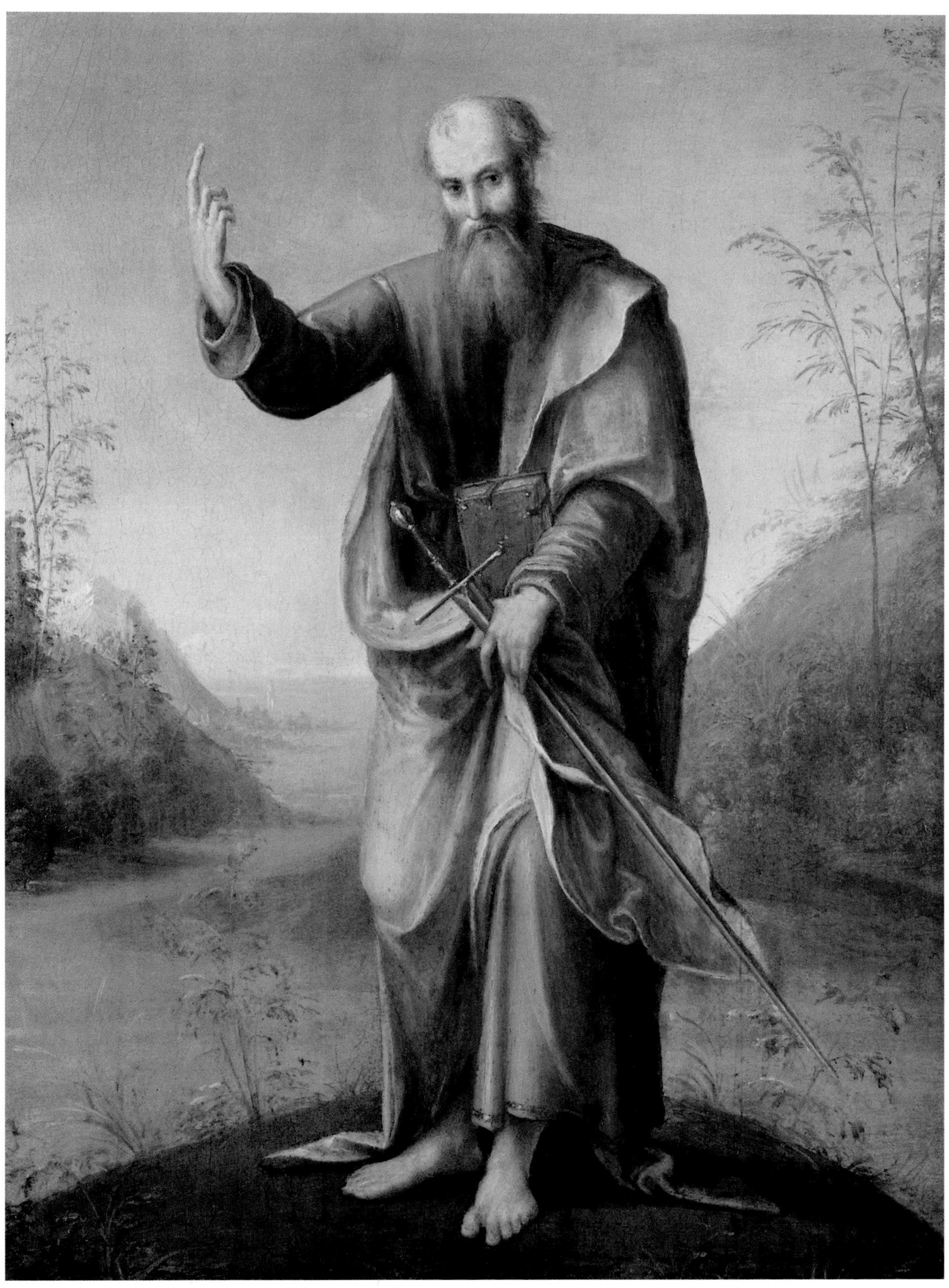

Fig. 252 Lorenzo di Ottavio Costa: *St. Paul*. Collection of Memphis Brooks Museum of Art, Memphis, Tennessee; Gift of the Samuel H. Kress Foundation, 61.194.

DUCCIO DI BUONINSEGNA, C. 1255–BEFORE 1319; FOLLOWER; SIENESE

Madonna and Child with Saints and Crucifixion (61.200; K 1289) 26.4 X 42.5 CM, TEMPERA ON PANEL

MEMPHIS, TENNESSEE. MEMPHIS BROOKS MUSEUM OF ART

Scholars have debated the attribution of this small, portable triptych. Bernard Berenson (1930; 1930) published it as a work of the Tuscan School, dating it to the early fourteenth century; he later (1963) listed it among works by Giotto's (1266/7–1337) anonymous contemporaries and immediate followers. When the altarpiece was exhibited at the National Gallery of Art (*Preliminary Catalogue* 1941), it was attributed to a contemporary of Duccio. Fern Rusk Shapley (1966) gave it to a follower of Duccio whose style was close to that of the Goodhart Master (active 1300–1325). Burton B. Fredericksen and Federico Zeri (1972) categorized it simply as Sienese, from the fourteenth century. Luciano Bellosi (1974) argued convincingly that the author was the Master of San Gaggio (active 1300), whose eponymous work is the *Madonna and Child Enthroned with Four Saints* (Accademia, Florence; 6115; formerly, San Gaggio, Florence). Bellosi's attribution was endorsed by Miklòs Boskovits (in Offner, Steinweg, and Boskovits 1984). A comparable work is this master's portable triptych in Berlin (Staatliche Museen, Gemäldegalerie; 1047).

The monogram on the placard above Christ's head reads "IC - XC" (Jesus Christ). Sts. Peter and John the Baptist appear on either side of the Madonna and Child, and an anonymous bishop saint occupies the upper register of the left-hand wing. Below him is an unidentified supplicant.

PROVENANCE

Paolo Paolini, Rome; American Art Galleries, New York, December 10, 1924, lot 91; E. L. Craven; Mortimer L. Schiff, New York; Christie, Manson & Woods, London, June 24, 1938, lot 83; Count Alessandro Contini-Bonacossi, Florence; Samuel H. Kress, New York, acquired 1939; National Gallery of Art, Washington, D.C., exhibited 1941–1952; Memphis Brooks Museum of Art (Brooks Memorial Art Gallery), acquired 1961

BIBLIOGRAPHY

Bernard Berenson, "Quadri senza casa: Il Trecento senese, I," *Dedalo* 11 (1930): 266, 269; Bernard Berenson, "Missing Pictures of the Sienese Trecento," *International Studio* 97 (1930): 32-33; National Gallery of Art, *Preliminary Catalogue of Paintings and Sculpture* (Washington, D.C.: National Gallery of Art, 1941), 61, no. 510; *The New Bulletin, Staten Island Institute of Arts and Sciences* 5 (1955): 25; Bernard Berenson, *Italian Pictures of the Renaissance: A List of the Principal Artists and Their Works with an Index of Places. Florentine School*, 2 vols. (London: Phaidon Press, 1963), 1:83; *The Samuel H. Kress Collection* (Memphis, Tenn.: Brooks Memorial Art Gallery, 1966), 25; Fern Rusk Shapley, *Paintings from the Samuel H. Kress Collection: Italian Schools*, vol. 1, *XIII–XV Century* (London: Phaidon Press, 1966), 15; Burton B. Fredericksen and Federico Zeri, *Census of Pre-Nineteenth-Century Italian Paintings in North American Public Collections* (Cambridge, Mass.: Harvard University Press, 1972), 240, 595; Luciano Bellosi, *Buffalmacco e il Trionfo della Morte* (Turin: G. Einaudi, 1974), 77; Richard Offner, Klara Steinweg, and Miklòs Boskovits, *A Critical and Historical Corpus of Florentine Painting*, sec. 3, vol. 9, *The Painters of the Miniaturist Tendency* (Florence: Giunti, 1984), 335 n. 3; Sally Palmer Thomason, *Painting and Sculpture Collection: Memphis Brooks Museum of Art* (Memphis, Tenn.: Memphis Brooks Museum of Art, 1984), 25-26; Enrico Castelnuovo, ed., *La pittura in Italia. Il Duecento e il Trecento*, 2 vols. (Milan: Electa, 1986), 2:625; Marilena Tamassia, *Collezioni d'arte tra Ottocento e Novecento: Jacquier fotografi a Firenze, 1870–1973* (Naples: Electa, 1995), 185, no. 50299.

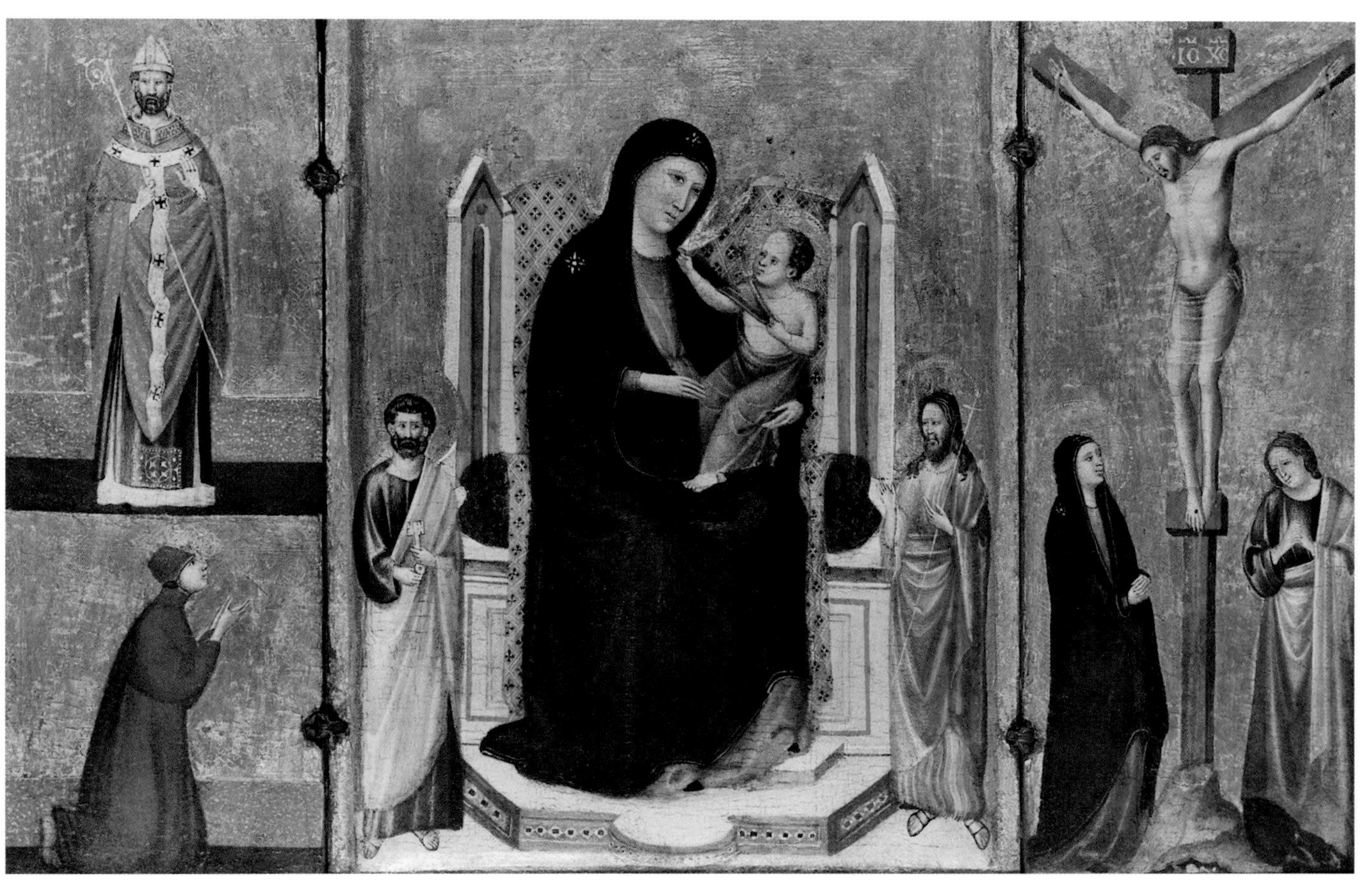

Fig. 253 Duccio di Buoninsegna (follower): *Madonna and Child with Saints and Crucifixion*. Collection of Memphis Brooks Museum of Art, Memphis, Tennessee; Gift of the Samuel H. Kress Foundation, 61.200.

GIOVANNI DEL BIONDO, ACTIVE 1356; DIED 1399; FLORENTINE

Madonna and Child with St. John the Baptist and St. Catherine of Alexandria (61.191; K 259) 86.1 x 76.9 cm, tempera on panel

MEMPHIS, TENNESSEE. MEMPHIS BROOKS MUSEUM OF ART

Published by Bernard Berenson (1931) as the work of Giovanni del Biondo, this small altarpiece was reattributed to the Master of the Prato Annunciation (active fourteenth century) by Richard Offner and Klara Steinweg (1969). Miklòs Boskovits (1972) proposed instead that the painting represented the collaboration of Giovanni del Biondo, Jacopo di Cione (1320/30–before 1400), and the Master of the Ashmolean Museum Predella (active c. 1365–c. 1390); in his opinion, Giovanni was responsible for the design and part of the execution, Jacopo for the heads of the Virgin and St. John. He dated the work 1385–1390.

"SCS JOHES BAPTISTA AVE DULCIS VIRGO MARIA SUCCHURRE NOBIS MATER PIA SCA KATERINA VIRG" ("St. John the Baptist; Hail, sweet Virgin Mary; succor us, pious Mother; St. Catherine, Virgin") is inscribed on the base of the frame, which is original to the panel. At the top appears the Annunciation. Depictions of the Madonna teaching the Christ Child to read the Gospels are rare in devotional art, as is the language of the inscription. In keeping with iconographic tradition, the Baptist points to Christ as the Lamb of God. "AG," the first two letters of the Latin word *agnus*, meaning lamb, appears on the verso in the open book. St. Catherine may have been included because of her association with scholarship.

PROVENANCE

Prince Galitzin, St. Petersburg; L. Currie, Combe Warren, Kingston Hill; Count Alessandro Contini-Bonacossi, Florence; Samuel H. Kress, New York, acquired 1933; National Gallery of Art, Washington, D.C., exhibited 1941–1952; Memphis Brooks Museum of Art (Brooks Memorial Art Gallery), acquired 1961

BIBLIOGRAPHY

Bernard Berenson, "Quadri senza casa: Il Trecento fiorentino, III," *Dedalo* 11 (1931): 1290, 1292; *An Exhibition of Italian Paintings Lent by Mr. Samuel H. Kress of New York to California Palace of the Legion of Honor, Lincoln Park, San Francisco, California* (San Francisco: Palace of the Legion of Honor, Burland Printing Co., 1934), 12; "San Francisco Sees Famous Kress Collection of Old Masters," *The Art Digest* 8 (1934): 32; Bernard Berenson, *Pitture italiane del Rinascimento* (Milan: U. Hoepli, 1936), 208; National Gallery of Art, *Preliminary Catalogue of Paintings and Sculpture* (Washington, D.C.: National Gallery of Art, 1941), 81-82, no. 238; Helen Comstock, "The Connoisseur in America," *The Connoisseur* 142 (1958): 203; William E. Suida, *The Samuel H. Kress Collection, Brooks Memorial Art Gallery* (Memphis, Tenn.: Brooks Memorial Art Gallery, 1958), 20; Bernard Berenson, *Italian Pictures of the Renaissance: A List of the Principal Artists and Their Works with an Index of Places. Florentine School*, 2 vols. (London: Phaidon Press, 1963), 1:86; *The Samuel H. Kress Collection* (Memphis, Tenn.: Brooks Memorial Art Gallery, 1966), 26; Fern Rusk Shapley, *Paintings from the Samuel H. Kress Collection: Italian Schools*, vol. 1, *XIII–XV Century* (London: Phaidon Press, 1966), 37; Richard Offner and Klara Steinweg, *A Critical and Historical Corpus of Florentine Painting*, sec. 4, vol. 5, pt. 2, *The Fourteenth Century. Giovanni del Biondo* (New York: Institute of Fine Arts, New York University, 1969), 36 n. 1; Miklòs Boskovits, "Review of Richard Offner and Klara Steinweg, *Giovanni del Biondo*," *Art Bulletin* 54 (1972): 206 n. 20; Burton B. Fredericksen and Federico Zeri, *Census of Pre-Nineteenth-Century Italian Paintings in North American Public Collections* (Cambridge, Mass.: Harvard University Press, 1972), 88, 595; Fern Rusk Shapley, *Paintings from the Samuel H. Kress Collection: Italian Schools*, vol. 3, *XVI–XVIII Century* (London: Phaidon Press, 1973), 383; Miklòs Boskovits, *Pittura fiorentina alla vigilia del Rinascimento, 1370–1400* (Florence: Edam, 1975), 226 n. 65, 227 n. 68, 312, 327, 374; Richard Fremantle, *Florentine Gothic Painters from Giotto to Masaccio: A Guide to Painting in and near Florence, 1300 to 1450* (London: Secker & Warburg, 1975), 253; Richard Offner and Hayden B. J. Maginnis, *A Critical and Historical Corpus of Florentine Painting: A Legacy of Attributions* (New York: Institute of Fine Arts, New York University Press, 1981), 49; Sally Palmer Thomason, *Painting and Sculpture Collection: Memphis Brooks Museum of Art* (Memphis, Tenn.: Memphis Brooks Museum of Art, 1984), 6, 29; Marilena Tamassia, *Collezioni d'arte tra Ottocento e Novecento: Jacquier fotografi a Firenze, 1870–1973* (Naples: Electa, 1995), 186, 50320; Mojmír S. Frinta, *Punched Decoration on Late Medieval Panel and Miniature Painting*, pt. 1 (Prague: Maxdorf, 1998), 506.

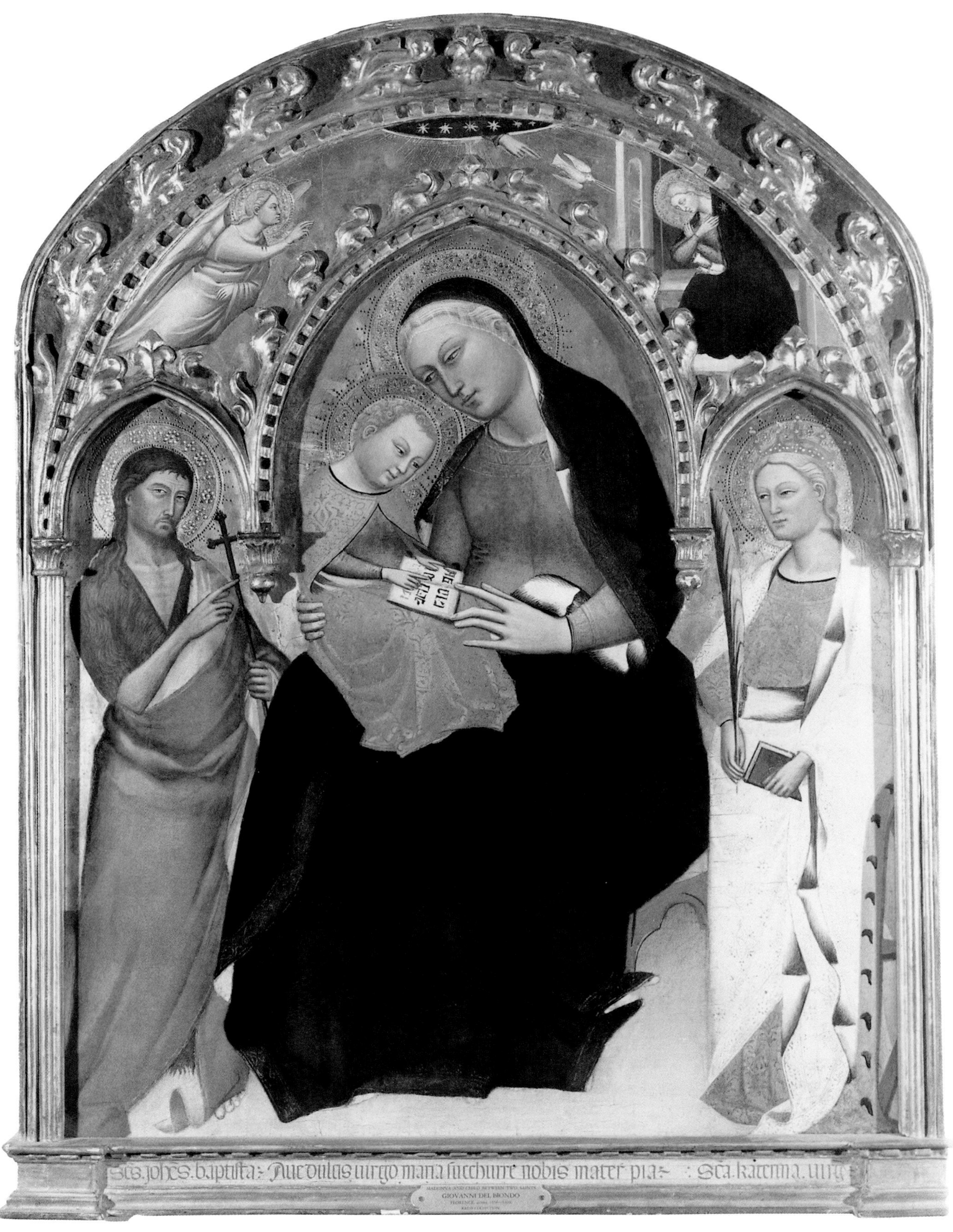

Fig. 254 Giovanni del Biondo: *Madonna and Child with St. John the Baptist and St. Catherine of Alexandria*. Collection of Memphis Brooks Museum of Art, Memphis, Tennessee; Gift of the Samuel H. Kress Foundation, 61.191.

LIPPI, FILIPPINO, C. 1457–1504; WORKSHOP; FLORENTINE

St. Francis in Glory (61.190; K 209) 179.1 X 148.6 CM, TEMPERA ON PANEL

MEMPHIS, TENNESSEE. MEMPHIS BROOKS MUSEUM OF ART

Katharine B. Neilson (1938) published the panel as a copy, by an unidentified artist, of a lost painting by Filippino; subsequent scholars rejected her hypothesis, with the notable exception of Carmen C. Bambach (in Goldner and Bambach 1997). Alfred Scharf (1950) believed the painting to be a late work by Filippino, left unfinished at his death and completed by an assistant, perhaps Raffaellino del Garbo (c. 1466–1524); he identified an autograph drawing by Filippino as a preliminary study for the composition (Gabinetto Nazionale delle Stampe, Villa Farnesina, Rome). Scharf's attribution and dating were generally accepted until recently, when Jonathan Nelson (1992; Zambrano and Nelson 2004) reassigned the panel to an independent personality active after the death of Filippino; he initially called this artist the Moses Master because of his *Moses Brings Forth Water out of the Rock* (National Gallery, London; 4904), but he later renamed him the Memphis Master in honor of this, his most important painting. William E. Suida (1958) suggested that the panel was one of the altarpieces mentioned by Vasari as having been painted by Filippino for the Franciscan church of San Salvatore, Florence. On the basis of the unique imagery, Perri Lee Roberts (1999) proposed an alternative venue, the Florentine hospital of San Paolo, which was affiliated with the Franciscan Third Order.

Although the preliminary drawing for the painting shows St. Francis confirming the rule of the Third Order, the Franciscan brotherhood of lay penitents, the panel itself depicts Francis with the stigmata, standing within a *mandorla* of seraphim. This unusual motif first appears in the late thirteenth century on Franciscan seals. Francis is accompanied by four saints intimately associated with the Franciscan Third Order, from left to right, the Blessed Lucchesius of Poggibonsi; St. Louis IX, king of France; St. Elizabeth of Hungary; and, probably for the first time in Italian art, the Blessed Bona of Poggibonsi, Lucchesius's wife. Reinforced by the exhortation on Francis's scroll, "VENITE FILII AVDITE ME TIMORE DNI DOCEBO VOS" ("Come, O sons, listen to me. I will teach you the fear of the Lord"), from Psalms 34:11, the image provides a model for meditation and imitation.

PROVENANCE

Stefano Bardini, Florence; Count Alessandro Contini-Bonacossi, Florence; Samuel H. Kress, New York, acquired 1932; National Gallery of Art, Washington, D.C., exhibited 1941–1952; Memphis Brooks Museum of Art (Brooks Memorial Art Gallery), acquired 1961

BIBLIOGRAPHY

Katharine B. Neilson, *Filippino Lippi, a Critical Study* (Cambridge: Cambridge University Press, 1938), 216 n. 20; National Gallery of Art, *Preliminary Catalogue of Paintings and Sculpture* (Washington, D.C.: National Gallery of Art, 1941), 107, no. 208; Alfred Scharf, *Filippino Lippi* (Vienna: Anton Schroll, 1950), 42-43, 46, 58; George Kaftal, *Iconography of the Saints in Tuscan Painting* (Florence: Sansoni, 1952), col. 212, no. 56; Maria Fossi Todorow, *Mostra di disegni di Filippino Lippi e Piero di Cosimo* (Florence: L. S. Olschki, 1955), 25; Luciano Berti and Umberto Baldini, *Filippino Lippi* (Florence: Arnaud, 1957), 56, 97-98; William E. Suida, *The Samuel H. Kress Collection, Brooks Memorial Art Gallery* (Memphis, Tenn.: Brooks Memorial Art Gallery, 1958), 24; "A Double Benefaction," *Arts* 32 (1958): 35; Bernard Berenson, *Italian Pictures of the Renaissance: A List of the Principal Artists and Their Works with an Index of Places. Florentine School*, 2 vols. (London: Phaidon Press, 1963), 1:110; *The Samuel H. Kress Collection* (Memphis, Tenn.: Brooks Memorial Art Gallery, 1966), 30; Fern Rusk Shapley, *Paintings from the Samuel H. Kress Collection: Italian Schools*, vol. 1, *XIII–XV Century* (London: Phaidon Press, 1966), 137-38; P. Martino Bertagna, "S. Lucchese da Poggibonsi, Note storiche e documenti," *Archivum franciscanum historicum* 62 (1969): 18 n. 1; Burton B. Fredericksen and Federico Zeri, *Census of Pre-Nineteenth-Century Italian Paintings in North American Public Collections* (Cambridge, Mass.: Harvard University Press, 1972), 105, 595; Innis H. Shoemaker, "Filippino Lippi as a Draughtsman" (Ph.D. diss., Columbia University, 1975), 342, no. 100; Enrichetta Beltrame Quattrocchi, *Disegni toscani e umbri del primo Rinascimento: Dalle collezioni del Gabinetto Nazionale delle Stampe* (Rome: De Luca, 1979), 32-33; John Pope-Hennessy, "Thoughts on Andrea della Robbia," *Apollo* 109 (1979): 197 n. 32; Sally

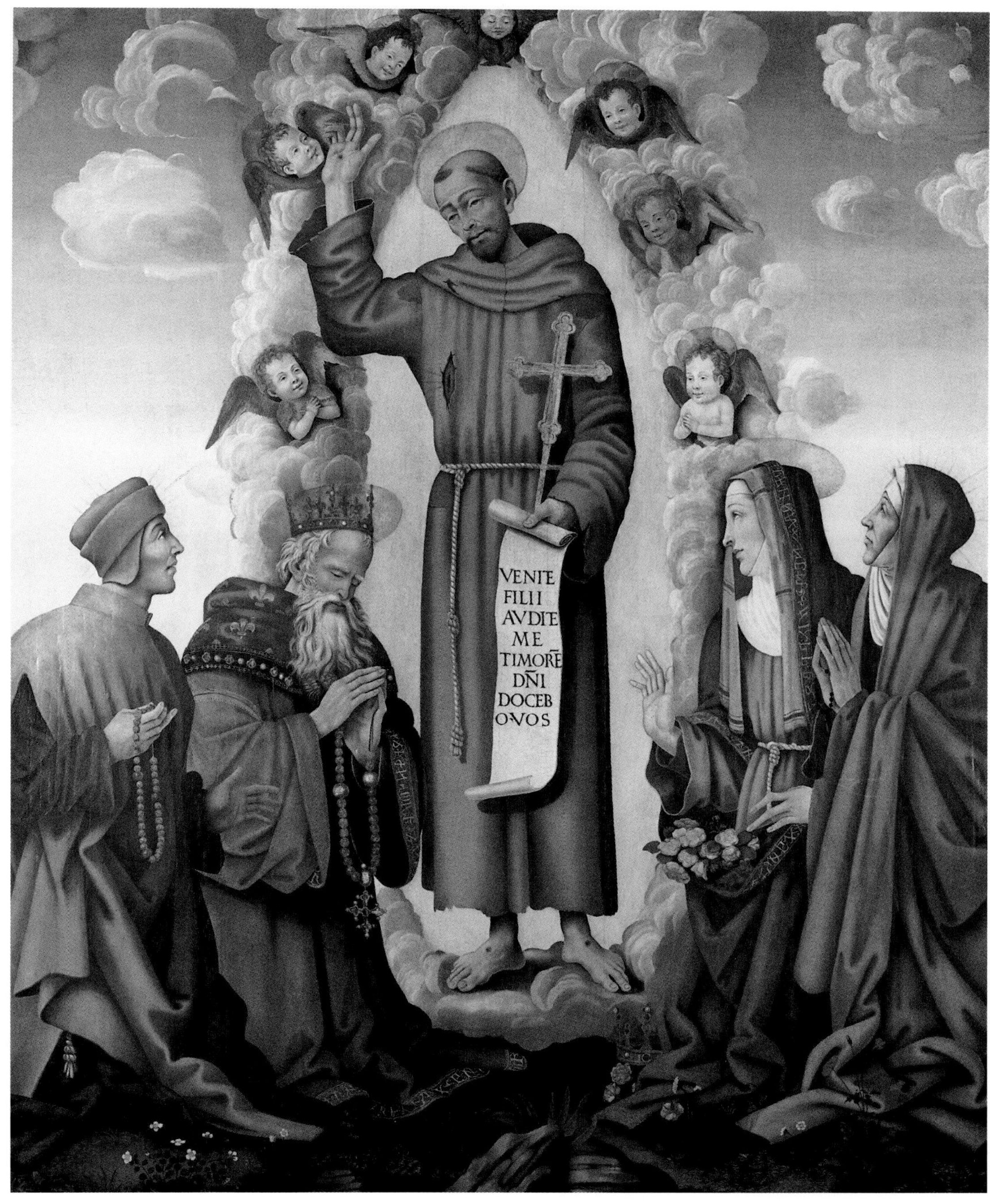

Fig. 255 Filippino Lippi (workshop): *St. Francis in Glory*. Collection of Memphis Brooks Museum of Art, Memphis, Tennessee; Gift of the Samuel H. Kress Foundation, 61.190.

Palmer Thomason, *Painting and Sculpture Collection: Memphis Brooks Museum of Art* (Memphis, Tenn.: Memphis Brooks Museum of Art, 1984), 43; Fiorenza Scalia and Cristina De Benedictis, eds., *Il Museo Bardini a Firenze*, 2 vols. (Milan: Electa, 1984), 1:102, 125; Luciano Berti and Umberto Baldini, *Filippino Lippi* (Florence: Edizioni d'arte Il Fiorino, 1991), 227; Jonathan Nelson, "The Later Work of Filippino Lippi: From His Roman Sojourn until His Death" (Ph.D. diss., New York University, 1992), 275, n. 11, 338; Marilena Tamassia, *Collezioni d'arte tra Ottocento e Novecento: Jacquier fotografi a Firenze, 1870–1973* (Naples: Electa, 1995), 194, no. 50548; George R. Goldner and Carmen C. Bambach, *The Drawings of Filippino Lippi and His Circle* (New York: Metropolitan Museum of Art, 1997), 264; Perri Lee Roberts, "New Observations on *Saint Francis in Glory*," *The Brooks Museum Bulletin, Essays on the Collection* 3 (1999): 6-15; Patrizia Zambrano and Jonathan Nelson, *Filippino Lippi* (Milan: Electa, 2004), 610.

LIPPO DI BENIVIENI, ACTIVE 1296–1320; ATTRIBUTED; FLORENTINE

Crucifixion; Scenes from the Passion and the Life of St. John the Baptist (61.201; K 1430) 64.8 X 34.3 CM (CENTRAL PANEL WITH MOLDINGS); 64.8 X 17.5 CM (LEFT WING); 62.9 X 16.5 CM (RIGHT WING), TEMPERA ON PANEL

MEMPHIS, TENNESSEE. MEMPHIS BROOKS MUSEUM OF ART

The attribution of this altarpiece has been the subject of scholarly discussion for many years. The work has generally been associated with the Giottesque School of the early fourteenth century, but it has also been assigned to trecento Umbria, by Burton B. Fredericksen and Federico Zeri (1972). More recently, Angelo Tartuferi (1986) and Andrew Ladis (1996), working independently, connected the triptych with Lippo di Benivieni. They based their opinions on its stylistic similarity, first observed by Zeri (1957 correspondence with the Kress Foundation), to Lippo's *Albizzi-Alessandri Altarpiece* (private collection, Milan) of c. 1315 and his *Lamentation* (Fogg Art Museum, Cambridge; 1917.195). Tartuferi placed the Brooks ensemble within the "close circle" of Lippo, whereas Ladis considered it to be a largely autograph, mature work, designed and, at least with regard to the *Crucifixion*, painted by the artist himself. Ladis also emphasized the influence of Giotto's *Crucifix* (Santa Maria Novella, Florence) from 1290–1300 and his *Lamentation* (Arena Chapel, Padua), from c. 1304–1306, on the imagery.

St. John the Baptist in the Wilderness, the *Baptism of Christ*, and the *Beheading of St. John* are depicted on the left wing; *Christ at Gethsemane*, the *Flagellation*, and the *Lamentation* are on the right. The Dominican monks who join the Virgin Mary, Mary Magdalen, and John the Evangelist at the foot of the cross are probably St. Dominic (left) and St. Peter Martyr (right). Norman E. Land (1995) suggested the kneeling female saint may be Catherine of Alexandria. Given the inclusion of the Dominicans, this small, portable triptych was probably commissioned by a member of that order or by a donor with Dominican sympathies.

PROVENANCE

Reverend Dr. Ash, Hungershall Park, Tunbridge Wells, England, 1880s; Arthur Brentano, New York; Samuel H. Kress, New York, acquired 1947; National Gallery of Art, Washington, D.C., exhibited 1951–1955; Memphis Brooks Museum of Art (Brooks Memorial Art Gallery), acquired 1961

BIBLIOGRAPHY

Algernon Graves, *Century of Loan Exhibitions 1813–1912*, 5 vols. (London: Graves, 1913–1915), 1:423; Bernard Berenson, *Italian Pictures of the Renaissance* (Oxford: Clarendon Press, 1932), 9; *Paintings and Sculpture from the Kress Collection* (Washington, D.C.: National Gallery of Art, 1951), 30, no. 3; Helen Comstock, "Connoisseur in America," *The Connoisseur* 142 (1958): 203; William E. Suida, *The Samuel H. Kress Collection, Brooks Memorial Art Gallery* (Memphis, Tenn.: Brooks Memorial Art Gallery, 1958), 18; Bernard Berenson, *Italian Pictures of the Renaissance: A List of the Principal Artists and Their Works with an Index of Places. Florentine School*, 2 vols. (London: Phaidon Press, 1963), 1:83; *The Samuel H. Kress Collection* (Memphis, Tenn.: Brooks Memorial Art Gallery, 1966), 22; Fern Rusk Shapley, *Paintings from the Samuel H. Kress Collection: Italian Schools*, vol. 1, *XIII–XV Century* (London: Phaidon Press, 1966), 31; Burton B. Fredericksen and Federico Zeri, *Census of Pre-Nineteenth-Century Italian Paintings in North American Public Collections* (Cambridge, Mass.: Harvard University Press, 1972), 243, 595; Sally Palmer Thomason, *Painting and Sculpture Collection: Memphis Brooks Museum of Art* (Memphis, Tenn.: Memphis Brooks Museum of Art, 1984), 28; Angelo Tartuferi, "*Corpus of Florentine Painting*: Nouveautés sur le Trecento," *Revue de l'Art* 71 (1986): 44-45; Norman E. Land, "Petrarch's Eye and a *Crucifixion* by Lippo di Benivieni," *Southeastern College Art Conference Review* 12 (1995): 391-98; Andrew Ladis, "An Early Fourteenth-Century Triptych in Memphis and Florentine Painting in the Glow of Duccio," *The Brooks Museum Bulletin, Essays on the Collection* 2 (1996): 1-10; Mojmír S. Frinta, *Punched Decoration on Late Medieval Panel and Miniature Painting*, pt. 1 (Prague: Maxdorf, 1998), 59.

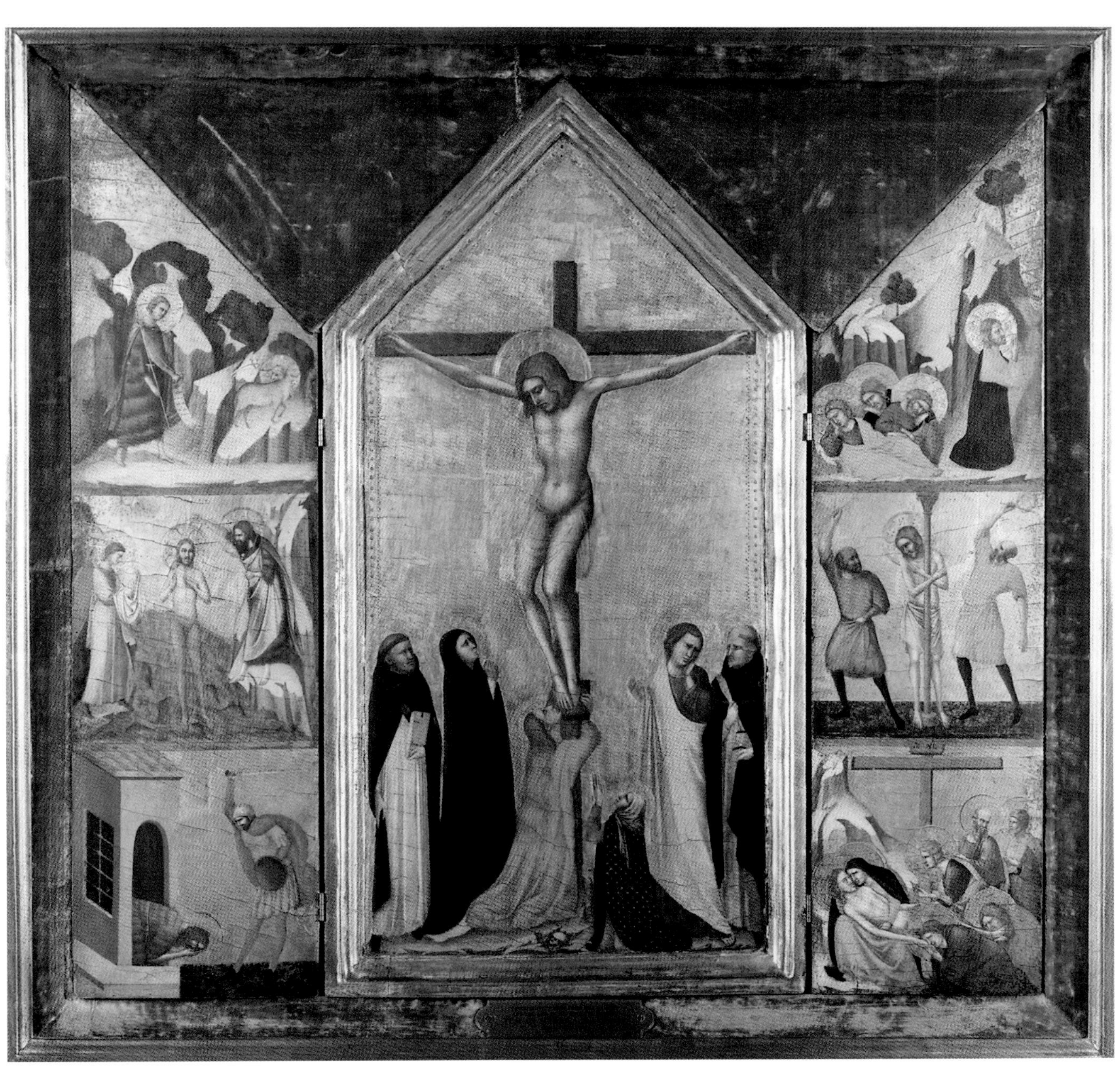

Fig. 256 Lippo di Benivieni (attributed): *Crucifixion; Scenes from the Passion and the Life of St. John the Baptist.* Collection of Memphis Brooks Museum of Art, Memphis, Tennessee; Gift of the Samuel H. Kress Foundation, 61.201.

LORENZO DI CREDI, C. 1456–1536; FOLLOWER; FLORENTINE

Madonna and Christ Child with St. John the Baptist (28.1; K B-1) 129.2 CM (DIAMETER), TEMPERA AND OIL ON PANEL

MEMPHIS, TENNESSEE. MEMPHIS BROOKS MUSEUM OF ART

This is one of a number of devotional *tondi* with similar compositons associated with Lorenzo di Credi and his followers in the early sixteenth century. Bernard Berenson (1909) initially attributed it to Piero di Cosimo (1462–1521), subsequently (1932) assigning it to a follower of Lorenzo di Credi, whom he called Tommaso. William E. Suida (1958) gave it to the Master of the Tondi. Fern Rusk Shapley (1968) preferred the generic "follower of Lorenzo di Credi." Gigetta Dalli Regoli (1966) identified the artist as the Master of the Santo Spirito *Conversazione*, his eponymous work being the *Madonna and Child Enthroned with St. John the Evangelist and St. Jerome* (Santo Spirito, Florence); she tentatively connected this altarpiece with Credi's collaborator, Giovanni di Benedetto Cianfanini (1462–1542). Burton B. Fredericksen and Federico Zeri (1972) considered the Memphis *tondo* to be a school, studio, or shop work. The Museum attributes it to a follower of Lorenzo di Credi, from c. 1500.

The subject of the Madonna adoring the Christ Child, in the company of the infant St. John the Baptist, originated in the middle of the fifteenth century in the work of Fra Filippo Lippi (c. 1406–1469) and, thereafter, became very popular in Florentine painting. Shapley observed that the poses of the Madonna and Child may derive from one of Leonardo's (1452–1519) many drawings of the Adoration, with Lorenzo di Credi's own *Adoration of the Child* (current location unknown; formerly, Staatliche Museen, Gemäldegalerie, Berlin) providing the model for St. Joseph leading the donkey in the left background.

PROVENANCE

John Stogdon, Harrow-on-the-Hill, Middlesex; Christie, Manson & Woods, London, July 14, 1922, lot 39 (not sold); Christie, Manson & Woods, London, February 12, 1926, lot 39; Sampson; Count Alessandro Contini-Bonacossi, Rome; Samuel H. Kress, New York, acquired 1927; Memphis Brooks Museum of Art (Brooks Memorial Art Gallery), acquired 1928

BIBLIOGRAPHY

Bernard Berenson, *The Florentine Painters of the Renaissance* (New York and London: G. P. Putnam's Sons, 1909), 164; Bernard Berenson, "Disegni inediti di Tommaso," *Rivista d'Arte* 14 (1932): 255; Alan Burroughs, *Art Criticism from a Laboratory* (Boston: Little, Brown, and Co., 1938), 82; William E. Suida, *The Samuel H. Kress Collection, Brooks Memorial Art Gallery* (Memphis, Tenn.: Brooks Memorial Art Gallery, 1958), 28; Helen Comstock, "The Connoisseur in America," *The Connoisseur* 142 (1958): 203; Bernard Berenson, *Italian Pictures of the Renaissance: A List of the Principal Artists and Their Works with an Index of Places. Florentine School*, 2 vols. (London: Phaidon Press, 1963), 1:208; Gigetta Dalli Regoli, *Lorenzo di Credi* (Milan: Edizioni di comunità, 1966), 191, no. 232; *The Samuel H. Kress Collection* (Memphis, Tenn.: Brooks Memorial Art Gallery, 1966), 34; Fern Rusk Shapley, *Paintings from the Samuel H. Kress Collection: Italian Schools*, vol. 2, *XV–XVI Century* (London: Phaidon Press, 1968), 114-15; Burton B. Fredericksen and Federico Zeri, *Census of Pre-Nineteenth-Century Italian Paintings in North American Public Collections* (Cambridge, Mass.: Harvard University Press, 1972), 110, 594; Sally Palmer Thomason, *Painting and Sculpture Collection: Memphis Brooks Museum of Art* (Memphis, Tenn.: Memphis Brooks Museum of Art, 1984), 40.

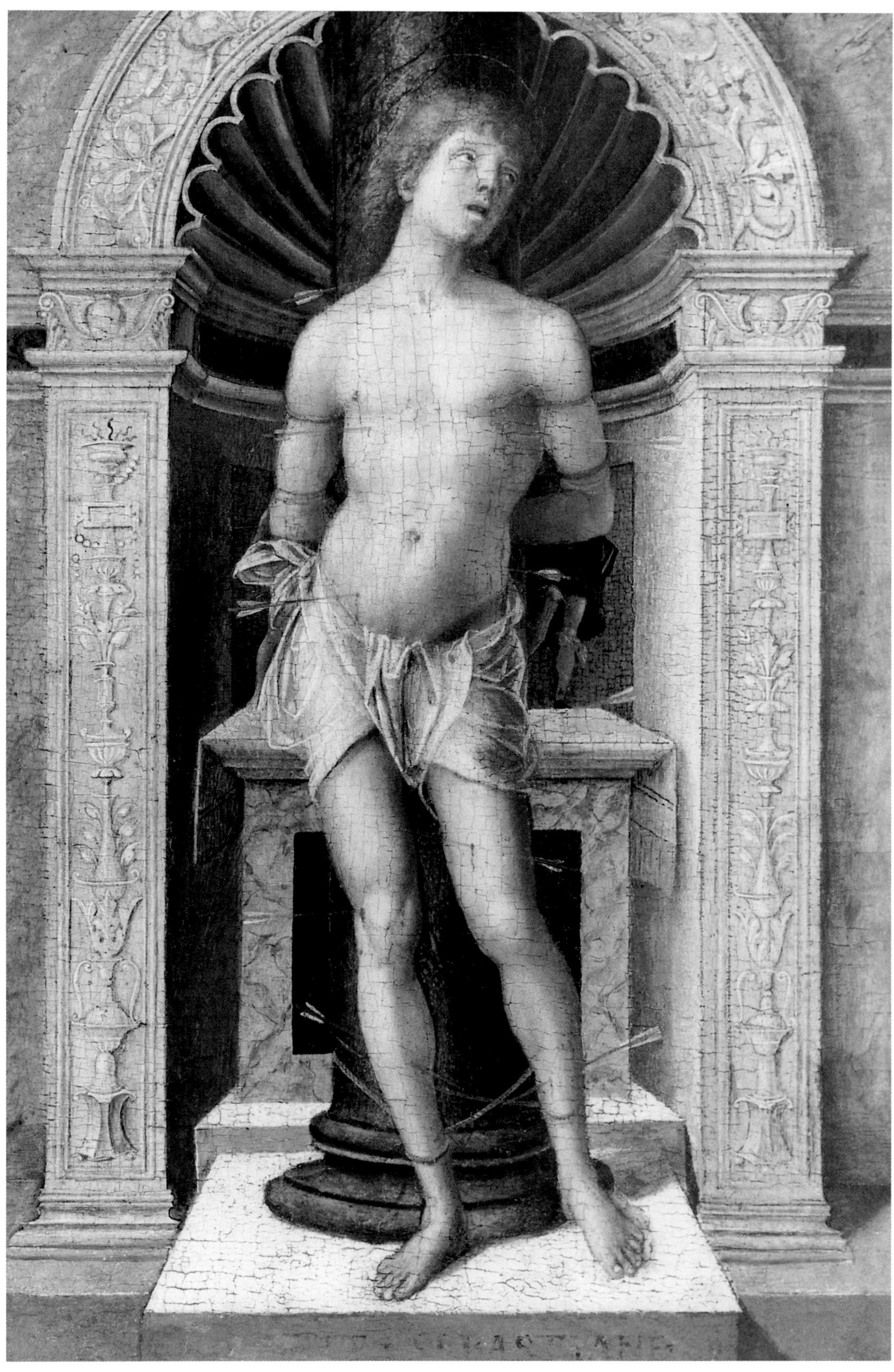

Fig. 258 Gian Francesco de Maineri (attributed): *St. Sebastian*. Collection of Memphis Brooks Museum of Art, Memphis, Tennessee; Gift of the Samuel H. Kress Foundation, 61.199.

MASTER OF THE CLARISSE PANEL, ACTIVE 1275–1300; SIENESE

Madonna and Child with Four Saints (61.210; K 1930) 100.3 X 191.1 CM, TEMPERA ON PANEL

MEMPHIS, TENNESSEE. MEMPHIS BROOKS MUSEUM OF ART

The painting is a type of altarpiece known as a dossal. Originally published by Raimond van Marle (1938) as the work of Guido da Siena (active c. 1250–1300), it was ascribed to the Guidesque Master of Montaione (active c. 1275–1285) by Edward B. Garrison (1949). James H. Stubblebine (1964) convincingly associated it with a group of paintings attributable to the Clarisse master and dating to the 1280s.

The figures flanking the Virgin, from left to right, have been identified tentatively as Mary Magdalen; St. Sabinus, a patron of Siena; John the Evangelist; and St. Margaret of Antioch. The poses and figure styles of the Madonna and Christ Child derive from late Byzantine icons.

PROVENANCE

Palazzo Piccolomini, Siena; Odescalchi, Rome (?); Stettiner, Rome; Principe del Drago, Rome; Lodovico Rosselli, Rome; Dedalo Gallery, New York; Samuel H. Kress, New York, acquired 1952; Memphis Brooks Museum of Art (Brooks Memorial Art Gallery), acquired 1961

BIBLIOGRAPHY

Raimond van Marle, *Gemme d'arte antica italiana* (Milan: Alfieri & Lacroix, 1938), pl. 46; Edward B. Garrison, "Post War Discoveries, Early Italian Paintings, IV," *Burlington Magazine* 89 (1947): 300-3; Edward B. Garrison, *Italian Romanesque Panel Painting* (Florence: Leo S. Olschki, 1949), 23, 167, no. 434; Richard Offner, "Guido da Siena and A.D. 1221," *Gazette des Beaux-Arts* 37 (1950): 65; "A Double Benefaction," *Arts Magazine* 32 (1958): 34; Helen Comstock, "The Connoisseur in America," *The Connoisseur* 142 (1958): 203; William E. Suida, *The Samuel H. Kress Collection, Brooks Memorial Art Gallery* (Memphis, Tenn.: Brooks Memorial Art Gallery, 1958), 8; Guy Emerson, "The Kress Collection—A Gift to the Nation," *National Geographic* 12 (1961): 837; *Exhibition of Art Treasures for America from the Samuel H. Kress Collection* (Washington, D.C.: National Gallery of Art, 1961), no. 68; "Art Treasures for America at the National Gallery of Art," *Arts Magazine* 36 (1962): 55; James H. Stubblebine, *Guido da Siena* (Princeton: Princeton University Press, 1964), 89-91, nos. 50, 51, 122; *The Samuel H. Kress Collection* (Memphis, Tenn.: Brooks Memorial Art Gallery, 1966), 10; Fern Rusk Shapley, *Paintings from the Samuel H. Kress Collection: Italian Schools*, vol. 1, *XIII–XV Century* (London: Phaidon Press, 1966), 13; Burton B. Fredericksen and Federico Zeri, *Census of Pre-Nineteenth-Century Italian Paintings in North American Public Collections* (Cambridge, Mass.: Harvard University Press, 1972), 127, 595; Sally Palmer Thomason, *Painting and Sculpture Collection: Memphis Brooks Museum of Art* (Memphis, Tenn.: Memphis Brooks Museum of Art, 1984), 2, 25; Mojmír S. Frinta, "The Decoration of the Gilded Surfaces in Panel Painting around 1300," in *Europäische Kunst um 1300,* ed. Elisabeth Liskar (Vienna: H. Böhlau, 1986), 70; Mojmír S. Frinta, *Punched Decoration on Late Medieval Panel and Miniature Painting*, pt. 1 (Prague: Maxdorf, 1998), 94.

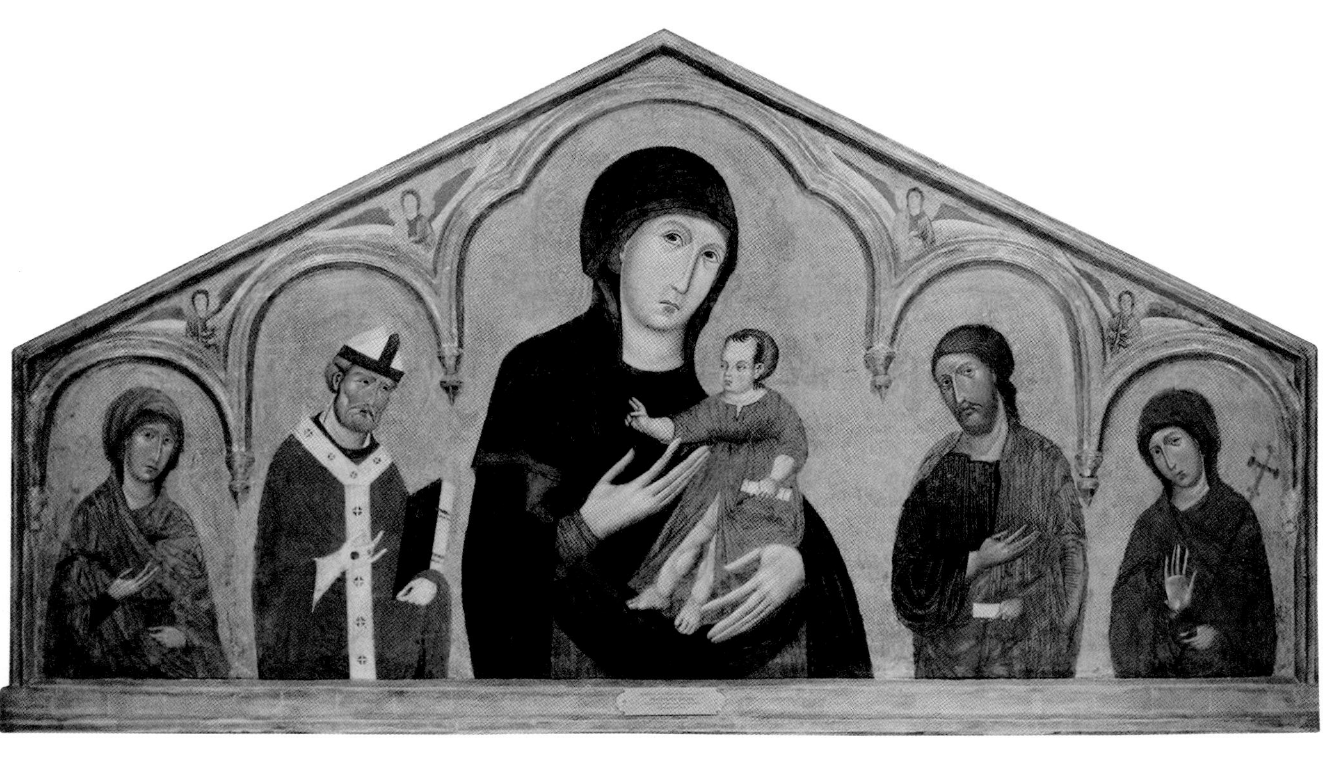

Fig. 259 Master of the Clarisse Panel: *Madonna and Child with Four Saints*. Collection of Memphis Brooks Museum of Art, Memphis, Tennessee; Gift of the Samuel H. Kress Foundation, 61.210.

PAOLO DI GIOVANNI FEI, C. 1345–C. 1411; SIENESE

Christ on the Road to Calvary (61.188; K 38) 26.7 X 21.3 CM, TEMPERA ON CANVAS, TRANSFERRED FROM PANEL

MEMPHIS, TENNESSEE. MEMPHIS BROOKS MUSEUM OF ART

Published as the work of Simone Martini (c. 1284–1344) by Adolfo Venturi (1906), the painting was attributed to the Bolognese School by Raimond van Marle (1934). When it was exhibited at the National Gallery (*Preliminary Catalogue* 1941), it was reassigned to Paolo di Giovanni Fei. This opinion has been accepted by scholars, with the notable exception of Michael Mallory (1976), who believed it to be by a follower of the artist. Based on stylistic affinities with Fei's *Assumption of the Virgin* (National Gallery of Art, Washington, D.C.; K 1547), Fern Rusk Shapley (1966) dated it c. 1385.

The composition derives from Simone Martini's painting of the same subject (Louvre, Paris; 670) of c. 1335. The Memphis work was originally part of a Passion cycle, appearing in the upper tier of an unidentified polyptych that probably had the Crucifixion as its central image. The polyptych's other panels may have included the *Flagellation* (current location unknown; Christie's, London, July 6, 1984, lot 49 [not sold]), attributed to Fei.

PROVENANCE

Giulio Sterbini, Rome; Count Alessandro Contini-Bonacossi, Rome; Samuel H. Kress, New York, acquired 1927; National Gallery of Art, Washington, D.C., exhibited 1941–1952; Memphis Brooks Museum of Art (Brooks Memorial Art Gallery), acquired 1961

BIBLIOGRAPHY

Adolfo Venturi, *La Galleria Sterbini in Roma: Saggio illustrativo* (Rome: Casa editrice de l'Arte, 1906), 26, no. 4; Raimond van Marle, *The Development of the Italian Schools of Painting*, vol. 2, *The Sienese School of the Late Fourteenth Century* (The Hague: M. Nijhoff, 1924), 248; Raimond van Marle, *Le scuole della pittura italiana*, vol. 2, *La scuola senese del XIV secolo* (The Hague: M. Nijhoff, 1934), 256-57 n. 1; *Preliminary Catalogue of Paintings and Sculpture* (Washington, D.C.: National Gallery of Art, 1941), 62, no. 137; *The Samuel H. Kress Collection* (Memphis, Tenn.: Brooks Memorial Art Gallery, 1966), 12; Fern Rusk Shapley, *Paintings from the Samuel H. Kress Collection: Italian Schools*, vol. 1, *XIII–XV Century* (London: Phaidon Press, 1966), 51; Bernard Berenson, *Italian Pictures of the Renaissance: A List of the Principal Artists and Their Works with an Index of Places. Central Italian and North Italian Schools*, 3 vols. (London: Phaidon Press, 1968), 1:128; Burton B. Fredericksen and Federico Zeri, *Census of Pre-Nineteenth-Century Italian Paintings in North American Public Collections* (Cambridge, Mass.: Harvard University Press, 1972), 69, 595; Michael Mallory, *The Sienese Painter Paolo di Giovanni Fei (c. 1345–1411)* (New York: Garland Pub., 1976), 212; *Important Paintings by Old Masters* (New York: Christie's New York, 6 June 1984), 81, no. 49; Sally Palmer Thomason, *Painting and Sculpture Collection: Memphis Brooks Museum of Art* (Memphis, Tenn.: Memphis Brooks Museum of Art, 1984), 29; Mojmír S. Frinta, *Punched Decoration on Late Medieval Panel and Miniature Painting*, pt. 1 (Prague: Maxdorf, 1998), 223, 368.

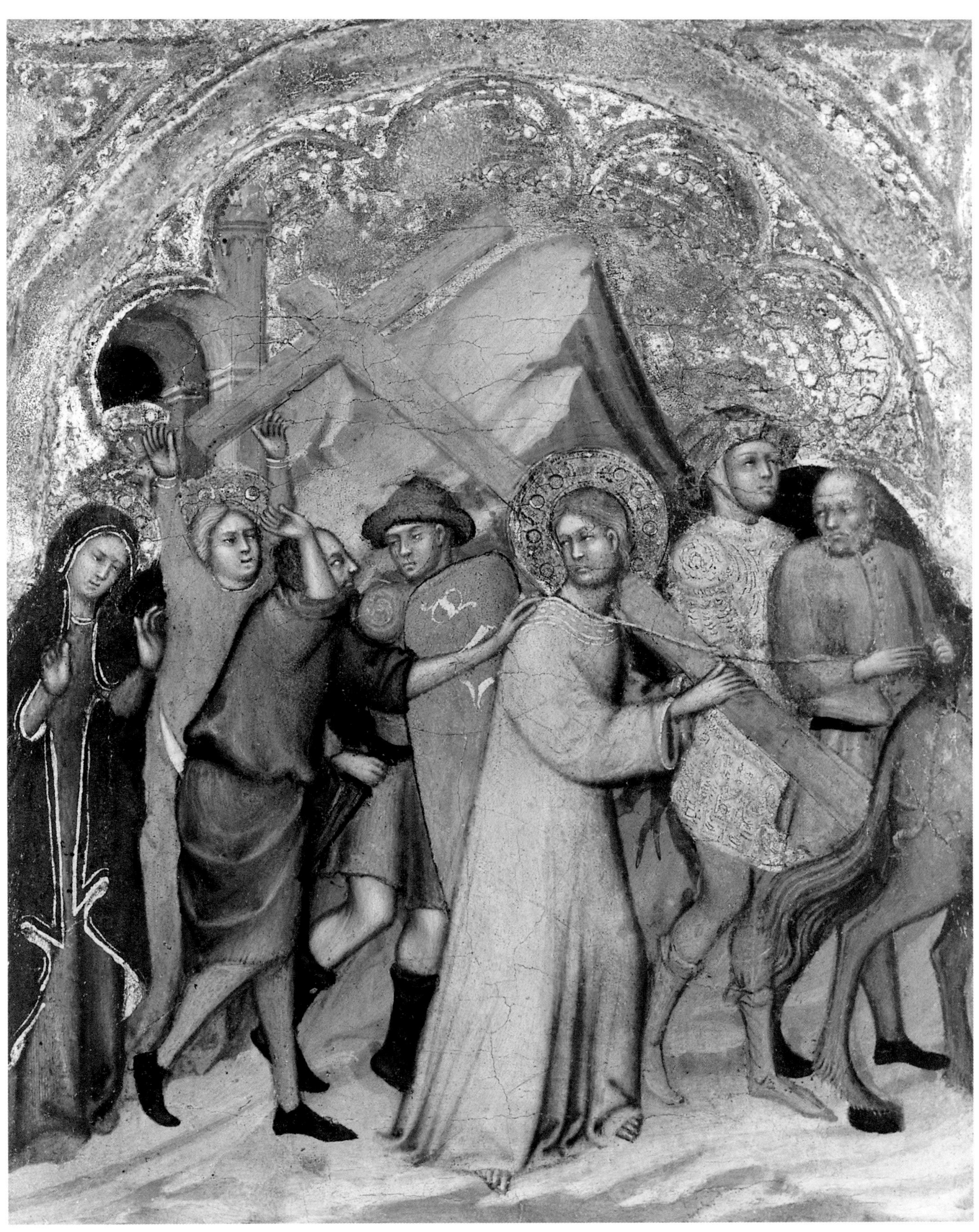

Fig. 260 Paolo di Giovanni Fei: *Christ on the Road to Calvary*. Collection of Memphis Brooks Museum of Art, Memphis, Tennessee; Gift of the Samuel H. Kress Foundation, 61.188.

PELLEGRINO DI MARIANO ROSSINI, ACTIVE 1449; DIED 1492; SIENESE

Madonna and Child with St. John the Baptist and St. Bernardino of Siena (61.198; K 1120) 58.4 x 41.9 CM, TEMPERA ON PANEL

MEMPHIS, TENNESSEE. MEMPHIS BROOKS MUSEUM OF ART

As Pellegrino's only signed and dated work, this small devotional altarpiece is important for the reconstruction of the artist's career. Fern Rusk Shapley (1966) suggested the commission for the work may have been connected with the canonization of St. Bernardino in 1450, the date that appears on the frame.

"ECCE AGNUS DEI" ("Behold the lamb of God"), from John 1:29, is inscribed on St. John's scroll. "YHS," the monogram of Christ, appears on St. Bernardino's plaque. The artist's signature and the presumed date of the panel, 1450, are written along the bottom edge of the frame, which is original to the work: "OPVS PELLEGRINVS . MARIANI . DE . SENIS . M. CCCC . L." The Virgin hands the Christ Child a pomegranate, a symbol of the Resurrection. In the lunette at the top of the panel the Virgin and John the Evangelist contemplate and grieve for the dead Christ. Usually these figures stand beside the cross, instead of sitting humbly on the ground; this alternative iconography was employed, albeit rarely, in fourteenth-century Tuscan painting.

PROVENANCE

Giuseppe Toscanelli, Pisa; Giulio Sambon, Florence, April 9, 1883, lot 116; Charles Fairfax Murray, London, 1914; Achillito Chiesa, Milan; Count Alessandro Contini-Bonacossi, Florence; Samuel H. Kress, New York, acquired 1937; National Gallery of Art, Washington, D.C., exhibited 1941–1952; Memphis Brooks Museum of Art (Brooks Memorial Art Gallery), acquired 1961

BIBLIOGRAPHY

Joseph A. Crowe and Giovanni B. Cavalcaselle, *A New History of Painting in Italy from the Second to the Sixteenth Century*, 3 vols. (London: John Murray, 1866), 3:81 n. 1; Joseph A. Crowe and Giovanni B. Cavalcaselle, *A New History of Painting in Italy from the II to the XVI Century*, 3 vols., ed. Edward Hutton (London: J. M. Dent; New York: E. P. Dutton, 1909), 3:127-28 n. 3; Joseph A. Crowe and Giovanni B. Cavalcaselle, *A History of Painting in Italy, Umbria, Florence and Siena, from the Second to the Sixteenth Century*, 6 vols., ed. Tancred Borenius (New York: C. Scribner's Sons, 1914), 5:179, n. 1; F. Mason Perkins, "Dipinti senesi sconosciuti o inediti," *Rassegna d'Arte Antica e Moderna* 1 (1914): 165-68; Raimond van Marle, *The Development of the Italian Schools of Painting*, vol. 9, *Late Gothic Painting in Tuscany* (The Hague: M. Nijhoff, 1927), 375-76; Bernard Berenson, "Quadri senza casa: Il Quattrocento senese, I," *Dedalo* 11 (1931): 632; Bernard Berenson, "Lost Paintings of XV-Century Siena—Part I," *International Studio* 98 (1931): 28; John Pope-Hennessy, *Giovanni di Paolo, 1403–1483* (New York: Oxford University Press, 1938), 159; John Pope-Hennessy, *Sassetta* (London: Chatto & Windus, 1939), 172; John Pope-Hennessy, "The Panel Paintings of Pellegrino di Mariano," *Burlington Magazine* 74 (1939): 212, 214; National Gallery of Art, *Preliminary Catalogue of Paintings and Sculpture* (Washington, D.C.: National Gallery of Art, 1941), 150, no. 479; William E. Suida, *The Samuel H. Kress Collection, Brooks Memorial Art Gallery* (Memphis, Tenn.: Brooks Memorial Art Gallery, 1958), 14; *The Samuel H. Kress Collection* (Memphis, Tenn.: Brooks Memorial Art Gallery, 1966), 17; Fern Rusk Shapley, *Paintings from the Samuel H. Kress Collection: Italian Schools*, vol. 1, *XIII–XV Century* (London: Phaidon Press, 1966), 151; Henk W. van Os and H. K. Gerson, eds., *Sienese Paintings in Holland* (Groningen: Wolters-Noordhoff, 1969), no. 32; Burton B. Fredericksen and Federico Zeri, *Census of Pre-Nineteenth-Century Italian Paintings in North American Public Collections* (Cambridge, Mass.: Harvard University Press, 1972), 160, 595; Sally Palmer Thomason, *Painting and Sculpture Collection: Memphis Brooks Museum of Art* (Memphis, Tenn.: Memphis Brooks Museum of Art, 1984), 34; Federico Zeri, ed., *La pittura in Italia. Il Quattrocento*, 2 vols. (Milan: Electa, 1987), 2:730; Keith Christiansen, Laurence B. Kanter, and Carl Brandon Strehlke, *Painting in Renaissance Siena, 1420–1500* (New York: Metropolitan Museum of Art, 1988), 243; Giulietta Chelazzi Dini, Alessandro Angelini, and Bernardina Sani, *Sienese Painting from Duccio to the Birth of the Baroque* (New York: Harry N. Abrams, 1998), 250; Mojmír S. Frinta, *Punched Decoration on Late Medieval Panel and Miniature Painting*, pt. 1 (Prague: Maxdorf, 1998), 47, 118, 193, 262; Maria Pia Mannini, ed., *Da Bernardo Daddi a Giorgio Vasari* (Florence: Edizioni Polistampa, 1999), 124; Perri Lee Roberts, Bruce Cole, and Hayden B. J. Maginnis, *Sacred Treasures: Early Italian Paintings from Southern Collections* (Athens, Ga.: Georgia Museum of Art, 2002), 28, 136-39.

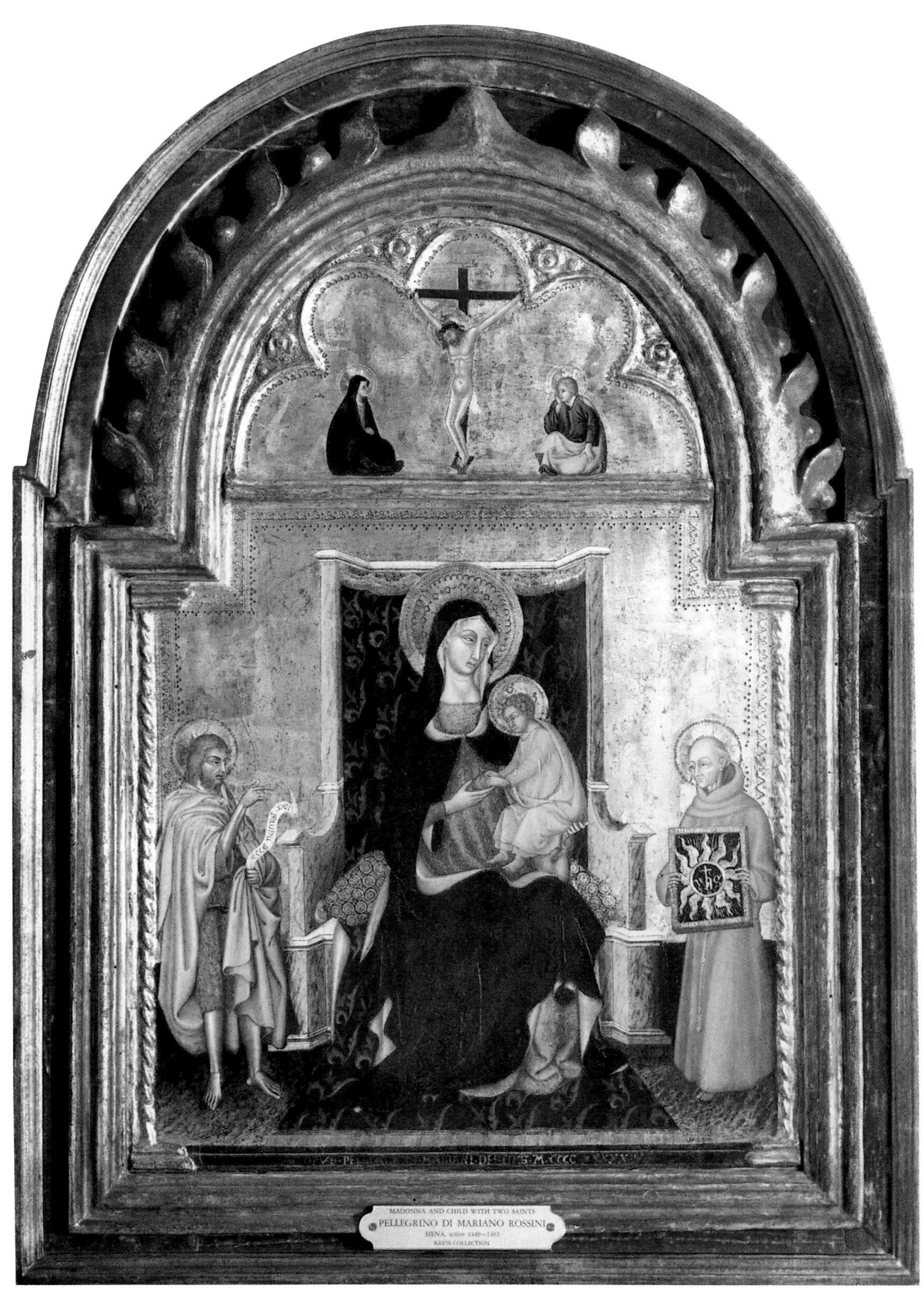

Fig. 261 Pellegrino di Mariano Rossini: *Madonna and Child with St. John the Baptist and St. Bernardino of Siena*. Collection of Memphis Brooks Museum of Art, Memphis, Tennessee; Gift of the Samuel H. Kress Foundation, 61.198.

PREVITALI, ANDREA, C. 1470–1528; BERGAMASQUE

Annunciation (61.197; K 1118) 155.6 X 161 CM, TEMPERA ON PANEL

MEMPHIS, TENNESSEE. MEMPHIS BROOKS MUSEUM OF ART

The painting has always been considered an autograph work by Previtali, dating late in his career, c. 1520–1525. Pietro Zampetti (cited in Dell'Acqua 1975) observed that the composition was influenced by Titian's *Annunciation* (Cathedral, Treviso) of c. 1520–1523. The setting, the still-life detail, and the just-extinguished candle on the *prie-dieu*, alluding to the advent of the "true light," Christ, as opposed to artificial light, reveal the influence of Netherlandish painting.

PROVENANCE

Count Alessandro Contini-Bonacossi, Florence; Samuel H. Kress, New York, acquired 1937; Philadelphia Museum of Art, exhibited 1950–1953; Memphis Brooks Museum of Art (Brooks Memorial Art Gallery), acquired 1961

BIBLIOGRAPHY

William E. Suida, "The Samuel H. Kress Collection," *Philadelphia Museum Bulletin* 46 (1950): 10, no. 7; Bernard Berenson, *Italian Pictures of the Renaissance: A List of the Principal Artists and Their Works with an Index of Places. Venetian School*, 2 vols. (New York: Phaidon, 1957), 1:149; William E. Suida, *The Samuel H. Kress Collection, Brooks Memorial Art Gallery* (Memphis, Tenn.: Brooks Memorial Art Gallery, 1958), 38; Fritz Heinemann, *Giovanni Bellini e i Belliniani*, 3 vols. (Venice: Neri Pozza, 1962), 1:139, S.321; *The Samuel H. Kress Collection* (Memphis, Tenn.: Brooks Memorial Art Gallery, 1966), 44; Bernard Berenson, *Italian Pictures of the Renaissance: A List of the Principal Artists and Their Works with an Index of Places. Central Italian and North Italian Schools*, 3 vols. (London: Phaidon Press, 1968), 1:149; Fern Rusk Shapley, *Paintings from the Samuel H. Kress Collection: Italian Schools*, vol. 2, *XV–XVI Century* (London: Phaidon Press, 1968), 63; Burton B. Fredericksen and Federico Zeri, *Census of Pre-Nineteenth-Century Italian Paintings in North American Public Collections* (Cambridge, Mass.: Harvard University Press, 1972), 170, 595; Jürg Meyer zur Capellen, "Andrea Previtali" (Ph.D. diss., Julius Maximilianus University, Würzburg, 1972), 181, no. 75; Giovanni Alberto Dell'Acqua, ed., *I pittori bergameschi dal XIII al XIX secolo*, vol. 3, pt. 1, *Il Cinquecento* (Bergamo: Poligrafiche Bolis, 1975), 137, no. 57; Sally Palmer Thomason, *Painting and Sculpture Collection: Memphis Brooks Museum of Art* (Memphis, Tenn.: Memphis Brooks Museum of Art, 1984), 46; Fritz Heinemann, *Giovanni Bellini e i Belliniani*, 3 vols. (Venice: Neri Pozza, 1991), 3:51, S.321.

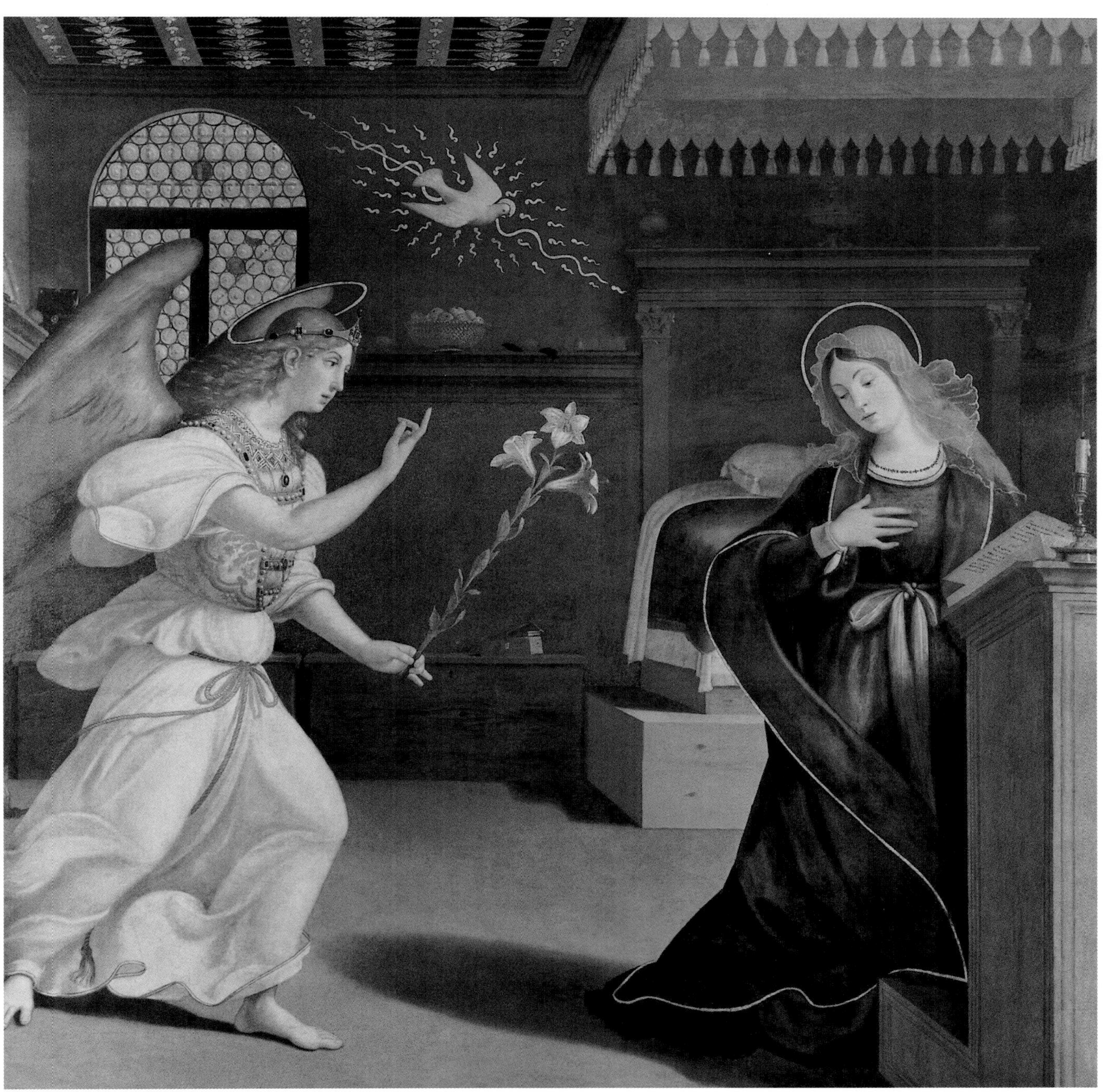

Fig. 262 Andrea Previtali: *Annunciation*. Collection of Memphis Brooks Museum of Art, Memphis, Tennessee; Gift of the Samuel H. Kress Foundation, 61.197.

SELLAIO, JACOPO DEL, C. 1441–1493; FLORENTINE

Adoration of the Magi (61.193; K 316) 89.2 X 170.8 CM, TEMPERA ON PANEL

MEMPHIS, TENNESSEE. MEMPHIS BROOKS MUSEUM OF ART

The painting has always been considered an autograph work. Its size, its format, and the intricacy of its composition suggest it served as a *spalliera*. In Fern Rusk Shapley's opinion (1966), it was created under the influence of Sandro Botticelli (1444/5–1510), with whom Sellaio collaborated in 1483 on the Nastagio degli Onesti series of *spalliera* panels (Museo del Prado, Madrid). The Museum dates the painting c. 1480–1490.

The Adoration of the Magi was an extremely popular painting subject in Renaissance Florence, where the Company of the Magi, dominated by the Medici after 1434, staged an enormous festival dedicated to the trio on the feast of the Epiphany. The processions associated with the celebration influenced Florentine Adoration iconography, with its teeming crowds, courtiers, domestic and exotic animals, and other trappings of court life. An *all'antica* ruin symbolizing the "old order" was also a common feature. Sellaio's work demonstrates the centralized compositions that became the norm in the 1470s.

PROVENANCE

Édouard Aynard, Lyons; Georges Petit Galleries, Paris, December 1, 1913, lot 64; Marczell von Nemes, Munich; Frederik Muller & Cie., Amsterdam, November 13, 1928, lot 14 (not sold); Frederik Muller & Cie., Munich, June 16, 1931, lot 20; Kleinberger Galleries, New York; Count Alessandro Contini-Bonacossi, Florence; Samuel H. Kress, New York, acquired 1935; National Gallery of Art, Washington, D.C., exhibited 1941–1951; Memphis Brooks Museum of Art (Brooks Memorial Art Gallery), acquired 1961

BIBLIOGRAPHY

Bernard Berenson, *The Florentine Painters of the Renaissance* (New York and London: G. P. Putnam's Sons, 1909), 183; August L. Mayer, "Zur Auktion Nemes. I. Die Gëmalde," *Pantheon* 2 (1928): 450; Raimond van Marle, *The Development of the Italian Schools of Painting*, vol. 12, *The Renaissance Painters of Florence in the Fifteenth Century, The Third Generation* (The Hague: M. Nijhoff, 1931), 421; National Gallery of Art, *Preliminary Catalogue of Paintings and Sculpture* (Washington, D.C.: National Gallery of Art, 1941), 183, no. 278; William E. Suida, *The Samuel H. Kress Collection, Brooks Memorial Art Gallery* (Memphis, Tenn.: Brooks Memorial Art Gallery, 1958), 22; Helen Comstock, "The Connoisseur in America," *The Connoisseur* 142 (1958): 204; Bernard Berenson, *Italian Pictures of the Renaissance: A List of the Principal Artists and Their Works with an Index of Places. Florentine School*, 2 vols. (London: Phaidon Press, 1963), 1:198; *The Samuel H. Kress Collection* (Memphis, Tenn.: Brooks Memorial Art Gallery, 1966), 28; Fern Rusk Shapley, *Paintings from the Samuel H. Kress Collection: Italian Schools*, vol. 1, *XIII–XV Century* (London: Phaidon Press, 1966), 134; Burton B. Fredericksen and Federico Zeri, *Census of Pre-Nineteenth-Century Italian Paintings in North American Public Collections* (Cambridge, Mass.: Harvard University Press, 1972), 186, 595; Sally Palmer Thomason, *Painting and Sculpture Collection: Memphis Brooks Museum of Art* (Memphis, Tenn.: Memphis Brooks Museum of Art, 1984), 36; Perri Lee Roberts, Bruce Cole, and Hayden B. J. Maginnis, *Sacred Treasures: Early Italian Paintings from Southern Collections* (Athens, Ga.: Georgia Museum of Art, 2002), 180-83.

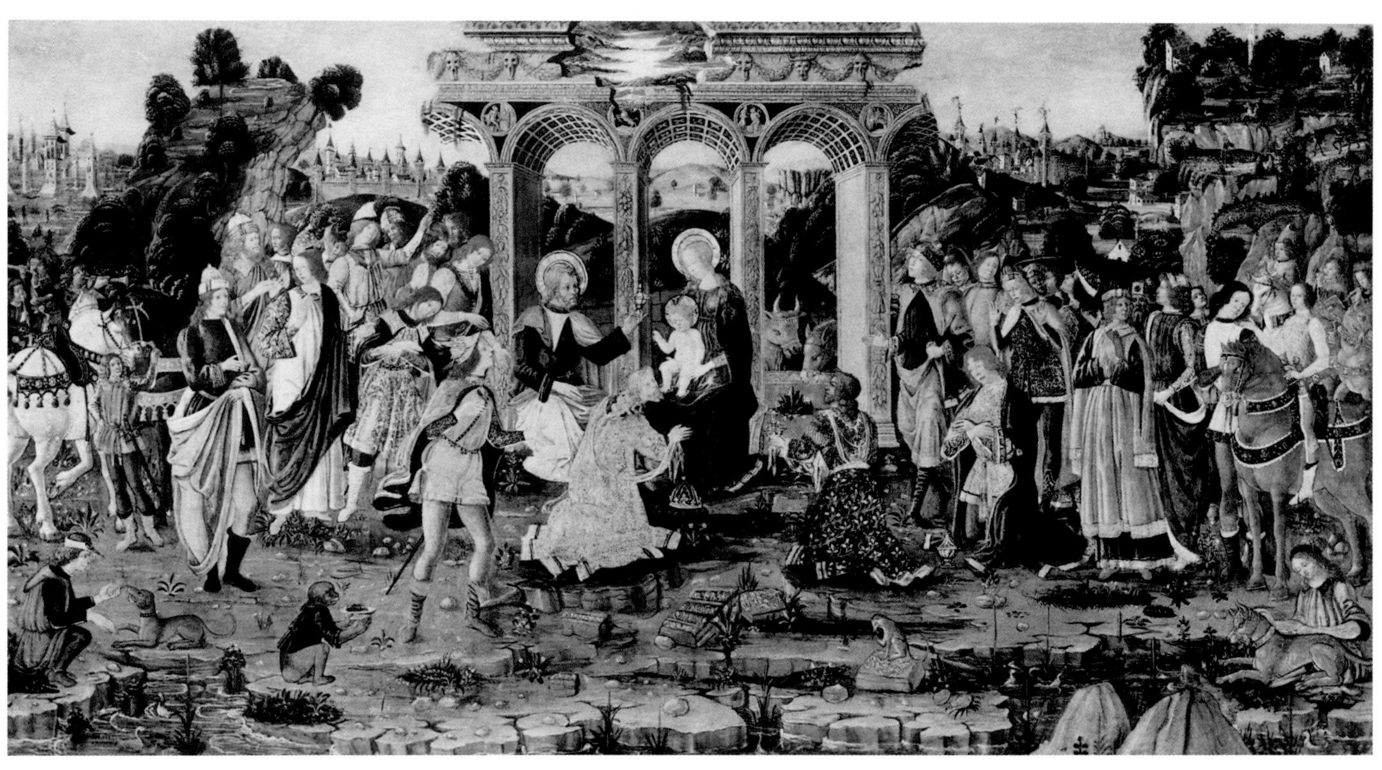

Fig. 263 Jacopo del Sellaio: *Adoration of the Magi*. Collection of Memphis Brooks Museum of Art, Memphis, Tennessee; Gift of the Samuel H. Kress Foundation, 61.193.

TADDEO DI BARTOLO, C. 1362–C. 1422; SIENESE

St. James Major; St. John the Baptist (61.196; K 551/2) 149.6 x 43.5 CM (K 551); 148.6 x 43.8 CM (K 552), TEMPERA ON PANEL

MEMPHIS, TENNESSEE. MEMPHIS BROOKS MUSEUM OF ART

The panels have long been recognized as the wings of a large altarpiece by Taddeo di Bartolo, which also included *St. Catherine of Alexandria* and the *Bishop Saint* (New Orleans Museum of Art; 61.63/4, K 553/4; see pages 572-73); F. Mason Perkins (1908) dated the work to c. 1410, Sibilla Symeonides (1965) to c. 1400–1405. On the basis of stylistic affinities, as well as substantial circumstantial evidence, Gail E. Solberg (1991) hypothesized that the four paintings constituted the lateral portions of Taddeo's polyptych for San Domenico, Gubbio, dated 1418. According to her reconstruction, *St. John the Baptist* and *St. James Major* flanked the *Madonna and Child* (Fogg Art Museum, Cambridge; 65.2) to the left and right, respectively, while the *Bishop Saint* and *St. Catherine of Alexandria* were on the far left and right, respectively; eight three-quarter-length saints (current location unknown; ex-Serristori Collection, Florence) comprised a second register, and the *Blessing Redeemer* (Collegio Teutonico, Vatican) served as the central pinnacle.

The Baptist's scroll is inscribed "ecce agnus dei ecce qui tollit pecca mundi" ("Behold, the Lamb of God, who takes away the sin of the world!"), from John 1:29.

PROVENANCE

Dan Fellows Platt, Englewood, N.J., by 1908; Samuel H. Kress, New York, acquired 1939; Memphis Brooks Museum of Art (Brooks Memorial Art Gallery), acquired 1961

BIBLIOGRAPHY

F. Mason Perkins, "Ancora dei dipinti sconosciuti della scuola senese," *Rassegna d'Arte Senese* 4 (1908): 8; Joseph A. Crowe and Giovanni B. Cavalcaselle, *A New History of Painting in Italy from the II to the XVI Century*, 3 vols., ed. Edward Hutton (London: Dent; New York: Dutton, 1909), 2:123; Bernard Berenson, *The Central Italian Painters of the Renaissance* (New York and London: G. P. Putnam's Sons, 1909), 256; F. Mason Perkins, "Dipinti italiani nella raccolta Platt," *Rassegna d'Arte* 11 (1911): 5; Raimond van Marle, *The Development of the Italian Schools of Painting*, vol. 2, *The Sienese School of the Late Fourteenth Century* (The Hague: M. Nijhoff, 1924), 556; Luigi Dami, "Taddeo di Bartolo a Volterra," *Bollettino d'Arte* 4 (1924–1925): 70; Bernard Berenson, *Italian Pictures of the Renaissance* (Oxford: Clarendon Press, 1932), 551; George H. Edgell, *A History of Sienese Painting* (New York: Dial Press, 1932), 180; Raimond van Marle, *Le scuole della pittura italiana*, vol. 2, *La scuola senese del XIV secolo* (The Hague: M. Nijhoff, 1934), 611-12; Bernard Berenson, *Pitture italiane del Rinascimento* (Milan: U. Hoepli, 1936), 474; *The Samuel H. Kress Collection in the Isaac Delgado Museum of Art* (New Orleans: Isaac Delgado Museum of Art, 1953), 14; Helen Comstock, "The Connoisseur in America," *The Connoisseur* 142 (1958): 203; William E. Suida, *The Samuel H. Kress Collection, Brooks Memorial Art Gallery* (Memphis, Tenn.: Brooks Memorial Art Gallery, 1958), 10; Sibilla Symeonides, *Taddeo di Bartolo* (Siena: Accademia senese degli Intronati, 1965), 97-98, 211-12; Fern Rusk Shapley, *Paintings from the Samuel H. Kress Collection: Italian Schools*, vol. 1, *XIII–XV Century* (London: Phaidon Press, 1966), 63-64; *The Samuel H. Kress Collection* (Memphis, Tenn.: Brooks Memorial Art Gallery, 1966), 14; Bernard Berenson, *Italian Pictures of the Renaissance: A List of the Principal Artists and Their Works with an Index of Places. Central Italian and North Italian Schools*, 3 vols. (London: Phaidon Press, 1968), 1:420; Burton B. Fredericksen and Federico Zeri, *Census of Pre-Nineteenth-Century Italian Paintings in North American Public Collections* (Cambridge, Mass.: Harvard University Press, 1972), 194, 595; Sally Palmer Thomason, *Painting and Sculpture Collection: Memphis Brooks Museum of Art* (Memphis, Tenn.: Memphis Brooks Museum of Art, 1984), 30; Gail E. Solberg, "Taddeo di Bartolo: His Life and Work" (Ph.D. diss., New York University, 1991), 466-71; Gail E. Solberg, "Taddeo di Bartolo: A Polyptych to Reconstruct," *Brooks Museum Bulletin: Essays on the Collection* 1 (1994): 1-16; Mojmír S. Frinta, *Punched Decoration on Late Medieval Panel and Miniature Painting*, pt. 1 (Prague: Maxdorf, 1998), 391, 518.

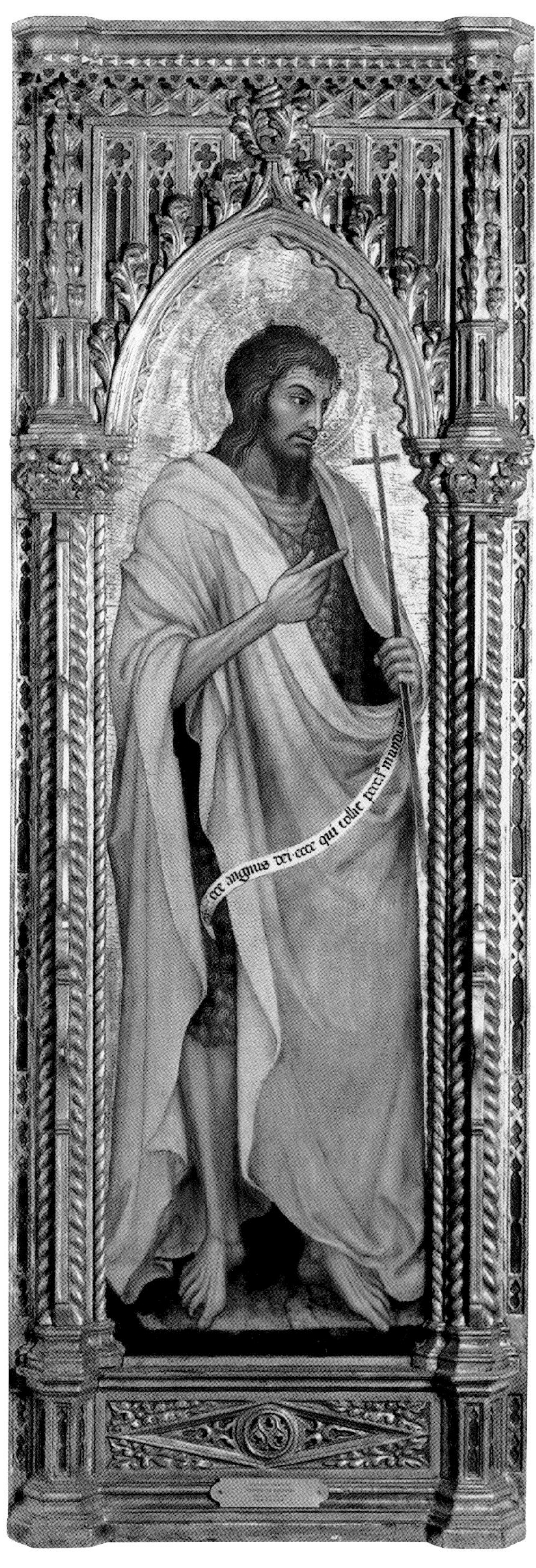

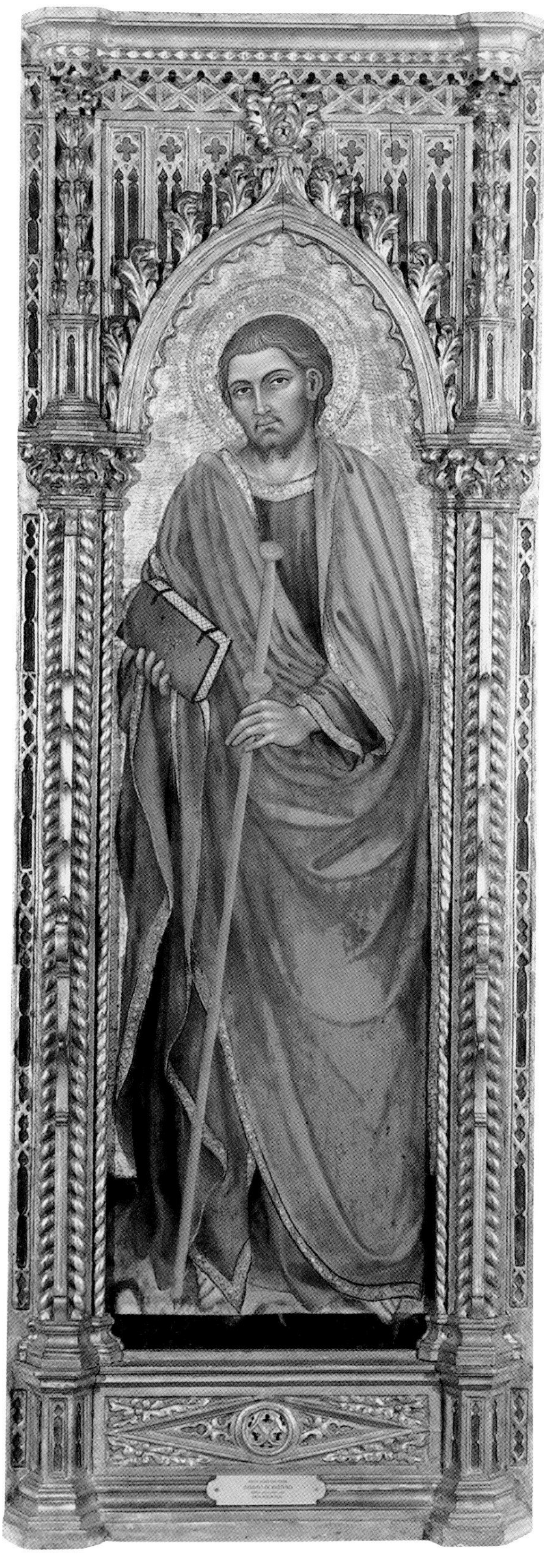

Fig. 264 (left) Taddeo di Bartolo: *St. John the Baptist*. Collection of Memphis Brooks Museum of Art, Memphis, Tennessee; Gift of the Samuel H. Kress Foundation, 61.196.

Fig. 265 (right) Taddeo di Bartolo: *St. James Major*. Collection of Memphis Brooks Museum of Art, Memphis, Tennessee; Gift of the Samuel H. Kress Foundation, 61.196.

BOTTICELLI, SANDRO, 1444/5–1510; FLORENTINE, AND GHIRLANDAIO, DOMENICO, 1449–1494; FLORENTINE

Coronation of the Virgin with Four Saints and a Donor (63.1) 270 X 176 CM, TEMPERA WITH OIL (?) ON CANVAS, TRANSFERRED FROM PANEL

MIAMI BEACH, FLORIDA. BASS MUSEUM OF ART

The design of the lower half of the painting recalls that of the bottom portion of Ghirlandaio's altarpiece for the Badia of Volterra, *Christ in Glory with St. Benedict, St. Actinia, St. Greciana, St. Romuald, and the Donor Abbot Giusto de' Bonvincini* (Pinacoteca Comunale, Volterra) of 1492. The upper half of the Bass picture mirrors Botticelli's *Coronation of the Virgin* (Florence, Uffizi; 8362) of c. 1488–1490, formerly in San Marco; the figures of Mary and God the Father are identical in the two works. In the early literature, the Bass painting was generally associated with the school or shop of Botticelli, but, since 1972, it has been recognized as a product of collaboration on the part of Botticelli and Ghirlandaio. In fact, the work, which may be dated c. 1492 on the basis of stylistic and circumstantial evidence, is the artists' only jointly produced panel painting and the sole surviving example of their co-participation in the design of a work. Because the surface is in poor condition, it is impossible to determine the exact roles of the artists as individuals, or of the members of their shops, in the execution. The two standing saints are Justus of Volterra, in a bishop's robes, and his brother Clement, who is dressed as a magistrate; they were the co-patrons of the city of Volterra, as well as the dedicatees of the churches of San Giusto and San Clemente in the precinct of the Camaldolese Badia of Volterra. The kneeling figure at the left is St. Romuald, the founder of the Camaldolese Order. On his right is the Beato Jacopo Guidi da Certaldo, the late-thirteenth-century abbot of San Giusto and San Clemente and a focus of cult-worship in Volterra; his relics resided in San Giusto, together with those of St. Justus and St. Clement. The Camaldolese supplicant in the lower right-hand corner has not been identified. The iconography of this large altarpiece reflects visionary experiences in late-fifteenth- and early-sixteenth-century Florentine painting, except in its unprecedented inclusion of three angels, below the Virgin and God the Father. Dressed in white, green, and red, they represent the cardinal virtues of Faith, Hope, and Charity, respectively.

PROVENANCE

Badia of San Giusto e San Clemente, Volterra; San Salvatore, Volterra, by 1650; Cavaliere Toscanelli, Pisa, c. 1880; Giulio Sambon, Florence, April 9, 1883; Baron von Anrep, Ringen, Latvia; Öffentliche Kunstsammlungen, Basel, c. 1909–1936 (on loan); Schneeli Collection, Vuippens, Fribourg, Switzerland, c. 1936; John and Johanna Bass, New York, by 1963; Bass Museum of Art, acquired 1964

BIBLIOGRAPHY

Joseph A. Crowe and Giovanni B. Cavalcaselle, *A New History of Painting in Italy from the Second to the Sixteenth Century*, 3 vols. (London: John Murray, 1864), 2:425; Giorgio Vasari, *Le vite de' più eccellenti pittori, scultori ed architettori* (1568), 9 vols., ed. Gaetano Milanesi (Florence: G. C. Sansoni, 1878), 3:273, 318 n. 3; Annibale Cinci, *Storia di Volterra: Memorie e documenti* (Bologna: A. Forni, 1885), 9; Hermann Ulmann, *Sandro Botticelli* (Munich: Verlagsanstalt für Kunst und Wissenschaft, 1893), 75; Corrado Ricci, *Volterra* (Bergamo: Istituto italiano d'arti grafiche, 1905), 82, 120; *Katalog der Öffentlichen Kunstsammlung in Basel* (Basel: E. Birkhäuser, 1908), 48, no. 213; Joseph A. Crowe and Giovanni B. Cavalcaselle, *A History of Painting in Italy, Umbria, Florence and Siena from the Second to the Sixteenth Century*, 6 vols., ed. Langton Douglas (London: John Murray, 1912), 4:208-9; Carlo Gamba, *Botticelli* (Milan: U. Hoepli, 1936), 262; Bernard Berenson, *Italian Pictures of the Renaissance: A List of the Principal Artists and Their Works with an Index of Places. Florentine School*, 2 vols. (London: Phaidon Press, 1963), 1:37; Gabriele Mandel, *L'opera completa del Botticelli* (Milan: Rizzoli, 1967), no. 100; Burton B. Fredericksen and Federico Zeri, *Census of Pre-Nineteenth-Century Italian Paintings in North American Public Collections* (Cambridge, Mass.: Harvard University Press, 1972), 34, 82, 595; *The John and Johanna Bass Collection at Miami Beach, Florida* (Miami Beach, Fla.: Bass Museum of Art, 1973), 1-5, no. 1; Ronald W. Lightbown, *Sandro Botticelli*, 2 vols. (Berkeley: University of California Press, 1978), 2:143-44; Margarita A. Russell, *Paintings and Textiles of the Bass Museum of Art: Selections from the Collection* (Miami Beach, Fla.: Bass Museum of Art, 1990), 14-17; Cristina Acidini Luchinat, "Gli artisti di Lorenzo de' Medici," in *'Per bellezza, per studio, per piacere': Lorenzo il Magnifico e gli spazi dell'arte*, ed. Franco Borsi (Florence: Cassa di Risparmio di Firenze, 1991), 187; Mina Gregori, Antonio Paolucci, and Cristina Acidini-Lucinat, eds., *Maestri e botteghe: Pittura a Firenze alla fine del Quattrocento* (Milan: Silvana, 1992), 42, 274.

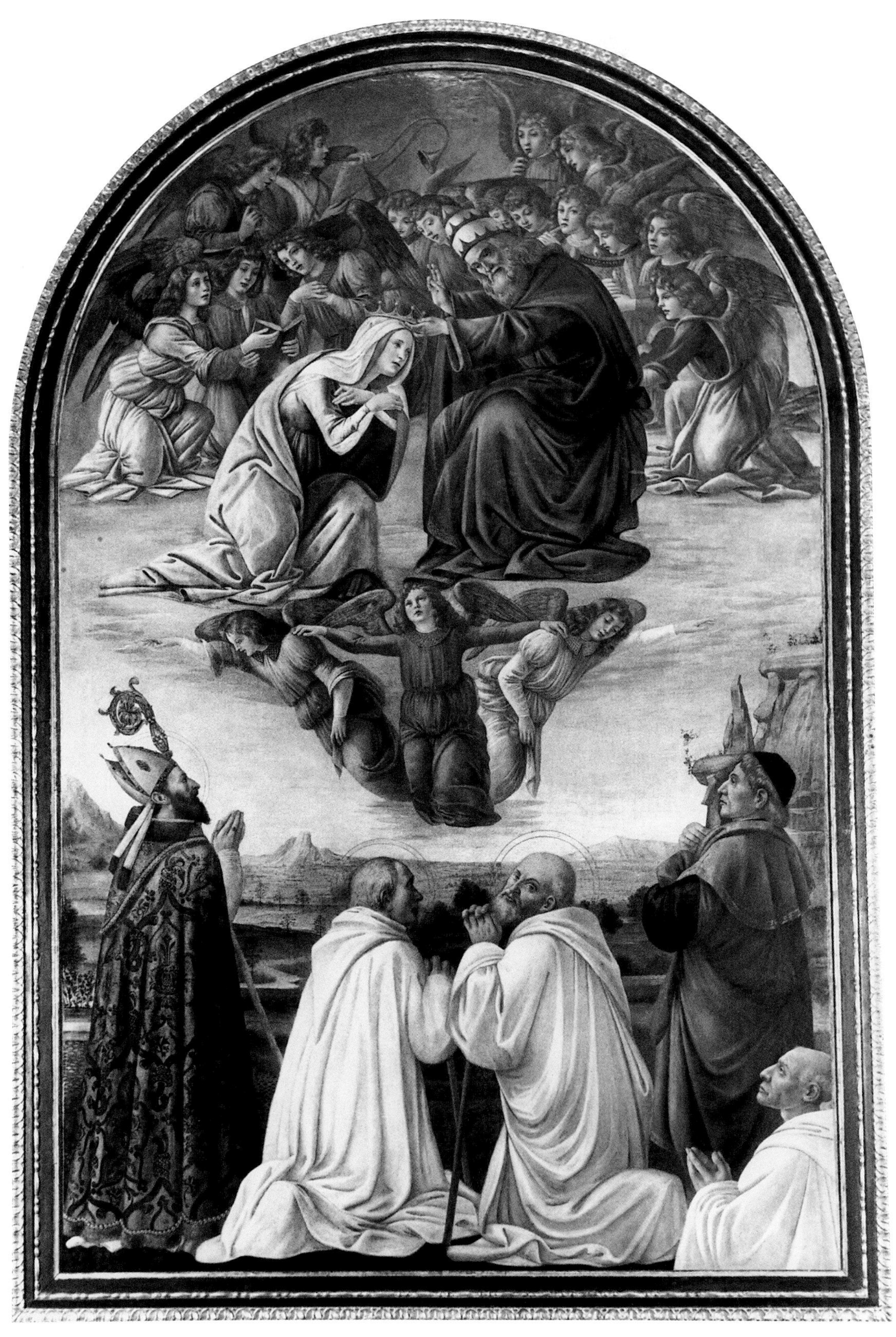

Fig. 266 Sandro Botticelli and Domenico Ghirlandaio: *Coronation of the Virgin with Four Saints and a Donor*. Collection Bass Museum of Art, Miami Beach; Gift of John and Johanna Bass, 63.1.

BOTTICELLI, SANDRO, 1444/5–1510; WORKSHOP; FLORENTINE

Mystic Marriage of St. Catherine of Siena (68.100) 73.5 X 49 CM, TEMPERA ON PANEL

MIAMI BEACH, FLORIDA. BASS MUSEUM OF ART

The entire surface is heavily overpainted and retouched, with details and facial features outlined. The figures of the Madonna and Child replicate those in Botticelli's *Madonna and Child with St. John the Baptist* (private collection, New York) of c. 1490–1495; they relate, as well, to a drawing by the master that was kept in his shop. They appear again in two contemporary workshop pieces, the *Adoration of the Magi* (Simon Collection, Berlin) and the *Madonna and Child with San Giovanni Gualberto* (current location unknown; sold, Christie's, New York, May 31, 1989, lot 111A); the architectural backdrop in the latter is identical to that in the Bass painting. The anatomical peculiarities of St. Catherine suggest that her figure does not derive directly from a drawing by the master, but is based instead on a representation of the Annunciate Virgin or of Mary kneeling in adoration, as may be seen, for example, in the *Madonna Adoring the Christ Child* (National Gallery of Art, Washington, D.C.; 1087, K 1432), attributed to the circle of Botticelli.

The Bass painting is the only surviving representation of the mystic marriage of St. Catherine from Botticelli's shop; no treatment of the subject seems to have been produced by the master himself. St. Catherine of Siena, canonized in 1461, although her cult was much older, was not especially popular in Florence. The unusual subject was probably chosen by the patron, who may have commissioned the work for a nun's dowry.

PROVENANCE

Ferdinand von Quast, Radensleben, Ruppin, c. 1914; John and Johanna Bass, New York, by 1963; Bass Museum of Art, acquired 1964

BIBLIOGRAPHY

Die Kunstdenkmäler des Kreises Ruppin (Berlin: Vossischen Buchhandlung, 1914), 197; Bernard Berenson, *Italian Pictures of the Renaissance: A List of the Principal Artists and Their Works with an Index of Places. Florentine School*, 2 vols. (London: Phaidon Press, 1963), 1:37; Burton B. Fredericksen and Federico Zeri, *Census of Pre-Nineteenth-Century Italian Paintings in North American Public Collections* (Cambridge, Mass.: Harvard University Press, 1972), 34, 595; *The John and Johanna Bass Collection at Miami Beach, Florida* (Miami Beach, Fla.: Bass Museum of Art, 1973), 27, no. 100; Ronald W. Lightbown, *Sandro Botticelli*, 2 vols. (Berkeley: University of California Press, 1978), 2:85; Margarita A. Russell, *Paintings and Textiles of the Bass Museum of Art: Selections from the Collection* (Miami Beach, Fla.: Bass Museum of Art, 1990), 18.

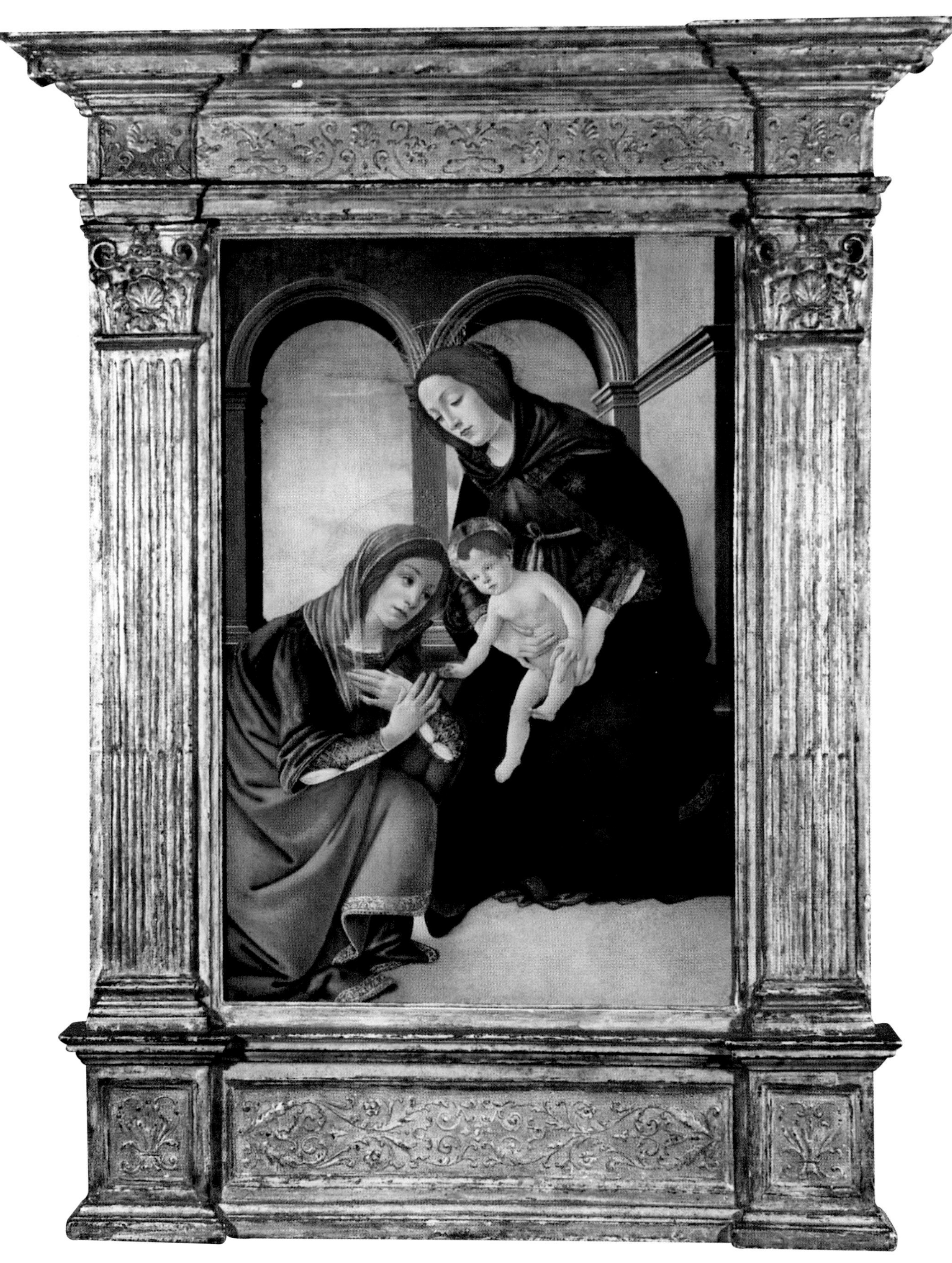

Fig. 267 Sandro Botticelli (workshop): *Mystic Marriage of St. Catherine of Siena*. Collection Bass Museum of Art, Miami Beach; Gift of John and Johanna Bass, 68.100.

LEONARDO DA VINCI, 1452–1519; FLORENTINE; COPY

Portrait of a Lady (Mona Lisa) (63.46) 65 X 52.5 CM, OIL ON CANVAS

MIAMI BEACH, FLORIDA. BASS MUSEUM OF ART

The Museum considers this to be a sixteenth- or seventeenth-century French copy of the original painting (Louvre, Paris; 779). The sitter in Leonardo's original has been identified as Lisa Gherardini, the wife of the Florentine silk merchant Francesco del Giocondo.

PROVENANCE

Mrs. Maximo Scioletti, Paris; John and Johanna Bass, New York; Bass Museum of Art, acquired 1963

BIBLIOGRAPHY

Burton B. Fredericksen and Federico Zeri, *Census of Pre-Nineteenth-Century Italian Paintings in North American Public Collections* (Cambridge, Mass.: Harvard University Press, 1972), 104, 595.

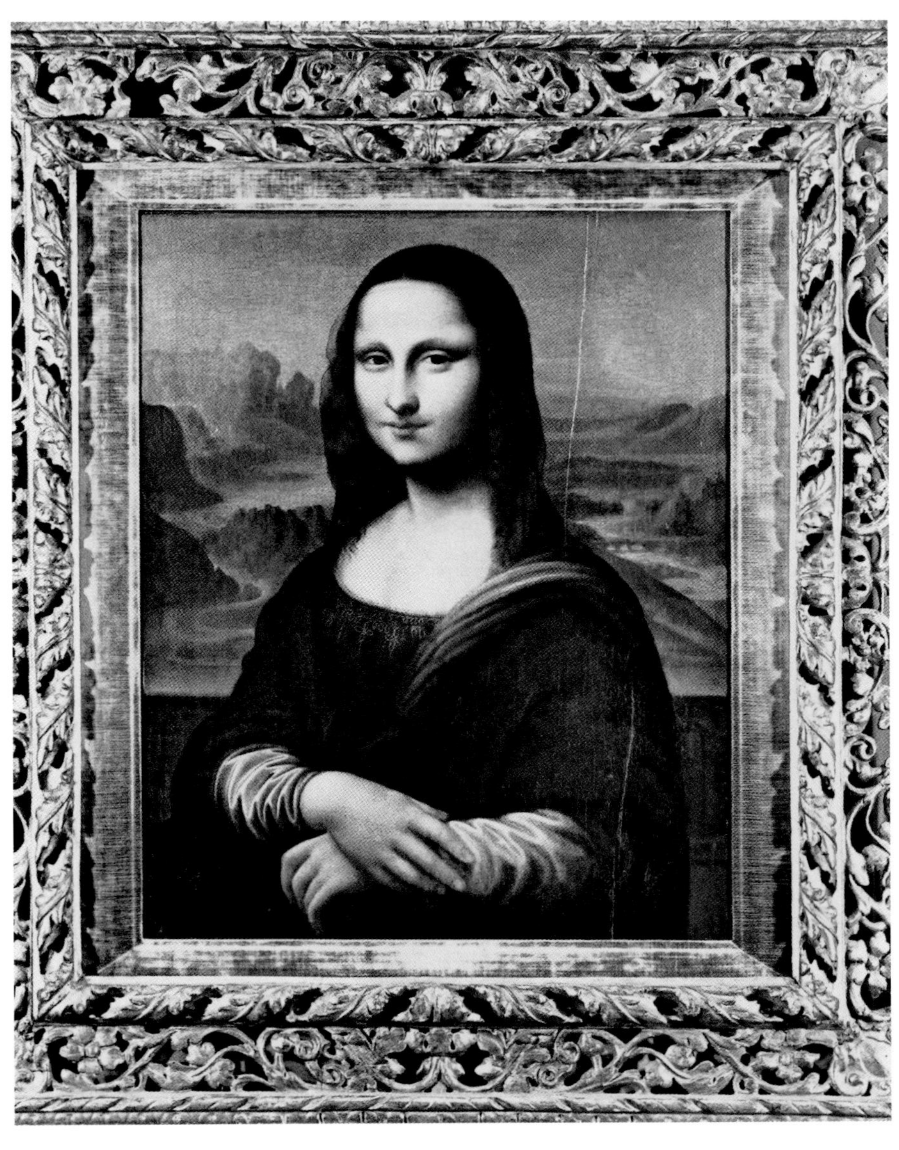

Fig. 268 Leonardo da Vinci (copy): *Portrait of a Lady (Mona Lisa)*. Collection Bass Museum of Art, Miami Beach; Gift of John and Johanna Bass, 63.46.

MASTER OF THE BORGHESE TONDO, ACTIVE 1490–1500; FLORENTINE

Virgin Adoring the Christ Child with Angels and the Infant St. John the Baptist (63.25) 94.8 CM (DIAMETER), OIL AND TEMPERA ON PANEL

MIAMI BEACH, FLORIDA. BASS MUSEUM OF ART

Burton B. Fredericksen and Federico Zeri (1972) attributed the painting to Bastiano Mainardi (1466–1513). Everett P. Fahy (1976) assigned it to a minor follower of Domenico Ghirlandaio (1449–1494) known as the Master of the Borghese Tondo, whose eponymous work is the *Madonna Adoring the Child with St. Joseph and the Infant St. John the Baptist* (Galleria Borghese, Rome; 352). A similar Virgin and Child pairing may be found in the *Nativity* (Bob Jones University Museum & Gallery, Greenville; 52.27; see pages 324-25) also attributed by Fahy to the Master of the Borghese Tondo.

The Baptist's banderole is inscribed "ECCE [Agnus Dei]" ("Behold, the Lamb of God"), from John 1:29. This *tondo* is one of many representations of the Adoration produced by Ghirlandaio, members of his shop, and followers. The Madonna and Child repeat, in reverse, the same figures in Ghirlandaio's *Adoration of the Shepherds*, painted c. 1485 for the Sassetti Chapel, Santa Trinità, Florence. The landscape, the ruinous wall, and the angels have parallels in other paintings by Ghirlandaio, for example, the *Adoration of the Magi* (Museo dello Spedale degli Innocenti, Florence) of 1488.

PROVENANCE

Sir Henry H. Howorth, London; Christie, Manson & Woods, London, December 14, 1923, lot 105; John and Johanna Bass, New York, by 1963; Bass Museum of Art, acquired 1964

BIBLIOGRAPHY

Burton B. Fredericksen and Federico Zeri, *Census of Pre-Nineteenth-Century Italian Paintings in North American Public Collections* (Cambridge, Mass.: Harvard University Press, 1972), 34, 82; *The John and Johanna Bass Collection at Miami Beach, Florida* (Miami Beach, Fla.: Bass Museum of Art, 1973), 13, no. 15; Everett P. Fahy, *Some Followers of Domenico Ghirlandajo* (New York: Garland Press, 1976), 167-68; Margarita A. Russell, *Paintings and Textiles of the Bass Museum of Art: Selections from the Collection* (Miami Beach, Fla: Bass Museum of Art, 1990), 38; Luisa Venturini, "Un altro pittore fiorentino nell'appartamento Borgia: Il Maestro del Tondo Borghese," in *Maestri e botteghe: Pittura a Firenze alla fine del Quattrocento*, ed. Mina Gregori, Antonio Paolucci, and Cristina Acidini-Lucinat (Milan: Silvana, 1992), 283, 286, no. 6; Sylvia Ferrari and Jean-Claude Bloch, *Trente-trois primitifs italiens: De 1310 à 1500, du sacré au profane* (Paris: G. Sarti, 1999), 196.

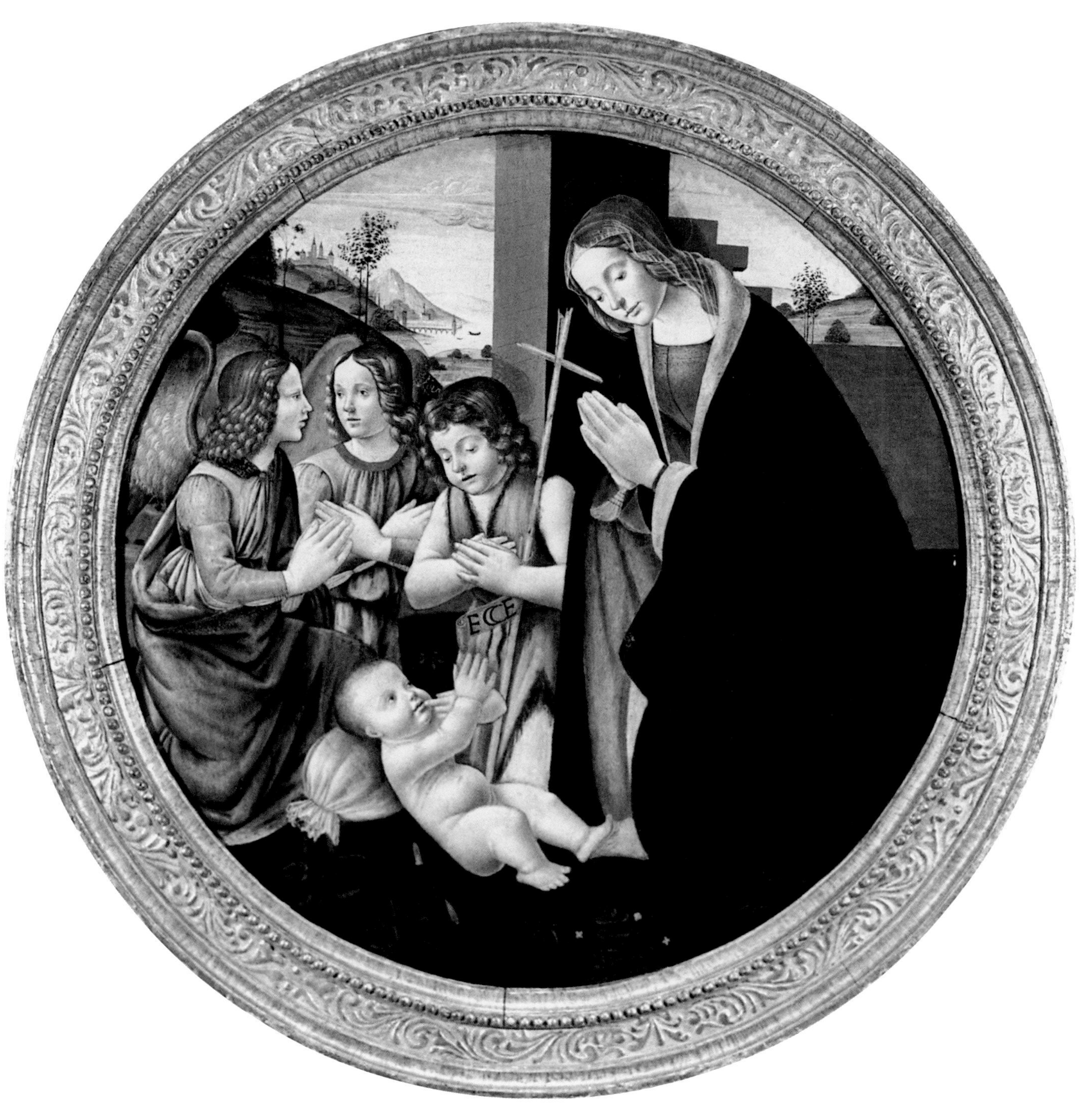

Fig. 269 Master of the Borghese Tondo: *Virgin Adoring the Christ Child with Angels and the Infant St. John the Baptist*. Collection Bass Museum of Art, Miami Beach; Gift of John and Johanna Bass, 63.25.

MAZONE, GIOVANNI, C. 1433–C. 1512; LIGURIAN

Madonna and Child with Four Angels; St. Francis, St. Anthony of Padua, and St. Peter; St. John the Baptist, St. Bernardino of Siena, and St. Louis of Toulouse; Crucifixion; Annunciation (63.17)

279.9 X 224.3 CM (OVERALL), TEMPERA ON PANEL

MIAMI BEACH, FLORIDA. BASS MUSEUM OF ART

Roberto Longhi (cited in *The John and Johanna Bass Collection* 1973) ascribed the work to Giovanni Mazone. Miklòs Boskovits (1987) dated it c. 1480 on stylistic grounds; he compared the panels with other works by the artist from the same period, including the *Annunciation* (Santa Maria di Castello, Genoa) and the *Madonna and Child* (Nostra Signora delle Vigne, Genoa). Margarita A. Russell (1990) reattributed the Bass work to Mazone's presumed student Giovanni da Barbegelata (active 1484–1508). Giuliana Algeri and Anna De Floriani (1991) assigned it to an anonymous Ligurian master active in the 1480s who was perhaps a follower of Mazone, but certainly not a close collaborator.

The Recollects, a reformed branch of the Franciscan Order, commissioned the altarpiece, motivating the inclusion of St. Francis himself and three prominent Franciscans, St. Anthony, St. Bernardino, and St. Louis of Toulouse, on its wings. The Virgin, depicted as the Queen of Heaven and the *Mater sapientiae*, the Mother of Wisdom, holds open the Book of Wisdom for the Christ Child's perusal.

PROVENANCE

Convent of the Recollects, Corbara, Sardegna; Galerie Heim, Paris, 1959; Galerie Charpentier, Paris, March 16, 1959, lot 77; John and Johanna Bass, New York, before 1963; Bass Museum of Art, since 1964

BIBLIOGRAPHY

Anna Maria Folli, "Giovanni Mazone pittore genovese del Quattrocento," *Studi Genuensi* 7 (1970–1971): 170; Burton B. Fredericksen and Federico Zeri, *Census of Pre-Nineteenth-Century Italian Paintings in North American Public Collections* (Cambridge, Mass.: Harvard University Press, 1972), 123, 595; *The John and Johanna Bass Collection at Miami Beach, Florida* (Miami Beach, Fla.: Bass Museum of Art, 1973), 11, no. 17; Miklòs Boskovits, "Nicolò Corso e gli altri: Spigolature di pittura lombardo-ligure di secondo Quattrocento," *Arte Cristiana* 75 (1987): 362, 382 n. 47; Margarita A. Russell, *Paintings and Textiles of the Bass Museum of Art: Selections from the Collection* (Miami Beach, Fla.: Bass Museum of Art, 1990), 8-9; Giuliana Algeri and Anna De Floriani, *La pittura in Liguria: Il Quattrocento* (Genoa: Gruppo Carige, Cassa di risparmio di Genova e Imperia, 1991), 300; Fabrizio Moretti, ed., *Da Ambrogio Lorenzetti a Sandro Botticelli* (Florence: Edizioni polistampa, 2003), 182, 185 n. 3.

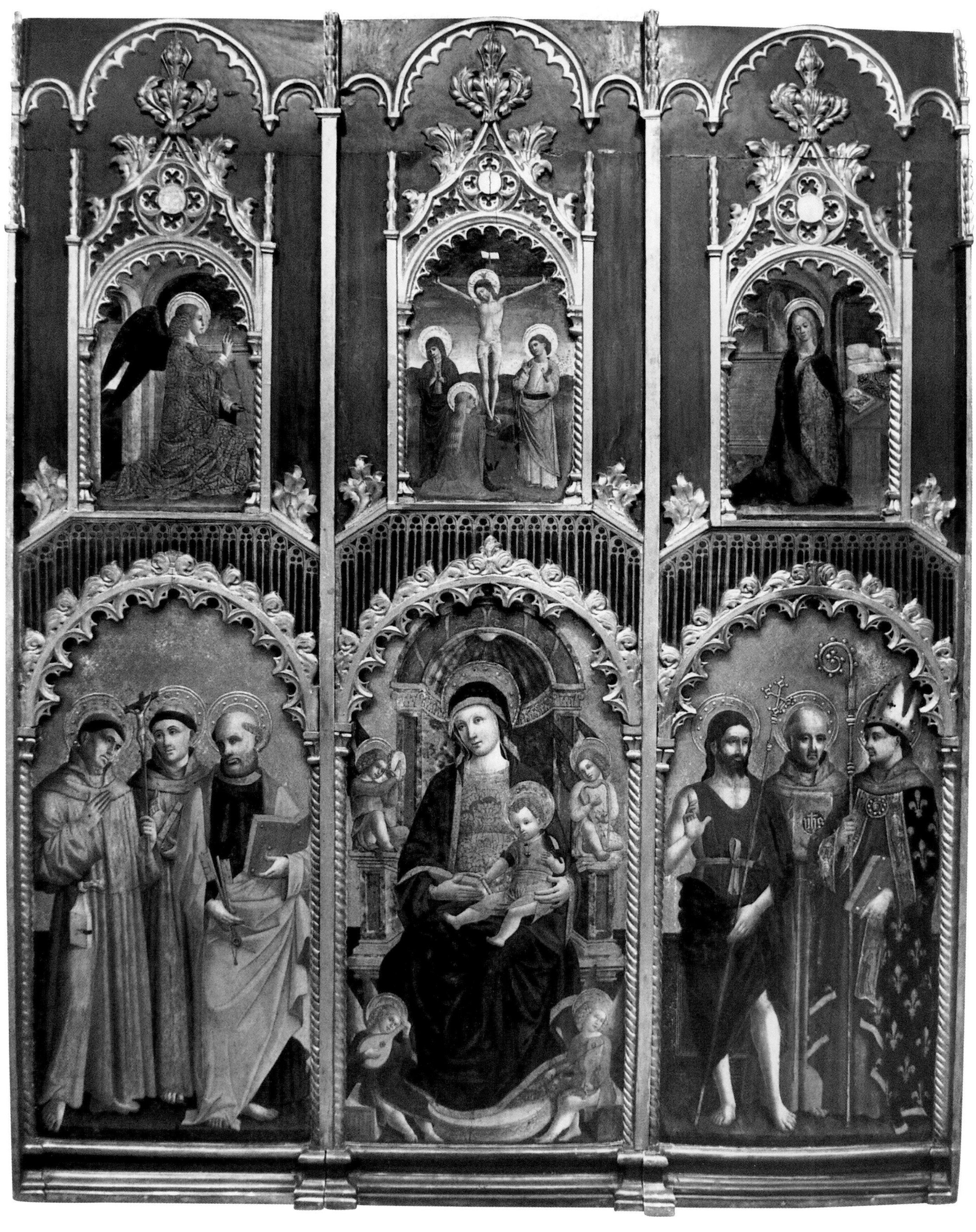

Fig. 270 Giovanni Mazone: *Madonna and Child with Four Angels; St. Francis, St. Anthony of Padua, and St. Peter; St. John the Baptist, St. Bernardino of Siena, and St. Louis of Toulouse; Crucifixion; Annunciation.* Collection Bass Museum of Art, Miami Beach; Gift of John and Johanna Bass, 63.17.

SELLAIO, JACOPO DEL, C. 1441–1493; ATTRIBUTED; FLORENTINE

Portrait of a Young Man (63.24) 47.5 X 77.5 CM, OIL AND TEMPERA (?) ON PANEL

MIAMI BEACH, FLORIDA. BASS MUSEUM OF ART

The painting is in ruinous condition. It has generally been attributed to Jacopo del Sellaio. Everett P. Fahy (Frick Art Reference Library photo mount), however, reassigned it to Francesco Botticini (1446–1497).

The composition reflects the conventions of Netherlandish portraits, particularly those by Hans Memling (1430/40–1494), which appeared in Florentine painting by the 1480s.

PROVENANCE

William Beattle, Glasgow, Scotland; John Levy Galleries, New York (?); William Salomon, New York; Duveen Brothers, New York, 1923; Edwin D. Levinson, Esq., New York, by 1935; John and Johanna Bass, New York; Bass Museum of Art, acquired 1963

BIBLIOGRAPHY

Fifteenth Century Portraits (New York: M. Knoedler & Co., 1935), no. 12; Bernard Berenson, *Italian Pictures of the Renaissance: A List of the Principal Artists and Their Works with an Index of Places. Florentine School*, 2 vols. (London: Phaidon Press, 1963), 1:198; Burton B. Fredericksen and Federico Zeri, *Census of Pre-Nineteenth-Century Italian Paintings in North American Public Collections* (Cambridge, Mass.: Harvard University Press, 1972), 186, 595; *The John and Johanna Bass Collection at Miami Beach, Florida* (Miami Beach, Fla.: Bass Museum of Art, 1973), 12-13, no. 24; Meryle Secrest, *Duveen: A Life in Art* (New York: Alfred A. Knopf, 2004), 184-85.

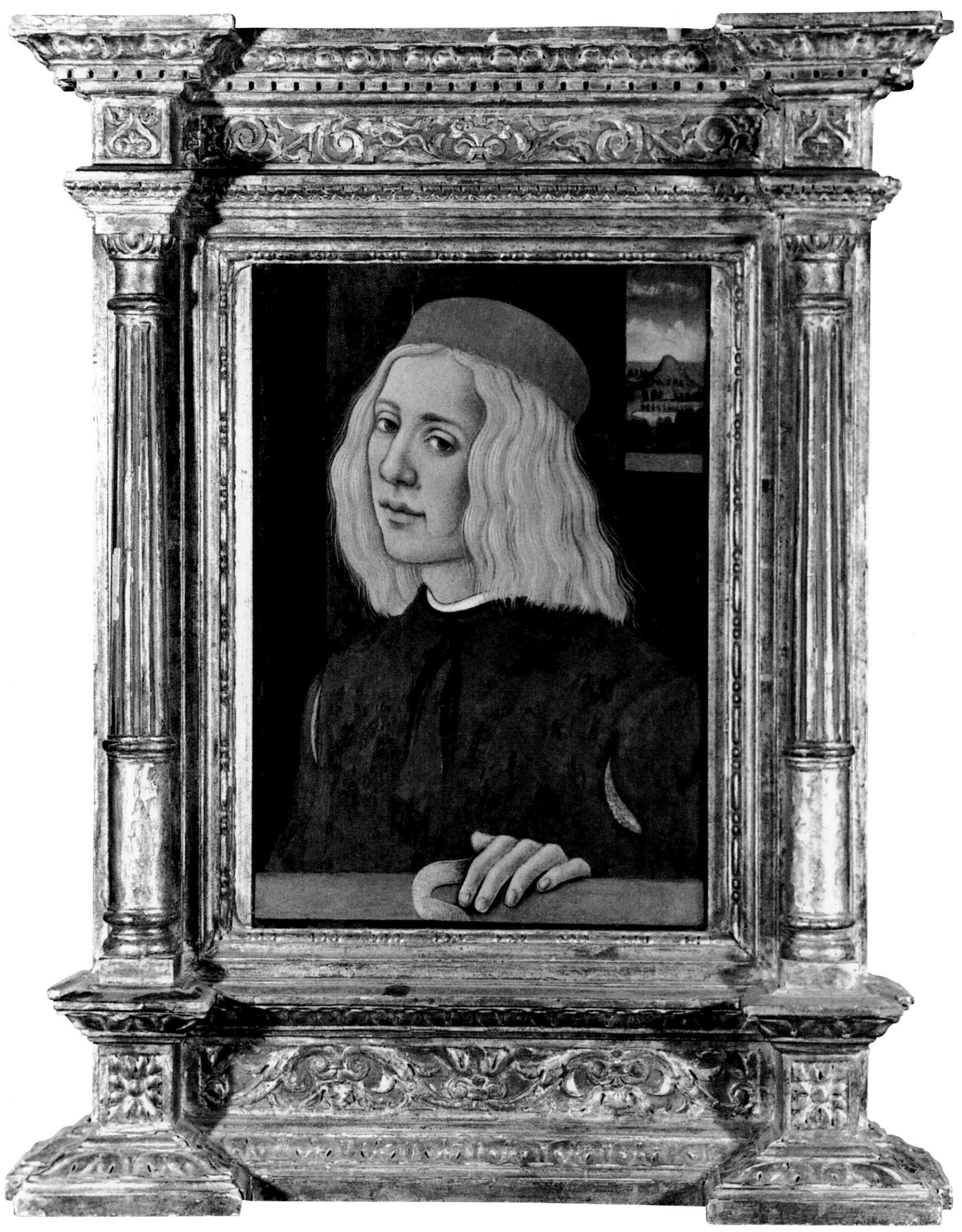

Fig. 271 Jacopo del Sellaio (attributed): *Portrait of a Young Man*. Collection Bass Museum of Art, Miami Beach; Gift of John and Johanna Bass, 63.24.

CENNI DI FRANCESCO DI SER CENNI, ACTIVE 1396–1415; FLORENTINE

Madonna and Child (K 1072) 57.3 X 34.5 CM, TEMPERA ON PANEL

MONTGOMERY, ALABAMA. HUNTINGDON COLLEGE, HOUGHTON MEMORIAL LIBRARY

Bernard Berenson (1963) ascribed the painting to an anonymous follower of Orcagna (1315/20–1368), while Fern Rusk Shapley (1966) and Burton B. Fredericksen and Federico Zeri (1972) assigned it to the Florentine School of the early fifteenth century. Miklòs Boskovits (1968) proposed the attribution to Cenni di Francesco, dating the work c. 1400. The same figural group appears in Cenni's fresco of the *Madonna and Child with Saints* in the Palazzo Comunale, San Miniato al Tedesco, which dates to 1393.

PROVENANCE

Frascione, Naples; Count Alessandro Contini-Bonacossi, Rome; Samuel H. Kress, New York, acquired 1929; Huntingdon College, acquired 1936; Birmingham Museum of Art, Birmingham, Alabama, on loan, as of 2000

BIBLIOGRAPHY

Bernard Berenson, *Italian Pictures of the Renaissance: A List of the Principal Artists and Their Works with an Index of Places. Florentine School*, 2 vols. (London: Phaidon Press, 1963), 1:215; Fern Rusk Shapley, *Paintings from the Samuel H. Kress Collection: Italian Schools*, vol. 1, *XIII–XV Century* (London: Phaidon Press, 1966), 91; Miklòs Boskovits, "Ein Vorläufer der spätgotischen Malerei in Florenz: Cenni di Francesco di Ser Cenni," *Zeitschrift für Kunstgeschichte* 31 (1968): 287; Burton B. Fredericksen and Federico Zeri, *Census of Pre-Nineteenth-Century Italian Paintings in North American Public Collections* (Cambridge, Mass.: Harvard University Press, 1972), 51, 597; Fern Rusk Shapley, *Paintings from the Samuel H. Kress Collection: Italian Schools*, vol. 3, *XVI–XVIII Century* (London: Phaidon Press, 1973), 385; Miklòs Boskovits, *Pittura fiorentina alla vigilia del Rinascimento* (Florence: Edam, 1975), 290; Richard Offner and Hayden B. J. Maginnis, *A Critical and Historical Corpus of Florentine Painting: A Legacy of Attributions* (New York: Institute of Fine Arts, New York University, 1980), 4.

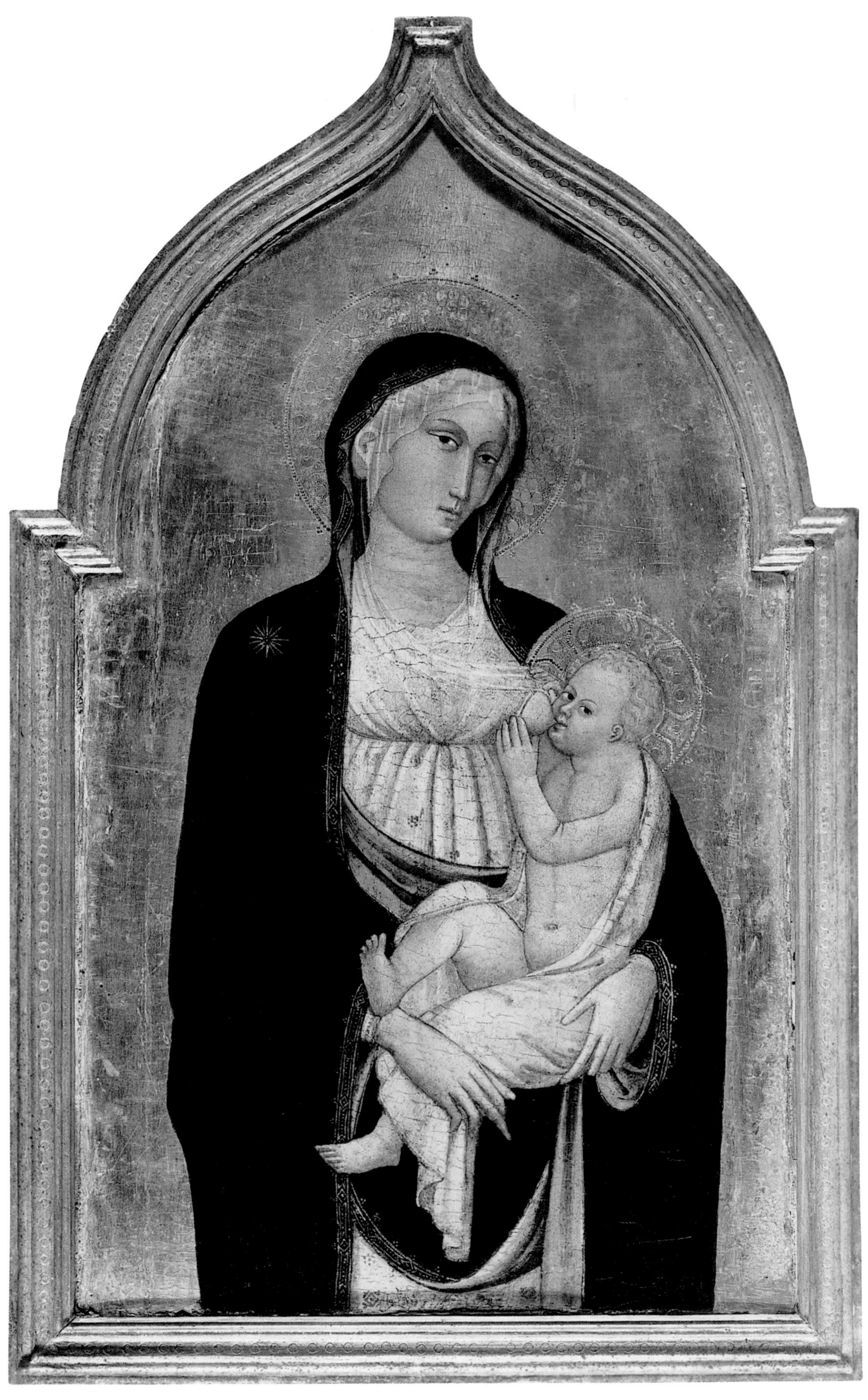

Fig. 273 Cenni di Francesco di Ser Cenni: *Madonna and Child*. Houghton Memorial Library, Huntingdon College, Montgomery, Alabama, K 1072.

FRANCESCO DI ANTONIO DI BARTOLOMEO, ACTIVE 1393–1433; FLORENTINE

Annunciation, Crucifixion, and Saints (1937.1; K 1046) 70.8 x 44.5 cm, tempera on panel

MONTGOMERY, ALABAMA. MONTGOMERY MUSEUM OF FINE ARTS

Roberto Longhi (1940) dated this small personal devotional panel 1425–1430. Its style resembles that of Francesco di Antonio's fresco of the *Crucifixion with Saints* in San Francesco, Figline.

Inscribed beneath the *Crucifixion* is "H OPVS FECIT FIERI MAESTRO ANTONIO DE GVARGVAGLI DA LVCHA MEDICO" ("Master Antonio de Guarguagli of Lucca, physician, had this work made"). St. Lucy, St. Catherine of Alexandria, the Virgin Mary, Mary Magdalen, John the Evangelist, St. Francis of Assisi, and St. Lawrence flank the crucified Christ from left to right. St. Michael, St. Leonard, St. Cosmas, St. Damian, St. Christopher, St. James Major, St. Anthony Abbot, St. Julian, and St. George appear in the bottom register.

PROVENANCE

Colonel C. J. Fergusson-Buchanan, Auchentorlie, Bowling, Dumbartonshire, Scotland; Giuseppe Bellesi, London; Samuel H. Kress, New York, acquired 1936; Montgomery Museum of Fine Arts, acquired 1937; Birmingham Museum of Art, Birmingham, Alabama, on loan, as of 2000

BIBLIOGRAPHY

Alfred M. Frankfurter, "Nationwide Gifts of Italian Art by the Kress Foundation," *Art News* 36 (1938): 15; Roberto Longhi, "Fatti di Masolino e di Masaccio," *Critica d'Arte* 5 (1940): 187; Bernard Berenson, *Italian Pictures of the Renaissance: A List of the Principal Artists and Their Works with an Index of Places. Florentine School*, 2 vols. (London: Phaidon Press, 1963), 1:63; Fern Rusk Shapley, *Paintings from the Samuel H. Kress Collection: Italian Schools*, vol. 1, *XIII–XV Century* (London: Phaidon Press, 1966), 93; Burton B. Fredericksen and Federico Zeri, *Census of Pre-Nineteenth-Century Italian Paintings in North American Public Collections* (Cambridge, Mass.: Harvard University Press, 1972), 73, 597; Richard Fremantle, *Florentine Gothic Painters from Giotto to Masaccio: A Guide to Painting in and near Florence, 1300 to 1450* (London: Secker & Warburg, 1975), 432; Perri Lee Roberts, Bruce Cole, and Hayden B. J. Maginnis, *Sacred Treasures: Early Italian Paintings from Southern Collections* (Athens, Ga.: Georgia Museum of Art, 2002), 126-29.

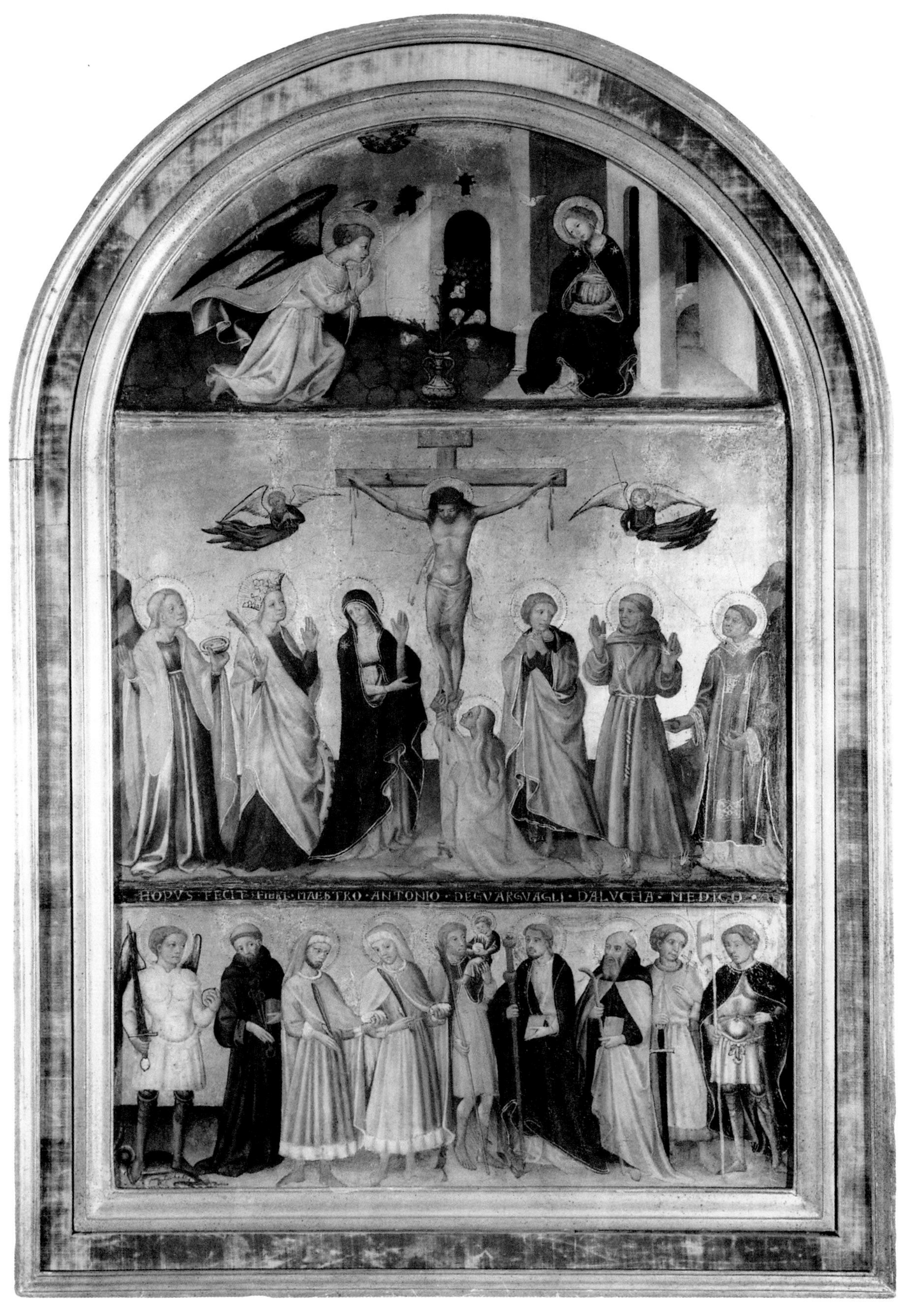

Fig. 274 Francesco di Antonio di Bartolomeo: *Annunciation, Crucifixion, and Saints*. Collection of the Montgomery Museum of Fine Arts, Montgomery, Alabama; Gift of the Samuel H. Kress Foundation, 1937.1.

ANDREA DI BARTOLO, ACTIVE BY 1389; DIED 1428; SIENESE

Crucifixion with the Virgin, St. Mary Magdalen, and St. John the Evangelist (1979.0.649 P; K 1014)

42.1 X 38.9 CM, TEMPERA ON PANEL

NASHVILLE, TENNESSEE. VANDERBILT UNIVERSITY FINE ARTS GALLERY

The shape of the panel and its subject matter indicate its probable role as the central pinnacle of an unidentified altarpiece. In imagery, function, and style, it resembles the *Crucifixion* in Andrea di Bartolo's triptych of the *Madonna and Child Enthroned with Saints, Angels, and a Dominican Donor* (Staatliche Museen, Gemäldegalerie, Berlin; 1995), which dates to the first decade of the fifteenth century. The Gallery dates its work c. 1400.

The placard at the top of the cross bears the inscription "I. N. R. I.," an acronym for "Jesus Nazarenus Rex Judaeorum" ("Jesus of Nazareth, King of the Jews"). The pelican at the apex of the panel, who gives her life-blood to feed her young, symbolizes Christ's sacrifice.

PROVENANCE

Count Alessandro Contini-Bonacossi, Florence; Samuel H. Kress, New York, acquired 1936; National Gallery of Art, Washington, D.C., exhibited 1951–1952; George Peabody College for Teachers, Nashville, 1961–1979; Vanderbilt University Fine Arts Gallery, acquired 1979

BIBLIOGRAPHY

Fern Rusk Shapley, *Paintings from the Samuel H. Kress Collection: Italian Schools*, vol. 1, *XIII–XV Century* (London: Phaidon Press, 1966), 66; Burton B. Fredericksen and Federico Zeri, *Census of Pre-Nineteenth-Century Italian Paintings in North American Public Collections* (Cambridge, Mass.: Harvard University Press, 1972), 6, 598; Robert L. Mode, *Old Master Paintings from Vanderbilt University* (Athens, Ga.: Georgia Museum of Art, 1991), no. 12.

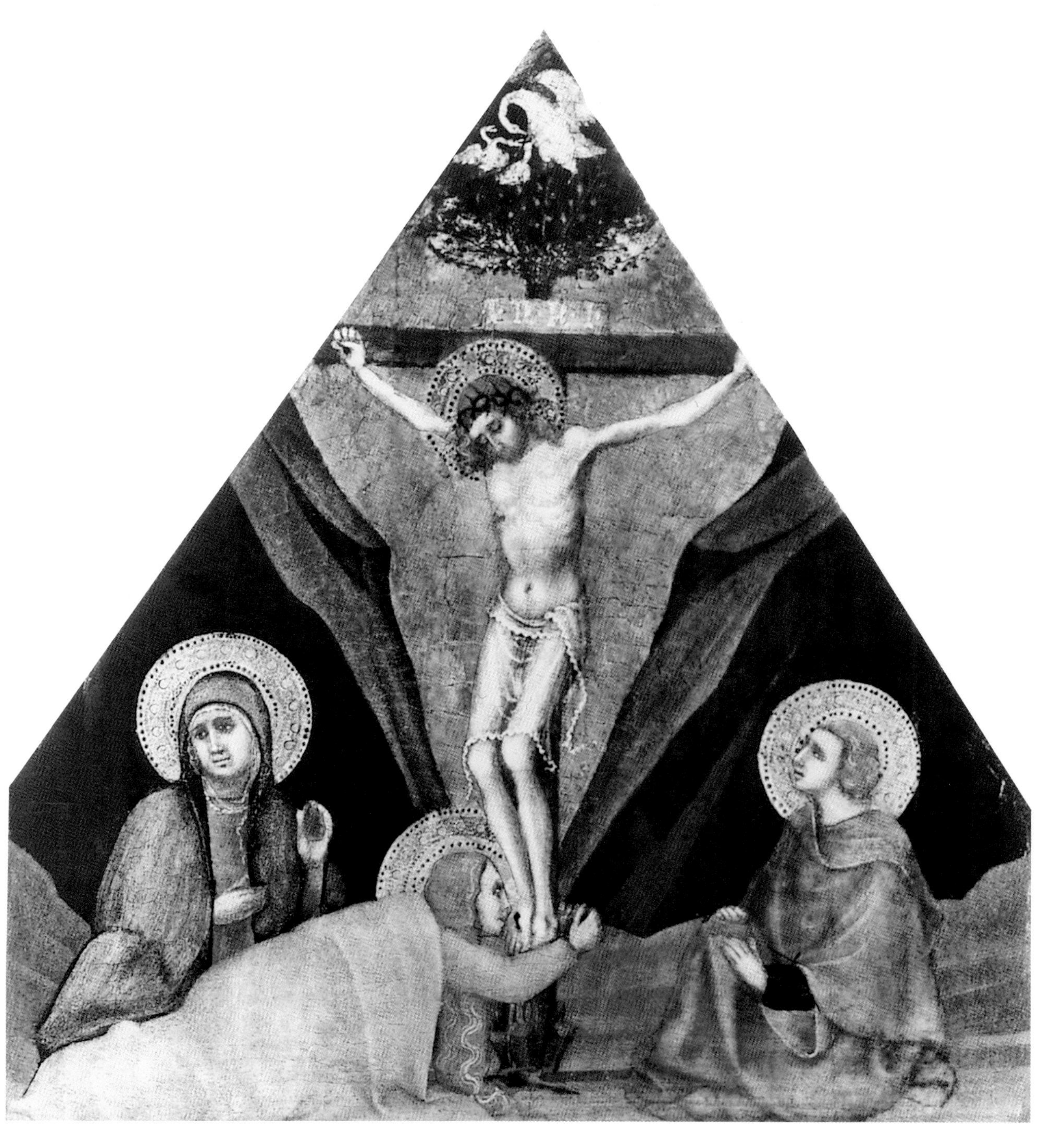

Fig. 275 Andrea di Bartolo: *Crucifixion with the Virgin, St. Mary Magdalen, and St. John the Evangelist*. Vanderbilt University Fine Arts Gallery, Nashville, Tennessee, 1979.0.649 P.

ASPERTINI, AMICO, 1474/5–1552; ATTRIBUTED; BOLOGNESE

Baptismal Ceremony (1979.0.648 P; K 78) 62.9 X 73.7 CM, TEMPERA ON PANEL

NASHVILLE, TENNESSEE. VANDERBILT UNIVERSITY FINE ARTS GALLERY

Roberto Longhi (cited in Shapley 1968) tentatively attributed the work to Amico Aspertini, c. 1515–1520, on the basis of stylistic affinities with his frescoes in San Frediano, Lucca, from c. 1506. Fern Rusk Shapley associated the panel with the Ferrarese-Bolognese School of the early sixteenth century, specifically with a follower of Lorenzo di Ottavio Costa (c. 1460–1535) and Aspertini. Burton B. Fredericksen and Federico Zeri (1972) assigned it to "Johannes Hispanus" (Juan de España), a Spanish artist active in the early sixteenth century.

Fredericksen and Zeri identified the subject as the baptism of St. Augustine by Ambrose, the Bishop of Milan, in the presence of Augustine's mother, Monica. The infant depicted beside the baptismal font may allude to Augustine's encounter with a child on a beach, as recounted in Jacobus de Voragine's *Golden Legend*. When the saint remarked on the futility of the child's attempt to dig a hole in the sand with a shell, he, the Christ Child, responded that his task was easier than Augustine's attempt to understand the mystery of the Trinity.

PROVENANCE

Spinelli, Florence; Volterra, Florence; Samuel H. Kress, New York, acquired 1930; George Peabody College for Teachers, Nashville, 1961–1979; Vanderbilt University Fine Arts Gallery, acquired 1979

BIBLIOGRAPHY

Fern Rusk Shapley, *Paintings from the Samuel H. Kress Collection: Italian Schools*, vol. 2, *XV–XVI Century* (London: Phaidon Press, 1968), 70-71; Burton B. Fredericksen and Federico Zeri, *Census of Pre-Nineteenth-Century Italian Paintings in North American Public Collections* (Cambridge, Mass.: Harvard University Press, 1972), 102, 598; Robert L. Mode, *Old Master Paintings from Vanderbilt University* (Athens, Ga.: Georgia Museum of Art, 1991), no. 11; Marilena Tamassia, *Collezioni d'arte tra Ottocento e Novecento. Jacquier fotografi a Firenze 1870–1935* (Naples: Electa, 1995), 219, no. 51372.

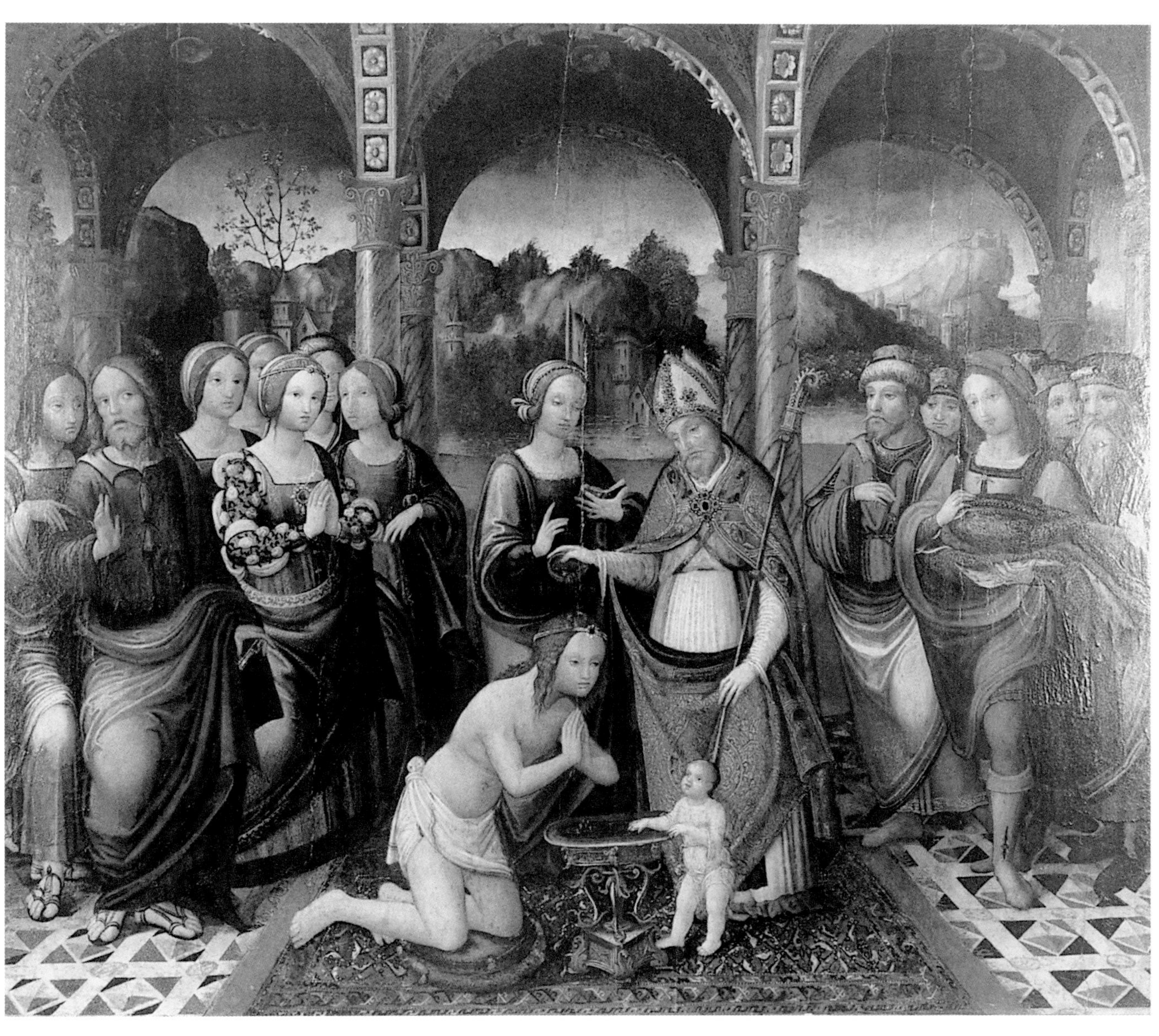

Fig. 276 Amico Aspertini (attributed): *Baptismal Ceremony*. Vanderbilt University Fine Arts Gallery, Nashville, Tennessee, 1979.0.648 P.

CRIVELLI, VITTORE, C. 1444–1501 OR LATER; VENETIAN

St. Louis of Toulouse (1979.0.651 P; K 1141) 117 X 41.5 CM, TEMPERA ON PANEL

NASHVILLE, TENNESSEE. VANDERBILT UNIVERSITY FINE ARTS GALLERY

This work and *St. Francis of Assisi* (El Paso Museum of Art; 1961–6/23; see pages 244-45) were together in the collection of Sir Archibald Buchan-Hepburn; they originally served as the right-hand panels of an unidentified polyptych that was similar to Vittore's *San Severino Altarpiece* (Pinacoteca Comunale, San Severino, Macerata). The panels are equivalent in terms of size and style, and they exhibit a punchwork pattern distinct from the others employed by Vittore, according to Sandra Di Provvido (1972). The inclusion of Francis and Louis, a member of the Order of Friars Minor, suggests that the altarpiece was painted for a Franciscan foundation. The Amandola provenance was listed in the 1929 catalogue of the Archibald Buchan-Hepburn sale, where it was also mentioned that the altarpiece was signed "Carlus Crivelli" and dated 1483. No documents, however, indicate Amandola was the altarpiece's original location. Di Provvido dated the work late in Vittore's career, probably after 1490.

Bernard Berenson (1957) identified the saint as Bonaventure, while Burton B. Fredericksen and Federico Zeri (1972) recognized him tentatively as Augustine. Di Provvido reidentified him as Louis of Toulouse because of his Franciscan habit and cord belt, the Angevin (French) *fleurs-de-lys* on his cope, and the association of the panel with the El Paso *St. Francis of Assisi.*

PROVENANCE

Franciscan convent, Amandola (Marches) (?); art market, Rome, 1845 (?); Sir Archibald Buchan-Hepburn, Sematon-Hepburn, Prestonkirk, East Lothian; Puttick and Simpson, London, July 31, 1929, lot 142; Fenouil; Count Alessandro Contini-Bonacossi, Florence; Samuel H. Kress, New York, acquired 1935; National Gallery of Art, Washington, D.C., exhibited 1941–1951; George Peabody College for Teachers, Nashville, 1961–1979; Vanderbilt University Fine Arts Gallery, acquired 1979

BIBLIOGRAPHY

Archibald Buchan-Hepburn and Other Collections Sale (London: Puttick and Simpson, 1929), no. 142; Raimond van Marle, *The Development of the Italian Schools of Painting*, vol. 18, *The Renaissance Painters of Venice: Antonio Vivarini, the Bellini, Cima, Basaiti* (The Hague: M. Nijhoff, 1934), 85 n. 1; National Gallery of Art, *Preliminary Catalogue of Paintings and Sculpture* (Washington, D.C.: National Gallery of Art, 1941), 50, no. 320; Bernard Berenson, *Italian Pictures of the Renaissance. A List of the Principal Artists and Their Works with an Index of Places. Venetian School*, 2 vols. (New York: Phaidon, 1957), 1:72; *George Peabody College for Teachers, Acquisitions* (Nashville: George Peabody College, 1961), 8-10; Fern Rusk Shapley, *Paintings from the Samuel H. Kress Collection: Italian Schools*, vol. 1, *XIII–XV Century* (London: Phaidon Press, 1966), 38; Luigi Dania, *La pittura a Fermo e nel suo circondario* (Fermo: Cassa di Risparmio di Fermo, 1968), 19; Burton B. Fredericksen and Federico Zeri, *Census of Pre-Nineteenth-Century Italian Paintings in North American Public Collections* (Cambridge, Mass.: Harvard University Press, 1972), 60, 598; Sandra Di Provvido, *La pittura di Vittore Crivelli* (L'Aquila: Japadre, 1972), 214-15; Pietro Zampetti, *Pittura nelle Marche*, vol. 1, *Dalle origini al primo Rinascimento* (Florence: Nardini, 1988), 339; Robert L. Mode, *Old Master Paintings from Vanderbilt University* (Athens, Ga.: Georgia Museum of Art, 1991), no. 8; Stefano Papetti, ed., *Vittore Crivelli e la pittura del suo tempo nel Fermano* (Milan: Federico Motta, 1997), 171, 247 no. 71, 250, 251.

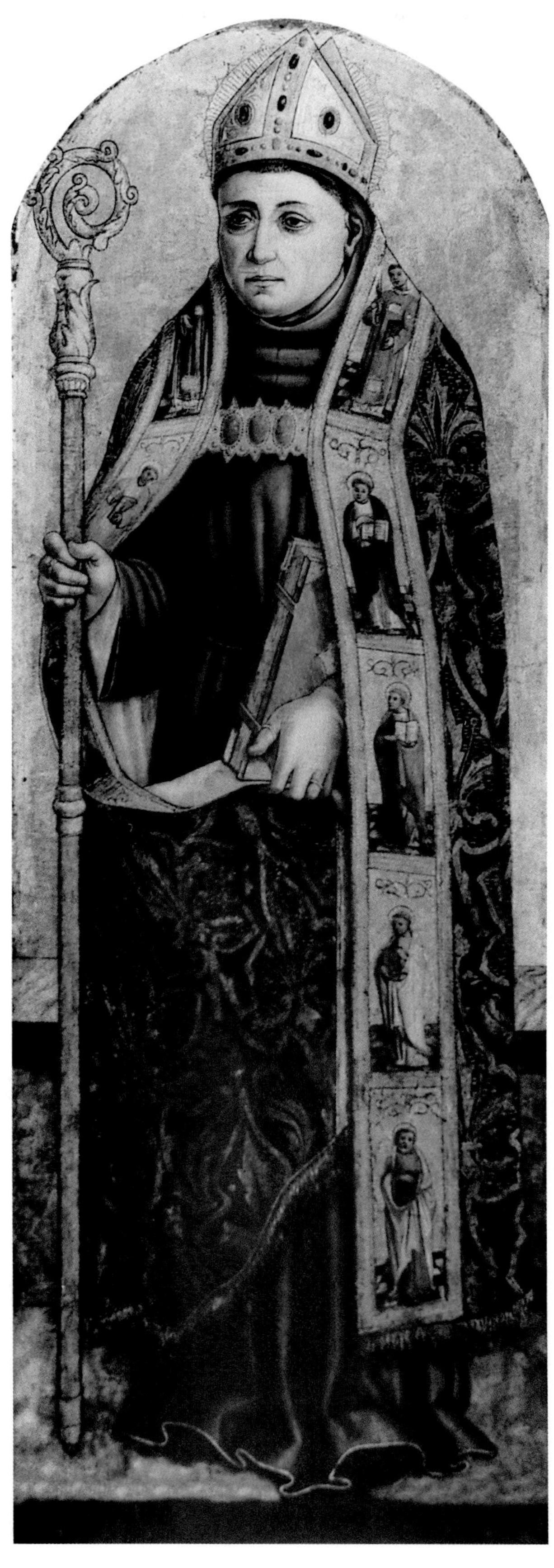

Fig. 277 Vittore Crivelli: *St. Louis of Toulouse*. Vanderbilt University Fine Arts Gallery, Nashville, Tennessee, 1979.0.651 P.

JACOPO DI PAOLO, ACTIVE 1371–1426; BOLOGNESE

Crucifixion with the Virgin Mary, St. Mary Magdalen, St. John the Evangelist, and a Female Saint
(1979.0.653 P; K 1209) 53.3 X 29.9 CM, TEMPERA ON PANEL

NASHVILLE, TENNESSEE. VANDERBILT UNIVERSITY FINE ARTS GALLERY

Fern Rusk Shapley (1966) dated the panel c. 1400 because of stylistic and iconographic affinities with the artist's signed *Crucifixion* (Pinacoteca Nazionale, Bologna; 191).

Burton B. Fredericksen and Federico Zeri (1972) identified the small female figure kneeling in the foreground as the donor. Her halo, however, and the deference shown to her by the Magdalen suggest instead that she is the patron or name saint of a donor who commissioned this small, votive work for penitential reasons.

PROVENANCE

Achillito Chiesa, Milan; Count Alessandro Contini-Bonacossi, Florence; Samuel H. Kress, New York, acquired 1939; National Gallery of Art, Washington, D.C., exhibited 1951–1952; George Peabody College for Teachers, Nashville, 1961–1979; Vanderbilt University Fine Arts Gallery, acquired 1979

BIBLIOGRAPHY

Fern Rusk Shapley, *Paintings from the Samuel H. Kress Collection: Italian Schools*, vol. 1, *XIII–XV Century* (London: Phaidon Press, 1966), 72; Burton B. Fredericksen and Federico Zeri, *Census of Pre-Nineteenth-Century Italian Paintings in North American Public Collections* (Cambridge, Mass.: Harvard University Press, 1972), 102, 598; Robert L. Mode, *Old Master Paintings from Vanderbilt University* (Athens, Ga.: Georgia Museum of Art, 1991), no. 1; Mojmír S. Frinta, *Punched Decoration on Late Medieval Panel and Miniature Painting*, pt. 1 (Prague: Maxdorf, 1998), 129, 147; Victor M. Schmidt, *Painted Piety, Panel Paintings for Personal Devotion in Tuscany, 1250–1400* (Florence: Centro Di, 2005), 139, n. 78.

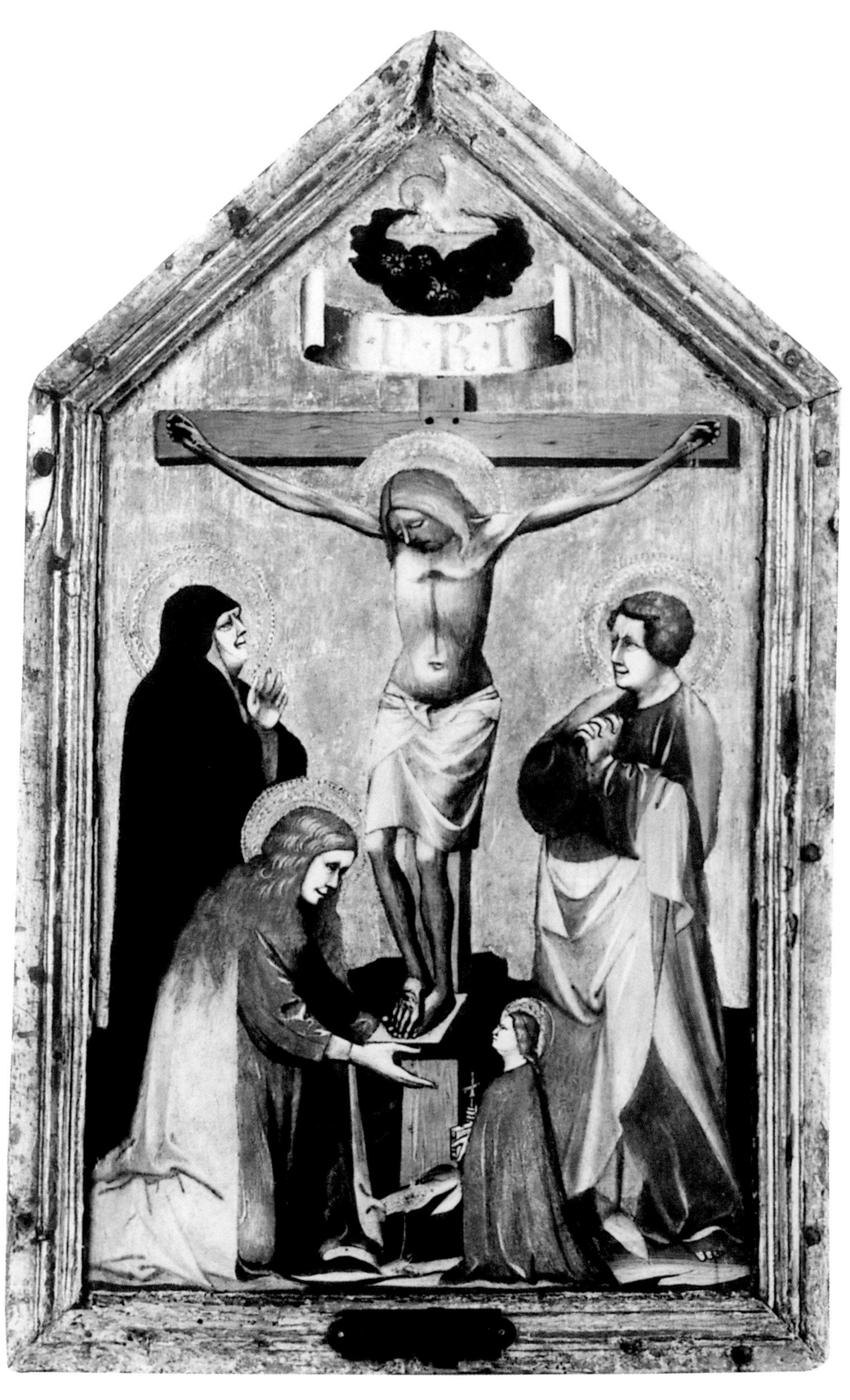

Fig. 278 Jacopo di Paolo: *Crucifixion with the Virgin Mary, St. Mary Magdalen, St. John the Evangelist, and a Female Saint.* Vanderbilt University Fine Arts Gallery, Nashville, Tennessee, 1979.0.653 P.

LIBERALE DA VERONA, C. 1445–C. 1526; VERONESE

St. Sebastian (1979.0.656 P; K 1267) 67.3 x 48.3 CM, TEMPERA ON PANEL

NASHVILLE, TENNESSEE. VANDERBILT UNIVERSITY FINE ARTS GALLERY

The panel has been considered an autograph work by Liberale da Verona, except by Fern Rusk Shapley (1968), who assigned it to a follower of the artist. She identified Liberale's full-length *St. Sebastian* (Brera, Milan; 177) as a model, which itself derives from Antonio Rizzo's statue of Adam for the courtyard of the Ducal Palace, Venice. Shapley dated the Vanderbilt picture, a personal devotional image, to the first quarter of the sixteenth century.

PROVENANCE

Count Alessandro Contini-Bonacossi, Florence; Samuel H. Kress, New York, acquired 1941; George Peabody College for Teachers, Nashville, 1961–1979; Vanderbilt University Fine Arts Gallery, acquired 1979

BIBLIOGRAPHY

Carlo Del Bravo, *Liberale da Verona* (Florence: Edizioni d'Arte Il Fiorino, 1967), 205; Fern Rusk Shapley, *Paintings from the Samuel H. Kress Collection: Italian Schools*, vol. 2, *XV–XVI Century* (London: Phaidon Press, 1968), 93-94; Burton B. Fredericksen and Federico Zeri, *Census of Pre-Nineteenth-Century Italian Paintings in North American Public Collections* (Cambridge, Mass.: Harvard University Press, 1972), 104, 598; Pierpaolo Brugnoli, ed., *Maestri della pittura veronese* (Verona: Banca mutual popolare di Verona, 1974), 110; Robert L. Mode, *Old Master Paintings from Vanderbilt University* (Athens, Ga.: Georgia Museum of Art, 1991), no. 10.

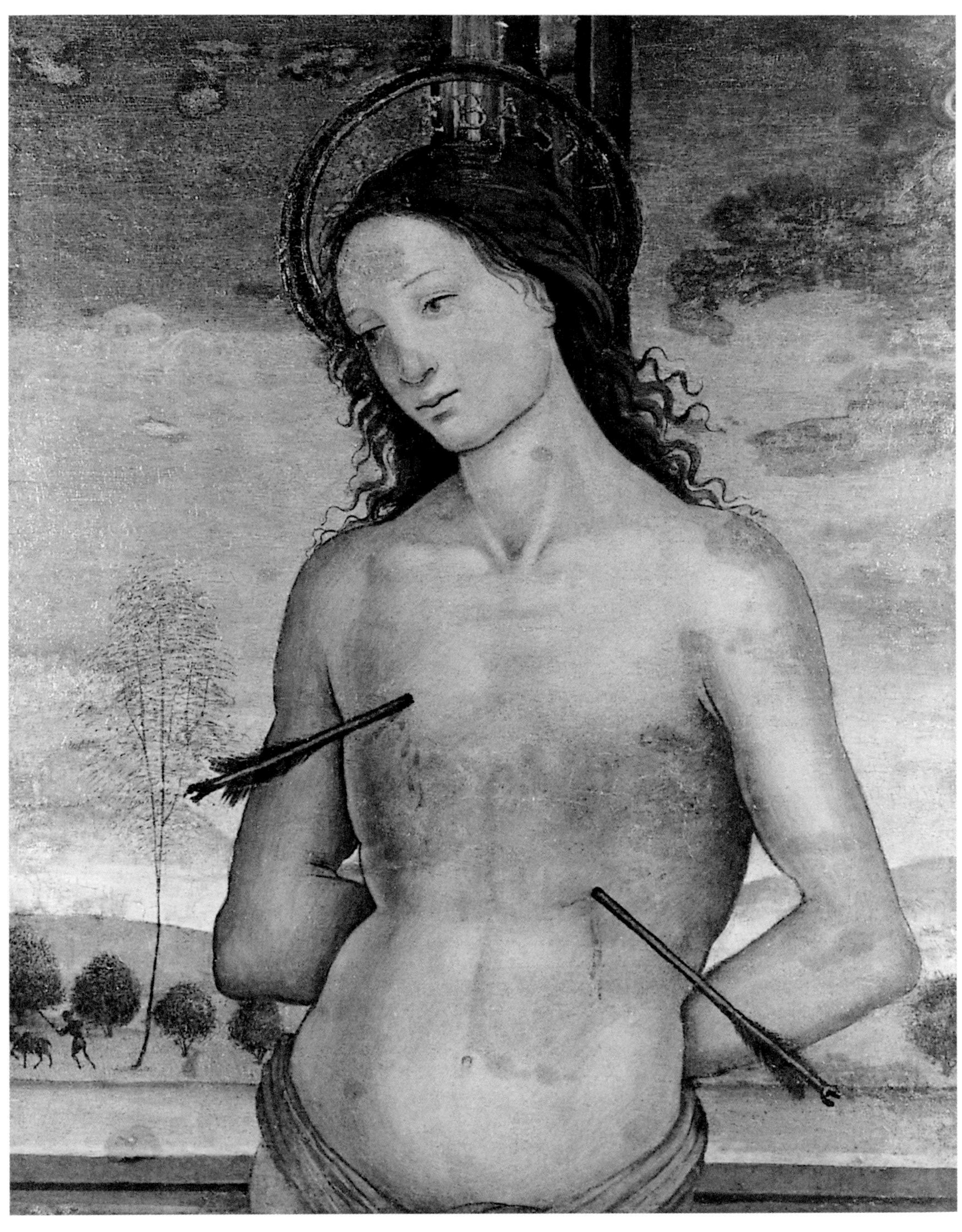

Fig. 279 Liberale da Verona: *St. Sebastian*. Vanderbilt University Fine Arts Gallery, Nashville, Tennessee, 1979.0.656 P.

LODI, GIOVANNI AGOSTINO DA, C. 1467–C. 1524; MILANESE

Madonna and Child (1979.0.654 P; K 1217) 52.1 X 38.1 CM, TEMPERA ON PANEL

NASHVILLE, TENNESSEE. VANDERBILT UNIVERSITY FINE ARTS GALLERY

William E. Suida (1956) published this devotional image as the work of Giovanni Agostino da Lodi, then known as Pseudo-Boccaccino; he dated it c. 1520 on the basis of the rocky terrain in the background, which he considered a characteristic feature of the artist's late work.

The apples and quinces represent the fruit of the Tree of Knowledge and, hence, the Fall of Man. The fruit held by Christ alludes to his roles as the new Adam and the Savior of mankind. Fern Rusk Shapley (1968) suggested the bas-relief on the parapet shows a bound prisoner brought before a judge, but it probably presents Adam and Eve after the Fall, given the feminine appearance of the so-called bound prisoner, the barren tree, and a third figure, who may be the Angel of the Lord.

PROVENANCE

Don Jaime de Bourbon, Duke of Madrid, Castle Frohsdorf, Austria; Kelly, Paris; Count Alessandro Contini-Bonacossi, Florence; Samuel H. Kress, New York, acquired 1939; George Peabody College for Teachers, Nashville, 1961–1979; Vanderbilt University Fine Arts Gallery, acquired 1979

BIBLIOGRAPHY

William E. Suida, "Pitture lombarde del Rinascimento: I, Lo pseudo-Boccaccino," *Arte Lombarda* 2 (1956): 91; Fern Rusk Shapley, *Paintings from the Samuel H. Kress Collection: Italian Schools*, vol. 2, *XV–XVI Century* (London: Phaidon Press, 1968), 20; Burton B. Fredericksen and Federico Zeri, *Census of Pre-Nineteenth-Century Italian Paintings in North American Public Collections* (Cambridge, Mass.: Harvard University Press, 1972), 125, 598; Robert L. Mode, *Old Master Paintings from Vanderbilt University* (Athens, Ga.: Georgia Museum of Art, 1991), no. 4.

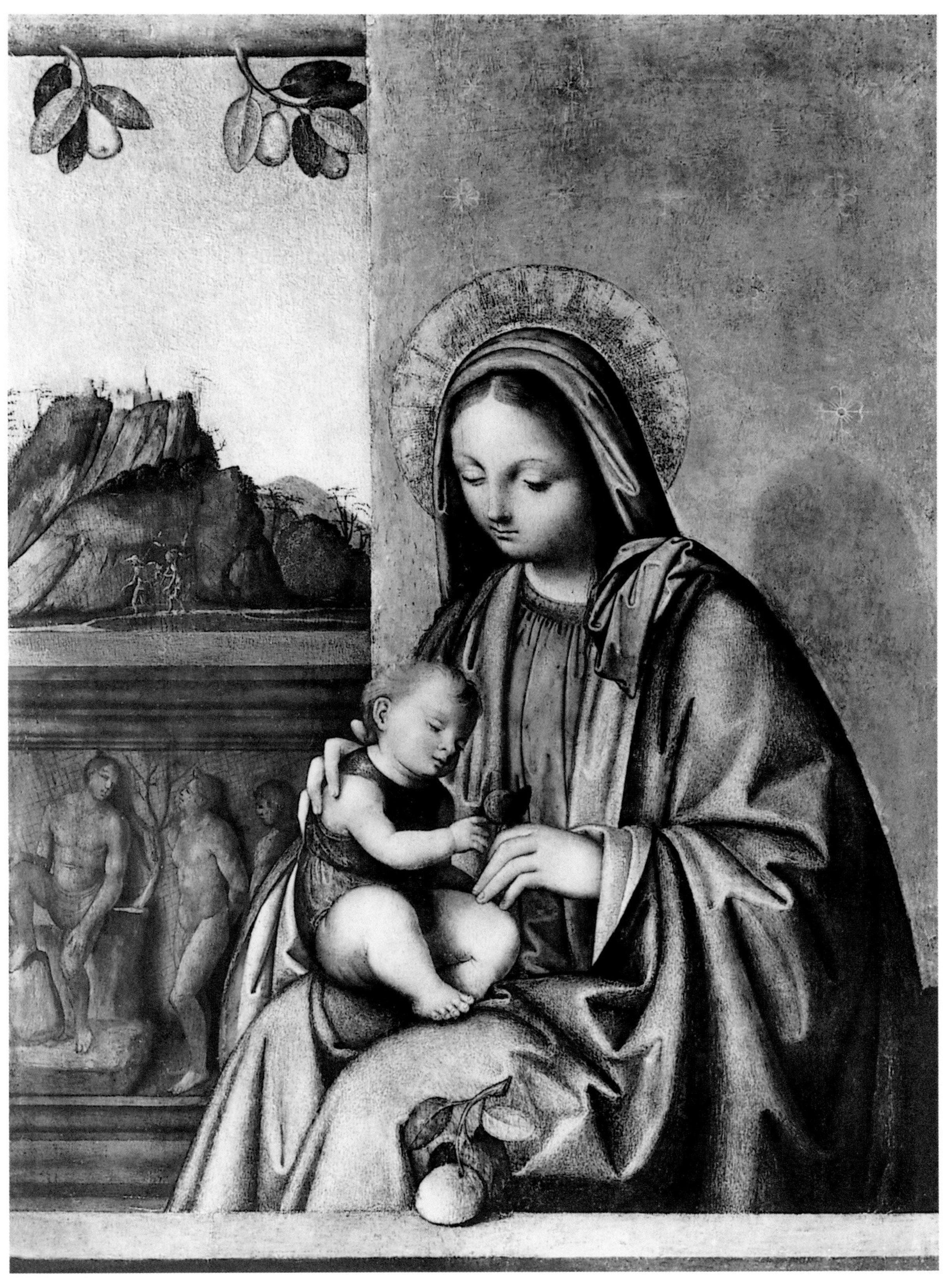

Fig. 280 Giovanni Agostino da Lodi: *Madonna and Child*. Vanderbilt University Fine Arts Gallery, Nashville, Tennessee, 1979.0.654 P.

LORENZO DI BICCI, C. 1350–1427; FLORENTINE

Madonna and Child with the Trinity and the Annunciation; Anonymous Martyr Saint; Resurrection; Noli me tangere (1979.0.652 P; K 1190) 70.2 X 52.1 CM, TEMPERA ON PANEL

NASHVILLE, TENNESSEE. VANDERBILT UNIVERSITY FINE ARTS GALLERY

Bernard Berenson (1963) ascribed this small devotional altarpiece to a Florentine artist close to Bicci di Lorenzo (1373–1452), working between 1350 and 1420. Fern Rusk Shapley (1966) assigned it to a follower of Bicci di Lorenzo. Federico Zeri (1967) reattributed it to Lorenzo di Bicci, associating it with similar panels in the Museo di Palazzo Venezia, Rome (10210), the Pinacoteca Vaticana (207), and the Art Institute of Chicago (1937.1004). Miklòs Boskovits (1975) endorsed this opinion and dated the panel 1370–1375.

The Madonna of Humility was a subject frequently chosen for autonomous altarpieces in trecento and early-quattrocento Tuscany. The inclusion of other images, in this case, the Trinity, the Annunciate Angel, and the Annunciate Virgin, as well as the scenes in the predella, however, is rare, perhaps a response to the patron's wishes.

PROVENANCE

Private collection, Milan; Count Alessandro Contini-Bonacossi, Florence; Samuel H. Kress, New York, acquired 1939; National Gallery of Art, Washington, D.C., exhibited 1945–1952; George Peabody College for Teachers, Nashville, 1961–1979; Vanderbilt University Fine Arts Gallery, acquired 1979

BIBLIOGRAPHY

Bernard Berenson, *Italian Pictures of the Renaissance. A List of the Principal Artists and Their Works with an Index of Places. Florentine School*, 2 vols. (London: Phaidon Press, 1963), 1:215; Fern Rusk Shapley, *Paintings from the Samuel H. Kress Collection: Italian Schools*, vol. 1, *XIII–XV Century* (London: Phaidon Press, 1966), 47; Federico Zeri, "Early Italian Pictures in the Kress Collection," *Burlington Magazine* 109 (1967): 477; Burton B. Fredericksen and Federico Zeri, *Census of Pre-Nineteenth-Century Italian Paintings in North American Public Collections* (Cambridge, Mass.: Harvard University Press, 1972), 110, 598; Miklòs Boskovits, *Pittura fiorentina alla vigilia del Rinascimento, 1370–1400* (Florence: Edam, 1975), 335; Richard Offner and Hayden B. J. Maginnis, *A Critical and Historical Corpus of Florentine Painting. A Legacy of Attributions* (New York: Institute of Fine Arts, New York University, 1981), 41; Robert L. Mode, *Old Master Paintings from Vanderbilt University* (Athens, Ga.: Georgia Museum of Art, 1991), no. 2; Mojmír S. Frinta, *Punched Decoration on Late Medieval Panel and Miniature Painting*, pt. 1 (Prague: Maxdorf, 1998), 96, 99, 103.

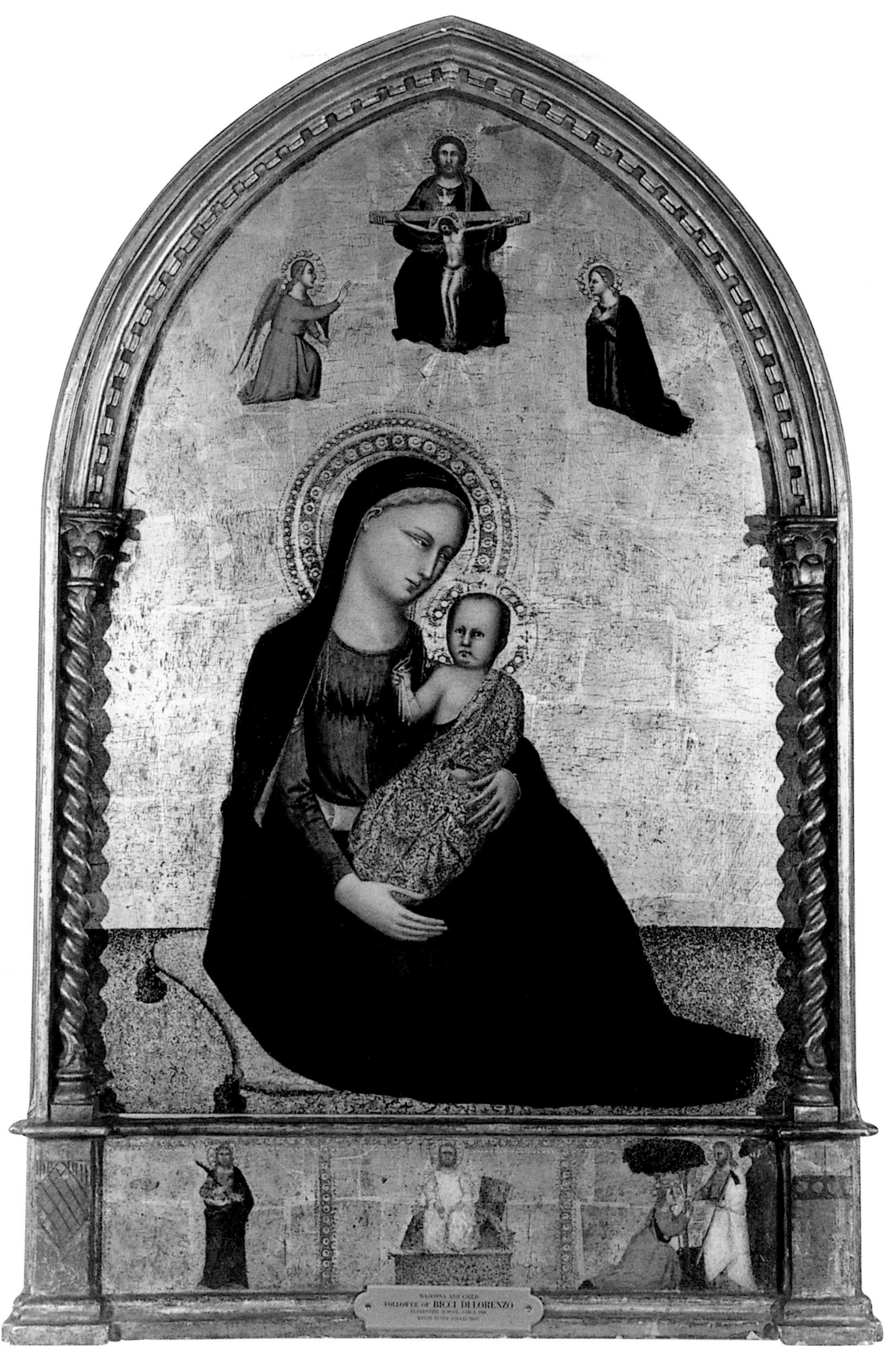

Fig. 281 Lorenzo di Bicci: *Madonna and Child with the Trinity and the Annunciation; Anonymous Martyr Saint; Resurrection; Noli me tangere.* Vanderbilt University Fine Arts Gallery, Nashville, Tennessee, 1979.0.652 P.

ORIOLI, PIETRO DI FRANCESCO DEGLI, 1458–1496; SIENESE

Madonna and Child (1979.0.650 P; K 1095) 36.5 x 27.3 CM, TEMPERA ON PANEL

NASHVILLE, TENNESSEE. VANDERBILT UNIVERSITY FINE ARTS GALLERY

Gustavo Botta (1936) published this personal devotional image as a work by Benvenuto di Giovanni (1436–c. 1518). It was assigned to Giacomo Pacchiarotti (1474–1539/40) when it entered the Kress Collection (*Preliminary Catalogue* 1941). Pacchiarotti's entire oeuvre was reattributed to Pietro di Francesco degli Orioli in 1982 by Alessandro Angelini.

PROVENANCE

Mendoza, Italy; Galleria Pesaro, Milan, December 25, 1936–January 2, 1937; Count Alessandro Contini-Bonacossi, Florence; Samuel H. Kress, New York, acquired 1937; National Gallery of Art, Washington, D.C., exhibited 1941–1952; George Peabody College for Teachers, Nashville, 1961–1979; Vanderbilt University Fine Arts Gallery, acquired 1979

BIBLIOGRAPHY

Gustavo Botta, *Le collezioni Agosti e Mendoza* (Milan: Tumminelli & C. Editori, 1936), no. 259; National Gallery of Art, *Preliminary Catalogue of Paintings and Sculpture* (Washington, D.C.: National Gallery of Art, 1941), 147, no. 463; Fern Rusk Shapley, *Paintings from the Samuel H. Kress Collection: Italian Schools*, vol. 1, *XIII–XV Century* (London: Phaidon Press, 1966), 110; Bernard Berenson, *Italian Pictures of the Renaissance. A List of the Principal Artists and Their Works with an Index of Places. Central Italian and North Italian Schools*, 3 vols. (London: Phaidon Press, 1968), 1:309; Burton B. Fredericksen and Federico Zeri, *Census of Pre-Nineteenth-Century Italian Paintings in North American Public Collections* (Cambridge, Mass.: Harvard University Press, 1972), 153, 598; Alessandro Angelini, "Da Giacomo Pacchiarotti a Pietro Orioli," *Prospettiva* 29 (1982): 72-78; Robert L. Mode, *Old Master Paintings from Vanderbilt University* (Athens, Ga.: Georgia Museum of Art, 1991), no. 3; Mojmír S. Frinta, *Punched Decoration on Late Medieval Panel and Miniature Painting*, pt. 1 (Prague: Maxdorf, 1998), 539, 540.

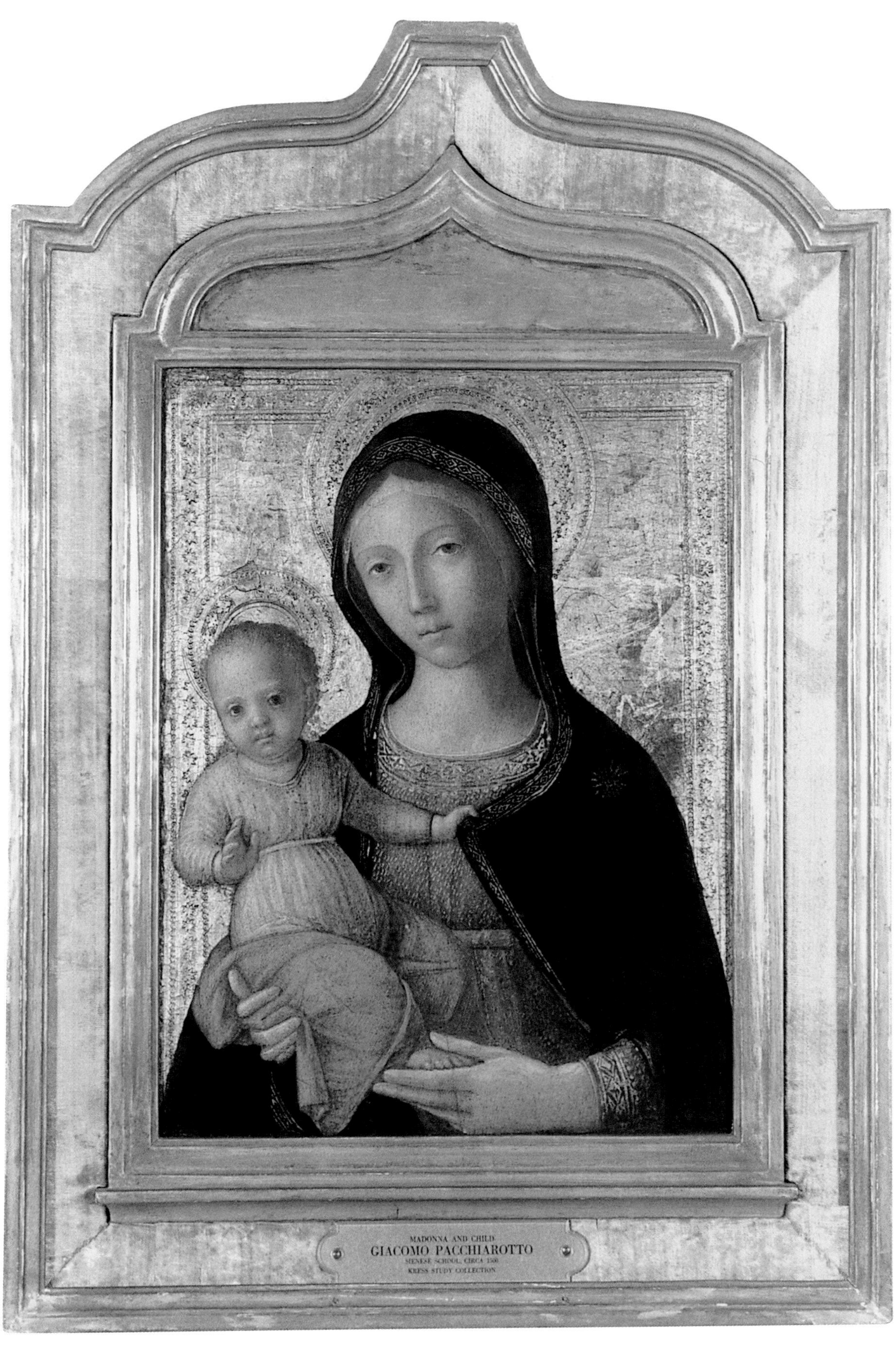

Fig. 282 Pietro di Francesco degli Orioli: *Madonna and Child*. Vanderbilt University Fine Arts Gallery, Nashville, Tennessee, 1979.0.650 P.

PSEUDO GRANACCI, ACTIVE C. 1490–1525; FLORENTINE

St. Sebastian (1979.0.655 P; K 1229A) 49.8 X 41 CM, TEMPERA WITH OIL ON PANEL

NASHVILLE, TENNESSEE. VANDERBILT UNIVERSITY FINE ARTS GALLERY

This painting and *St. Mary Magdalen* (Walker Art Museum, Brunswick; 1961.100.6; K 1229B) are the upper portions of larger panels that presented full-length figures and came from the same unidentified altarpiece; they probably flanked an image of the Madonna. Fern Rusk Shapley (1968) ascribed the work to the Umbrian painter Giovanni Battista Bertucci I (c. 1465–1516). Burton B. Fredericksen and Federico Zeri (1972) listed it as a fifteenth-century Florentine work. Everett P. Fahy (1976) reattributed it to an anonymous follower of Domenico Ghirlandaio (1449–1494), known as Pseudo Granacci, formerly called the Master of the Spiridon Story of Joseph, who was active in Florence in the late fifteenth and early sixteenth centuries.

"S. [S]EBASTIA[N]" is inscribed on the saint's halo.

PROVENANCE

Private collection, England; Christie, Manson & Woods, London, March 5, 1937, lot 77; Count Alessandro Contini-Bonacossi, Florence; Samuel H. Kress, New York, acquired 1939; George Peabody College for Teachers, Nashville, 1961–1979; Vanderbilt University Fine Arts Gallery, acquired 1979

BIBLIOGRAPHY

Fern Rusk Shapley, *Paintings from the Samuel H. Kress Collection: Italian Schools*, vol. 2, *XV–XVI Century* (London: Phaidon Press, 1968), 104; Burton B. Fredericksen and Federico Zeri, *Census of Pre-Nineteenth-Century Italian Paintings in North American Public Collections* (Cambridge, Mass.: Harvard University Press, 1972), 221, 598; Fern Rusk Shapley, *Paintings from the Samuel H. Kress Collection: Italian Schools*, vol. 3, *XVI–XVIII Century* (London: Phaidon Press, 1973), 391-92; Everett P. Fahy, *Some Followers of Domenico Ghirlandajo* (New York: Garland Press, 1976), 199; Robert L. Mode, *Old Master Paintings from Vanderbilt University* (Athens, Ga.: Georgia Museum of Art, 1991), no. 9.

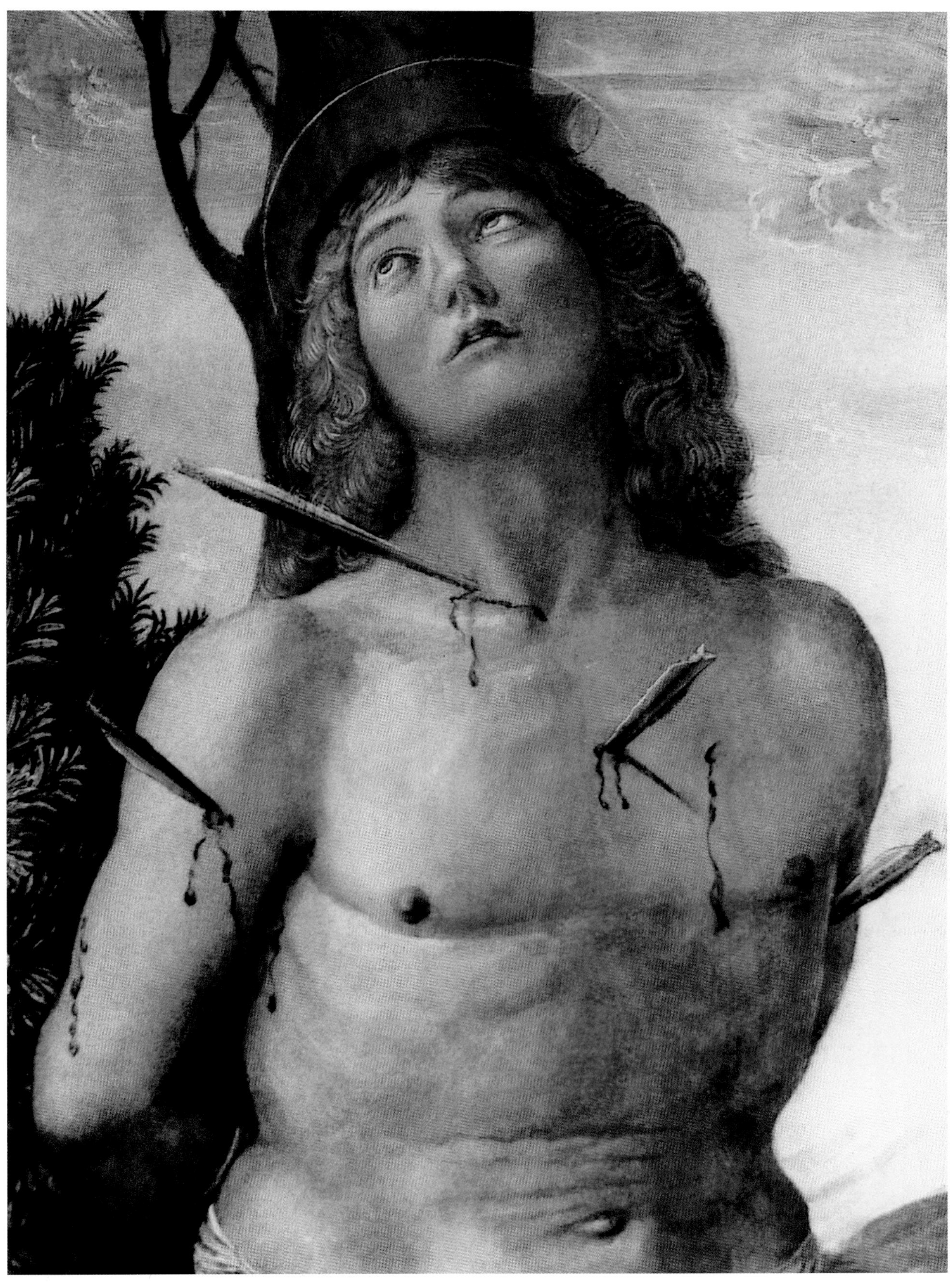

Fig. 283 Pseudo Granacci: *St. Sebastian*. Vanderbilt University Fine Arts Gallery, Nashville, Tennessee, 1979.0.655 P.